Volume 39

THE SIXTH INTERNATIONAL CONGRESS ON ACCOUNTING 1952

T0384424

THE SIXTH INTERNATIONAL CONGRESS ON ACCOUNTING 1952

VARIOUS

Routledge
Taylor & Francis Group

LONDON AND NEW YORK

First reissued in 1984 by Garland Publishing, Inc.

This edition first published in 2021
by Routledge
2 Park Square, Milton Park, Abingdon, Oxon OX14 4RN

and by Routledge
52 Vanderbilt Avenue, New York, NY 10017

Routledge is an imprint of the Taylor & Francis Group, an informa business

© 1952 The Sixth International Congress on Accounting

British Library Cataloguing in Publication Data
A catalogue record for this book is available from the British Library

ISBN: 978-0-367-33564-9 (Set)
ISBN: 978-1-00-304636-3 (Set) (ebk)
ISBN: 978-0-367-51279-8 (Volume 39) (hbk)
ISBN: 978-0-367-51280-4 (Volume 39) (pbk)
ISBN: 978-1-00-305313-2 (Volume 39) (ebk)

Publisher's Note
The publisher has gone to great lengths to ensure the quality of this reprint but points out that some imperfections in the original copies may be apparent.

Disclaimer
The publisher has made every effort to trace copyright holders and would welcome correspondence from those they have been unable to trace.

The Sixth International Congress on Accounting 1952

GARLAND PUBLISHING, INC.
NEW YORK & LONDON
1984

For a complete list of the titles in this series
see the final pages of this volume.

This facsimile has been made from a copy in the library of
the American Institute of Certified Public Accountants.

Copyright, 1952, by The Sixth International Congress
on Accounting.
Reprinted by permission of the Institute of Chartered
Accountants in England and Wales.

Library of Congress Cataloging in Publication Data

International Congress on Accounting
(6th : 1952 : London, England)
The Sixth International Congress on Accounting, 1952.

(Accounting history and the development of a profession)
Reprint.
Includes index.
1. Accounting—Congresses.   2. Comparative account-
ing—Congresses.   I. Title.   II. Series.
HF5603.I62   1952   657   84-13535
ISBN 0-8240-6335-X (alk. paper)

The volumes in this series are printed on acid-free,
250-year-life paper.

Printed in the United States of America

THE ROYAL FESTIVAL HALL

THE SIXTH
INTERNATIONAL CONGRESS
ON ACCOUNTING
1952

16th, 17th, 18th, 19th and 20th June, 1952

ROYAL FESTIVAL HALL
SOUTH BANK, LONDON

Printed by
GEE & COMPANY (PUBLISHERS) LIMITED, LONDON AND ST. ALBANS

FOREWORD

Nearly fifty years have passed since the first International Congress on Accounting was held at St. Louis in the United States of America in 1904. Prior to the 1952 Congress the last International Congress on Accounting to be held in England took place in 1933.

It was a great honour to the accountancy bodies of Great Britain and Ireland to sponsor the Congress in June, 1952, and it was our privilege, as President and Vice-President of that Congress, to welcome to London a great gathering of delegates and visitors from overseas and of members of the sponsoring bodies. We were especially pleased that so many were accompanied by their ladies.

The subjects selected for discussion at the Congress were, we thought, those which were, and still are, uppermost in the minds of accountants in all countries. In the preface to the programme we expressed the hope that all attending would find interest and benefit not only at the sessions but also at the informal talks arising out of them. We trust that this hope has been fulfilled and that the business sessions and the social events of the Congress have helped to cement old friendships and have been the means of making many new ones.

103 societies from 35 different countries accepted invitations to the Congress and 490 delegates and visitors from abroad attended. In addition there were 1,009 members of sponsoring bodies. These figures will give some indication of the international character of the Congress. The pages which follow will help to show the many and varied contributions which have been made to the business sessions. Our warmest thanks are extended to all who attended. We believe the Congress to have been a success and it is to delegates, visitors and members alike that the success is to be attributed.

There may be those who will wish to add this book to their collection to remind them of happy times. To all who read it, whether or not they attended the Congress, we hope that the book will be regarded as a contribution towards right thinking on some of the most important financial and economic problems of our day and generation.

H. G. HOWITT,
President.

C. PERCY BARROWCLIFF,
Vice-President.

London,
December, 1952.

TABLE OF CONTENTS

OTHER EVENTS OF THE CONGRESS

CLOSING OF THE CONGRESS

VISITS TO SCOTLAND AND IRELAND

APPENDICES

LIST OF ILLUSTRATIONS

SPONSORS OF THE CONGRESS

THE INSTITUTE OF CHARTERED ACCOUNTANTS OF SCOTLAND
27 Queen Street, Edinburgh, 2

President: SIR DAVID ALLAN HAY, K.B.E., C.A.

Secretary: E. H. V. MCDOUGALL

THE INSTITUTE OF CHARTERED ACCOUNTANTS IN ENGLAND AND WALES
Moorgate Place, London, E.C.2

President: T. B. ROBSON, M.B.E., M.A., F.C.A.

Secretary: ALAN S. MACIVER, M.C., B.A.

THE SOCIETY OF INCORPORATED ACCOUNTANTS AND AUDITORS
Incorporated Accountants' Hall, Temple Place,
Victoria Embankment, London, W.C.2

President: C. PERCY BARROWCLIFF, F.S.A.A.

Secretary: I. A. F. CRAIG, O.B.E., B.A.

THE INSTITUTE OF CHARTERED ACCOUNTANTS IN IRELAND
7 Fitzwilliam Place, Dublin

President: H. E. A. ADDY, F.C.A., F.S.A.A.

Secretary: W. E. CRAWFORD, F.C.A.

THE ASSOCIATION OF CERTIFIED AND CORPORATE ACCOUNTANTS
22 Bedford Square, London, W.C.1

President: THE RT. HON. LORD LATHAM, F.A.C.C.A.

Director and Secretary: J. C. LATHAM, D.L., F.S.A.A., F.A.C.C.A.

THE INSTITUTE OF MUNICIPAL TREASURERS AND ACCOUNTANTS
1 Buckingham Place, Westminster, London, S.W.1

President: C. H. POLLARD, O.B.E., F.S.A.A., F.I.M.T.A.

Secretary: L. F. CHEYNEY, F.S.A.A., F.I.M.T.A.

THE INSTITUTE OF COST AND WORKS ACCOUNTANTS
63 Portland Place, London, W.1

President: S. C. TYRRELL, F.C.W.A.

Director and Secretary: STANLEY J. D. BERGER, M.C.

OFFICERS

President
SIR HAROLD GIBSON HOWITT, G.B.E., D.S.O., M.C., F.C.A.

Vice-President
C. PERCY BARROWCLIFF, F.S.A.A.

Chairman of Council
H. GARTON ASH, O.B.E., M.C., F.C.A.

Vice-Chairman of Council
A. STUART ALLEN, F.S.A.A.

Secretary
ALAN S. MacIVER, M.C., B.A.

Chief Executive Officer
BRIGADIER S. O. JONES, O.B.E., M.C.

Honorary Public Relations Officer
DEREK DU PRÉ

Honorary Auditors
HAROLD G. JUDD, C.B.E., C.A.
J. C. BURLEIGH, C.A.

MEMBERS OF COUNCIL AND COMMITTEES

Council

H. GARTON ASH, O.B.E., M.C., F.C.A., *Chairman*

A. STUART ALLEN, F.S.A.A., *Vice-Chairman*

Representing The Institute of Chartered Accountants of Scotland
CHARLES D. GAIRDNER, C.A.
SIR DAVID ALLAN HAY, K.B.E., C.A.
JOHN L. SOMERVILLE, F.R.S.E., C.A.

Representing The Institute of Chartered Accountants in England and Wales
CHARLES W. BOYCE, C.B.E., F.C.A.
SIR HAROLD HOWITT, G.B.E., D.S.O., M.C., F.C.A.
T. B. ROBSON, M.B.E., M.A., F.C.A.
GILBERT D. SHEPHERD, M.B.E., F.C.A.
SIR NICHOLAS WATERHOUSE, K.B.E., M.A., F.C.A.

Representing The Society of Incorporated Accountants and Auditors
SIR FREDERICK ALBAN, C.B.E., F.S.A.A., F.I.M.T.A.
C. PERCY BARROWCLIFF, F.S.A.A.
BERTRAM NELSON, F.S.A.A.

Representing The Institute of Chartered Accountants in Ireland
H. E. A. ADDY, F.C.A., F.S.A.A.
JOHN BAILEY, F.C.A.

Representing The Association of Certified and Corporate Accountants
T. EDGAR KILLIP, F.A.C.C.A.
J. C. LATHAM, D.L., F.S.A.A., F.A.C.C.A.
THE LORD LATHAM, F.A.C.C.A.
FREDERICK WILSON, O.B.E., F.A.C.C.A.

Representing The Institute of Municipal Treasurers and Accountants
JACK WHITTLE, B.COM., A.C.A., F.I.M.T.A.

Representing The Institute of Cost and Works Accountants
STANLEY J. D. BERGER, M.C.

Entertainments Committee

J. C. LATHAM, D.L., F.S.A.A., F.A.C.C.A., *Chairman*

Representing The Institute of Chartered Accountants of Scotland
SIR DAVID ALLAN HAY, K.B.E., C.A.

Representing The Institute of Chartered Accountants in England and Wales
H. GARTON ASH, O.B.E., M.C., F.C.A.
CHARLES W. BOYCE, C.B.E., F.C.A.

Representing The Society of Incorporated Accountants and Auditors
A. STUART ALLEN, F.S.A.A.
C. PERCY BARROWCLIFF, F.S.A.A.

Representing The Institute of Chartered Accountants in Ireland
G. BROCK, F.C.A.

Representing The Institute of Municipal Treasurers and Accountants
L. F. CHEYNEY, F.S.A.A., F.I.M.T.A.

Representing The Institute of Cost and Works Accountants
STANLEY J. D. BERGER, M.C.

Golf Committee

D. V. House, F.C.A., *Chairman*

L. R. Elcombe, F.C.A.
Charles D. Gairdner, C.A.
Arthur E. Middleton, F.S.A.A.

Percy Toothill, F.S.A.A.
James Wood, C.A.

Ladies' Committee

Lady Howitt, *Chairman*

Mrs. C. Percy Barrowcliff
Mrs. Stanley J. D. Berger
Mrs. Charles W. Boyce
Mrs. E. Cassleton Elliott
Mrs. C. I. R. Hutton

Mrs. J. C. Latham
Miss Phyllis E. M. Ridgway,
B.A., F.S.A.A.
Mrs. T. B. Robson
Mrs. Jack Whittle

ACCOUNTANCY ORGANISATIONS REPRESENTED

(In alphabetical order)

ARGENTINA
Federación de Colegios de Doctores en Ciencias Económicas y Contadores Públicos Nacionales.

AUSTRALIA
Association of Accountants of Australia.
Australasian Institute of Cost Accountants.
Commonwealth Institute of Accountants.
Institute of Chartered Accountants in Australia.

AUSTRIA
Kammer der Wirtschaftstreuhänder.

BELGIUM
Collège National des Experts Comptables de Belgique.
Institut Belge des Reviseurs de Banques.
Société Royale Chambre Belge des Comptables à Bruxelles.

BOLIVIA
Federación Nacional de Contadores.

BRAZIL
Federação dos Contabilistas do Estado de São Paulo.

BURMA
Burma Accountancy Board.
Burma Society of Accountants.

CANADA
Canadian Institute of Chartered Accountants.
Institute of Chartered Accountants of Alberta.
Institute of Chartered Accountants of British Columbia.
Institute of Chartered Accountants of Manitoba.
Institute of Chartered Accountants of Ontario.
Institute of Chartered Accountants of Quebec.
Society of Industrial and Cost Accountants of Canada.

COLOMBIA
Instituto Nacional de Contadores Públicos.

DENMARK

Foreningen af Statsautoriserede Revisorer.

EAST AFRICA

Association of Accountants in East Africa.

FINLAND

K.H.T.-Yhdistys: Föreningen C.G.R.

FRANCE

Chambre Nationale des Experts-Comptables Diplômés par l'Etat.
Compagnie des Chefs de Comptabilité.
Compagnie Nationale des Experts Comptables.
Conseil Supérieur de la Comptabilité.
Fédération des Associations de Commissaires de Sociétés Inscrits par les Cours d'Appel.
Ordre National des Experts Comptables et des Comptables Agréés.
Société de Comptabilité de France.
Union Professionelle des Sociétés Fiduciaires d'Expertise Comptable.

GERMANY

Bundesverband der Vereidigten Buchprüfer.
Institut der Wirtschaftsprüfer.

GREAT BRITAIN AND IRELAND

Association of Certified and Corporate Accountants.
Institute of Chartered Accountants in England and Wales.
Institute of Chartered Accountants in Ireland.
Institute of Chartered Accountants of Scotland.
Institute of Cost and Works Accountants.
Institute of Municipal Treasurers and Accountants.
Society of Incorporated Accountants and Auditors.

INDIA

Institute of Chartered Accountants of India.
Institute of Cost and Works Accountants (India).

ISRAEL

Association of Public Accountants and Auditors in Israel.

ITALY

Consiglio Nazionale dei Commercialisti.
Istituto di Ricerche Economico-Aziendali: Università degli Studi di Torino.
Mutual Security Agency.

JAPAN
  Nihon Konin Kaikeishi Kyokai.
  Nippon Keirishi Kai.
  Shadan Hojin Nihon Keirishi Kyokai.

MALTA
  Malta Institute of Accountants.

MEXICO
  Instituto de Contadores Públicos Titulados de México.

NETHERLANDS
  Nederlands Instituut van Accountants.
  Vereniging van Academisch Gevormde Accountants.

NEW ZEALAND
  Incorporated Institute of Accountants of New Zealand.
  New Zealand Institute of Cost Accountants.
  New Zealand Society of Accountants.

NORWAY
  Norges Statsautoriserte Revisorers Forening.
  Revisorforeningen i Oslo.

PAKISTAN
  Pakistan Council of Accountancy.

PERU
  Colegio de Contadores Públicos del Perú.
  Instituto de Contadores del Perú.

PHILIPPINES
  Philippine Institute of Accountants.

PORTUGAL
  Sociedade Portuguesa de Contabilidade.

RHODESIA
  Rhodesia Society of Accountants.

SOUTH AFRICA
  Cape Society of Accountants and Auditors.
  Institute of Municipal Treasurers and Accountants, South Africa.
  Natal Society of Accountants.
  Transvaal Society of Accountants.

SWEDEN

Föreningen Auktoriserade Revisorer.
Svenska Revisorsamfundet.

SWITZERLAND

Schweizerische Kammer für Revisionswesen.
Verband Schweizerischer Bücherexperten.

UNITED STATES OF AMERICA

American Accounting Association.
American Institute of Accountants.
Arkansas Society of Certified Public Accountants.
California Society of Certified Public Accountants.
Colorado Society of Certified Public Accountants.
Connecticut Society of Certified Public Accountants.
Georgia Society of Certified Public Accountants.
Illinois Society of Certified Public Accountants.
Institute of Internal Auditors.
Kansas Society of Certified Public Accountants.
Kentucky Society of Certified Public Accountants.
Maine Society of Public Accountants.
Maryland Association of Certified Public Accountants.
Massachusetts Society of Certified Public Accountants.
Michigan Association of Certified Public Accountants.
Missouri Society of Certified Public Accountants.
National Association of Cost Accountants.
New Jersey Society of Certified Public Accountants.
New York State Society of Certified Public Accountants.
Ohio Society of Certified Public Accountants.
Oklahoma Society of Certified Public Accountants.
Oregon Society of Certified Public Accountants.
Pennsylvania Institute of Certified Public Accountants.
Rhode Island Society of Certified Public Accountants.
Society of Louisiana Certified Public Accountants.
Texas Society of Certified Public Accountants.
Virginia Society of Public Accountants.
Wisconsin Society of Certified Public Accountants.

URUGUAY

Colegio de Doctores en Ciencias Económicas y Contadores del Uruguay.

VENEZUELA

Colegio Nacional de Técnicos en Contabilidad.

TIME-TABLE OF EVENTS

MONDAY, 16TH JUNE

10.30 a.m.   Westminster Abbey
             SPECIAL CONGRESS SERVICE (by kind permission of the Dean
             and Chapter). Sermon by the Very Reverend A. C. DON,
             K.C.V.O., D.D., Dean of Westminster.
                                      or
10.30 a.m.   Westminster Cathedral
             SOLEMN HIGH MASS for Roman Catholic delegates, visitors,
             members and their guests.

3.15 p.m.   Royal Festival Hall
    to   OPENING OF THE CONGRESS by the President.
4.0 p.m.

9.0 p.m.   Royal Festival Hall
    to   CONGRESS RECEPTION.
12.0 mid-   Reception; dancing; demonstrations of Scottish reels and
  night   square dances.

TUESDAY, 17TH JUNE

10.0 a.m.   Royal Festival Hall   FIRST SESSION
    to   Subject: '*Fluctuating Price Levels in Relation to Accounts*'
12.30 p.m.   (i) Summary of papers by the rapporteur, A. C. VELLING,
                   Denmark.
               (ii) Discussion.
              (iii) Summing-up by the introducer, C. PERCY BARROWCLIFF,
                   F.S.A.A.

2.15 p.m.   Royal Festival Hall   SECOND SESSION
    to   Subject: '*Accounting Requirements for Issues of Capital*'
4.45 p.m.   (i) Summary of papers by the rapporteur, A. A. FITZGERALD,
                   B.COM., F.I.C.A., F.C.A.A., Australia.
               (ii) Discussion.
              (iii) Summing-up by the introducer, IAN W. MACDONALD,
                   M.A., C.A.

2.45 p.m.   Royal Festival Hall
    to   DRESS SHOW for ladies of delegates, visitors and members.
4.0 p.m.

7.0 p.m.   THEATRE PARTIES.

WEDNESDAY, 18TH JUNE

10.0 a.m.   Royal Festival Hall   THIRD SESSION
to   Subject: *'The Accountant in Industry'*
12.30 p.m.   (i) Summary of papers by the rapporteur, N. R. MODY, B.COM., F.C.A., India.
                 (ii) Discussion.
                 (iii) Summing-up by the introducers, F. R. M. DE PAULA, C.B.E., F.C.A., and W. S. RISK, B.COM., C.A., F.C.W.A.

2.15 p.m.   Royal Festival Hall   FOURTH SESSION
to   Subject: *'The Accountant in Practice and in Public Service'*
4.45 p.m.   (i) Summary of papers by the rapporteur, PROFESSOR A. M. VAN RIETSCHOTEN, Netherlands.
                 (ii) Discussion.
                 (iii) Summing-up by the introducers, A. H. MARSHALL, B.SC., PH.D., F.S.A.A., F.I.M.T.A., and G. F. SAUNDERS, F.C.A.

7.0 p.m.   Guildhall.
            BANQUET.

7.0 p.m.   THEATRE PARTIES.

THURSDAY, 19TH JUNE

1. Visit to Windsor Castle and Hampton Court Palace. Luncheon at the Castle Hotel and the White Hart Hotel, Windsor.

2. Visit to places of interest in London, including the Houses of Parliament, Guildhall, Tower of London, St. Paul's Cathedral and Goldsmiths' Hall. Luncheon at the Holborn Restaurant.

3. Visit to Oxford University. Luncheon at the Randolph Hotel.

4. Visit to Cambridge University. Luncheon at Trinity Hall and Gonville and Caius College.

5. Tour of the Port of London on board *S.Y. Katherine* and *M.V. Fordson* (kindly arranged by the Port of London Authority). Luncheon at the National Maritime Museum, Greenwich.

6. Golf competition at Wentworth, near Virginia Water. Luncheon at the club house.

9.0 p.m.   Tate Gallery.
to   GOVERNMENT RECEPTION for delegates and their ladies, by
10.30 p.m.   BRIGADIER H. R. MACKESON, M.P., Secretary for Overseas Trade.

FRIDAY, 20TH JUNE

10.0 a.m.
to
12.30 p.m.
	Royal Festival Hall
	Subject: '*The Incidence of Taxation*'
	  (i) Summary of papers by the rapporteur, PERCIVAL F. BRUNDAGE, C.P.A., United States of America.
	  (ii) Discussion.
		FIFTH SESSION

2.15 p.m.
to
3.45 p.m.
	Royal Festival Hall
	  (ii) Discussion (*continued*).
	  (iii) Summing-up by the introducers, G. B. BURR, F.A.C.C.A., and THOMAS J. GREEN, C.P.A., United States of America.
		FIFTH SESSION (*continued*)

4.0 p.m. to 4.30 p.m.	Royal Festival Hall CLOSING OF THE CONGRESS by the President.	
6.0 p.m.	Grosvenor House COCKTAIL PARTY at the invitation of the Editor-in-Chief and the Editor of *The Accountant*.	
10.0 p.m. to 2.0 a.m. (June 21)	Savoy Hotel CONGRESS BALL.	

MONDAY TO WEDNESDAY, 23RD–25TH JUNE

PROGRAMME IN SCOTLAND

Monday, 23rd June

10.45 a.m. to 12.30 p.m.	COACH TOUR of Edinburgh, including the Castle, St. Giles Cathedral, the Thistle Chapel, Parliament House, John Knox's House, Holyrood House, Burns Monument and the Scott Monument.
12.45 p.m.	LUNCHEON at the George Hotel.
8.0 p.m. to 10.0 p.m.	CIVIC RECEPTION by the Corporation of the City of Edinburgh.

Tuesday, 24th June

8.45 a.m. to 6.0 p.m.	COACH TOUR of Loch Lomond, Loch Long and Gareloch. Luncheon at Balloch.
6.30 p.m.	DINNER at the St. Enoch Hotel, Glasgow.
9.30 p.m.	Return to Edinburgh.

Wednesday, 25th June

1.45 p.m. to 6.15 p.m.	COACH TOUR of the Scott country. Tea at Dryburgh.
7.0 p.m.	DINNER at the North British Hotel, Edinburgh.

PROGRAMME IN IRELAND

Monday, 23rd June

12.30 p.m.   RECEPTION by the Lord Mayor of Dublin.

1.0 p.m.   LUNCHEON at the Shelbourne Hotel, Dublin.

2.30 p.m.   COACH TOUR of Dublin, including Trinity College, the Botanic Gardens and Phœnix Park.

7.0 p.m.   THEATRE PARTY.

Tuesday, 24th June

10.15 a.m.
to
7.0 p.m.   COACH TOUR of County Wicklow, visiting Glendalough and Vale of Avoca. Luncheon at Glendalough. Tea at Greystones.

7.30 p.m.   DINNER at the Royal Marine Hotel, Dun Laoghaire.

9.30 p.m.   Return to Dublin.

Wednesday, 25th June

12.45 p.m.   LUNCHEON at the Shelbourne Hotel, Dublin.

2.30 p.m.   COACH TOUR of the Boyne Valley.

7.30 p.m.   RECEPTION AND DINNER at the Shelbourne Hotel, Dublin.

PROCEEDINGS
OF THE SIXTH
INTERNATIONAL CONGRESS
ON ACCOUNTING
1952

MONDAY, 16th JUNE, 1952

SERVICE IN WESTMINSTER ABBEY

SERVICE IN WESTMINSTER CATHEDRAL

OPENING OF THE CONGRESS

SERVICE IN WESTMINSTER ABBEY

More than one thousand members of the Congress, many accompanied by their ladies, attended a special service held in Westminster Abbey at 10.30 a.m. on Monday, 16th June, by kind permission of the Dean of Westminster, the Very Reverend A. C. Don, K.C.V.O., D.D. The Dean conducted the service and was assisted by the Precentor, the Reverend C. T. H. Dams.

ORDER OF SERVICE

When the Dean and Chapter and the other Officers of the Establishment of the Collegiate Church of St. Peter in Westminster had entered the Dean said:

We are gathered together, brethren, in this historic Church, surrounded by memorials of men who have served their generation faithfully in every department of our varied life, and helped to build up our manifold inheritance; and we are here to witness to our belief in the providence and continuing love of Almighty God and to ask his blessing upon the counsels of those whose business in different parts of the world is for the welfare of men in their dealings one with another.

First let us join with all angels, all men and all creatures in worshipping the King of Heaven.

Hymn

Bright the vision that delighted
   Once the sight of Judah's seer;
Sweet the countless tongues united
   To entrance the prophet's ear.

Round the Lord in glory seated
   Cherubim and seraphim
Filled his temple, and repeated
   Each to each the alternate hymn:

'Lord, thy glory fills the heaven;
   Earth is with its fulness stored;
Unto thee be glory given,
   Holy, Holy, Holy, Lord.'

Heaven is still with glory ringing,
   Earth takes up the angels' cry,
'Holy, Holy, Holy', singing,
   'Lord of Hosts, the Lord most high.'

4

With his seraph train before him,
With his holy Church below,
Thus unite we to adore him,
Bid we thus our anthem flow:

'Lord, thy glory fills the heaven;
Earth is with its fulness stored;
Unto thee be glory given,
Holy, Holy, Holy, Lord.'

Richard Redhead (1820-1901)   *Bishop R. Mant* (1776-1848)

Let us pray.

Lord, have mercy upon us.

Christ, have mercy upon us.

Lord, have mercy upon us.

Our Father, which art in heaven, Hallowed be thy Name. Thy kingdom come; Thy will be done; in earth as it is in heaven. Give us this day our daily bread. And forgive us our trespasses, As we forgive them that trespass against us. And lead us not into temptation; But deliver us from evil. Amen.

Almighty God, our heavenly Father, who of his great mercy hath promised forgiveness of sins to all them that with hearty repentance and true faith turn unto him; Have mercy upon us; pardon and deliver us from all our sins; confirm and strengthen us in all goodness; and bring us to everlasting life; through Jesus Christ our Lord. *Amen.*

V. O Lord, open thou our lips.

R. And our mouth shall show forth thy praise.

V. O God, make speed to save us.

R. O Lord, make haste to help us.

All standing

V. Glory be to the Father, and to the Son: and to the Holy Ghost;

R. As it was in the beginning, is now, and ever shall be: world without end. Amen.

V. Praise ye the Lord.

R. The Lord's Name be praised.

Psalm CXI

Confitebor tibi

I will give thanks unto the Lord with my whole heart: secretly among the faithful, and in the congregation.

The works of the Lord are great: sought out of all them that have pleasure therein.

His work is worthy to be praised, and had in honour: and his righteousness endureth for ever.

The merciful and gracious Lord hath so done his marvellous works: that they ought to be had in remembrance.

He hath given meat unto them that fear him: he shall ever be mindful of his covenant.

He hath showed his people the power of his works; that he may give them the heritage of the heathen.

The works of his hands are verity and judgment: all his commandments are true.

They stand fast for ever and ever: and are done in truth and equity.

He sent redemption unto his people: he hath commanded his covenant for ever; holy and reverend is his Name.

The fear of the Lord is the beginning of wisdom: a good understanding have all they that do thereafter; the praise of it endureth for ever.

Glory be to the Father, and to the Son: and to the Holy Ghost;

As it was in the beginning, is now, and ever shall be: world without end. *Amen.*

The Lesson

St. Matthew VI, 19-34

Anthem

Let thy merciful ears, O Lord, be open unto the prayers of thy humble servants; and that they may obtain their petitions make them to ask such things as shall please thee; through Jesus Christ our Lord. Amen.

Thomas Weelkes (c. 1574-1623)   *Book of Common Prayer*

Let us pray.

O Lord, who hast set before us the great hope that thy kingdom shall come on earth, as it is in heaven, make us ever ready to thank thee for the signs of its dawning.

For the work of thy Spirit within and beyond the bounds of thy visible Church,

     We thank thee, O Lord.

For the work of thy spirit in the history of the world, through peaceful advance, and through pain and tumult,

> *We thank thee, O Lord.*

For all thou art and ever hast been to us and all believers, and for the sure and certain hope of thy continued help,

> *We thank thee, O Lord.*

O God, who has taught us to live in the cities of this world as knowing our citizenship to be in heaven: guide, we pray thee, with thy heavenly wisdom, all who are in positions of responsibility and trust; that they may keep ever before their eyes the vision of the heavenly kingdom; for the sake of Jesus Christ our Lord. *Amen.*

Almighty God, who by thy Son Jesus Christ hast taught us to seek first thy kingdom and righteousness: take from us, we beseech thee, the spirit of covetousness, and give us the spirit of service; so that none may suffer want, but each according to his need may share in thy wealth; through Jesus Christ our Lord. *Amen.*

Eternal God, in whose perfect kingdom no sword is drawn but the sword of righteousness, and no strength known but the strength of love: so mightily shed abroad thy Spirit, that all peoples may be gathered under one banner of the Prince of Peace, as children of one God and Father of all, to whom be dominion and glory, now and for ever. *Amen.*

May the Lord bless us all, preserve us from every evil, and bring us to everlasting life. *Amen.*

Hymn

Teach me, my God and King,
In all things thee to see;
And what I do in anything
To do it as for thee.

A man that looks on glass,
On it may stay his eye;
Or, if he pleaseth, through it pass,
And then the heaven espy.

All may of thee partake;
Nothing can be so mean
Which, with this tincture, *For thy sake,*
Will not grow bright and clean.

A servant with this clause
Makes drudgery divine;
Who sweeps a room, as for thy laws,
    Makes that and the action fine.

This is the famous stone
    That turneth all to gold;
For that which God doth touch and own
    Cannot for less be told.

Harmonischer Liederschatz, 1738   *George Herbert* (1593-1632)

The Sermon

The sermon was delivered by the Very Reverend Alan Campbell Don, K.C.V.O., D.D., the Dean of Westminster, who took as his text St. Matthew VI, verse 33: 'But seek ye first the kingdom of God, and his righteousness; and all these things shall be added unto you'.

THE DEAN said:

It is always comforting to me to think how very human Our Lord's disciples were. In due course through their companionship with Jesus they became changed men. They were converted, all except Judas Iscariot, but to start with they were much like the rest of us—very ordinary men.

Think, for example, of the two brothers, James and John, the sons of Zebedee. They were young enthusiasts—hot-heads perhaps—'sons of thunder' Our Lord called them. Once they had become convinced that Jesus was the Messiah, the Christ, they kept thinking about the good times coming, for they had heard tell of the glory of the Messianic kingdom that was to be and of the Messianic banquet that was to usher in the golden age for Israel. So they came one day to Jesus and tried to stake a claim for their share, and more than their share, of the benefits that would fall to the lot of the followers of the Messiah. 'Grant unto us', they naïvely said, 'that we may sit one on thy right hand and one on thy left in thy glory'. No wonder that they were taken aback when Jesus told them in effect that they did not know what they were talking about. 'Ye know not what ye ask' he said. 'You do not understand the kind of Messiah I am or the nature of the kingdom that I have come to found, nor do you grasp the conditions that must be fulfilled if you are to have any share in it. Are ye able to drink the cup that I drink of, or be baptised with the baptism that I am baptised with? That is what I want to know.' 'Like the Gentiles,' he said, 'you think that greatness consists of getting something for yourselves in the way of money or power or authority over other people, but you have yet to learn that God thinks otherwise. Whosoever will become great among you shall be your minister, and whosoever will be first among you shall be servant of all. When you have grasped that truth you will begin to understand what the kingdom, the reign of God, really means and the conditions that must be

SIR HAROLD GIBSON HOWITT, G.B.E., D.S.O., M.C., F.C.A.
President of the Congress

fulfilled by those who would hasten its coming, for the kingdom of God is within you.'

What Our Lord wanted to impress upon his disciples was that God's kingdom is the product of spiritual forces operating within the hearts of men and women, or, as St. Paul says, 'The kingdom of God is not eating or drinking, but righteousness and peace and joy in the Holy Ghost'.

If Our Lord's original disciples in the first century had to be taught to think less materialistically and not to worry overmuch about secondary things, may it not be so with us today? Let us by all means dream dreams and see visions of a better world, but what right have any of us to anticipate the coming of a golden age or the building of a better England or a better world except on the terms and the conditions laid down by Our Lord 1,900 years ago? 'Seek ye first the kingdom of God, and his righteousness' and then—and not till then—all the other things will be added unto you.

We sing about building Jerusalem in England's green and pleasant land but we are apt to forget what Blake had in mind when he penned those familiar words. He was thinking of the Holy City, the new Jerusalem, of which we read in the Book of Revelation. This Jerusalem of which Blake sang was no mere human structure devised and planned in the brains of politicians and economists and reproduced in a series of reports and blueprints. What Blake saw was the Holy City coming down out of Heaven from God. It was God's creation, not man's.

Similarly, the Jerusalem of our dreams, a world-wide society of peace-loving peoples, cannot be built of bricks and mortar or of any material things. It can only be built of living stones; that is, of men and women whose minds are akin to the mind of Christ, whose standards are his standards and who find their perfect freedom in the service of God and in obedience to his righteous laws.

That, I submit, is one of the truths which the bitter experience of the past few decades has brought home to the consciousness of thinking people in many parts of the world—the importance of the moral and spiritual factor in every department of life. In these post-war days it is becoming increasingly clear that religion and the moral standards that go with it, so far from being a private affair between the individual and God, are a public concern of the most far-reaching importance. For what will determine the future of this and every other country is not how much money we get per day or how many hours we work per week, nor yet how many gadgets we are provided with in order to make life easy and comfortable; what will determine the future is the character of men and women, that is to say, how people like ourselves behave and what spirit and outlook we manifest in the ordinary activities of daily life.

In the great profession to which you belong you are brought into close contact with a large variety of people of one sort or another, and I do not doubt that you would agree with what that great accountant, Lord Plender, once said when speaking at a dinner in the Mansion House about the City of London. 'What is the key,' he said, 'to the position which the City holds? Not entirely its command of money, its stock of gold and its unequalled resources; not entirely its position as a great shipping, railway and dis-tributing centre; not entirely its embrace of banking, commercial and financial institutions; but, more than anything else, its credit, its honouring of obligations, its fulfilment of contracts.' 'But credit,' he added, 'is not a flower that blossoms untended. It has to be watched, it has to be shielded from the blighting winds and storms. And this great asset, the greatest that the City can have, is but another word for character, the highest virtue man can possess and without which little else matters.'

What Lord Plender said so truly about the City of London is true every-where. We are living in an age of revolution, the most disturbing feature of which is the prevailing sense of insecurity. This arises from the fact that immense power has been seized in the modern world by men who openly repudiate the Christian God and the Christian way of life. They dismiss the idea that there are any absolute standards of right and wrong based upon the laws of God as Sovereign Ruler of this universe, for they do not believe in God and have, therefore, no fixed standards except those dictated by the expediency of the moment. So long as this materialistic philosophy prevails over large areas of the world, mutual trust and confidence is impossible and the prevailing sense of insecurity will continue to bedevil our lives and frustrate our hopes.

Religion is, then, as I have said, a concern of the utmost public import-ance, for it matters supremely how men think and how they act, and experi-ence proves that what we are and what we do depends in the long run upon what we believe about God and about man. Leave God out of account, treat him as an optional extra or a mere appendix who has nothing to do with politics or industry or social life and the result will be—indeed, the result has already been—the chaos and confusion with which we are surrounded today.

Your presence here in this ancient place of worship is, if I am not mistaken, an indication that you are keenly alive to the vital importance of these intangible things, the things of the spirit which determine the quality of all human life and on which the whole future of mankind depends. Therefore, 'Seek ye first the kingdom of God, and his righteousness', and all these other things shall be added unto you.

Hymn

Thy Kingdom come! on bended knee
   The passing ages pray;
And faithful souls have yearned to see
   On earth that Kingdom's day:

But the slow watches of the night
   Not less to God belong;
And for the everlasting right
   The silent stars are strong.

And lo, already on the hills
  The flags of dawn appear;
Gird up your loins, ye prophet souls,
  Proclaim the day is near:

The day in whose clear-shining light
  All wrong shall stand revealed,
When justice shall be throned in might,
  And every hurt be healed;

When knowledge, hand in hand with peace,
  Shall walk the earth abroad:
The day of perfect righteousness,
  The promised day of God.

Hymns and Sacred Poems   *Frederick Lucian Hosmer*
(Dublin, 1749)   (1840-1929)

A General Thanksgiving

Almighty God, Father of all mercies, We thine unworthy servants do give thee most humble and hearty thanks For all thy goodness and loving-kindness To us, and to all men; We bless thee for our creation, preservation, and all the blessings of this life; But above all, for thine inestimable love In the redemption of the world by our Lord Jesus Christ; For the means of grace, And for the hope of glory. And, we beseech thee, give us that due sense of all thy mercies, That our hearts may be unfeignedly thankful, And that we shew forth thy praise, Not only with our lips, but in our lives; By giving up ourselves to thy service, And by walking before thee in holiness and righteousness all our days; through Jesus Christ our Lord, to whom with thee and the Holy Ghost be all honour and glory, world without end. Amen.

The Blessing

B

SERVICE IN WESTMINSTER CATHEDRAL

By kind permission of the Very Reverend Monsignor C. Collingwood, Administrator of Westminster Cathedral, a service was held in the Cathedral at 10.30 a.m. on Monday, 16th June. The mass was celebrated by Father Pilkington assisted by Father Wright (Deacon) and Father Aylward (Subdeacon).

ORDER OF SERVICE
Monday within the Octave of the Feast of Corpus Christi

Introit
Psalm lxxx, 17

Full ears of wheat are the nourishment he gives them, and honey dripping from the rock to their hearts' content, alleluia, alleluia, alleluia.

Rejoice we all in honour of the God who aids us: cry out with gladness to the God of Israel.

Glory be to the Father, and to the Son, and to the Holy Ghost. As it was in the beginning, is now, and ever shall be, world without end. Amen.

Collect
Let us pray.

God, who in this wonderful sacrament hast left us a memorial of thy passion enable us, we pray thee, so to venerate the sacred mysteries of thy Body and Blood that we may constantly feel in our lives the effects of thy redemption: thou who art God, living and reigning with God the Father, in the unity of the Holy Spirit, for ever and ever. Amen.

Epistle
1 Corinthians xi, 23-29

Brethren: The tradition which I received from the Lord, and handed on to you, is that the Lord Jesus, on the night when he was being betrayed, took bread, and gave thanks, and broke it, and said, Take, eat; this is my body, given up for you. Do this for a commemoration of me. And so with the cup, when the supper was ended. This cup, he said, is the new testament, in my blood. Do this whenever you drink it, for a commemoration of me. So it is the Lord's death that you are heralding, whenever you eat this bread and drink this cup, until he comes; and therefore, if anyone eats this bread or drinks this cup of the Lord unworthily, he will be held to account for the Lord's body and blood. A man must examine himself first, and then eat of that bread and drink of that cup; he is eating and drinking damnation to himself if he eats and drinks unworthily, not recognising the Lord's body for what it is.

Gradual

Psalm cxliv, 15-16

Lord, all creatures raise their eyes to thee, and thou grantest them, in due time, their nourishment. Thou art ready to open thy hand and fill with thy blessing all that lives.

Alleluia, alleluia.

John vi, 56-57

My flesh is real food, my blood is real drink; he who eats my flesh and drinks my blood, lives continually in me, and I in him.

Sequence

Laud, O Sion, thy Salvation,
Laud, with hymns of exaltation,
Christ, thy King, and Shepherd true;
Bring Him all the praise thou knowest;
He is more than thou bestowest;
Never canst thou reach His due.

Special theme for glad thanksgiving
Is the Living and Life-giving
Bread, to-day before thee set;
From His hands of old partaken,
As we know by faith unshaken,
Where the twelve at supper met.

Full and clear ring out thy chanting,
Joy nor sweetest grace be wanting,
From thy heart let praises burst:
For to-day the Feast is holden
When the Institution olden
Of that Supper is rehearsed.

Here the new law's new oblation,
By the new King's revelation,
Ends the form of ancient rite;
Now the new the old effaces,
Truth away the shadow chases,
Light dispels the gloom of night.

What He did, at supper seated,
Christ ordained to be repeated,
His Memorial ne'er to cease;
And His rule for guidance taking,
Bread and Wine we hallow, making
Thus our Sacrifice of peace.

Wondrous truth by Christians learned,
Bread into His Flesh is turned,
Into precious Blood the Wine.
Sight hath failed, nor thought conceiveth;
But a dauntless faith believeth,
Resting on a Power Divine.

Here beneath these signs are hidden
Priceless things, to sense forbidden:
Signs, not things, are all we see;
Flesh from bread, and Blood from wine,
Yet is Christ in either sign,
All entire confess'd to be.

Whoso of this Food partaketh
Rendeth not the Lord, nor breaketh;
Christ is whole to all that taste;
Thousands are, as one, receivers:
One, as thousands of believers,
Eats of Him who cannot waste.

Bad and good the Feast are sharing:
O what diverse dooms preparing,
Endless death or endless life!
Life to these, to those damnation:
See how like participation
Is with unlike issues rife.

When the Sacrament is broken,
Doubt not, but believe 'tis spoken,
That each severed outward token
Doth the very Whole contain,
Naught the precious Gift divideth,
Breaking but the sign betideth,
Jesus still the same abideth,
Still unbroken doth remain.

Lo, the Angels' Food is given
To the pilgrim who hath striven;
See the children's Bread from Heaven
Which on dogs may ne'er be spent:
Truth the ancient types fulfilling,
Isaac bound a victim willing:
Paschal Lamb its Life-Blood spilling:
Manna to the Fathers sent.

Very Bread, Good Shepherd tend us,
Jesu, of Thy love befriend us;
Thou refresh us, Thou defend us,
Thine eternal goodness send us.
In the Land of life to see:

Thou who all things canst and knowest,
Who on earth such Food bestowest,
Grant us with Thy saints, though lowest,
Where the Heavenly Feast Thou showest,
Fellow-heirs and guests to be. Amen.

Gospel
John vi, 56-59

At this time: Jesus said to the Jewish crowd: My flesh is real food, my blood is real drink. He who eats my flesh, and drinks my blood, lives continually in me, and I in him. As I live because of the Father, the living Father who has sent me, so he who eats me will live, in his turn, because of me. Such is the bread which has come down from heaven; it is not as it was with your fathers, who ate manna and died none the less; the man who eats this bread will live eternally.

Offertory
Leviticus xxi, 6

It is for the priests of the Lord to offer their God incense and consecrated loaves: they are men set apart for God, and must never bring reproach upon his name, alleluia.

Secret

Lord, be gracious to thy Church, we pray thee, and grant her those gifts of unity and peace of which our offerings here are symbols: through our Lord Jesus Christ, thy Son, who is God, living and reigning with Thee, in the unity of the Holy Spirit, for ever and ever. Amen.

Communion
1 Corinthians xi, 26-27

It is the Lord's death that you are heralding whenever you eat this bread and drink this cup, until He comes; and therefore, if anyone eats this bread and drinks this cup of the Lord unworthily, he will be held to account for the Lord's body and blood, alleluia.

Postcommunion
Let us pray

Grant us, Lord, we beseech Thee, through all eternity that enjoyment of Thy godhead which is foreshadowed in this life by our partaking of thy precious body and blood: Thou who art God, living and reigning with God the Father, in the unity of the Holy Spirit, for ever and ever. Amen.

OPENING OF THE CONGRESS

The President of the Congress, Sir Harold Gibson Howitt, G.B.E., D.S.O., M.C., F.C.A., was introduced by Sir David Allan Hay, K.B.E., C.A., President of The Institute of Chartered Accountants of Scotland.

SIR DAVID ALLAN HAY:

The first on the list in your programmes of the sponsoring bodies of accountants who have undertaken the organisation of the Congress is The Institute of Chartered Accountants of Scotland, which was incorporated by a Royal Charter in 1854 and is not only the oldest incorporated body of accountants in Britain but is the oldest existing incorporation of accountants in the world.

The duty and privilege which has been assigned to me today as President of this Scottish Institute is to call upon the President of the Congress, Sir Harold Howitt, a very distinguished member of The Institute of Chartered Accountants in England and Wales, to take the chair and to address a message of welcome to the delegates and visitors and their ladies.

THE PRESIDENT:

Thank you, Sir David, and all of you for the warmth of the introduction. During the current week I shall try to deserve it.

Before I deliver my opening remarks I should like to have the pleasure of introducing you to each other. First, I propose to introduce to the body of the hall certain of us on the platform, these being the Vice-President of the Congress, the Presidents of the seven sponsoring bodies, the Chairman and the Vice-Chairman of the Council of Congress, the Secretary, the Chief Executive Officer and the Honorary Public Relations Officer.

I also want to introduce the members of the sponsoring bodies to our delegates and visitors and their ladies from overseas. There are a large number from overseas. There are over one hundred accountancy bodies represented and there are about thirty countries, and it would be quite impossible to ask each delegation to stand in turn and be welcomed in the way we should like. If I did that, the warmth of the welcome we wish to give them might vary inversely with the length of the proceedings and not in relation to the importance of the delegation concerned.

I shall ask all overseas delegates, visitors and their ladies to stand and be welcomed by the members of the sponsoring bodies. It is impossible to mention people individually. I should like to mention the names of the Presidents of the various accountancy bodies the world over who are represented here but it is impossible. For example, we have with us from the United States of America no fewer than eight Past Presidents, as well as the present holder of that office.

I should also like to introduce you to the members of the sponsoring bodies. We have received various messages of greeting, and some people have expressed a desire to get up and present them here, but that also, in view of the numbers involved, is quite impossible. Therefore, at the end I shall ask the members of the sponsoring bodies, with their ladies, to stand and accept the greetings which are being offered by those who come from overseas.

I should like to present to you from the platform Mr. C. Percy Barrowcliff, F.S.A.A., Vice-President of the Congress and President of The Society of Incorporated Accountants and Auditors; Sir David Allan Hay, K.B.E., C.A., President of The Institute of Chartered Accountants of Scotland; Mr. T. B. Robson, M.B.E., M.A., F.C.A., President of The Institute of Chartered Accountants in England and Wales; Mr. H. E. A. Addy, F.C.A., F.S.A.A., President of The Institute of Chartered Accountants in Ireland; the Rt. Hon. Lord Latham of Hendon, F.A.C.C.A., President of The Association of Certified and Corporate Accountants; Mr. C. H. Pollard, O.B.E., F.S.A.A., F.I.M.T.A., President of The Institute of Municipal Treasurers and Accountants; Mr. S. C. Tyrrell, F.C.W.A., President of The Institute of Cost and Works Accountants; Mr. H. Garton Ash, O.B.E., M.C., F.C.A., Chairman of the Council of Congress; Mr. A. Stuart Allen, F.S.A.A., Vice-Chairman of the Council of Congress; Mr. Alan S. MacIver, M.C., B.A., Secretary; Brigadier S. O. Jones, O.B.E., M.C., Chief Executive Officer; and Mr. Derek du Pré, Honorary Public Relations Officer.

At the invitation of the President, first delegates and visitors and their ladies from abroad stood and were welcomed with applause, and then the members of the sponsoring bodies and their ladies stood and were greeted with applause.

OPENING ADDRESS BY THE PRESIDENT

It is my great privilege on behalf of the sponsoring bodies of qualified accountants in Great Britain and Ireland to welcome you all to this International Congress. Some of you have come great distances—some from foreign parts and some from the British Commonwealth overseas; some by yourselves and some with your families and friends; and there are many of you, members and students of the sponsoring bodies, who have come partly on your own account but also, I am sure, with intent to help in the welcome we offer to our visitors.

It may, then, be of interest to you to know, however roughly, the numbers and categories of those attending the Congress. Judged by the tickets issued, we are a total of 2,510 made up as follows: sponsoring bodies 1,450 members, of whom 494 are ladies and friends; Commonwealth accountancy bodies overseas 196 members, of whom 64 are ladies and friends; other accountancy bodies overseas 668 members, of whom 196 are ladies and friends; and there are also 196 students.

There are representatives from 10 territories of the British Commonwealth and from 23 other countries. I should be rash indeed if I attempted to assess

Photo Annan, Glasgow

SIR DAVID ALLAN HAY, K.B.E., C.A.
President of The Institute of Chartered Accountants of Scotland

the antiquity or the relative size or importance of the various accountancy bodies here represented. Suffice it to say that so far as the sponsoring bodies are concerned, as you have just heard from Sir David, our oldest is the Institute of Chartered Accountants of Scotland, whose earliest Charter dates from 1854. We are, however, brought up in this country to believe that the first association of accountants of which a record exists was founded at Venice in 1581 but at that point one may get controversial, so I will not pursue that theme further. At any rate, in our present form we are a comparatively young profession.

I wish to stress that it is the most earnest desire of all the sponsoring bodies that our visitors shall be made to feel completely at home. We have endeavoured to ensure this by our various arrangements and personal contacts, but should anyone at any time wish for assistance or for company I hope he or she will not hesitate to approach me or any member of our various committees. I emphasise this as my opening remark so that in case any of our plans miscarry you may know that both remedy and will to welcome are available.

This is the sixth of these International Congresses, and it is perhaps interesting to recall where and when the others were held. The first was in 1904 at St. Louis, the second was in 1926 at Amsterdam, the third was in 1929 at New York, the fourth was in 1933 at London and the fifth was in 1938 at Berlin.

I have no doubt that some here today have attended several of these earlier Congresses. I have myself read papers at two of them and know, therefore, from experience how much we are indebted to all those who have taken the trouble to prepare papers for our edification this week. It is a much easier and much more pleasurable task to act as President.

I cannot hope to refer by name to all our distinguished visitors and it would be invidious to try. You would, however, I am sure, expect me to give a special welcome to anyone who attended the first Congress. I know of only one such, though if there are others I should like to be informed. We are proud indeed to have with us Mr. G. O. May who was present and took a leading part in 1904—nearly fifty years ago—both in the organisation of the Congress and in the reading of a paper prepared by one of his partners. Mr. May is well known to accountants the world over, and, I am glad to say, a frequent visitor to his old homeland. We much appreciate the compliment he pays us in honouring us with his presence. Perhaps Mr. May would stand up and take a bow.

Having opened our Congress with services at Westminster, the remaining functions may be divided broadly into those of a social and those of an educational nature. He would be a bold man who would venture to assess the relative values of each but in the presence of the ladies who have been good enough to join us, it is perhaps fitting that I should first mention the social engagements. I very much hope you will enjoy all the arrangements which have been made and I assure you that it is our intention and hope that you should take back with you the happiest of memories.

On the educational side, the selection of papers is designed in order to collect ideas on some of the pressing subjects of the day. I suppose each succeeding generation thinks it has been born to face the most difficult era in history and perhaps, if progress is to mean something more than taking life more easily, this is natural and is to be expected. It is certainly true of accountancy which, indeed, would not be much of a profession if this were not the case.

Apart, however, from the formal conferences, at which, admittedly, it is difficult to arrive at agreed conclusions, I hope that much use may be made of this week for private discussions—not only on the subjects covered by the papers, but on others, and also on the relationship of accountancy bodies with each other the world over. It is common knowledge, and it is natural, that on occasion there should in all countries be a conflict between the interests of nationals and of those from overseas. If we can do anything during this Congress or afterwards to resolve our respective problems I am quite sure the sponsoring bodies would be very happy to try. I am also sure I can speak for them in saying that we shall welcome visits by any of you to our various headquarter buildings where contact with our chief executives will provide that personal touch which so often helps in subsequent discussions. So far as concerns this country, whilst the sponsoring bodies are, of course, bound by the terms of their various documents of incorporation as to admission to their own membership, there is no restriction against those from overseas in respect of practice or employment; and only in regard to the audit of certain companies is there the statutory requirement that the auditor in question shall have proper qualification such as membership of a responsible overseas body.

I have run my eye over the proceedings of the earlier Congresses and cannot help reflecting how much the scene has changed even within the limited span of life which they cover. In 1904 we lived in comparatively stable times. We all had our upheavals, no doubt, but we were able to take them in our strides and recover from them. They were more local than world-wide. They left us able, and indeed obliged, to look after our own destinies and we worked to simple and well-understood economic rules. Due largely to the advent of wars, to the march of science and to the ease and speed of communication, all this is changed and not in all respects for the better.

If I were to attempt to review the special features facing accountants gathered for the present Congress, I would emphasise the following points. First, although all countries represented here today have, in varying degrees, suffered from changes in the value of money, we have not yet reached agreement as to how this problem is best dealt with in periodical accounting statements. Secondly, although taxation is no new subject, it is today so heavy in most countries that the State is, in effect, the major partner in enterprise; and it is probably true to say that without the help of the professional accountant and the trust imposed in him, the State revenues could not be raised, and Government, therefore, could not function. Thirdly, the difficulty of raising or retaining capital for development or even for existence is materially enhanced by these two factors. Fourthly, whereas the accountant in public practice has to direct his thoughts and certainly his certificates primarily to the past and to the present, the professional accountant who has entered the commercial field, and indeed the practising accountant who helps him therein, thinks even more of the future.

It will not have escaped your notice that the selection of papers for this Congress has been made with these special features of the accountant's responsibilities chiefly in mind. I hope that the papers so carefully prepared and the discussions on them will contribute materially to a clarification of the problems involved. As a background—perhaps even as a relaxation—I commend to your attention the historical exhibition of books on accountancy which has kindly been arranged by the City authorities at Guildhall.

I feel, at this stage, I should perhaps offer a word of apology that, for reasons beyond the control of the Congress staff, the papers and programmes did not in all cases reach overseas delegates and visitors before they left their homes. Even if this may have enabled them the more to enjoy their journeys, I realise it may have imposed on them an added burden of reading on arrival here.

Progress there must be in the help given to management, in mechanisation and other improvements in accounting technique, in methods of audit and in the form of presentation of final accounts, and yet the twin purpose of these final accounts remains the same as it has always been, namely, to show whether and to what extent a surplus or a deficit has accrued over a period of time, and to show the financial position at the end of that time. We claim no magic for our art. It is as old as the hills and both nations and individuals are in the long run subject to its inexorable laws. If I may use an expression of our friends from France, and if they will excuse my pro- nunciation, '*Plus ça change, plus c'est la mê.ne chose*'.

But it is not quite so easy as that, for although, as we say in this country, the object of accounts is to present a true and fair view, different people have different views as to what is 'true and fair', and the ends they seek to achieve are often conflicting. We are, in consequence, subjected to requests that accounts should serve many purposes, perfectly legitimate in them- selves, but not always capable of being reflected in the same document. I refer to requests as diversified as those from proprietors, temporary investors, wage earners, creditors, economists, tax collectors and even politicians; and I am not forgetting the special requirements of government accounting, whether central or municipal. It is not surprising that a single form of accounts cannot stand the stresses involved in attempting to satisfy all these interests. The difficulty has recently become much accentuated by inflation and high taxation. I must not, however, at this stage anticipate the discussions which will arise on these contentious issues.

Apart from attempting to hold the balance fairly between contemporary interests such as I have mentioned above, correct accounts should have also in mind their effect on succeeding generations. I mention this because in periods of intense financial strain such as we are at present experiencing there is a risk of taking the easy course and of passing on to posterity liabilities against which we ought ourselves to provide. I refer in particular to pension obligations which tend to be taken on light-heartedly, whether by governments or individuals, and with no real assurance that posterity will foot the bill. On the other hand, it may be said that this generation, having borne the cost of two wars, is being too kind to the future in endeavouring to replace its assets at inflated costs out of resources which might otherwise have been distributable. Accountants must endeavour to apply sound and impartial judgment to such issues and not to be influenced by political considerations one way or the other.

I doubt if any other profession has increased numerically as ours has done over the last half century. I hope the quality of our work has kept pace with our growing numbers and, though it is not for us to appraise ourselves in such a matter, it is perhaps a fair test to mention that the demand for our services has never been so great. The demand comes for professional services and also for the supply of our members for government, industrial and financial appointments. It is the privilege of the profession to supply members for these specialised demands, and in turn to benefit from the research and professional skill which they promote in those surroundings. One of the main objectives of a Congress such as this is to stimulate the search for an even higher technique in all branches of the accountant's work.

Finally, I cannot help recalling that the last Congress at Berlin was held almost on the eve of war. It is sad to reflect that, although the tragedies of two world wars are within the memories of most of us, we do not even yet seem to have learnt our lesson. Is it too much to hope that a gathering such as this, of peoples from many countries exchanging ideas in common, and understanding each other's points of view, even when we differ, may be some small contribution to that peace and fellowship which we all so ardently desire? Is it presumption further to hope that qualified accountants throughout the world should have a material influence towards right thinking on all those financial and economic problems which are normally at the root of international disputes and wars? If such hopes are even partially justified, a Congress of this nature must be abundantly worth while, quite apart from any progress it may achieve in the technique of accountancy and quite apart from the pleasure it gives the sponsoring bodies to meet our friends from overseas.

TUESDAY, 17th JUNE, 1952

FIRST SESSION

FLUCTUATING PRICE LEVELS IN RELATION TO ACCOUNTS

FLUCTUATING PRICE LEVELS IN RELATION TO ACCOUNTS

by

C. PERCY BARROWCLIFF, F.S.A.A.
Society of Incorporated Accountants and Auditors

SYNOPSIS

I The monetary unit as the basis of accounting measurements.

II Price Levels, Industrial Profits and Wages:

(*a*) Wholesale price level indices from 1880 to 1951.

(*b*) Profit Indices from 1908 to 1951.

(*c*) Wages Indices from 1880 to 1951.

(*d*) The relation between profits and wages and their contribution to National Income.

(*e*) Indices of Replacement Costs.

III Is the fluctuating price level of sufficient permanency and effect to disturb current accountancy conventions?

IV Effect of fluctuating price levels on:

(*a*) Profit ascertainment.

(*b*) Fixed assets.

(*c*) Current assets.

(*d*) Asset and liability claims.

V Types of businesses affected by fluctuating price levels.

VI What are business profits?

(*a*) The Accountant's view.

(*b*) The Economist's view.

(*c*) The Lawyer's view.

(*d*) The Business Man's view.

VII British accounting views on changing price levels.

VIII The effect of fluctuating price levels on the value of long-term trends.

IX Special considerations affecting Nationalised Undertakings.

X Special considerations affecting Local Authorities.

XI Open questions:

(*a*) Is there a satisfactory alternative basis to the monetary unit for accounts?

    (b) How should fixed assets be treated in the accounts?
        (1) Stated at original costs or revalued annually.
        (2) Depreciated on the principle of:
            (a) original cost;
            (b) current value.
        (3) Where improved replacement takes place at lower *real* cost owing to technical development.
    (c) Should securities be taken into account on the basis of current values?
    (d) Can the existing accountancy basis of measuring business profits be varied in any way?
    (e) What practical means are available to accountants to enable them to measure change in asset values?
    (f) What are proper standards of accounting comparisons?

XII Conclusions.

INTRODUCTION

In submitting this paper I desire to make it clear that all the views expressed are personal views and do not necessarily represent the opinions of the Council of The Society of Incorporated Accountants and Auditors.

I am deeply conscious of the shortcomings and imperfections of the paper, but if it stimulates and contributes to thought on this important question, it will have achieved its purpose. It is my view that the accountancy profession must make up its mind, one way or the other, on the validity of existing conventions to meet present conditions. It may well be that before this paper is discussed in June, some pronouncement may have been made by the British accountancy profession.

I am greatly indebted to my colleague, Mr. F. Sewell Bray, who is Senior Nuffield Research Fellow in the Department of Applied Economics, University of Cambridge, for his invaluable support and collaboration in the preparation of this paper. Two other of my colleagues on the Council of the Society have kindly contributed special sections of the paper, Mr. L. C. Hawkins, Member of the London Transport Executive, Section IX, and Mr. J. Ainsworth, City Treasurer of Liverpool, Section X.

I also acknowledge with thanks the assistance of Mr. Leo T. Little, Lecturer in Economics, University College of the South West, Exeter, and Editor of *Accountancy*, in the preparation of the tables in Section II, and for the contribution 'The Economist's View' of 'What are Business Profits?' Similarly, my thanks to Mr. T. W. South, M.A., Barrister-at-Law, for his contribution 'The Lawyer's View' in the same section.

I. THE MONETARY UNIT AS THE BASIS OF
ACCOUNTING MEASUREMENTS

At the very outset of this paper it appears necessary to plunge into a quasi-philosophical discussion which has its roots in what is more or less a first principle of civilised economic society. I refer to the adoption of the monetary unit as the basis for accounting measurements. Most of us, at one time or another, have been schooled in concepts which clearly perceive the convenience of the monetary unit as a medium of exchange, a standard of value, and so on. It is not difficult to see the cumbrous inconveniences associated with even limited systems of barter exchange. Indeed, a review of economic history suggests that the early adoption of money as a medium of exchange marked a distinct advance in the evolution of economic society.

As soon as money became the medium of exchange, the price of any one good or service was implicitly representative of its value in exchange for other goods and services; goods or services commanded goods or services by reference to a common measure. The monetary unit was both the scale and the earnest which very quickly endeared itself to recorders of transactions as a means of adding and subtracting unlike things. But these were not the days of imputed transactions and few were found to question the standard of value. Money, although useful as a common measure, was itself a real and relatively scarce commodity and in this way one reality was exchanged for another. Only with the progress of the ages did the measure begin to lose its reality and become a symbol. As a veiler of intrinsic worth the symbol has turned out to be a provoker of trouble.

In this context Adam Smith saw the trend of events when he said that

'money has become in all civilised nations the universal instrument of commerce, by the intervention of which goods of all kinds are bought and sold, or exchanged for one another'.[1]

It is of interest to note the words 'civilised' and 'universal'. Freedom to exchange goods and services as welfare dictates is surely a mark of civilised society. What could be more natural than that the common unit of exchange should serve as the measure to indicate a rise or decline in entity wealth? It was obvious that values would come to be measured in terms of quantities of monetary units. Inventories of wealth valued in such a manner, and available either for consumption utilisation or accumulation, were both serviceable and essential. They seemed to indicate a power of economic survival, and if only the common unit of measure was itself a commodity stable in value and available in supply adequate to the volume of transactions, all would be well. As

[1] *The Wealth of Nations*, Everyman Edition, Vol. I, page 24.

is well known, there was a commodity at hand which seemed to approximate to this ideal, but its universal use in times of rapid development
imposed too great a strain, and fiats of government have minimised its
use. Thus, the commodity gave place to the symbol.

The civilised world has always been aware that

'a commodity which is itself continually varying in its own value, can
never be an accurate measure of the value of other commodities'.[1]

How much more so then when the symbol takes pride of place over the
commodity. Adam Smith thought that

'at the same time and place the real and the nominal price of all commodities
are exactly in proportion to one another. . . . At the same time and place,
therefore, money is the exact measure of the real exchangeable value of all
commodities.'[2]

But he was most careful to add that this proposition held 'at the same
time and place only'.

Money has continued to regulate the *business* of everyday life. The
recording function of accounting received a pronounced stimulus with
the advent of the merchant, and the whole spirit of modern attachment
to monetary accounting has its origin in this source. To quote once
more from Adam Smith:

'Though at distant places, there is no regular proportion between the
real and the money price of commodities, yet the merchant who carries
goods from the one to the other has nothing to consider but their money
price.'

And again,

'As it is the nominal or money price of goods, therefore, which finally
determines the prudence or imprudence of all purchases and sales, and
thereby regulates almost the whole business of common life in which
price is concerned, we cannot wonder that it should have been so much
more attended to than the real price.'[3]

There appears to be little reason to dissent from the content of these
quotations. Small wonder, then, that money is the unit of record, and
accounting measurement largely a process of counting.

There is another and more fundamental reason why the monetary
unit is at the very heart of accounting practice. It rests in the fact that,
at bottom, the practice of accounting is firmly wedded to economic
concepts of income and wealth. Accounting in all its forms is always
concerned with measurements of income and wealth. For this purpose
it must have a unit of value as a standard of reference in order to add

[1] Op. cit., page 28.
[2] Op. cit., page 32.
[3] Op. cit., page 33.

up and take away unlike things, a situation inherent in those problems which are associated with income and wealth calculations.

Measurement presupposes universality in diversity; only thus can we symbolise unlike transactions. But the very moment a symbol is found to achieve this very necessary function, critics are not wanting to emphasise the essential difference between the nature of things and their conventional modes of measurement. On the deeper philosophical plane Professor Ritchie has commented thus:

'it is true that measurement is the most powerful of all scientific tools because it gives precision of statement and makes available all the resources of mathematics. Nevertheless, measurement is not the only tool and it cannot be used except on the basis of previous non-metrical notions and operations, which are qualitative, not quantitative.'[1]

In the immediate context of our own pursuit we have had Canning saying that

'if "assets" are different from "liabilities" one cannot be subtracted from the other'.[2]

Or, rather more precisely,

'A numerical difference between two quantities can have a substantive meaning only when the two quantities are homogeneous.'[3]

And yet Canning took the point, and towards the end of his critical analysis of accounting theory we find him concluding that

'in a régime in which the institution of private property and private enterprise and the money and credit economy prevail, a money-valued accounting only may be expected. Values not conveniently and reliably convertible into money equivalents are excluded from modern accounting.'[4]

He might well have added *must* be excluded from modern accounting, for what other common mediator can be found to record, classify and epitomise the exchange of that wide variety of goods and services which constitute the input and output resources of modern economies?

All of us are familiar with a natural reckoning of inputs and outputs. Tons, yards, mileage, hours and such-like units are natural enough, but we can only deal with them *together* in terms of their prices at some defined point in time. We cannot add up tons, yards and hours in one aggregate with any show of meaning, but we can add up the units of money into which they may be converted. Fixed assets are even less susceptible to reckoning in terms of natural units. There have been

[1] A. D. Ritchie, *Reflections on the Philosophy of Sir Arthur Eddington* (Cambridge University Press, 1948), page 33.
[2] *The Economics of Accountancy*, by J. B. Canning (Ronald Press, New York, 1929), page 11.
[3] Op. cit., page 58.
[4] Op. cit., page 315.

schools of thought which have sought to measure all values in terms of the average price of a man-hour of labour, only to be met with the insuperable problem of the relative variability of wage rates for different types of labour. If we could overcome the improbability of invariable labour, no doubt we might attempt a partial accounting in terms of labour units.

The notion of reality underlying incomings and outgoings is both useful and instructive, but we can never get away from the monetary attachments. The financial consequence of money-flows lies too close at home for most of us to ignore it. Current money values determine profitability. Payments for goods and services can only be met out of receipts, whether from goods and services or from borrowing, and relative prices are still a major factor in the economics of substitution. The convenience of money as a unit of measurement assails us from every side, but it has one serious weakness; it is buoyant, flexible and subject to change over time.

NOTES TO TABLE ON FACING PAGE

Col. 2. Statist/Sauerbeck index of wholesale prices converted to base 1938.

Col. 3. Parkinson's index of company profits for 1908–37 converted to base 1937. (*The Economist,* 17th December, 1938.) Cmd. 8203 for profits of companies and public corporations for 1938 and 1946–50, recalculated on base 1938. (*N.B.*—'Profits' includes non-trading revenue.)

Col. 4. Calculated from White Paper on National Income and Expenditure of the United Kingdom, 1946–50. (Cmd. 8203.)

Col. 5. Bowley's *Index of Money Wages* (Wages income since 1860, p. 30, for 1880–1914, recalculated to base 1938). London & Cambridge Economic Service *Bulletin,* Vol. 29, No, 4, November, 1951, for 1919–51.

Col. 6. 1880 and 1913, Pigou, *Wages Statistics and Wage Policy,* Appendix II, p. 40, 1924, from Bowley's *National Income,* pp. 58 and 82, 1938 and 1946 to 1950 calculated from Cmd. 8203.

Col. 7. (*a*) 1875, 1885, 1895, 1900, 1905 and 1914 from Lenfant, 'Great Britain's Capital Formation', *Economia,* Vol. XVIII, No. 70, May, 1951, recalculated to base 1914.

(*b*) 1938–46 calculated from Prest, 'National Income of the United Kingdom', *Economic Journal,* Vol. LVIII, No. 229, March, 1948, p. 55.

(*c*) 1947–50 from Economic Commission of Europe, *Economic Survey of Europe, 1949,* page 236, and *Economic Survey of Europe, 1950,* page 238.

N.B.—(*a*) Is a simple index of capital goods prices (machinery and buildings).

(*b*) is calculated index of depreciation allocations necessary for replacement at current prices of fixed assets (machinery and buildings).

(*c*) is calculated index of machinery and vehicle prices and of building costs.

II. PRICE LEVELS, INDUSTRIAL PROFITS AND WAGES

(Col. 1) Year	(Col. 2) Wholesale Prices 1938=100	(Col. 3) Profits 1937=100 1938=100	(Col. 4) Profits as Percentage of National Income	(Col. 5) Money Wages 1938=100	(Col. 6) Money Wages as Percentage of National Income	(Col. 7) Replacement Costs 1914=100 1938=100	(Col. 8) Year
1880	98			36	37·3	90†	1880
1885	80			37		81	1885
1890	80			42			1890
1895	69			42		78	1895
1900	83			47		92	1900
1905	80			45		93	1905
1908	81	27·3		47			1908
1909	82	28·5		47			1909
1910	87	32·4		47			1910
1911	89	33·7		48			1911
1912	94	37·5		49			1912
1913	94	48·5		50	35·8		1913
1914	94	45·6		50		100*	1914
1915	120	54·7					1915
1916	151	63·6					1916
1917	194	64·1					1917
1918	213	67·4					1918
1919	229	81·6		105			1919
1920	279	89·0		125			1920
1921	172	51·0		137			1921
1922	146	59·2		105			1922
1923	142	66·1		94			1923
1924	154	72·8		96	38·3*		1924
1925	151	78·3		96			1925
1926	139	76·6		96			1926
1927	136	81·1		96			1927
1928	132	82·4		96			1928
1929	127	85·6		95			1929
1930	107	73·0		94			1930
1931	91	53·7		93			1931
1932	88	50·3		92			1932
1933	87	56·6		90			1933
1934	90	67·7		90			1934
1935	92	76·1		91			1935
1936	98	88·1		93			1936
1937	113	100·0*		97			1937
1938	100	100·0	18·6	100	36·8	100	1938
1939	104			101		100	1939
1940	142			112		163	1940
1941	158			122		175	1941
1942	168			131		183	1942
1943	182			138		189	1943
1944	178			146		182	1944
1945	183			154		179	1945
1946	207	193	19·2	167	37·3	180*	1946
1947	256	232	21·1	175	38·8	212	1947
1948	289	248	20·6	188	40·0	229	1948
1949	304	242	19·4	193	40·2	234	1949
1950	360	270	20·2	197	40·0	238	1950
1951 Jan.	450			208			
Feb.	467			209			
Mar.	466			211			
April	473			212			
May	467			212			
June	450			213			
July	438			214			
Aug.	431			214			
Sept.	440			216			
Oct.	436			216			
Nov.	441			—			

* Indicates break in series. † Year 1875. Blank spaces—not available.

III. Is the Fluctuating Price Level of Sufficient Permanency and Effect to Disturb Current Accountancy Conventions?

During the First World War wholesale prices (Sauerbeck) rose from 94 (1938=100) to 213 in 1918, 229 in 1919, and to 279 in 1920. From then, however, wholesale prices started to decline and by 1931 had fallen to 91 ; therefore, despite the increase in wholesale prices occasioned by the First World War, prices gradually returned to a pre-1914 level, and so they continued until 1939. Reviewing the period 1880–1939, there appears to be no reason to question the validity of the assumption that the price level was a fairly constant factor and even when events temporarily caused fluctuation the original price level was restored in due course. The impact of the Second World War in 1939 disturbed the price level once again. It is interesting to note that the effect during the Second World War was not so serious as in the First World War. In 1918 wholesale prices were 213, whereas in 1945 they were 183. In the two years following 1918 the prices rose by 16 and 50 points and in the two years following 1945 prices rose by 24 and 49 points.

It is, however, from that point that the marked difference can be seen. In the earlier period the price level declined gradually to about normal, whereas in the latter period prices continued to increase. In fact, from the level of 183 in 1945 it reached 441 by November, 1951.

The profits indices shown in Column 3 of the table give 48 (1937=100) for 1913 and 81 for 1919, representing an increase of 70 per cent. Profits broadly continued at this level until 1938, whereas in 1950 the index had risen to 270 (1938=100) which indicated a much greater increase over 1938 than 1919 had shown over 1913. This trend followed closely the wholesale price level.

It is worth noting that with an increasing price level and profits following the same course, the relation of profits and wages to national income remained in about the same proportion. In 1938 profits were 18·6 per cent. and in 1950, 20·2 per cent. Wages were 36·8 per cent. in 1938 and 40 per cent. in 1950.

Replacement cost indices also emphasised the same general upward trend. From 1938 (100) the costs mounted to 180 by 1946 and have continued to rise since that time.

It follows that the course of events to-day is quite different from that following the First World War and that there is no sign of any stabilisation of the pre-Second World War price level. All the indications appear to make it clear that the present level has little relation to the price level which in the past was accepted as a constant basic factor.

In surveying the problem of trends in the price level the views of economists are of importance and the following might be taken as a short summary of the general view of economists.

Most economists are agreed that there is a strong probability of a continued rise in prices during the next few years (though perhaps with slight intermittent recessions which would not affect the general trend). Many economists would be prepared to argue that the price rise is likely to be of quite long duration, say, at least a decade.

For this, the following main reasons may be cited:

(1) The outstripping of the production of primary products by the growth of population (especially in the East). For the United Kingdom, particularly, this implies a continued deterioration in the terms of trade and rising prices.

(2) Continued heavy expenditure upon rearmament.

(3) The maintenance of 'full employment' policies, leading to over-investment.

(4) Pressures for higher money wages, facilitated by full employment and the intensification of collective bargaining.

(5) Over-investment resulting from attempts to make good deficiencies of capital goods and to expand capital equipment.

(6) Long-term tendencies towards a reduction in the propensity to save and an increase in the propensity to consume.

(7) The maintenance, for fiscal reasons, of low interest rates, and the avoidance of deflationary pressure commonly associated with unemployment—implying expansive monetary policies.

The steep rise in prices during the past five years as shown in the foregoing table has thus brought about a complete change in the position, as the present level has little relation to that prevailing before 1939, and many economists feel there is little hope of the general trend being reversed. In the light of these factors, it would appear there is an element of permanency and effect in the present price level which seriously disturbs current accountancy conventions.

Accountancy practice in this country over the past seventy years has been firmly wedded to original costs. There have been fluctuations in the price level over that period of time, but it has always been assumed that prices would find their level again and, therefore, fluctuations in the long term had no consequence. If, as has happened now, fluctuations had taken place in the past, carrying the price level to ever-increasing heights with little evidence to suggest that in a reasonable period the old price level would be restored, then some variation in accountancy conventions would have been necessary much earlier. The whole question seems to rest fairly and squarely on the one issue—will the present increased price level prove to be temporary? The answer from the evidence available appears to be that the conditions are not temporary. The pre-war (1939) price level will not be restored and an altogether different and higher price level has to be accepted as the normal standard.

The main convention or practice called into question is that which requires financial accounts to be based on historical or original costs. The profit statement and balance sheet are both affected by adherence to this convention.

Adherence to the historical or original cost basis involves a lower depreciation charge on fixed assets in a period of rising prices than would be the case if that charge were measured in terms of current value. Therefore, it has to be decided which charge should strictly be made against current profits to give a true measure of the profits. A charge which does not provide replacement in full must surely be leaving out of account some element of loss or wastage occurring in the current period and really incurred in earning the profit of the period. It would seem essential to charge against a current profit statement all costs and expenses of earning profits or income. The failure to do so must result in an overstatement of profit or, to put it another way, the amount shown as profit will include the real profit plus an amount of capital used up and not made good out of current earnings. This process has two most serious consequences: the distortion of the profit, with all the implications which flow therefrom, and the gradual decrease in the effective capital of the undertaking.

Many accountants hold the view that original costs provide the only true factual basis for the accounts—facts established by actual expenditure as distinct from estimates or valuations of replacements. They suggest that to base depreciation upon anything else but a known factor introduces into the accounts that element of uncertainty which accountants are not justified in adopting. They submit that accounts based on historical or original costs, and following conventional practices, are well established and well understood by the various sections of the community. Any alteration in practice would, it is said, confuse the minds of those using the accounts and would raise issues of interpretation and generally disturb all comparison with previous periods.

There is much to be said for this point of view, but the question is— are the results thrown up by existing practices and conventions correct? Do the accounts prepared in such a way indicate a real profit? Do they show that any loss of capital, by usage or wastage of fixed assets in earning the profits, has been made good during the period?

It is submitted the answer to these questions is clearly 'No'! There seems little doubt that existing accountancy conventions do not give an accurate measurement of profit in present circumstances.

It should be pointed out that profit statements at the present time are prepared showing depreciation charges calculated on original costs

T. B. ROBSON, M.B.E., M.A., F.C.A.

President of The Institute of Chartered Accountants in England and Wales

incurred at varying dates and on different price levels. The only uniformity is in the term of 'original cost', but there is not necessarily any uniformity in the price level of the historical or original cost. The best that can be said is that the original money capital is being preserved, yet in result the depreciation charge is a varying factor depending on the price ruling at the date of purchase of the asset. The current depreciation charge could include different amounts for similar types of assets in the same undertaking, and as between one concern and another using the same type of asset, there need be little consistency in the depreciation charge owing to a difference in the basic cost. Hence, the present profit statements are subject to the same degree of variation from a consistent measurement of profit as may be indicated by this variation in the depreciation charge.

It would appear clear that we have now reached an altogether new permanent price level far in excess of that previously accepted as normal, and the effect is of sufficient importance to disturb current accountancy conventions. Events appear to have caught up with the accountancy profession and demand that existing practices shall be varied to meet present conditions; varied in so far as workable procedures can be formulated to meet the situation.

IV. EFFECT OF FLUCTUATING PRICE LEVELS ON . . .

(a) Profit Ascertainment

Matters already reviewed have included certain considerations appropriate to the ascertainment or measurement of profit. But other considerations will be brought under review in this section. Our present accountancy conventions provide that profit shall consist of the surplus of current income over current outgoings, provided that in the latter case this means using original costs for short- or long-term expenditure carried over from one period to future periods. It is in this proviso that the point of difficulty arises in periods of fluctuating value.

Obviously some convention or acknowledged practice is required to meet the case of expenditure incurred in one period and having an effective and useful life over several future periods—a convention unnecessary if accounts were drawn up once-for-all during the whole existence of the business or enterprise, because all expenditure would be finalised and completed within that given period. It is because short-period reports are required for all sorts of practical purposes that in many businesses it is quite impossible to relate all expenditure exclusively to the operating income of the period in question. Thus, it becomes essential to establish a convention or practice for dealing with these suspended items.

It has been the practice in Great Britain to spread out the short- or long-term expenditure over the respective periodic accounts on the basis of the actual original outlay.

So long as the price level remains on a stable basis over the effective life of the suspended expenditure, the use of the original cost gives a fair measurement of the charge to revenue. On the other hand, when the suspended expenditure is carried into periods of a different price level, the question of the correct treatment of this expenditure or original cost arises. If, as is claimed, the measure of charge is the cost of renewal at current values, an altogether higher cost would, at present, be charged against operating income, with a corresponding reduction in the operating profit.

It is well to have in mind the real significance of profit and the importance of an accurate measurement of profit. Profit statements have an effect upon:

(1) The correct determination of the earning capacity of an enterprise.
(2) The accountability of directors and others for true results.
(3) The taxation liability.
(4) Government policy in relation to price regulation, limitation of profits, etc.
(5) The respective claims of capital and labour.
(6) The wisdom and legality of dividend declarations.
(7) The preservation of the capital of the concern in terms of current value.
(8) Public opinion with regard to profits, prices and wages.

In the light of these considerations, the importance of correctly measuring profits cannot be over-estimated. Profits touch and influence practically all phases of life.

It is submitted that existing accountancy practice, in so far as it relates to depreciation based on original costs, is giving an inaccurate measurement of profit. Depreciation should be based on the current replacement value of the asset and form the proper charge to operating profit. Until this has been done, there has not been a true measurement of the profit of a concern.

It is said that the difficulty of using current replacement value rules out this method as impracticable. This is not strictly true, although of course there are difficulties.

In many cases, it is possible to keep detailed schedules of all fixed assets showing original costs, dates of purchase and so on. These schedules are often capable of being repriced exactly on current replacement values. The life of each asset can be reviewed yearly or at other intervals, and with all this information there should be little difficulty in arriving at the appropriate depreciation charge based on the current replacement value. In cases where the foregoing is not practical, it should be possible to apply a percentage figure of increase based on various known costs, i.e. building, engineering materials, and so on. With a reasonably detailed schedule of fixed assets, a percentage adjustment to bring up the figures to the approximate current price level will enable the appropriation for replacement to be made. It may be that statutory indices could be established over a reasonable range of capital goods. It may well be that all assets purchased prior to 1939 will have to be taken as being purchased on the same common price level and percentages applied for the later price increases will operate on this defined price level.

Surely it cannot be argued that the foregoing methods are too much in the realms of estimates for the accountancy profession. The methods indicated do give figures based upon facts and must give the profit statement that element of reality which it could not possess by existing accountancy conventions.

Undoubtedly criticisms will be offered because, in adopting a new convention so far as depreciation is concerned, losses in earlier periods will not have been provided. It does not fall into the requirements of measuring profits by charging depreciation at replacement cost that earlier deficiencies in such depreciation be provided in a period when they did not occur. These earlier deficiencies would have to be treated as losses of capital under the then prevailing accountancy conventions. In fact, did not these amounts actually represent capital used as profits? However that may be, they would have to be accepted on a change over as capital losses. It would, of course, be possible to deal with this item by present and future appropriations of profit if the circumstances permitted.

It might well be asked what happens when prices fall. Adjustments to the depreciation charge would be related to the current replacement charge and if, at the end of the life of the asset, there was an excess, then this could be treated as a balancing charge to be written back. At the same time, it would probably be necessary to protect contributed money capital by pegging depreciation rates at original cost, although if prices fell below the original cost, the depreciation charge would still appear to be properly calculated on the current replacement cost. If the principle of protecting the original contributed capital is abandoned, in measuring profit, for the principle of protecting the physical asset, then consistency would appear to demand the use of current replacement cost in calculating depreciation, whether this cost was higher or lower than the historical cost.

There is also the somewhat difficult case of technological development. It may well be that a business will not replace its worn-out equipment exactly in the form of the original. Newer and sometimes cheaper forms of equipment performing similar functions more effectively may be purchased. In such cases, it would seem clear that the fixed asset costs recovered by way of operating accounts should not fall below the allocations based upon the money expended as capital on the original assets. At the same time, it would possibly be more appropriate if it could be urged that the purchasing power in real terms, which was the equivalent of the money cost of the original asset at the time of its acquisition, might be validly provided on the basis of the trend of the general price level at accounting dates.

It would no doubt be argued by some that to treat the whole problem as one of replacement of the original asset does not go far enough. If there are technological developments envisaged, then, so it is said, it would be a matter of thinking of replacements in terms of the cost of the replacing asset rather than of the replacement cost of the original asset. Such a submission would create the utmost difficulty in its practical application. There would be the difficulty of getting the real facts upon a reasonably indisputable basis, to enable the depreciation charge to be calculated. It would be a problem to determine the precise kind of replacement so far ahead and its possible cost. So that if the case in general could be made out, it would appear to fail on the ground that it would be impossible of practical application. It really seems to come back clearly to accepting the original assets as the basis for the depreciation charge adjusted to the appropriate price levels.

It is no part of the duty of this paper to examine the various methods of apportioning depreciation. Whether the straight-line method, the reducing-balance method, the sinking-fund method, or, finally, the renewals reserve method (which is not generally used in industrial and commercial undertakings) is adopted would normally depend to a large extent on the nature of the assets. But if a change is made from historical to replacement cost in computing depreciation, consideration would need to be given to the mechanics of applying any of these methods.

There are three factors involved in determining the depreciation: the cost of the asset, its ultimate disposal value and its probable life. Will, then, a change in the variable basic value, i.e. cost to a variable current value, seriously affect the use of any one of the foregoing methods of applying depreciation? Obviously the straight-line method presents little difficulty in its application. The reducing-balance method would occasion more calculations, but there should be no insuperable difficulty in using this method whenever thought suitable. Equally with the sinking-fund method, there is no serious difficulty except for the extra work and calculations required to bring it into effect. The fourth method would not be affected by a change, because apparently in most cases it has no precise relation to the value of the assets.

The second important question affecting the profit statement is the much debated one of valuation of inventories, or in other words the valuation of stocks. It is maintained that capital invested in stock should be preserved intact at the current price level. The capital invested therein should, at the end of a period, be capable of the same purchasing power as it had at the beginning of the period. The case rests on the principle that if money values have increased during the year, the capital invested in the foregoing current assets has depreciated, and this depreciation has arisen in earning profits and is therefore a proper charge against profits.

In 1950, the British national income calculation was adjusted by the deduction of £350 million as the estimated appreciation in the value of stocks due to rising prices. In the Economic Survey for 1951, the estimated figure is £700 million, and this figure is likely to be exceeded. The reason for the deduction is the computation of real wealth as distinct from rising prices. Under present accountancy conventions, the foregoing £350 million of rising prices is treated as profit, with all the implications attaching thereto, and similarly with the £700 million.

It is also urged that costs should be calculated on the same price level basis as the revenue to which they relate. In other words, the cost of the stock sold in the current period is its replacement cost, not its original cost. The process consists of repricing the closing stock at a first original cost or, alternatively, repricing the opening stock to the current price level. In America, this procedure is known as LIFO (last in—first out) as opposed to the older method which still prevails in England of FIFO (first in—first out). As an alternative to the LIFO principle, the following method has received a fair amount of support:

(1) Opening inventory. Write this up to cost from the lower of cost or market value. This should require little or no adjustment to work-in-progress figures.

(2) Value the closing inventory at current cost, or as near to current cost as is practicable. In general, identify current costs for this purpose as:

(i) The most recent price paid for goods and the conversion factors of production.

(ii) The identified cost of the most recent acquisition considered in relation to the end date of account.

Again value the closing inventory at the costs applied to the opening inventory. Even where stocks have changed and where work in progress is of a different order it should not be impossible to value the closing inventory at opening inventory costs. It only amounts to revaluing the closing inventory as if it were being taken at the previous accounting date. The difference in the two values for the closing inventories gives the price movement for the period, which can be expressed as a percentage of the value of the opening inventory.

(3) The difference between the opening inventory and the closing inventory value at opening inventory costs gives the movement in volume.

(4) If the volume of the closing inventory is less than the volume of the opening inventory, the closing inventory may be deemed to consist wholly of the opening inventory. In these circumstances, a reserve should be created by debit to profit and loss account equal to the difference between the value of the closing inventory valued at closing costs and the closing inventory valued at opening costs.

(5) If the volume of the closing inventory is greater than the volume of the opening inventory, then the closing inventory may be deemed to consist of the opening inventory plus additions at cost. In these circumstances, a reserve should be created equal to the difference in value between a volume of inventory equal to the opening inventory valued at closing costs and at opening costs.

(6) The inventory should be stated at its closing cost figure in the balance sheet and a reserve should be passed to a price change account to be shown separately and related to stocks.

Many in Britain who are prepared to accept the logic of the position when related to fixed assets cannot accept the foregoing views regarding stock. This may seem somewhat odd, as the arguments accepted in the case of fixed assets should, on the face of it, be as effective when applied to stock. Although the same effect is produced in the case of stock, i.e. replacement at original cost instead of current cost with a consequential deficiency in the charge to revenue of the difference between the original and replacement cost—yet it is important to see if the conditions are in every respect the same. On careful consideration, a very important difference emerges in the relative life of the assets in question. Fixed or capital assets are expected to have many years of life, whereas stock has a comparatively short life and the effect of rising or decreasing prices is quickly brought into account. This is a distinguishable feature as in a period of stabilised prices there would be no effective difference between the older and the newer method of stock valuation.

There is, however, still the problem of the rise from one stabilised level to another very much higher stabilised level. For instance, a later period may be stabilised at a price level twice as high as that prevailing in the earlier period, in which case should the effect of the price increase on the stock from one stabilised level to another be treated as profit? Could it not, in fact, be argued that the difference is purely a price increase and not a profit at all? Whatever view is taken, it would no doubt be agreed that the effective capital had decreased by the foregoing difference, and then comes the all-important question: Does a profit statement ignoring this difference present a true measurement of the real profit?

It would be foreign to accountancy concepts to follow swiftly fluctuating values which do not appear to suggest any material change in the eventual stabilised price level. Minor fluctuations or still more serious fluctuations, if only temporary, would hardly justify any change in current accountancy conventions because the original cost level would still, in the long view, give the more consistent and accurate results.

On the other hand, if the fluctuations were of such a character as to indicate clearly an eventual stabilised price level far removed from the one previously known, then consideration probably should be given to this important factor. Would it not be essential to see what effect this change had upon accounts prepared according to existing conventions? That there would be an effect seems obvious, and if it is agreed that the effect is material, then existing accountancy conventions would not reflect the implications of the change in the price level.

At the same time, there will always be difficulties of practical application. If it is agreed that minor or temporary fluctuations do not justify recognition in accountancy conventions, then at what point could a decision be made that a change was not of this character? It would appear that this would be mostly only when all the effect had already been absorbed in earlier accounts and thus could not be taken into account in any current measurement of profit. Differences arising in the past could only be dealt with as a matter of policy and not as a profit measurement. These would be capital losses and, as a matter of policy, could only be dealt with by appropriations of profit.

In Britain, wholesale prices had risen from 100 in 1938 to 436 in October, 1951 (Statist/Sauerbeck) and, consequently, profit statements based on present conventions will already have included this increase as profit. It would thus be quite impossible to get this increase excluded from the current or future measurement of profit. It relates to past measurements of profit and is no concern in the measurement of present or future profits. The past loss on the stock could only be dealt with by appropriations of profit in the future. To bring into account future fluctuations in value would mean adopting a figure of, say, 436 as a basic figure to start with.

The general conclusions would appear to be that logically the stock position should follow the same principle as that adopted for fixed assets, yet the rapid increase in the price level in Britain had already occurred and, broadly, a change now in our accountancy conventions could not bring into account the present increase (based on 1938) and could only affect future fluctuations. These fluctuations do not appear as if they were likely to vary the existing price level to any considerable extent, otherwise than in a downward direction.

(b) Fixed Assets

Fixed assets represent the expenditure of capital moneys on assets not purchased for resale and with a life extending over a number of future accounting periods. It is this latter factor of expenditure made in one period and carried over to subsequent accounting periods which raises the question of how far a fluctuating price level could affect the assessment of the value of such expenditure in the balance sheets of later periods. Little difficulty, therefore, generally arises in the first accounting period as the cost broadly is the current value. The difficulty arises in subsequent accounting periods which are enjoying the benefit of the earlier expenditure. The two issues emerging are, first, the measurement of the value of the usage in the respective periods of enjoyment of use, which is fully considered elsewhere in this paper, and, second, the statement of such expenditure in succeeding balance sheets when the value of the assets represented by the foregoing expenditure has materially increased. Can it be maintained that balance sheets showing original costs in such cases are truly representing the position of the undertaking? Or would the position be more accurately shown if the fixed assets were shown at current values?

Different considerations appear to arise in connection with the balance sheet than with the profit statement. In the balance sheet the existing practice of stating assets at original cost, less depreciation where it applies, is based on sound reasoning. It clearly shows how the contributed money capital of the business has been expended, and may be regarded as a document which reports on the stewardship of contributed money capital, capital gains and savings. Realisation of the capital structure is not an objective of a continuing business, and therefore it would appear artificial to write up the values in the balance sheet when realisation is not contemplated and when, in fact, the values could not be realised without prejudicing the continuance of the business. These considerations appear to be sound sense if the balance sheet is supposed to be a statement of fact as to the contributed money capital of the business and the use to which it has been put. Variations from year to year in the intrinsic value of assets which are not turning over would create difficulties in keeping a consistent and readily understandable balance sheet. Contributed money capital invested in a business has its original stated value and everyone understands that is the precise value at that moment of time. Thereafter, the original stated value is maintained in the balance sheet, but its precise value would then depend on a variety of factors not least among which is the earning capacity of the business. These factors are not valued and assessed at the date of each balance sheet. The balance sheet does not, therefore, take note of these influencing factors any more than it does of the current value of the assets.

On the other hand, new contributed capital, capital gains and savings would be reflected in the balance sheet and in the last category would be profits ploughed back into the business. It would not be the same thing to say that a book increase in the value of fixed assets (which in fact are not available for realisation at the current value) increased the contributed capital and savings of the concern.

It has to be conceded, however, that there is quite a strong opinion in favour of showing assets at current values in the balance sheet. It is argued that in the same way as it is important to measure profits accurately, it is equally important to give an accurate measurement of the capital of the concern. It is said that to show in the balance sheet the capital of the concern at some value quite unrelated to current values cannot give a true picture of the capital structure at the current date. It is related only to the value at the moment of time when the capital was contributed or profits ploughed back. The answer to the problem, so it is claimed, is the virtual restatement of carried-over costs in terms of current standards of money value. The problem does not extend to keeping pace with the purchasing power of money for all purposes, neither does it involve any departure from the objectively dependable basis of accounting record in terms of original costs. It is merely a question of converting those original costs, which are out of time relationship, into current costs in order that in the statements of measurement all significant entries shall rest on the same plane of reference.

(c) Current Assets

In Britain the term current assets includes: (i) stock, (ii) debtors, (iii) cash. Consideration has already been given to stock in the measurement of profit and little further need be said now on its relation to capital measurement. It is a well-established practice that stock should be shown at its original cost unless the market value is lower, in which case the latter value should be used. The basis for this practice is that

c

stock, being a current asset, is held for realisation. Therefore, regard would be had to its realisable value, always providing that it is not stated above the cost price to avoid taking an unrealised book profit into account.

The American LIFO method would not be appropriate here, as it shows an undervaluation in the balance sheet of assets whose main purpose is to be realised.

Thus, even if the case were made out for the treatment of stock on the basis of a current renewal value for the purposes of measuring profit, it would still be necessary to bring into the balance sheet the stock on the basis of cost or market value, whichever was lower. It would not be in accord with British views on the accuracy of balance sheets to undervalue the stock deliberately to some earlier basis of original capital cost.

Debtors, bills receivable, prepayments, cash and other such items represent claims for money in respect of which payment can only be demanded in current units of money. They therefore generally create no measurement problem at all and would not be affected by a fluctuating price level.

(d) Asset and Liability Claims

As has already been indicated in the preceding section, monetary claims, whether to be received or demanded, are payable in current units of money and are correctly shown in the balance sheet at that value. No question of profit or capital measurement arises in ordinary circumstances.

V. TYPES OF BUSINESSES AFFECTED BY FLUCTUATING PRICE LEVELS

It follows from the consideration already referred to that undertakings with no fixed assets or stock would be unaffected by any change in the price level. Where transactions are normally started and completed in a current period and are not using any expenditure incurred in previous periods, then the price level can have little or no effect on the accounts of the current period. Any undertaking, therefore, which by its nature is able to match its revenue with costs on the same current price level would be unaffected by price level changes.

Alternatively, undertakings which are not matching their revenue with costs on the same current price level are affected to the degree of the gap between the foregoing current price level cost and the cost actually computed under existing conventions. The extent of the gap depends on the amount and the date of the expenditure, influencing the current results, incurred out of the current period.

Fixed assets represent one type of such expenditure, the outlay having been incurred years previously at the price level then prevailing. A proportion of such expenditure written off on the basis of the particular price level of the year of purchase introduces this element of unmatched costs and revenue. In such undertakings, the fluctuations in the price level are a matter for serious consideration. Similarly, it is urged, undertakings having expenditure on stocks in a period prior to the current period are not matching costs with revenue on the same price level. Therefore, the results of all such undertakings would also be affected by fluctuations in the price level.

It can therefore be seen that a change in the price level affects a very large majority of trading undertakings, the degree of effect being dependent upon the capital involved in fixed assets and stock.

VI. WHAT ARE BUSINESS PROFITS?

(a) The Accountant's View

The accountant's conception of 'business profits' is well known and really needs little elaboration to an audience of accountants. At the same time, it is worth recording in a paper of this kind exactly what accountants really do mean by 'business profits'.

It might be summarised as the surplus of revenue (which would include the term income) over the costs and expenses related to and associated with such revenue.

The Committee on Company Law Amendment in Great Britain recommended in 1945 that the profit and loss account should give a true and fair indication of the earnings or income of the period covered by the account and that it should plainly disclose and distinguish any items of a non-recurring, exceptional or extraneous character.

Mr. George O. May, in his *Business Income and Price Levels—An Accounting Study*, says:

> 'Business income is broadly an excess of revenue over costs and expenses. As a rule, the problem of measuring the revenue attributable to a given period gives rise to little difficulty or disagreement. It is the allocation of costs and expenses that constitutes the major problem.'

He goes on to quote from a letter from the Special Committee on Co-operation with Stock Exchanges of the American Institute of Accountants to the New York Stock Exchange, dated 22nd September, 1932, which said:

> 'In an earlier age, when capital assets were inconsiderable and business units in general smaller and less complex than they are to-day, it was possible to value assets with comparative ease and accuracy and to measure the progress made from year to year by annual valuations. With the growing

mechanisation of industry, and with corporate organisations becoming constantly larger, more completely integrated and more complex, this has become increasingly impracticable. From an accounting standpoint, the distinguishing characteristic of business to-day is the extent to which expenditures are made in one period with the definite purpose and expectation that they shall be the means of producing profits in the future; and how such expenditures shall be dealt with in accounts is the central problem of financial accounting. How much of a given expenditure of the current or a past year shall be carried forward as an asset cannot possibly be determined by an exercise of judgment in the nature of a valuation.'

The problem lies in the fact that business is a long-term matter and must in general be treated on the principle of a going concern. Dicksee's *Advanced Accounting* (sixth edition, page 227) stated the position thus:

'The true profits of an undertaking can only be that surplus that remains after providing for all expenses of carrying on the undertaking *upon a permanent basis*.'

The last four words are significant.

The need for charging costs or expenditure against the appropriate profit or period involves a practice or convention.

Mr. F. Sewell Bray says, in *The Accounting Mission*:

'. . . the essence of the accounting problem, as related to homogeneous measurements of capital and income, is largely centred upon those costs applied to *real* assets (as distinct from what might be called natural financial claims), which are carried over from one accounting period to another as short-term and long-term charges against the future operations of continuing enterprises.'

So far as existing British practice is concerned, the position is clearly defined. Expenditure upon a fixed asset is shown at original cost and this amount is allocated over the several financial periods of its useful life.

(b) The Economist's View

In periods when there is no marked instability in the value of money, economists' views on the measurement of business profits do not significantly differ from those of accountants. Thus, in the nineteenth century in Great Britain, when the price level was not very variable, economists here were mostly content to accept without question the accountants' version of business profits. But it is otherwise when the value of money is changing drastically. During the inter-war inflations on the Continent of Europe, and in smaller degree in the U.S.A. and Great Britain at that time, economists became concerned at what they considered to be shortcomings in the accounting interpretation of profits; and after the Second World War these criticisms were reviewed and extended as the general inflationary trend gathered momentum.

The broadest argument put forward by economists against the traditional accounting view of business profits, as elaborated in the preceding subsection of this paper, is that it is 'backward-looking' instead of 'forward-looking'. It has prime regard to the proprietor's capital expressed in terms of the monetary unit at the time the capital was subscribed, and deems the preservation of this money capital to be the accountants' predominant concern. Consistently with this, conventional accounting looks backward to the original or historical cost of fixed assets in determining current depreciation charges, and normally charges for stock usage on a FIFO basis. But these methods of accounting for depreciation or stock usage necessarily mean that charges are made in the current period in terms of money units of preceding periods—the money units obtaining when the fixed assets were originally installed or the 'first-in' portions of stock were acquired—while the other main elements of cost (for example, wages) are charged in terms of money units of the current period. If the value of money has changed between the earlier and current periods, this 'backward-looking' view means that money units of different values are combined in the accounts to make up total costs charges. This, say the economists, is illogical. Money units may be added together if they are of the same value, but a meaningless result is arrived at if their values differ. The 'backward-looking' approach is permissible only if the monetary unit is invariable.

Instead of this 'backward-looking' approach the economist adopts a 'forward-looking' one. He regards the proprietor's money capital, as originally subscribed, as having legal rather than practical importance. Economically, it is a bygone with which one does not have to be much concerned. Similarly, there is little or no economic significance in the original or historical cost of fixed assets or in the cost of acquiring the 'first-in' portions of stock. They, too, are economic bygones which should have no influence upon current issues—issues such as the determination of the profits of present business activities and, through the results of that determination, other essentially current issues, like the assessment of taxes upon business profits, the fixing of shareholders' dividends, and decisions whether or not to install new equipment. It is current issues such as these which determine the trend in the business sector of the economy, which itself is a main determinant of the future state of the economy at large, and the economist is interested in these current issues precisely because, broadly speaking, he considers the future state of the economy—immediate and more remote—as his main concern. Anxious that accounting should assist in the attainment of correct decisions on current issues such as those mentioned, the economist urges that accountants should abandon their 'backward-looking' approach.

This means that the economist considers that charges in the profit and loss accounts of businesses should be as nearly as possible in current money and not in the money of previous periods; more specifically, depreciation should be computed on the current or replacement costs of fixed assets and stock usage should be calculated on current costs of stock. The latter requirement may be rather differently expressed by saying that the economist would like to exclude from the profits of current operations the element of 'inventory profit'. This 'inventory profit' is the amount by which the opening stock appreciates in times of rising prices between the beginning of the accounting period and its end. The economist regards it as no part of operating profits but simply as capital appreciation, which should be dealt with by entering it as a 'capital surplus' in the balance sheet.

The economic argument this broadly expresses has one particular implication upon which most economists place emphasis, particularly in times such as the present. This is the necessity of 'maintaining capital intact'. Businesses should allow, it is contended, for the preservation of their fixed assets and stocks at a constant level in physical terms, as distinct from money terms, before striking profits derived from current activities. They will allow for this preservation of productive capacity only if the charge in the profit and loss account for depreciation of fixed assets is based on the current costs of the assets and if the charge for stock usage is calculated on the current prices of the items concerned. Otherwise, profits will be over-stated, and moneys may be distributed and paid away in tax instead of being retained in the business to finance the maintenance of fixed assets and stocks. At worst, the productive capacity of industry will run down; at best, resort will have to be had to outside sources of finance, not to extend productive capacity, but merely to keep it at a constant level. In any event, the profit figure will be incorrect and misleading. In other words, the business must ensure that it earns from current activities sufficient to keep its productive potential intact, before it deems itself to have made any profit.

The economist supports this view by the thesis that a business is to be regarded as a continuous entity, whose productive capital—using 'capital' in its economic meaning of real assets—should, as a first consideration, be maintained. If the business has shrunk during the accounting period, in the sense that there has been a diminution, in physical terms, in its productive capital (fixed assets and stock) greater than the amount, again in physical terms, that can be made good from money sums provided out of revenue during the period, then those responsible for the accounting of the business have not put uppermost the desideratum that the business should end the accounting period in no worse position to produce than it was at the beginning. This is the dominant desideratum from the economist's point of view, because if it is not observed the business is in danger of dissipating its productive capital. On the broader plane, the community may in consequence be drawing upon its social capital, or be failing to enlarge it as rapidly as it otherwise would, and the serious economic effects of this are self-evident.

Some economists, while not dissenting from the general lines of the 'maintenance-of-capital-intact' argument, point to some difficulties which it involves when more precisely examined. Thus, when technological conditions are changing, keeping physical assets intact is not synonymous with keeping productive capacity intact. Again, it may well be undesirable that each and every business should set out to keep its same physical assets at a constant level. For example, if the prices of a particular kind of fixed assets are rising faster than wages, it may be economically desirable that the given business should allow its fixed assets to run down and employ more labour instead.

Points such as these may be regarded as demanding only qualifications to the economic argument that has here been stated. Or they may be avoided if the economist's case is put in a rather different way—as it sometimes is. Some economists would place the stress upon the necessity to allow for maintenance of the physical assets, not in order to keep productive capital intact, but in order to preserve the proprietors' investment in the business in real terms, rather than in money terms. They would share the traditional accounting view that the proprietors' interest must be safeguarded, but they would depart from that view by contending that the safeguard is seriously lacking unless their interest is maintained after any change in the general level of prices is taken into account. As thus given, this argument leaves to be settled such questions as whether the term 'proprietors' includes or excludes the preference shareholders. But the broad conclusion is plain: namely, that depreciation of fixed assets and stock usage should be taken at current prices in order that the value attaching to proprietorship be maintained.

Often economists do not confine their argument to the measurement of business profits. They also contend that assets in the balance sheet should all be entered at current prices—that they should not be a mixture of items evaluated on historical and current (and anticipated) prices, as in traditional accounting practice. They would maintain that what is of significance is the up-to-date value of the assets—that the balance sheet should give the current value of the business, as it would be in the event, for example, of its being sold. The proprietors always have the alternative, so this argument would run, of disposing of their business, so that it is misleading to place a value upon it in the balance sheet other than the current one. This argument is thus derived from the economic principle of 'opportunity' or 'alternative' cost—an asset or collection of assets is worth in its present use X no less than it would be worth in its alternative use Y, to which it can freely move. There follows a conclusion of importance to the measurement of business profits, as well as to the drawing up of the balance sheet. For if assets are valued at their current prices, a logical corollary is that the rate of depreciation—the rate at which fixed assets are being worn out in production—should be applied to those current prices and, similarly, stocks should be taken at current prices. Thus the argument via 'opportunity' or 'alternative' cost leads to the same result for profits measurement as the other arguments earlier set out—but that result does not depend upon acceptance of the economist's view of the balance sheet.

(c) The Lawyer's View

1. To the question, '*What are business profits?*' the law returns no answer, not because it could not do so—some answer would have to be given if the question were one of the issues to be decided in some case before the Court—but because the question is never put to it in this abstract and generalised form. The law is asked, not 'What are business profits?' but, 'In this particular case, and under the articles of *this* company, what are the profits available for dividend?' or, 'In *this* partnership deed, what is meant by "the profits of the business"?' or, 'In *this* service agreement, what are the "net profits" out of which the employee's salary or commission is payable?' The question always arises as a matter of construction of a document or a statute or a regulation, and always in a given context. It is not possible to divorce the answer given from its context. Nevertheless, the law has elaborated the answer to certain questions which are constantly arising and has established some principles of general interest to the business community as well as of specialised interest to lawyers and draftsmen.

2. The question, 'What are business profits?' resolves itself for the lawyer into three questions:

   (*a*) What is the meaning of the phrase 'the profits of the business'?

   (*b*) When are profits 'available for distribution' in the sense that the distribution will not be out of capital and *ultra vires*?

   (*c*) When are the profits 'available for distribution' under the usual article giving the directors power to set aside reserves and to carry forward amounts which they do not think it prudent to distribute?

The last two questions are sometimes confused, though really distinct —see the judgment of Maughan, J., in *Long Acre Press Ltd. v. Odhams Press Ltd.* ([1930] 2 Ch. 196).

3. The question (*a*), 'What are "the profits of the business"?' has provoked what seems to be the only attempt made by the Bench to provide a generalised definition of the word 'profits', namely, the first part of the judgment of Fletcher-Moulton, L.J., in *Re Spanish Prospecting Co. Ltd.* ([1911] 1 Ch. 92 (C.A.) at pages 98-101). This is a *locus classicus* for accountants and auditors, but it is perhaps not so well remembered as it ought to be that the learned Lord Justice expressly said that his remarks did *not* apply to the question of what profits were distributable in dividend and had no bearing on cases such as *Lee v. Neuchatel Asphalte Co. Ltd.* and *Verner v. General & Commercial Investment Trust Ltd.*

The question came up as a matter of construction of a service agreement with a company which provided that the salary of two technical advisers to the company, Mr. Punchard and Mr. Vivian, was to be payable only out of the profits, if any, arising from the business of the company, though the salary was to be cumulative and arrears payable out of the profits of succeeding years. In well-known words, the Lord Justice said:

> 'The word "profits" has in my opinion a well defined legal meaning. The fundamental meaning is the amount of gain made by the business during the year. This can only be ascertained by a comparison of the assets of the business at the two dates. For practical purposes these assets must be valued and not merely enumerated ... if the total assets of the business at the two dates be compared, the increase which they show at the later date as compared with the earlier date (due allowance being made for any capital introduced into or taken out of the business in the meanwhile) represents in strictness the profits of the business during the period in question.'

He went on to point out that, to simplify the comparison, it is customary to make what he called 'certain assumptions', e.g.:

(i) to exclude gains and losses from causes not directly connected with the business of the company;

(ii) to show trade buildings and plant at actual cost less depreciation by a certain percentage each year, though this does not necessarily give their true value either in use or in exchange.

'These, however,' he says, 'are merely variations of practice by individuals. They rest on no settled principle.' He touches on the difficulty of valuing all assets in money, no matter what their nature, and draws a distinction between the wide field for variation of practice in the estimation of profits in the 'domestic documents' of a firm or company, and the stricter practice which must apply when the rights of third parties, such as the Revenue or employees paid by a percentage of profits, intervene. This last distinction probably needs reconsideration in the light of the statutory principle of the 'true and fair view' and the stricter legal requirements with regard to the accounts of companies, but it is probably still true that the word 'profits' by itself in a service agreement is all-inclusive and, prima facie, means 'actual profits' (including capital profits), not merely the balance on the profit and loss account, unless the context otherwise requires, e.g. by speaking of 'trading profits', 'net profits', etc.

This part of the judgment, if it is an accurate statement of the law of the subject, appears to establish two propositions:

(i) That the ascertainment of the periodical profits of a business rests upon a genuine comparison of the value of the total assets at two different dates, due allowance being made for increases or decreases in the capital in the meanwhile;

(ii) That, in carrying out the valuation, the customary and reasonable practices of business men and accountants (within the general framework of any specific legal requirements) may properly be used.

The law thus states the principle on which profits are to be ascertained, but leaves most of the practical problems involved to be solved by the business community and their financial advisers.

(One word of warning may be uttered about this part of the judgment. The passage referred to appears to be *obiter*, since the case could be and was decided on the basis that the £3,000 surplus in liquidation had been realised by the sale of debentures which were part of the stock-in-trade of the company, and therefore unquestionably represented profits of the business, to which Punchard and Vivian were entitled as their salaries were £8,000 in arrear. Farwell, L.J., referred to his own distinction between fixed and floating capital in *Bond v. Barrow Haematite Steel Co. Ltd.*, and equated 'profits arising from the business of the company' with the profits made by the use of its floating or circulating capital. Moreover, Fletcher-Moulton, L.J., seems to have been rather bold in saying that 'The word "profits" has in my opinion a well-defined legal meaning'. In 1901, only ten years before, Lord Halsbury, L.C., had said in the House of Lords:

'I doubt very much whether such questions can ever be treated in the abstract at all. The mode and manner in which a business is carried on, and what is usual or the reverse, may have a considerable influence in determining the question what may be treated as profits and what as capital. Even the distinction between fixed and floating capital, which may be appropriate enough in an abstract treatise like Adam Smith's *Wealth of Nations*, may with reference to a concrete case be quite inappropriate.' (*Dovey v. Cary* ([1901] A.C. 477 at pages 486-7).)

And Farwell, L.J., who sat beside Fletcher-Moulton, L.J., on the bench in *Re Spanish Prospecting Co. Ltd.*, had said nine years before, in *Bond v. Barrow Haematite Steel Co.* ([1902] 1 Ch. 353, at page 364):

'There is no hard and fast rule by which the Court can determine what is capital and what is profit. ... There is no single definition of the word which will fit all cases.'

He did not find occasion to go back on this remark in *Re Spanish Prospecting Co. Ltd.*

Finally, it may be pointed out that in the ascertainment of profits, ' "profits" means profits after deducting the expenses of earning them' (per Scrutton, L.J., in *Vulcan Motor & Engineering Co.* (1906) *Ltd. v. Hampson* ([1921] 3 K.B. 597 (C.A.) at page 606)). Excess profits duty and excess profits tax are, in effect, part of the expenses of earning them, though income-tax is not. National defence contribution and profits tax are somewhat anomalous in this respect, and it does not seem possible to say with certainty whether or not they are an expense for this purpose.

4. The question (*b*) 'When are profits available for distribution in the sense that the distribution will not be out of capital and *ultra vires*?' is answered by reference to the well-known cases which are in all the auditing and company law text-books.

There does not appear to be much to comment on here, except the doubt whether an *unrealised* capital profit may be distributed, assuming that the directors have bona fide revalued the assets and liabilities and ascertained that the share capital is intact. There is no authority against crediting such a profit to profit and loss account, and such opinion as has been expressed seems to be in favour of the legality of doing so. These remarks only apply where there is nothing in the articles to prevent the distribution of capital profits. If the articles provide that dividends are only to be distributed out of 'profits arising from the company's business', capital profits must be credited to a capital reserve; though even in this case they may be used to wipe out a capital loss, realised or unrealised, and may probably be applied in writing down intangible assets commonly written off by appropriation of profits, e.g. goodwill, preliminary expenses, expenses of an issue, former debit balance on profit and loss account. Since a premium payable on redemption of redeemable preference shares must come out of profits or the share premium account (Companies Act, 1948, Section 58 (i) (*c*)), capital accretion, whether realised or unrealised, cannot be used for this purpose. For the rest, the cases have established the well-known principles:

(i) That, subject to its articles, a company may distribute a dividend out of its profits without first making good a loss on capital account (*Lee v. Neuchatel Asphalte Co. Ltd.* ([1889] 41 Ch. 1)) but after making reasonable provision for bad debts.

(ii) That, in ascertaining whether profits have been made in the year, a loss of circulating capital must be made good, though a loss of fixed capital need not be made good (*Verner v. General & Commercial Investment Trust* ([1894] 1 Ch. 239))—which may be simply another way of saying, with Scrutton, L.J., that ' "profits" means profits after deducting the expenses of earning them'. The 1948 Act now requires depreciation to be shown, and *Verner's* case is perhaps a rather special case, which ought not to be pressed too far.

(iii) That before a capital profit is distributable, it must be ascertained by a bona fide consideration of the whole position of the company that the liabilities are covered and the issued share capital is intact (*Foster v. New Trinidad Asphalt Co. Ltd.* ([1901] Ch. 208)).

It is evident that, even when considering the question of an *ultra vires* distribution, the law leaves considerable room for manoeuvre to the directors, the company and their financial advisers. The Statute has not basically altered the position except to make the share premium account a capital reserve no longer distributable as dividend (Companies Act, 1948, Section 56 (1) and (2)) and to add excess profits tax post-war refund to the same category. The capital redemption reserve fund to be created when preference shares are redeemed out of profits has existed since 1st November, 1929 (Companies Act, 1929, Section 46).

5. The question (*c*) 'What profits are available for distribution when the directors have a power and a duty under the articles to set aside reserves and to carry forward undistributed profits?' is answered, under Table A, 1929 or 1948, and the articles of most companies, in the board room. Table A so provides in express terms, '*The directors* may, before recommending any dividend, set aside out of the profits of the company, etc.' Even without a power in the articles, reserves may be created and either used in the business or invested at discretion by the directors, as this is a business question for decision by the company (*Burland v. Earle* ([1902] A.C. 83)).

In spite of careful drafting, questions sometimes arise whether the divisible profits of a company, under its articles, are its general profits, i.e. the credit balance on the profit and loss account, or the profits available after reserves, etc., have been set aside. The law shows a distinct tendency to answer this question in the more restricted sense, since it has been held that, in an article dealing with dividend rights, 'profits of the company' prima facie means 'profits available', not the balance on profit and loss account (*Dent v. London Tramways Ltd.* ((1881) 16 Ch. 344), *Fisher v. Black and White Publishing Co. Ltd.* ([1901] 1 Ch. 174), *Long Acre Press Ltd. v. Odhams Press Ltd.* ([1930] 2 Ch. 196), *Re Buenos Ayres Great Southern Railway Co. Ltd.* ([1947] 1 All E.R. 729)). The fact that the reserves may be used, *inter alia*, for dividend equalisation which may only benefit the ordinary shareholders is no argument in favour of the preference shareholders that 'profits of the company' means the balance on the profit and loss account, because the reserves may usually be used for other purposes as well, which are beneficial to the company as a whole, preference shareholders included. Nevertheless, these words must be carefully considered in their context, particularly if special and unusual articles define the rights of shareholders to the profits and make no mention of a reserve fund. (*Paterson & Sons v. Paterson* ([1917] S.C. (H.L.) 13).) *Erling v. Israel & Oppenheimer Ltd.* ([1918] 1 Ch. 101) provides an English example of this.

With regard to the capitalisation of profits, the legal position seems to be that it is a question of fact answered mainly by reference to the intention of the company. The use of a reserve fund in the company's business does not by itself show that it has been capitalised so as not to be available for dividend (*Re Hoare & Co. Ltd.* ([1904] 2 Ch. 208)). The usual course is to pass a resolution in general meeting capitalising a portion of the profits and then to distribute fully-paid bonus shares or debentures. Table A, 1948, now allows capitalisation, by resolution of a general meeting, and also subject to the recommendation of the directors, of any amounts standing to the credit of a reserve account or the profit and loss account, or otherwise available for distribution. The amount capitalised may be applied either in paying up fully-paid shares or debentures for issue to the members (the share premium account and capital redemption reserve fund being only applicable for an issue of fully-paid bonus shares) or in paying up uncalled share capital, or partly in one way and partly in another. The article in Table A (paragraph 128) reads rather as if it is laying down the only method by which a company working under that table may capitalise its profits, although the opening phrase, 'The company in general meeting *may* . . . resolve that it is desirable to capitalise . . .' is permissive in form.

6. So far as a single phrase can sum up the answer of the law to the question, 'What are business profits?' it seems to be: Business profits

are whatever the company (which really means the board) says are the profits of the business, subject to its own articles, and subject to the rule that its issued share capital must be kept intact. The law is quite prepared to apply the current reasonable practice of accountants and business men to the matter, indeed regards the inquiry as peculiarly one for them. As Lindley, L.J., said in *Lee v. Neuchatel Asphalte Co. Ltd.* ([1889] 41 Ch. at page 21):

> 'There is nothing at all in the Acts about how dividends are to be paid, nor how profits are to be reckoned; all that is left, and very judiciously and properly left, to the commercial world.'

If, therefore, the commercial world and the accountancy profession can arrive at any conclusion as to the effect of replacement cost, for example, upon the measurement of trading profits, the law is not likely to have any preconceived notions upon the subject.

7. One thing the law clearly cannot do. It must assume that £1 is £1 at all times. We are here in the realm of legal tender. The law cannot engage in speculation as to the rising or falling value of the currency. The financial unit for the measurement of profits may in fact be elastic, but the law must assume it to be static and leave it to the business world to devise any new methods of measurement rendered necessary by that fact.

(d) The Business Man's View

A great deal has been said and written on this vital subject by business men. There appears to be an overwhelming body of opinion amongst them that in one respect at least existing accountancy conventions are not giving an accurate measurement of profit. It is stressed on almost all hands that to charge depreciation based on the original cost grossly understates the current value of the wastage of the asset in earning revenue, and prevents the accumulation of the necessary funds charged against revenue to replace the asset which is being depreciated. Profit is thus overstated and capital resources are depleted.

Whilst there are many who also favour the replacement cost basis in the case of stock, there is nothing like the same concensus of opinion as there is in the case of fixed assets. In fact, it is extremely doubtful that if such an issue were to be determined by business men there would be a sufficient weight of opinion in favour of the change.

On the question of restating the items in the balance sheet to give a measurement of capital based on current values, there is by no means any general claim that this should be done. There are some important concerns which do in fact carry out this procedure, but they are few.

The following view by a well-known business man sets out the view fairly widely held in business circles.

Mr. John P. Bibby, of J. Bibby & Sons Ltd., Liverpool, issued in June, 1950, a booklet entitled, *A Plea for Some Reform in the Conventional Methods of Computing Profits.*

In the introduction he says:

'During pre-war days it would have been difficult to raise much enthusiasm for such a cause as the reform in the method of computing industrial profits.

'It is true that under conventional methods of accounting inflation has always resulted in some overstatement of profits, but while taxation remained relatively low, neither industrialists nor their accountants had much cause to worry about the matter.

'Circumstances have changed, however, during recent years, in that the rate of inflation has increased and taxation has risen to a much higher level. The effect of these changes is disturbing and I think it is true to say that during the period 1939-49, although excellent profits were shown in the profit and loss accounts, industrial concerns, speaking generally, were poorer in real assets at the end of the period than at the beginning.

'It is clear that a method of computing profits that is capable of leading directors, shareholders, employees and the general public into a belief that good profits are being made, while in fact inroads are being made into capital, is sadly in need of some reform.'

After examining the problem in detail, he concludes:

'The case for reform in the method of computing profits may now be summed up in very few words.

'It is agreed by most people that the main practical purpose for which traders and industrialists compute their profits is that they may be kept informed of the amounts that become available for distribution as dividends and for expansion of business, as a result of their business activity during each succeeding accounting period. This indeed may be said to be the economist's definition of profits.

'It has been shown, and it is not disputed, that the profit and loss account as drawn up on conventional lines produces a figure for "profit" during periods of changing prices levels which bears no relationship whatever to the amount available for distribution and expansion of business.

'Such a profit and loss account fails, therefore, in its main purpose. It has been mentioned, too, that the profits shown in profit and loss accounts of industry are used in computing national income, and it is obvious that (unless corrections are made) their use during periods of inflation introduces considerable error into these estimates. They are used, too, by various negotiating bodies dealing with wages and profit margins, and here again they mislead rather than inform those who use them.

'They are used, too, in computing income-tax and profits tax on industrial and trading profits, and it has been shown that great inequity as between one company and another results from their use for this purpose.

'It is clear that a method of computing profits which produces a figure which misleads those who use it as a guide to the amount available for dividends, and which results in false conclusions and inequity when used for other purposes, is in urgent need of reform.'

Mr. Frank Bower, C.B.E., M.A. (Unilever Ltd.), in an address on 'Inflation' to The Corporation of Certified Secretaries on 21st September, 1951, said:

'The conventional basis of . . . accounting postulates that business is entitled only to recoup its past costs and that anything over and above is a profit. Where the value of money is stable there is no material difference between current costs and past costs. Where prices rise permanently, the recovery and retention of current costs keeps the business intact. To recover only past costs injures the business to the extent of the difference between the two costs during the time which it takes to turn the capital asset over. In the case of stocks, this happens quickly and repeatedly; in the case of fixed assets the turnover is spread over more years.

'The kernel of the problem therefore lies in relating current costs to current receipts. An accounting . . . technique is needed which will produce this result.'

After a detailed survey, Mr. Bower sums up:

'In conclusion we must accept the position that money has permanently lost in value and that pre-war levels of prices will not recur. The present prospect is that its value will fall still lower. The argument on the principle of maintaining conventional profit accounting or of reflecting the changing value of money in the calculation of profit is fast moving in favour of change.

'The immediate practical need is to translate the principle into precise accounting techniques which can command general acceptance.'

In 1951 The Federation of British Industries published a booklet entitled *The Effects of Inflation on Industrial Capital Resources*. The following extracts are of interest:

'1. It is frequently contended amongst industrialists that the capital resources of industry are not merely being strained but are in danger of exhaustion as the result of combined inflation and high taxation. Yet at the same time complaints are repeatedly heard from other quarters at what are described as the excessive profits being made by industry.

'2. The twin questions of the erosion of capital and the adequacy of profits are clearly inter-related, for unless industry is able to provide from its own resources for the maintenance intact of its productive capacity, it is, in effect, living on capital. The maintenance of capital intact, in the sense of preserving the productive capacity of the enterprise, is, in fact, one of the most important responsibilities of management. For the fulfilment of this responsibility, only the balance remaining after provision has been made for the maintenance of capital can be regarded as "profit" and as available either to meet taxation or for distribution as dividends.

'3. If the value of money remained constant, an increase or decrease in the capital resources of industry would be fairly easy to measure. But when the value of money is changing as progressively as it has done in recent years, then there is great difficulty in interpreting the published accounts of public companies so as to measure changes in capital. This difficulty arises from the use, in a long period of rising prices, of accounting methods which assume a stable value of money. Since 1938 the money cost of maintaining intact a given volume of real capital including fixed assets, stocks and book debts has greatly increased. Despite this, balance sheets by tradition treat all £s as being of equal value, whether they are £s of 1951, 1938 or 1900. The convention is that in calculating profit it is sufficient to put aside a sum equal to the cost of the asset whenever it was bought, despite the fact that the replacement will actually cost much more. The connection between the maintenance of capital and the level of profits is clear; in so far as the published accounts of companies understate the requisite provision for maintenance of assets, they correspondingly overstate the real profits earned.'

Finally, a short extract from a speech delivered by Mr. J. B. Braithwaite (Chairman of the London Stock Exchange) at a Luncheon Club meeting of the Incorporated Accountants' London and District Society on 6th November, 1951:

'I ... am troubled by the results that flow from the present system of relating depreciation allowances to the historical cost of the asset to be depreciated. ... Of course the arguments for the present system are quite clear and one must have a considerable degree of sympathy with them, because the accountant feels—and I should feel it myself—that while he sticks to the historical cost of the asset he has his feet planted firmly upon the ground, whereas if he departs from it he enters at once the debatable region of estimates and of rapidly moving values. Probably he feels also that, in the long run, the present system does do substantial justice. I agree that in the long run it does, but as a business man and as something more than that—a citizen—I feel that the system has two very serious defects. First from the purely business point of view, whilst over the average of a pretty long period of time substantial justice may be done, yet the result is that profits are grossly distorted in many cases, over many if not all the individual accounting periods. It is difficult for me to see how the accounts of a business can be said to present a true and fair and proper picture of the affairs of a company unless assets have been depreciated in a reasonable proportion to their correct replacement value.

'I start from the point that I think a company cannot be said to have made a profit at all until it has dealt realistically and not academically with this problem of depreciation. In all those years when old assets are being depreciated on the historical cost basis you get a distortion of the profit figure for the business. That, of course, leads to excessive taxation and distortion in a good many other ways. This applies not only to accounts, but to a great many things in business and in life generally. If you start with a wrong picture, no matter what fairly reasonable grounds there are for it, the distortion grows and grows as it might be from mirror to mirror, and all sorts of bad results flow from it. In particular, I would suggest that extravagance in administration flows from an unduly large profit figure. You also get a dissatisfaction amongst employees, a wrong idea of what a business is earning, requests for higher wages than can reasonably be paid, and things of that kind.

'I believe it is of the first importance to the sound conduct of business that profits shall be accurately shown, computed upon a true and realistic basis in accordance with the conditions prevailing at the time.'

The British Bankers' Association submitted a memorandum dated July, 1951, to the Royal Commission on the Taxation of Profits and Income, and the following are extracts from it:

'In seeking to explain the development of financial stringency, it is impossible to isolate the influence of taxation from that of other factors. We feel no doubt, however, that the existing systems of basing depreciation allowances for fixed capital on original cost, and of levying taxation on "profits" which reflect merely an inflationary rise in the price of stock that has to be replaced at the inflated price, are elements of overwhelming importance. We take it as self-evident that both profits tax and income-tax as applied to companies are intended to be taxes on income and not on capital. To the economist, if not to all accountants, it appears equally self-evident that the true profits for any period cannot exceed the receipts accruing from the year's trading after providing for the replacement of the physical capital used in earning the profits for the period, i.e. after allowing for the wearing out of fixed assets and replacing circulating capital embodied in the output for the period, both of which, in a continuing business, have to be maintained.

'There can be no question that remedies which are practicable in administration can be found, since, as the Committee point out, action has been taken to deal with the problem in France and Belgium. Beyond a certain point, indeed, it becomes impossible to cling to ordinary accountancy principles in the face of inflation. Had the inflation experienced in this country been even a little more rapid than has been the case hitherto, there seems no doubt that the problem would already have been faced and dealt with.'

These extracts do emphasise the grave concern of the business world with the working of some of our existing accountancy conventions.

VII. British Accounting Views on Changing Price Levels

The British views which influence existing practice here are to be found in recommendations issued by the Institute of Chartered Accountants in England and Wales. Recommendations IX and X issued in 1945, dealing with fixed assets and stock, stated that in both cases the normal basis of valuation for accounting purposes should be the historical cost (or, in the case of stock, the market value if lower). Further recommendations (Fourth Supplement, Recommendation XII) were issued by the Institute in January, 1949, and extracts from the statement accompanying the recommendations bearing on the question were:

'180. The combined effect of the rise in price levels and the oppressive burden of taxation has led a number of business men and their advisers to question the validity of the methods of profit ascertainment hitherto generally followed by industrial and commercial undertakings. They do not challenge the generally accepted accounting principle that the profit of a period can be ascertained only after providing, by way of charges against revenue, adequate sums for remedying any impairment of the capital of a business which may have occurred in the ordinary course of trading in that period. Opinions differ, however, as to whether capital for this purpose means (a) the money contributed by the proprietors, including profits left by them in the business for financing it, or (b) the power of that sum of money to purchase a particular volume of goods or equipment. Some business men have adopted the latter conception and accordingly maintain the proposition that profit can be stated correctly only if it is ascertained after treating as revenue charges sums sufficient to provide the increased funds necessary for replacing the stocks consumed or sold and for providing an appropriate proportion of the prospective enhanced cost of replacing the fixed assets used up in carrying on the business.

'181. This proposition is at variance with the accounting practice hitherto generally followed of treating as charges to revenue the actual monetary cost of the stocks consumed or sold and depreciation provisions representing the appropriate proportion of the amounts carried in the books for fixed assets (usually their historical cost). Those who maintain the view hitherto accepted, point out that logical application of the method advocated by those who desire a change would require them in ascertaining profit not only to make charges against revenue on new bases in respect of stocks and fixed assets, but also to provide for the diminished purchasing power of cash and other liquid assets to be used in the business. They put forward the criticism that it would be illogical, in ascertaining profit, to treat as a necessary charge the cost of maintaining the purchasing power of money provided by the issue of fixed preference or loan capital, whilst ignoring the corresponding diminution in the obligation, expressed in terms of purchasing power, to the holders of that capital. They emphasise that if the new conception were adopted the holders of preference shares might be deprived of dividends without acquiring any capital benefit. Moreover, they point out, as regards goods consumed or sold, that those who desire the change have not yet been able to devise a satisfactory method, suitable for general use, of applying the principle advocated and, as regards fixed assets, that, owing to improved processes of manufacture, plant which becomes worn out or obsolete is not invariably replaced. Further, they claim that not only is the suggested change wrong in principle, but also that it strikes at the root of sound and objective accounting because of the practical difficulties of assessing the amounts which would be treated as charges to revenue if the new conception were adopted.

'183. Apart from the question of depreciation, the writing-up of the fixed assets itself involves practical difficulties, including, inter alia, those which arise because relative stability of prices on a new level has not yet been attained, the invalidation of comparisons with figures of previous periods and, in many cases, the lack of data on which satisfactory revaluations could be achieved.'

The recommendations were:

'192. (1) Any amount set aside to finance replacements (whether of fixed or current assets) at enhanced costs should not be treated as a provision which must be made before profit for the year can be ascertained, but as a transfer to reserve. If such a transfer to reserve is shown in the profit and loss account as a deduction in arriving at the balance for the year, that balance should be described appropriately.

'193. (2) In order to emphasise that as a matter of prudence the amount set aside is, for the time being, regarded by the directors as not available for distribution, it should normally be treated as a specific capital reserve for increased cost of replacement of assets.

'194. (3) For balance sheet purposes fixed assets should not, in general, be written-up on the basis of estimated replacement costs, especially in the absence of a measure of stability in the price level.'

And further, in Recommendation XIII, dealing with accountants' reports for prospectuses, where the prospectus contains an expert valuation of fixed assets in excess of the book value and this valuation is to be incorporated in the books, it is recommended that:

'207. (5) Where a valuation of fixed assets is adopted for the purposes of the books and accounts:

    (a) It is not normally appropriate or practicable, in a report dealing with a period during which there have been material changes in price levels, to make consequential adjustments in the depreciation provisions for past years;

    (b) The report should, however, indicate the approximate future annual provision computed on the basis of the valuation and should give a comparison thereof with the actual provision made in arriving at the profit or loss shown in the report for the last year covered thereby.'

These recommendations set out the current accountancy practice in Great Britain and, up to the present time, may be taken as representing the accountant's view of the changing price level in relation to the accounts.

VIII. The Effect of Fluctuating Price Levels on the Value of Long-term Trends

The first and most obvious point is the fact that long-term trends depend upon a time series. In the case of accounting, the series must come from and be constituted by a set of formally related accounts, prepared for specific periods and marked off at definite points in time, i.e. the accounting dates. It is clear that if the series is to be of any use at all for the purpose of discerning a trend, then the underlying accounts must be prepared with an eye to exactness of form in order to preserve identical types of relationship between the intrinsic aggregates which constitute the items in those accounts. Standardised accounts are essential for the investigation of long-term trends.

It appears to be equally plain that the content of each set of accounts entering into the series must be kept on the same plane of reference if the relationships in the series are to have any meaning at all. This is quite primary, and the failure to observe its purport will lead considerations astray by inferring wrong conclusions from ill-founded trends.

Prediction lies at the root of the establishment of all trends, and surely accountancy is only in its infancy so far as this subject is concerned. All are familiar with pre-determined estimates based on experienced observation entering into the techniques of standard costing and budgetary accounting. Many who have had experience in these techniques know only too well what a time it takes to reach reliable measurements of normal and effective standards against which to set actual performances. If there was greater knowledge of mathematical methods of prediction from trends, we should have some means, at least, of testing the validity of those empirical standards devised too early on in schemes of cost control.

It should never be denied by any accountant that, apart from reports of stewardship, all good accounting designs are formed with the object of providing a quick means of understanding past happenings in the hope that this understanding will help forward such policy decisions as may bear upon, and perhaps shape, the course of future probabilities. In this context the interpretations to be drawn from both short- and long-term trends are of paramount importance. Nevertheless, it has always to be remembered that, by themselves and taken alone, accounts of actual transactions can be little more than historical documents, and the policy uses to which they can be put must still depend upon the judgment and ideas of those who are called upon to interpret them. Yet it is well known that no proper judgments can be formed from data which are intertwined with different measurements occasioned by different price-level scales brought into use at the same time.

To interrupt these considerations temporarily, it might be remarked that the overall problems, for which long-term trends are meant to point solutions, extend well beyond those of the individual enterprise. One quotation will suffice to emphasise the point:

> 'Undistributed corporate earnings have been widely discussed in connection with cyclical fluctuations in business activity, long-run trends in investment and employment, changes in the economic functions of the securities markets, and other economic problems.'[1]

The greater part of all sections of this paper has been designed to consider the necessity for measuring those aggregates which enter into the accounting assessment of periodic income and capital on the same plane of reference. As is well known, it is these short-period measures

[1] *Corporate Income Retention, 1915-1943*, by Sergei P. Dobrovolsky, page 1. Financial Research Program, Studies in Business Financing (National Bureau of Economic Research, New York, 1951).

and their constituents which must form the basis of a time series designed to establish long-term trends. Even though these short-period measures *are* put on a proper foundation so far as concerns their ascertainment at accounting dates, they are still only *reliable money* measurements at those dates. As everyone is aware, money measurements at different dates in a long-term series do *not* mean the same thing, and to that extent they are not comparable. To make them comparable we still need some adjustments to set them forth in terms of constant prices. The calculation of these adjustments is never an easy matter. No long-term trend, for example, which depends upon operating profit as a function of *real* assets employed, can have much meaning to establish the changing effectiveness of an entity's resources, unless both the profits and the asset valuations are set by measures which themselves purport to be constant. There are many other functions inferrable from accounts which lose all significance over time unless they are formulated in like content measures.

All adjustments to money measures over long periods are awkward and difficult, for once again we have to summon to our aid general averages, weighted or otherwise, expressed in the form of indices, and it can never be certain that the base data of the index are representative of the underlying data in the monetary measures. Nevertheless, we must strive to approximate to this correspondence in selecting the index.

One last thought on these particular issues. Capital measures are frequently at the base of long-term trends. If we think of capital as a store of resources having *alternative* uses, then there may be something to be said for such adjustments to money capital measures at defined dates as depend upon an index of the general price level of capital goods. And so, a plea can properly be entered for a central and official formulation of such an index.

IX. SPECIAL CONSIDERATIONS AFFECTING NATIONALISED UNDERTAKINGS

The undertakings which have now been nationalised were largely undertakings providing public utility service. Before nationalisation, the practices followed by these public utility undertakings in relation to depreciation and renewals frequently differed from what was then known as commercial practice, i.e. from the practice followed by the generality of limited liability companies.

Many of the public utility undertakings were owned by local authorities, who usually set up sinking funds, related to assumed asset lives, for the redemption of the capital, fixed and wasting, invested in such undertakings. In some cases, additional provisions were set aside for the renewal of wasting assets, but this amounted to a double provision.

In the case of statutory companies, that is to say companies constituted not under the Companies Acts, but by special Acts of Parliament, practices varied. Some of them adopted the normal commercial practice of providing for depreciation on original cost spread over assumed effective lives. In other instances, and the main-line railways were an outstanding example, it was accepted that the 'like-for-like' cost of replacing wasting assets should be met out of revenue account. Renewal funds were therefore set up and the provisions carried to their credit were calculated on the estimated replacement cost of the assets concerned for the year in respect of which the provision was set aside (after taking account, of course, of the assumed useful life of the assets); that is to say, each year's revenue was charged with a renewal provision related to current replacement costs. It was not the practice to adjust the accumulated balance on these renewal funds to current replacement values year by year. Having set aside a provision based on current replacement cost, and having charged the renewal fund with the appropriate expenditure, the net balance of the fund was carried forward unchanged from year to year.

It is probably fair to say that the depreciation and renewal policy followed by the nationalised bodies after they had been constituted was influenced to some extent at least by the past history of each industry concerned. Very broadly, it is true to say that the nationalised bodies have followed the principles laid down by the Institute of Chartered Accountants. That is to say, they have calculated depreciation by reference to book cost.

National Coal Board

The reports indicate that the National Coal Board has not yet finalised its depreciation and renewal policy, and the position is summed up in the report for the year 1950 in the following words:

'Depreciation provisions have again been based on the cost of the assets to the Board (using estimates where necessary) and not on replacement values. There is no doubt that replacement values now exceed cost because of increases in prices since 1947. Further consideration will be given to the Board's depreciation policy when the major part of the compensation payable is determined and can be allocated to the various types of assets.'

British Transport Commission

The policy followed by the Commission is fully and clearly stated in paragraph 74 (pages 44 and 45) of their annual report for the year 1948, which is as follows:

'CHAPTER FIVE

'FINANCE: THE CONSOLIDATED POSITION

'*Basis of Account*

'74. The underlying assumption of the double account system is that capital is something which can be permanently maintained by renewal, and which changes neither up nor down unless the undertaking itself expands or contracts. Changes in price levels are accordingly ignored when capital assets wear out and are replaced, the cost of the new assets being charged to revenue (or to reserve created out of revenue). The so-called "Commercial" basis of account has a less static conception of capital. The capital assets, at least so far as they require individual replacement, are regarded as undergoing a steady process of change, and when an asset is scrapped it is written out of capital; any new asset provided, whether as a replacement or otherwise, is written into capital at its actual cost. Under this system the capital expenditure relating to the assets in question reflects the cost when acquired of the assets actually in use, and revenue is charged with the annual instalments needed to write off this capital cost, as distinct from the provision which would have to be made to buy a replacement if price levels changed.

'In respect of assets requiring individual replacement, the Commission decided to employ the "commercial" basis and, notwithstanding the exceedingly great volume of accounting work involved in the change, the former railway companies' assets—in the category of rolling stock, ships and plant (as distinct from permanent and fixed works such as ways and structures which are renewed rather than replaced)—now appear in the accounts at their full cost when acquired, whether by the vested undertakings or by the Commission, and will continue to do so in future. The effects of this change are explained in the Notes on Accounts, and the main considerations which influenced the decision were as follows:

(*a*) It was essential to establish a common basis for the accounting.

(*b*) It is desirable (1) that the book records of the assets in existence at any time should, as a general rule, be related to their actual cost rather than to the cost of the original assets which they replace, and (2) that depreciation provided on such assets should also be related to the firm fact of their actual cost rather than to estimates of current costs of replacement, which may vary greatly from year to year.

(*c*) An annual provision based on actual cost of the assets is likely to be steadier from year to year than any other basis of provision.

(*d*) Asset accounts maintained on this basis reflect more accurately the changes in the capital position and the extent to which the assets have been written down out of revenue.

(*e*) Changes in the forms and techniques of transport may mean that much of the Commission's existing equipment will never be replaced.

(*f*) Leading accountancy bodies in this country and the United States have recommended that depreciation provisions should be based on actual cost of the assets in use, and that any further provision towards replacement cost should be regarded as a matter of financial appropriation rather than as a process of accounting charge.

There is the further consideration that the employment of actual cost as a basis is in line with Inland Revenue practice.'

In a note to the accounts (page 196 of the 1948 report) it is stated that:

'... This (depreciation) provision has been calculated by spreading the gross book values of the assets by equal annual instalments over their assumed useful lives. ...

'As and when earnings are available for the purpose, it is intended to make further allocations out of profits year by year to a replacement reserve towards meeting the increased cost of replacement as compared with the gross book values upon which the depreciation provision is computed.'

It is also to be noted that, in presenting the Commission's case to the Transport Tribunal for an increase in fares and charges, the Commission included in their assessment of the amount of money to be raised an allowance for the increased cost of replacement compared with depreciation provisions calculated on book costs.

British Electricity Authority

The depreciation policy of the British Electricity Authority is fully explained in paragraphs 523 to 529 of its first annual report. The more important of these paragraphs, numbered 526 to 529, are as follows:

'CHAPTER EIGHT

'FINANCE AND ACCOUNTS: THE NEW FINANCIAL STRUCTURE

'*Depreciation and Redemption of Capital*

'526. In considering the principles to be applied in computing the total amount of the annual provision for discharge of capital expenditure, regard was had to the practices of the transferred undertakings and to the best current commercial practice in measuring depreciation. For capital expenditure after vesting day and for assets acquired after vesting day, the "straight-line" method of depreciation has been adopted, the periods or lives of the assets being fixed according to the classes or types of capital expenditure and their expected periods of usefulness. Periods or lives of different kinds of assets were formerly reflected in the maximum periods allowed by the Electricity Commissioners for the redemption of loans raised for capital purposes by public authorities (see Appendix 43). Before vesting day there was a substantial body of opinion in favour of the revision of certain of these periods, in the light of experience gained of the effective working lives of the corresponding assets; and accordingly an inquiry has been set on foot to examine, from the point of view of future policy, the appropriate periods of usefulness to be assumed as reasonably conservative, having regard to physical efficiency and the possibility of obsolescence, for different classes or types of capital expenditure.

'527. If practicable, the principles adopted for measuring depreciation of newly-acquired assets would also have been applied to the vested assets. Depreciation of these assets would then have been calculated on values representing the original cost of assets actually in use, reduced by a notional accumulation of depreciation provision built up by applying the straight-line method to each asset from the date of its original acquisition. But this, as has been explained, proved to be an impracticable task. It was therefore decided that provision for depreciation of vested assets should be calculated on the basis of the values of the assets as disclosed in the balance sheets of the transferred undertakings, after deducting the total provision already made for depreciation by the former undertakers.

'528. This has meant very largely the continuance of the practices of the former undertakers. In the case of assets inherited from public authorities, upon which amortisation was in course of being provided within the appropriate maximum loan periods allowed by the Electricity Commissioners (see Appendix 43), the amount of the expenditure remaining undischarged at vesting day was ascertained, together with the unexpired period of discharge. In each case the provision to be made for depreciation in each remaining year was computed by applying the straight-line method to the amount of undischarged expenditure. In the case of assets inherited from company undertakings, similar treatment was accorded in so far as the necessary particulars were available; where, however, it had been the practice to make lump-sum provision for depreciation, it was not possible to ascertain in detail the extent to which the depreciation of individual assets had been provided for. In such case the scales upon which the reduced values should be written off were fixed on the same bases as the scales appropriate to comparable assets for which the full facts were known. The result is that the annual revenues of the Authority and the area boards will be charged, in respect of all vested assets not fully amortised before vesting day, with provision for depreciation which is in effect the sum of the individual amounts representing one year's proportion of the net book value of each asset, computed by reference to the remainder of its assumed useful life. The annual provision for depreciation of vested assets will gradually diminish as individual assets are wholly written off.

'529. From a scrutiny of past records of the treatment of depreciation and provision for redemption of capital by their predecessors, the Authority and the area boards are satisfied, on the criterion of the straight-line method of amortisation, that the aggregate provision made before vesting day was adequate. An important contribution to this satisfactory condition had arisen from the practice followed by many undertakers of meeting substantial amounts of capital expenditure out of revenue, thus making full provision for depreciation at the time of acquisition of the assets. Further, the Authority and the boards are satisfied that their annual revenues will be charged with provision for depreciation and redemption certainly no less than would have been set aside had there been no change in the ownership of the industry.'

General

This study could be carried further through the accounts of the remaining nationalised bodies, but enough has probably been said to indicate that, in general, the position of the nationalised bodies on this question of depreciation and replacement cost provisions does not differ materially in relation to present practices from the position of commercial undertakings in this country generally.

X. Special Considerations Affecting Local Authorities

In any consideration of this subject, it is essential to keep in mind the fundamental difference between the methods of financing the operations of a local authority and those employed in a commercial undertaking, and also the consequent difference in the structures of their respective accounts and balance sheets.

The Local Government Act, 1933, and ministerial regulations and orders lay upon local authorities the necessity of maintaining their records of capital expenditure and loan borrowings absolutely separate and distinct from their revenue transactions.

Having regard, therefore, to the legal requirements laid on local authorities in the matter of their capital transactions, it has been found advantageous to adopt a variation of the 'double account' system in some form or other, with separate accounts for capital and revenue and separate balancings of capital and revenue items in the balance sheet.

In private enterprise the share capital is applicable to all purposes of a company's business (subject, of course, to the limitation that dividends can only be paid out of profits) and it is not restricted to capital expenditure. In the event of continuous overall losses occurring, those losses must fall ultimately on the shareholder.

In the case of a local authority, the merging of capital and revenue moneys is not permissible and it is a fundamental principle that capital shall not be borrowed except for permanent works. Furthermore, the necessary Government sanction to borrow is granted with the obligation to repay the amount so borrowed out of revenue over a period of years which is usually somewhat less than the life of the asset. No power to borrow again for the renewal of the asset is granted until the full amount of the original loan has been provided and repaid to the loan holder.

There is always, therefore, just sufficient capital money raised to meet the cost of permanent works. The loan holders always receive the repayment of their capital in the given period, whilst revenue deficiencies are met by the ratepayer.

Local authorities therefore finance the cost of permanent assets and their replacement by borrowing and provide for the redemption of the capital by annual sinking fund contributions from revenue, i.e. the rates. A local authority's loan debt is therefore of a temporary nature and is merely 'deferred revenue' and it is the continuous amortisation of that capital out of the rates which merits attention in the present consideration.

In a period of rising price levels, the increased cost of replacement of assets or acquisition of new assets is met by a corresponding increase in the capital debt, and is reflected almost immediately in the increased debt charges, which are again met out of the local rate.

Broadly speaking, local authorities have been overcoming the difficulties created by increased price levels by increased local taxation, whereas the commercial undertaking and the equity shareholder are confronted with the problem of solving the same difficulty either by profit appropriations or by creation of new capital or otherwise.

It is doubtful whether local authorities in any case have the legal power to set aside replacement reserves, but if they wished to do so, it could only be by providing such reserves from the rates in addition to the sinking fund provisions already being made, and it is doubtful whether such an additional burden could be borne in view of the already high level of rates prevailing. However, a local authority is a taxing body in contrast to a trading company, and if the local authority fails to create such replacement reserves, it does not avoid raising the necessary taxes when the replacement occurs; that action is merely deferred.

To a certain extent efforts can be made to render the replacement cost problem less acute and to reduce borrowings. As has been mentioned, loans are repaid well within the life of the asset, and in certain cases steps can be taken to bring the period of repayment required by the loan sanction more in line with the life of the asset. Where possible a policy of 'pay as you go' can be adopted whereby the smaller items of capital expenditure are charged direct to revenue, and again debt redemption may be accelerated.

Generally speaking, however, it may be argued that a local authority is justified in leaving over the problem of meeting the increased cost of replacement of old assets until the new ones are to be provided. The cost has to be met by the ratepayer at some stage and it is the old question whether the present or future generations should pay.

On the question whether or not the fixed assets should be revalued at their increased worth in the balance sheet, it is doubtful whether this would serve any purpose in the case of local authorities. As continuous equilibrium is maintained between capital expenditure and loan borrowings, the historical figures of cost and debt appearing in the balance sheet are continuously adjusting themselves as price levels vary. Admittedly, the older provision remaining in the permanent assets would possibly be undervalued, but a revaluation of the old assets would not require an increase in the loan capital, but would only create a corresponding capital account surplus.

With regard to current assets, local authorities' services require the carrying of extensive stocks and the rise in prices of stores has, therefore, a corresponding effect, as they are charged out, upon the revenue expenditure, with a relatively short time-lag. In the meantime, the money necessary to finance the purchase of stocks will require an increased working balance, but local authorities, with the diminishing reserves which serve as their working capital, must possibly finance the increased cost through bank overdrafts, unless the increased working capital is raised by an additional rate levy.

Stocks are bound to be carried which are both fast- and slow-moving, and this, coupled with the method of pricing out, will decide how quickly the rising prices will have their effect on the revenue expenditure. FIFO will delay the increase until the last possible moment. A policy of LIFO will bring the increases into effect immediately, whereas some process of averaging—which it is thought the majority of authorities adopt—produces a gradual increase in the impact on the rate charge.

To summarise the position, the problem of rising price levels in relation to the accounts of both commercial businesses and local authorities is one of under-capitalisation.

The problem may be resolved in companies either by obtaining new capital which is permanent or by appropriations from profits. But there are obstacles to these solutions. On the one hand, equity share-holders may be apprehensive of the effect of the introduction of new capital on their equity; on the other hand the scale of present taxation may so restrict profits that there may not be sufficient available to permit of appropriation to redress the measure of under-capitalisation.

Local authorities are not faced with these difficulties. Under-capital-isation arising from the enhanced cost of either fixed or current assets is overcome almost immediately by the raising of capital or levying of additional rates.

The amount of capital which may be raised is comparatively unlimited (subject to the capacity to pay the interest rates involved) and, being temporary, is amortised from revenue. The embarrassment caused to local authorities by this problem is the mounting burden of local taxation they must perforce levy.

XI. OPEN QUESTIONS

In the synopsis which was issued last year, the following open questions were propounded with a view to giving a general indication of the scope of the paper and of assisting in the preparation of supplementary papers:

(a) Is there a satisfactory alternative basis to the monetary unit for accounts?

(b) How should fixed assets be treated in the accounts?
   (i) Stated at original costs or revalued annually.

(ii) Depreciated on the principle of:
    (*a*) original cost;
    (*b*) current value.
(iii) Where improved replacement takes place at lower *real* cost owing to technical development.
(*c*) Should securities be taken into account on the basis of current values?
(*d*) Can the existing accountancy basis of measuring business profits be varied in any way?
(*e*) What practical means are available to accountants to enable them to measure change in asset values?
(*f*) What are proper standards of accounting comparisons?

They will no doubt serve to assist the discussion by focusing attention on to the principal points which seem to emerge in any consideration of this subject.

XII. CONCLUSIONS

There is little more to say, but I would summarise my own views as follows:

(1) In the measurement of profit, depreciation of fixed assets should be based on the current replacement cost and not on the original or historical cost. The practical application of this principle is not insuperably difficult.
(2) In the measurement of profit, the same type of principle should apply to inventories. I concede, however, that at this time inventory profits have largely been absorbed in published reports of profits. We are now in the situation when there is a possibility of a fall in the price level. This would certainly have unfortunate repercussions if a change had to be made in the treatment of inventories. It may be that when a stabilised price level has been reached, the principle should be adopted.
(3) The balance sheet should be treated as a document reporting on the stewardship of contributed money capital, capital gains and savings. Therefore I am in favour of following the existing convention of adherence to original costs in statement of the balance sheet.

FLUCTUATING PRICE LEVELS IN RELATION TO ACCOUNTS

by

A. GOUDEKET
Nederlands Instituut van Accountants

I. INTRODUCTION

It is impossible to consider the problem of fluctuating price levels in relation to accounts without first defining the terms to be used. There must be a clear appreciation of the meaning of the words 'profit' and 'value' and a real understanding of the function of accounting and financial statements.

Again, no definitions of 'profit' and 'value' can be attempted without first formulating a sound theory of their economic significance. These terms have an economic significance only and it follows that any definition which associates them with an accounting or calculating technique will not lead to the proper conclusion. Improper conceptions of 'profit' and 'value' may have serious consequences for the individual enterprise, and ultimately for the national economy. There are great issues at stake which demand imaginative decisions.

If the conventional conceptions of profit and value are found to be inappropriate there must be no reluctance to abandon traditional accounting and calculating techniques. The accounting and financial statements are not ends in themselves; they are designed to serve the needs of managements at all levels and the business community as a whole, and therefore their traditional form should be changed to ensure that their function is properly fulfilled.

The auditor is concerned with this problem within the scope of his direct function, because in certifying the financial statements he expresses his opinion upon the profit and capital disclosed in the statements. In so far as the auditor is required to advise on the organisation and development of an accounting system, the problem is of equal importance.

Space does not permit an exhaustive analysis of the subject and many side-issues must be left undeveloped if a general review of the problem is to be attempted within the limits of this paper.

II. PROFIT AND VALUE

It would be impracticable to use this opportunity to develop a complete theory of profit and value, particularly in relation to an industrial or commercial enterprise, and it will only be possible to refer to the principles upon which the theory is based. The principles first put forward by Professor Limperg in the 1920s are accepted by the majority of the members of the profession in the Netherlands, and it has since been proved in practice that the application of the theory based on these principles provides the solution to this important and pressing problem. The comments on 'profit' and 'value' which follow have, for the greater part, been developed from a treatise on the subject written by Professor Limperg in 1937 following the devaluation of the Netherlands currency in the previous year.

At that time the change in the price level originated in the currency itself, but the nature of the problem remains the same if changes in the price level are due to changes in the real value of goods and services.

Economically, profit has only one meaning—it must be the basis for the rational satisfaction of the needs of those whose incomes depend upon the results of business activities. Proper planning of expenditure depends upon knowledge of the level of the 'spendable income'.

The economic view is that income is that part of the capital which can be spent. It follows that profit is the spendable income arising from a business and accruing to those whose incomes depend upon the results of the business. Profit is therefore the income which may be spent without trespassing on the capital of the business, which is the source of the income. The fruit may be picked but the tree may not be felled.

The fact that the taxation authorities of most countries do not recognise this conception of profit is no reason for business managements to ignore the proper principles of profit measurement. The calculation of taxable profits is a separate problem, which need not be considered here.

In a business transaction the value of the goods surrendered in an act of exchange is the basis for determining the profit. Value is the quantitative assessment of the *significance* of the goods exchanged, to the owner of the business.

In practice the valuation problem arises in two stages, first at the time of the exchange and secondly in the composition of the financial statements.

The difference between the value at the time of exchange and the proceeds of the goods is the spendable income, but the value of the goods exchanged is not in any way determined by the price originally paid for the goods or for the means of their production. No matter what the original expenditure may represent it is certainly not the value of the goods at the time of the exchange. Within the period of a wholly stable price level the historical expense and the replacement value would, of course, be the same but the principle is not affected. The difference between proceeds and historical expense cannot therefore be the profit on the transaction, and because in a going concern there is an economic obligation to replace the goods exchanged, it follows that the profit from the transaction is determined by the value represented by the cost of replacing the goods.

When price levels are rising it is well understood that higher replacement costs will eventually have to be recovered from consumers, but this elementary truth is less generally accepted in so far as goods in stock are concerned. It must be pointed out, however, that any selling price policy based on historical expenditure necessarily involves a sacrifice of profit arising on the exchange of goods. The goods surrendered have to be replaced, and if the consumer does not compensate the vendor for the increased cost of replacement, the vendor encroaches upon his capital to the extent of the difference.

On the other hand, if selling prices are based on replacement costs, but the vendor does not realise that the value of the goods is higher (and by implication his sacrifice greater in the exchange) the spendable income will be calculated on too high a level. If the vendor believes he can profit partly by reason of the favourable circumstances by measuring his profit against the original expense, the spendable income will be overstated, and as a result he may spend that part of the proceeds required to replace the goods.

The same considerations apply to the permanent means of production. Misconceived considerations in this connection will have still more serious repercussions than in the case of raw materials. Mistakes may persist for years because the replacement of the permanent means of production invariably takes place some considerable time after the rise in prices; consequently the effect of the rise in prices only becomes apparent when replacement has in fact to be made. The technique by which fixed amounts of depreciation are calculated as part of the expenses of the production obscures a true appreciation of the problem. Depreciation represents the value of the units of work consumed during a prescribed period of time. Because replacement will eventually be made on a higher price level, depreciation must be based on the replacement value. It is true that the actual replacement is long deferred, but the economic obligation to replace is present from the very beginning. The degree of the obligation is determined by the new price and therefore the value of the units of work consumed in the production is again the replacement value.

In considering the permanent means of production, two problems must be solved. First the significance of the effect of the increase in prices with reference to the units of work consumed in the production during the past year (and to be consumed in the future) and secondly the units of work consumed in previous periods. The increasing cost of replacement must necessarily lead to a revision of past provisions for depreciation in order to correct past calculations when the replacement price of the means of production was under-estimated. It is obvious that these corrections must be made before spendable income (profit) can be measured.

What is the significance of the difference between the replacement value of the goods exchanged and the historical expense? The appreciation is certainly not spendable income; the increase of the historical expense to the higher replacement value is no more nor less than the increase of the replacement value between the time of acquisition and the time of the exchange. The appreciation may be claimed only by the economic obligation to replace. If this fictitious income is taken as spendable income, the process would involve a dissipation of capital. By the same reasoning it follows that this appreciation of goods in stock at the time of making up the financial statements is not spendable income either. In actual practice these tenets are instinctively implemented, but when this happens the appreciation is called 'non-realised profit'. This exposition shows, however, that an increase in the value of stocks and the permanent means of production does not create

D

a profit, either realised or non-realised. It is an important conclusion because the economic function of the financial statements is to show the *spendable income* arising from the business activities.

The ultimate conclusion is therefore that the growth of capital arising from an increase in the replacement value of both stocks and the permanent means of production leads to an appreciation of capital, but this increment is not spendable income. It does not represent profit arising from an exchange, and from the outset it must be recognised as being required to meet the economic obligation to replace at higher prices. If the appreciation of capital is treated as distributable profit, the business can no longer be maintained at the former level of activity, and it follows from this conclusion that a rational selling-price policy must be based on replacement value.

In the social economic sphere there is a real danger that a considerable part of the national wealth will be expunged because, if selling-prices are not increased, the consumer will not immediately realise that, with the same nominal income, he can no longer make the same demands on the national income. On the other hand, if selling prices are increased, the overstatement of business profits would encourage excessive expenditure by those who have a title to the profits.

Finally, it must be realised that a selling-price policy based on historical expense always tends to work against the best interests of the vendor; when prices are rising, he is always a few rounds behind, and when prices are falling the consumer is not interested in the vendor's historical expense.

III. Accounting

Theoretically, it is of little importance whether the appreciation of stocks and the permanent means of production is taken into the books or not. If it is brought into the books it does not matter what the account in which the appreciation is recorded is called, as long as the designation is clear and unambiguous; in particular the title of the account must not give the impression that it represents a profit.

If it is agreed that the function of accounting is to record and provide the basis for the interpretation of the economic affairs of the enterprise, then it is necessary to bring the appreciation into the books. The mere recording of nominal increases in capital is not enough because the management of the business cannot be properly conducted if acts of management are based on this misleading evidence. A differentiation between economic income and the growth of capital arising from price increases is essential for proper planning in all its aspects, the establishment and maintenance of a rational commercial policy, the sound judgment of results, and ultimately the determination of distributable profit and dividend policy. It might be deduced that this differentiation has a purely negative application to the maintenance of capital, but it can be positively interpreted to lead to a true appreciation of the capital employed and the earning capacity of the business. It can be argued that the function of accounting is to record what has happened and it can be maintained that the recording of events excludes all economic considerations. This is quite a fallacious argument. The registration of historical expense alone does not disclose the full implications of an act of exchange.

It is not possible within the limits of this paper to devote further consideration to the problem of deciding upon the actual moment of exchange, or the extent of the influence of replacement value in those cases where there is no economic obligation to replace. It must be enough merely to refer to these matters, but they must be studied before they are thoroughly understood. Similarly it is not possible to do more than comment on some of the aspects of the accounting technique.

It is often pointed out that it is impracticable to incorporate the replacement value in the accounting by charging all the items consumed in the manufacturing process at their individual replacement value. This contention will in general be advanced by a business which cannot justify the employment of modern accounting machines. The issue, however, is not a mathematical one demanding an arithmetically precise computation, but an economic one which demands an efficient solution. It is only necessary to guarantee that degree of accuracy which does full justice to the principles.

An acceptable solution to the problem of stock valuation can be reached where standard prices are used in the stock administration. Where stocks can be subdivided into groups which are characterised by more or less homogeneous price movements, the differences between purchase price and standard price can be recorded for each group. Such a system has certain distinctive features:

(a) the account of the price difference can be regularly compared with the purchases at standard price, and from this comparison the price difference in each group can be expressed as percentages. At this stage the price difference account contains two elements—the influence of changes in price and the measure of the efficiency of the purchasing activity. An analytical survey of market price levels enables the elements in the price difference account to be separately identified.

(b) The fact that stocks are recorded in the books at pre-determined standard prices enables fluctuations in prices to be expressed as group-indices, and the application of these indices converts the standard price valuation of the stocks and the goods consumed to their respective replacement values. The nature of the business will determine whether it is necessary to calculate indices for each of the elements in the several phases of the manufacturing process or whether it is sufficient to calculate one index for each of the basic elements represented in the standard price of the finished goods.

(c) Within the period of a rising price level, when the volume of stock is unchanged, the price difference on purchases will be recovered by the application of the indices to consumption. When the level of stocks is increasing, the recovery of the price difference will be made by the application of the indices to consumption and to the increase in stocks. When the level of stocks is decreasing, the surplus on the price difference account must be transferred to a reserve account to meet the higher cost of the eventual replacement of the stock level. The term 'stock' should be used in an economic and not in a physical sense. Outstanding orders in the hands of suppliers and unexecuted commitments to consumers (to the extent that the prices have been agreed) form part of the economic stock. This is the stock which is liable to the risks of price movements. As soon as the economic obligation to replace is ignored, a speculative element is introduced no matter whether the decision is involuntary or deliberate. The character of the speculation depends upon the reasons for the repudiation of the obligation, which may be due to a decision of the business itself or to quite extraneous circumstances. In both cases the result of the effect of the price movement should be booked and brought into account in the measurement of profit or loss where it should be distinguished as the results of the speculation.

The accounting for the permanent means of production must follow the same considerations. One further problem arises, as the period of time between the inception of the consumption and replacement may be quite considerable, and the replacement value at every stage of the consumption may have been lower than at the time of the actual replacement or at those times during the consumption when consideration had to be given to the distribution of profits and the determination of capital. It is stated under the heading 'profit and value' that a revision of past provisions for depreciation must be made before distributable profits can be calculated.

Consideration has so far been limited to the consequences of a rising price level, but it is obvious that the same principles apply to a falling price level. It is just as important to distinguish the results of the activities of the business from the incidence of falling price levels as it is from that of rising price levels. In principle it is not important to know whether the losses arising from a falling price level can be met by charging them to reserves.

IV. FINANCIAL STATEMENTS

As with the accounting itself, it is theoretically of little importance to show the result of price increases in the financial statements. If it is shown, then it must be shown in such a way that the headings and annotations are fully understood, and the impression that the result of price increases gives rise to a profit must be avoided. It is therefore inappropriate to describe the depreciation required to restore the increase of the replacement price of the permanent means of production as 'extra depreciation', because such a description would suggest that an unnecessarily prudent policy is being followed when in fact no more is being provided than the economic obligation demands.

It is equally misleading to disclose a profit in the financial statements and appropriate part or all of it to specific reserves to meet the incidence of an increasing price level, because such a policy confuses the determination of profits with the destination of profits.

Because the financial statements are the media by which the managers of an enterprise account for their stewardship, they must disclose the amount and composition of the capital and profit. It follows that if the profit is incorrectly calculated, the earning capacity in relation to the capital will also be miscalculated. Improper acts of management will succeed the improper appreciations which follow the miscalculations. In such circumstances the whole purpose of the financial statements will be negatived.

In those countries where the composition of the financial statements is governed by law, they are required to be drawn up in such a way that the prescriptions are observed. Legal provisions generally stipulate the minimum obligations so that the practical application of these theories should always be possible. In this connection it should not be forgotten that legal prescriptions invariably follow the development of economic principles and the demands of society, and for this reason it would be wrong to go no further than the existing law. The fact that the taxation authorities in the Netherlands have already accepted a limited application of the replacement value theory in relation to the determination of taxable income is evidence that the persistent and emphatic presentation of well-founded principles will result in their ultimate recognition.

V. CONCLUSION

(1) It has been established that the replacement value is an essential element in the calculation of profits and in the computation of capital employed. The inflationary trends in the last few decades have given practical emphasis to the theory of replacement value.

(2) The results of the application of the replacement value theory must be brought into the books of the business. The books and accounts provide information for management and all others interested in the affairs of the business, and therefore the financial statements must show the nominal increase of capital distinguished between profits and differences in value.

(3) Accounting technique has progressed to such a degree that rational methods are available, both for the recording of mass data and for the fundamental solution of the problem.

PRICE LEVEL CHANGES IN RELATION TO ACCOUNTS

by

PROFESSOR WILLARD J. GRAHAM
American Accounting Association

Seldom has an accounting subject been so fiercely debated over so long a period as the one at issue here—the effect of price level changes on the determination, reporting and interpretation of income and of financial condition. But the issues in this controversy are still not very clearly defined.

Those demanding a change—the 'challengers'—'view with alarm' the inadequacies of accounting reports showing only historical costs, but their proposed substitute bases for reporting are too often revolutionary and impracticable, or too vague and indefinite for evaluation.

The 'defenders' of the *status quo*, on the other hand, while they freely admit that the historical cost base is far from perfect, maintain stoutly that it is better than the 'visionary schemes' proposed by the advocates of 'current cost'.

Neither 'challengers' nor 'defenders' can 'point with pride' to a design for completely satisfactory corporate reports as an accomplished fact.

I. AREAS OF AGREEMENT

Out of the noise and smoke of battle—the multitude of speeches, articles, monographs and books which this controversy has produced—there have emerged a few fundamental conclusions on which there seems to be substantial agreement.

(1) *The monetary unit is not 'stable'; it does fluctuate in value—materially; there is general and grave concern that these fluctuations are not now compensatory over time.*

Under the more-than-one-hundred-year reign of the gold standard in the United States and England, the ever-changing value of the monetary unit reverted periodically to approximately the same point. Beginning in 1933, the value of the dollar has been declining almost continuously, with minor interruptions in 1938 and 1949; its value now is less than 40 per cent. of the value in 1932. With inflationary forces still at work—uncontrolled money supply, large government debt, deficit spending to avoid 'recessions', union demands for wage increases in excess of the gain in productivity, support of farm prices, the mobilisation programme, etc., together with accounting methods that fail to reflect adequately the impact of inflation on profits— a recovery of any substantial portion of this loss of value is highly improbable; indeed, a continuing decline in value appears to be the far more likely prospect.

The significance of the decline in the value of the monetary unit to the problem of corporate reporting may be stated in various ways:

(a) The profits of all United States corporations for the past five years, when adjusted to reflect the effect of price change, are about 30 per cent. less than the profits actually reported.

(b) These adjusted profits, related to invested capital also stated in common dollars, indicate a per cent. return perhaps not much more than one-half of that actually reported.

(c) The impact of price change varies greatly among corporations, depending upon the nature of their assets and their financial structure; this results in a lack of uniformity and complicates still further the interpretation of conventional income statements and balance sheets.

(2) *At the present stage of accounting development, corporate reports must include financial data based on historical costs, either in the principal statements or as 'supplementary' information.*

The case for continuing to include historical cost data in financial statements is well stated by the American Accounting Association's Committee on Accounting Concepts and Standards.[1]

'Conventional accounting practices, which include adherence to historical dollar costs in financial reporting, have evolved over a long period. The usefulness for certain purposes of data so derived is well established. A complete and abrupt shift to an alternative basis at the present time is believed to be both inappropriate and impractical for several reasons:

(1) A vast body of common and statutory law and legal precedent, innumerable contractual and business relationships, and many regulatory provisions are presently founded on existing accounting practices.

(2) Although the upward movement of prices has occasioned an increasing general awareness of the instability of the dollar as a unit of value measure, there is no clear indication that business men, stockholders, employees, and the general public either desire or could now accept, without considerable confusion, any departure from historical cost.

(3) There is a lack of substantial agreement as to methods by which purchasing power adjustments may be accomplished; experimentation with specific methods has been inadequate. General acceptance of a proposal that present accounting methods be changed demands a clear demonstration of practical utility, which in this case is not yet available.

(4) Recorded and summarised historical dollar costs appear to provide the only adequate starting point for the development of information which will reflect the effects of changes in the value of the dollar.

'These reasons are deemed sufficient to sustain the conclusion that, at the present stage of accounting development, the primary financial statements should continue to reflect historical dollar costs.'

It should be noted, however, that only the *first* of the foregoing reasons (that relating to laws, regulations, contracts, and precedent) points to the

---

[1] 'Changing Price Levels and Financial Statements'. Supplementary Statement No. 2 of the Committee of Accounting Concepts and Standards Underlying Corporate Financial Statements of the American Accounting Association. Published in the *Accounting Review* of October, 1951. In the opinion of the writer, this statement presents a most carefully reasoned recommendation for meeting the reporting problem resulting from price change. It represents the considered opinion of members of the accounting profession, both educators and public accountants—the members of the Committee. In the present paper the writer quotes extensively from this statement, referring to it as 'The A.A.A. Committee Statement'. His justification lies in the fact that he was chairman of the committee during the two years the statement was in preparation.

conclusion that the corporate report should include financial statements based on historical dollar cost. The second and third reasons relate only to the *'timing'* of the change; they describe the difficulty of developing satisfactory methods of computing and presenting data which reflect the effect of price change—and the problem of educating readers to understand such data. And the fourth reason demonstrates only that the *'books'* must be kept on the basis of historical dollar costs to provide a starting point for the preparation of information reflecting the effect of price change.

(3) *Corporate reports which include* only *financial statements which are based solely on historical dollar costs—which ignore the changing value of the monetary unit—have severe limitations and are not satisfactory for all purposes for which corporate reports are used.*

Here again sound reasons for the inclusion of statements which reflect the changing value of the monetary unit are presented by the A.A.A. Committee on Accounting Concepts and Standards.

'While corporate reports are typically prepared primarily for stockholders, the information therein presented becomes, in effect, public property, and may enter quite generally into the formation of judgments. Financial statement data expressed in uniform ''current'' dollars would seem to be useful for the following purposes:

(1) The appraisal of managerial effectiveness in terms of the preservation of the current dollar equivalent of the capital invested in the business and not merely its initial dollar amount;
(2) The analysis of earning power in terms of the current economic backdrop;
(3) The determination and justification of sound wage policies; negotiations with labour unions;
(4) The determination by government of long-range policies with respect to ''control'' of the economy through monetary policy, price regulation, limitation of profits, taxation, etc.;
(5) The creation of an informed public opinion with respect to profits, prices, wages, etc., and the effect of inflation (or deflation) upon financial relationships generally;
(6) The determination and evaluation of managerial policies with respect to pricing, credit, dividends, expansion, and the like.'[1]

An analysis of the various uses of the information presented in corporate reports requires separate consideration of:

(1) the report of a single corporation;
(2) aggregates for an industry;
(3) aggregates for the economy as a whole.

Reports for a single company are normally read and used by the following: stockholders; short-term and long-term creditors; financial editors; financial services; employees; union leaders; the public; regulatory agencies such as the Security and Exchange Commission, the Wage Stabilisation Board; the Office of Price Stabilisation, etc.; and to some extent by management to get an overall picture of operations and 'financial condition'.

Aggregate reported figures for an industry are compiled by or reported to such users as: many of the foregoing public agencies; the top management of

[1] Op. cit.

labour unions; trade associations; financial services; forecasters; the public; and the top management of individual companies in the industry.

Aggregate figures for all business—for the total economy—are used by the Council of Economic Advisers, the Committee on the Economic Report to the President, financial and reporting agencies, forecasters, the Federal Reserve Board, and by management for an overall picture of the total economy.

A close analysis of the uses of the information presented in corporate reports demonstrates rather forcefully the desirability of presenting financial data reflecting the effect of price change. For many of these purposes historical cost data alone leads to erroneous conclusions.

It is almost certainly true that during the past decade the reporting of income based almost entirely on historical dollar costs has resulted in exaggerated impressions of corporate prosperity. Examples are these rather widely held opinions:

(1) That corporate profits generally are large—perhaps 'excessive', both in relation to sales and to invested capital, particularly the latter;

(2) That corporations generally have the 'ability to pay' higher wages without increasing prices;

(3) That dividends represent far too small a percentage of profits;

(4) That the portion of 'profit' retained in the business is used largely for 'expansion' of the business; actually much of it is required to maintain the same physical capital at higher prices;

(5) That rising prices result in higher profits—that a little inflation may be 'good for business'.

It must be noted, however, that special consideration must be given to situations in which conclusions to be drawn or decisions to be made from corporate reports *must* be based on historical dollar cost because it is so *specified* by law, contract or regulation. Examples lie in the determination of surplus legally available for dividends; taxable income; amount available for a corporation's purchase of its own stock; 'fair' rates for public utility services; prices under 'cost-plus' contracts; net income for profit-sharing plans, and many others.

This is not to say that the use of historical dollar cost secures the 'best', the most accurate, the most equitable results for all of these purposes. It is only to say that since the law, or the regulation, or the contract specifies historical dollar cost, results must be determined and interpreted accordingly. It is undoubtedly true that for many of these foregoing purposes the application of a current cost would be preferable—if permissible.

II. AREAS OF DISAGREEMENT

Here the area of agreement would seem to end. Still unresolved are many questions about which there are substantial differences of opinion. Predominant among them are these:

(1) Should the data reflecting price change be 'value' data—specific replacement cost or its equivalent—or should they be 'adjusted cost' data—historical dollar costs adjusted by a general price index? If the latter, what index is most appropriate for the purpose?

(2) Should the process of conversion to 'current cost' be applied only to a few items on the income statement which are affected most materially by price change, such as depreciation and cost of goods sold, or should the adjustment be all-inclusive—applied in a consistent manner to all items affected on both the income statement and the balance sheet?

(3) Should the *principal* statements in the corporate report be adjusted to reflect the effects of price change or should such 'current cost' data be presented only as supplementary information?

(4) In any case, is it possible to develop 'current cost' data on an 'objective' basis and with a reasonable degree of accuracy? And what degree of accuracy is necessary in order that the information be useful? Do existing accounting records contain in organised and accessible form the information necessary for the conversion of historical cost to a current dollar basis?

(5) Can current cost information be presented in such form that it will be understandable, and therefore useful, to the readers of financial statements? Can they be educated to recognise the value—and also the limitations—of such information?

Space does not permit a full discussion of all of these questions. To some of them, in fact, pending extensive investigation and experimentation, only tentative answers are possible. But a discussion of some of the issues involved may be of assistance in their ultimate solution.

III. Adjusted Historical Cost versus Replacement Cost

The distinction between 'adjusted historical cost' and 'replacement cost' has never been very clearly defined.

Adjusted historical cost is a definite objective concept—historical dollar cost adjusted to a current dollar basis by the application of a broadly accepted index of general prices. Given the dollar cost, the date of acquisition and the index, a clerk can make the required computation.

It follows that *net income* based on 'adjusted historical cost' is also a clear-cut definite concept—the excess of revenue, expressed in current dollars, over the incurred cost of the capital (assets and services) consumed in producing that revenue, expressed in the same sized current dollars. Under this concept net income is that portion of revenue not required to maintain intact the generalised, overall *purchasing power* of the capital investment—not just its *dollar* amount.

Replacement cost, on the other hand, 'means all things to all men'. It has been variously described as:

(1) what an identical asset *would* cost currently;
(2) what an identical asset *will* probably cost at the time of replacement;

(3) what the 'equivalent' of the asset *would* cost currently, 'equivalent' being none too clearly defined;

(4) what it *has already* cost to replace the asset, e.g. LIFO;

(5) historical cost adjusted by specific price indexes—many narrowly specialised indexes, or a few, or just one index specific to all of the expenditures of a company, or even of an industry.

All of these varieties of replacement cost are based on the concept that net income is the excess of revenue over some measure of the 'current cost' of replacing the *physical* capital (assets and services) consumed in producing that revenue—that net income is the portion of the revenue not required to maintain intact some *physical quantity* measure of invested capital.

It would appear that both of these concepts of 'current cost'—and the resultant concepts of income—are useful, but each for different purposes. Both concepts of income are in sharp contrast to the conventional one— that net income is the excess of revenue over the historical dollar cost of the capital (assets and services) consumed in producing the revenue, which implies that any excess of revenue over what is required to maintain the *dollar* amount of invested capital may be classified as income, even though the value of the dollar has declined materially since its investment.

IV. Adjusted Historical Cost

For a good presentation of the case for 'adjusted historical cost' as the preferred basis for the periodic reporting of income, reference is made again to the statement of the A.A.A. Committee on Accounting Concepts and Standards:

'It has sometimes been suggested that the current or anticipated replacement cost of specific types of assets be used as a means of measuring the current dollar costs of capital "consumed". This, however, would represent a departure from recorded historical cost and thereby would destroy to a considerable degree the objectivity of accounting. The cost of "consuming" existing capital should be determined irrespective of the intention to replace in kind, to replace with a different type of capital, or not to replace at all. This conclusion appears to rule out, in the determination of income for periodic reporting to stockholders and other non-management groups, the use of either replacement costs or a price index specific to the particular kinds of assets "consumed" by a given corporation.

'In contrast, the adjustment of historical dollar costs—the restatement of these costs in current dollars of equivalent purchasing power as measured by a *general* price index—is independent of estimated replacement costs or replacement policy. It differs from the conventional original dollar cost concept only in that it recognises changes in the value of the dollar and reflects these changes in the amortisation of costs and in the determination of periodic income. Its application is independent of possible or probable future price changes, either upward or downward, since only past changes in the value of the dollar are reflected in the adjusted figures.

'The use of a measure of overall price levels as a basis for such adjustment is entirely consistent with the fact that initial investment is made as an alternative to all other possible business uses of funds and, as recovered, again becomes "free" for reinvestment or any other proper business use. While substantial portions of inflowing funds must be used to replace the capital "consumed" if the productive resources of the enterprise are to be maintained, management has considerable freedom of choice in selecting the new assets to be acquired.'[1]

V. UTILITY OF PRICE INDEXES

The preparation of such common dollar statements involves the choice of a particular general price index from those now available, or the preparation of a new one more suitable for the purpose in hand. Involved too is a demonstration that the index selected will yield results that are reasonably accurate. For a well-reasoned discussion of this issue, reference is made again to the A.A.A. Committee Statement No. 2:

'The most widely urged objection to the use of price indexes as a means of adjusting past dollar outlays to current dollar equivalents is their alleged inaccuracy. The Committee believes, however, that the errors inherent in index number construction are relatively unimportant where substantial changes in price levels are involved. The existence of such weaknesses in index number construction places practical limitations on the utility of index number adjustments but does not invalidate their use. Specifically, the practical limitations are: (1) Adjustments for very small changes in the general price level are ineffective, and (2) adjustments tend to become less accurate (because of changes in the real weights of index number elements) as the time period is extended.

'Generally speaking, any index number adjustment for change in the value of the monetary unit must be viewed, not as a fact, but as an indication of fact— although quite possibly a more accurate indication than is often possible in other accounting judgments as, for example, the periodic cost expiration of long-lived assets. That price indexes provide generally acceptable indications of fact is demonstrated by their increasing adoption as bases for wage payment contracts.

'The Committee believes that one reasonably accurate and objective instrument for adjusting original dollar costs to reflect changes in the value of the dollar is the Bureau of Labour Statistics index of wholesale prices. Undoubtedly a better index can be developed, and will be as the need becomes apparent. In the meantime, the B.L.S. index will serve reasonably well for experimental purposes; any degree of error introduced by its variation from the "ideal" index may be negligible as compared with the difference, given substantial price changes, between original dollar costs and their current dollar equivalents.'[2]

VI. REPLACEMENT COST

The choice of 'adjusted historical cost' as the *preferred* basis for reporting to investors and other non-management groups in current dollars does not gainsay the importance of replacement costs for many purposes. As indicated by the A.A.A. Committee in a footnote to the preceding quotation, comparisons of revenues with the current costs of replacing the capital consumed in producing such revenues may be highly significant. There can be no valid objection to the inclusion of such information in the corporate report if it enhances the comprehension of management problems on the part of stockholders and other non-management groups.

There are two major objections, however, to the reporting of income on the basis of specific replacement costs.

[1] Op. cit.
[2] Op. cit.

One of these is a matter of basic accounting principle and has been discussed earlier in this paper, viz. that the cost of 'consuming' existing capital should be determined irrespective of the intention to replace in kind, to replace with a different type of capital, or not to replace at all.

The other objection to specific replacement costs is a matter of practicability. It is highly improbable that there are many situations in which such costs can be determined objectively and with a sufficiently high degree of accuracy to inspire confidence in their validity on the part of readers of the corporate report. Exceptions would seem to be only where the turnover period is very short and replacements are normally made continuously and 'in kind'.

It should be recognised, therefore, that specific replacement costs have their greatest significance for those engaged in the active management of business. To a very large degree management should ignore, in its decisions, facts about historical cost, except as these costs are indicative of present or probable future costs. Management involves planning for the future, including the replacement of actual physical capital when it has been consumed. It follows that the plans for revenue—and other sources of capital—must take into consideration the present cost, and even the probable future cost, of the capital being consumed.

That such costs are not objective is not necessarily a bar to their usefulness to management. That they are frequently only broad estimates, and subject to varying degrees of inaccuracy may be unfortunate but unavoidable. Still, with allowances for their limitations, management must—and does— make its decisions on the basis of specific replacement costs rather than past costs.

VII. EXTENT OF ADJUSTMENT FOR PRICE CHANGE

While not altogether conclusive, the weight of the argument to this point seems to indicate that corporate reports should include, in addition to historical cost data, financial information in terms of adjusted historical cost rather than specific replacement cost, even though management must be provided with replacement cost data on which to base its decisions.

Irrespective of the type of 'current costs' to be reflected in corporate reports, there remain unresolved two important issues: (1) Should the adjustment for price change be all-inclusive or should it be restricted to a few income statement items materially affected, e.g. depreciation and cost of goods sold, and (2) should the adjusted data appear on the principal financial statements or as supplementary information?

In resolving these issues a distinction must be made between what may be a desirable long-range development and what is immediately practicable. Looking to the future—following 'intensive research and experimentation'— the A.A.A. Committee on Accounting Concepts and Standards makes this recommendation:

'Adjustments made for changes in the value of the dollar should be all-inclusive (i.e. should apply to all statement items). This is held to be essential to full disclosure. One of the most important effects of price level change, for example, may be its impact on the "net balance of fixed dollar items" (assets fixed in dollar amount minus claims fixed in dollar amount). When the general price level is rising, corporations derive gain (realised or unrealised as may be) from any excess of liabilities and non-participating preferred stock over assets fixed in dollar amount. (When the general price level is declining, this same relation of fixed-dollar items results in loss—realised or unrealised.) This gain (or loss, as the case may be), which typically moves inversely to the real cost of capital "consumed" and which may be of significant proportions, is revealed only by analysis and adjustment of balance sheet items.'[1]

Perhaps the most compelling reason for converting the balance sheet—the establishment of a proper basis for determining financial ratios—was not mentioned in the A.A.A. Committee Statement. For example, it was noted earlier that the ratio of net income to invested capital remains distorted even after elimination of 'price profits', unless the adjusted profit figure be related to invested capital *also* converted to current dollars. In the absence of complete balance sheet adjustment parenthetical notations on the balance sheet indicating approximations of present values—or 'adjusted cost'—of specific items would make possible the computation of more useful financial ratios.

Objections to an all-inclusive adjustment—including the balance sheet too—relate either to the lack of significance of an adjusted balance sheet or to the practical difficulties involved in effecting such adjustments.

In the first category are the objections of those who insist that over the years the balance sheet has lost much of its importance as a statement of financial condition. Recently it has been variously described as a 'statement of residuals', 'a statement of sources and investment of capital', and similar concepts that indicate its historical rather than current nature. As an historical statement showing on the right side the amount of capital received frcm various sources and on the left side the 'residual' of this capital—the amounts not yet consumed in operations—the statement has historical significance. Furthermore, while the working capital section does have current significance in the appraisal of short-term financial condition, the amounts here are already largely in current dollars.

It is doubtful that the usefulness of the rest of the balance sheet can be materially increased by full adjustment to current dollars. Such an adjusted statement would still not be a statement of financial condition—a statement of 'value'—but it would almost certainly be so interpreted by many readers; this would lead to many erroneous judgments.

In the second category are the objections of those who insist that the practical difficulties involved in the adjustment of the balance sheet far outweigh the usefulness of the adjusted statement. There is, of course, the problem of 'dating' the acquisition of all assets subject to adjustment, but this must be done anyway for inventories and depreciable fixed assets in the adjustment of depreciation and cost of goods sold for the income statement; the adjustment of accumulated depreciation does present special problems. Apparently, however, the difficulties envisaged are these, among others:

[1] Op. cit.

(1) What is an appropriate adjustment of stock investments, particularly those which represent majority holdings?

(2) How should the adjustment of paid-in-capital be reflected when the *legally* significant figure is the original dollar amount?

(3) What is the significance of 'adjusted retained earnings', unless the income figures of all past years are adjusted to eliminate 'price profits'— in many cases an impossible task?

(4) What is the nature of the loss or gain arising from 'the balance of fixed-dollar items'? And how is the accumulated amount to be determined and reflected in the balance sheet?

The foregoing questions present problems not subject to easy solution. Together with the doubtful significance of the adjusted balance sheet they present a strong case for at least deferring the all-inclusive adjustment approach to the problem and concentrating on the adjustment of the income statement.

VIII. METHODS OF PRESENTING COMMON DOLLAR DATA

Here reference is made again to the statement of the A.A.A. Committee. After insisting that 'at the present stage of accounting development . . . the primary financial statements should . . . continue to reflect historical costs'[1] this Committee makes the following recommendation:

'Management may properly include in periodic reports to stockholders comprehensive supplementary statements which present the effects of the fluctuation in the value of the dollar upon net income and upon financial position.

(a) *Such supplementary statements should be internally consistent; the income statement and the balance sheet should both be adjusted by the same procedures, so that the figures in such complementary statements are co-ordinate and have the same relative significance.*

(b) *Such supplementary statements should be reconciled in detail with the primary statements reflecting unadjusted original dollar costs, and should be regarded as an extension or elaboration of the primary statements rather than as a departure therefrom.*

(c) *Such supplementary statements should be accompanied by comments and explanations clearly setting forth the implications, uses, and limitations of the adjusted data.*'[2]

The all-inclusive adjustment of financial statements, even for presentation as supplementary information will probably make progress slowly, even though it appears to be a logical, conservative, and at the same time an extremely useful development. There are many handicaps to be overcome— incomplete accounting records, lack of completely satisfactory price indices, resistance to change, lack of general understanding of common dollar information, etc. Still further in the future is the 'stage of accounting development' when the *principal* financial statements may be in terms of common dollars. The educational programme that must precede such a development

[1] Op. cit.
[2] Op. cit.

represents a stupendous task. It must be admitted, however, that continued and rapid inflation—decline in the value of the dollar—might well hasten these developments.

IX. POSSIBLE SHORT-RUN ACHIEVEMENTS

This does not mean, however, that no immediate progress is possible in the solution of this important problem. A substantial improvement in reported income data can be achieved *now*, by adjusting for the income statement only the two expense items most materially affected by price change—depreciation and cost of goods sold. In most situations these two adjustments alone will account for most of the difference between 'conventional' income based on historical cost and income completely adjusted to a common dollar basis. Net income, thus adjusted, can be important supplementary information for the purposes described earlier in this paper. Granted that the adjustment is not complete, that it is only approximately correct (as are so many other items on financial statements) and that it is not 'at the present stage of accounting development' subject to verification by independent accountants, at least it will force upon the readers of the report a realisation that there are two concepts of income—that they are, or may be, substantially different in amount, and that each is useful for specific purposes. Thus there can be begun immediately the educational programme essential for the long-range developments discussed earlier as ultimate goals—*the all-inclusive adjustment of all items on financial statements, to reflect completely the effect of price change upon the determination, reporting and interpretation of income and financial condition.*

APPENDIX

Tentative Suggested Procedures for Determining Income on the Basis of 'Adjusted Original Costs'

In the foregoing pages the writer recommends research and experimentation leading eventually to the development of an appropriate method for the all-inclusive adjustment of the financial statements, with a view to segregating or eliminating the effect of changes in the general price level—conversely, changes in the value of the monetary unit.

But the writer also recommends that *immediate* steps be taken to adjust the items on the income statement most materially affected by price change—principally cost of goods sold and depreciation. For the time being, at least, the adjusted amounts should be presented in a supplementary income statement.

A preliminary analysis of possible procedures for making these adjustments has produced the following tentative suggestions. They are not intended in any sense as prescribed rules of procedure. Some of the suggested procedures will be found to be impracticable in many cases because of the lack of detailed records for past years. In many cases the suggested 'short-cut' methods may not produce results of sufficient accuracy. Each situation will present its own problems of adjustment.

Since the basic accounting records and (at least for the present) the primary financial statements are on the basis of historical dollar cost, the adjustments suggested here for changes in the value of the monetary unit will be reflected only on the supplementary statement of income; no changes need be made in the accounting records.

In theory, adjustment of expense items for changes in the value of the monetary unit requires that each item of cost that is not consumed as expense immediately upon its incurrence should be adjusted for the change in the value of money during the interim between incurrence and consumption. At one extreme are depreciation of fixed assets, amortisation of leaseholds and the like; at the other extreme are purchases of merchandise in a rapid turnover situation.

In such a supplementary statement of income the historical dollar costs of items such as the following would be subject to adjustment for purposes of the supplementary income statement:

(1) Cost of goods sold
    (a) For a merchandising company:
        1. Acquisition cost of merchandise.
    (b) For a manufacturing company:
        1. Acquisition cost of materials.
        2. Labour and other 'rapid turnover' costs.
        3. Depreciation, depletion, and amortisation of other long-term prepayments allocable to production cost.

(2) Depreciation, and amortisation of other long-term prepayments not allocable to production cost.

The Cost of Goods Sold

(a) For a merchandising company

In theory, the historical dollar cost of each item sold should be adjusted for the change in the value of the dollar between the date of its acquisition and the date

91

of its sale; under most circumstances, of course, this would be impossible—or at least far too costly to be practicable.

An approximate adjustment may be computed as follows:

(1) Multiply the historical dollar cost of the initial inventories by the percentage of net change in general prices from the dates of their acquisition to the beginning of the accounting period. This can be done approximately by applying one-half of the percentage of net price change for a 'turnover period' to total initial inventories, or more precisely by applying the proper percentage to each month's acquisition.

(2) Multiply the average inventories of the period priced at historical dollar cost adjusted to the price level at the beginning of the period, by the percentage of (net) change in general prices during the accounting period. The accuracy of this approximation may be substantially increased, in many cases, by making a separate computation for each month, and accumulating the amounts (algebraically, if both price increases and decreases are involved).

(3) Multiply the historical dollar cost of the final inventories by the percentage of net change in general prices from the dates of their acquisition to the end of the accounting period. As in the case of initial inventories, this can be done approximately by applying one-half of the percentage of net price change for a turnover period to total inventories, or more precisely by applying the proper percentage to each month's acquisitions.

(4) Counting price increases as positive amounts and price decreases as negative, the sum of the results in steps (1) and (2) above less the result in step (3) is the amount of the adjustment to cost of goods sold; if positive it should be added, if negative, subtracted. The cost of goods sold should then be a reasonably accurate estimate of the historical dollar cost 'adjusted' for changes in the general price level between the dates of acquisition and the dates of sale.

In many cases a result substantially equal to the above may be secured by dividing the percentage of net change in general prices during the accounting period by the number of 'turnovers' and applying the resulting percentage to increase (or to decrease, if negative) the cost of goods sold.

(b) For a Manufacturing Company

(1) *Acquisition cost of materials and supplies.* While detailed procedures may be different, the general principles underlying the adjustment of material cost for changes in price levels between the time of acquisition and the issuance into production are the same as those described above for a merchandising company. The specific procedures adopted would, of course, depend on the kind of records maintained—the availability of detailed information. The adjustment of material cost for the changes in price levels between the issuance of materials into production and the completion of the finished product should not ordinarily be combined with the adjustment of labour costs and other rapid turnover costs described below, for the reason that material is usually introduced at the beginning of the process while labour and other costs are incurred continuously throughout the process.

(2) *Labour, both direct and indirect, and other 'rapid turnover' costs.* Since adjustment of these 'rapid turnover' costs is made only for general and not specific price changes, the only variable to distinguish one element of cost from another is the time of incurrence and entry into the production process. The first adjustment involves the determination of the total amount of these costs in process, the length

of the production period, and the percentage of price change during this production period; on the assumption that these costs are introduced continuously throughout the production process one-half of the percentage of price change is applied to the total costs in process to determine the amount of the adjustment to the end of the production process.

The second adjustment involves the period of time between completion of the production and its final sale. There *may* be included here *all* costs of manufacture *adjusted* to the end of the production period, even depreciation and other long-term amortisations. (See below for discussion of these long-term adjustments.) Here again there is involved the determination of the total cost of the finished goods inventory (adjusted for price level changes to the end of the production period), the 'turnover period' of this inventory, and the percentage of price change during this turnover period. The application of the percentage of price change to the total 'cost' determines the amount of the adjustment.

The accuracy of these adjustments may be increased by separate adjustments of the initial and final inventories, as described in connection with the adjustment of merchandising company inventories.

It should be noted here that, for managerial purposes, as opposed to determination of income for the financial statements, the current costs of specific items of materials or merchandise, and specific revisions in wage contracts, will be more useful information than historical costs adjusted for changes in general prices. Furthermore, if the differences between adjusted historical costs and specific current costs are substantial—and if specific current costs can be determined objectively and with a reasonable degree of accuracy, perhaps both should be reflected on the supplementary income statement. For certain purposes the usefulness of the information is increased if there is first determined an 'operating income' based on the excess of revenue over the current costs of the specific capital consumed in earning the revenue. To this 'operating income' would be added 'other income' (or there would be deducted 'other expense') equal to the differences between adjusted historical cost and the specific current cost; the final result would be net income based on adjusted historical costs.

Depreciation and other Long-term Amortisations

The separate determination and adjustment of cost of goods sold for price level changes requires the separation of these long-term costs into two groups—those allocable to cost of goods sold and those chargeable to the period as non-manufacturing costs. The procedure of adjustment, however, is the same for both groups, except that the adjusted cost of those chargeable to cost of goods sold are subject to a second adjustment for price level changes in the period between the end of the production period and the time of sale—along with the other costs of finished goods. This procedure is explained in the foregoing section.

The adjustment, for price level changes, of an income statement on which the expenses are presented on a 'class' rather than on a 'functional' basis—where the cost of goods sold is not separately determined—can be made, of course, without separate adjustment of those items which are charged to the product from those which are not so allocated; in such a case, however, special care must be taken in the adjustment of inventories.

Depreciation

In theory the determination of depreciation on historical dollar cost adjusted for changes in the general price level requires the following procedure:

(1) The classification of the historical dollar cost of all items of depreciable property in existence at the beginning of the accounting period by year of acquisition, and sub-classification by depreciation rate.

(2) The application of the proper depreciation rate to the historical dollar cost of the property in each sub-classification.

(3) The sub-totalling of the resulting amounts of depreciation on each year's property acquisition. (A grand total of these amounts taken at this point as a check should be equal to the current period's depreciation charge based on historical dollar cost.)

(4) The application of the proper general price indexes to the total depreciation of each year's property acquisitions (i.e. multiplying the depreciation on historical dollar cost by the general price index of the current period and dividing by the index of the year of acquisition).

(5) The totalling of the 'adjusted' depreciation amounts for each year's property acquisitions, to secure the total 'adjusted' depreciation charge on all property for the current period.

In many cases the procedure outlined above may be feasible. Where property records are such that it is impossible or impracticable, a shorter procedure may be employed. It involves the following steps:

(1) The classification of the historical dollar cost of all items of depreciable property existing at the beginning of the current period by year of acquisition.

(2) The application of the proper general price indexes to the total of each year's acquisitions, to get the 'adjusted' cost, as at the beginning of the current period, of each year's acquisitions.

(3) The totalling of these amounts to get the total 'adjusted' cost of all existing property as at the beginning of the current period.

(4) The division of this 'adjusted' cost of property by its historical dollar cost to get a weighted index of 'adjusted' cost to historical dollar cost of total property.

(5) The application of this index to the current year's depreciation on historical dollar cost—to get depreciation on 'adjusted' historical cost.

Both of these procedures are based on the assumption that depreciation is computed on the balance in the property account at the beginning of the period. Otherwise modified procedures would be necessary.

In situations where existing property records are incomplete, a greater or lesser degree of estimating may be necessary to secure reasonably accurate approximations of depreciation based on 'adjusted' historical cost. Any reasonable estimate is more useful for many purposes than depreciation computed on historical dollar cost.

The Amortisation of Leaseholds, Wasting Assets and other Prepayments

The 'adjustment' of the amortisation of the historical dollar costs of leaseholds, wasting assets and other prepayments may be accomplished by the application of appropriate general price indexes. The current period's amortisation as computed on the historical dollar cost may be multiplied by the general price index as at the beginning of the current period and divided by the index at the date on which the prepayment was made, to get the amortisation on adjusted historical cost.

Bond discount is not a prepayment for purposes of adjustment for changes in the value of the dollar; it is best treated as a deduction from bonds payable; this net liability increases each year as the borrower defers (borrows) part of the interest chargeable against that year; it is considered as a part of the 'net balance of fixed-dollar items' discussed earlier in this statement.

Adjustment of Net Income

The net effect of all of the adjustments of items on the income statement to allow for changes in the value of the dollar is, of course, reflected in 'adjusted' net income. The difference between the 'adjusted' net income and the net income on the basis of historical dollar costs should appear on the balance sheet in the proprietorship section under the caption of 'Capital Adjustment Account', or 'Adjustment for Changes in the Value of the Dollar' or similar descriptive caption.

This item represents, in effect, an unallocated 'purchasing power' adjustment of all of the proprietorship accounts except retained earnings—positive if prices have risen, negative if prices have declined. It is in no sense income (or loss, if negative).

It should be noted that if the balance sheet is similarly adjusted for changes in the value of the dollar as at the end of the current period, the resulting adjustment of the proprietorship accounts includes, without separate computation, the adjustment of net income for the current period.

FLUCTUATING PRICE LEVELS IN RELATION TO ACCOUNTS

by

PROFESSOR DR. KARL HAX, DR. ERNST KNORR
AND DR. ALBERT MEIER
Institut der Wirtschaftsprüfer,
Germany

I. CONCEPTION OF THE EXPRESSION OF ALTERATIONS IN MONEY VALUE

We purposely do not speak of price fluctuations, but of alterations in the money value, because we are concerned not only with short-term price fluctuations, but with the primary problem of defining long-term development, i.e. the trend of price level. *Fluctuation* of prices which solely alters the price relations (fluctuation in real value) belong in our opinion to normal market conditions; to meet and to utilise those fluctuations is a matter for the undertaking concerned. In theory, completely separate treatment is necessary for *permanent* alteration of price levels which have their origin not in a shifting of price relations, but in an alteration of money value. In practice, however, it is seldom possible to separate the influence of fluctuations in real value from the influence of alterations in money value. As a rule, it must suffice to express both influences in one single figure. It should, however, be remembered that this is a figure of complex value which reflects both alteration in money value and fluctuation in real value. This should be borne in mind when considering the following calculations and their effect on commercial or tax incidence as well as on business conditions.

In what follows, the influence of alterations of money value is to be understood as the total difference between cost price and replacement price of the consumed goods (the using-up of plant and of materials). Replacement price, however, apart from goods officially quoted, can rarely be determined with accuracy. For this reason, calculations are in practice related to the price on which the seller bases his sales calculations. (The 'calculated price'.) This calculated price should, in principle, correspond to the replacement price on the day of the sale. In reality, it will frequently differ therefrom. This difference, however, is as a rule not ascertainable, so that our calculation at this point remains incomplete.

For the determination and neutralisation of the difference between cost price and calculated price we have in Germany developed special systems.

II. ASCERTAINMENT OF THE ALTERATIONS IN MONEY VALUE

To determine the alterations in money value we require two figures, i.e. the cost price of the goods consumed and the calculated price which will be returned to the firm in the profit of the products sold. The ascertainment of the cost price presents no special problems. More difficult, however, is the determination of the calculated price. It is necessary here to discriminate between the costs of long-term utilisation of invested goods and the consumption of materials.

Ascertainment of the Alterations in Money Value with Investments

If we wish to find the economically correct (objective) costs of utilisation of plant, we have to calculate the writing-off of the replacement price of the plant. This principle relates to the fixed as well as to the movable plant. For economic reasons the replacement prices can only be computed at long intervals. Consequently, the elements for the calculated depreciation are from time to time adapted to the altered price conditions. The new prices are either ascertained directly or with the assistance of indices from earlier prices. Both procedures suffer from certain imperfections. The results, however, suffice for practical purposes, all the more as constant practice develops a certain training and experience. It is, of course, well known that enterprises when computing calculated depreciation, frequently do not start with the replacement price of the plant but with the purchase price. In such cases, it should be noted that the influence of alterations of money value on the result of the balance must be taken into account, since in the calculations below the starting point will be the calculated value.

The influence of the alterations of money value on invested capital is dealt with outside the book-keeping. After primarily ascertaining the replacement prices and their alterations, the calculation would be approximately as follows:

Example 1				*Dm.*
Normal depreciation on cost price (historical costs)	..		..	100,000
Calculated depreciation on replacement costs	..	..	..	175,000
Influence of alteration of money value	..	..	..	.. Dm. 75,000

Ascertainment of the Alterations in Money Value with Stocks

Whilst the calculation of replacement prices on invested capital in Germany meets with opposition by the authorities it is, on the other hand, generally accepted when dealing with the costs of the raw material. In practice, the principle of calculation on the basis of replacement prices cannot, under the influence of competition, always be fully realised. In a rising market it is primarily calculated on the basis of so-called intermediate prices, whilst sinking prices involve a quick adoption of ruling prices. To determine the influence of alterations in money value on the balance, it is necessary to ascertain what price was used when the selling prices for the consumed goods were calculated. The fixing of this price is not always simple. The sellers must be requested to set out in figures the basis of their calculations used in fixing the selling prices for the finished article. If the selling price is altered during sales negotiations, it should be made clear whether an eventual price reduction is based on a reduction in the calculated price of the raw materials or on the reduction of the calculated profit. It will not be easy to educate the sellers to such exact reasoning.

If the manufacturer diverges intentionally from replacement price in his calculation—be it for reasons of competition or under the compulsion of official price rulings—we have to keep to the calculated price, although the total influence of the alterations in money value has not been retained.

If the calculated price is fixed, the influence of the alterations in money value on the costs of raw material may be found in a simple manner. The practical handling is shown by the following example in which the cost prices of consumed materials are compared to the prices forming the basis of the calculation of the finished product.

Example 2

CALCULATION OF THE RAW MATERIAL

(a) *Finding the consumption of raw material*

	Dm.
Stocks at the beginning of the accounting period (1st January) valued at purchase prices	500,000
Plus Goods received	750,000
	1,250,000
Less Stocks at the end of the accounting period (31st December) valued at purchase prices	600,000

Raw material consumption at actual purchase prices amounts to Dm. 650,000

(b) *Finding the consumption of raw material at calculated prices.* (Result of raw materials sale)

Item	Number of pieces	Per piece Dm.	Total Dm.
1	40,000	10.50	420,000
2	22,000	10	220,000
3	4,500	12	54,000
4	6,000	11	66,000
5	1,500	11	16,500

The calculated value of the raw material amounts to Dm. 776,500

The calculated value of the raw material per piece is to be taken from the calculation per item.

(c) *Finding the difference between consumption of raw material and return*

	Dm.
Consumption of raw material at cost price	650,000
Calculated result of raw material sales ..	776,500
Surplus (difference between cost price of the raw material and the calculated price)	Dm. 126,500

There can be a similar calculation as to the invested capital outside the book-keeping, with a reconciliation with figures in the book-keeping system (cost prices) or their calculated composition.

III. NEUTRALISATION OF THE ALTERATIONS IN MONEY VALUE

The examples show that it is desirable to ascertain the alterations in money value only in so far as they influence the profit returns. The principles of balance valuation remain unchanged. Hereafter, consideration will be given to methods necessary to neutralise sham profits and sham losses in the balance sheet as well as in the earnings statement.

Neutralisation of the Alterations in Money Value in the Balance Sheet

The German law relating to balances (not only commercial law, but also the law relating to taxation) starts with the nominal capital account. Profit is understood as being everything exceeding the original capital shown in money figures. Consequently the profit or loss shown in the balance sheet contains the realisable alterations in money value. These, however, are not to be considered as real profits or losses, since they have neither augmented nor reduced the quantity of the capital substance. We call them sham profits or sham losses. What consequences follow in drawing up the balance sheet?

Profits derived from alterations in money value (i.e. sham profits) should not be drawn out or distributed amongst the proprietors. Such profits should not be subjected to income-tax. Withdrawal or taxation both prevent the undertaking from replacing plant and re-stocking raw materials out of sales profit. A loss of substance with subsequent shrinking of business will be unavoidable if the undertaking cannot recover what it has lost through taxation and withdrawals by the issue of new capital. If new capital is not available (perhaps because of high taxation) liquidation is the unavoidable result of gradual exhaustion.

In addition to well-known methods of protecting the sham profits from withdrawal or taxation (for example LIFO and the 'base stock' procedure) the formation of plant renewal or re-stocking reserves has become a practice in Germany. In so far as it relates to the capital invested and to the compulsory closing of certain reserves (fire, expropriation and the like) it is recognised by the taxing authorities. Recently, such reserves have been formed on a wider basis to neutralise profits and losses resulting solely from alterations in money value. These 'substance maintenance reserves' are intended to prevent the exhaustion of the enterprise which would otherwise automatically follow continuously rising price levels. So far they are not acknowledged by the taxing authorities.

The substance maintenance reserve has to be credited with the excess profits obtained in consequence of the alterations in money value. (In Example 1, Dm. 75,000; in Example 2, Dm. 126,500.) Sham losses have to be debited. In this manner the influence of alterations in money value on profits is as far as possible neutralised.

Sham *profits* may in this manner be neutralised to any extent; with sham *losses* this procedure has limits. The neutralisation can then only be carried so far as earlier substance maintenance reserves permit. If the substance maintenance reserve has been consumed, sham losses can no longer be neutralised in the balance sheet, but must be shown as capital-reducing losses, since capital devaluation accounts are contrary to the law in Germany and are only admitted in exceptional cases.

Elimination of the Alterations in Money Value by Analysis of Results

In our reckoning, we only list a portion of the alterations in money value, since we cannot base our correction on the objective correct replacement price (current price): we have to hold on to the calculated price. Apart from this, the possibility of neutralising sham losses in the balance and in the earnings statement is limited. For this reason our reckoning has to be complemented by an analysis of results. With its assistance, the total profits or losses caused by alterations in money value are, as far as possible, separated. In that manner, the actual profit will appear.

This additional analysis of results is particularly important if genuine profits are compensated by sham losses due to alterations in money value. The example hereunder shows this:

Example 3   *Dm.*

Loss as per balance sheet	220,000
Excess of depreciation on replacement prices compared to the price as per balance sheet	100,000
Total loss	320,000
Loss of sales according to calculation of raw material (sham loss)	400,000
Actual profit in production	Dm. 80,000

The calculated prices of consumed raw material are lower by Dm. 400,000 because of the sinking of the prices for raw material compared to the cost prices. The neutralisation of this sham loss in the balance statement is often impossible because a substance maintenance reserve is not available. In this case there will be a loss shown in the balance of Dm. 220,000 and, after taking account of the excess amount of the calculated depreciations, a loss of Dm. 320,000. As shown in the analysis of results, the sham loss in the raw material is taken account of so that a real profit results. The example shows that by isolating sham profits or losses due to alterations in money value it is possible to form a judgment as to the actual earning power of the undertaking.

IV. LIMITS OF THE PROCEDURE (CRITICAL SURVEY)

Against the procedure as described, industry raises the objection that by using calculated figures for balance purposes, the taxation and the price authorities obtain an undesirable insight which they otherwise would not have. This objection, in view of the importance of a clear analysis of results, is not convincing.

Another criticism is that, under the procedure described, not only alterations in money value, but also genuine purchase profits are neutralised, whilst the profits from replacements remain unconsidered. A further point is that the formation of reserves would not suffice to protect the sham profits from distribution or taxation.

Limiting Profits on Purchase

The level of the purchase prices for investment goods or raw material depends not only on the general price situation, but also on the ability of the buyer. This buying profit or loss by favourable or unfavourable purchase is, however, contained in the difference between purchase or cost price and the calculated price of the consumed goods. It can only be ascertained where there is an objective purchase value, e.g. in the shape of prices quoted on exchange which can take the place of the individual purchase value.

Example 4	Dm.
(1) Actual purchase price	950
(2) Price quoted on exchange on the day of purchase	1,000
(3) Price quoted on exchange on the day of sale (calculated price) ..	1,200
Profit on purchase (difference between (1) and (2))	50
Excess profit due to alterations in money value (difference between (2) and (3))	200
Total difference between (1) and (3)	Dm. 250

If there is no objective purchase value, it is impossible to separate the purchase profit on the alterations in money value except approximately, i.e. in cases where the extent of the purchase advantages obtained can be fixed. Only in individual cases can it be decided if this fact carries sufficient weight to disturb the value of the calculation.

Limiting Profits on Repurchases and Speculation

In calculating prices, it is desirable to start with the current price of the consumed raw material or the utilisation of plant, that is to say of the replacement price on the day the deal is closed. It must be remembered, however, that it is not always possible to undertake replacement immediately. For this reason the effective replacement price deviates from the calculated replacement price. The difference between these two prices is the *profit or loss on replacement*. It depends in part on alterations in money value which may occur in the pèriod before the goods are repurchased; in part it depends on the ability of the buyer to choose the right time for repurchasing. Repurchase profits and losses are not shown by the described process of neutralisation of alterations in money value, since the procedure is based on the calculated price and not on the actual repurchase price.

This procedure can only be considered correct for two reasons: firstly, the calculated price (i.e. as far as possible the current price) is a better gauge of the monetary value on the day the deal is closed than an estimated repurchase price which possibly lies far in the future. Secondly, replacement profits or losses are the result of business measures arising in the future and, for that reason, should not affect the actual calculation for the current period.

With plant the period between the first utilisation and replacement often extends over years, or even tens of years. Within this period, considerable alterations in money values can appear. It should therefore not be overlooked that the replacement computation should be flexible. Amounts of depreciation are not, of course, accumulated for every single particular item of plant until it is replaced, but every year the accruing amounts of depreciation are used to build up an investment fund. For this reason the use of current prices in the valuation of plant utilisation is perfectly justified in relation to effective replacement.

The correct fixing of the calculated price is often difficult. There may be a divergence from current prices in speculative conditions when there is hope that it may be possible to purchase in a cheaper market. In this case, the calculated price may have to be fixed more or less arbitrarily and the value of the calculation may possibly be considerably lowered. If the current price can be assessed objectively (that is when dealing with goods quoted on exchange) these speculative differences may be eliminated by taking the prices quoted on exchange instead of the calculated values. With all other goods, the elimination of these speculative differences is difficult.

Similarly, there may be intentionally wrong calculated values, taken in order to inflate the profit. This danger exists particularly when the income of the sales staff is dependent on the sales profit.This danger can be met by letting the buyer fix the calculated items instead of the sales staff.

Building up of Reserves or Change in Capital?

It has been mentioned that a criticism of the suggested procedure is that the building up of substance maintenance reserves would not with certainty prevent the distribution or taxation of sham profits. It is wise not to distribute them or to pay them away in taxes; but neither commercial law nor tax law has yet recognised the procedure. It is to be hoped the proprietors will not use their rights to dispose of these reserves and will have regard to the importance of substance maintenance. It is further to be expected that the taxing authorities will some day drop their claim to full taxation on these sham profits, or at least not press their claims at the wrong time.

Capital owners and taxing authorities may, however, take the view that sham *losses* resulting from a rise in money value are not to be considered in the assessment of profit. In Example 3, instead of a loss in the balance sheet of Dm. 220,000, a profit of Dm. 80,000 might appear, which might be claimed by the tax authorities or the capital owners. Such a view would correspond with the principle of commercial caution that nominal losses are treated in the same way as real losses. This is no more inconsistent than the principle that in drawing up the balance sheet, it is proper that unrealised losses should be shown, but not unrealised profits. To prevent the distribution or taxation of sham profits, it has been suggested that the nominal profits or losses caused by alterations in money value should be adjusted on capital account. This proposal may hold good for merchants and associations, but not, however, for companies. With registered companies, alterations in the nominal capital can only be carried through under certain formalities. On account of the difficulties which arise on repeated changes in the capital of companies, the building up of reserves is the only practical course to pursue.

FLUCTUATING PRICE LEVELS IN RELATION TO ACCOUNTS

by

T. A. HILEY, F.C.A.(AUST.)
Institute of Chartered Accountants in Australia

It is quite unnecessary to examine at any length the detailed manner in which fluctuating price levels have played their part in distorting the results disclosed by our conventional accounting approach. The entire theory of historical cost is based upon a comparison of like with like, an accumulation over successive periods of money units of equal significance. Once currency values become unstable, accounts, of necessity, tend to lose their reliability.

But this difficulty is not entirely of recent growth. It is true that the growing concern of to-day is largely the product of what is best described as an erosion of capital—the process where an appearance of sustained or enlarged earning is encountered side by side with the certain knowledge that the replacement of each item of trading stock will entail a heavier outlay—frequently higher than the price at which the earlier article was sold; or where our judgment of the adequacy of amortisation of plant is sobered by the thought that replacement costs have doubled. But long before these days of mounting price levels there was one frequent criticism by the public. It was a criticism of the convention of historical cost as applied to freehold properties after a lengthy period of ownership.

The tendency of most countries has been to concentrate greater aggregations of their populations in cities. It is not my purpose to examine the reasons for or the consequences of that policy. It is sufficient to observe that this tendency has accelerated the growth in the value of real property, the unearned increment so common in a growing city where freehold titles are employed, and not entirely absent where freeholding has been abolished and all land is held on lease from the State. With rare exceptions, with which I shall deal subsequently, accountants have disregarded that increment.

It is not hard to discover the reasons for that disregard. Primarily, it obeys the very commendable convention that unrealised gains should not be included in any statement of the surplus, whether in its annual measure in the revenue account or in the overall review in the balance sheet. If any doubt remained, accountants were then influenced by the doctrine of conservatism which governed most accounting practice up to 1930. In the light of that outlook, the balance sheet which showed premises at historical cost but well under its present value was a most excellent document.

The cumulative effect of the passing years has been to accumulate a vast factor of distortion of the balance sheet. No longer does that document convey a reasonably true picture of the real worth of the assets; nor does it permit an accurate assessment of the real funds of the proprietor. If such a document is of reasonable satisfaction to the investor, it is of limited value to the banker who desires to value his security; or to the economist who seeks to compile tables measuring the movements in investment capital. But let us be quite clear about it—although these difficulties have existed, although their degree has grown with each passing year until they now assume very great dimensions, the growing weight of this criticism by the public has largely been ignored by the profession.

The new problems arising from fluctuating price levels commonly work in reverse. Instead of operating as a measure of conservatism, they mostly have the opposite effect. But it is well to remind ourselves that the profession chose largely to ignore the unearned increment and we might now look at both problems together in considering what we should do to outline any fresh approach.

Before we do so, let us survey what attempts have been made and examine the degree of their success or their failure. Then, in the light of those attempts, we can outline the main purpose to be sought in any fresh accounting approach.

In fairly rapid succession, the rise in values introduced four features, each of relative novelty. First, we had the storm of controversy over the valuation of trading stock, with LIFO and FIFO being vociferously argued in many tongues.

Then came a wave of fiscal provisions permitting heavy allowances for initial depreciation. In turn, these were followed by a practice, limited no doubt, but fairly common in Australia, where many joint stock companies revalued their assets and disposed of the valuation surplus in the form of an issue of bonus shares, or what our American cousins would describe as a 'stock dividend'. Finally, and quite currently, we find a school of thought which favours relating the annual charge for depreciation to the estimated replacement cost of the asset.

Now, one thing must be said of all these expediencies. No one is more than partial in effect; together, all fail to present a complete solution; at their best, they are a fixed stab at a target which is still moving; and, worst of all, they have done much still further to distort the accounting result.

The inadequacies of LIFO in a time of inadequate supply and excessive demand centre round the inability to maintain a basic stock. If, after two years of rising prices, the stock is completely cleared in the third, the protection afforded by LIFO is lost but, still worse, the surplus arising from a series of transactions over the three years is largely concentrated into the year of inventory clearance, with grave distortion of annual accounting of incomes.

Looking back on several years of initial depreciation, I consider that nothing has done more to distort accounting conclusions than has that practice. It was designed as a political appeasement to offset the growing discontent over the widening gulf between depreciation allowances based on historical cost and ever-rising prices. To the extent that it encouraged capital expenditure, it poured fresh oil on the fires of inflation, already burning over-brightly. Not infrequently, it halved the disclosed surplus of a year in which the accident of heavy outlays on capital goods happened to be possible. In some reprehensible cases, advantage was taken, for income-tax purposes, of the initial allowance, but the published accounts reflected neither the corresponding charge for extra depreciation nor the extra taxation which would be payable in subsequent years, reporting without comment merely the reduced requirement for taxation of the year.

Initial depreciation is in process of abandonment in many countries. Few will mourn its passing. In some hands, it has been plainly dangerous. It has provided only a partial answer to a small percentage of enterprise.

The revaluation of assets with the consequent issue of bonus shares has won a considerable following in Australia over recent years, but the dominating considerations have been those of income-tax expediency and of stock exchange convenience rather than accounting purity. The extent of the writing-up has more frequently been governed by the selection of a convenient proportion of the new issue to the existing capital rather than by the adoption of the fresh figures for land, building, plant, etc., disclosed by the expert valuers. Under taxation law in Australia, this remedy is available only to enterprises conducted in joint stock form. It has helped a little to offset the misconception of an apparent increase in the rate of earning. After a revaluation bonus issue of one for two, a 6 per cent. dividend on the new capitalisation is equal to 9 per cent. on the old. But this remedy has been applied to only a small percentage of cases. It provides no general answer as yet.

The relating of the annual charge for depreciation to the replacement cost of the asset is a newer cult and this, in turn, poses some real difficulties. It reverses the settled accounting convention that the cost of a machine with a five-year life is an expense which should be spread over the years in which the expense is suffered. If our accounting period were five years instead of annual, the principle of meeting in the period the exact cost consumed in the same period would be undoubted. I have yet to be persuaded that annual accounting should completely alter the foundation of such a soundly based accounting convention.

But, assuming that we do, let us consider at least two practical difficulties. What percentage of depreciated plant is replaced with even a remotely comparable unit? The rapid pace of new machine design, capacity and process, makes comparison almost impossible. The picture is one of the artist who paints a new picture over the old canvas, rather than touches up the faded spots on the old. The light engineering shop may replace its row of old presses with a set of roll formers. It may do so, quite apart from the exhaustion of the old plant and purely on account of the economy of the new operation. If we accept the new principle for depreciation, how do we apply it in such cases?

Then I ask you to consider the plant with a five-year life where price levels in fact rise at 20 per cent. per annum on the first-year base. The annual charge must not only be adjusted to a fresh target in each year but, if the purpose is to be attained, must overtake the deficiency of past years. The annual charge, in such a case, for every £100 of original cost is:

1st year	..	..	20	per cent.
2nd „	..	..	25	„
3rd „	..	..	31·6	„
4th „	..	..	41·7	„
5th „	..	..	61·7	„

The serious distortion of annual accounting is obvious. It marches ill with our published advocacy of straight-line depreciation.

For the reasons I have set out, I do not regard any of the reviewed methods as presenting a desirable answer to our problem. Before I examine possible remedies, let us state another most important angle to our problem. The most remarkable feature of the last generation of accounting has been its reorientation. The accountant of to-day is more concerned with looking forward than backward.

The budget, the estimate of production costs, the other instruments of managerial accounting have, for those who are charged with the responsibility of the conduct of enterprise, made the balance sheet a document, not of discovery, but of mere confirmation. Christopher Columbus set out on uncharted seas to discover America. The *Queen Mary* arrives regularly in New York merely to confirm what has been made certain by managed navigation.

No longer can the profession accept its conventions purely out of regard for what has gone. We must examine how our great responsibilities to current management are affected. And here let me say that I know of no really effective safeguard against unstable price levels. In Australia, we have seen the certainty of budgetary practice largely destroyed; we have seen programmes of capital expenditure call for revision after revision, whilst manufacturing costs and prices have called for multiple revision with every passing year.

If fluctuating price levels impair the quality of historical accounting, they play an even worse part in the field of managerial accounting, where calculations of sufficiency of funds, or surplus above the break-even point, may be a matter of very close tolerance.

Having broadly considered some aspects of the problem, let me briefly state my conclusions in the following terms:

(1) Permanent fluctuations in the price level can attain a degree where they can no longer be ignored by the profession.

(2) The permanent fluctuations should largely be those reflecting changes in the general purchasing power of currencies but the effect of the unearned increment should also be considered.

(3) Fluctuations of a temporary character, and particularly those reflecting the movements of a free commodity market, should be ignored.

(4) Consideration should be refused during a period of continuing movement and should be limited to a period of restored stability.

(5) Any device yet proposed for adjusting the basis of annual accounting is unworthy of general adoption.

(6) The pronouncements of the accountancy institutes of England and Wales, the United States of America and Australia content themselves with the observation that recorded profits, during a period of rising prices, contain an element of living on capital; and counsel those charged with the administration of commerce to avoid too great a current distribution and to arrange the addition to reserves of a greater portion of current earnings.

(7) These advices have been widely followed in Australia. Generally, they have failed to meet the entire need for expansion in the circulating capital, let alone provide for general extension of the enterprise. But they have, over the past ten years, made a most material contribution towards limiting what otherwise must have been a colossal need for extra circulating capital.

(8) When stability is restored there could be advantage in a complete revaluation of the assets of all enterprise, with the adoption of those revaluations.

(9) To be effective, within each currency area, any such revaluation should be simultaneous and universal. The personally conducted business should be dealt with in exactly the same manner as the joint stock enterprise. I can think of nothing more confusing to both owner and shareholder, to the economist and the tax-gatherer, than to make a patchwork quilt of commercial accounting.

(10) The revalued figures should be regarded as a modern yardstick of measurement and a new basis for depreciation charges and allowances, and should not be regarded as involving any capital profit for those countries which tax capital gains.

(11) Tax-free stock dividends on the Australian pattern should be the vehicle for adjusting the interest of shareholders.

(12) The position of fixed preferential shareholders and other special classes of shareholders calls for consideration. I can see no case for, nor means open to consider, even long-term debenture-holders, nor in any way to alter their fundamental position as fixed-sum creditors. It is probable that the preference shareholder, who has no right to participate in excess earnings or in a surplus during a winding-up, is similarly pegged to the strict money term of his contract. His is an ownership without the equities common to ownership.

(13) The importance and rarity of such a general revaluation are such as to warrant statutory authority in each country. The statute should fix the date of the valuation, the manner of its application, and should adopt the new basis for depreciation allowances. It should provide for the problem likely to arise with the holders of preference and other shares to which special rights are attached, the main purpose being to preserve equities between the different classes of shareholder.

(14) Statutory authority should only be sought following a full enquiry in each country by the accountancy institutes, such enquiry covering:
   (a) The need for revaluation;
   (b) Whether stability has been restored to currency values;
   (c) The local problem likely to arise; and
   (d) A fully detailed programme covering the accounting procedure to be followed in every class of undertaking.

I have no doubt that these proposals will excite a mixed reception. Disappointment from those who seek to command what they would describe as a corrected measure of the annual result; apprehension, from those who see danger in any interference with our historical convention.

8

To the first, let me say that I would welcome any device which would fully accomplish their purpose without reducing the value of published accounts for public consumption. I do not consider that replacement accounting is possible either for inventories or depreciable plant. There is the further suggestion by some of our economist friends that we should cling to our present conventions but employ an additional column to convert the cost figure to its equivalent present worth by measuring the movement in currency values between the date of acquisition and the date of present publication. I can conceive of some businesses where such a presentation would be convenient; but I shrink from endeavouring to apply such a remedy in a large departmental store, employing continuous stocktaking techniques; or in an engineering business with a plant accumulated by purchase and by reconstruction over, say, fifty years. The complications in such cases could be very real.

Quite apart from their difficulties, I am deterred by the aspect of taxing probabilities. We should never permit the expediency of taxing authorities to govern our assessment of what is sound accounting. But I hesitate to introduce a further feature in our annual reporting which is unlikely to be followed by taxation laws. All our endeavour must be concentrated on discovering a solution which is capable of common acceptance by accountant, tax-gatherer and economist alike.

To those who oppose any alteration, let me ask what attitude they would have adopted in a German corporation over the period when the old currency lost all significance. There must be a stage at which the accumulated decline in a currency value enforces recognition. The steady but slow inflation measured by Keynes at 2 per cent. per annum can be safely ignored for generations. The major dose of inflation during and since World War II in itself warrants an immediate examination of the problem. If most of us hope that the forces leading to further world inflation will be corrected, there will be few students of currency behaviour who will hope for any material ebbing of the tide which has already flooded our accounting basis. To count on a correction by a resoration of currency values is an unreal approach. The most we can hope for is stability on a new plateau.

If I do conclude that sufficient grounds exist for a completely fresh basis for accounting values, I decline to consider anything savouring of a regular process and look for a single answer, applied when stability of economic affairs warrants the belief that the new values will provide a stable accounting basis for years to come.

Apart from major crises, such as a world war, the cumulative effect of the unearned increment is a factor which will eventually compel the further consideration of changing values. If the deck is shortly cleared with a revaluation, I would expect that the accounting world could reasonably apply present conventions for the remaining part of this century. The remedy of a general revaluation should be a rare specific, applied only in the face of extraordinary need.

FLUCTUATING PRICE LEVELS IN RELATION TO ACCOUNTS

by

P. LAUZEL, J. POLY AND A. CIBERT
Conseil Supérieur de la Comptabilité
(Ministère des Finances et des Affaires Economiques),
France

INTRODUCTION

The object of this report is to describe and comment briefly on the means employed in France to adapt accounts to the very important problem of fluctuating prices.

We shall limit our report to the means applied or proposed with a view to correcting estimates of *fixed assets and stocks*.

In studying each of these questions the accountant first considers: the necessity of establishing a true balance sheet making allowance for real depreciation and ruling out any unrealised surplus from enhanced values; the advisability of segregating in the apparent total profit the part attributable to monetary depreciation, which needs special attention as regards taxation and distribution of profits; the advisability of incorporating in costing the costs of real consumption related to price increases so as to have a valid basis for fixing selling prices in accordance with market conditions.

It is of primary importance that the definition of a single and uniform notion of value (or cost) should be used in every case. But several considerations explain the serious difficulties this concept has to face; the diversity of the aims in view (sometimes juridic, sometimes fiscal, sometimes economic), this difficulty reflecting the opposing views of persons or entities using the accounts; and an increasing tendency to ask the book-keeping departments of undertakings to furnish valid data for the preparation of national accountancy.

DEPRECIATION OF FIXED ASSETS

1. A fiscal decree dated 13th February, 1939, had originally authorised the creation of *provisions for renewing plant* to be added to the usual depreciations calculated on original values. The calculation of such provisions obeyed the following principles:

   (*a*) replacement value is calculated by multiplying original cost by co-efficients;

   (*b*) at the end of each financial period, a ceiling figure is obtained by applying to the surplus arising from revaluation the ratio existing between the number of years elapsed and the total number of years corresponding to the probable life of the asset;

109

(c) the difference between the ceiling figure and the total of depreciation previously set aside gives the depreciation charges for the year under consideration.

In short, the constitution of reserves for replacements should be spread over the probable life of plant and equipment and through annual adjustments, the total depreciation plus reserves for replacement plus residual value should provide the theoretical replacement value at the end of each financial year.

2. This system was replaced from 1945 onwards by a system of complementary depreciation arising from the revaluation of assets (decree of 15th August, 1945).

The maximum value of each revalued fixed asset is obtained by multiplying the cost or purchase price by one of the coefficients fixed by the government department, the coefficient being the one corresponding to the year of acquisition of the asset in question.

Correlatively yearly accretions to the depreciation reserve are revalued by applying appropriate coefficients taken from the same schedule.

The difference between the two above-mentioned amounts gives the net written-up value on which new depreciations are based.

At first the government department stipulated that depreciation should be spread over a minimum period of eight years for plant and twenty years for buildings. Since 1948 these limitations have been suppressed and the remaining life of the asset is now the accepted basis.

3. The authors of the 'Standard Plan 1942' originally proposed to add to the depreciations calculated on original costs a replacement reserve calculated as follows:

(a) determination of surplus of revaluation represented by the difference between the replacement value and the original cost;
(b) calculation of the annuity of replacement by application to the surplus value or to the deficiency resulting from revaluation the appropriate rate of depreciation applicable to the assets under consideration.

During a period of continued rising prices, the total of the annuities of depreciation and replacement would be inferior to the replacement value. On the other hand, this total would be in excess of replacement value in a period of rapidly falling prices.

Precautions were taken to control the use of reserves thus created, which until re-employed had to be deposited in banks or otherwise blocked.

4. The Book-keeping Normalisation Committee has defined depreciation as being the accounting expression of the shrinkage in value of fixed assets which necessarily suffer depreciation with the passing of time. It is considered as a charge unrelated to profit-earning. In a resolution annexed to the standard plan of accounts it was proposed that following the revaluation of balance sheets and breaking away from the rules created by the decree of

15th August, 1945, new depreciations should be calculated taking into account a residual value determined as shown in the following example.

Revaluation of original value, 10,000 × 10 100,000

Time remaining to be covered .. .. 7 years

Residual value, $100,000 \times \dfrac{7}{10}$ 70,000

Depreciation annuity, $\dfrac{70,000}{7}$ 10,000

This system thus consists of applying to the theoretical replacement value the rate corresponding to the normal life of the asset.

5. Another solution consists in calculating the depreciation annuity in such a way that at the close of each financial period an equation is set up.

Depreciation fund + Residual value = Original value revalued.

6. Certain authors have suggested the following cumulations:

(a) a depreciation annuity calculated on the revalued original value (or replacement value);
(b) a replacement annuity calculated according to the following equation:

Depreciation fund + Replacement fund + Residual value
= Original value revalued

7. Concrete examples of the calculations corresponding to the above solutions are given in the Appendix taking into account certain hypotheses of price variation.

8. In the methods described in paragraphs 1 to 5 constant annuities are employed and depreciation takes the form of a fixed charge not depending on annual production.

Apart from these depreciations which generally follow fiscal regulations as regards both the value to be written off and rates of depreciation, enterprises often apply other *technical depreciations* in order to establish production costs more accurately. Nevertheless it must be noted that depreciations calculated on *machine hours* or on *the number of units produced*, thus causing annuities to vary with production, are not yet sufficiently developed in France.

The depreciations established by these two methods (fixed and proportional charges) sometimes co-exist in the same enterprise, from which it may be deduced that a difference exists between depreciations charged to the income statement and those included in costings. If the rules of the standard plan of accounts were used (that is to say, if the general accounting and the cost accounting were distinct but linked together by connecting accounts (*comptes refléchis*)) such variances would appear as variance accounts (*différences d'incorporation*).

9. The accelerated depreciation authorised in France since 1951 (fixed rate but first annuity doubled for certain recently acquired material) is less generous than that allowed in the U.S.A. and has not the same aims as the methods used by Chrysler and United States Steel—analysed in 1949 by Mr. McMullen and Mr. Bailey.[1]

Stocks

10. Several methods of fiscal origin have been used successively in order to identify that part of the revenue due to the effect of monetary depreciation on the stocks, the basis used being the weighted average price.

Provisions for renewal of stocks (1941)

11. The basic principle was that the opening stock was maintained at the end of each of the following trading periods by creating provisions equal to the appreciation due to inflationary causes.

The maximum amount of the provision was calculated by multiplying the value of the opening stock (at cost price) by a coefficient varying with the index of wholesale prices.

The objection to this system was that it did not take into account the time required to turn over the stocks, and it was cancelled in 1945.

Provision for technical supplies

12. Creation of a provision account:

(a) 1948. Amount limited to either the difference in value between the opening and closing stocks of the financial period, or half the value of the closing stock.

Deductions were provided for in the case of commercial undertakings, such allowances varying with the time required to turn over the stock.

(b) 1949. Provision calculated in relation to the time required to turn over the stock, restricted to the lesser of
   (i) either the difference in value between opening and closing stocks of the financial period; or
   (ii) the difference between the value of the closing stock reduced by 15 per cent.; and the same value reduced by a fraction representing the increase of the index of wholesale industrial prices.

Provision for fluctuation of market prices (1948 and following years)

13. This was additional to the foregoing provisions and limited to industries carrying out the first operation on certain imported raw materials.

Amount was based on the *notion of a basic stock* and calculated in total as the difference between closing value of the basic stock and value of the same stock, priced at the average of prices obtaining at the closing dates

[1] *Journal of Accountancy*, October and November, 1949.

of the 1945 to 1947 financial periods, revalued in accordance with the average exchange rate of the dollar.

Profits invested in stocks (1950)

14. This was a measure limited to certain products, applicable in one of two ways:

(*a*) reduction on the asset side of the value of the closing stock;
(*b*) creation of a provision account.

The amount involved was calculated as the lesser of the difference between opening and closing stocks, according to one of the two rules following:

General rule. Limited to the lesser of the values of closing or opening stocks, multiplied by arbitrary coefficients.

Special rule for undertakings keeping permanent stock records. Multiplication of the value of the opening stock by the difference between the price of the closing stock and the price of the opening stock increased by 10 per cent.

Solution proposed by M. A. Dubois

15. Before any comparisons are made, one must value at the final price c the opening quantity O, the value of which then becomes Oc instead of Oa, that is a 'change in price' equal to $O(c - a)$.

It is true that if the quantity O has been replaced before the end of the period at a price c then the closing value will be greater by $O\ (c - a)$ although the stock remains really unchanged.

M. Dubois calls this amount 'fictitious appreciation' and draws the conclusion therefrom that the 'true' value V of the closing stock, whatever the closing quantity P may be, is:

$$V = P \cdot c - O(c - a)$$

He suggests the following balance sheet presentations:

Either V on the asset side; or
$P \cdot c$ as an asset and $O(c - a)$ as a liability.

The only difference with the fiscal procedure for 1950 (paragraph 14) is that a is increased by 10 per cent.

Valuation of items included in manufacture

16. Although numerous accountants in France remain faithful to the classic rule of valuation (FIFO at average price), current cost is normally used when the goods are manufactured and sold at a contract price (estimate).

Various methods have been proposed to bring up to date the cost of sales by a more general use of a more recent cost—LIFO[1] or NIFO.[2]

M. Nataf, engineer, *expert comptable*, acting for the Conseil Supérieur

[1] G. Peauit, 1948 International Congress.
[2] Notably M. Pouivet (1950), A. Dime (1951).

de la Comptabilité, made a study of the use of current standards in 1950, but he hesitates before the necessity of frequent revisions, and judges the method to be complicated. In fact, all these suggestions involve the working out of the difference with the real cost normally when taken out of stores, this difference, which is included in the debit of the manufacturing account, being credited to a liabilities account.

Let us note that this accounting adjustment seems different from that proposed by Mr. J. W. McEachren.[1]

The incorporation of materials, priced at current rates, in the manufacturing cost should not cause any difference between balance sheet and operating accounts.

The following formula must therefore be respected:

Opening stock + Purchases — Closing stock = Materials used

The accounts show the first three of these items at actual costs. The use of fictitious costs for the fourth necessitates a variance account and the formula becomes:

Opening stock + Purchases — Closing stock =
Materials used, at fictitious cost — Variance account

The inclusion of the variance account on the liabilities side of the balance sheet reintroduces agreement with the manufacturing account.

The same considerations do not obtain, however, in the sales account; M. Nataf points out that the variance account relates to materials incorporated in *all* the manufactured goods, whether they are sold (realised profits) or in stock (realisable profits).

This affects the computation of profits realised on sales.

REVALUATION OF BALANCE SHEETS

17. In France, the rules now applicable for the revaluation of balance sheets were introduced by the ordinance dated 15th August, 1945 (articles 69 and following). At first limited to the balance sheet for the financial period ending before 1st January, 1947, the possibility of revaluation was afterwards extended to later periods.

Essential characteristics of the revaluation of balance sheets

18. The operation, instituted by an ordinance having as its object the establishment of a national solidarity tax, was and still is of a *predominantly fiscal character* designed to enable businesses subject to exceptionally heavy fiscal burdens to apply, free of tax, more substantial depreciations than previously.

The revaluation is *optional*, whether one is considering the subjects or the objects. Undertakings only revalue if they find it profitable. Moreover, they may select from the list of assets which may be revalued those whose revaluation will prove useful.

[1] *Journal of Accountancy*, July, 1949.

THE OPENING OF THE CONGRESS

The revaluation has a *limited application*. It applies to the following groups, with a right to exercise a free choice among the items of each group:

(*a*) fixed assets, both tangible and intangible, and to the depreciations provided in the past on these assets;

(*b*) investments, including participations in other businesses and shares held in other companies;

(*c*) balances receivable and payable in foreign currencies.

On the other hand, revaluation does not apply to balances receivable and payable in francs or stocks and work in progress.

It is to be noted that the share capital is not altered by the revaluation, unless the company decides to capitalise the revaluation reserve.

The revaluation reserve is equal, for each asset revalued, to the difference between the accounting value of the asset before and after revaluation.

EXAMPLE

	Asset	Depreciation	
After revaluation	100,000	21,000	79,000
Before revaluation	10,000	3,000	7,000
			72,000

The object of the rules prescribed is to fix *maximum values* but they do not preclude the use of values lower than these maxima.

These fiscal provisions have been accompanied by others of an accounting nature, which include definitions and a form of balance sheet inspired by the Standard Plan of Accounts 1947.

Criticisms of the method used

19. From a fiscal point of view it is certain that the revaluation of balance sheets by undertakings has earned them important exemptions from taxes in the increased depreciation.

From the *legal* point of view, the shareholders have been favoured by the fact that the whole of the revaluation reserve is incorporated in the capital instead of being divided in accordance with the nature of the various classes of capital used (share capital, reserves, loans).

From the *accounting* point of view, the administrative method adopted has not favoured the standardisation of balance sheets, firstly because of its optional character (both as to subjects and objects), and secondly because the residual values obtained have no valid economic significance and are not comparable.

Proposals of the Commission de Normalisation des Comptabilités

20. The Commission de Normalisation des Comptabilités has made the following proposals:

(*a*) compulsory general revaluation progressing by section in decreasing order of economic usefulness;

(*b*) adoption of a method of valuing assets which shows their net actual worth, by subtracting from the replacement value an amount corresponding to wear, without bothering to revalue the depreciation actually carried out (see paragraph 14).

Other proposals

21. After criticising the administrative system, M. Alexandre Dubois proposes the formula of revaluation presented under the heading 'Stocks' (paragraph 15).

The asset is shown in the balance sheet at its actual worth (column 6 of table given below) but a 'compensation for fictitious appreciations account' is shown as a liability. This account is equal to the increase in value of the asset through revaluation between the date of purchase and the date of the balance sheet.

The formula is applied not only to the fixed assets, but to the stocks and cash resources as well.

As far as fixed assets are concerned, the workings are presented as follows:

Year of purchase	Coefficient of revaluation	Purchase Price	Residual values (*a*)		
			Quantum	Gross	Revalued
1	2	3	4	5	6

(*a*) Depreciation deducted.

This procedure shows similarities with the proposals made by M. Burhenne, French expert accountant, before the 1948 International Congress; those made by Mr. James S. Lanham, professor of accountancy at the University of Florida (*Journal of Accountancy*, June, 1950), and also the system used for many years by the Office de Comptabilité Agricole de Soissons under the direction of M. Jean Ferte.

ORDER AND ACCURACY IN ACCOUNTS

22. When estimates either of fixed assets or of stocks are concerned, the preceding statement shows that the accountant is forced to submit to contradictory requirements. The desire to avoid distribution of 'fictive dividends' will sometimes compel him to decide in favour of the lowest stock valuation where the presentation of the balance sheet is concerned, but replacement value would be preferred for calculation of costs giving adequate security. By employing reserve or adjustment accounts these values may be harmonised to result in an optimum fiscal economy. Thus opportunism prevails.

23. It cannot be denied that fiscal pressure has occasioned the adoption or proposal of many of the afore-mentioned methods—often in contradiction to traditional accountancy rules.[1]

For example, such is the case with this underquoting of stocks which may be used directly in the inventory without figuring in the debit of the trading account and in a balance sheet reserve. Most accountants think that such a practice leads to the establishment of something resembling a fraudulent balance sheet.

Accountants are now strongly in favour of freeing accountancy from the too evident influence of much criticised fiscality. The Conseil Supérieur de la Comptabilité has become the champion of this movement by claiming that operating results should be determined by sound accounting rules and that corrections of a fiscal nature necessary for fixing taxed income should not be a part of accountancy as such.

24. How is agreement on sound accounting rules possible when basic notions of capital and revenue, cost and profit, are still uncertain? Those who, in a period of rising prices, propose to write down stocks for excess inflation value are the first, in a period of falling prices, to claim provision for stock depreciation.

This 'about turn' was observed in France in a period of six months. The accountant, when begged to modify his basic principles to uphold demands which vary with existing circumstances, can have no pretention to accuracy, he being perpetually in search of the approximate.

Fluctuating prices lead to corresponding accounting fluctuation
25. In France, the efforts made by the Conseil Supérieur de la Comptabilité toward a better conception and a better utilisation of accounting are considerably hampered by this situation.

The Standard Plan of Accounts has helped to elaborate a *terminology* and a logical *classification* of accountancy data. But in presence of price variations of great volume affecting in different ways the various branches of activity, it cannot resolve correctly valuation problems by general rules referring to an abstract notion of value. At least, by separating general accounting from cost accounting, it renders easier the valuation of the wear and tear of fixed assets and stock consumption which depends on different criteria, according to the aims in view.

THE ECONOMICAL POINT OF VIEW

26. The saving on taxes realised by the application of regulations based on the notion of replacement value represents certainly an important power of investment which has been very useful to enterprises, banking credit being limited in the present juncture.

The table below shows the results of a survey of the balance sheets of nine limited companies chosen from various fields of activity (iron and steel

[1] General situation contested by Mr. W. A. Paton, Professor at the University of Michigan (*Journal of Accountancy*, January, 1950).

industries, chemical works, mills, automobile works) representing in 1950 a capital of approximately 19 milliard francs, and investments (fixed assets and stocks) of approximately 162 milliard francs.

	1947		1948		1949		1950	
Profits before adjustment	2,105,000	100	13,312,000	100	8,855,000	100	8,936,000	100
Depreciation ..	1,264,000	60	2,929,000	22	4,111,000	46·4	5,128,000	57·4
Adjustment on stocks: Replacement reserve fund	—		7,684,000	57·7	1,837,000	20·8	518,000*	5·8
Fluctuating Price Provision ..	—		762,000	5·7	529,000	6	393,000	4·4
Profit (balance sheet)	841,000	40	1,937,000	14·6	2,378,000	26·8	2,897,000	32·4

27. The segregation of the results of monetary depreciation as included in the apparent profits has most certainly allowed directors to avoid exaggerated payments of dividends which might undermine the financial position of the enterprise.

The questions must be asked: Has not the use of replacement value in costs been too sudden? and, Has not self-financing, realised by a rise in consumer prices, caused inflationist tendencies without a corresponding rise in production? A conclusive statistical survey on this subject is, alas, lacking.

28. The accountant cannot be criticised for setting forth in his accounts the consequences of rising prices supported by the enterprise. It is his work but nevertheless he must take certain precautions. It would be undesirable if, under cover of seemingly truthful accounting, though really based on unreliable estimates, the head of a business should unduly increase his prices —sometimes thus unnecessarily anticipating an incipient and feeble rise.

Special attention must be paid to the psychologic role of accounting valuations and corrections. Experience has taught that excess of personal safety—certainly quite legitimate if taken separately—may lead to conditions of collective insecurity.

The parliamentary debate on the 'Sliding Scale of Prices and Wages' gives us something to think about.

29. Accounting can be something more than an automatic recording of price fluctuation. In inflationist conditions the accountant can help to direct the actions of the management towards compensation or restraint of increases.

The classical analysis of costs as fixed or proportional charges (or the study of break-even point) brings to light information which has perhaps been

* Three companies only. For the others, the use of stock reduction not figuring in books prevented the information from appearing in the balance sheet.

neglected in the past and the technique of rational charging should not be disregarded.

Accountants, by measuring and increasing productivity, have created another form of active intervention exceeding in interest the simple presentation of information based on replacement value. It is true that inflation by reducing the role of money as a standard of value deprives accounting of a part of its usefulness in this field.

Thus as a natural sequence it follows that accounting should participate in the efforts to stabilise prices.

30. On a general economic plan we must agree with Mr. A. Mey (Holland) and M. Uri (France) that, from a statistical point of view, it is better to employ replacement value to establish the necessary data for *national accounting* and the *economic budget*.

But here, as in the economy of private business, the principle of 'national charging' should guide the presentation of accounts and direct action against inflation. In short, it is not a question of being limited to a mechanical adjustment of public expenditure to rising prices. The information originating from *ex post facto* accounts must be utilised to promote reforms liable both to diminish service costs and, taking into account national income corresponding to a possible level of production, to distribute costs fairly in time and space so as to ensure a perfect balance of prices, wages and money.

SUGGESTIONS

31. In the presence of an inflation of such importance as that now existing in France, a general revaluation of balance sheets is probably desirable and possibly unavoidable. The use of the method specified by the Commission de Normalisation des Comptabilités would be a definite improvement on present practice.

If price fluctuations intervened subsequently, adjustment accounts might be created on the liabilities side as long as the total of these accounts did not exceed a figure which would justify a new revaluation. But in any case, it may be admitted that a more practical and less logical conception of accounting leads to a concomitant use of two kinds of documents:

  (a) Accounting statements following general rules fixed by requirements of a legal statistical and economic nature.
  (b) Economic statements adapted to a permanent and rapid survey of management, depending particularly on current economic conditions.

With this in mind, it will be seen that great interest is given to the realisation (recommended by certain authors) of an 'economic balance sheet' as distinguished from an 'accounting balance sheet'.

32. Compliments are due to the organisers of The Sixth International Congress for having chosen a subject of such wide interest.

It is to be hoped that such exchanges of opinion will not end here but will continue after the Congress.

APPENDIX (see paragraphs 1 to 6)

COMPARATIVE CALCULATION OF DEPRECIATION ANNUITIES (in thousands of francs)

For equipment acquired at the beginning of year 1 – at the price of 100,000 francs

Constant rate of depreciation, 10 per cent.

Hypothetical indices of price variation. First revaluation at the end of year 5, then annual revaluation

Financial periods	Indexes	New value	Surplus of valuation	Depreciation on original value	Para. 1 A	Para. 1 C	Para. 2	Para. 3 A	Para. 3 C	Para. 4	Para. 5	Para. 6 B	Para. 6 C
1	1	100	0	10	10		10	10		10	10	10	
2	2·5	250	150	10	10		10	10		10	10	10	
3	2·2	200	120	10	10		10	10		10	10	10	
4	2	200	100	10	10		10	10		10	10	10	
5	3	300	200	10	10	100	38·2	10	20	30	110	30	80
6	3·5	350	250	10	10	50	44·7	10	25	35	60	35	25
7	4·2	420	320	10	10	74	53·5	10	32	42	84	42	42
8	4·5	450	350	10	10	56	57·3	10	35	45	66	45	21
9	4·7	470	370	10	10	53	59·9	10	37	47	63	47	16
10	5	500	400	10	10	67	63·7	10	40	50	77	50	27
				100	100	400	357·3	100	189	289	500	289	211
						500			289				500

OTHER SYSTEMS

(A) Amortissements de la valeur d'origine = Depreciation on original value

(B)   ,,   réévalués = Depreciation after revaluation

(C)   ,,   complémentaires par Fonds de Renouvellement = Provisions for renewal

FLUCTUATING PRICE LEVELS IN RELATION TO ACCOUNTS

by

EDWARD B. WILCOX, C.P.A.

American Institute of Accountants

If there is one point on which both domestic and international agreement should be possible it is that, to be useful, modern financial statements must be expressed in terms of monetary units. That is not to say, however, that they must be measured in terms of such units. Conceivably the expression could be in currency units counted, not by their number, but by their buying power. Any proposal to do so would be inspired by the belief that a measurement in terms of buying power could be achieved which would be more stable and more useful than a measurement of currency units. Whether or not such a measure is practicable, it is certain that currency units are not stable.

In the United States of America there was, according to the best available statistics, a period of relatively stable prices from 1880 to about 1915, but before the effects of World War I subsided prices had more than doubled. They then fell back to a new period of stability in the 1920s. For this period, 1926 is generally used as a basis of comparison. The pre-war stability had been at a level of about 65 per cent of 1926 prices. In the depression which followed the 1929 collapse, prices dropped back briefly to something near the 1915 level. Thereafter they recovered, and, with and after the advent of World War II, they reached about 160 per cent of the 1926 level in 1948. For a short time it then appeared that the typical post-war decline had set in, but, with the current crop of world hostilities, prices began to rise again. There is here a clear and typical pattern of inflation during and following wars with lower levels in the intervals of peace, but with each cycle at higher levels than before.

Wartime inflation in the United States cannot be attributed to shortages of consumer goods. These were produced in increasing amounts during each year of World War II and thereafter. Rather it must be attributed primarily to the combination of war production and deficit spending by the Government. As wages and profits rose in response to defence needs, taxes did not take away enough to account for war production. There was, therefore, a widely spread and growing effective demand in the market which outstripped the growing production of consumer goods. That this situation resulted in an inflation which was less than disastrously explosive is due to the reasonably good success of rationing and price and wage controls while they lasted, the partial success of patriotic appeals for voluntary saving, and the persistence for a time of the psychology of caution which had been engendered during the depression of the 1930s.

For similar reasons it appears probable that price levels will continue to rise. For as long as the world is oriented toward military preparations, the ingredients of inflation are present. In the United States the present political outlook seems to indicate further deficit spending for defence preparations, and rather weak controls of rationing, prices, and wages, and there is now some popular distrust of savings. Powerful labour unions tend to uphold wages, and the large federal debt provides a governmental incentive to prevent the multiplication of that debt which could be caused by falling prices.

In some respects rising prices affect different businesses in different ways. A company holding tangible property and owing fixed monetary obligations during a period of rising prices is generally in a more advantageous position than one holding monetary claims. However, most business enterprises encounter the fact that increasing numbers of currency units are required to maintain a uniform volume of operations. The same stock of goods ties up more money at higher prices than at lower ones. The same volume of sales in terms of commodities requires more currency to carry customers' accounts. The same plant facilities require increasing investment in terms of monetary units. These requirements for increased financing as price levels rise must be met either from operations or from the addition of new capital.

The duty to provide increasing numbers of currency units obviously falls upon business management, and when profits are reported in accordance with historical cost in terms of money, management is apt to find itself in the midst of uncomfortable pressures. Total business profits in the United States in 1947 were about 17 billion dollars, of which it has been estimated that 7·3 billions were the result of inflation. That figure is an indication of the amount that should be retained for financial needs. Yet, looking at the profits, labour is prone to demand higher wages, customers lower prices, and shareholders higher dividends. Management must retain funds in the face of these pressures. Similarly, taxes based on income, political and economic policies, and the entire climate of public opinion are, to some extent, affected by reported business income.

It should be noted that the fact that there is a need to retain funds is not to be mitigated by increasing charges to income. Large charges to income do not produce money. The problem in accounting is not to provide funds, but rather to determine income and financial position. Any proposal, therefore, to depart from historical monetary cost in the determination of income must rest on some concept of how business income should be regarded. Two points are clear: first, income is and must necessarily be conceived differently for different purposes, and second, income determination rests, not on natural and discoverable law, but on artificial postulates and assumptions. The test of these postulates and assumptions is in the usefulness of the results they produce. The challenge is to find a concept of income which would be both practicable and more useful than that which reflects profits in terms of numbers of currency units.

Two practices have been adopted and accepted in the United States which have, at least temporarily, the effect of reducing reported amounts of income. They are LIFO for inventories of goods, and accelerated depreciation for plant utilisation. Neither is based on any departure from historical monetary cost, and both have been adopted only as permissible alternative methods and only to a limited extent.

LIFO means last-in, first-out. It is a method applied to stocks of goods on hand according to which the costs of the most recent purchases are charged against income so that, when prices rise, the amount appearing in a balance sheet represents, not current cost, but cost at some earlier date. Obviously the resulting charges to income are then higher than they would be under other methods, and the balance sheet figure is correspondingly lower. Originally this method was deemed to be appropriate only to stocks of interchangeable goods in cases where sales prices were promptly influenced by changes in costs. It was therefore widely considered as representing an assumption as to a certain flow of goods or cost factors. There is a growing body of opinion, however, to the effect that LIFO represents a basic concept of income according to which charges should represent current rather than historical costs. Thus it has even been applied, by the use of price index numbers, to retail stores where goods are often not interchangeable. Subject to certain restrictions it is permissible for use in taxation based on income.

Accelerated depreciation, as used here, means the otherwise abnormally rapid amortisation of a part of the cost of new plant construction or acquisition. In general, it is based on the representation that, in specific cases, construction costs were abnormally high, justified only because of a temporary market for products. The excessive costs are therefore written off over the period justifying them. Immediate write-off of costs deemed to be excessive, before usage, has been repudiated in the United States, but rapid amortisation of the same excessive costs has received acceptance in the preparation of financial statements for general use. It is not, however, permitted for income-tax purposes. Its obvious defect is that costs deemed to be excessive when incurred may, after still more currency inflation, be seen to be not excessive. Then the remaining unamortized monetary cost will afford but a small charge to income in subsequent years, and its purpose will ultimately be defeated.

The type of accelerated depreciation discussed in the preceding paragraph should not be confused with rapid amortisation of facilities acquired for national defence, which is permitted for income-tax purposes. This is in the nature of a tax incentive, not for general economic and industrial expansion, but strictly for defence. Although more often than not these permitted deductions from taxable income are used in financial reporting, there is no inherent reason why they should be.

The search for underlying postulates and assumptions which would eliminate the effects of inflation from financial reporting has led to consideration of the replacement theory for plants. The argument runs that accounting is on a going concern rather than a liquidation basis, that most businesses are operated in contemplation of indefinite continuance certainly longer than the life expectancy of their properties, and that, over a life indefinitely long, plant replacement is comparable to ordinary maintenance. It follows that provisions for plant replacements should be made by charges against income. The difficulty lies in knowing whether or not properties will be replaced in kind, and if so at what price levels, how to distinguish between replacement and expansion, and how to recognise the effect of technological increases in efficiency. Furthermore, if provisions are to be adjusted annually to reflect current or anticipated replacement costs, the resultant charges to income might, in a year of rapid change in price levels either up or down, be so great or so small as to invalidate the determination of income for any useful purpose. Largely for these reasons the strictly literal application of the replacement theory has not found much support.

The search has also turned to the idea of expressing economic rather than monetary income. It has been suggested that income be regarded as that which could be spent during a period and still leave the person as well off at the end as he was at the beginning. Presumably, all other things being equal, a person owing a fixed monetary debt throughout a year of rising prices would be better off at the end than he was at the beginning. His economic position improved and therefore he had income. On the other hand, the loss of economic position due to plant utilisation during any period would be the current value of the quantum of plant consumed. In 1936 a book was published in the United States entitled *Stabilised Accounting* by Professor Henry W. Sweeney, which set forth proposals designed to take these and related matters into consideration in adjusting accounts. The suggested techniques were rather complicated, and the proposal did not meet with general acceptance. It is now only of historical interest. Perhaps the fundamental difficulty is in the recourse to appraisals or specific price index numbers for adjustment of depreciation charges. When it is considered that the most significant value of plant assets is represented by earning power, it is obviously impossible to measure earnings in terms of expiring plant values. Simon-pure economic income seems to be an attractive but unattainable goal.

In 1947 the American Institute of Accountants and the Social Science Research Council, jointly financed a project known as the Study Group on Business Income. The group included accountants, lawyers, and economists drawn from business, professional and governmental occupations. Among the contributions to the study was one by Mr. George O. May who acted as research consultant for the group. His monograph contained a concrete proposal which, though not generally accepted, has won a number of supporters. In brief he recommends the LIFO method for inventories, which has been previously mentioned, and general price level adjustments of depreciation charges to income. Depreciation in excess of the amount related to monetary cost would be credited to a special reserve. There would be no adjustment of asset or liability items, and no recognition of the effect of inflation on monetary claims or debts. It is to be noted that this proposal avoids the basic faults of both the strictly replacement cost theory and the simon-pure economic income idea. Its purpose is to state revenues and charges against revenues in terms of units of the same purchasing power, in the belief that the greatest significance in accounts would thereby be attained.

Admittedly the results would be less than perfect, because of inherent defects in both the LIFO method and general price index numbers. LIFO eliminates only a part of the effects of inflation. In cases where prices change rapidly or buying is seasonal or speculative, it may eliminate only a small portion of these effects. Price indexes are statistical averages which include varying margins of error; they may be quite inappropriate to some specific properties, and they do not reflect technological improvements. On this latter point there is room for serious doubt about the true extent of inflation, at least in the United States, because no index numbers can measure either improvement in quality of consumer goods or improvement in efficiency of productive equipment. Rather recently Secretary of the Treasury Snyder has been quoted as saying that Americans get more for their money now than in 1939. Even aside from the difficulty of considerable inaccuracy, the significance which is claimed for accounts which state or purport to state revenues and charges in terms of the same purchasing power, may be questioned. It rests on no such clear concept of income as improvement in economic position, or the presently well-established relation to the monetary unit. And finally the proposal is open to the same serious objection which applies to others, namely the public confusion which would ensue from any basic but inadequately explored change which would for a time, at least, be inconsistently applied and widely misunderstood.

The final report of the Study Group on Business Income, published in 1951, is somewhat less conclusive with respect to price level adjustments, than the proposal in the monograph by Mr. May. It acknowledges the possible wisdom of continuing to prepare primary financial statements on bases now commonly accepted, and urges supplemental information and some sort of separation in reports of the effects of price changes from the other results of operations. However, its general tenor is favourable to the goal of expressing costs and revenues in terms of equal purchasing power, and it urges early attainment of that goal. Because of the controversial nature of this recommendation, several members of the group have dissented to it.

Also in 1951 a statement was issued by a special committee of the American Accounting Association, an organisation including in its membership a large number of university instructors in accounting. This report recommends that, at the present stage of accounting development, primary financial statements should continue to reflect historical dollar costs. It further recommends disclosure of the effects of price changes, in supplementary statements, and suggests that these effects should be measured by a consistent application of a general price index to all statement items affected. This means including the balance sheet, and, with respect to inventories, it does not mean LIFO.

The present position in the United States is that generally accepted accounting principles forbid the introduction of price level adjustments into the preparation of primary financial statements except in so far as the LIFO inventory method may be regarded as doing so. With respect to depreciation, the committee on accounting procedure of the American Institute of Accountants has taken the position that, for the time at least, increasing such charges is not a satisfactory solution to the problem. In this view it has had the support of the New York Stock Exchange, and apparently that of the Securities and Exchange Commission. These authoritative bodies clearly establish the present position.

For several years the literature of accounting in the United States has been crowded with comments, recommendations, and arguments on the subject, indicating a considerable disagreement as to what, if anything, should be done. In the meantime several research projects and experimentations with various possible methods have been carried out, and others are under way. Since the problem is of unquestioned importance and is continuing to cause deep concern, these projects are of unquestionable value, whatever their outcome. It should be borne in mind, however, that the trouble lies in inflation itself, and that prevention of inflation would not only eliminate the accounting problems which result from it, but would also be of greater social usefulness than any conceivable adjustment of accounts.

THE ANNUAL ACCOUNTS OF MANUFACTURING AND TRADING CONCERNS IN A PERIOD OF FLUCTUATING PRICE LEVELS

by

PROFESSOR B. J. S. WIMBLE, F.S.A.A., C.A.(S.A.)
Transvaal Society of Accountants

I. INTRODUCTION

Every accountant must, at some time in his life, have wondered why it is not customary for a balance sheet to show the true present value of all the assets. To answer this may seem trite but, as suggestions have been made that traditional accounting practices should be discarded, it may be worth while briefly to state what these practices are and why they have been adopted. The assets which are not shown at their true values can usually be divided into two categories: fixed assets and stock.

The normal method of dealing with fixed assets is to ignore fluctuations in price, to apportion their cost as equitably as practicable over their estimated useful lives and to regard the figures in the balance sheet, not as the values of the assets, but as expenditure to be charged to future operations. The reasons for doing this are well known. In the first place the true value of any article can be ascertained only when it is bought and sold and, in the absence of a sale, any valuation must of necessity be merely an expression of opinion that may or may not be reliable. Secondly, if an asset is not held for sale, any fluctuations in its saleable value are of no importance to its owner if he has no intention of selling it and is continuing to use it for the purpose for which it was bought.

The normal method of dealing with stocks is to charge sales with the cost of the stocks that have been sold and to value those on hand at cost, taking no account of any estimated appreciation. Again the reason is that accounting aims, as far as possible, at recording facts rather than opinions and, therefore, no profit is considered to have been earned until a contract of sale makes it reasonably certain that it will be realised. On the other hand, depreciation, to the extent that cost is estimated to exceed net realisable value, is allowed for but this apparent anomaly is, in reality, only the recognition of the fact that, once money is spent on the acquisition of unprofitable merchandise, a mistake has been made and nothing can be done to retrieve the situation except to sell it for what it will fetch.

Except in periods of rapidly changing money values, these accepted practices work well. They have stood the test of time. They have the virtue of simplicity. They result in the financial history of a concern being recorded as truthfully and objectively as possible. What has actually taken place is recorded—not what might have taken place if some other course of action had been followed. Sales are charged with the cost of the stocks that have actually been sold and with a fair proportion of the cost of the fixed assets

127

that have actually been used to carry on the business. The question of whether the prices of new stocks and new fixed assets have risen or fallen is not considered relevant. It is realised that the world is constantly changing, that no business can remain static and that the history of the future cannot be written in advance.

The methods outlined above are, as a general rule, adopted without modification in periods of considerable inflation. This has led to a great deal of adverse criticism but, while the critics are unanimous that what is being done is unsound and misleading, there is not the same degree of unanimity as to what ought to be done.

The main objection to orthodox accounts in a period of inflation is, apparently, that they tend to overstate profits. There are two separate and distinct reasons advanced as to why they do so, but the fact that these reasons are separate and distinct is not always appreciated. The first is that amounts charged against profits are insufficient to ensure that no distributions of profit will be made which will result in financial embarrassment if stocks are maintained at the same quantitative level or when the fixed assets have to be replaced. The second is that the profits shown in the accounts are money profits and not real profits.

II. REPLACEMENT ACCOUNTING

In order to produce more satisfactory accounts, numerous systems have been evolved such as basing depreciation on estimated replacement prices and issuing stocks on the last-in-first-out or next-in-first-out principle. The essence of all these systems is that sales are charged, not with the cost of the fixed assets and stocks consumed in producing them, but with the ascertained or estimated cost of replacing what has been consumed. It is argued that the adoption of these methods leads to the production of accounts that more nearly reflect true profits, and that it ensures that distributions of apparent profit will not be made that endanger the continued existence of the business at the same level of activity.

It is, of course, practicable for a concern that is constantly replenishing its stocks with others of an identical kind to issue them at current prices but, except in very rare cases, the merchandise in which any business deals is liable to change out of all recognition over a period of years and difficulties are bound to arise when new stocks differ from old. Even when there is no change in the kind of stock handled, there is practically certain to be a change in the volume held from time to time and, when a larger quantity than usual has been accumulated, the balance sheet will, if a system of replacement accounting is in force, reflect an amount made up of a meaningless conglomeration of figures relating to purchases made over a long period.

In the case of fixed assets, replacement theories are obviously more difficult to put into practice. Fixed assets are seldom, if ever, replaced by others that are identical in every respect. Nor is it possible to foretell what the price of an asset will be in the comparatively distant future when the one presently owned is expected to wear out. The best that can usually be done is to base charges for depreciation, not on the amount that will, in fact, be paid for the new asset, but on the present price of an asset similar to, but not identical with, either the one in use or the one that will be bought to take its place.

Quite apart from these practical difficulties, replacement theories of accounting are themselves so divorced from reality that they are worthless in all but the most exceptional circumstances. The last-in-first-out system has its uses. Where, for instance, a financial company that already holds a large block of shares in another company enters into speculative transactions in those shares, the application of the system may very well give a fair picture of the resulting profit or loss. In such circumstances the system is consistent with the facts. On the other hand, where stocks are being constantly turned over, a system that presupposes that a basic stock is held but never used, can never truthfully record what has really happened.

Even if it were feasible always to deal in commodities of the identical kind and to maintain a constant volume of merchandise on hand, and even if it were possible to foresee with some degree of accuracy what the cost of replacing fixed assets was going to be, and even if the new fixed assets were always identical with the old—even, in fact, if no progress were ever made— replacement accounting theories, while they would ensure that distributions of profit were not made that endangered the continued existence of the business at the same level of activity, would still not result in accounts which reflected true profits. These theories take no cognisance of the very sub- stantial profits or losses which sometimes result from real depreciation of liabilities and assets with fixed money values and ignore the fact that, in a period of changing prices, some invariably rise or fall more than others. True wealth is not necessarily maintained if one's possessions remain physically intact. They may lose or gain value in exchange just as much as money. Replacement accounting tries to measure true profits by substituting for the measure money only those commodities that each particular concern happens to own. One unreliable measure is being substituted for another.

III. CONVERSION ACCOUNTING

If money is a true measure of value at any moment, and if its value is constantly changing, it seems that the most promising way that has so far been suggested of preparing accounts in times of changing price levels must be to adopt the technique that has, for years, proved satisfactory for dealing with fluctuating foreign currencies. All that is necessary to make it possible to apply this theory is a measure of the extent to which the value of money has changed.

To calculate such a measure the prices of all commodities or, at any rate, a representative sample, would have to be taken into account. Whether it is possible to compile an 'index of inflation' and, if so, how it should be done, is beyond the scope of this paper and, in any case, it is a problem for the economist rather than for the accountant. It is, however, suggested that, if an official figure were published monthly for each country, and if the same index were generally applied to all businesses, the results, being comparable with each other, might be satisfactory for all practical purposes, even if the index itself were only more or less accurate.

In theory the system is sound. Accounts would still be historical documents but they would be based not only on the history of the concern to which they related, but also on the history of the value of the currency in which they were expressed and it would still, therefore, be possible to prepare them as objectively as orthodox accounts.

Two methods of applying this theory are possible. One is to convert all figures to the comparatively stable pre-inflation pound in exactly the same way as fluctuating foreign currencies are converted to the comparatively stable home currency. This method, although theoretically correct, would not be altogether satisfactory as the accounts produced would become less and less realistic as the meaning of the value of the pre-inflation pound faded from memory. People are naturally accustomed to think in pounds of present-day values. The preferable method is, therefore, probably to convert those figures in the accounts which represent pounds of the past to their equivalent values in pounds of the present. All revenue and expenditure items should be converted at the average 'rate of inflation' ruling during the year and all balance sheet items at the rate current at the year-end. If the equity shareholders' interest is converted at the year-end rate, the resulting figure is the minimum amount at which the net assets must be maintained before any profits are revealed. The balancing figure in the converted trial balance is the difference between the profit due to inflation and the required minimum increase in the equity shareholders' interest.

The adoption of this plan will not, in a period of rising prices, result in smaller profits being disclosed. More often than not, total profits will be larger; but a clear distinction will be drawn between trading profits and windfall profits attributable to the change in the value of money.

It may be argued that it is undesirable to adopt the same index of inflation without regard to whether the fixed assets and stocks owned by the concern have increased in value to a greater or lesser extent than the general average and that it would be preferable to use a different index for each category of asset. To do this is, however, to fall into exactly the same fundamental error as that committed by the advocates of replacement accounting when they assume that the maintenance of physical assets ensures the maintenance of real wealth.

It may also be argued that, if the prices of the stocks or fixed assets have risen by more than the general level, it may not be possible, if all profits revealed in the converted accounts are distributed, to maintain the business at its same level of activity and that, when the fixed assets have to be renewed, financial difficulties are bound to be encountered. This is quite true. The same thing can equally well happen in a period of steady price levels if accounts are prepared in the usual way, and if the prices of the stocks or fixed assets owned by the concern have risen.

If stocks rise in price by more than the general level, real wealth can be maintained by holding smaller quantities and, if it is desired nevertheless to

H. GARTON ASH, O.B.E., M.C., F.C.A.

Chairman of the Council of the Congress

hold the same quantities as before, it is necessary for those in control to provide the required finance, either by retaining profits or in some other way. If fixed assets rise in price by more than the general level, it means that the concern has acquired its assets relatively cheaply and, everything else being equal, it will make larger profits than those who are not so fortunately placed. It is for the owners of the business to decide whether they wish to distribute these profits immediately or to retain them with the object of enhancing their prospects for the future.

Accounting records, if they are to be prepared with the degree of objectivity that is essential if they are to be sufficiently reliable for their purpose, must be historical in nature. It is true that occasionally, as, for instance, in making a fair allocation between past and future trading periods, future probabilities must of necessity be taken into consideration, but this does not alter the fact that this is only a way of arriving at a fair statement of what is already past. Taking adequate steps to safeguard the future is one of the duties of management, not one of the functions of accounting. If it is decided not to distribute profits because of the probable future requirements of the business, the decision to withhold them, and the reason it was made, will be reflected in the accounts but the history of the eventuality that is foreseen cannot be written until it has actually taken place.

Illustration

As figures are, to the accountant, usually more expressive than words, an illustration of the various theories that have been discussed has been prepared and is included in an appendix.

The accounts relate to the first year of inflation after a period of stable prices. During this year, the general 'index of inflation' rose steadily from 100 to 140, the prices of the commodity in which the company dealt also increased steadily, but only by 20 per cent., while the prices of its fixed assets increased by 50 per cent.

At the end of the previous year, the company had distributed all available profits except £1,000, which had been placed to a reserve account. The company is accustomed to mark its stock up by 40 per cent. on cost. There is no price control and, in order to guard against the effects of inflation, it now marks it up by the same percentage on replacement value.

At the beginning of the year one article costing £5,000 was in stock and this was sold on the first day of the second quarter for £7,350. On the same day, a second identical article was bought for £5,250, which was sold on the first day of the third quarter for £7,700. Again, on the same day, a third identical article was purchased for £5,500 which was sold on the first day of the last quarter for £8,050. A fourth identical article was then bought for £5,750 and this last purchase was still in stock at the end of the financial year.

In paragraph (i) of the appendix is set out the trial balance of the company. The left-hand group of columns shows the balances extracted from the books which have been written up in the normal way. The middle group of columns shows the balances converted to pre-inflation currency in exactly the same way as is customary when dealing with the conversion of foreign currencies. The right-hand group shows the balances converted to present-day currency in the manner suggested above, the revenue items being converted to the average rate of inflation for the year and the balance sheet items to the rate ruling at the financial year-end. It will be noted that the two last groups are comparable, the revenue figures in present-day currency being exactly 20 per cent. higher than the corresponding pre-inflation figures and the balance sheet items being exactly 40 per cent. higher. The present-day currency figures have the advantage, however, that items such as sales, purchases, expenses, creditors, debtors and bank remain at their book values.

In paragraph (ii) of the appendix the usual detailed annual accounts have been compiled and, in addition to those prepared in the orthodox way and two sets prepared from the converted trial balances, a set has been included that has been drawn up in accordance with the principles of replacement accounting that are usually advocated.

In paragraph (iii) is shown a calculation of the true gross profit realised, firstly in pre-inflation pounds and secondly in pounds of the average value for the year. These results do not differ substantially from the more approximate figures appearing in the trading accounts, but they illustrate how the gross profit is affected by the change in the value of money during the time-lag between a purchase and a sale.

A scrutiny of this example, which is, admittedly, an extreme case, will emphasise the danger of regarding not only orthodox profits, but also profits revealed by adopting replacement accounting methods, as trading profits available for dividend.

IV. CONCLUSION

It is possible, if only the economist can provide a suitable 'index of inflation', to prepare accounts in a period of fluctuating price levels that are quite as satisfactory as are orthodox accounts in a period of steady price levels. This does not mean, however, that any businesses that do not wish to prepare such accounts should be compelled to do so. The fundamental reason why companies with limited liability are not permitted by law to declare dividends out of capital is the need to protect the interests of creditors, and creditors, it is suggested, are entitled to have their interests protected only in terms of the money in which their debts are measured. Profit is a relative concept. There is no known way of ensuring that real wealth does not diminish and, if some companies choose to regard as profit the amount by which their position is better than it would have been had they left their money idle in the bank, there is no reason why they should not do so, provided their creditors do not suffer, and provided all concerned are aware of what is being done.

For the sake of uniformity, therefore, it is most desirable that the accounts of public companies should continue to be prepared in the traditional way. Those who wish to give their shareholders more information can append supplementary accounts drawn in the way that has been outlined.

If many of them did so, it would undoubtedly lead to a better understanding of the effects of inflation. It would probably result in dividends being restricted in prosperous times and to a more liberal dividend policy being followed in times of depression. As a consequence of this, disputes with labour might, in a period of inflation, be avoided.[1] It might lead to a proper understanding of the extent to which our present laws regarding the taxation of income really result in a tax on capital. It is, perhaps, too much to hope that the laws themselves might be changed.

---

[1] I am indebted to my colleague, Mr. J. C. Laight, for drawing my attention to this aspect of the matter.

APPENDIX

(i)

TRIAL BALANCES

Account	Orthodox		Converted to pre-inflation currency			Converted to present-day currency			
	Dr.	Cr.	Rate to 100 from	Dr.	Cr.	Rate From	To	Dr.	Cr.
	£	£		£	£			£	£
Profit and loss items									
Stock at start ..	5,000		100	5,000		100	120	6,000	
Purchases ..	16,500		120	13,750		120	120	16,500	
Sales		23,100	120		19,250	120	120		23,100
Stock at end ..		5,750	130		4,423	130	120		5,308
Expenses ..	3,000		120	2,500		120	120	3,000	
Depreciation ..	600		100	600		100	120	720	
Taxation ..	1,000		120	833		120	120	1,000	
Balance sheet items									
Fixed assets, at cost	6,000		100	6,000		100	140	8,400	
Provision for depreciation ..		2,400	100		2,400	100	140		3,360
Stock at end ..	5,750		130	4,423		130	140	6,192[1]	
Debtors and bank	7,400		140	5,286		140	140	7,400	
Capital ..		10,000	100		10,000	100	140 ⎫		10,000 ⎧
Reserve ..		1,000	100		1,000	100	140 ⎬		5,400 ⎨
Sundry creditors		2,000	140		1,429	140	140		2,000
Provision for taxation ..		1,000	140		714	140	140		1,000
	45,250	45,250		38,392	39,216			49,212	50,168
Loss on inflation				824				956	
£	45,250	45,250		39,216	39,216			50,168	50,168

[1] Not reduced to replacement value as realisable value exceeds cost.

(ii)

TRADING ACCOUNT

	Orthodox	Replace-ment	Pre-inflation currency	Present-day currency		Orthodox	Replace-ment	Pre-inflation currency	Present-day currency
	£	£	£	£		£	£	£	£
Stock at start ..	5,000	5,000	5,000	6,000	Sales	23,100	23,100	19,250	23,100
Purchases ..	16,500	16,500	13,750	16,500					
	21,500	21,500	18,750	22,500					
Less Stock at end	5,750	5,000	4,423	5,308					
Cost of stock sold	15,750	16,500	14,327	17,192					
Gross profit ..	7,350	6,600	4,923	5,908					
	£23,100	£23,100	£19,250	£23,100		£23,100	£23,100	£19,250	£23,100
Percentage gross profit to turnover	32	29	26	26					

PROFIT AND LOSS ACCOUNT

	Orthodox	Replace-ment	Pre-inflation currency	Present-day currency		Orthodox	Replace-ment	Pre-inflation currency	Present-day currency
	£	£	£	£		£	£	£	£
Expenses ..	3,000	3,000	2,500	3,000	Gross profit ..	7,350	6,600	4,923	5,908
Depreciation ..	600	900	600	720					
Net trading profit	3,750	2,700	1,823	2,188					
	£7,350	£6,600	£4,923	£5,908		£7,350	£6,600	£4,923	£5,908

APPROPRIATION ACCOUNT

	Orthodox	Replace-ment	Pre-inflation currency	Present-day currency		Orthodox	Replace-ment	Pre-inflation currency	Present-day currency
	£	£	£	£		£	£	£	£
Taxation ..	1,000	1,000	833	1,000	Net trading profit	3,750	2,700	1,823	2,188
Arrear depreciation		900			Profit on inflation				3,444
Transfer to reserve				4,400					
Loss on inflation			824						
Balance available for dividend ..	2,750	800	166	232					
	£3,750	£2,700	£1,823	£5,632		£3,750	£2,700	£1,823	£5,632
Taxation per £ of trading profit .	5s. 4d.	7s. 5d.	9s. 2d.	9s. 2d.					

BALANCE SHEET

	Orthodox	Replace-ment	Pre-inflation currency	Present-day currency		Orthodox	Replace-ment	Pre-inflation currency	Present-day currency
	£	£	£	£		£	£	£	£
Capital	10,000	10,000	10,000	10,000	Fixed assets ..	6,000	6,000	6,000	8,400
Reserve	1,000	1,000	1,000	5,400	*Less* Depreciation	2,400	3,600	2,400	3,360
Appropriation Account ..	2,750	800	166	232		3,600	2,400	3,600	5,040
	13,750	11,800	11,166	15,632	Stock	5,750	5,000	4,423	6,192
Provision for Taxation ..	1,000	1,000	714	1,000	Debtors and bank	7,400	7,400	5,286	7,400
Sundry creditors	2,000	2,000	1,429	2,000					
	£16,750	£14,800	£13,309	£18,632		£16,750	£14,800	£13,309	£18,632
Possible dividend— per cent. ..	27	8	1	2					

(iii)

CALCULATION OF GROSS PROFIT

(a) In Pre-inflation Currency

	Money cost	Rate at purchase date	Money selling price	Rate at sale date	True cost	True selling price	True gross profit
	(a)	(b)	(c)	(d)	(e)	(f)	(g)
					$(a \times 100 \div b)$	$(c \times 100 \div d)$	$(f-e)$
	£		£		£	£	£
First article	5,000	100	7,350	110	5,000	6,682	1,682
Second article	5,250	110	7,700	120	4,773	6,417	1,644
Third article	5,500	120	8,050	130	4,583	6,192	1,609
	£15,750		£23,100		£14,356	£19,291	4,935

Error due to approximation 12

Gross profit, as reflected in trading account .. £4,923

(b) In Present-day Currency

	Money cost	Rate At purchase date	Rate At sale date	True cost at sale date	Money selling price	Gross profit realised at sale date	Rate at sale date	Equivalent gross profit at rate of 120
	(a)	(b)	(c)	(d)	(e)	(f)	(g)	(h)
				$(a \times c \div b)$		$(e-d)$		$(f \times 120 \div g)$
	£			£	£	£		£
First article	5,000	100	110	5,500	7,350	1,850	110	2,018
Second article	5,250	110	120	5,727	7,700	1,973	120	1,973
Third article	5,500	120	130	5,958	8,050	2,092	130	1,931
	£15,750			£17,185	£23,100	£5,915		5,922

Error due to approximation 14

Gross profit, as reflected in trading account .. £5,908

DISCUSSION

MR. A. C. VELLING, *Foreningen af Statsautoriserede Revisorer, Denmark, the rapporteur, summarised the contents of the papers:*

On the subject of this morning's proceedings eight papers in all have been submitted and the task has fallen to me of presenting a summary thereof.

It is not possible, in the short time allowed me, to do justice to the wealth of information and comment, of observations, opinions, and conclusions contained therein. I can but point to some of the main lines of thought and argument.

Each in their own way, the authors have dealt with various fundamental questions: money as a measure in accounts; the purpose of accounts and financial statements; the difference between temporary fluctuations of prices, and permanent changes in money values; the theory underlying historical cost; and others. But the weight of argument centres round the criticism directed against existing accounting conventions, and the various measures evolved for the production of more satisfactory accounts.

The critics charge that in times of rising prices existing accounting conventions fail to provide adequately for the replacement of assets consumed; thereby causing profits to be overstated. The result is excessive taxation and payments of dividends with a consequent depletion of capital resources. In defence, it is stated that accounting should be objective and concerned with facts, not estimates; that historical accounting being well established and well understood, any alteration of practice would only cause confusion, the more so, as there does not seem to be any agreement as to what procedure should take its place.

The criticism has, however, resulted in various corrective measures being suggested. As outlined by the authors of the papers submitted, they are generally: (*a*) the use of replacement costs; (*b*) an adjustment of historical costs; (*c*) various methods, partly of a fiscal nature, for dealing with depreciation of fixed assets; (*d*) special methods for dealing with inventories; and (*e*) a revaluation of assets. In reviewing these measures, the contributors do not contend that no change should be made in conventional accounting. On the contrary, they are all agreed that some change is necessary. They differ only as to the extent and degree thereof.

Much argument revolves round the theory of replacement costs, a term that, according to Professor Graham, has no precise meaning and therefore is liable to be variously interpreted.

The idea behind the theory is that depreciation should be computed on the current or replacement value of the fixed assets and that stock usage should be calculated on the current costs of stock. Costs and revenues should be matched on the same level.

The theory is opposed chiefly by Professor Graham, Mr. Hiley, and Professor Wimble. A principal objection would seem to be the difficulty of determining the appropriate replacement values to be used. Merchandise

137

stocks are liable to undergo considerable change over a period of years. Fixed assets are not always replaced in kind, and technological improvements exert an influence that cannot be measured. Even if replacement is made, at what price level will it be effected? And if specific replacement costs are used, there is the added difficulty of handling the multitude of costs involved. The critics, while conceding that replacement costs may be important for some purposes, contend that for the purpose of reporting profit the theory is impracticable; difficult to apply with a degree of accuracy sufficient to inspire confidence; or, even, that it is so divorced from reality as to be worthless in all but exceptional circumstances. In the opinion of Mr. Wilcox, the strictly literal application of the theory has for these reasons not found much support.

Mr. Barrowcliff, on the other hand, holds the opinion that in the measurement of profits, depreciation should be based on current replacement costs, and thinks that in many cases specific replacement values may be determined without undue difficulty. Should this prove impractical, it should at least be possible to apply a percentage figure of increase based on various known costs. The same type of principle should, logically, apply also to inventories; but as we are in a situation where there is a possibility of a fall in the price level, and as inventory profits have by now been largely absorbed in published reports of profits, it might be unfortunate if a change in method were now made. In the preparation of the balance sheet, existing conventions of original cost should be adhered to.

Mr. Goudeket's paper is a condensed exposition of, and strongly supports, the theory of replacement costs which would seem to have found favour amongst accountants in the Netherlands. The criticism of impracticability is, in Mr. Goudeket's opinion, largely due to a lack of modern accounting equipment. It is, however, not a question of arithmetical exactness, but only of such a degree of accuracy as will do justice to the economic principles involved. To that end, Mr. Goudeket considers that the use of standard costs will prove an acceptable solution where stock valuations are concerned, similar methods to be used in dealing with depreciation of permanent means of production.

Replacement costs have found favour also in Germany, and the paper by Professor Dr. Hax, Dr. Knorr and Dr. Meier demonstrates through practical examples the calculation and elimination of unearned, or sham, profits and losses from the income accounts, such profits being shown in the balance sheet as special 'substance maintenance reserves'. At the same time, it is emphasised that as long as fiscal authorities do not recognise the procedure, it cannot by itself provide any protection against excessive taxation.

In France, on the other hand, it is the fiscal authorities who have taken the lead in the use of replacement costs by providing definite rules, based on index figures, for calculating replacement values both for stocks and fixed assets. In their paper, Mr. Lauzel, Mr. Poly and Mr. Cibert explain the working of the French fiscal system, mentioning also various other methods that have been suggested; and pointing out that the difficulty of reconciling the fiscal rules with those of traditional accounting imposes conflicting demands on the accountant.

Several of the contributors have referred to the case where insufficient provision for depreciation of fixed assets may have been made in previous periods. In Mr. Goudeket's opinion, this must of necessity be corrected before there can be any question of stating profits. Mr. Barrowcliff, Mr. Hiley and Mr. Wilcox are all opposed to this, pointing to the resulting distortion of annual accounting; Mr. Barrowcliff further contending that it does not fall into the requirements of measuring profits that earlier deficiencies should be provided in a period when they did not occur. Such deficiencies are in the nature of capital losses and should be dealt with by appropriations of profit where circumstances permit.

Professor Graham, in his paper, refers to adjusted historical cost, a method recommended by the American Accounting Association's Committee of Accounting Concepts, of which he was chairman. While it is advisable that financial statements should continue to reflect historical cost, it is unsatisfactory if they ignore the changing value of the monetary unit. To that end, historical costs should be adjusted to current cost basis by the application of a broadly accepted index of general prices, the resulting information to be shown in supplementary statements. While the ultimate goal should be the all-inclusive adjustment of all items on the financial statements, this is not practical at present; but adjustment for the income statement of depreciation and cost of goods sold could with advantage be introduced immediately. In an appendix to his paper, Professor Graham has outlined tentative suggestions for procedures to be employed in making such adjustments.

Professor Wimble is also strongly in favour of the adjustment of historical cost by means of an 'index of inflation', comparing the procedure to that of the conversion of foreign currencies by means of rates of exchange. In an appendix to his paper, Professor Wimble has shown the practical application of conversion to a full set of financial statements, showing also the figures obtained by means of the usually advocated principles of replacement accounting.

In the papers submitted, reference is made to various methods dealing specifically with depreciation of fixed assets. While partly of a fiscal nature, they have been used also in the preparation of financial reports. Initial depreciation has been tried out in Australia, but has, in the opinion of Mr. Hiley, resulted only in serious distortions of accounting conclusions and is now in process of abandonment. Mr. Wilcox mentions accelerated depreciation as having received acceptance in the United States, also in the preparation of financial statements for public use; pointing out the inherent defect that the resulting smaller depreciation charges in subsequent years might well defeat the original purpose.

From the United States has come the LIFO inventory method dealing specifically with merchandise. It is not a departure from historical cost but makes use of the convention that the last merchandise to come into stock may be regarded as the first to go out. While originally deemed to be appro-

F

priate only with certain limitations, it would appear from the paper presented by Mr. Wilcox that LIFO is now being used more extensively, and that there is a growing body of opinion to the effect that LIFO represents a basic concept of income. In the United States, generally accepted accounting principles do not prohibit its use in preparing primary financial statements.

Mr. Barrowcliff observes that for balance sheet purposes LIFO would not be appropriate in Britain as it shows an undervaluation of realisable assets. For that same reason it is criticised also by Mr. Lauzel, Mr. Poly and Mr. Cibert. Mr. Hiley and Professor Wimble are opposed to the LIFO theory of a basic stock. Mr. Hiley points to the loss of protection and the consequent distortion of profits that would result from inability to maintain this stock. Professor Wimble, while conceding that LIFO may have its uses, contends that where stocks are constantly turned over, a system that presupposes that a basic stock is held but never used, cannot truthfully record that which has actually happened.

In the opinion of Mr. Hiley, none of the suggested methods provide a complete solution, and all of them tend to distort accounting conclusions. While there are sufficient grounds for a fresh basis for accounting values, the correction should be applied, not as a continuous process but as a single measure. A complete revaluation of all assets should be undertaken only at such time as a new price level may have become stabilised, and depreciation should be based upon the revalued figures thus obtained. To be effective, it should be applied simultaneously and universally within each currency area. The valuation surplus should not be subject to taxation. In the case of joint-stock companies, tax-free bonus shares should be issued to shareholders, a method already used, and in favour, in Australia.

A revaluation of assets is used in France as part of the fiscal provisions. While originally applicable only to a single year, it has later been extended to subsequent years. The revaluation is optional, and it is limited to certain types of assets, including fixed assets, investments, and balances receivable and payable in foreign currencies, but excluding stocks, work in progress and balances receivable and payable in French francs. The valuation surplus is shown in the balance sheet as a 'revaluation reserve'. Mr. Lauzel, Mr. Poly and Mr. Cibert express the opinion that the revaluation of assets should be general and compulsory, progressing by sections in decreasing order of usefulness.

In conclusion, it is appropriate to refer to the official attitude of responsible organisations of accountants. While no definite pronouncements are quoted, I understand that the principles of replacement costs are generally accepted in France, Germany, and the Netherlands, although there may be some discussion as to details. In Britain, the Institute of Chartered Accountants in England and Wales has pronounced against treating provisions for the replacement of assets at enhanced costs as charges before profits; and in the United States, the American Institute of Accountants has made a similar pronouncement in respect of depreciation of fixed assets. The official attitude in Australia would appear to be the same as in Britain.

I have endeavoured in this survey to give a brief summary of the main lines of thought and argument as I see them. If in doing so I have unduly condensed, or inaccurately reported, views and comments as expressed by the writers of the papers submitted, my apologies are due to them and to this congress.

DR. ERNST KNORR (Germany):

Practising accountants in Germany, as well as lecturers in commercial economics, have closely studied the question of fluctuating price levels in relation to accounts and have gained considerable experience on the subject. We in the Institut der Wirtschaftsprüfer have read with great interest the large number of ideas and proposals contained in the reports of our colleagues abroad and believe that the question is important for all countries taking part in world trade and affects them in the same way and, consequently, the same or similar solutions are needed.

In general, we agree with the recommendations issued by the Institute of Chartered Accountants in England and Wales. In the event of the historical costs being the basis on which annual accounts should be prepared, it will be necessary to analyse the profits and to separate the real profits from the sham profits. But we would prefer the replacement costs to be the basis for preparing annual accounts so far as current assets are concerned.

We feel that it is equally important for sham profits to be duly recognised by the partners or shareholders and for the companies not to distribute them to their disadvantage, just as the taxation authorities should not submit such sham profits to taxation, thus having a similar harmful effect. The taxation authorities in Germany have lately declared themselves willing to give due consideration to the danger involved in recording sham profits and in submitting them to taxation, as has long been the case in France.

The German Government has submitted a draft law to Parliament whereby, in the case of fluctuating prices, it will be possible to establish reserves on the basis of the replacement costs for current assets, especially material. These reserves are to-be dissolved in a few years, thus meeting the demand of the economy for avoidance of any unhealthy intervention on the part of the taxation authorities. It goes without saying that the partners or shareholders of such companies cannot receive any dividends on sham profits.

The German scientific and trade journals will give a full report on the outcome of these legislative measures, and we shall be glad to place this report at the disposal of our colleagues abroad. We are of the opinion that the discussion of this important question will not be confined to this Congress but will be continued after its conclusion. If foreign colleagues wish, we will certainly participate in the further discussion.

PROFESSOR DR SCOTT (United States of America):

The papers disclose the influence of conflicting points of view. This conflict divides accountants into opposing groups. It is my purpose to try to point out the nature of the conflict and its bearing on the problem we are discussing.

We are all familiar with the fact that the community in which we live has expanded so much that in some respects it includes the whole world. We are not so familiar with the fact that the expansion has been accompanied by an expansion of time, which is no less significant. Time expansion is universally recognised in concrete areas of action. Both in public economic policy and in the private management of business enterprise we consistently and continuously apply a time perspective. In fact, our universal practice of doing our economic thinking in such terms is the strongest influence bearing upon accounting today. It has given us a consistency and is a source of particular rules and techniques, especially those dealing with the accrual of income and expense.

Accounting has never made an overall adjustment to this powerful trend. Instead, resistance to such an adjustment has concentrated in the development of a doctrine that accounting is and must be preserved as essentially a record of historical costs. The issue thus joined is illustrated in the dictum that costs obtained by cost accounting methods must be adjusted to the actual costs, that is, traditional costs, before the preparation of periodic statements.

Cost accounting has had an era of experimentation outside the system of accounts and it is now proposed that the problem before us be given similar treatment. There are other areas of experimentation which could be cited. If we, as accountants, hold to a fixed notion of accounting and undertake to treat new problems outside a fixed system, the inevitable result will be that the outside exception will become the rule and the tail will be wagging the dog.

The nature of the conflict is essentially one between tradition and the growing science of accounting. The doctrine of historical costs, which represents tradition, is essentially a defensive and restrictive device. It is like the doctrine of the divine right of kings, which was evolved only when the absolute authority of the monarchy was being effectively challenged by Parliament. When we have abandoned the doctrine of historical costs, as we surely shall in the course of time, we shall find that the problem we are discussing here will have ceased to exist. It will have been absorbed in the problems which we are now developing in what we call 'cost accounting'.

DR. FRANCO ANTOLINI (Italy):

Italy is one of the countries most affected by deterioration of money especially since the Second Great War. After the war price levels were 50 to 60 times higher than in 1938 but with important variations between different products, for in our economy some prices have increased only 40 times while others have done so 100 to 120 times. Problems of scarcity, dealt with by Professor Robbins, problems of imperfect competition, dealt with by Professor Joan Robinson, and difficulties of international trade, dealt with by Professor Chamberlain, are at the basis of these different levels of price in the same market.

In a country with cheap money, fluctuations in price levels are especially fluctuations of a pathologic character, and relations among price levels and accounts are also of particular importance.

A law made by my Government in February, connected with the fiscal 'reform' commenced last year, consents to statements being founded on original cost of fixed assets and of depreciation funds augmented as a maximum 40 times in relation to levels of 1938. Original costs of 1913 are augmented as a maximum about 400 times.

It is thus impossible for us in practice to apply Mr. Barrowcliff's conclusions about depreciation based on current replacement cost. For inventories, the Italian general law confines the accountant to the lesser value between cost and current value. A modification has been introduced by a recent special law which allows the reconstitution of the permanent stock on the basis of the pre-war level. Thus, in Italy the application of the LIFO system is very difficult for that part of the inventory exceeding permanent stocks.

In the long run, it should be possible to measure assets, liabilities and profits in real terms, and in this connection it ought to be possible to keep in mind statistics on real national income studied by Professors Bowley and Pigou and the stability, in real terms, of relative redistribution for profits and for wages; but, as Keynes said, 'In the long run, we shall all be dead'.

MR. O. BIRLEY (Great Britain and Ireland):

The problem before the Congress is to discover a principle, and unless we do so we are back again into the ordinary everyday affairs of life and shall carry on exactly as we did before.

That people are thinking about the problem very seriously is evidenced in this morning's *Times* in the report of a very large company. The headline is 'Effect of inflated price levels on industrial operations'. In relation to the problem of inflated costs, the chairman of the company says, 'In my opinion such a course is essential if the physical capital of the undertaking is to be kept intact and its earning power maintained'.

When 'the maintenance of capital' is mentioned, it is very often assumed that it is quite impossible to do that for various reasons. But it does not mean maintenance of the fixed assets or any of those things. It means, as the chairman of the company says, the maintenance of earning capacity. From an economic point of view, what we are trying to do is to retain in the community a system whereby all the available resources are still there. Unless it is clearly in mind that these resources must be there for the purposes of continuing the productive capacities of the community, we might as well resolve ourselves into mere recording arithmeticians.

The Congress has before it the question: What are the sound principles of commercial accountancy? Unless we have regard to these sound principles, I am afraid that we shall get into great difficulties. We can more easily discover those sound principles if we take a phrase from ordinary economics. Let us tear aside the paper curtain of the balance sheet and forget about it, and let us look clearly at the industry or undertaking and report on it and not merely on the figures in the balance sheet. Let us say precisely what its assets are worth. When we have done that we can go to the statistician, the economist and to members of the community with a clear picture of what is happening. We can do that in regard to the inflation of costs; it is something that we ought seriously to consider.

MR. F. L. BOULY (France):

Since the publication of the paper submitted by Messrs. Lauzel, Poly and Cibert, which relates, *inter alia*, to stocks, a further French decree has been issued providing relief from taxation of that part of the revenue which is due to the effect of monetary appreciation of stocks.

I must state the principles adopted without comment owing to lack of time. The system is a permanent one, subject to revision every four years. It allows commercial and industrial concerns to set aside an amount to represent the increase in value of what is described as the indispensable or basic stock, before arriving at the figure of taxable income. This object may be attained either by deducting the amount from the figure of stocks or by creating a provision on the liabilities side of the balance sheet.

The amount of the deduction or provision depends essentially on the basic stock which is based on the average stock held in 1950; it has no connection with the quantities in stock at the end of the financial year. It therefore enables concerns either to maintain the basic stock or to renew it at a later date, should prevailing economic conditions not permit of an immediate renewal, without liability to tax on a paper profit produced by inflation. The methods available under the decree are twofold. Basic stocks of raw materials are represented by the average number of units at the end of 1949 and 1950, multiplied by the increase in cost prices per unit during the financial year to be considered, as shown by the company's own stock records.

The measures taken, although of fiscal origin, constitute an attempt to calculate and set aside the increase in the monetary value of stable stocks as measured either by the increased price level or by arbitrary indices.

I now wish to suggest on behalf of the Company of Chief Accountants, France, that the opinions expressed today should not end here but should continue after the Congress. Indeed, we should not limit our efforts to what has been admitted up to the present. Various countries have, in fact, voted laws relating to changing price levels as affecting fixed assets and stocks but, at least in the case of France, such legislation is more of a fiscal nature rather than the official recognition of revised accounting principles, and these laws have usually appeared in countries where inflation has been sufficiently severe to make the remedies imperative.

We feel that all the delegates of the associations represented at the Congress should, upon their return to their respective countries, form committees with a view to defining their point of view on a national basis. Such committees could originally consist of all delegates who have taken part in today's discussion and then they could be extended to all the accounting bodies in each country.

The suggestions made in each country could then be co-ordinated and reconciled during annual meetings of an international council. Thus motions could be carried which would bear the weight of international approval of the accounting profession. Lastly, it should be possible to take action in each country, with a reasonable chance of success, with a view to obtaining official recognition of the principles suggested by the international council.

MR. SAMUEL J. BROAD (United States of America):

Throughout the world, and certainly in the United States, the importance of the accountant is being recognised.

Three or four reports have been published in Britain and the United States in the last few months dealing with the effect of inflation on income and suggesting disclosure. If we have to disclose, we must be able to measure and we can have difficulty in doing that. It would be comparatively easy to say what was the price last year of the equivalent amount of goods that we have on hand this year and include that figure in the profits for the current year, but you give important information in disclosing that. The LIFO system which is being used more and more in the United States has proved very useful, although it is not theoretically perfect. It has been suggested that the LIFO method would not do in England because of the effect on the balance sheet, which shows a residual figure. The trend in the United States is to show the current value of the inventory as one of the items disclosed on the balance sheet.

Accountants deal primarily with the past. They have to look to the future on questions of useful life and estimated salvage value, but they deal primarily with the past, and they should not have to deal with the future too much. That is one reason why we have difficulty about replacement costs. We do not know what replacements will cost and when they will be made, and we do not know whether the goods are going to be replaced at all.

We ought to determine replacement costs today by applying a price index to the original cost of the plant. You have replacement costs and replacement of currency. Our income status today is real income. Accountants should display the extent to which they can do this. As disclosure has been made, it is the task of the accountant to push it along.

MR. R. D. BROWN (New Zealand):

It will be generally agreed that the question of accounting procedure in times of rising prices can be reduced to two factors, that is, whether to use LIFO or FIFO for stock inventories, and how to make a proper charge in the accounts for the year's use of wearing assets. I believe that in all other respects it may be claimed for the profession that the principles and standards which have guided us in the past are perfectly sound today.

I propose to touch only on inventories. In discussing a choice between FIFO and LIFO for stock inventories, two factors play a most important part in the decision which has to be made; first, the present-day high rate of taxation, and, second, the fact that the emphasis is now on the accuracy of the profit and loss account rather than on the balance sheet as hitherto.

With regard to the first of these factors, it was Mr. Gilbert D. Shepherd who, when addressing the Australian Congress on Accountancy at Sydney in 1949, made a comment to the effect that taxation in Great Britain had reached the stage when its effect coloured practically every business transaction, a viewpoint which is true in my own country and would apply, I should think, to all countries. Its effect must be a vital consideration to all concerned with the financial affairs of any enterprise.

The second factor, the final balance of money profits shown in the profit and loss account, governs the first and fixes the rate of and amount of tax payable.

Bearing these two factors in mind, I would say that LIFO is a safe, sound and sensible method to adopt for stock inventories, notwithstanding that it has certain faults and that its use can be complicated. I say this because (1) it keeps the cost of sales in line with current prices in a rising market; (2) it gives a true profit for a given period; and (3) it avoids the declaration of profits on inventories before they are realised, it avoids taxation on such profits, and it avoids the possible declaration of a dividend out of capital. Its principal fault is that it tends to create a possible secret reserve, thus infringing one of the profession's more recently enumerated principles. I say 'possible' because such reserves may never be real.

FIFO, on the other hand, throws into the profit and loss account all unrealised profits carried in the stock inventory due to higher cost values, it inflates the profit and loss account to that extent, and involves taxation on profits not yet earned. It does avoid the creation of a possible secret reserve. Of the two evils, LIFO seems to be the lesser.

It is significant that in my country the first paper issued by my society's accounting practice and procedure committee, prepared by Mr. E. D. Wilkinson, is on the question of the determination of business profits in times of rising prices. This is evidence of the fact that even far-away New Zealand cannot escape world trends. The author concludes by recommending caution in departing from the generally accepted principles of accounting and states that the course which it is proposed to follow must be clearly defined and likely to yield useful results which may be expected ultimately to meet with general acceptance. Until that time it is suggested that the use of supplemental statements will best meet the need for a more realistic figure of business profits. It is necessary to have a solid base from which to take off and to which to return.

MR. PERCIVAL F. BRUNDAGE (United States of America):

The problem can be approached from several points of view. It seems to me that the accountant's responsibility is to present financial statements as clearly and in as informative a manner as possible. It is a case of adding together apples, pears and bananas and expressing them in some common medium. It is like taking marks, sterling, dollars or lire and converting them into some common medium.

Income is the most important matter, and it should be expressed in some common current medium. Inventories and depreciation are two items in respect of which different media are employed. The depreciation of fixed assets over many years is really in different kinds of dollars, sterling or lire, and there are several methods of making the conversion. The easiest method is to measure the fluctuations in the value of the medium one is using and use an index number for the consumer's price and convert it into the current dollar or sterling value. The simplest procedure is to convert the depreciation of the original cost of the acquisition of the fixed assets into the current medium of exchange by such an index number. The difference between the costs computed in original dollars and current dollars or original sterling and current sterling would be credited to a separate replacement reserve in the balance sheet and the amount deducted from the fixed asset account.

A balance sheet is a residual figure today. We have costs of assets and charges and investments and it is impossible to try to adjust all the items year by year in your current medium. I would limit my adjustment to the income statement and clearly explain it as such.

MR. W. H. LAWSON (Great Britain and Ireland):

The Council of the Institute of Chartered Accountants in England and Wales issued, on 30th May this year, Recommendation No. XV in their series of Recommendations on Accounting Principles. This new statement is an amplification of an earlier Recommendation (No. XII) on 'Rising Price Levels in relation to Accounts', which was issued by the Institute in January, 1949.

The time-limit allows me to give only a very brief indication of the contents of Recommendation XV, but anyone attending this Congress can, if he wishes, obtain a copy of it from the offices of the Institute at Moorgate Place and I would like, if I may, to put in a copy as part of the record of these proceedings. This statement recognises that the significance of accounts prepared on the basis of historical cost is subject to limitations, not the least of which is that the monetary unit in which the accounts are prepared is not a stable unit of measurement. In consequence, the results shown by accounts prepared on the basis of historical cost are not a measure of increase or decrease in wealth in terms of purchasing power; nor do the results necessarily represent the amount which can prudently be regarded as available for distribution, having regard to the financial requirements of the business. Similarly, the results shown by such accounts are not necessarily suitable for purposes such as price fixing, wage negotiations and taxation, unless in using them for these purposes due regard is paid to the amount of profit which has been retained in the business for its maintenance.

On the other hand, the statement summarises the alternatives to historical cost which have so far been suggested and they appear to have serious defects; in addition, their logical application would raise social and economic issues going far beyond the realm of accountancy. The Council of the Institute is, therefore, unable to regard any of the suggestions so far made as being acceptable alternatives to the existing accounting principles based on historical cost. Unless and until a practicable and generally acceptable alternative is available, the Council recommends that the following accounting principles should continue to be applied: (1) historical cost should continue to be the basis on which annual accounts should be prepared; (2) any amount set aside out of profits in recognition of the effects which changes in the purchasing power of money have had on the affairs of the business should be treated as an appropriation out of profits, that is, as a transfer to reserve and not as a charge in arriving at profits; (3) in order to emphasise that as a matter of prudence the amount so set aside is, for the time being, regarded by directors as not available for distribution, it should normally be treated as a capital reserve; (4) except in special circumstances which are mentioned in the Council's statement, fixed assets should not be written up for balance sheet purposes, especially in the absence of monetary stability.

Those are the recommendations on accounting. In view, however, of the limitations on the significance of profits so computed, the Council's statement draws attention to the desirability of three things. First, the desirability of setting amounts aside from profits to reserve in recognition of the effects which changes in the purchasing power of money have had upon the affairs of the business.

Second, the desirability of showing in the directors' report or otherwise the effects which those changes have had on the affairs of the business, including in particular the financial requirements for its maintenance and the directors' policy for meeting those requirements either by setting aside to reserve or by raising new capital.

Third, the desirability of experimenting with methods of measuring the effects of changes in the purchasing power of money on profits and on financial requirements. If the results of such experiments are published as part of the documents accompanying the annual accounts, the Council recommends that the basis used for the calculations and the significance of the figures in relation to the business concerned should be stated clearly.

After the conclusion of this Congress the Council hopes to continue its study of this problem in consultation with other professional bodies in this country.

MR. J. DE JONG (Netherlands):

In his admirable review, Mr. Barrowcliff states: 'The broadest argument put forward by economists against the traditional accounting view of business profits is that it is "backward looking" instead of "forward looking".'

On reading this, I could not help recalling a definition of a penguin, that it is a bird that only walks backwards because it does not want to know where it is going but only where it comes from. It may be that in the days of yore a penguin was one of the ancestors of accountants, but nowadays it is quite certain that in the last decade the profession has gradually shaken off that streak of this inheritance. When forming our opinion as accountants we are well aware that we have to include the present and the future in our considerations.

I am glad that I have been allowed to say a few words about one of the features that is closely connected with fluctuating price levels of fixed assets and that has hardly been touched upon in the papers, namely, the influence of the diversity factor.

In order to give you some idea of its implications, I should like to put before you the example of someone who wants to start a bus service and who therefore buys five brand-new coaches. Let us assume that these buses have a lifetime of five years and no residual value and that in the course of those five years there is a steady increase in the cost of replacing the consumed transport capacity. In each year, one-fifth of the total transport capacity of each of the five coaches is used up, so in all this exactly equals the total capacity of one coach. The actual replacement of this capacity must, however, be postponed till all coaches are worn out. Even if the owner computes the yearly cost of the used capacity correctly on the basis of current values—the cost of a new coach—he will find that, since prices have risen, after the elapse of five years he is not able to replace the worn-out coaches for new ones unless the appropriations of his operating and other income are such as to make up for the deficiencies in depreciation in earlier periods.

What would have happened, however, if our man had not started his business with five brand-new but with only one new and four second-hand coaches of identical capacity, respectively one, two, three and four years old? In this case he would have been obliged to replace one coach every year and by so doing he would have actually replaced the capacity that factually had been used up during the year. The cost of each new coach would then have equalled the amount that on the basis of current values had been calculated for the yearly depreciation on his five coaches. At the beginning of each ensuing year, he would have found himself in this respect in exactly the same position as when he started his business.

From this example it may be concluded that in a period of rising costs no decrease in the effective capital of the undertaking will result if from year to year the investments necessary to keep the productive capacity on the same level can be met out of the amounts which, on the basis of current values, have been charged to the profit and loss account for depreciation. This will be more likely to occur in those corporations where a great variety of fixed assets with a diversity in age-distribution are in use. Each delay in the factual replacement of used capacity results in a speculation which is likely to have an unfavourable result since the price level is apt to show an upward trend.

I am glad to have had this opportunity to say a few words about this aspect of the problem which I feel ought not to be underestimated.

MR. J. CLAYTON (Great Britain and Ireland):

Accounting—essentially a system of recording—is by its very nature factual and objective. It is now proposed, however, that, at the point at which the results of this factual accounting see the light of day, we should abandon objectivity and present those results adulterated by speculation and conjecture. The road to hell is paved with good intentions and, of course, we are given many reasons for this fall from grace; but none of them is convincing.

Inflation, we are told, is rampant. But, as indicated by Mr. de Blank in last winter's issue of *Progress*, inflation has been a constant feature of civilised life; and the reason is not far to seek. Government is the arch-debtor in civilised society, and inflation represents the expropriation by the debtor of the creditor. Is it this aspect of inflation that the advocates of the new accounting seek to redress, or at least to depict? No, their various proposals do not touch upon monetary debts, nor do their revised balance sheets reflect the devaluation of the creditor.

In periods of rising prices, we learn, businesses tend to become under-capitalised. But why? Is it, perhaps, that the prior-chargeholder, squeezed by inflation, thinks 'once bitten twice shy'? In its pamphlet *The Effects of Inflation on Industrial Capital Resources*, the Federation of British Industries demonstrated, by summarising the consolidated balance sheets of 80 companies, that between 1939 and 1949 an almost doubling of the historical cost of assets reflected no significant increase in volume. But the F.B.I. omitted to add (an omission which I ventured to correct in *The Accountant* on 1st March last) that, whereas the creditors and prior-chargeholders had more than doubled their stake in the businesses, their interest in the similar volume of assets had actually declined from 50 per cent. to 40 per cent. Had it been possible to persuade the unfortunate creditors and prior-chargeholders to treble their stake, and thus preserve their 50 per cent. in the assets, there would seemingly have been no shortage of capital.

Is it to show the role of tangible assets as a 'hedge' against inflation? Here again the answer is 'No', except—and most significantly—to the extent that this 'hedge' is lost by the assets being absorbed in production. Could there be any more violent departure from objectivity than the proposal that fixed assets should be carried in the balance sheet at historical cost but charged to profit and loss account at 'current' or at 'replacement' cost!

Is it to advocate tax concessions for those who have suffered from inflation? No, the plea is for tax concessions for those who have benefited from inflation at the expense—presumably—of its victims.

We are told that the transition from objectivity to subjective speculation is in pursuance of a conception of 'true profit'. But this ignores the fact that there is no true profit. Profit is always a convention: 'For what shall it profit a man, if he shall gain the whole world and lose his own soul?'

Speculation has even gone so far as to seek philosophical justification in the 'postulate of permanence'. But this 'postulate' is quite contrary to fact. The life of man is sufficiently impermanent. But whereas the annual mortality rate in the United Kingdom is of the order of 12 per thousand, the annual death rate of limited companies in Great Britain, which has risen sharply in the last few years, is now of the order of 40 per thousand—more than treble the human death rate.

Two simple facts emerge from this controversy. First, taxation, on its present swingeing scale, is crippling the economy of many countries, and, secondly, currency units are, as ever, losing their purchasing power. The former calls for a pruning of taxation and the latter for a reconsideration of currency units. But real currency units will remain the counters of commerce and not some hypothetical mystical currency unit deemed to possess the immortal attribute of constancy. Above all, neither of those salient facts justifies a departure from that objectivity in accounting which is enshrined in the motto of my Institute.

The 'replacement cost' and 'current cost' concepts do not withstand factual examination and cannot become viable alternative systems of accounting to the traditional historical cost method. They are no more than fig-leaves with which the results of factual objective historical accounting are dissembled.

MR. L. R. DUCHESNE (France):

The subject of this session nearly brought about a revolution in France, because at least six bodies were ready to write something on the subject!

In his excellent study, Mr. Barrowcliff with his associates has given four points of view on this question—the accountant's, the economist's, the lawyer's and the business man's.

In my opinion, we should also take other viewpoints into account. What about the company debenture-holder's point of view? What about the point of view of the public? And we know that there is also the State's point of view. Yes, accounting has a social responsibility, and I sincerely regret that this was not sufficiently underlined in the papers and the 'blitz' speeches that we have heard.

Can a balance sheet satisfy so many people? Personally, I share the opinion of presenting as many balance sheets as there are interests to be informed. We have first—and probably the only right one—the orthodox or the historical cost balance sheet, the book balance sheet. I think we should try to maintain its character; it must be a true and fair document. It must remain a summary of facts. We should also try to prepare a more subjective statement, the economic balance sheet. And we know at least a third one, the taxation balance sheet.

In expressing the hope that this third statement will become a fair and true expression of the situation, I shall deal with the economic balance sheet and, in fact, this is the very subject before this meeting. I read with interest Professor Graham's paper and the report prepared on behalf of the French official Supreme Council for Accountancy by my French colleagues on this subject. The economic balance sheet must be a realistic document. We must make it a reliable document, giving an accurate measure of all assets and liabilities and not only of the capital of the concern. The economic profit and loss account should give the accurate measure and the origin of profits and losses.

We know in France, by experience, that through the application of accelerated amortisation, of permanent revaluation of cost of production means, and also in respect of self-financing principles, the interest of the general public is not always safeguarded. Some people in my country consider that these methods have very bad effects and bear a part of the responsibility for the creation of an inflationary trend.

In this respect I should like to mention some recent French steps. As a consequence of the loss suffered by company debenture-holders in the purchasing power of their capital and interest, France is beginning to try to meet the problem. I have heard, for instance, that some French companies are giving their debenture-holders an option, in certain conditions, to have their bonds replaced by the new French Government loan, that is, bonds based on the rate of the gold louis.

The other news is that our French political bodies are at present examining a law, which is more or less ready now, on the 'mobile scale of salary', which is a flexible basis for workers' salaries. It will be assessed according to the French so-called 'family consumption index', subject to certain control by interested parties. If I underline this fact, it is only because I think it could become an excellent means of revaluation of a part of the assets and liabilities of our economic balance sheet, that is, the floating capital, and also for ascertaining the origin of profits and losses. I should also like to point out that the French revaluation law provides for a special tax on the revaluation reserve according to companies' fixed liabilities.

PROFESSOR AXEL GRANDELL (Finland):
The central point in the discussion is the question of the measurement of profit during times of fluctuating prices.

As to method, we can define the profit or net income as either the difference between the capital at the beginning and the end of a business period or the difference between revenue and expenditure during a given time. The first method can be used satisfactorily only if the capital at the beginning and the end of the period is composed of ready money or liquid means. The more the capital is invested in real capital the more difficult the measurement of profit becomes, because in that case the latter assets must be evaluated. Thus, in most cases the second method must be used when the profits of enterprises are measured.

When this method is used, three problems appear: first, to ascertain the quantities of expenditure in terms of goods and services on one hand and the quantities of revenue in the same terms on the other hand for a certain period of accounting; second, to evaluate these quantities; and, third, to divide the income and costs on the different products or branches of the enterprise. I shall talk only about the problem of evaluation, because it is the most difficult one at fluctuating currency values.

As the measurement of profit requires a comparison of revenue and expenditure, this comparison must be done with the same measure of value in order to give a correct result. If we evaluate the output, both goods and services, according to the actual currency value at the time of selling, the expenditures for this output must accordingly be evaluated in the same currency value. By applying this principle, we endeavour to maintain the enterprise at an undiminished purchasing power. This means that the capital which was invested in the enterprise is kept intact—undiminished— in spite of the fluctuations of the currency value. Profit is then only that which can be taken out from the enterprise without reducing the purchasing power of the invested capital.

MR. C. L. S. HEWITT (Australia):

I wish to criticise the arguments put forward in the papers in justification of the new conventions. I do not agree that there is a choice to be made between the existing conventions and the new conventions. I regard the new conventions as a supplement to the existing ones. The arguments in the papers are open to serious criticism and I wish to restate some of them with a view to determining whether they are as acceptable as they appear on the face of them.

It is suggested that taxation should be levied on profits against which there has first been charged a sufficient sum to ensure that the proprietors of the existing capital equipment shall be in a position to perpetuate their possession and always to replace their equipment. That argument could be applied equally to all income earnings. A man might simply state that he wished to put aside from his income a certain sum with which to purchase a small piece of capital equipment in the future and that it should be free from income-tax.

Another argument was that a criticism of existing conventions was that in the recording of high money profits embarrassment was created in relation to negotiations over wages. As a corollary, the new conventions which would allow a substantial writing down of money profits would be advantageous and the accountant as such is asked to say that that is the only method of measuring profit. Without wishing to question the wisdom of that judgment in relation to wage negotiations, I suggest that it is a form of special pleading akin to that relating to taxation which the accountant would prefer to leave to others.

On the vexed question of maintaining real capital, if the proprietor of an existing piece of capital equipment wished to replace a machine and was short of funds, he would borrow money in the market. That was described recently by an eminent contributor to the *Manchester Guardian* as 'preposterous'. I suggest that it is a great deal more preposterous if the accountant as such is to say that the new conventions are the only conventions and that these require prices to be charged to the consumer calculated to enable sufficient sums for ever to perpetuate the existing proprietors of capital equipment in their present position.

As a consumer, I should much prefer that I should pay a price calculated in accordance with existing accounting conventions. I should then have left from my income a small margin of savings which I would hope in future to contribute to the capital needs of industry and become a small proprietor of a small amount of capital equipment. I do not wish to hand over my savings to the proprietors of existing capital equipment so that they may use what would have been my savings to buy capital equipment for themselves. If the accountant is to judge this question between different sections of the community in the way suggested in the papers, he will receive neither gratitude nor respect.

MR. L. KENNETT (Great Britain and Ireland):

The subject-matter of our discussion is the role which money is called to perform in the system of accounts. During the long regime of the gold standard monetary stability was so much taken for granted that no distinction was made between the two main functions for which money was used in the accounts.

But after thirty years of monetary instability and after ten years of continuous inflation there is a general consensus of opinion among accountants and economists, to which the present session of the Congress bears witness, that the monetary unit has ceased to function as an efficient and reliable 'standard of values' and that where money stands in the accounts for real goods, where its function is to serve as a yard-stick for a given quantum of real goods, this function is not performed satisfactorily and it ought to be replaced by some more accurate and more reliable method of measurement. On this there is a fairly general agreement.

Some accountants and economists in this country and the U.S.A., while admitting the existence of this problem, prefer to defer its solution until some later time, hoping that this period of inflation and monetary instability will come to an end and that then money will again become the useful and serviceable standard of values. This expectation may or may not be realised. But even if inflation were eventually stopped, it is very doubtful whether it would not be resumed again. Therefore, I see no virtue in delaying a reform which many accountants and business men feel is already long overdue.

The recommendations which have been made recently in the U.S.A. and in this country recognise the necessity of adjustments. But it is proposed that such adjustments should be made outside the framework of the accounts in the form of supplements to the primary accounts. It should not be too difficult to bring these supplementary adjustments into the general framework of the accounts in such a way that the historical basis will not be impaired, and if this were achieved a solution would be found which satisfies all the interests concerned.

It has also been proposed that the adjustments in the supplementary statements should be all-inclusive; in other words, that they should be applied to all items in the financial statements, whether they represent real goods or merely money claims. I suggest that this proposal would really go beyond the scope of a reform of accountancy conventions and would imply a reform of the monetary system. We should restrict ourselves to those uses of money where the purpose represents real goods.

MR. E. R. KERMODE (Great Britain and Ireland):

Is it true that the inflationary profits are fictitious and that to maintain existing conditions we must adopt replacement standards? When new capital equipment is wanted, you can capitalise. Why not borrow as suggested? If the money is borrowed by charging it out to the customers, the structure is changed and the greater proportion of capital is in the hands of existing shareholders and not investment companies. If the profits are fictitious, presumably the losses are fictitious as well.

The Economist said recently that to tax profits was like taxing a man on the increased value of a season ticket. It is a good analogy but it is the wrong way round. He should be allowed to charge the cost of the new ticket. It is the railway people who made the loss by selling future travel at a low rate; the man who bought the ticket made a profit. Is it fair that shareholders should have real income taxed? If they wish to maintain revenue, they should save out of profits which they have made and increase the savings. They may maintain their real income by technological improvements. We should not be anxious about them in the event of prices falling.

By all means show the effect of inflation by adjusting the statement of accounts or by means of supplementary statements such as have been suggested. If it is in the national interests that the continuity of business should be recognised, do that and give relief from taxation to businesses, but do it openly, as France has done, and do not say that profits do not exist. Do not ask for inflation, in the case of public undertakings, by charging replacement costs out, when the losses you make are falling on capital creditors and not on the general undertaking.

MR. A. MACBEATH (Great Britain and Ireland):

The papers submitted to the Congress have dealt so thoroughly with the points in this problem that my remarks are mainly of a general nature based on my favouring the use of replacement costs for fixed tangible assets and for stock-in-trade.

The Congress which met at New York City in 1929 discussed 'Historical versus Present Day Costs', very largely the same subject as we are discussing today. I read in the report of the Congress that the adoption of present-day valuation seemed to be gaining more friends from Congress to Congress; that the use of present-day cost was recommended by the economist, Ricardo, after the reign of Napoleon I (1815) and by the American economist, Carey, after the American Civil War (1865). Present-day value was thus recommended in 1815, endorsed in 1865, gaining more friends in 1929, and now, in 1952, the papers seem to suggest that we are as far as ever from reaching agreement. It is argued that all the methods so far proposed have grave limitations. Surely it must now be evident that if the profession has not been able to find an acceptable solution after so many years it is unlikely that a solution will be found which will satisfy everyone.

Our problem seems to be similar to the one which the motor-car manufacturer faced and solved. Historical costs have carried us along a period of relatively stable currency conditions like a motor-car travelling along a flat road in top gear. When the motor-car reached a gradient similar to our inflation gradient it could not climb in top gear. Alternative gears were therefore devised which, rather cleverly, not only helped the car to climb hills but assisted it also on going downhill; in other words, in a period of steep deflation.

The lower gears in the motor-car have obvious limitations and the driver welcomes the return to a level surface and to top gear, but the car is practically helpless without those alternative gears. At present we have only one accountancy gear which becomes of diminishing worth as fluctuations in values grow. Today, whatever our academic prejudices may be, we need at least one alternative gear, and those which have been made available to us so far have been fully discussed in the papers.

It seems to me significant that action has taken the place of discussion where the inflation has been most severe—again proving that 'necessity is the mother of invention'. The papers have suggested on the one hand that we need concern ourselves with fixed assets and stock-in-trade only and on the other hand that any new method of accounting should take in all items in the balance sheet.

Mr. Barrowcliff has pointed out that all businesses are not affected by fluctuating values in the same way—one readily thinks of banks, discount houses and insurance companies—and I feel, therefore, that we gain in simplicity by limiting ourselves to those assets which affect the revenue profit or loss for the year. In the complex world of today simplicity has become a major virtue.

It seems to me also that if we tried to revalue all assets and liabilities we should be as far as ever from a satisfactory solution. For example, goodwill and other intangible assets are written off by the prosperous business but kept in the balance sheet of the business struggling to make ends meet. Yet the written off assets have more present-day value than those which appear in the balance sheet.

How could we revalue securities which are not quoted on any stock exchange? Replacement costs have been recommended as the basis for calculating the charge against profits for fixed assets. These costs will vary between industries and between countries but there will be a basic general change caused by fluctuating currency values.

Our first requirement seems, therefore, to be an acceptable currency index for universal adoption. If none exists, let us make one for ourselves. Perhaps the International Monetary Fund could publish half-yearly a currency index going back as far as, say, 1935. The information to compile the index could be supplied by each country, perhaps through their central bank, and be prepared from internal indices which the accounting bodies considered suitable.

A further point which has been raised is that assets are seldom replaced with exactly similar assets. I do not think this point is important in considering fluctuating values. The endeavour of replacement cost accounting as I see it is to charge against profit the correct cost for the year and that correct cost is the replacement cost of the asset used up. The fact that the charge may not produce the exact sum required for replacement because of obsolescence or replacement by a different asset at a higher or lower cost does not seem to be any more relevant than it is in historical costing.

If a form of replacement costing is, as I hope, adopted, protection should be given to those whose rights would be prejudiced by such a change. Preference capital could be given cumulative right to the lesser of the dividend lost or the amount by which available profits were reduced by the change.

MR. F. R. M. DE PAULA (Great Britain and Ireland):
We have heard various new conceptions of profits. We must come to the root of all the troubles, and that is inflation itself. Professor T. H. Sanders, of Harvard University, a few years ago put this extremely well:

'The evils of the inflation itself should not escape notice, and proposals to adapt accounting to inflation should not divert attention from the more important task of controlling and limiting it. . . .

'The most needed and the most fruitful policy is for economists and account-ants to unite in explaining to all groups the baleful results of the inflationary process and in urging the government to control it. Advantages are claimed for a moderate inflation, but we pay a dangerous price for these advantages. The well-known tendency of governments to regard inflation as an easy way out o their dilemmas is not one which accountants will wish to encourage. Another reason for not accepting the proposal on depreciation on the present inflated price levels is that such a step might in itself have inflationary tendencies of its own and make accountants party to the next inflationary spiral. The write-ups of the nineteen-twenties were afterwards regarded as having contributed their share to the inflation, and accountants did not escape criticism by saying that they merely recorded what had happened, without endorsing it. It will be more constructive if accountants now stand their ground. . . .'

This same fundamental point about inflation being the root was made in the leading article of *The Accountant* in its issue of 31st May last.

The papers submitted, however, are mainly confined to the arguments for or against the continuance of our ancient basic principle of historical cost. In this connection, I would suggest that progress towards a solution of this vexed question will not be made unless and until we clear our minds upon a number of basic factors, of which the following are but four examples.

First, are sums set aside for the estimated increased cost of replacement of assets to be regarded as matters of financial policy and, therefore, as appro-priations of available profits? If the answer were in the affirmative, then, I think, most of our difficulties would disappear. But if the answer were in the negative our troubles begin and the following further questions arise.

Second, would it not be necessary to alter the existing company laws in this country, and perhaps in others, in order to make such sums legal charges against earnings?

Third, if such sums were a legal charge, then, as *The Accountant* pointed out in its leader referred to, 'Would not all industrial, commercial and similar undertakings be trading with an unlimited liability in this regard, as it is impossible to forecast the future replacement cost of industrial assets? . . . Might it not be argued that an industrial company, having a high proportion of its capital invested in fixed assets and inventories, could not, over the long term, safely carry the replacement cost risk regarding its assets? The future might well prove that the company had assumed an impossible burden.'

Fourth, if the replacement cost basis were accepted as a charge against earnings for taxation purposes, then, in the words of *The Accountant*, 'Would that be fair and equitable to the other sections of the community—would not the inevitable result be, in times of inflated prices, that the taxation of industrial profits, in the aggregate, would be reduced by a vast amount, at the expense, presumably, of other sections of the community?'

MR. GEORGE O. MAY (United States of America):

I have decided not to discuss any controversial questions here because I have done so in writing elsewhere. I decided to talk about a broad aspect.

First, what is the role of the accountant? I have heard it suggested that it is comparable to that of a nurse rather than that of a physician. There is justification for that in history for the accountant has been concerned more with book-keeping and the auditing of the balance sheet and less with accounting and economic theory. I should like to see the role changed. If the accountant thinks that the patient-investor is suffering from the effects of inflation in that the income reported to him represents inflation and not the result of healthy activities, he should be free to say so and he should recognise his duty to see that the investor is so informed and not put on the management the responsibility for saying what should be said to the poor patient-investor.

In any study we must start with an historical retrospect. The suggestion in the report of the study group is that we should segregate the two elements of present-day income into the part that is the result of activities and the part that reflects only inflation, which is a valuable first step, and that the accountant should assume a large measure of responsibility for that. In that I differ from the recent recommendations.

The statement that historical cost is an established tradition is wrong in its implication. I say that after sixty years' experience and after having listened to reports at various Congresses during that period. Mr. Barrowcliff stated the case of those opposed to the change in its most plausible form in the sentence saying that accounting practice in this country over the past thirty years has been firmly wedded to original costs. That suggests a lifetime of devotion to a single idea, that costs are a family consisting of many genera and many species and that what the accountant deals with is a pool of costs and that there is a wide range of choice as to which should be drawn from the pool.

The suggestion that original costs is factual and objective is a myth. It is a term which covers up a lot of insecurity and uncertainty in accounting. We must get down to more fundamental considerations. One accounts system, which was the most logical produced, failed because it was imperfectly implemented due to the weakness of the accounting profession. Knowing how much stronger the accounting profession is today than when I joined it in 1892, I realise how it should pursue larger and greater responsibilities today. We must have further study, but it should be based on a study of law, and income accounting is the basis of statistical conventional law. Many people have said that conventional and natural law has its root in custom and that custom is based in the first instance on tradition. That is not the basis of our system. Accounting has reached the age when it can revise tradition in the light of reason, and this is the great task that faces us in the future. I hope we shall make full use of it in the small amount of time left to me and that I shall live to see the accountant dealing with theory in the broader and more effective way.

Income today is a political concept. We must recognise that. We must choose a narrower definition and we should try to distinguish between income in good business practice and what is treated as income by the politicians for their own purposes. There is a large field for further development of accounting. It is a field which must be left for the younger members of the profession to exploit in order to make the profession greater than it is today.

MR. S. K. OJHA (India):

Before coming to any discussion I should like to congratulate the sponsoring bodies of this Congress on behalf of India and Indian accountancy bodies for giving a new life to this international organisation during this spring after its long winter of more than a dozen years. At this critical hour not only the accountant but also the economist, the trader, the investor and, indeed, the whole of the industrial and financial world is perplexed to see the colossal Himalaya of money value moving to and fro in an unpredictable way. Here are assembled the best brains from every part of the globe to untie the Gordian knot. I hope that their efforts will be crowned with glorious success.

No doubt Mr. Barrowcliff has produced a masterpiece on the subject and he rightly deserves the congratulations of the assembly for its excellence. He has blended the most modern and the most conservative views on the subject, yet I doubt if this patchwork quilt will ultimately solve the problem. My personal reaction to the paper is that it has not gone as far as it should have done.

Mr. Barrowcliff agrees that 'in the measurement of profit, depreciation of fixed assets should be based on the current replacement cost, and not on the original or historical cost'. He also feels that 'the practical application of this principle is not insuperably difficult'. He suggests that 'the same type of principle should apply to inventories'. Thus he is prepared to make allowance for the alteration in money value in the profit and loss account for ascertainment of the profits.

The only item where he is not prepared to compromise is the balance sheet. But if he agrees to the immediate implementation of the principle suggested by him in the ascertainment of profit as a short-term plan and to make a change in the balance sheet in the light of the alteration in money value as an ultimate goal and a long-term plan I think an easy reconciliation between the extremist groups of challengers and defenders can be found.

Professor Graham also holds almost similar views. He claims that an 'immediate progress is possible, by adjusting for the income statement only the two expense items most materially affected by price-change depreciation and cost of goods sold'. His long-range development as ultimate goal is the all-inclusive adjustment of all items on financial statements. In the opinion of his committee also adjustments made for changes in the value of the dollar should be all-inclusive.

Mr. Wilcox says 'that total business profits in the United States in 1947 were about 17 billion dollars of which 7·3 billion were the result of inflation'. Looking at this 75 per cent. inflated profit, the labourer is prone to demand higher wages, customers lower prices and shareholders higher dividends.

If the wholesale price index can give some indication to the alteration in money value, it shows that in April, 1951, it shot up to 473 per cent. in Great Britain, and to 457 per cent. in India if 1938 be taken as a pre-war basis. It reveals a really horrible state of affairs. The pound today is not even worth a crown compared to the pound of 1938, and the accountant who reports on the basis of all pounds at all times being the same merely keeps the management in a fool's paradise where all the flowers bloom during the winter.

The French and Belgian Governments have taken certain steps in this matter, and in this country the matter was taken up by the Research and Technical Committee of the Institute of Cost and Works Accountants, which has published its views in a book under the title of *The Accountancy of Changing Price Levels* in May last. Its recommendations can be summarised for our purpose as follows. First, the profit and loss account should accompany a memorandum profit and loss account giving the figures of actual value, basic value and the current value. Second, the historical balance sheet should also accompany a memorandum balance sheet giving the figures at basic value and current values.

The Research Committee claims that these methods are capable of general application. I feel at one with the recommendations of the Research Committee and, with it, I am prepared to say that 'what is advocated is nothing more than the extension of a trend in accounting technique which is already apparent'.

Before concluding my argument I should like to appeal to our accountants to learn to walk on the escalator of fluctuating price levels and to banish the backward-looking tendency from the accounting world. This is the age of budgetary control, standardisation, short and long term plans and variances. Now let us go from price variance to price level variances. It is no use being a square peg in a round hole. We must round off the edges.

MR. C. PERCY BARROWCLIFF, *the introducer, summed up the discussion:*

It is clear that there is still a variety of views on this very difficult question.

I suggest that the convention of historical costs would not have been in existence at all if we had not had price stabilisation. If we had had fluctuating price levels in the early days of the accountancy profession we should certainly have had to face the effect of the fluctuations and we should have had to adapt our convention at that time to the conditions then existing.

There has been the suggestion that any change brings in personal opinion and that the accounts will have impressed upon them personal opinion in place of fact. Our present method of depreciation is based on the historical or original cost, but there is a personal opinion in judging its useful life, for that is purely a matter of opinion. It may be broadly drawn on experience from various places, but it is clearly a matter of opinion. So our existing convention is not free from opinion.

In my view, business is fundamentally a continuing enterprise and we accountants have not only to recognise that it is a continuing enterprise but we must apply that in practice. Whatever may be implied by a continuing enterprise must be implemented by us in the accounts that we produce. Surely continuity means continuity; it means preserving at any rate the physical assets of the concern. If we are content to allow exhaustion of the physical assets over a period of years, it means that the concern may go completely out of business unless fresh capital is produced. Therefore, I believe that continuity means that we have to preserve intact the physical assets, and that means correct measurement of the earnings of the undertaking. That is the crux of the whole problem.

I disagree with the view that this is only a matter of taxation. There is much more to it than taxation. One speaker asked why there should be any difference between business and private income. There is a great deal of difference when we realise that what accountants certify as profit is taken and used for all sorts of purposes, taxation included, I agree. But it is also taken into account in Government regulations, and the claim by workers in undertakings for their share in what the undertakings can stand. If we have a false measurement of profits and do not show the correct amount for them, we are then inflating the profits. We are allowing the Government to exact a greater amount in taxation. We are allowing the workers to get a false impression of the profits of the undertaking so that, in consequence, they make their claims higher.

The answer to the gentleman who raised the question of the private income is that if the business is gradually skimmed by the Government for taxation and the workers for increased wages from profits, he may not get the dividends or income from the investment to enable him to save at all. I emphasise that we should address ourselves to the question of the measurement of profit.

There are two things here to match our revenue and our expenditure. Stocks and depreciation are the two vital matters. They are the two things which are out of step with the rest of the revenue account. I suggest to those who are still in doubt that they should seriously reconsider the position in the light of presenting an income account, a profit and loss account, which consists of different currencies. Most of the items will be at the current rate, but two items will necessarily be unrelated to it. We must decide in our own minds whether we are prepared to go on certifying accounts which do not tune up to the correct position.

I should also like to refer to the statement and recommendations issued by the Institute as late as 30th May, which I was unfortunately unable to get into the paper to be circulated. I am glad that it has been brought to your attention this morning. It is a very valuable addition to our literature. In particular, I would stress paragraph 315 which was read to you. The Council also recommends to members who are directors or officers of companies, or who are asked to apply for advice, to stress the limitations on the significance of profits computed on the basis of historical costs.

I leave that with you. There is a plain statement of doubt about the 100 per cent. value of accounts prepared on the historical costs basis. As one of those who have been rather keen on some change in this convention, I have been hoping that we might have pushed our friends off the fence which they decorate so well. Unhappily, up till now we have done no more than get part of the second leg over the fence. Another little push and I think it would be there.

There is this to be said. At any rate, we are all of one mind in this. We are trying seriously to find the right conclusion, a conclusion which can have great effects. We do not want anything transitory which may have to be altered within a generation. We must adopt some principle that will stand the strains of whatever the circumstances may be. The whole case for advocating a change in our existing convention is that it has not stood up to the strain of the prevailing conditions.

There seems little likelihood that we shall revert to the old state of affairs. We are certainly at a much higher level of prices in this country than we were before 1939, and we are not likely to go back for a very long time, so we are in an entirely changed condition. It seems to me that our existing conventions do not meet us sufficiently, and I hope that before too long we shall be able to convert all of you to that point of view.

A vote of thanks to the authors of the papers, the rapporteur and those who had taken part in the discussion was accorded with acclamation.

TUESDAY, 17th JUNE, 1952

SECOND SESSION

ACCOUNTING REQUIREMENTS FOR ISSUES OF CAPITAL

164

ACCOUNTING REQUIREMENTS FOR ISSUES OF CAPITAL

by

IAN W. MACDONALD, M.A., C.A.
Institute of Chartered Accountants of Scotland

INTRODUCTION

Issues of capital are made in so many different circumstances that it is not possible to generalise to any extent on this subject as a whole. An early step must be an attempt to classify the situations which give rise to the event. Before doing so, it may be advisable to say a word about proposed definitions and indicate broadly the method of treatment.

'Requirements' will not be construed in the narrow sense of an imperative demand, but in the broader sense of what is called for or needed. 'Capital' throughout will include shares, stock, medium and long-term indebtedness. 'Issues' will be deemed to include cases where an 'offer for sale' or 'placing' is associated with an issue by the company.

As to treatment of the subject, it is proposed to adopt a broad basis and consider the part the accountant may play in each of the classified situations where issues of capital may arise. We shall find that he usually takes some part, but that his duties and functions vary considerably and depend largely on the type of case.

The following classification is thought to cover the different types which commonly arise in practice in the United Kingdom.

(1) Public subscription.
(2) Private placing.
(3) Offer to members for cash.
(4) Bonus to members.
(5) Reconstruction.
(6) Amalgamation.
(7) Conversion of private business.
(8) New company for new venture.

It is not proposed to give equal space to all of these headings. 'Public subscription' is the most important as regards accounting responsibility and contains more open questions than any other. It therefore merits special consideration. Moreover, by developing certain specific questions under this first heading which are common to others, repetition is avoided. 'Reconstruction' and 'amalgamation', although properly included, are subjects where the primary purpose is not usually an issue of capital, and comment on these matters will be restricted to one or two selected accounting features.

I. PUBLIC SUBSCRIPTION
(*Prospectus or Offer for Sale*)

In this field accountants carry considerable responsibilities, particularly in relation to their reports on profits and on assets and liabilities which appear in the published documents. Accounting conventions are now fairly well established and a study of published reports over the last few years shows a marked degree of consistency as regards both form and content. There is still evidence of variation in some matters of importance and no authorities yet exist covering the whole subject. The practical difficulties have been lessened by the passing of the Companies Act, 1948, which prescribes a full measure of disclosure in financial accounts. Moreover, Government control of new issues (presently over £50,000) has improved the quality of public issues and indirectly eased the burden on accountants. The majority of cases in practice are now fairly straightforward in essentials but each case has its individual problems.

(a) *Report on Profits and Losses* (*10 years*)
General

This report normally presents a figure of profit or loss for each of the ten years. The basis on which the figures are computed is invariably the audited accounts. Clearly any report covering a decade of business activity must be historical and factual. However much the expected future is to be different from the established past, it would be quite impossible to attempt to re-create the past on a might-have-been basis. Any large-scale attempt would only produce a dangerous and misleading fiction.

This does not mean that every single historical fact must remain undisturbed or be accepted without comment. A fact may have been recorded in a manner unsuitable for the present purpose; isolated facts may have a significance which merits comment or special treatment; a particular experience may have an exceptional quality with little chance of recurrence; an accounting practice may have created distortion. These are all grounds for adjustment or comment. At the end of it all, however, the report will remain essentially a factual statement.

Within a strictly limited range there is opportunity usefully to introduce the fiction element, and to calculate and submit one or two specific would-have-been figures. These are not substituted for the historical results but are stated separately by way of contrast. Moreover the contrast is usually limited to the final year of the period covered. The most common example in this category is the treatment of directors' remuneration which must now be featured in that way to comply with Stock Exchange rules.

Where the issuing company is a parent with one or more subsidiaries, the profits shown in the report will be those of the group in so far as attributable to the parent company. If the issue arises from a recent amalgamation involving a new company as the parent, then the profits of each of the combining units may be set forth separately and aggregated in a total column.

It is accepted practice to make particular reference to certain standard items. Depreciation and taxation (other than income-tax) are frequently shown in separate columns. If not shown separately, there will always be reference to the basis of charge of these items. As mentioned above, directors' emoluments are separately stated, for the final year at least. A specific comment will be made on any major abnormality or unusual feature of particular significance.

United Kingdom Taxation

United Kingdom taxation is usually divided into two categories: (1) national defence contribution, excess profits tax, profits tax; (2) income-tax. The charge for each year in category (1) is listed in the report. Income-tax on the other hand is excluded entirely from the figures so that reported profits are subject to charge for this tax. This practice was established in the days when income-tax alone was levied on company profits. The new taxes (category (1)) have all been introduced since 1937. The Finance Acts provide that these taxes are allowable deductions from the profit on which income-tax is assessed. Accountants have tended to follow this pattern in reports for prospectuses. It is rather difficult, however, to find a principle which justifies the fundamental distinction made between two groups of taxes, each based on income and each representing the severance of a proportion of computed earnings. So far, however, the practice has worked fairly well, as it has the merit of excluding wartime excess profits from any final figure of earnings. The introduction in 1947 of a two-stage profits tax, which is building up an ever-increasing contingent liability on undistributed profits, will before long compel a reconsideration of the whole treatment of taxation in profit reports for a prospectus.

Another possible criticism of the usual treatment of taxation is the incidence of capital allowances on profits tax and more particularly on income-tax. In recent years the substantial initial allowance available for set-off against computed profits has afforded considerable tax relief to many businesses. The extent to which this relief has been absorbed into profits has varied. Some companies have taken credit for the full benefit as received, others have spread it over a period of years. The taking of the benefit is likely to be expressed in the accounts by lower provisions for both profits tax and income-tax. The profits tax actually charged may, therefore, require adjustment so as to eliminate the bumps caused by these special allowances.

The effect on income-tax is not, however, brought within the scope of the figures since the profits are stated before making any provision for this tax. If a substantial benefit has already been taken in the accounts, the future burden of income-tax will be correspondingly greater. This question, however, cannot be considered in isolation from the depreciation method followed in the accounts. It is also related to the future programme of capital expenditure and to government policy on initial tax allowances. The point is merely noted that capital allowances raise special problems for the reporting accountant and that current practice in dealing with the tax benefit does not always give an entirely satisfactory solution.

In several reports within the past year, the profits have been submitted before making any provisions for home taxation, and no figures have been given for excess profits tax or profits tax. This method avoids making the somewhat artificial distinction between two groups of taxes based on earnings. It may be suitable in cases where profits in the war years were not abnormally high and where post-war earnings (before tax) are above the earlier level. If this method is followed, it is customary for the reporting accountants or the directors to state the current rates of profits tax on distributed and non-distributed profits.

Depreciation

On this part of the subject guidance has been given by the Recommendations (No. XIII) published by the Institute of Chartered Accountants in England and Wales and much of what follows is in effect an expression of like views.

In the normal case where depreciation has been charged on a consistent basis throughout the ten years, and where no question of revaluation arises, it is usual to compare the amounts charged in the accounts with the sums allowed for taxation. Where the aggregate charge in the accounts exceeds the aggregate taxation allowances, a statement to that effect will be included in the report. In such circumstances the actual taxation figures will not be given. Where the taxation aggregate is the greater, it is usual to make reference, in figures, to the excess. In exceptional cases it may be advisable to substitute the taxation figures for the amounts charged in the accounts. The taxation allowances referred to above are usually interpreted as the annual allowances granted for income-tax (or profits tax).

Where for any reason depreciation has not been charged throughout the period on a consistent basis, it will be advisable to take steps to achieve consistency. This may involve the substitution of tax allowances for amounts charged in the accounts, or, less frequently, a recalculation of depreciation charges based on normal rates. The inconsistency may have been caused by exceptional depreciation charges as a form of initial provision on new expenditure, thus keeping the total charge in line with aggregate tax allowances. If this has happened, it is advisable to disclose the sums involved in these extra charges over normal consistent rates. It may also be advisable to make a comment on future depreciation charges bearing in mind that these will be comparatively low owing to the heavy amounts previously charged.

Where a revaluation of fixed assets has been made for inclusion in the prospectus, the accountant's course of action will depend on whether the new values are to be incorporated in the books or merely quoted and used in the prospectus. Where there is effective booking, the additional depreciation required will be reported—and also tax on any excess depreciation disallowed in the tax computations. Where there is no booking, there is no call to make any special adjustments or comments in the report, but steps should be taken to see that the directors do not boost the assets cover and then fail to make adequate provision out of reported earnings to maintain that cover.

More difficult questions arise in groups of companies where shares in subsidiaries have been acquired at a cost in excess of the book values of the underlying assets. It may be difficult or impossible to determine how much of the excess should be regarded as applying to fixed assets and how much to goodwill. If the group accounts disclose the excess entirely as goodwill, there will probably be no support for any adjustment or comment on depreciation. If an asset valuation has been made for the prospectus, then the same principles should be applied as for a single company.

The topical problem of attempting to express depreciation in terms of current money costs does not arise directly in profit reports unless it has been tackled by way of revaluation. Otherwise, as accountants, we are not yet agreed on the merit of hypothetical depreciation. There is, however, one angle to this question which deserves thought. While the immediate purpose of the issue may not be specifically related to an asset replacement or extension programme, it may well be that the new money will enable such a programme to be undertaken without financial embarrassment. The view as seen from the board room may, therefore, contain a foreground of rising depreciation with only a distant prospect

of extra profit. As yet there is no recognised obligation—moral or legal
—to paint this kind of picture into the prospectus, although the disclosure of capital commitments is perhaps the first outline.

Stock Valuations

These valuations do not often call for either comment or adjustment. In most cases an approved method will have been consistently
followed. Where there has been a change in the basis of valuation
during the ten-year period, it will be necessary to assess and report
on the significance of the change. Any such alteration is also likely to
have had an influence on the disclosed tax liability, equally calling for
comment.

In Britain the tax authorities have successfully resisted methods such
as base stock, or last-in-first-out, as being suitable for general application. As a result the vast majority of businesses have followed the cost
principle of first-in-first-out (modified to average cost where suitable)
both for accounts and for taxation. This method, of course, gives the
least possible advantage during a period of rising prices, and many
companies have felt it necessary to establish stock replacement reserves
out of taxed profits. For the prospectus report these would be regarded
as appropriations of profit and not brought into charge.

Abnormal or Non-recurring Income and Expenditure

Difficult questions may arise in determining the exceptional. Every
business has transactions which are abnormal or transactions which
produce an exceptional or non-repeating result. It would be improper,
as well as difficult, to attempt to ascertain, adjust and report on all
such experiences. The aim is an ascertainment of factors having a
material influence on results, abnormal and non-recurring for the
trade, fortuitous and beyond the control of management. This is a
rigorous test which few transactions may pass. It is proper that it should
be so, as otherwise the factual statement will drift into the realms of
fiction. A study of prospectuses published in recent years supports the
view that reporting accountants are applying rigid tests. Comparatively
few transactions or experiences are exposed and listed as non-recurring.
Those which have been so classified are usually described and the sums
involved are stated.

This heading includes income and expenditure not relating to the
years of booking and thus creating distortions. Such items should be
adjusted by appropriate spreading. Special comment may not be necessary unless there has been a major distortion.

There is a further type of transaction which, owing to changes in the
capital structure of the business, may properly be regarded as non-

recurring. Interest on loans to be repaid out of the proceeds of the issue, and income from investments later used to satisfy a reduction of capital are examples in this class. The expenditure or income would properly be excluded from the profits computation, and a statement made to that effect.

War circumstances, of course, created abnormal conditions for most of British industry. It would serve no useful purpose to attempt to segregate war influences on a particular business at a time when the whole economy was controlled and geared to the war effort. There was, however, considerable variation in the degree of control on prices and profits. In some trades the Government acted as principals for all buying and selling, the traders being agents remunerated on a quota/commission basis. Where an issue is being made by a company whose wartime profits depended primarily on pre-war quotas, it is to be expected that the directors will disclose this situation in the prospectus and the accountant's report will also make reference to it. Apart from these extreme cases, it is unusual to find any particular reference to the abnormal trading conditions prevailing during the war period. The later readjustment to post-war conditions caused further abnormalities, but here again it is the exception rather than the rule to find any reference to this factor in the accountant's report.

Deferred Repairs

In the years following a war the question of deferred repairs may bulk large. It did so in many industries in Britain—particularly those which did not have a high war priority for materials and labour. The principle usually followed in the accountant's report is a levelling of charges by the backward spread of post-war expenditure. It may also be necessary to spread the provisions made for the repair programme not yet overtaken at the date of the report. Some adjustment may also be necessary in the excess profits tax or profits tax figures to keep these in line with the revised spreading.

Bad and Doubtful Debts

In some cases in practice this question causes much needless argument and discussion. Perhaps the business man regards most bad debts as abnormal while the accountant is not easily persuaded that any bad debt is a non-recurring experience!

This heading may conveniently be divided into two categories: (a) home debts and (b) foreign debts. With home debts the question is usually one of determining whether the experience over the ten-year period has given rise to excessive charges. If so, there may be cause for

G

adjustment. It is probably true to say that over British business as a whole the past ten years show lower than average bad debt losses. The accountant may, therefore, recognise particular losses as abnormal and yet be reluctant to make any disclosure or adjustment if the aggregate position is considered unusually favourable.

Foreign debts give rise to much more difficult questions. In the past ten years losses have been incurred through political causes in Europe and Asia, through the freezing of foreign currencies, through fluctuations in foreign exchanges and through refusal to implement bargains. It is not easy to discuss in general terms the treatment of losses from these varied causes. If a business is dependent on foreign trade, then such risks may not be avoidable. Reference might be made in the report to the facts of any material losses from foreign debts, but a particularly strong case would be required to merit the actual adjustment of profits.

Directors' Remuneration

This heading does not often give rise to special problems. In most cases the actual emoluments are left undisturbed as a charge against profits. It is necessary, however, in terms of Stock Exchange rules, to state the aggregate emoluments paid to the directors by the company during the last period for which accounts have been made up, and to state the amount, if any, by which such emoluments would differ from the amounts payable under arrangements in force at the date of the prospectus. In the case of parent company directors, it is not unusual to find that the emoluments for the last period are stated at the aggregate amount paid by the company *and* its subsidiaries. This is in line with the disclosure in the annual accounts although it goes beyond the minimum prospectus requirements.

If an examination of directors' emoluments over the ten-year period shows that the charges have not been related to the quality or market worth of services rendered (e.g. in a family business) it may be advisable to show the profits *before* directors' remuneration and give the required special information for the last year.

Pension Funds

In recent years many British companies have established or extended their arrangements for the payment of pensions to staff and officials. The schemes take many forms but in the majority of cases money goes out of the business to trustees or assurance companies. The setting up or extending of a fund will probably involve an ascertainment of the amount required to make the fund actuarially solvent. The whole of this sum may be found out of reserves or profits or may be spread as a charge on profits for several years after the date of the ascertainment. There may accordingly be abnormal charges in some years and no charges in others. These circumstances will call for adjustment or disclosure in the report.

Foreign Branches and Subsidiaries

It would not be appropriate to embark on a lengthy discussion of the many and varied problems which arise in connection with the ascertainment of profit from foreign trade. Most of these questions have to be determined when preparing annual accounts and the solutions accepted for that purpose are likely to be followed in the prospectus report—frequently without comment. Indeed the 'Notes' on this subject in the annual accounts may be more numerous and involved than the comments in the prospectus report. In the latter case the accountant is permitted to exercise his judgment as regards the form and content of the ten-year statement. The annual accounts, on the other hand, are entangled in the mesh of the most recent Companies Act, particularly of the Eighth Schedule thereto.

One finds, however, that reference is frequently made in the prospectus report to one or two foreign trading matters, provided these are a material part of the total activities.

First, the method of treatment of foreign taxation and of the corresponding relief from United Kingdom taxation is stated. A measure of relief from double taxation is now available in respect of all foreign profits. This, however, was not the position throughout the whole of the past ten years and many businesses with overseas interests have experienced a diminishing burden of double taxation during that period. The weight of this factor cannot easily be assessed in view of the complicated relationship between foreign and home taxation and numerous changes in taxes and the basis of computation. Accordingly, two methods of treatment are open to the reporting accountant. All charges for foreign and home taxation (including profits tax) may· be eliminated from the profit statement. This is not a recommended course but may have to be followed if year-by-year figures are of little value. Such a course should, if possible, be supported by a statement that the aggregate taxation provisions made by the company over the years have been adequate. The alternative method—and the one more commonly adopted—is to charge all foreign taxation and credit all United Kingdom relief. Theoretically this restores the adjusted profit to the figure on which the full rate of United Kingdom income-tax would be chargeable.

Secondly, reference may be made to the rates of exchange used to convert currencies to sterling. If only one or two foreign currencies are involved, the actual rates used may be stated in a note. If many currencies are involved, the basis adopted will be described.

The devaluation of sterling in 1949 produced a crop of special problems in the accounts immediately following this event. The conversion of net current assets from 'hard' currencies to sterling gave rise to certain exceptional profits which were so classified in the annual accounts and merit similar treatment in the prospectus. In a group of companies some part of these exceptional profits would only emerge on consolidation, e.g. net current assets owned by foreign subsidiaries. In many cases a practical difficulty arose in distinguishing between the recurring element, due to the existence and continuation of earnings in 'hard' currencies and the non-recurring element arising from the ownership of net current assets in 'hard' currencies at the date of devaluation.

Expenditure on Development

In a company which is extending its activities, a major question may lie in the distinction between capital and revenue expenditure, and in the continuing worth of sums charged to development account. The traditional tests of assessing the value and duration of the resultant benefit will have to be applied throughout the ten-year period and more particularly at the date of the issue. For expenditure to be charged to capital in the first instance there must be a strong expectation of a continuing value to the business. Moreover, it should have been specifically incurred with such an end in view. It is proper to charge to capital all expenditure on major development schemes aimed at advancing the company's existing position in industry or increasing its overall activity. In some of the newer industries where rapid scientific progress is the normal experience it may be difficult to make this assessment. In these cases considerable expenditure on research and development must be incurred merely to maintain a competitive place in the industry. The bulk of such expenditure may therefore properly be regarded as a normal element of cost.

Of the sums properly charged to capital in the first instance, the appropriate parts deemed to be consumed during the ten-year period will be charged against profits. The balance of the development expenditure remaining on capital account at the date of the prospectus will again be tested for continuing value as meriting inclusion in the asset statement. Any part of the balance which should properly be excluded will be written off either out of reserves or as spread charges against past profits, depending on the history and circumstances of the project.

There remains for consideration the future writing down of development expenditure included in the asset statement. The need for a reduction will, of course, depend on the nature of the development and the probable duration of the benefit, but some indication may have to be given of the effect on future profits of any such reduction.

Statement of Adjustments

The Stock Exchange requires a written statement to be available for inspection, signed by the reporting accountants, setting out the adjustments made in the report and giving the reasons therefor. The Stock Exchange has also made certain suggestions as to the form of this statement. It is recommended that the first part of the statement should reconstitute the profit and loss accounts as though the Companies Act, 1948, had been in force throughout the whole period. The second part of the statement will show the actual adjustments made specially for prospectus purposes.

(b) Report on Assets and Liabilities

In the absence of special circumstances the standard practice is to incorporate in the report the figures of assets and liabilities appearing in the most recent audited balance sheet. An aggregation is made of the net assets, followed by details of the issued capital and reserves representing these assets. If the issuing company is a holding company, the statement will list the assets and liabilities of the parent and, separately, of the group.

This report does not often give rise to any special difficulties. The audited balance sheet on which the report is based will already have passed the tests provided by the Companies Act, 1948. The decisions then reached on such matters as reserves, provisions, depreciation, and value of current assets will, in the normal case, be accepted and followed in the prospectus report. Where the reporting accountant has made adjustments to profits, it is necessary to consider whether any of the adjustments has a counterpart which calls for an alteration in an asset or liability at the terminal balancing date. It is not customary to try to adhere rigidly to the double-entry principle as between the profit report and the statement of assets and liabilities. Each has its separate purpose and these purposes may best be achieved without the strict application of a book-keeping rule which is conventionally applied in preparing the accounts of a single year. While this is so, there is not likely to be any radical departure from the conventional link between the two statements. Any adjustment on profits which materially influences assets or liabilities at the last balancing date will normally call for a corresponding adjustment in the net assets statement. A case where the double adjustment is not usually made is a substitution of taxation allowances in lieu of depreciation, while still submitting balance sheet figures for fixed assets.

(c) *Report on Dividends*

This is a factual statement which normally covers the ten-year period. It only applies to dividends declared by the issuing company—not, for example, by a company to be acquired out of the proceeds of the issue. Where the capital has altered during the period, it will be necessary to associate amounts of capital with rates of dividend in a suitably tabulated statement.

(d) *Commitments for Capital Expenditure*

It is customary to include in the report the estimated amount at the date of the last balance sheet. This will repeat the figure noted in the annual accounts in accordance with the Companies Act, 1948.

(e) *Net Assets at Date of Issue*

The published report does not often make reference to the net assets position at the date of the report unless some material change has taken place since the most recent balance sheet. Whatever may be the legal obligations of the accountant as regards the intervening period, steps should be taken to test the profit-earning capacity during that period. The directors will probably express an opinion (in the prospectus) on the rate of current earnings and the accountant should independently satisfy himself that the figures support the directors' opinion. Moreover, the accountant is well advised to make specific inquiries about changes in assets and liabilities due to any cause other than normal business activity. A further precaution is to try to verify that the list of special contracts published in the prospectus is correct and complete. One may find other contracts relating to factory extensions, purchase of plant, etc., which the directors regard as being in the ordinary course of business. While this view may be technically correct, it is necessary to consider whether these contracts increase materially the amount of capital commitments as stated at the date of the most recent balance sheet. If so, a revised figure should be given. The influence of these commitments on future depreciation is not a matter on which it is yet customary to make any comment in the prospectus.

II. PRIVATE PLACING

This heading includes the placing of new issues—usually by a finance house—and also the taking up of the whole or part of a new issue by a financial institution specialising in that class of business. These specialist institutions have grown steadily in recent years and are taking the place formerly occupied by private sources of capital, no longer available owing to high taxation and death duties.

It is likely that an accountant's investigation and report will be required before final agreements are completed. In some cases the accountant's investigation will be the last step in the procedure— everything being agreed subject to a satisfactory report from the accountant. In a strongly established and well-known business such an order of procedure may be followed. In most cases, however, the accountant's report will be made before final terms are discussed and frequently it will be made immediately after a preliminary scrutiny of the proposition.

The purpose of the investigation might be expressed in general terms as follows: to amplify information contained in the annual accounts; to disclose and adjust abnormalities; to probe for latent weaknesses or concealed strength; to assess financial requirements, covering both fixed assets and working capital; to express past earnings, suitably adjusted, in a form which will disclose significant trends. Most of the special points discussed in relation to prospectus reports will require similar consideration and treatment.

In this field, however, we find more cases of private companies— often family concerns—seeking outside capital for the first time. Special care may, therefore, be necessary on a number of questions which arise less frequently in connection with public issues. Personnel of management; levels of directors' remuneration and expenses; adequacy of accounting and costing systems; possible under-valuations of stocks; liability to sur-tax; estimate of working capital requirements; these are matters which may be of special importance in the smaller company. Moreover, the fixed assets may have been written down to nominal amounts, thus distorting both profits and assets. A valuation of the business or of the equity capital may also be required.

The accountant's aim is to give a comprehensive report on the state of health of the business. His approach must not be too narrow or technical. While he must cover pure accounting questions such as costing and taxation, he should constantly be trying to assess the real strength of the case in terms of production, selling and management. His knowledge and experience of other businesses should help him to measure standards of ability and efficiency. His awareness of the importance of supplies of raw material and availability of labour will influence his inquiry programme. His report on working capital requirements will contain a note of warning on the unpredictability of future costs.

As regards the form and terms of new capital to be taken up or 'placed', this is a matter primarily for negotiation between the company and the financial specialists. The accountant, however, will probably have a say in these negotiations since capital structure considerations involve accounting questions. In Britain the incidence of taxation varies with different forms of capital structure, and in a choice between, say, debentures and preference shares the tax question may have relevance. Tax matters also arise on the issue of bonus shares and on certain forms of reconstruction of share and loan capital. In some cases in this field the most convenient way to deal with the financial situation would be the liquidation of the old company and the formation of a new company (with the desired capital structure). This may have to be ruled out because of the extra tax burden which might arise on a liquidation. If the transaction involves the issue of redeemable capital, the method of redemption raises accountancy questions. Should there be annual appropriation of profit? If so, what burden might the profits be expected to carry after allowing for tax and dividends? Should appropriations be invested outwith the business? If so, is this likely to result in the uneconomic situation of investing and borrowing at the same time? What will be the tax burden, if any, caused by the act of redemption (assuming to-day's tax laws)? These and other questions show that the clear-cut distinction between company finance and accountancy is a thing of the past. The financier must have accounting knowledge or advice. Equally, the accountant, to be effective, must understand and appreciate the principles and methods of financial institutions which provide or 'place' capital for industry. It is likely that in the future—in Britain at least—an increasing amount of capital for industry will have to be found through financial institutions.

III. Offer to Members for Cash

This type of issue is fundamentally different from a public issue or a placing in that the bulk of the money is expected to come from existing shareholders who are presumed to have knowledge of the company's history and present effectiveness. In some cases the issue may be underwritten—in part at least—and this may call for an accountant's report.

Accounting matters arise in determining the amount of additional capital required. Estimates of overall capital requirements for some years ahead may have to be computed. There should be an understanding between directors and the accountant as to assumptions on cost and price levels. There is usually a desire that the issue should provide adequate capital for several years ahead. On the other hand, it is not prudent to raise capital merely in anticipation of further expected inflation. In practice calculations are probably anchored at or slightly above current price levels. Where new capital is required to cover a major development scheme, the accountant will rely on officials of the company to give him estimates of future capital expenditure and of production and sales.

The accountant may also be asked to report on current trading results since the date of the last balance sheet. This may be difficult if stocks and work in progress have to be included at estimated figures.

The company's requirements having been determined, the next step will be to consider the terms of offer to members in so far as the capital is to be raised from that source. In a public company this is primarily a financial matter which involves questions of share-premiums, 'rights', etc. The accountant as such will not be in the picture at this stage, although he may be asked for comments on the taxation or accounting implications of specific proposals. In a private company, however, the situation may be quite different. Here a gauging of the public investment market does not arise and the accountant may be the person on whom the directors and shareholders rely for advice as to the type of capital, rates of dividend, voting rights, conditions of redemption, etc. The ages of shareholders, the balance of control (now and in the future), income of controlling directors, death duties and sur-tax are factors which may have an important bearing on the form and rights of the new capital. The accountant and, to a lesser extent, the company's solicitors, are the persons best qualified to prepare and negotiate a scheme which will meet the company's needs and balance the rights and interests of participating shareholders.

IV. BONUS TO MEMBERS

New capital may be issued as a free bonus to existing shareholders in accordance with the provisions of the company's articles of association. The directors will take the initiative in determining the amount of the bonus issue, the reserves to be capitalised to achieve it, and the form and rights of the bonus capital. In a company with quoted equity shares it is usual to issue exactly the same kind of share as presently held and entitled to the bonus. In a private company the field of choice is open for any kind of debenture or share thought suitable, subject perhaps to an alteration of the articles.

The reserves to be utilised may offer scope for accounting advice. If there are capital reserves such as share premiums or excess profits tax refunds which cannot be used for any other purpose, these would probably be used first. At the other extreme, if there are capital reserves built up out of realised capital profits (tax free), these would not readily be recommended for conversion since a distribution to shareholders in cash without any sur-tax liability may be made therefrom. In between there may be a motley collection of reserves having labels which disclose excessive conservatism or distant hopes. Perhaps the labels now have little significance and, generally speaking, if the historical source is taxed profit, may be classed as general reserves suitable for conversion into capital.

If the historical source is a revaluation or writing-up of assets, it may be necessary, as a matter of law, to consider how much of the reserve may properly be capitalised. If the assets involved have been written up to a figure in excess of the historical cost to the company, the whole of the resultant reserve may not be available. One would also bear in mind the danger of unduly inflating the capital structure by a conversion of reserves from such sources.

The accountant may also be asked to give his views on the total amount which may prudently be capitalised. Several matters are relevant in making this assessment. Firstly, reserves invested in assets which are employed in the business may be regarded as suitable for incorporation in the capital structure. Secondly, the capital should not be increased beyond the point where reasonable rates of earnings and dividend can be maintained in the future. Thirdly, a fair reserve should be maintained as a cover for future contingencies and against the embarrassment of a profit and loss account in the red. Fourthly, the aggregate amount should have a convenient arithmetical relationship to the issued capital whose holders will receive the bonus.

As indicated above, the form of the bonus capital may be an open question in private or non-quoted companies. The factors mentioned in connection with a cash issue to members will again apply. An additional point is the possibility of a future sale of the bonus capital to outside investors to provide funds towards death duties. Sometimes the bonus is issued for immediate sale by the proprietors to a finance house who will have to be satisfied as to the form and conditions of the new capital—usually medium-term redeemable debentures or similar preference shares. If a future but not immediate sale is contemplated, the bonus should be in a form capable of later conversion into an investment meeting the then requirements of the purchasers.

V. RECONSTRUCTION

A reconstruction of capital may be associated with a new issue in a variety of circumstances. In the conversion of a private company to a public company involving new outside capital, the existing capital structure may require overhaul and changes in form. There may be small blocks of preference shares with rights which are unsuitable for further *pari passu* issues. These may have to be redeemed or converted. Equally there may be family loans or debentures calling for similar treatment. In some of these cases the best solution may be liquidation of the existing company and the flotation of a new company with a structure suitably geared to the new circumstances of ownership. In these cases the reconstruction is incidental to the new issue and is only made because the existing structure fails to match up to the new financial requirements.

In the other class of reconstruction the primary cause is a maladjustment of capital related to earnings and assets. Either some of the capital has been absorbed by trading losses or the original structure has proved to be inflated and normal earnings have not given a fair return on the amount issued. These reconstructions essentially involve an ascertainment of the capital lost, or not represented by assets, followed by a scheme which fairly spreads the loss against the owners of the capital. A new issue is not necessarily involved, although a company in need of a capital rearrangement may also be in need of fresh capital, and the reconstruction may be delayed until the assets and earning position have settled on a level which enables lost capital to be determined with some precision and the situation is attractive for new investment. The terms for the issue of new capital may be arranged conditionally on the reconstruction being approved by present holders and by the Court. Alternatively, the method most appropriate may involve liquidation and flotation, the present holders being offered a reduced stake in the new company.

The first practical question is the timing of such a reconstruction. If there is a history of losses, it is fruitless to attempt a reconstruction until the tide has turned. If there is a history of profits, though insufficient to cover dividends and reserves, the reconstruction itself may be tackled at any time. Putting it generally, the reconstruction may take place when earnings are sufficient to offer scope for the resumption of dividends on a reduced structure.

The accountant will be in the picture from the beginning. He will be asked to prepare statements of maintainable revenue, and of assets and liabilities valued in mutual relationship with the estimated profits.

The maintainable revenue computations may rest entirely on the assumption that recent trading conditions represent a normal expectation of the future. The accountant himself may not have enough knowledge of the trade to judge the fairness of such an assumption. In such a situation he will take steps to safeguard his position and will not allow his report to be misrepresented as an expert opinion. The profits computation need only include charges for depreciation on the basis of revalued fixed assets. These revised charges may be materially less than the sums allowed for taxation. Moreover, the lightened burden of depreciation will only be a true measure until the replacement of fixed assets begins to have an influence. While the reconstruction may technically justify a depreciation holiday, it is evident that dividend policy should not be equally care-free. This point is of importance, as the directors in submitting the scheme to the proprietors may give some indication of the dividend on equity capital which they hope to pay for a period following reconstruction.

In framing the assets and liabilities valuation, the accountant may have the support of expert valuers. It may be found that a writing-down of fixed assets to the levels recommended still leaves a net asset position which the maintainable revenue does not adequately cover. Further reduction may be accepted on the recommendation of the accountant. This question cannot, however, be finally judged in isolation from the capital structure. If the existing structure contains preference and equity capital, both calling for reduction, the total amount to be written off the fixed assets may be influenced, within limits, by the equitable rights present and future of the two classes of shareholders. If there is only one class of capital, the precise amount of the writing-down is of less importance since an under- or over-valuation of assets will affect all shareholders equally.

The final step in preparing the reconstruction scheme is the spread of the total reduction. Here again the accountant will be asked for views or comments. He may also be asked to tabulate appropriations of profits at various levels for several possible schemes of reconstruction. These tables can be most illuminating in demonstrating the comparative fairness of different proposals at different levels of prosperity. One feels that some reconstruction schemes, involving a reduction of preference capital, get into print without facing an accounting searchlight. It is fair to say, however, that there is now widespread recognition of the need to give preference shareholders, who suffer a reduction, some share in the equity capital as a means of compensation should prosperity come again to the company.

VI. AMALGAMATION

This is a wide field and clearly the subject which we are discussing was not intended to cover the many and varied activities of accountants in advising on merger schemes. It will be necessary to limit this discussion to a general outline of accounting requirements and to the development of one or two particular matters selected on grounds of interest rather than of importance.

An issue of capital will be made in every holding company scheme and in every complete amalgamation scheme unless the purchasing company has existing cash resources sufficient to finance the merger transactions. In the case of a partial merging of interests such as the formation of a central selling company there will also be an issue of capital.

The issue of capital will involve two-way valuations of shares (and possibly debentures) if there is to be an exchange of shares or stock between two or more operating companies. A one-way valuation meets cases where settlement is in cash or by the issue of capital at par in a newly-formed company. It is probable that several accountants will have a hand in the valuations. There may well be an accountant acting for each of the merging units and also an independent accountant who will have the final word in recommending comparative or absolute valuations of all blocks of capital throughout the proposed group. The primary task of the independent accountant is to establish consistent methods of valuation and ascertainment which may fairly be applied to all units. He is likely to have the support of independent valuers for fixed assets and perhaps for stocks, who will also apply consistent methods of valuation. The final stage in the valuations will be the computation of goodwills (or 'badwill') and on this question the independent accountant has to satisfy his accountant associates not only that he is consistent but also that he is producing results which individually and in aggregate avoid distortions.

These valuations of capital will probably be the main accounting activity in a holding company or complete amalgamation scheme. There may, however, also be scope for accounting advice in determining the best method of amalgamation. In many cases, of course, the attitude of the board of directors is the overriding factor and the form of merger is virtually settled in the early negotiations. If method is an open question, then factors such as taxation, security cover for existing loans and debentures, and redemption dates of prior capital may point to one type of scheme in preference to another.

On occasion accountants may be asked to express the money value of economies and savings which may be expected to result from reorganisation made possible by a merger. A tabulated statement of estimated savings may even be used to promote or sell the scheme to diffident or sceptical adherents! While such calculations provide an interesting exercise, the finished product may have to be enshrined in reservations.

One particular matter of special interest which arises in valuations of two or more operating units is the liberality or otherwise of goodwill assessments. This question may be much in the foreground in cases where little or no cash will pass and where the transaction is essentially an exchange of paper. In favour of liberal valuations is the psychological factor of boosting somewhat the value of each block of equity capital. A generous but not unreasonable valuation may prove to be a mild tonic for acceptance. On the other hand liberal valuations will reduce the percentage yield shown by the expected maintainable revenue, and increase the money cost of each unit rate of future dividend. Moreover, a liberal valuation may not act fairly as between one company and another. Goodwill may be a negligible asset in one company and a major asset in another. Any deliberate upward valuation may then distort the true relationship of two such companies.

Another matter of interest, perhaps more financial than accounting, is the security standing of different blocks of capital before and after the merger. A proposal involving acceptance of shares or stock in a company having two or.more classes of capital may raise this issue. The ingoing shareholders will contrast their standing *before* merger with their position *after* merger. Ingoing preference holders will assess the change in asset and dividend covers. Ingoing ordinary shareholders will assess the burden of prior rights, old against new. If prior capital in proposed subsidiary companies is to be left with present holders, it is likely that the parent company will give some guarantee as to future dividends. The parent company members in turn will assess the weight of the guarantee against the additional profits likely to flow from the acquisition.

VII. CONVERSION OF PRIVATE BUSINESS

Nowadays these conversions are not often large-scale affairs. Most personal businesses are driven into a corporate state by the vicious effect of sur-tax when profits become sizeable for each partner. Apart from the professions which are compulsorily exposed to the full blast of taxation, there is a marginal point beyond which it no longer pays to conduct one's business on a personal or partnership basis. Here is the first opportunity for accounting advice in this field. Rapidly changing tax laws have complicated this assessment in recent years. At present partners are exposed to income-tax and sur-tax on total earnings but are free from profits tax, whereas a limited company as a corporate body is liable to income-tax and profits tax. Part of the profits tax is contingent on distribution and this element has been increased twice in four years. Moreover, in certain circumstances the limited company itself may be liable for sur-tax in lieu of profits tax. Accordingly the simple question, 'at what point in the earnings scale does it pay to convert?' no longer has a single simple answer. It is dependent on proprietors' needs as reflected in distributions and even if this hypothesis is established, the answer may only hold good until the next Finance Bill becomes law! Fortunately, other considerations such as the advantage of limited liability and the chance of creating a more permanent and more varied capital structure often outweigh the importance of the tax factor.

The accountant acting for a comparatively small private business is likely to be the only professional adviser who has the technical knowledge, allied with an understanding of the proprietors' needs, to enable him to give the right advice at the right time. In many cases the initiative must be taken by the accountant. It is within his province not only to consider such matters as taxation benefits but also to anticipate difficulties or embarrassments which may arise if death or retiral should happen with a business structure ill-designed to withstand such an event.

One effect of high taxation (if expected to endure) is to reduce or even destroy the market value of goodwill in the medium/small business. The cash value of goodwill has always been dependent on the prospect of recovering the price out of profits over a comparatively short period of years. Nowadays the net profit, after meeting all taxation, may not even maintain the volume of physical assets, quite apart from any redemption of goodwill. This loss of marketable goodwill makes it all the more difficult to find the capital for a small family business to replace sums due to a deceased or retiring partner. In many cases the only solution lies in the formation of a limited company and a spreading of the shares (by sale or gift) over members of the family. The choice of capital structure and the spreading of shares will have several objectives —to avoid a 50 per cent. (or greater) interest held by one person (in this country a 50 per cent. interest in a company may increase the death duty burden by causing the deceased's interest in the company to be valued on the basis of the actual worth of the net assets of the company including goodwill); to have the balance of control in suitable hands; to avoid a forced sale of shares to meet death duties. Clearly these objectives are most likely to be attained if there are timely anticipation of events and wise guidance by the accountant.

It is difficult to generalise further on questions of capital structure as this may well depend on the pattern of the family tree. One might say that a non-voting preference share is often suitable for issue or transfer to members or branches of a family not expected to be engaged in the management of the business. Such preference shares might be redeemable at the company's option, although this may raise a future difficulty since by law such shares can only be redeemed out of profits or out of the proceeds of a new issue of shares. An alternative is the issue of unsecured debentures. If these are redeemable at the company's option, the legal restriction on redemption does not arise. Against that the creation of a debt may impair the credit standing of the company. The former partners, if still actively engaged in the business, will usually retain the bulk of the equity capital, whilst always trying to avoid individual control. If there are two equal partners, the danger of an assets valuation on death may be avoided by allowing two entirely independent shareholders to come in as original subscribers for one share each, the former proprietors thereafter taking the balance of the issue equally.

It will be evident from this brief discussion that taxation and death duties are the two compelling factors in this branch of the subject. The family business which contributed so much to our industrial and commercial development and strength is now disappearing from the medium-size class. As accountants, we may slightly retard this process but only by applying an intimate and up-to-date knowledge of the tangles and twists of the revenue code.

VIII. New Company for New Venture

The flow of capital into entirely new ventures is now confined to one or two types of channels. It comes mainly from established companies who branch out into a new activity and form a new company to handle the business. The new company may be a wholly-owned subsidiary or there may be associated ownership by two or more founders. The other type of channel flows from private individuals to a company usually of modest proportions. Public investment has for the time being virtually disappeared. The financial houses take little part in this movement of capital, except perhaps in cases where a foreign corporation of high standing wishes to establish a plant in this country and desires to raise part of the capital here.

Accordingly, under present conditions, this is not an extensive branch of accounting practice.

The promoters of the new venture may require accounting assistance in building up estimates of capital requirements—particularly working capital. The basic information will be supplied by the promoters or their technical experts. The estimated production, the cost of the various ingredients, the length of time each is immobilised, the stocks carried and the credit terms are factors in the computation. These factors may all have to be supplied while the accountant acts merely as a computer.

A provisional budget may also be prepared. Much of the cost information used in the working capital estimate will be repeated in the budget statement. The effect of any proposed royalty, licence or commission arrangements will also be incorporated. If the budget statement is likely to be used to attract capital to the venture, the accountant will 'gang warily' in any report he may give on the estimated results.

The form of capital structure may be an open question on which the accountant is asked for views or comments. If the promoters have a single common interest in the new venture, the new company need not have more than one class of share. Such a structure is perhaps the ideal for a new venture. It gives the maximum flexibility for future issues. It does not create any priorities which may prove to be awkward or restrictive at a later stage of development. The circumstances of the flotation may, of course, make it impossible to start on the simplest of structures. There may be interests behind the venture which are not identical. If it is a co-operative scheme between the owner of patent rights and the owners of capital, the acceptable structure may involve two classes of equity shares, the owner of the patent taking a major block of deferred shares. If the promoters have to seek capital from private sources, high-rated cumulative preference shares or debentures plus a portion of equity may be the price which has to be paid to get the initial amount required.

The existence of two classes of equity shares—preferred and deferred —is apt to give rise to a conflict of interest in the building of reserves. It is probable that sums set aside to reserve will primarily come out of the fund available for deferred dividends. Once established, however, the reserve will probably be a cover mainly for the preferred shares as strengthening both their capital and dividend position for the future. It may not be possible to introduce any condition into the terms of issue which will avoid this conflict, but the promoters should have in mind that a later simplification of equity structure may have to be faced to resolve this conflict and thus allow adequate reserves to be retained without prejudice to any one class of holder.

CONCLUSION

In dealing with a large subject in a single paper, it is not possible to combine breadth and depth. One or other of these dimensions must largely be sacrificed. The choice here has favoured a wide treatment and the aim throughout has been to cover the ground, take note of the contours and landmarks, and point to some of the areas where a more detailed exploration has not been possible. This broad survey does, however, enable one to draw certain conclusions as to the qualifications and qualities required of those who work in this accounting territory. Its varied nature calls for experience and sound judgment more than highly specialised knowledge. There may be need for the specialist in particular questions such as taxation; there is continuous need for a common-sense application of accounting knowledge to the facts and circumstances of each case. There is also need for wider knowledge— of business, of finance and of some branches of law. We need that knowledge to meet the cases where we occupy a central position as investigator and adviser and where we may have a major influence on the size and shape of the capital issue. These opportunities come to us because we are accountants, but the degree of our success may depend on the extent to which we have grown and developed beyond our original technical qualification.

ACCOUNTING REQUIREMENTS FOR ISSUES OF CAPITAL

by

W. L. BIRNIE, B.COM., F.I.A.N.Z.
Incorporated Institute of Accountants of New Zealand

Introduction

At the outset, may I express my appreciation of the opportunity to prepare a paper on this subject, my main regret being that the time available has been so short.

Although the subject is an extremely wide one, it would be possible to make a detailed survey of accounting requirements from the New Zealand viewpoint: however, the excellent synopsis of Mr. Macdonald's paper clearly shows that every main aspect of the subject is being covered, and it is therefore much more appropriate that my comments should be confined to those features which are particularly affected by New Zealand conditions, developments and methods.

The requirements outlined in the balance of Mr. Macdonald's paper are equally and fully applicable to New Zealand conditions.

The Responsibilities of Accountants

The world-wide improvement in the acceptance of proper accounting principles, and the improvement in form and presentation of published statements, has been well reflected in New Zealand, and, particularly since the war, the business community generally has placed increasing emphasis on the need for proper accounts and reports. This is regarded in the Dominion as part of an actual urge towards the greater *accountability* of the profession towards the matters with which it deals, and, in particular, it reflects the increasing responsibilities of the accountancy profession towards the investor.

To-day's thought being to-morrow's practice: we can and should look forward to adopting in New Zealand every possible improvement which is available from overseas, and I may say that some of the most stimulating thoughts on improvement in accounting principles in recent years have come from papers presented at congresses or similar gatherings of the profession in New Zealand and abroad.

Comparisons between the London and the New Zealand Money Markets

A brief comparison of the markets is necessary to an appreciation of capital issue conditions in the Dominion.

New Zealand has a population of just under two million people and, while its manufacturing industries are growing, the major portion of its income is derived from its primary produce. There are no large corporations even distantly comparable to the size of those known overseas—not surprising really in a country whose actual settlement is only 100 years old. It naturally follows that the money market in New Zealand is proportionately small, and while the London money market is international in character, not only in the source of sums that come there for investment, but in the places in the world in which such investment is made, the New Zealand money market is almost solely confined to the placing of investments within New Zealand from sources of funds available also within our country.

This applies substantially to all the normal sources of funds, whether share capital, loan capital or from bank borrowing. There certainly has been, over the last several years, investment by overseas companies in New Zealand branches or associate companies, but the proportion of this investment, while certainly growing, is yet small compared with the total.

Investment and insurance companies play a large part in the New Zealand financial market, and their requirements have quite a substantial bearing on the type of investments made, and as the wartime surplus of liquid funds becomes less and less, the amount available for investment from time to time from such companies has an increasing effect on the success of share issues.

One noteworthy feature of our market is that, since the country is so relatively small, in size and population, most projects which become available to investors are known to some greater or lesser extent to most investors. This leads perhaps to the investor taking a lot for granted, and in my view rather emphasises the need for greater care as far as accounting investigation goes. A greater degree of responsibility is placed on an investigating accountant, to make sure that disadvantages which an investor may tend to gloss over, because of his assumed knowledge of a project, are fully pointed out in any reports which are prepared.

Again, the size of the New Zealand market is such that, by overseas comparisons, it could be easily saturated, this feature being not peculiar to the money market alone. The market for most things in New Zealand is naturally small, being in proportion to its population, and the difference between an excess of supply or demand in most things is not very great.

Like most other countries there was practically no new issue investment during the war, but since 1945, and particularly in the last two years, there has been a steady flow of new capital issues.

The need for additional capital has been further brought about by heavily increased costs in all directions, not only of capital assets but of raw material stocks, and as New Zealand has to compete in the markets of the world for many of the raw materials which she uses, she has had to pay full prices, and it has been necessary for many businesses to provide sufficient further capital to finance the increased investment in the assets necessary to carry on trading of the same volume that, prior to the war, was financeable on a fraction of the capital. This particularly affects the accountant in his report on such an issue of additional capital, to ensure that the reduced rate of return on investment is clearly demonstrated and related to the general soundness of the proposals being considered.

Sound Capitalisation

Whether an issue of capital—or the acquisition of further funds which can effectively be regarded as capital—is offered for public subscription or to existing members or in any other form, it means, essentially, that the business or the proposal has reached the stage where it requires money, and I feel personally from the New Zealand viewpoint that too much emphasis cannot be placed on the need for the most careful possible calculation of an adequate amount of capital on which a business should be started or continued.

A feature of New Zealand's finance which has often appeared unusual to overseas visitors is that we make considerable use of bank overdraft finance, and this circumstance also is quite common in Australia. In fact, it could be said that we lean much more on the bank than businesses in other countries do. In both Australia and New Zealand, the banks have played a major part in developing both primary and secondary industries, and have provided much intermediate finance between various stages of capital development. Taxation rates have been a principal reason for this tendency to make the maximum possible use of the overdraft finance. Company taxation quickly reaches the maximum rate of—at present—11s. in the £1, and this means that it would cost a company approximately 13 per cent. to provide funds from shareholders to whom, say, a 6 per cent. dividend is paid, compared with 4 per cent. on best rates to a bank. The short-term advantages of these savings are obvious.

While many banks have encouraged substantial use of overdraft funds, and while the national business outlook has been, generally, to take full advantage of this finance which has been freely available, I feel that it is a clear responsibility on our profession to make a particular point, in any reports in which we are concerned connected with capitalisation, or with the alteration of the finances of a business, to see that a good and safe balance is preserved between fixed and working capital.

I would go so far as to say that this is the real and main accounting requirement for any issue of capital or in any consideration in the finance of a business—that the accountant concerned should advise fully and most carefully as to whether the proposed capital structure is a proper and adequate one, and this should apply equally whether the advice is prepared for the management of the business or for the intending investor.

The considerations, in judging the adequacy of a capital structure, are naturally well known, but are worth repeating—firstly, that fixed capital should be properly covered by shareholders' funds; secondly, that there should be a proper and adequate balance of working capital available; and, thirdly, in addition, that the dependence of a business on outside overdraft or similar finance should not be too great compared with the interest which the shareholders themselves have in the business, taking all things into consideration. From the local point of view, one feature emerges, and that is that, in such a comparatively small money market, care should be taken to see that provision can be made for obtaining additional capital in a period in which the market is likely to be able to supply it. The accountant should take care to stress the need for sufficient liquidity in a business, so that when further capital is required it does not have to be obtained at short notice and possibly in difficult circumstances.

Effect of Controls

Another major feature, which no doubt has its counterpart in many other countries, is that New Zealand has for a number of years been a controlled economy. The very existence of controls has had a definite effect on the considerations to which the accountant should give thought, in his recommendations on the capitalisation of a business. Like most countries in the British Commonwealth, we have seen a change of government in the last few years, and many controls have consequently been thrown in the melting pot. The continuation of some of these controls could mean the very difference between the future success or failure of a business which may have been established under semi-monopoly conditions; consequently if a new business is being contemplated, one of the first things which the accountant should consider, in assessing estimated future profits and returns on investment, is the likely effect of the removal of controls, whether the controls be over price, importation or any other aspects of the business. The effects of tariffs are equally important.

Again, with the world-wide tendency to inflation, New Zealand authorities have not been slow to put in train various checks on the too-free availability of capital. There has been control over the issue of capital since the beginning of the war, and the Government has always reserved to itself the right to nominate the issue price at which an issue can be made. The nomination of too great an issue price could, of course, kill the success of a capital issue and, bearing this in mind, the accountant should, in his recommendations to his client company, suggest, if possible, alternative methods of obtaining finance in case such a difficulty is met. The long-term secured loan capital obtained from financial institutions is a growing feature here, and is typical of alternative means of finance available if such a difficulty should arise.

New Companies Act

New Zealand operates under the New Zealand Companies Act, 1933, which parallels closely the English Companies Act of 1929, and over the last three years a committee appointed by the Government has been working on recommendations for a revised statute; it is expected that the resulting new Act will closely follow the English Act. The main aspect which deserves comment is that the general effect of a greater legal requirement of *disclosure* of results of companies' operations will be that stricter attention will be required from an accountant in making recommendations for capital structure of a company. If the capital structure of a company is soundly based, then the wisdom of it will be reflected in subsequently published balance sheet and revenue accounts. If it is not soundly based, then the effect on both capital and income will be disclosed equally fully.

The fact that the last ten years has been a particularly favourable period for commercial enterprises, which has contributed to a record low percentage of failures in business, should not call for the relaxation of effort in the care taken by accountants when investigating and reporting on proposals for any alteration to a capital structure. The responsibility of the investigating accountant in this matter is indeed an onerous one, and it is clear that his services will continue to be required and should be encouraged in reporting fully on new proposals for the raising or issue of capital.

ACCOUNTING REQUIREMENTS FOR ISSUES OF CAPITAL IN SWITZERLAND

by

DR. KARL KAEFER

Verband Schweizerischer Bücherexperten,
Switzerland

I. GENERAL REMARKS

The functions of independent accountants and auditors in their role of economic advisers are essentially the same in all countries where the system of free enterprise is predominant. During the course of his activities concerning the promotion, formation and financing of a limited company, a Swiss accountant will proceed on the same lines as his colleagues in other countries. His ultimate goal is to determine whether or not the prospective enterprise will be profitable. This involves the estimation of annual sales and costs. In the case of a new venture, the first step is to forecast the demand, taking into consideration all forms of competition. The estimated volume and price of yearly sales will give the basis for fixing the most efficient methods of production, the size of the plant, the requirements of capital and the probable costs of the annual output. The conversion of a private business into a limited company leads to a valuation of the tangible assets of the firm, an investigation of the true profits of the previous years, an estimation of future profits and, on the basis of these elements, a determination of the value of the business, including goodwill.

The next step is to investigate the adequacy of organisation and financing. In addition to economic considerations, there are many legal and customary restrictions which influence the financial plan. These regulations of state statutes vary from country to country. It is the aim of the following pages to describe briefly the influence of Swiss company law and Swiss financial practices on the issue of shares and debentures of limited companies.

In Switzerland, the Companies Act, 1936, constitutes a small part of the general Civil Act (143 short paragraphs and 35-40 pages of print). On the whole it is a liberal law, although there are several regulations and restrictions regarding the issues of capital and the presentation of balance sheets and of profit and loss accounts. Limited companies are considered to be private businesses which account only to their members and, with the exception of banking and insurance companies, etc., are not required to publish or register their annual statements. The act is based on the conviction that the very great majority of honestly managed limited companies must not be hampered by regulations designed only to limit opportunities for abuse.

There are only few requirements as to the contents of the balance sheet and the profit and loss account; usually these statements do not give the shareholders very much information. In addition, the directors of the

193

company are entitled by law to create secret reserves (e.g. to avoid fluctuations in dividends).

In Switzerland, the financial practice shows a tendency towards simplicity and conservatism. Generally, new companies have only one type of share, issued at par and fully paid; very often these are bearer shares with a nominal value of 500 or 1,000 francs.

II. ISSUE OF SHARES ON FORMATION OF A LIMITED COMPANY

In Switzerland a limited company becomes a body corporate by registration in the Register of Commerce. There are two ways of founding a company. The first is called '*Sukzessivgründung*' (formation by successive steps) and provides for public subscription, a prospectus and, in certain cases, a report by promoters. The overwhelming majority of limited companies are, however, created by '*Simultangründung*' (simultaneous formation), that is a registered agreement of all promoters and shareholders, without subscription, prospectus or any statutory accounting report.

When a single proprietorship or partnership is transformed into a limited company, a basis for the agreement will be the balance sheet of the existing business. This balance sheet may be prepared by an independent auditor investigating the last annual statements, to ascertain, on behalf of the parties, the correct value of the current assets, liabilities and, especially, of the goodwill; the land, buildings and plant may, in rare cases, be estimated by a professional valuer. The procedure in such an investigation is essentially the same as in other countries.

The consideration given to a member in the form of cash or shares, as payment for his invested assets, must be shown in the memorandum of the company. Profits and losses before the date of incorporation are not mentioned in Swiss company law, and it seems that the problem has never been discussed in Swiss accounting practice and literature.

During the formation of a new company, notice has to be taken of several special regulations of the Companies Act. The issue of shares at a discount or without nominal value is prohibited, the minimum par value of a share being 100 francs. Preliminary expenses, such as initial legal charges and expenses of formation, must be treated as a loss; but the organisation costs and stamp duty can appear as a separate item in the balance sheet and must be written off to revenue account over a period of five years. A profit made by the reissue of forfeited shares must be transferred to general reserve, in addition to a minimum of 5 per cent. of the yearly profits. The payment of dividends out of this legal reserve is prohibited until the reserve exceeds 50 per cent. of the share capital.

III. RAISING OF SHARE CAPITAL

A prosperous company annually expands its assets and has, therefore, need for additional capital, either from retention of earnings or from outside the business. The Swiss law facilitates withholding of profits and accumulation of open and hidden reserves upon decisions by directors *or* shareholders. This widely used method of retaining funds is, however, often insufficient, and it then becomes necessary to consider the desirability of a proportional increase in share capital. The expansion of a limited company by means of the sale of new shares has certain well-known advantages over financial expansion by other means.

Swiss company law provides that the decision to augment the share capital is reserved for shareholders at general meetings. Ordinarily, the new shares are offered exclusively to existing members, with or without public subscription. In the case of a public issue, the directors are obliged to publish a prospectus containing certain parts of the memorandum and articles of association, and also certain statements of accounts, such as the last balance sheet, the profit and loss account, and the controllers' report. These statements are precisely the accounts of the previous year, drafted by the directors without any adjustments, a special report from an independent auditor not being required.

The balance sheet, which in Switzerland is usually an actual account of the ledger, must comply with a number of regulations of the Companies Act, 1936. The share capital, special funds and debentures must be stated separately. The assets may be valued very conservatively. The valuation of current assets is based on the rule, 'Cost or market, whichever is lower', but securities listed on exchange may be valued at market price. Tangible and intangible fixed assets are stated at cost less adequate depreciation. The cost of goodwill is regularly written off in a few years. The disclosure of share transactions by remuneration of and loans to directors is neither compulsory nor usual.

There are few requirements as to form and content of the profit and loss account. Ordinarily there is nothing stated other than the gross profit and certain administration and financial charges, with perhaps also the distribution of profit as proposed by the directors.

The report of the controllers of the company has to be inserted in the prospectus. The report must state whether the balance sheet and the profit and loss account are as shown by the books of the company and are drawn up in accordance with the law. Anyone, whether qualified or not, may be elected controller by the general meeting. In addition, the directors of companies having a share capital of five million francs or more are obliged to appoint independent and qualified auditors who report each year to the directors and controllers, but not to the members.

The prospectus must contain a report of the rates of dividends paid by the company for the five financial years preceding the issue.

Prospering companies whose outstanding shares are priced by the market well above par usually issue new shares at a premium. Again, the directors may ask advice of an expert accountant, e.g. regarding the difference between the market and subscription prices. The amount of the premium is used to write down certain assets and to create funds for the benefit of employees; or, being capital, it must be transferred to general reserve account. To simplify the legal proceedings, the new shares are usually first taken and paid in by the bankers of the company, who are obliged to accept applications from shareholders or buyers of rights.

The distribution of profits and the raising of share capital may be combined with the issue of bonus shares. In Switzerland, this transformation of undistributed profits and free reserves into shares has recently lost favour on account of heavy special taxation.

IV. ISSUE OF DEBENTURES

Companies acting in well-established fields of enterprise, whose earnings are comparatively stable, generally take advantage of the issue of debentures. The debentures are usually bearer securities with coupons, redeemable upon maturity or callable at some earlier date; they contain occasionally a specific, but never a floating, charge on the assets of the company. To comply with the Swiss Companies Act, the actual amount to be repaid must be shown as a separate item in the balance sheet, the difference between the price of issue and the amount repayable being written down yearly until maturity, repayment or refunding of the debentures.

The public issue of debentures in Switzerland involves the issue of a prospectus as a source of information for investors; its contents are again the balance sheet and the profit and loss account of the preceding financial year. It must include the report of the controllers and a statement of the rates of dividends paid during the last five years. Registration is unnecessary.

Usually the company sells the issue outright at a fixed price to a syndicate of bankers, who invite the public to buy the securities from the issuing houses at a price augmented by the underwriting, purchasing and selling commissions and expenses.

The buyers of debentures or shares prefer marketable securities. Therefore the prospectus often contains a promise to apply for permission to deal at certain mentioned stock exchanges. The Swiss Stock Exchange regulations as to the accounting information to be inserted in the prospectus are similar to the legal regulations, but they require, in addition, the disclosure of the subsidiaries of the limited company and a short report by the directors concerning the operations of the current financial year. Every company whose securities are listed is obliged to publish annually its financial statements and a comprehensive directors' report.

V. RECONSTRUCTIONS AND AMALGAMATIONS

Investigations on company reconstructions constitute a broad and difficult field of activity for qualified accountants and auditors. The investigator should have a wide knowledge of economic affairs and business psychology, especially when an arrangement between a company and its creditors is proposed. The Swiss Companies Act requires that as soon as the share capital of a limited company has been diminished by 50 per cent., on account of losses, a general meeting of the shareholders is to be called to consider measures for reorganisation.

The appointed expert must try to find out the relevant causes which have led to the failure and to discover the means by which the company can be turned into a profitable business. Perhaps some fundamental readjustment of the capital structure of the enterprise may be necessary. The scheme of resonstruction should be clear and easy to be understood. The fact that Swiss companies prefer to have a simple capital structure facilitates the preparation of plans to secure the harmony of all important interests.

In the case of a reduction of share capital, the Swiss Companies Act orders a special investigation, made by an officially recognised auditor, who is asked to certify that the liabilities of the company will be fully covered by the assets if the reconstruction is completed.

Reorganisation of a limited company often involves imposition of some sacrifice, not only on members but also on creditors, including debentureholders. In exchange for debentures and to procure new money, the issue of preference shares is necessary in certain cases. Practically all Swiss preference shares have been issued in the course of reconstructions. The preference shares carry the same voting power as the common shares and are noncumulative, unless the articles of the company especially provide for the contrary. Swiss preference shareholders usually take their share of additional earnings with the common shareholders.

Other opportunities for accountants to make investigations in relation to issues of capital arise on the amalgamations of limited companies. In Switzerland, companies are generally combined by absorption, the corporation whose shares are highest priced absorbing the others without their liquidation. The remaining company issues common shares which are exchanged for the shares of the absorbed companies, the calculation of the relative value of the shares being the point of major importance. The accounting problems are complicated by the regulations of the Swiss Companies Act, which orders a separate administration of the properties of each company, until the liabilities of the absorbed companies are paid or secured. Not until then should a consolidating balance sheet be drafted. Usually the directors do not observe this regulation, in spite of their civil liability resulting from breach of the regulation.

ACCOUNTING REQUIREMENTS FOR ISSUES OF CAPITAL

by

F. M. RICHARD

Compagnie Nationale des Experts Comptables, France

I. INTRODUCTION

Position of Companies in French Economy

There are two classes of companies adopted by the industrial and capitalistic world since the mid-nineteenth century: one based on the *intuitus materiae*, the other on the *intuitus personae*.

The public limited company,[1] the most widely employed of the first class, made it possible in France (a liberal country where savings were high and sound) until World War I, to raise large amounts of capital from public sources for large concerns which developed through the industrial evolution of the late nineteenth and early twentieth century. Furthermore, it made it possible to evolve from an 'ownership-capital' to a 'control-capital' structure by opening up family business to public participation.

In the twenty years between the two world wars, large ventures were financed by public subscriptions for securities of corporate organisations under the form of public limited companies.

Finally in France, the public limited company was also often used in lieu of partnership (either limited or general) based on the *intuitus personae*, until in 1925 an Act was passed organising a new type of company of a mixed nature: the private limited company.[2]

*General Characteristics of the Role of the Public Accountant
in Large French Corporations*

We will not consider here the place and duties of the accounting personnel of a large company, whatever their rank—accountant, manager of the accounting department, treasurer, etc.—all these being essentially internal functions.

The role of the accountant in corporations is compulsory concerning his mandate as auditor and optional regarding the economic and accounting missions which are freely entrusted to the public accountant.

But large companies in France, issuing from and still patronised by a domineering form of capitalism, are averse to external control and audit and prefer supervision from their own internal organisation.

Law and Doctrine on Company Accounting

French company legislation never aimed at promoting the legal structure of an institution that would keep pace with the needs of the modern business world, but rather tried to protect the public against dishonest practice in corporate organisation.

[1] Société Anonyme.
[2] Société à responsabilité limitée. (S.A.R.L.).

198

Doctrine has always been ahead of legislation, which has taken a repressive character. But the strictness of this repressive legislation, although theoretically sufficient, has caused no significant practical transformation in accounting control; and it seems that the only possible way to bring into full effect the intended meaning of the law is through the strict discipline of public accountants and corporate auditors themselves.

II. HISTORY OF LEGISLATION REGULATING FRENCH COMPANIES

Public Limited Companies—Act of 1867

Among the group of joint-stock companies, the public limited company ranks first in numbers (more than 50,000) and in the amount of capital this class of company has been able to raise.

The original law dates back to the Act of 1867, which first authorised the formation of companies formerly submitted to a governmental incorporation, and also enacted their pattern of rules, still enforced to-day.

Amendments

This original Act, dating back almost a century, has been amended through several important Acts, but the defects of the main law have only partially been remedied.

The most important amending Acts were passed during the last fifteen years to adapt the original Company Act of 1867 to political and economic circumstances and principally amended or re-enacted is the qualification, rights and duties of auditors; the control of stock issued for property; the protection of bondholders; the regulation of public subscription issues; the organisation of the board of directors; the rights and responsibilities of the president, general manager, etc.

Tendency of French Legislation

This legislation, intended to protect public savings, has provided Courts of Justice with heavy penal means of repression, but has not entirely succeeded in organising the joint-stock companies so that they become an instrument of economic development in a new industrial society.

These preliminary remarks are essential to the understanding of the limitations of the role of the accountant with regard to the control of corporations.

The Private Limited Company

The form of public limited company, originally conceived for concerns with large capital, was soon used for the partnership of only few persons, often of the same family, tied together more by their desire to associate (*affectio societatis*) than by the necessity to merge important funds; but the juridical frame of the public limited company, rigid and formal, was not suited to this type of partnership.

The Act, 1925

The Act of 1925 created the private limited company, a mixed type of stock company and partnership.

Differences between French Private and Public Limited Companies

In a private company the number of partners may be of only two (instead of a minimum of seven in the public company). One manager is sufficient (instead of a board of a minimum of three directors for the public company). Shares are not represented by negotiable title-deed or certificates and their transmission to a non-member is restricted by the approval of the other partners; some regulations prescribe *per capita quorum* leading to maintaining a fair balance between the rights of persons and those of capital; and the rules concerning the constitution and management of the company are very simplified, but prohibit any invitation to the public to subscribe for any shares or debentures of the company.

Finally, public limited companies can be of right converted into private limited companies and vice versa.

III. MAIN DIFFERENCES BETWEEN THE ENGLISH LIMITED COMPANY (PUBLIC AND PRIVATE) AND THE FRENCH LIMITED COMPANY

It is necessary to underline here a few of the differences between companies governed by the English legislation and the French public limited company; otherwise some French regulations would seem meaningless or unexplainable.

There is only one class of French company limited by shares,[1] no matter how many shareholders there may be (minimum seven) instead of the two English types of companies (private, with a limit of fifty partners, and public).

The formation of a limited company in France is absolutely and positively dependent upon the full subscription of the total capital. There are therefore no unissued shares in France, nor any possibility of reduction of the formerly agreed capital to the amount actually subscribed.

One-fourth of the capital subscribed in cash must be paid up upon subscription and the remaining three-fourths must be called up within five years. In cases where shares of capital stock are issued for property, such property must immediately be transferred to the corporation.

Issues of shares below par are strictly prohibited.

Auditors are appointed for three years and their remuneration is fixed by the shareholders' general meeting. Auditors report for their mandate to the annual meeting. In addition to their report on the balance sheet, auditors must report on all contracts concluded directly or indirectly between the directors and the company.

Reciprocal shareholding between two companies is prohibited whenever one company holds 10 per cent. or more of the other's capital stock.

IV. OBLIGATIONS REGARDING AUDITORS OF COMPANIES OFFERING SUBSCRIPTION TO THE PUBLIC

Meaning of 'Offer to the Public for Subscription'

There is no very definite description in the Act of what must be considered

---

[1] The French 'Société à responsabilité limitée' which has been translated 'private limited company', is essentially different from the 'Société Anonyme' which is primarily the province of this paper.

as invitation or offer to the public for subscription, but a company is considered as calling upon the public when its stocks are listed on the Stock Exchange, or whenever they are offered to the public either by prospectus, posting up in banks, advertisement in newspapers, bank's propositions to clients, letters, and generally whenever the founders do not know personally those to whom the offer is made.

Auditors to Capital Stock Issued for Property
Auditors to capital stock issued for property are appointed at a first general statutory meeting of shareholders; they are nominated to audit the value of property for which the shares are issued; they must report on this audit to a second statutory meeting of shareholders held to approve or reject such valuation.

A person is not qualified for appointment as auditor of this class whose independence is not guaranteed; for instance, all persons related to, or in the employment of a subscriber (for property), a founder or a director of a company, are not eligible as auditors of that company.

Special Regulations for Companies issuing to Public Subscription
To protect the public against over-valuation or misstatement of property for which capital stock is issued, the choice of the auditor is made with even greater care in order to ensure increased security regarding their experience and integrity; companies, calling upon the public, must select at least one of the appointed auditors (for property) from a list of auditors agreed by the Courts of Appeal.

Duties of the Auditors
The chief duty of the auditor is to examine the books and accounts of the company, to check the cash, receivables and securities, and to control the correctness and sincerity of inventories and balance sheets; and also to check the accuracy of information of an accounting nature on the company's financial position given by the board of directors in its report to the annual meeting.

General Rule
Appointment of auditors is not subject by law to any regulations, except in the case of companies offering stock to the public. Nevertheless, auditors must be fully independent of the company and its directors. For example, a person is not qualified for appointment as auditor if he is a servant of the company or of the directors or of another concern holding 10 per cent. of the company's capital, or if he is a relative of the company's directors or subscribers (having received stock for property).

Special Regulations for Companies Calling upon the Public
According to the Act of 1935, companies calling upon the public must select at least one auditor with recognised knowledge, experience and independence.

The auditor or auditors must be selected from a list drawn by the Courts of Appeal.

Method of Listing Auditors by the Courts of Appeal

Lists of the names of auditors are drawn up for each Court of Appeal by a commission composed of three judges and one civil servant.

Candidates have to pass a technical examination, chiefly on accounting, commercial law, and company law; they also have to fulfil certain conditions that will establish their knowledge, experience and integrity.

These 'chartered' (or agreed) auditors are compelled to join a body endowed with disciplinary authority. Practically all French certified public accountants are members of this body.

V. PROCEEDINGS OF CONTROL OF CAPITAL ISSUED FOR PROPERTY AND OF OTHER SPECIAL PRIVILEGES

Basis

According to French law, shares of capital stock may be issued either for cash or for other property, real or personal, tangible or intangible, goodwill, etc., actually conveyed or transferred to the company.

Such a practice is rather common in France and in most cases these shares are subscribed by the founders of the company. The law aims at protecting partners subscribing in cash from deliberate over-valuation of property often difficult to estimate.

The proceedings of audit call first for a report from the auditor; secondly, for subsequent approval of the subscription at a statutory general meeting at which the subscribers receiving such shares[1] have no voting right.

Over-valuation of property is not only a fraud against cash subscribers; it endangers the life of the company, for the company has thus acquired assets at a price superior to their real value.

Procedure of Control

The duty of the special auditor for issuance of stock against property is to estimate the value of all such property and the reasons for special privileges granted to promoters.

The auditor has full authority to appraise the value of the property; in other words, the amount of the consideration paid for the stock; he is entitled to make any investigations, consult other experts at will and, according to the various kinds of property, apply principles admitted generally with respect to valuation.

The auditor must make a report which is put at the disposal of the shareholders.

He is liable for his errors or neglects.

VI. PUBLICITY UPON ISSUES

Notice.

Certain legal formalities of publicity are compulsory only when the promoters of a company invite the public to subscribe for shares or debentures. (See *supra*.)

[1] Actions d'apport.

The companies must comply with the publication of a notice in the annex to the official journal.[1] The chief matters to be disclosed in the notice are name, object, corporate office, end of the existence of the company, etc.

Relating to accounting information, the notice should state the registered capital, the value of each class of stock, the fraction of capital still uncalled, the privileges granted to directors or any other persons, and the capital stock issued for property.

The same regulations apply to issuance of stock for increase of capital, but in this case the last balance sheet should also be published.

Prospectus

The prospectus is the document used on solicitation of subscriptions; it should disclose the same information as is published in the notice and, in addition, should state the names of the founders.

Large companies also include in the prospectus issued appreciation and references about the possibilities of the enterprise.

Disclosure of Information to the Public

The notice and prospectus are intended to inform the public invited to subscribe to stock. But we have to admit that the information of an accounting and financial nature brought to the attention of subscribers is highly inadequate; a new organisation, based on the principle of a broad circulation of complete and clear information, seems desirable. The certification of financial statements and financial reports by certified public accountants is one answer to the various aspects of gaining the confidence of the public.

VII. INCREASE OF CAPITAL—PRE-EMPTION RIGHT

Rights of Stockholders to Subscribe New Capital

When an increase of capital involves new subscriptions, the new stocks have a *pro-rata* right on the reserve fund existing at the time of issue of additional capital, earned surplus accumulated through previous deductions from profits.

The actual shareholders should not therefore be deprived of their own portion of this earned surplus and, consequently, they are entitled to the privilege of priority in the subscription to the new issues of capital.

Waiving of Pre-emption Right

This pre-emption right can be totally or partly waived by the existing shareholders to the benefit of another party, for the company's own sake; for example, in order to bring in a new financial group to give needed financial or industrial assistance, or in case of merging.

This renunciation can only be authorised by the general meeting of shareholders, duly informed by a report from the board of directors and a report from the auditor.

---

[1] *Bulletin Officiel d'Annonces Légales.*

H

Report from the Auditor

The auditor's duty is essentially to estimate if the basis determined by the board of directors for computation of the premium on new capital stock issued, or the issuance at par, is correct and sincere.

Boards of directors usually refer in advance to their auditors or public accountants for this calculation.

Calculation of the Premium on Issue

In theory, if the new shares are of equal par value with the old ones, the premium on the new issue is equal to the amount of the reserve fund of earned surplus divided by the total number of old shares.

There are no special problems as to the fixation of the reserve funds appearing on the balance sheet; but the valuation of hidden reserves and of surplus of assets in nominal value specially due to currency devaluation, offers many difficulties and calls for the accountant's full care and competence.

Negotiation of the Right to Subscribe

If the issue of additional capital has to be paid for in cash, the right to subscription can be negotiated, that is, sold by the holder of old shares, for instance on the Stock Exchange if the shares are listed.

Computation of the Right on New Issue

The theoretical value of the subscription right depends upon the conditions of the issue; if the new shares are treated like the old ones, this value would in principle be derived from the following formula:

$$v = (A - N) \frac{n}{a+n}$$

in which:

A = the quotation or value of old shares with right attached.
N = the value of new shares at issue.
n = the quantity of new shares.
a = the quantity of old shares.

VIII. REVALUATION OF ASSETS AND INCREASE OF CAPITAL

General Principles of the Revaluation of Assets

Following currency devaluations, revaluation of assets is the accounting operation through which the various items of assets, mainly fixed assets, appear in future at their actual value or at a value arbitrarily fixed by legislation. Through this accounting adjustment, the increase of value of the assets is arrived at by the difference as compared with the nominal value.

This operation is recommended:—

(a) for greater clearness and accuracy in the balance sheet where assets include items entered at highly different monetary values;
(b) in order to allow the computation of depreciation on the basis of values theoretically closer to the cost of replacement, and the inclusion of

such depreciation in costs to arrive at more accurate current production costs;

(c) in order to make possible financial reorganisation of some companies by disclosing the real and actual value of their assets;

(d) to enable enterprises, through adequate tax regulations:

> (i) to deduct from profits the depreciation based on these new revalued amounts;
>
> (ii) to capitalise, tax free or at a reduced rate the increase of value of assets, due to revaluation;
>
> (iii) to exempt from taxation the profit made when selling part of fixed assets, as this is of purely monetary origin.

Regulations arising from the Finance Acts, 1945, 1946, and Amendments

The general principle consists in multiplying each of the items of fixed assets by an index number. This index represents the supposed variation of prices from the date of their acquisition to the date of revaluation of assets.

The revaluation of depreciation accounts is computed in the same way.

The surplus of the new residual value over the old one is the 'increase in value due to revaluation' to be listed among the liabilities, as a special reserve.

The coefficients set by Finance Acts are only maximum limits and companies are free to adopt lesser marks and even not to revalue at all.

All companies revaluing their assets are compelled to adopt for their balance sheet a uniform model designed by the Treasury Department derived from a uniform official accounting system.

Increase of Capital by means of Capitalisation of the Reserve Fund
representing 'Increase of Value due to Revaluation'

Although they were of a purely fiscal nature, the Finance Acts, 1945, 1946 and amendments, have provided for the capitalisation of the revaluation reserve fund.

But tax regulations, especially those fixing the indexes of revaluation, do not supersede the provisions derived from commercial law and Companies Acts concerning the sincerity and fairness of balance sheets; therefore it is recommended to companies that they operate reasonable revaluations within the limits set as maxima by the fiscal regulations. Should the special reserve for revaluation be capitalised, companies, in order to avoid serious criticism, should have their new values appraised by experts.

We are faced here with a juridical problem of importance: how are we to determine who owns this reserve revaluation fund? As long as it is listed among liabilities, it belongs to the company and no one can claim it; but when it is converted into shares—either new shares or an increase of the nominal of old ones—these new shares should, in theory, be distributed according to the statutory clauses of the by-laws of the company governing the bonus of winding-up of the company. Accordingly, they would be assigned not only to the shareholders, but also to the holders of no par value stocks. No par value stocks (*parts de fondateurs*) are stocks without nominal value, having no voting right at the shareholders' meeting but being entitled to a portion of the annual earnings and of the bonus of liquidation. No par value stocks are generally issued for promotional services. Such a rule, although satisfying from a legal aspect, can be of serious consequences to various parties concerned within the company, because holders of no par value stocks, without voting right, will receive an important portion of common stock with voting right.

Some writers argue that this surplus from revaluation cannot be directly or indirectly capitalised because such a surplus account has not the required characteristics of a definite, earned and unrestricted reserve fund.

The great majority of authors think that, provided that the revaluation was reasonably conducted, and bearing in mind that a return to a former monetary situation is unfortunately highly improbable, the provision can be considered as sufficiently consolidated, and therefore as being definite. Besides, capitalisation cannot strictly be viewed as a distribution of dividends followed by a subscription but more like a modification of statutes or by-laws.

The French doctrine is almost unanimously opposed to the payment of cash dividends of this surplus from revaluation and even to its appropriation to the purpose of writing off previous company losses.

IX. BOND ISSUES

General Remarks

As long as the monetary situation was sound, bonds played an important part in the financing of large corporations: they were a means of obtaining long-term funds while restricting the lender's rights to those of a creditor instead of a partner.

On account of unending devaluation of the national currency, investors are no more interested in the kind of security which will not increase in value in the event of further monetary devaluations.

As a result, most of the issues of bonds in France are made at a discount. The practice of reporting this discount on the asset side of the balance sheet is universal and objectionable. This bond discount is amortised each year; several accounting and mathematical methods are used in practice to absorb this charge.

Protection of Bondholders

As the bondholders' security depends on the general credit of the issuer, formal legal procedure must be followed by corporations issuing bonds.

The balance sheet for the first financial year (or period) must have been drawn up and approved by the annual meeting of shareholders; the registered share capital stock must have been fully paid up; finally, the company must comply with certain publicity regulations.

Publicity Regulations

Before offering an issue of bonds to the public, companies must publish in the *Bulletin Officiel d'Annonces Légales* (see *supra*) a notice similar to the one described for the issuance of shares. The notice must state the amount of bonds previously issued and the guaranties, mortgages, collateral, etc., securing them, also the number of bonds presently issued and their value, the interest to be paid, the conditions and date of refunding or redemption, the guarantees covering the current issue, the last certified balance sheet, etc.

X. AMALGAMATION OF COMPANIES

This subject is so wide and so complex that it is impossible to cover it in such a limited paper.

Amalgamation can be analysed as the transfer of the assets of the absorbed company to the absorbing company with the provision of payment of the liabilities. The technical difficulty which the certified public accountant will help to solve is the objective valuation of the property and business acquired and the equitable treatment of the shareholders of the absorbed company.

XI. CONCLUSION

Role of the Accountant in Issues of Capital

The accountant, especially the public accountant, takes part in issues of capital, either as adviser appointed by the company or as commissioned representative of the shareholders, compulsorily appointed in accordance with company legislation.

Role as Adviser

The determination of the necessary capital is the initial and primordial action of the company; some concerns have utterly failed because of insufficient capital or of lack of proportion between cash and fixed assets (property). It is of the utmost importance, even more so for new ventures, to forecast, to budget what the balance sheet would be at the end of the first financial period and of following periods.

Excess corporate capital does not imply as many risks, but if the funds raised are out of proportion with the needs of the company, their normal remuneration is impossible and their insufficient return will bring a depreciation of the stocks.

The utilisation of various means of raising capital, such as shares and bonds, and the attribution of profits to the different categories of beneficiaries entail problems with which the accountant is highly qualified to deal.

In the course of its operations, a company must necessarily, to keep pace with economic developments and monetary changes, call on its shareholders or other investors to increase its resources. This necessitates building a policy of confidence which is conditioned by circulation among shareholders and the public of detailed information, balance sheets, reports and results made easy to understand by all, and certified by an independent public accountant to guarantee their reliability.

If the public, nowadays, is not interested in investments in major companies, it is largely due to the inconsiderate manner with which shareholders have been ignored or treated in most countries.

Juridical Function of the Accountant

'Custom', says Edward Jenks, 'is the earliest known stage of Law; it is not enacted, nor even declared: it establishes itself as the result of experience.'

In France, where the notion of law is inflexible, the juridical function of accountants comes first in his economic function.

In the theoretically perfect juridical structure of auditor of accounts and of property (see *supra*), there is a lack of custom and acceptance of technical experience on the part of all concerned.

Free enterprise, even of gigantic size, if it wants to survive, must be strengthened by a new capitalism derived from workers' savings. But this new form of capitalism cannot come into existence without a radical change of mind in the relations between the companies' delegates and the shareholders.

Accountants, especially the public accountants, must in the future play a much more important part, through their technical development and the self-discipline they inevitably acquire in the fulfilment of missions they are entrusted with.

ACCOUNTING REQUIREMENTS FOR ISSUES OF CAPITAL: A CANADIAN VIEWPOINT

by

J. R. M. WILSON, F.C.A.(CANADA)
Canadian Institute of Chartered Accountants

No subject is more appropriate for the consideration of accountants than that of 'Accounting Requirements for Issues of Capital'. In most capital issues the prime interest of the prospective investor revolves about the accounting statements included in the prospectus. It is only a truism to say that the acceptance of these statements by investors, and therefore the ability of modern business to obtain capital in the amounts it requires, is dependent upon a faith by the investing public in the accounting profession—a faith that its members have the technical skill to enable them to assay whether or not the financial statements do fairly show the financial position and earnings of the enterprise and that they have the independence of mind which enables them to withhold that opinion when such is not the case. Our responsibility is correspondingly great and the position which the accounting profession has attained to-day reflects in large measure the response which it has made to the challenge presented to it in this field.

My comments will be restricted to the position of the accountant in reporting to prospective purchasers as to the reliability of the financial data included in a prospectus, although, in doing so, you will appreciate it is with no intention to deprecate in any way the role of the accountant as an adviser. On the contrary, some of the most useful work that accountants are called upon to do in their day-to-day practice is to advise their clients on the financial effects of certain transactions or proposed transactions. I do not propose to develop this familiar idea further, however, as it is obviously one which is difficult to generalise about, each situation necessarily calling for its individual treatment based not only on the facts of the case but frequently on the accountant's knowledge of the personality traits of his client. At the same time it must surely follow that when the accountant is acting in an advisory capacity he is performing the same functions whether he is practising in Europe, America or Asia.

Turning to the position of the public accountant as one who expresses an independent opinion for the benefit of a prospective purchaser we are in a field where the practices in different countries will vary depending on the laws and customs of each country. Each of us is necessarily most familiar with the requirements of his own country. Mr. Macdonald, in his paper, has appropriately dealt with the law and practice in Great Britain. My commentary will deal primarily with practice in Canada and, if I could, I would gladly do so without inflicting on you a recognition of our local problems

209

and, instead, discuss merely those developments in Canada which may be of interest to accountants in other countries as providing a basis for comparison with their own experience. But nothing exists in a vacuum and when considering accounting practices in Canada one must take into account at the very least three conditions which have affected, are affecting and will continue to affect them. First, there is our proximity to the United States and our cultural ties with England and France. Each of these factors exerts an influence on every aspect of Canadian life, but with differing intensity in different parts of the country and with different individuals. Secondly, there is the large amount of United States and United Kingdom capital invested in this country which has required a knowledge on the part of Canadian accountants of what United States and United Kingdom investors want to know. It has also resulted in several of the larger firms of public accountants in the United Kingdom and United States having Canadian associated firms of the same or somewhat similar name. And then there is the fact that Canada is not a unitary state but a federal one with a central government and ten provincial governments. The division of legislative powers between federal and provincial governments has resulted in a division of authority in many fields but possibly in no field is it more confused than in the field of capital issues. For example, some companies are incorporated under our federal Companies Act, others under provincial acts; the criminal code is enacted by the federal government and deals with certain aspects of fraud and conspiracy which are pertinent to trading in securities; but the licensing of security dealers comes under provincial jurisdiction which also deals with fraud in trading in securities.

The federal Companies Act requires companies incorporated under it to meet certain minimum accounting requirements in prospectuses or offering circulars. They are applicable, however, only to companies incorporated by the federal government and there are not corresponding provisions in all provincial companies acts. In any case, while a copy of the prospectus must be filed with the Secretary of State, the latter appears to take no action to ensure that the information called for is included and that it correctly complies with the Act. In Ontario, however, there is a very active Securities Commission which passes on all prospectuses for the sale of securities to the public in that province. Ontario is the most populous province in Canada and contains the head office of many of the larger financial institutions, so that any issue for which it is wished to have more than a local distribution must be registered with the Ontario Securities Commission. As a result, the Commission has come to act as guardian for all larger issues in Canada. The Ontario Commission's requirements are to some extent the same as those of the federal Companies Act, but the approach differs in the fact that the Commission insists on a close scrutiny of the prospectus before it is accepted for filing and, consequently, before the securities may be sold.

The federal Companies Act has been in force in its present form since 1935, and while the Ontario Securities Commission has existed for some time, its present standards and procedures are a product of the last few years. Until shortly after the end of the war there was very little guidance to the accounting

Photo Hay Wrightson

C. PERCY BARROWCLIFF, F.S.A.A.
Vice-President of the Congress
President of The Society of Incorporated Accountants and Auditors

profession or anyone else as to what were the accounting requirements for issues of capital. In 1946, however, the Canadian Institute of Chartered Accountants authorised its Committee on Accounting and Auditing Research to study matters of interest to the profession and to issue bulletins from time to time to the membership. In doing so, it was paralleling the work begun earlier by the accounting and auditing committees of the American Institute of Accountants and the Council of the Institute of Chartered Accountants in England and Wales. The first bulletin issued by the Canadian committee did not deal specifically with prospectuses, but rather with standards of disclosure in annual financial statements of manufacturing and mercantile companies. While it did not purport to deal with other than these annual statements, many of the opinions expressed would obviously be equally applicable to balance sheets included in prospectuses. The bulletin went somewhat further than the requirements of the Companies Acts and was received with general approval by the profession and all business. The largest stock exchange in Canada sent copies to all listed companies, suggesting to them that they make sure that their annual statements conformed to this bulletin.

Having completed this first task, the committee then turned its attention to minimum standards of professional practice which should apply in respect to prospectuses. This culminated in a bulletin which set out certain principles which it felt should be generally followed by all practising accountants in this connection and was issued in April, 1947. The effectiveness of the bulletin was greatly increased when the Ontario Securities Commission adopted both it and Bulletin 1 almost verbatim and issued them as their accounting regulations. While Bulletin 2 represents what the accounting profession in Canada felt should be the accounting regulations for the issue of capital, it also has become in effect the regulations which govern all the larger issues. Any study of accounting regulations for issue of capital in Canada can, therefore, largely be confined to Bulletin 2. It is not my purpose to summarise the entire bulletin, but included in it are the following conclusions:

(1) It was the opinion of the Committee that the accountant should review the entire circular before it was printed in order to ascertain that in his opinion the contents so far as they related to matters with which he was familiar as a result of his examination were not misleading and, unless he was given such an opportunity, he should not permit the use of his opinion in the offering circular. This was definitely a bolder step than many wished to take, for fear that it could be construed as implying that the accountant should be responsible for the veracity of the circular as a whole. No such construction was intended nor would it be warranted. In practice, it has ensured that the accountant is able to help the underwriters and solicitors in seeing that the offering circular as a whole is true and fair, and that references throughout the circular to the accountant are correct.

(2) In dealing with the accountant's report it was stated that it should be printed in full and that it should contain an expression of his opinion concerning the statements presented; that it should not be so qualified as to be

useless to an investor and that an opinion should not be given unless a sufficient examination had been made to warrant it.

(3) Consideration was given to the extent to which accountants can properly rely on the work performed by other members of the profession not employed by them or acting as their agents and by public accountants practising in other countries. While no hard and fast rules were suggested, and it was considered that it was a matter which would have to be decided in each particular case, it was pointed out that a chartered accountant should not sign any opinion unless he had some knowledge of the company's affairs and had made some direct examination himself. In other words, it would not be appropriate for an accountant to express an opinion on a consolidated statement of a holding company and its operating subsidiaries where he had done nothing more than add together the figures of various operating companies, each of which had been reported on by some other accountant.

(4) It was pointed out that the statement of earnings should be for a sufficient number of years to give a reasonable picture of the operations of the business. The federal Companies Act requires that the earnings be shown for three years, and it was recognised that this was not a sufficiently long period to present to a prospective investor. In recognition of this, even before the bulletin was issued, many firms of chartered accountants had been insisting that the earnings of ten years be shown, although they had no legal authority to require any such period. Shortly after the bulletin was issued, the Ontario Securities Commission decided to insist on ten years' earnings in every case except where there were special circumstances which would make it impracticable to do so. At that time there seemed to be a considerable advantage in requiring earnings for such a long period, as it extended back into pre-war years and gave a picture of the company's earnings under peacetime conditions. To-day, the ten-year period dips back into the war years and, in many cases, the earnings of the earlier years are meaningless to an investor. It may be that a shorter period would provide sufficient useful information, but it appears that the absence of a strict rule as to how many years are to be included places a heavy burden on the issuing company, and possibly on the accountants, in asking them to decide which years are significant from the standpoint of a prospective investor.

(5) It was pointed out that the statement of earnings was an historical statement and that changes in the figures to reflect changes or expected savings were dangerous. At one time it had been usual to adjust statements of earnings in prospectuses to reflect retroactively changes in depreciation, income-tax rates, interest, management salaries, etc. The committee felt, however, that to attribute to a former period certain conditions presently existing and at the same time to ignore other changed conditions was likely to be misleading. For this reason it recommended that such adjustments to earnings should ordinarily be avoided, but if used, the statements should set out clearly all such adjustments which had been made. The recommended practice has generally been followed and the statements of earnings included in the Canadian offering circulars in most cases set out the earnings as they

actually were, corrected only for adjustments made in subsequent years, either through profit and loss account or surplus. When this practice results in a lack of comparability within the period or with conditions as they will exist in the next fiscal period, it is usual to draw attention to such differences by way of a footnote.

(6) Lastly, in dealing with *pro forma* statements, it was set out that an opinion should not be expressed on a *pro forma* balance sheet unless there were firm commitments from responsible parties and a reasonable assurance that the company's position would in fact resemble that shown by the statement. This was designed to prevent an underwriter who held only an option on securities which could be taken up in whole or in part from setting out a balance sheet showing what the company's position would be were he to take up all of the shares.

Since the bulletin was issued the underwriting of securities of all existing companies has complied with its recommendations. Whether it would have been possible to achieve such a unanimous result without the backing of the Ontario Securities Commission is possibly doubtful, but the combination of the accounting profession and the Commission together has provided Canada with its accounting regulations for issues of capital, at least so far as larger public issues are concerned.

There are, of course, some unsolved problems which we still must face. Like accountants the world over, we have divided opinions on how, if at all, accounting techniques should be modified to meet the problems of the depreciating purchasing power of the monetary unit. Occasionally, in the case of new issues of securities the fixed asset accounts are revalued in terms of the current price level. Such a change in balance sheet valuations would require, in my judgment, adequate disclosure of the depreciation to be charged on the new basis, if not a restatement of recent years' profits. This is not always furnished and, in the absence of such information, the earning statement may well be misleading. There is also the problem of what foreign subsidiaries should be consolidated and the extent of disclosure required as to the financial condition and earnings record of a guaranteeing company or one whose ability to carry out a contract may be vital to the security being offered. These and many other problems are, however, merely indicative of the limitation of accounting regulations. Individual judgment based on sound training and wide experience is still required to determine whether any statements do fairly present the financial position and earnings of the enterprise.

DISCUSSION

MR. A. A. FITZGERALD, B.COM., F.I.C.A., F.C.A.A., *Commonwealth Institute of Accountants, Australia, the rapporteur, summarised the contents of the papers:*

The papers to be submitted at this session cover a very wide area. Each of the five papers distinguishes between two main functions of the accountant: one is the function of providing information, the other is the function of advising upon financial structures, financial policy, and prospective earnings.

Mr. Macdonald's comprehensive paper, necessarily concise, discusses both functions, as performed by accountants in the United Kingdom; Mr. Wilson's paper deals mainly with Canadian law and practice relating to the presentation of accounting information; Mr. Birnie describes some of the peculiar features of business finance in New Zealand, and comments on the advisory role of the accountant; and Dr. Kaefer and Mr. Richard describe legal requirements and professional standards in Switzerland and France respectively.

The papers of Messrs. Macdonald, Birnie and Wilson show that there is a substantial degree of uniformity in legal requirements and normal practice in the United Kingdom, Canada and New Zealand. Legal background and standard practice in Australia are modelled on similar lines, and doubtless law and practice in U.S.A. are not markedly different in essentials. So it appears that, in English-speaking countries, accounting for capital-issue purposes is meeting its problems with much the same outlook and in much the same ways. Dr. Kaefer's paper, and that of Mr. Richard, however, bring out sharply important differences, arising partly from legal requirements and partly from a different philosophy of accounting. In English-speaking countries, much greater use is made of independent accounting reports; and the legal requirements are founded upon acceptance of the accounting philosophy of disclosure, consistency and objective expression of opinion. English accountants doubtless appreciate the extent to which their professional status has been raised by recent legislation, as well as by their own performance. Those of them who, in Mr. Macdonald's picturesque phrase, have become 'entangled in the mesh of the most recent Companies Act' may have momentary feelings of nostalgia for the 'good old days' of secret reserves and go-as-you-please balance sheets, and of envy for the comparative simplicity of the company laws of Switzerland and France, as described by Dr. Kaefer and Mr. Richard. But Mr. Macdonald's and Mr. Wilson's papers show conclusively that voluntarily-accepted standards of presentation of accounting information are still in advance of minimum legal requirements, such as those of the United Kingdom and Canadian Companies Acts, or of the regulations of the Ontario Securities Commission, complex and exacting though those requirements may be.

214

Dr. Kaefer and Mr. Richard each emphasise, against the legal background, the importance of the role of the accountant as adviser, and this is stressed also by Mr. Birnie. Mr. Richard describes the nature of the responsibilities of the accountant as an 'adviser appointed by the company or as commissioned representative of the shareholders, compulsorily appointed in accordance with company legislation'. Dr. Kaefer mentions the report of an elected controller which must be included in a Swiss company prospectus. These normal procedures may be compared with the references by Mr. Macdonald to special-purpose procedures, such as the preparation of a provisional financial budget for new ventures or the advisory services of accountants in connection with capital reconstructions or amalgamations of businesses.

Within the field of information-providing services, Mr. Macdonald and Mr. Wilson both stress the point that accounting reports for capital-issue purposes must be historical and factual, and that the introduction of hypothetical figures should be avoided. For example, Mr. Macdonald says that, in deciding whether a transaction is abnormal or has produced an exceptional or non-repeating result, which should be excluded from the record of past earnings, a rigorous test is applied, which few transactions may pass. Similarly, Mr. Wilson says that 'changes in the figures to reflect changes or expected savings are dangerous', and that 'such adjustments to earnings should ordinarily be avoided'. Each of these contributors, of course, recognises the possibility that adjustment of past figures may be necessary in special circumstances. But, in this field of reporting to prospective investors, they see accounting as an historical record primarily, and not as predictive.

The question of the length of the past period of which the history is to be reported is also raised by Mr. Macdonald and Mr. Wilson. Mr. Macdonald says that the report *normally* presents a figure of profit or loss for each of ten years. Mr. Wilson refers to the general adoption by accountants in Canada of the ten-year convention, but makes the reservation that this practice developed at a time when the ten-year period reached back into pre-war years and so gave a picture of earnings under peacetime conditions: today it 'dips back into the war years' and 'it may be that a shorter period would provide sufficient useful information'.

On some other conventional practices, Mr. Macdonald expresses uneasiness—particularly the tendency to follow a 'pattern' in distinguishing between two categories of taxation, each based on income, and the usual method of treating 'initial' depreciation allowances and tax relief resulting therefrom.

All the papers refer to the need for the exercise of sound judgment by the accountant, whether he is acting as provider of information or as financial adviser. This need is illustrated by many parts of Mr. Macdonald's paper, especially in his discussion of the treatment of depreciation provisions, stock reserves, deferred charges, taxation and directors' remuneration, as well as in his comments on the circumstances in which, and the extent to which, 'abnormal' items should be the subject of adjustment or special reference in the report.

Two other points should be mentioned. One is that Mr. Macdonald, Mr. Richard and Mr. Birnie all draw attention to the change which has come about in the sources of business capital. Mr. Richard calls the change the 'new capitalism, derived from workers' savings'; Mr. Macdonald speaks of the growth of specialist financial institutions, 'taking the place formerly occupied by private sources of capital'; and Mr. Birnie refers to the importance in New Zealand of investment in business by investment and insurance companies—a new feature which has become important in recent years in Australia also. Evidently this is a widespread change, which may be of great significance for accounting.

The other point is the thorny question of accounting for price-level changes. As everyone knows, this has been the subject of controversy for many years, and it is listed for discussion at another session of this Congress. Little has hitherto been said about its relationship to reports for capital-issue purposes. It is referred to in the papers of Mr. Macdonald and Mr. Wilson, and Mr. Richard has briefly described the French method of revaluation of 'fixed' assets by means of index numbers.

MR. F. M. RICHARD (France):

Judging by the limited number of papers submitted on this subject, I was under the impression that we were the poor relations of the Congress. But, giving it a second thought, I believe that the reason is that we all agree on the general principles regarding the functions and the responsibility of accountants in connection with issues of capital. This proves also that it is easier to come to an agreement on such problems than on counting from one to seven.

To come back to our subject, the possible area of diversion is to decide how the functions of accountants are to be organised when related to issues of capital—by law, or voluntarily, or a combination of the two. In France we have resolutely turned to the first solution because, as you say in England, 'he who pays the piper calls the tune'. It is therefore necessary to define the activities of the independent piper, and we strongly rely upon legal regulations.

But we admit that it is not enough, for it would give only a mimicry of an organisation or, as a speaker said this morning, it would be the 'fig-leaf' covering the nudity and indecency of bad intentions. My opinion, which is shared by a number of my colleagues, bears on several points. First, the provision by our professional bodies of auditors and public accountants of recommendations on standards and procedure of audit, and I believe that on this ground international co-operation would prove to be to the benefit of everyone.

Secondly, the reinforcement of legal requirements not only concerning corporations calling upon the public but also closed or private corporations. Thirdly, an educational programme to convince the public of the necessity of the functions of auditors and their responsibility in building the confidence of the public, in order to create what you have in the English-speaking countries—a state of tradition.

This leads me to my final point. We accountants and auditors, in public practice or in private, should be more than controllers of the exactitude and sincerity of balance sheets and profit and loss. I believe we have a special part to play in a moving, industrial world, moving from technical, economical and political angles; we have to be the link, the trustee, between capital and the public.

MR. S. V. AIYAR (India):

I consider it a great honour to have been called upon to take part in the discussion. This is a very important subject. The papers have dealt with the problem exhaustively and indeed they leave very little scope for further contribution. They have also thrown some light on provisions in the statutes of the several countries for securing full and complete disclosure in the documents issued by companies.

In my own country the Government found it necessary, in the light of wartime experience of company formations and management, to appoint a committee to go into these and cognate matters and make proposals for the overhaul of the present unsatisfactory system. The committee, of which the President of our Institute and leader of our delegation to this Congress was a distinguished member, has only recently published the report. The report is now engaging the attention of our Government and we hope that without further loss of time proposals made by the committee will be translated into law.

One of the recommendations made is that auditors' reports as to profits and losses and dividends paid by the companies should relate to a period of five years instead of three as at present, and they should also relate to the assets and liabilities at the last date to which the accounts of the company are made up. It has also been suggested that similar reports should be made by qualified accountants to be named in the prospectus, if the proceeds of the issue are to be applied in the purchase of any business or any interest therein exceeding 50 per cent., with the exception that the report as to assets and liabilities must be on a date not more than 120 days before the date of the issue of the prospectus. This recommendation is perhaps in advance of the English schedule.

In this, as in other matters, the law can lay down the minimum. But the profession should aim at the maximum—complete and full disclosure of all the particulars necessary in this connection. No profession can ever make any progress by merely complying with the formalities of law to the letter. It is only by the voluntary acceptance of unwritten obligations that the progress of a profession can be measured.

A speaker this morning said that the mortality rate among companies was greater than among humans in the United Kingdom. I am not sure whether there is not a cut-throat competition between the two in my country. Capital has become once again shy and scarce and difficult. And if these conditions are to be removed, we cannot be too strict in the matter of the accounting requirements for issues of capital.

MR. F. J. BOUTIN (France):

As a result of the rapid expansion of world industry and commerce since the war, a large number of businesses have found themselves with limited financial resources. They have to turn, therefore, to seeking means of financial aid which will permit them to undertake the new investment required for the increased production necessary to satisfy national and international markets and to place them in a favourable position in the export market. It is on the subject of the particular conditions of financing laid down by regulations made in France in December, 1945, that I especially desire to address you.

It is an undisputed fact that, as a consequence of the war, most businesses have been faced with very heavy repair programmes. In addition, large reconstruction projects have been required and, in many cases, it has been necessary to extend and modernise existing factories. These needs, in the most part, are covered in France by a nation-wide plan called the 'Plan Monnet' financed by Crédit National which has set up, in addition to the War Damage Reconstruction Fund, a separate fund for the extension and modernisation of factories. This fund is known as 'Fonds de Modernisation de l'Equipement'. It is thus that the French Government has entered, through this intermediary, into the industrial field for the execution and conduct of projects recognised to be in the national interest.

The big banks, when approached by industrial concerns, make representations on their behalf to Crédit National. This new function has necessitated the development by the banks of their department known as 'Service Risques', who undertake all financial inquiries. It is necessary for personnel of this department to have a high degree of financial training. Where necessary, the staff are assisted by technical experts.

An undertaking seeking a loan (short, medium or long term) furnishes the bank with a dossier containing balance sheets and profit and loss accounts covering up to five years. A very thorough financial examination of the situation is made. Attention is focused mainly on the value of the fixed assets, current assets and liabilities (having regard to their term) and, naturally, the capital structure and various reserves. A study of the possibility of increasing production by the intended modernisation is made, and the capacity of the market to absorb such production is studied.

The banks' 'Service Risques' have established ratios which enable them to ascertain and compare the risk element of similar industries. They carry out the most complete inquiry possible to investigate and audit the documents and satisfy themselves as to arguments put before them by the undertaking.

When the dossier is complete, and the bank is satisfied as to its investigation, the loan is granted by Crédit National on the recommendation of the bank, which is required to guarantee its customer's credit.

Although, to a greater or lesser degree, all countries have faced similar problems since the war, I have tried to give you some idea of the method by which we, in France, have sought a solution.

It is with deep interest that we have listened to the different addresses. There is no doubt that our experience at this Conference will enable us to carry out our duties the better and to advise, with a greater understanding, on problems concerning issues of capital.

MR. E. J. CARROLL (Great Britain and Ireland):

I regret that we have not an American with us, because if we had he might have enlarged on a subject of which I and perhaps most members in the British Isles are somewhat ignorant—shares of no par value. It would be of absorbing interest to many of us, when the provision of further capital arises, to know what is the significance of these shares, what are their rights and to what extent they participate in profits.

I want to join issue with Mr. Macdonald in his views on the treatment of income-tax in the ten-year reports on profits and losses. He says:

'The Finance Acts provide that these taxes are allowable deductions from the profit on which income-tax is assessed. Accountants have tended to follow this pattern in reports for prospectuses. It is rather difficult, however, to find a principle which justifies the fundamental distinction made between two groups of taxes, each based on income and each representing the severance of a proportion of computed earnings.'

Later he says:

'In several reports within the past year, the profits have been submitted before making any provisions for home taxation, and no figures have been given for excess profits tax or profits tax. This method avoids making the somewhat artificial distinction between two groups of taxes based on earnings.'

I think the distinction is not artificial at all and it is of interest to see that this matter was touched upon in the *Notes on statistics relating to income of and capital employed by companies*, issued by the Institute of Chartered Accountants in England and Wales in December, 1950. There was a tendency for figures to appear in company reports showing a break-down of each £1 of gross income, and the reports were showing a tendency to be what our American friends would call 'slanty'. I am not aware of the value of these notes north of the Tweed but they say:

'Dividends so expressed in relation to equity capital and reserves should be stated at the gross amount before deduction of income-tax and if the dividends are expressed free of income-tax the amount should be increased to the equivalent gross amount.'

I am sure the Institute did not issue those notes without feeling that there was a grave necessity to do so.

Mr. Richard, with non-Gallic bluntness, states:

'The role of the accountant in corporations is compulsory . . . but large companies in France, issuing from and still patronised by a domineering form of capitalism, are averse to external control and audit and prefer supervision from their own internal organisation.'

Even though accountants in practice are not subject to that internal pressure, the pressures none the less exist and I am grateful to my own Institute for having recognised and resisted these pressures by issuing the notes I have mentioned, and also that which we discussed this morning.

Mr. Richard has said that we appear in these matters in the capacity of trustee. I think we do, not only in relation to the public, but that we are also trustees for the reputation of the profession. Let us not, therefore, be *ex officio* spokesmen for any interests but remain above the battle.

MR. ANSON HERRICK (United States of America):

It is impossible in my allotted time to discuss the papers which have been presented other than to express commendation for the complete presentation by Mr. Macdonald of the requirements, and the related accounting responsibilities, under English regulations and the interesting and informative papers concerning the requirements in New Zealand, Switzerland, France and Canada. The variations in extent of data required and in the evident responsibilities of the accounting profession are most interesting.

I regret the absence of a paper relating to the requirements in the United States for, from the standpoint of the extent of disclosure and the responsibilities of the independent accountant, they go farther, I believe, than the regulations of other countries. While I cannot describe our regulations even in outline, I must at least point out that the registration statement which must be filed with respect to every issue of a significant amount of securities requires particularly a full disclosure of all financial and related data. Further, the independent accountant who is required to attach his certificate to the registration statement becomes responsible not only for the integrity and fairness of the accounting statement but also for the assurance that no related information is omitted the inclusion of which is required to make the statements not misleading.

I find one responsibility of our profession, which I believe it should recognise, is not stressed or particularly mentioned in any of the papers except that of Mr. Wilson of Canada. I refer not to any legal or technical responsibility but to the *moral* responsibility to take the lead in the establishment of adequate regulations relating to the content and manner of presentation of financial data to be provided to prospective investors for their consideration of an offer of capital securities. In this, except in Canada, it would seem that the profession has been derelict, or at least it has failed to take leadership. It may be that there has been and may still be a fear of extension of existing regulatory controls. If so the profession has not realised that its failure to advocate reasonable requirements may result in sudden enactment of unreasonably harsh regulations designed upon the basis of a pure political background. Such was our experience in the United States. Except for a short but important statement of certain accounting principles made by the profession in co-operation with the New York Stock Exchange, and effective only as to corporations with securities listed on that exchange, there were no nationally recognised regulations relating to data to be presented to prospective investors until 1933.

In that year, as a result of the depression which began with the collapse of security prices in 1929 and the obvious deficiencies in earlier financial statements, the Securities Act was adopted by Congress. This Act suddenly placed upon the profession new and heavy responsibilities and penalties.

The Act also implied that its regulation body, the Securities and Exchange Commission, had broad powers to determine accounting procedures and principles, a power which, wisely, the Commission has not assumed. On the contrary, it has in general left with the profession the responsibility of determining accounting principles and extends to the profession the privilege of co-operating with it in the preparation of such special rules as have from time to time been issued with respect to the form and content of registration statements.

If I can contribute anything to this Congress, it will be the suggestion that the profession everywhere actively takes the lead in the development of such improvements in existing regulations, relating to data to be provided to prospective investors, as will prevent unreasonable regulations from being initiated by others.

MR. CONRAD F. HORLEY (Australia):

The papers have shown, if nothing else, the growth in importance of the profession over the last thirty years. The whole of the discussion deals with the responsibilities which have arisen as a result of accountants being placed in the position of advisers, as interpreters of the law and of assisting their clients to deal with the regulations which arise and alter the preconceived ideas which have been held for many years. In particular, we have had no reference to the actual machinery, no reference to the requirements under capital issues controls. That is one of the later requirements, particularly of Australia, where accountants are being called upon to master it. It is in addition, of course, to the requirements of the various Companies Acts.

One has to present the information in such a way that the necessary permission is obtained. We have tried to find out what are the things which the capital issues control want, and to help them by showing them what they want. That, I think, requires certain modifications in accounting which are not to be found in text-books. A certain amount of diplomacy is required and a rearranging of facts so as to present them in the way required—which may be entirely different from the presentation of facts which industry wants.

Our profession has grown out of recognition in the past thirty years but we still see prominent in the profession the names of people we knew thirty years ago. There are many newcomers, too. There can be no doubt but that the expansion of the duties and responsibilities of the profession have grown out of the standards of integrity and dependability which the public and the government and others who require information on capital issues place upon the certificates issued by reputable firms of accountants.

PROFESSOR GEORGE R. HUSBAND (United States of America):

At yesterday's meeting the President of the Congress stated that accounting is largely concerned with the measurement of acquired surplus. As a general matter, acquired surplus is measured by deducting incurred costs from realised revenues. The two main accounting statements are largely conditioned by this endeavour. To a considerable extent the statement of financial position consistently reflects incurred costs that are designed to be deducted from revenues which it is hoped will be subsequently realised.

By and large, the statements geared to the purpose of surplus measurement are the statements which the papers devoted to the consideration of this afternoon's topic accept as valid support of public appeals for capital. In general these statements meet the requirements of Company Acts. They exhibit historical facts.

The writer of the first paper, however, defines requirements as used in the general topic 'Accounting requirements for issues of capital' as meaning 'what is called for or needed'. It is a serious question whether conventional statements geared to the measurement of realised surplus fully meet the requirements of new investors. The new investor is a purchaser or quasi-purchaser of a business. He buys in terms of the present rather than in terms of the past. It is therefore present rather than past values that are of importance.

Present values, however, rest upon future expectations rather than upon past performance. Past performance has significance only in so far as it lends support to future expectation. Statements geared to surplus measurement are therefore serviceable only to the extent that they support the belief that the organisation which has kept its financial house in order in the past will continue to do so in the future. To the extent that this belief fails to be generated, the appeal for funds will be less successful.

There are deficiencies, however, from the point of view of investment usefulness in conventional statements exhibiting past experience. To a considerable extent the investment of funds is an alternative use of funds. Social purposes are best served when the investment funds are attracted to the most economic alternative use. Since statements exhibiting the past experiences of different firms do not all rest on common price level bases, comparison of the relative success attained in maintaining the order of respective financial houses is difficult. Statements exhibiting present values would therefore appear to be of greater potential service.

Secondly, so-called comparative statements for the individual firm are in truth not comparable. That they are is fiction rather than fact. In periods of radically changing price levels the significance of money costs incurred in different periods varies greatly. The longer the period for which the statements are exhibited, the greater are the discrepancies. Comparability requires correction for the changed significance of the monetary unit.

Thirdly, the profit or loss depicted by the income statement is, with exception, assumed to be operating profit. Often this is not the whole case. In conducting operations most businesses implicitly engage in a number of speculations, chief among which, in addition to the speculation in the supplying of a utility, are the speculation in the changing values of assets and the speculation in the changing value of money. A distinct service would be rendered the new investor if the accountant segregated the profits or losses realised in these respective speculations. Segregation of implicit capital gains and losses and of money gains and losses from true operating results would aid the investor to make his projections for the future.

It is my opinion that the endeavour to secure new capital is an end differing greatly in requirement from the end of measuring realised surplus, and that it is therefore better served by the provision of different statements.

MR. N. KARLGREN (Sweden):

It is not customary in Sweden for auditors to be called upon to sign prospectuses or offers relating to public subscriptions, whether it concerns the issue of shares, bonds or debentures.

As a rule, quite new firms are founded in the following manner—that one or more capital-owners put up as much capital as they themselves consider sufficient for the purpose in mind. In the case of the firm being founded as a limited company, the Royal Recording Board for limited companies controls that the necessary legal formalities are observed. These refer to company statutes, subscriptions lists, payment of the subscribed shares, etc. Such formal documents are generally prepared by a solicitor, entrusted with the company's legal affairs. If the company is founded by cash payments of stock capital, the auditor first comes into the picture at the initial general shareholders' meeting, when the board of directors and the auditors are to be elected. On the other hand, according to the Companies Act of 1944 which came into force as from 1st January, 1948, if the stock capital shown in the deed of foundation shall be liquidated wholly or partly otherwise than in money, the founders may employ special examiners appointed by the local Chamber of Commerce.

The main task of these examiners is to draw up a special examination report in which they express their opinions regarding the value of the contributed property. As it is not compulsory to make such a request to the Chamber of Commerce, this alternative so far has not been made much use of to any great extent. Corresponding regulations apply to the increasing of joint-stock capital by means other than money. In this case, however, the examinations are compulsory and if the local Chamber of Commerce is not consulted, then the checking should be carried out by the company's auditors.

When one or more persons have decided to invest money in a business, the estimates of the firm and the judgment of its prospects are, in most cases, placed in the hands of a professional auditor, usually an authorised public accountant. This occurs irrespective of it being a question of either a limited company, a partnership or a private firm or the reorganisation of a private firm or a partnership into a limited company or a private firm into a partnership or into a limited company.

The methods and principles employed seem to be mainly much the same in all countries—whether it concerns material assets or goodwill, or the determination of a firm's commercial value with regard to profit earned, or, in other words, by capitalisation of profit exceeding normal interest and risk-premium of the working capital of the company.

In his paper, Mr. Macdonald has very concisely and excellently covered all the main aspects of this rather wide subject, in relation to conditions in the United Kingdom. Therefore, I only mention here a few features most characteristic to Sweden in valuation of companies.

In adjusting the audited accounts over a period of years, one must pay special attention to the following details when dealing with Swedish firms, because the adjustments in question could be more considerable with Swedish companies than with companies in other countries:

1. Writing off of machinery and furniture fixtures.
2. Writing off of raw materials and stock.
3. Directors' salaries.
4. Reserves for pension funds.
5. Adjustment of subsidiary or affiliated companies' profits.

During the period 1938-50, according to the valid taxation laws (though not the wartime super-tax law 1939-45), Swedish companies had the right to write off entirely machinery, cars and furniture and fixtures as well as freely to reduce the balance sheet value of their merchandise stock to 15 per cent. or 30 per cent. of its cost price or market value, whichever was the lower. These possibilities have been of much value to Swedish firms, to stabilise and consolidate their financial positions, but to some extent the laws have been declared invalid for the period 1951-53.

Furthermore, there is no legal taxable limit as to what amount a company owner who is, at the same time, its managing director, may utilise for himself as salary from his company. Progressive tax on a private man's income is, however, very great in the higher income brackets.

Firms which have had large profits over the period in question have, moreover, transferred considerable sums to pensions funds. It is usual for the capital of these funds to remain in the company, but of course, there is no objection raised to it being detached and managed separately.

Since affiliated or subsidiary concerns are a most outstanding feature of Swedish business organisation, there occurs with valuations of the type in question the important task for accountants of adjusting any possible inter-concern profits. Many interesting problems can arise in this connection; for instance, in the case where a firm calls on its parent, sister or daughter company to be contractor for building a new factory—how great would be the resulting inter-concern profit?

It is the practice in Sweden, in the valuation of companies, that the accountant, upon the wish of his client, does not only state the official figures in the balance sheets and the profit and loss accounts and report the equivalent adjusted figures together with relevant remarks, but also gives his general impression of the company as a whole. Hereby can occur the question of certain necessary specifications such as the total amount of existing orders, or in the case of industrial companies, the idle capacity as well as the actual tendencies relative to both of these factors. The accountant should also endeavour to give his own opinion of the capability of the business's management, its reputation and personal character. An enterprise's prosperity, as is well known, often depends on it having or obtaining the right man as its leader.

Finally, to this audience, I should like to take the opportunity of mentioning that those who study business economics at either Stockholm's or Gothenburg's University of Commerce and have to acquire a theoretical background on the subject of 'goodwill', are firstly recommended to read an English text, namely, *Goodwill and Its Treatments in Accounts*, by L. R. Dicksee, London, 1920. Furthermore, another English text-book is recommended to the Swedish University of Commerce students, this one being in connection with the amalgamation of concerns—it is Cutforth's *Amalgamations*, London, 1933.

MR. GEORGE L. WEISBARD (United States of America):
The papers seem to underscore the function of financial statements in providing information to prospective investors. Obviously the keystone of that information is the terminology employed. Anyone who has troubled to read financial statements, prospectuses, annual reports, in various parts of the world will find significant differences in terminology. It seems to me that the need for a more free movement of capital on an international basis suggests that these differences in accounting terminology should not exist.

I understand that industry is setting an example in standardisation on a world-wide basis. For example, only last week in New York the international organisation for standardisation started a three-weeks' meeting at which industrial standards are being set, uniformly, on an international basis. Standards of accounting terminology are, in my humble opinion, equally necessary on an international basis. Please do not misunderstand me: I am not suggesting an accounting Esperanto. I think if we work within existing language groups we can have a simplification and standardisation which will make for greater information. Perhaps this should be considered by a committee of this Congress, and I make the suggestion for further study as time goes on.

MR. T. H. WHITE (Australia):
In the last few years in my country there have been a considerable number of private companies turned into public companies, calling for new issues of capital, either in the form of new shares or the sale of existing shares. As an investor from time to time in a number of these companies, I have always looked at the certificates given by the auditors or the investigating accountants and have taken note of the average profits over the preceding number of years. In Australia there have not been a great many prospectuses going back as far as ten years, and in most cases they have covered not more than five years. These certificates of profits are based on the profits shown by the books and accounts of the respective private companies and they do not always give an indication of the amount that would be available for distribution, to the prospective shareholders, on the capital that they may subscribe.

A direction has been issued by the Australian Institute of Accountants to the effect that accountants must never turn themselves into prophets and must concern themselves solely with what has happened, not with what is going to happen. But a statement of profits relating to a number of previous years is obviously only of value in so far as it may give an indication to the prospective investor of the profits which he may expect to be available in the future. In the case of debentures or preference shares, the usual thing he wants to know is how many times his dividend will be covered by the average profits —that is, in the case of shares where there is a fixed return. In the case of the ordinary shareholder, he wants to know the chance of a dividend being available to him out of the profits.

There are two special considerations in Australia, which also apply in England—depreciation and taxation. In my country the Government did allow a 20 per cent. initial depreciation allowance, which subsequently was increased to 40 per cent. That is obviously above the true amount of diminution of value, and above what is a fair amount charged against revenue for depreciation. Consequently, in considering what is likely to be available by way of profits, it is only reasonable to adjust the profits shown by the books of the company, not by the amount actually written off by them but by an amount which is a reasonable commercial charge against profits for that particular year.

Turning to taxation, in my country, in the case of private companies, the practice of providing for each year's tax from each year's profits was virtually abandoned, and the amounts taken into account were debited in order to get a fair amount of distribution. The principle is to charge those profits which would be equivalent in the case of a public company, if it had been formed.

MR. IAN W. MACDONALD, *the introducer, summed up the discussion:*

The first observation one must make is on the comparative tranquility of the afternoon after the controversy of the morning. I am in a difficulty in that about ten of the eleven or so speakers dealt with conditions prevailing in countries of which I have no professional experience. That makes it almost impossible for me to take up many of the points, for I am not qualified to deal on level terms with matters which are essentially of practice and not accounting principles. I speak within the limitations of my own experience in my own country.

Mr. Carroll challenged a view I had expressed on a technical point, when I suggested that there was no fundamental reason in prospectus reports to make any distinction between two types of taxation. He made the point, which I appreciate, that in this country there is a difference between profits tax and income-tax in that the latter has a bearing on the dividend paid to the shareholder whereas the former has not. I still adhere to the view that for prospectus purposes the potential investor is interested essentially in the total tax burden likely to fall on the business. He should be given information either about the total tax or about none at all; for it cannot be entirely satisfactory to give information about part of the tax burden and be silent about the other part.

Perhaps I may say a few words about our activity in making reports to the public. All the papers and most of the discussion bore out the growing

THE NORTH BANK OF THE THAMES
from the Royal Festival Hall

recognition of the need for adequate accounting information for the public, in public reports. There have been two stages in the development of public opinion in relation to these accounting reports.

The first stage grows out of a drive by financial or government authorities to establish certain accounting safeguards and protection for the investor. Some countries may be assisting that strongly, but they are at the first stage and you find that the accounting information given is rather sparse in its content, while the accountants in that country strive to extend the contents of their reports.

The second stage, which has been reached in this country and probably in the North Americas, is that of not merely trying to provide something to protect the investor but rather of trying to supply information which will enable investors to assess the merits of offers made. We have not progressed far in that second stage. One significant point about it is that the initiative in the second stage undoubtedly lies with the accountants, and we are striving to grasp it. The whole of the discussion today is evidence of the way in which we, on the one hand, recognise the limitations, and, on the other hand, try to take the techniques further ahead.

On the question of giving advice, the papers and the discussion were necessarily descriptive, because the advice which we give depends largely on the law and customs of the country and on the circumstances of the case. There is evidence that the scope for accounting advice in relation to capital increases as the taxation burden increases. From what we have heard, it is clear that accountants in various parts of the world are concerned with giving such advice for one reason if for no other—the burden of taxation.

The major tasks in this field—reports to the public, amalgamations, reconstructions, big jobs—do not happen very frequently in the average professional office, and probably when these occasions arise much of our work tends to follow the pattern which has been set by the leaders of the profession. But in the field of advice opportunities knock on almost everyone's door almost every day. The opportunity to give advice to clients, probably small clients, on such vital questions as capital structure, is at our door daily. Probably we are the only professional advisors able to give it, and probably it is advice which may have a vital influence on the health or well-being of our clients. I suggest that probably the aggregate influence of this advice which we can daily give on the body economic, the body corporate, will be greater than our influence in the more formal and more spectacular forms of public reports.

A vote of thanks to the authors of the papers, the rapporteur and those who had taken part in the discussion was accorded with acclamation.

WEDNESDAY, 18th JUNE, 1952

THIRD SESSION

THE ACCOUNTANT IN INDUSTRY

THE ACCOUNTANT IN INDUSTRY

by

F. R. M. de PAULA, C.B.E., F.C.A.

Institute of Chartered Accountants in England and Wales

INTRODUCTION

In the industrial world of to-day, the accountant is playing an increasingly important part in the management field. In this country this significant development has been most marked during the past two or three decades, and is evidenced by the

> 'considerable extent to which members of the Institute have taken whole-time appointments in industry and commerce after qualification, instead of practising as public accountants. The accountancy profession now embodies a much wider field than that of public accountants. . . .'[1]

It is the purpose of this paper broadly to outline this development and attempt to make clear its main purposes and objectives. But before doing so, it may be helpful to trace briefly the growth of the accountancy profession in this country; as to this, the writer can speak only from his own limited experience and as a member of the Institute of Chartered Accountants in England and Wales.

The art of book-keeping can be traced back to medieval times, but accountancy, as an organised profession, is very young and emerged here during the second half of the nineteenth century. Thus the birth of our profession took place during the prosperous Victorian era, when England was the richest and most powerful country in the world. Her industries were expanding rapidly, serious competition from abroad was not yet felt, for she was first in the field of industry, and thus had a flying start. The Royal Navy controlled the Seven Seas, and our commerce was backed by our vast mercantile marine; thus, in that age of great progress, our trade followed our flag to all parts of the globe. The pulse of industry was running fast and a period of great expansion lay ahead.

During that period, the individual business concerns were growing in size and private partnerships were being converted into private companies under the Companies Acts. Thus the opportunities for accountants were opening out.

---

[1] *Members' Handbook*, August, 1950. The Institute of Chartered Accountants in England and Wales, page 13.

The Institute of Chartered Accountants in England and Wales was incorporated by Royal Charter on the 11th May, 1880. Its objects were modest and were described in the original petition as follows:

'The profession of public accountants in England and Wales is a numerous one and their functions are of great and increasing importance in respect of their employment in the capacities of liquidators acting in the winding-up of companies and of receivers under decrees and of trustees in bankruptcies or arrangements with creditors and in various positions of trust under Courts of Justice as also in the auditing of the accounts of public companies, of partnerships, and otherwise.'

It will be noted that the main emphasis is upon liquidation and receivership work and that auditing is the last item upon the list. It is significant also that accounting is not even mentioned.

Looking backwards, it is clear that the Institute has developed in many directions never contemplated by its founders.

During the Victorian age, the rapid and extensive expansion of industry and commerce and particularly the growing size of the individual business unit, created the need for accurate and improved records. The old-fashioned methods were very slow and cumbersome and commonly the books of account were written up by the proprietor of the concern himself. But as the business grew this became impossible and part, at least, of the book-keeping had to be delegated, and when private firms were converted into companies under the Companies Acts, accounting assumed an added importance.

In this way the need arose for skilled accountants to help business men to organise their book-keeping records and the practice grew rapidly for public accountants to prepare and audit the annual accounts of industrial and commercial concerns.

During this stage in the development of the profession the emphasis was, to a large degree, upon recording. The practitioners of those days were extensively engaged in introducing sound systems of double-entry book-keeping into industry and commerce, and the auditor generally balanced the books and himself prepared the annual balance sheet and profit and loss account. So much time and energy were devoted, by the auditor and his staff, to the actual preparation of the accounts, that this accounting work, some may think, was carried out at the expense of the true audit work.

During this period, the profession undoubtedly rendered valuable service in raising the general standard of recording and accounting in this country.

The profession developed, at this time, upon an individualistic basis, that is to say, that each accountant decided for himself his basic accounting and auditing principles and procedures. The Council of the English Institute did not commence to issue recommendations on accounting principles for the guidance of its members until 1942.

During the second half of the nineteenth century, the profession grew very rapidly and extensively, audit practices expanded and many other fields of opportunity were opening out. Succeeding generations of accountants were building up upon the firm and sound foundations laid by their predecessors. It was a period of consolidation, and thus confidently the profession moved forward into the fateful twentieth century.

THE IMPORTANT EFFECTS OF THE COMPANIES ACT, 1900

Upon the turn of the century, this country was involved in the South African War, Germany and America were becoming serious trade competitors in both our home and foreign markets, and the ominous clouds of war had commenced to form in the skies over Europe. But the most important landmark at that time for the profession, in this country, was the coming into force of the Companies Act, 1900, which for the first time provided for the compulsory audit of the accounts of all companies, both public and private. Prior to this the field of opportunity for the public accountant was limited, but the passing of the Act of 1900 immediately expanded audit practices enormously, as auditors had to be appointed by countless numbers of companies that had never employed professional auditors before.

The coming of the auditor to every company had several important effects, e.g. many strange and inadequate accounting systems came under the review of the skilled accountant; and thus a large section of industry and commerce was persuaded to improve and modernise its system of records. The professional auditor rapidly proved his usefulness to his clients and became, in most cases, the financial adviser to the boards of the companies, and to the partners of the firms of which he was auditor.

Thus the coming into force of the Companies Act, 1900, was responsible for the first great step forward of the accountancy profession in this country.

THE EFFECTS OF WORLD WAR I

The World War of 1914-18 had profound effects upon the profession, as new fields of activity developed, which vastly widened the whole scope of the profession's activities.

Prior to the outbreak of the South African War in 1899, the rates of income-tax were very low; from 1879-80 to the year 1899-1900, the rates had varied between a minimum of 5d. and a maximum of 8d. in the £. During the South African War the rate rose to 1s. 3d. in the £ and after the war fell to 11d. in the £.

Sur-tax, profits tax, and excess profits duties and taxes had not been born. As, therefore, the direct tax burden was very light, the individual taxpayer was not greatly concerned regarding his tax assessments; consequently taxation work represented a negligible proportion of the earnings of public accountants in those days. But when during the 1914-18 War, the rate of income-tax rose to 6s. in the £ plus a heavy excess profits duty, a vast change came about and the individual tax-payer and the management of all companies and partnerships became acutely concerned with their tax assessments.

Public accountants undertook this work for their clients and thus an enormous field of activity developed. This work, which is highly specialised, must to-day represent a considerable proportion of the earnings of the profession in this country.

During the 1914-18 War many members of the accountancy profession served in various of the government departments and services and thus, in many cases, for the first time, became concerned with the problem of administration upon a very big scale. In this way, the outlook of many accountants was broadened greatly.

The vast armament programme raised the problem of the costing of government contracts both for the accountants serving within the government departments concerned, and for the public accountants outside, acting for their clients. In this way many professional accountants, for the first time, had to consider seriously the whole problem of costing, which up to that time had received little attention from the profession.

Thus a further new field of activity was developed and one which has since been greatly expanded. This also is a highly specialised subject, in which many accountants have now become expert.

Starting with costing only, this technique has since been expanded into what is now known in industry as management accounting. It is this field within industry and commerce that has attracted the interest of increasing numbers of professional accountants; and many of them have become specialists in the modern methods and practice of management accounting.

THE PERIOD BETWEEN THE TWO WORLD WARS

The period between the two world wars was one of great activity in the profession; audit practices grew rapidly and extensively, taxation work became evermore important and specialised. Professional accountants, in increasing numbers, were appointed to the boards of companies, on government committees and as advisers to trade associations and other bodies. At the same time great numbers of professional accountants took up full-time appointments in industry and commerce and thus were forced to study closely the whole field of management accounting. Thus accountants found themselves playing an increasingly important part throughout the economic life of the nation.

After World War I management consultants commenced to practise in this country; their techniques and procedures were obviously founded upon the teachings of the late F. W. Taylor, and as subsequently developed in the U.S.A. during the past fifty years.

Their object was to help industry to improve its whole organisational methods with a view to raising efficiency and consequently productivity, in the interests of all concerned, including, of course, the whole of the personnel employed. Thus, when engaged upon the reorganisation of an industrial concern, their report covered all of the functions of the business, e.g. production, technical, engineering, sales, personnel, finance, accounting, organisation and methods, etc. Management consultants are generally engineers and they employ skilled accountants to help with the financial and accounting parts of their investigations. Thus some accountants became interested in the financial and accounting parts of these new techniques.

These management consultants gain great experience as the result of investigating numbers of business concerns, and the successful practitioners undoubtedly render very valuable services to industry and commerce.

But the most significant landmark in the life of the profession during this period was the *Kylsant* case, which fell like an atomic bomb, and changed the face of the world of accounting.

Up to that time, both business leaders and the majority of accountants held the view that secret reserves were justified, upon the grounds of prudent financial policy, but this case gravely challenged the practice of drawing upon secret reserves for the purpose of bolstering up current earnings without revealing these facts. The public conscience was gravely shocked by the disclosures in this case, as also were many accountants. In consequence, a careful reconsideration of basic accounting principles commenced in the 1930s, in the first place by individuals and subsequently in 1942 the English Institute commenced to issue recommendations on accounting principles for the guidance of its members. This was an event of deep significance and many of these recommendations found their way into the Companies Act, 1948.

THE EFFECTS OF WORLD WAR II

The profession had grown to maturity and, strangely enough, in the midst of World War II had paused to take stock of its position and to think out its basic principles. The Council of the English Institute thus gave an invaluable lead and one which has had profound effects.

In the aftermath of World War II, this country found herself in extremely difficult circumstances; her vast overseas investments had, to a great extent, been liquidated to pay for the costs of the two World Wars, she was unable to balance her international accounts, her industrial equipment was run down and badly needed replacement and reconditioning, her citizens were fatigued and were staggering under a stupendous burden of taxation, together with a rapidly rising cost of living. However, her industries have made a supreme effort in turning over from war to peacetime production and have succeeded in vastly increasing the country's export trade. Now she is involved in a huge rearmament programme.

In these acutely complex times, the overall burdens of the accountancy profession have risen greatly and naturally its staff requirements increased proportionately. But, at this same time, an insatiable demand has arisen, from industry and commerce, for skilled accountants to help to reorganise our industrial and commercial concerns upon the most efficient basis and thus help to increase productivity. This demand for accountants, expert in the modern management accounting techniques, is acute and the prospects of an adequate supply for the future are not assured.

This problem is of great concern, in this country, both to industry and to the accountancy profession. Both are deeply concerned as regards the general significance of the subject as a whole and as to whether in the future there will be available a sufficient number of suitably skilled accountants to supply the needs of both the public accountants in general practice and those of industry and commerce. The fact that it has been included in the agenda of this Congress clearly indicates that this problem is of general interest not only here but in other parts of the world.

THE PLACE THAT ACCOUNTANTS ARE REQUIRED TO FILL IN INDUSTRY

It is proposed, therefore, to attempt to make clear what the writer considers to be the place that accountants are required to fill in industry and commerce, to outline the broad basis upon which management accounting is founded and how it is operated. The need is not merely one of providing numbers but accountants of the right type and with adequate preliminary training in these new and specialised techniques, for the whole outlook and practice of accountants in industry are very different from those of accountants in general practice.

The difference in the outlook of the auditor and that of the modern accountant within industry is a fundamental one. The accounts for last year reflect the results of transactions of the past; they are of great value, but they are of limited value to management for the purpose of deciding future policy and for controlling the day-to-day operations of a business. A comparison of this year's operating results with those of the preceding year may represent comparison of two inefficient operations. Thus the achievements of the past are not a safe and sure measuring stick. The position may be likened to the navigation of a ship across the seas. The log is kept written up recording every happening and the position of the ship from hour to hour, and valuable lessons are to be learned by the captain from a study of the factors that caused the misadventures of the past. But to navigate his ship safely over the Seven Seas, the captain requires his navigating officer to work out the course ahead and constantly to check his ship's position against the predetermined one. If the ship is off its course, then the navigating officer must report immediately so that the captain may take prompt action to regain his correct course.

Exactly so is it with the industrial ship; the past records represent the log and the auditor is responsible for verifying, so far as he can, that those records are correct and reveal a true and fair view of the financial position of the concern. But what modern management requires, for day-to-day operating purposes, is forecasts showing in detail the anticipated course of the business for, say, the coming year. During the course of the year management requires immediate reports of any material variances from the predetermined course, together with explanations of the reasons for them. This enables prompt action to be taken to rectify the position. By these means effective control can be maintained over the affairs of a business concern, as upon the happening of any adverse factors prompt action can be taken to rectify such faults before they reach serious proportions. By no other means, it is submitted, can widespread groups of companies be controlled. It is of no value to bring to the notice of management inefficiencies and losses long after the event, when it is too late to take remedial action. Water over the dam can never be put back.

THE MAIN REQUIREMENTS OF TOP MANAGEMENT

In the first place it would seem desirable to attempt to sketch, in very broad outline, the main requirements of top management for the purposes of controlling an industrial undertaking; and then to consider the modern methods by means of which those requirements can be effectively met.

For the purposes of illustration, it is proposed to take the most complicated example, i.e. a large group of companies with ramifications all over the world. In such circumstances, it is impossible for top management, personally, to supervise and control the vast number of individual transactions scattered over so world-wide a field. Decentralisation and delegation of responsibility become essential. Under such conditions effective control is impossible without an efficient system of organisation, and one by means of which essential information can be reported promptly from every part of the whole organisation to headquarters, in order that immediate action can be taken. That does not mean that every local action should be cabled to headquarters; were that done the organisation at headquarters would be completely choked. On the contrary, the system must be designed and operated so that only important information reaches headquarters and such as needs action; furthermore, headquarters must have some measures by means of which the results of operations can be judged before action is taken. It is obvious, therefore, in circumstances such as are envisaged, that every part of such a vast organisation must be closely studied in order to design a system that will provide, with the utmost promptness, all the necessary information required at the top, with extreme clarity and simplicity of form. But at the same time there must be available great detail at the base. Furthermore, at every level of management, from the shop floor up to the chief executive, there must be available the necessary information to enable each part of the operations to be controlled. Only in this way can prompt remedial action be taken immediately any inefficiency arises.

The basis of such a system is to provide the manager of every section of the operations with the information by means of which he, or she, can effectively control the activities for which he or she is responsible. The manager must also have a 'yardstick' by means of which to measure achievement; thus the manager is immediately aware of variances from normal. In this way, each level of management acts as a sieve—so far as possible all adverse factors are dealt with 'on the spot' by local management, but if that cannot be done, then the facts and the position of affairs are reported upwards via the 'chains of command', and it may be ultimately to the chief executive. By this means the chief executive is burdened only with matters of importance that require action from him.

What top management requires to know is when operations are not proceeding according to plan. This information is required promptly in order that immediate action may be taken. This is referred to as 'management by exception'. Where operations are proceeding according to plan, no action from management is required. Top management should, therefore, not be flooded with unnecessary detail upon which no action is required. A very common defect in many organisations is the clogging of the organisational machine with superfluous information —accountants have a weakness in this direction. Only too commonly, in practice, effective control becomes hopelessly lost in a wilderness of detail.

For those without experience, these new techniques generally appear to be alarmingly complicated and expensive to operate. They may be costly to install, but their subsequent operation often proves to be less costly than the system superseded. However, experience has clearly proved that the whole of the costs involved are infinitesimal when compared to the managerial and financial advantages that are to be derived from these methods. In fact the writer would venture the opinion that it is impossible effectively to manage a large group of companies without a system of control broadly upon the lines under consideration.

FORWARD PLANNING

The basis of this technique is merely forward planning—a word which strikes an apprehensive note in the ears of many industrialists in this country—but in truth and in fact forward planning must be the basis of all successful operations in every walk of life. Industrial concerns must and always have had to plan ahead. Before manufactured goods can be sold plans have to be made for the provision of production capacity, raw materials, consumable stores, labour, power, storage capacity, transportation facilities, lighting, heating, supervision, sales staff and innumerable other items. The whole operation must be carefully surveyed and planned and if miscalculations are made the results may be very serious.

In small businesses, there are to be found managers who do not work out their future plans in great detail but rely largely upon intuition and judgment; many most successful enterprises have been built up in this way. But in the case of the large groups of companies, such rough methods are fraught with great danger and in the past have resulted in many industrial shipwrecks. Wise management, therefore, sets up a system of organisation for working out plans (called budgets) for the future in great detail, and as the operations develop, management constantly checks actual achievement against the plan. Within the factory the overall plan is broken down into 'yardsticks' (called standards) by means of which each sectional operation is measured daily. The standard of measurement is in terms of time and money, thus embracing the two basic factors necessary in order to judge true production efficiency.

As these 'yardsticks' are used to judge the actual results achieved by the particular manager and his team and also to assess emoluments, it is essential that all concerned shall agree that the target thus set is fair and attainable. Management must be prepared to prove the reasonability of the standard by demonstration, otherwise it will not act as an incentive to endeavour.

Naturally the volume of production or activity must affect the final costs of production, but the factory is not responsible for that volume, which is the concern of the sales division of a business. In order, therefore, that production efficiency can be properly and fairly judged the budgets should be made flexible. This means that the 'yardsticks' or 'standards' must be calculated for various levels of activity, in order that management may be judged by the correct gauge.

The setting up of a system, upon the lines broadly indicated, is a highly difficult and complicated problem, based upon a technique that has been hammered out and proved upon the anvil of practice by engineers and accountants.

The Introduction of a System of Management Accounting

The problem now arises as to how such a reorganisation should be introduced to an individual industrial concern and by whom? Is it a matter for the accountant, the engineer, or the management consultant?

The setting up and operating of such a system of budgetary control and standard costing affects every division and section of an industrial concern. In order that forecasts may be reasonably reliable and that the standards set may be fair and acceptable targets, it has already been pointed out that the co-operation of management, at all levels in the factory, is essential. Furthermore, engineering and technical considerations play a very important part in the working out of these plans. The sales division, and in fact many other divisions and sections of the concern, must co-operate in the working out of the budgets.

It will, therefore, be appreciated that the success of such a system must be based upon team work. All divisions and sections must co-operate in the building up of the whole plan and in its operation.

It may be asked: 'What part does the chief accountant or comptroller play in connection with this matter?'

The whole of such plans are expressed in financial terms and often involve the handling, analysing and focusing of a mass of detailed figures; and in operation require prompt comparisons of actual achievement with the targets set. As accountants are specially qualified in the handling of masses of figures rapidly and accurately, they can render an invaluable service in designing the system for operating this part of the work.

The budgets are not those of the chief accountant or comptroller; their preparation represents a united effort of all sections and divisions concerned; the departments supply all of the pieces of the jig-saw puzzle which the comptroller fits together and thus reveals the complete picture.

The comptroller has not the necessary experience and information to enable him to make either the necessary forecasts for the budgets or to fix standards of measurement. It is very common in practice to hear the budgets referred to as being those of the comptroller, no doubt because it is he who generally presents them to the board of a company, but in the writer's submission it is a thoroughly bad practice. If this belief is allowed to grow, it implies that the comptroller has assumed responsibilities that he does not and cannot properly carry out, and the result will be loss of faith by the departments in the budgets. On the contrary, it should be made clear to all concerned that they themselves have been largely responsible for fixing their own sections of the budgets and standards. Only in this way can success be achieved.

Regarding the inauguration of such a system, in a business that had not previously practised these methods, it is submitted that the following are factors worthy of consideration:

(a) The person responsible for the inauguration of the new system should be someone thoroughly experienced in this technique.

(b) It is very difficult for an officer in a business, with other executive responsibilities, at the same time to control so complicated a reorganisation. It is suggested, therefore, that the person responsible for the reorganisation should work upon a full-time basis; either by detailing a suitably experienced member of the staff of the business or employing someone from outside, upon a professional basis.

(c) As the qualifications needed for this work embrace both engineering and accounting, it is a matter of opinion whether the most suitable person would be:

(1) An accountant with a working knowledge and experience in engineering.

(2) An engineer with a working knowledge and experience in accounting.

(3) An accountant in co-operation with an engineer.

(4) A practising management consultant.

(5) A practising public accountant who had specialised in management accounting.

(6) An accountant detailed from the staff of the business concerned.

Industry has drawn from all the sources available but there is every indication that there will be difficulty, in the future, in recruiting the right types of executives in the required numbers for this particular work.

The problem also arises as to whether there should be available facilities for preliminary training in management accounting for those accountants intending to enter industry. In the past those who have done so have learned this new technique empirically.

The viewpoint of the industrial accountant is from an entirely different angle from that of the accountant in general practice. Whereas the auditor is looking backwards, the industrial accountant is ever looking forward when assisting in the preparation of plans for the future operation of his company.

For the purposes of operating these new techniques very specialised systems and practices have been devised, and they are interlocked with engineering. The accountant has to approach this whole problem from the point of view of the engineer, and thus he finds himself in a new world. Preliminary training in these new techniques would be of the greatest value; it would seem, therefore, that this problem is worthy of the closest consideration, for the empirical approach must prove to be a slow and faltering one.

THE PLACE AND FUNCTIONS OF THE FINANCE DIVISION

Assuming that a modern system of budgetary control and standard costing has been inaugurated in an industrial group of companies, it is now proposed to consider the place and functions of the finance division in such an organisation.

If the finance division, headed by the comptroller, is to play an effective part in the operation of the group, then this division must be placed upon an equality with the other main divisions, such as production, technical and research, sales, personnel, etc. The comptroller's status must be level with that of the heads of the other divisions, and he must report direct to the managing director of the holding company. The comptroller should be in a position to represent finance at the board and all other meetings where policy decisions are made, as he should be in a position to voice the financial implications of any proposal before the decision is made.

The functions embraced by the finance division, in this country, commonly are finance, accounting, recording, costing, statistics, organisation and methods, and internal audits. The basis of the organisation it is submitted should be centralised control and decentralised responsibility.

The comptroller would be responsible for the basic principles upon which all accounts, costs, statistics, and returns, etc., should be prepared throughout the whole group of companies and for laying down the forms of presentation to headquarters of all accounts and returns and the dates for their submission. He would also be responsible for the general standard of organisation and the methods used throughout the group and for the internal audits. Some authorities hold that the chief internal auditor should be independent of the comptroller and report direct to the board of directors. However, it is thought that in this country the most common practice is for the chief internal auditor to report to the comptroller.

Regarding the accountants upon the staffs of divisions and subsidiary companies, they would report to the appropriate executive above them in their division or company. But they would be responsible to the comptroller for the functional technique and methods used within the local accountant's department and also for all the returns, reports, etc., sent by them direct to the comptroller. The annual reports and accounts of subsidiary companies, in the form approved by the comptroller, would be submitted to the comptroller by the managing director of each subsidiary.

A wise practice is to provide that there should be attached to the annual report and accounts of each subsidiary a questionnaire, in a form drawn up by the comptroller, to be completed and certified by the chief accountant of each subsidiary. The questions asked would cover all the important matters regarding the balance sheet and profit and loss account and would inquire whether the accounts had been drawn up strictly in accordance with the principles laid down by the comptroller and that the local accountant approved of the accounts without reserve. Another question would be as to whether the report and accounts included all of the information required by the comptroller. By this means the accountant of the subsidiary is made responsible for verifying that the accounts are in fact prepared upon correct principles and for bringing to the comptroller's attention any variations or points with which the local accountant is not in agreement. The questionnaire, signed by the local accountant, would be sent to the comptroller by the managing director of the subsidiary, with the annual report and accounts, thus passing through the proper channels and keeping the managing director of the subsidiary fully informed.

In the same way regarding costing and works accounting, the comptroller would be responsible for the general system and for the detail methods used, but the local works accountant in each factory would report to the works manager of that factory. Were the comptroller of the holding company to give executive orders to the works accountant in the factory of a subsidiary company, that comptroller would be cutting across the 'chains of command', which in administration is an unforgivable sin.

The internal audit department is a most important and helpful one if it is wisely operated, but if it is not it may act like sand poured into running machinery and lead to endless trouble.

The work of the internal auditor is largely of a critical nature and thus he and his staff may become regarded as spies and trouble makers. He certainly will be most unpopular if he makes adverse reports, however well justified, direct to the comptroller of the holding company, without reference to the head of the subsidiary or department under audit. If an internal auditor is not satisfied regarding any matter he should discuss it fully with the manager of the subsidiary or department, note in his audit report the manager's explanations and (if any) promises of corrective action. Before sending his audit report in to the comptroller, the internal auditor should show the draft to the manager of the subsidiary or department under audit, so that the manager may be fully informed as to the exact contents of the report. Except in special cases, this practice, in the writer's submission, should invariably be followed, as only in this way can the internal auditor hope to gain the confidence of the departments he audits. His objective should be to 'sell a service' to the departments and aim to prevent managers from getting into trouble with higher authority. Proof that the internal auditor is working in the right way is if it is found that managers of departments are calling for the internal auditor to make special investigations for them. Managers of subsidiaries and departments should regard the internal auditor as a functional expert available to help keep the administrative organisation of the particular subsidiary or department in good running order and also available to carry out special investigations on behalf of the manager.

The internal auditor and his staff should be most carefully chosen as great tact combined with skill and firmness of purpose are essential. The attitude of the stage policeman inevitably would result in great harm to the whole organisation.

ORGANISATION AND METHODS

Organisation itself, it is submitted, is a distinct and separate function and furthermore, administrative methods, practices, procedures and facilities are constantly changing in this progressive and restless age.

In this connection it is interesting to note that the Civil Service here has set up a separate functional branch, known as the 'Organisation and Methods Branch', the purposes of which are to watch the working of the organisation and administrative methods, in order to note defects and inefficiencies and. to make recommendations for improvements. This division keeps in touch with all developments in the field of organisation, including mechanical facilities, etc. Furthermore, individual government departments appoint, from time to time, special organisation committees to review and report upon the whole of the organisation of the particular department. Such a committee was recently appointed to review and report upon the organisation and administrative methods of the Inland Revenue Department. By coincidence the Bureau of Internal Revenue in Washington was, at that same time, being subjected to a similar review. These two committees visited each other and compared notes.

The development within the Civil Service of an organisation and methods branch is extremely interesting and the writer understands that it has been fully justified by the successful results that have been achieved.

It is suggested that there are lessons to be learned by industry from these examples, viz. the allocation of the responsibility for organisation and administrative methods to a separate branch or executive and for the holding of periodic reviews of the whole organisation of a business concern.

In fact, movement in the above direction can be observed in industry, though, in the writer's opinion, industry would be greatly benefited by the further development of these principles and their general application.

One of the responsibilities of the internal auditor of many companies is to watch the organisational machinery and to make recommendations for improvements, much in the same way as is the practice of the organisation and methods branch of the Civil Service.

In a large group of companies this function is of great importance; however, in order to gain full benefits, it is necessary to employ highly skilled and experienced staff. An accountant, in every way competent to carry out an internal audit, does not necessarily have either the skill or experience to deal successfully with the difficult problems of organisation. This subject, therefore, it is submitted, is worthy of far more consideration by industry and accountants than it has received in the past.

THE BROAD BASIS OF THE SCHEME OF ORGANISATION AND ITS EFFECTS

To summarise—the scheme of organisation, as outlined above, is upon a functional basis, with centralised control and decentralised responsibilities, thus it is very similar to that of a fleet fighting at sea. Each ship is under the sole command of the commander of that ship, but the exact part that each ship is to play in the operation is laid down by the admiral of that fleet; within those orders each commander operates and fights his ship.

The complement of each ship includes several specialised techniques, e.g. navigation, engineering, electrical engineering, gunnery, signalling, personnel, medical, paymasters, Royal Marines, etc. Each branch has its own techniques laid down by the command of its branch of the Service, but all on the ship are under the direct orders of the ship's commander. Thus, for example, the commander gives the guns their target and orders them when to fire and the number of rounds, but the drill for firing the guns, the design of the guns, ammunition, etc., have all been laid down by the gunnery branch of the Service.

In exactly this same way should a group of companies be operated. The managing director of the holding company, acting in accordance with the policy laid down by his board, approves the detailed plans for the group, as a whole, for (say) the year ahead, and instructs each unit within the group accordingly.

During the course of the year the managing director of the holding company requires reports in very broad outline, showing how the plan is proceeding. This overall picture is commonly in terms of geographical or trade groups. Actual performance will be compared with the plan and any important variances will need to be explained. If the variance is serious then the root causes must be located and they will lie with individual companies or departments within the group.

In this way the managing director and the board of the holding company watch progress and, in particular, variations from the predetermined plan. These variations, if material in amount, may entail a readjustment of the plan itself, in order to maintain a correct balance throughout the whole operation.

As the overall plan will have been built up from the detail plans of each subsidiary company or department, each manager will watch the progress of his company or department in exactly the same way as described above. Thus the whole of the plan both in the aggregate and in detail is under constant observation. Within a unit the variances can quite easily be traced down to the shop floor, as every operation, as it proceeds through the works, is measured against a set standard as it passes through each process. Thus every level of management watches progress and is instantly aware of all variations from normal as they occur, and therefore is enabled to take corrective action. In this way inefficiencies and losses are promptly rectified before they can rise to serious proportions. The effects upon the plan of changes of circumstances are likewise promptly observed, so that appropriate action can be taken, and thus the consequences of such dislocations are greatly minimised.

THE SETTING OF STANDARDS

The setting of the standards of measurement throughout a factory is a very complicated and arduous task; this work requires close co-operation between the engineers and the accountants. Production has to be measured in two dimensions, i.e. time and money cost. Time and motion study, therefore, play an important part in establishing the standards. Standards must be reasonable and based upon actual performances and management must be prepared to demonstrate that the times are reasonable. In order to arrive at the cost element very close and complicated investigations must be made by the accountants.

In this way 'standard costs' are arrived at and every operation is measured in terms of standard cost units. Thus a common factor is arrived at by means of which a variety of types of articles can be measured.

It is not the purpose of this paper to describe the details of standard costing procedures; that will be dealt with in Mr. W. S. Risk's paper.

From the practical point of view the great benefit of this system is that it saves management from having to wade through masses of figures to find out what needs attention and action. The system automatically throws out all abnormal items, and those are the ones of particular concern to management. As this operates in every level of management, the system must greatly increase the effectiveness of control and the promptness of action. Furthermore, the setting of targets not only acts as a measure of achievement but as an incentive to endeavour, in exactly the same way as does the setting of 'bogey' on a golf course.

One clear lesson that the writer's experience teaches is that this new technique should never be forced down from above upon staff and employees without full explanation. The whole system should be discussed in detail at every level of management and great patience is needed. In the writer's opinion, it is most unwise to make so fundamental a change unless and until it is thoroughly understood by all levels of management down to foremen and chargehands and until all have agreed to give the new system a fair trial. If the inauguration of the system is properly handled, experience proves that all levels of management soon begin to appreciate how greatly the system helps them to control their sections and with increased benefit to the whole team. One of the greatest advantages of this technique is that it makes every manager cost-conscious, and in consequence the beneficial results are often astonishing. A further lesson is the importance of making vividly clear to all that the figures are not prepared for the benefit of the accountants, but for management to take action upon. Therefore, management must thoroughly understand the system and use it for the day-to-day control of every section of the concern. The writer has known of cases where an excellent system has been installed, but the full benefits have not been derived from it because management did not completely understand and use it. The reason for this is that managers have not had the system thoroughly explained to them and they have not been convinced of its merits. Thus they do not appreciate the advantages to be gained from it. Under such circumstances the costs of installation of this technique have been largely wasted. Success can only be achieved if management believes in the system and does in fact use it for control purposes at every level.

Accountants can play an invaluable part in designing the system, explaining it to all concerned, installing it and seeing that it runs smoothly and efficiently. When the system is operating the accountants read the figure statements and bring to the notice of management the abnormal trends that require the consideration of management. In this way accountants in industry render great service to management by relieving executives from having to study masses of figures in order to find the information required for control purposes. The system automatically shows up 'the red lights' and thus the accountant signals management. Such a system reduces greatly the burdens of management, whose whole time can be devoted to productive work.

The Main Purpose of Management Accounting

The main purposes of an organisation, upon the lines described above, are to provide the organisational machinery by means of which an industrial concern, or a group, can be controlled by its management. The basis is the detailed planning of future operations and the checking of progress. The only means by which that can be done effectively is by building up a detailed system of records, which must be crisp, clear, accurate and very prompt in action. The overloading of management returns with detail defeats their purpose; it has been said that for management purposes every figure statement should be written upon 'a half-sheet of notepaper', and that no report for the board of a company should exceed two sheets of foolscap. It is in connection with the design and operation of such a system of records that we accountants can render invaluable service to industry.

From the point of view of top management some of the factors that need to be considered, planned and watched in operation are as follows:

(a) Before productive capacity is provided it is necessary to plan and consider carefully its siting with regard to such factors as availability of labour, raw materials, power, transportation facilities, access to markets, rating, etc. But above all the most important decision is the initial quantitative capacity to be installed and this should be based upon careful market research. If the capacity provided proves to be inadequate then the concern is immediately faced with the necessity for expansion of capacity and the consequential dislocations and expense. If the capacity is too great then the business will be burdened with the costs of idle capacity which may prove to be like a millstone round the neck. The wisdom or unwisdom of these decisions will have vital influences upon the subsequent welfare of that concern.

It is of great importance that management may be enabled to see clearly at all times the degree of utilisation of available capacity. Sales and production policies will be directly influenced by this position.

(b) The calculation of the financial capital required and the form in which it shall be provided is another fateful decision. The two factors are (i) the capital required for the provision of fixed assets; and (ii) for adequate working capital. These two figures in the aggregate, may vary considerably from time to time; therefore they require to be under constant observation. Long term capital budgets are, therefore, essential, together with a strict system for controlling capital expenditure and working capital.

(c) The production programme must be carefully planned and based upon the sales programme, and have regard to the productive capacity and facilities available. The sales budget will be broken down into sales areas and by products, and targets will be set. Selling and distribution expenses will be dealt with in a similar manner. Thus the progress of sales and selling and distribution charges can be checked constantly against the plan.

(d) The production budget will be broken down firstly in terms of facilities, raw materials, consumable stores and labour requirements, and compared with availabilities. Production will then be planned throughout the whole of each factory. Standard costs should be available for every process or operation and calculated for all likely levels of activity. By these means any 'bottlenecks' would be revealed and management at every level can watch progress against the plan and note all variances, and thus be in a position to take prompt corrective action.

(e) Administrative and all other expenses and charges would likewise be estimated and actual expenditure watched against the budgets.

(f) The position of the order book and its relationship to the plan should be under constant observation, as also should the position of inventories of raw materials, stores, manufactured and partly manufactured goods. Other important items are the amounts owed by debtors and on the other hand the current liabilities and commitments. In other words the whole of the details of the current balance sheet position must be watched against the planned position, thus the significant trends can be observed.

(g) Throughout the group monthly profit and loss accounts should be prepared, and individually, or by groups, submitted to headquarters. These accounts would be in a condensed and summarised form showing comparisons with previous years and with the budget. Other key information is generally furnished with such returns.

It is the responsibility of the comptroller to organise such a system and to see that all levels of management receive all the information that is required for control purposes. The comptroller would also study all of the returns and reports coming in to his headquarters, and he would point out to top management any significant trends and facts that indicate the need for action.

It would be the responsibility of the comptroller to watch closely the whole of the finances of the group of companies and he would act as financial adviser whenever matters of policy are under consideration. For these purposes he would make all necessary investigations and prepare special reports for top management. His association with the managing director and, through him, with the board of directors, is a very close one indeed, and he is thus in a position to make a most valuable contribution towards the efficient management of the group of companies with which he is concerned.

Industry in this country is awakening to the vital importance of improving its systems of control upon modern lines. This new technique has been proved out over a wide field in this country, the U.S.A., and many other parts of the world. The productivity report on *Management Accounting* issued by the Anglo-American Council on Productivity,[1] should be studied by all who are interested in this subject. This report makes clear that this technique is thoroughly understood by a portion of British industry, but this technique, it is thought, should be adopted far more generally in this country than is the case at the present time. Substantial progress will not be made unless and until the great benefits of the modern methods of management accounting are widely appreciated and understood by industrialists, engineers and accountants throughout this country. Herein lies a challenge for British accountants.

The fact that the problem of the accountant in industry has been

[1] Published by the Anglo-American Council on Productivity, United Kingdom Section, 21 Tothill Street, London, S.W.1; United States Section, 2 Park Avenue, New York, N.Y.

included in the agenda of this Congress is proof that the accountancy profession is keenly interested. But the writer would suggest that the profession has not yet made up its mind as to the part that it should play regarding the development of management accounting, which is the technique upon which the work of the industrial accountant is based. The following are some of the many points that, it would seem to the writer, need consideration:

(a) Does management accounting represent a new and specialised technique within the field of accounting?; or

(b) Is it a specialised technique outside the field of general accounting, but embraced within the field of engineering?

(c) If management accounting is a specialised technique:

(1) from what sources should industry draw the necessary specialists for work within industry?

(2) Is there a need for public accountants in general practice, specialised in this new technique, to advise industry in the installation of systems of management accounting?

(3) Should there be facilities for providing specialised training for such specialists, required under (1) and (2) above? If so, how should such training be provided?

(4) Is it necessary for accountants taking up this technique to have a working knowledge of engineering? If so, how should that knowledge be obtained?

(5) Is there a need for full-time research work in the field of management accounting? If so, how and by whom should such research be undertaken and organized?

(6) If the need for research (as in (5) above) were agreed, would it be necessary to obtain the co-operation of engineers and industrialists?

The need within industry for accountants skilled in management accounting is, in the writer's opinion, clear and experience already gained has proved that this technique is capable of increasing productivity in a marked degree. There is, therefore, a challenge to accountants to help this movement in every way that they can, and thus increase their services to the community.

THE VITAL FACTOR OF LEADERSHIP

In conclusion the writer begs leave to quote from a paper that he delivered in 1946.

'In conclusion I would like to sound one word of warning. It is very easy for all of us who become enthusiastic supporters of these modern management methods to lose sight of the most important factor in this whole management problem. We so easily overlook the vital factor of leadership which is the only means by which the breath of life can activate what otherwise is an inanimate body. Only by inspired leadership from the top can any group of men and women be fired with the impulse to co-operate fully and to give of their best. A faulty system of planning and control combined with brilliant leadership will result in great success in achievement. But the best system in the world with bad leadership will probably result in dismal failure. How to obtain full co-operation through-out an organisation is the great unsolved problem facing society all over the world. Upon this all-important point may I read to you three quotations.

'The first is from a brilliant paper by Lt.-Col. L. Urwick read before the conference held in London in October last, of the Institute of Industrial Administration. In this paper he stated that the central problem facing society to-day was how "to correct the terrible lack of balance between our technical knowledge of how to make this and that, of how to conquer space and time, and our ignorance of how to organise even the smallest system of co-operation so that men are satisfied in their work and happy to give of their best. We have learned how to split the atom and thus release its destructive energy. We do not know even the beginning of putting our social groups together so as to release a tithe of the constructive energy which is possible with true co-operation."

'My second quotation is from an article in the *Sunday Express* on the life of Field-Marshal Montgomery. In this article there are quoted prin-ciples that he enunciated before the war when instructor at a military staff college in India. The basic principles of military operations he laid down as follows:

' "No. 1. MORALE. Study the individual soldier. Create the atmosphere of success. Morale means everything.

' "No. 2. SIMPLIFY THE PROBLEM. Sort out the essentials which must form the basis of all future action, and once you have decided upon them, ensure that those essentials stand firm and are not swept away in a mass of detail.

' "As a commander, lay down the general framework of what you want done—and then within that framework allow great latitude to your subordinates. Stand back yourself.

' "No. 3. You must learn how to pick a good team of subordinates, and once you have got them stick to them and trust them.

' "No. 4. Make yourself know what you want and have the courage and determination to get it. You must have the will to win."

'If you change the word "soldier" for "employee" and the word "com-mander" for "manager", how surprisingly those principles apply to industrial operations. And note that he places morale as No. 1, and says that "morale means everything".

'My third quotation is from a recent statement by Sir Stafford Cripps which is that "morale in industry can be studied as scientifically as was the morale of the troops in time of war".

'There, I am sure you will all agree, is the key to nearly all our social and industrial problems. We have not found that key yet but we must hope that we shall before it is too late.'[1]

[1] *Developments in Accounting*, by F. R. M. de Paula. Pitmans, pp. 201-2.

THE ACCOUNTANT IN INDUSTRY

by

W. S. RISK, B.COM., C.A., F.C.W.A.
Institute of Cost and Works Accountants

INTRODUCTION

Much has been said and written about accountants in industry and many conflicting opinions have been expressed about their function and the contribution they can make to industry. It can, however, be claimed with reasonable assurance that those who manage industry, and make the decisions, are becoming increasingly aware of the value of the accountant's services in assisting them to make better and quicker decisions and to measure and present the results of these decisions.

The main purpose of this paper is to consider by what means the manager and the accountant in industry can, in co-operation, improve the service given by the accountant and advantageously extend the use made of the service by the manager. It is necessary, therefore, for these purposes to define the terms 'manager', 'industry' and 'accountant'.

Management[1] has been described by Sir Charles Renold, the first Chairman of the British Institute of Management, as being 'the process of getting things done through the agency of a community'. A manager, therefore, is taken to mean anyone at any level of the organisational structure from a charge-hand to a managing director who is concerned with the making of decisions (policy or otherwise) and with ensuring that these decisions are implemented by those under his control.

Industry is taken to mean the entire industrial community engaged in the processes of extraction, manufacture and distribution. It is interesting to note in this connection that according to the Ministry of Labour's figures for June, 1950, out of a total of 55,129 establishments, 41,423 (i.e. 75 per cent.) employed less than 100 people.

The accountant is the executive responsible for producing accounts, facts and figures (statutory or otherwise) relating to the organisation for the use of management and employees, customers and suppliers, shareholders and the State. His functions may be concerned with financial accounting, cost accounting and internal auditing and his

[1] An address on 'The Functions of Management' delivered by Sir Charles Renold at a meeting of the London and District Society of Chartered Accountants in London on 17th November, 1948. Published in *The Accountant* (Gee & Co (Publishers) Ltd.) of 27th November, 1948, page 434.

title, the scope of his activities and his responsibilities vary widely as between one organisation and another.

The accountant in this context does not include practising public accountants and auditors nor, unless specifically stated in the paper, does it include the accountant who holds a managerial position other than that of the financial executive of the organisation.

This last-named executive function, however, will be dealt with more fully in the complementary paper submitted by Mr. F. R. M. de Paula, C.B.E., F.C.A., with whom the author is happy once more to be in collaboration.

The opinions expressed in this paper derive from the experiences of others, as published in numerous accounting and other journals in this country and elsewhere, combined with the personal experience of the author who has been fortunate in that his work has brought him in contact with accountants and accounting organisations in firms of different sizes on a wide range of industries in this country.

It is fully realised that these opinions may be challenged, that they may be wrong and that British methods and techniques may differ from those in use in other countries. Nevertheless, objective examination, comparison and discussion of technique and experience between one firm and another and between one country and another can hardly fail to be for the benefit of all concerned and these are indeed the objects of the Congress which it is hoped this paper will, in some small measure, help to advance.

FUNCTIONS AND RESPONSIBILITIES
Basic Functions
Basically the function of the accountant in industry is to record events as they affect the organisation of which he forms a part.

Mr. W. W. Fea, in an excellent article[1] in *The Accountant* of 27th August and 3rd September, 1949, said:

'Accounting is both a science and an art. To use accepted definitions, the science consists in recording, classifying and summarising in a significant manner, transactions, operations and events, in terms of quantity, time and money; the art consists in interpreting the results thereof.'

It has long been accepted that the role of the accountant in industry goes beyond this primary conception, but while acknowledging the wider aspects of control through accounts, it should not be forgotten that the effectiveness of the application of the accountant's work will

[1] An address on 'The Presentation of Accounting Statements for Management' by Mr. W. W. Fea, B.A., A.C.A., to the Summer Course of the Institute of Chartered Accountants in England and Wales on 16th July, 1949. Published in *The Accountant* (Gee & Co. (Publishers) Ltd.) of 27th August, 1949, and 3rd September, 1949, page 220.

depend in no small measure upon the extent to which the initial recording is effectively organised to meet the demands to be made upon it.

Thus the accountant's function may conveniently be subdivided into two main categories:

(1) Executive,

(2) Informative,

and it is proposed to consider each of these in turn.

Executive Function

The executive function comprises mainly the responsibility for recording transactions to which reference has already been made. Originally these records consisted of those denoting amounts due to and by the concern, and of amounts received or paid by it. We have travelled far from the days of such simplicity and the demands made upon the accountant *qua* accountant in industry have grown steadily in amount and in complexity. They have resulted in the development of modern techniques of financial and cost accounting and the integration of accounting records, for all of which the accountant is naturally responsible.

In most small or medium-sized firms the accountant (acting also, perhaps, as secretary of the company) is responsible also for all office organisation and all clerical work. This carries with it the responsibility for the choice of staff and office machinery necessary to perform the work. It requires in the accountant the ability to choose and keep staff and to this end he must be capable of applying, consciously or otherwise, such techniques as job evaluation and merit rating in so far as they apply to clerical and administrative staff.

This responsibility requires also a general knowledge of the principles of machine accounting and a particular knowledge of the different types and makes of machines and the uses and capabilities of as many of them as possible. Calculating, typing, telephone and stationery staff and equipment also commonly come within the executive control of the accountant.

Employee services such as the calculation and payment of wages are not the least of the accountant's additional responsibilities. In many industries this task is neither onerous nor difficult and involves only simple calculations by office staff and an understanding by the accountant or his deputy of trade union or other relevant agreements.

In some industries in Great Britain, such as certain branches of engineering and textiles, however, wages calculation is extremely complicated, often as a result of unintelligible wages awards which are anomalous and cumbersome in their operation or because of technicalities within the industry. Wages incentive schemes based on individual or group outputs have been increasingly employed and as a rule responsibility for their successful operation is eventually laid upon the accountant. Too often such schemes are devised and agreed without the knowledge of the accounts department which is left with the responsibility of operating a scheme that is unworkable in practice. It is the experience of the author that it is generally advisable for the accountant to be represented at the inception of these schemes. This calls for co-operation between him, the other executives and the employees concerned. Apart from the direct results achieved, such a procedure gives the accountant a useful opportunity of obtaining first-hand information about production problems and employees and their reactions, an experience which may well stand him in good stead in carrying out the interpretative part of his functions.

Additional employee services involve the creation and disbursement of sickness, savings and pension funds, holiday, social, sports and other welfare funds, and, sometimes, the operation of the canteen facilities.

Credit and discount control, insurance arrangements, complying with the requirements of company law, knowledge of the law relating to industrial injuries and kindred subjects are other matters for which the accountant and his department are normally responsible.

This list is an impressive one and in considering the knowledge required successfully to discharge all the duties involved, one may well echo Goldsmith's words 'and still they gazed and still the wonder grew that one small head could carry all he knew'. It is, however, only a beginning for the accountant seeks to render service to industry and to do so effectively he must apply to his own department the same tests of efficiency that he would himself apply to a production department, continually striving to improve his methods and his results.

Informative Function

It is, however, mainly in management's use of accounting results that the accountant's efforts reach fruition and this is brought about through the informative function. Any business which seeks to become or to remain efficient must have a plan or a policy that is capable of being expressed in some coherent manner. Once the plan has been made, control can be exercised by comparing actual results with the plan.

Henri Fayol,[1] the French industrialist, said:

[1] An article on 'Inventory Management Know How' by Harold E. Bliss, published in the National Association of Cost Accountants' *Bulletin* of August, 1951, page 1476.

'The control of an undertaking consists of seeing that everything is being carried out in accordance with the plan which has been adopted, the orders which have been given and the principles laid down. Its object is to point out mistakes in order that they may be rectified and prevented from recurring again.'

Normally a plan or policy is built from, and is dependent upon, the interaction of a variety of facts and circumstances which it is necessary to express in a common medium. Sir Charles Renold,[1] to whom earlier reference has been made, said:

'The extreme importance of the technique of accountancy lies in the fact that it works in the most nearly universal medium available for the expression of facts so that facts of great diversity can be represented in the same picture.'

It follows, therefore, that the role of the accountant is to express the plan and the digressions from it in a medium and a manner in which both can be clearly recognised. Perhaps it is not too much of a simplification to say that planning necessitates the translation of facts (or estimates) into terms of money, whereas control, or, more correctly, the means of control, is obtained by turning money values into facts.

Management in Balance

There are, however, always influences tending to disturb either the plan or the performance and not the least of these influences derive from the personalities and prejudices of the executives within a business. Some of these prejudices and their effects are as follows:

First there is the financially-minded manager (often an accountant), penny wise and pound foolish, who tends to live with his head in the petty cash book from which he emerges only to refuse requests for expenditure on plant, expansion or research.

Secondly, there is the sales-minded manager (inevitably a former salesman), an extrovert who plans and dreams, to whom the grass on the other side of the fence is always greener and who is prepared to sell anything and everything except that which can be economically produced.

Thirdly, there is the factory-minded manager (usually a production engineer), obsessed with the idea of new plant, regardless of cost, who insists on special purpose equipment without consideration of the market available, the sales policy and the finances of the firm.

Fourthly, there is the product-minded manager who, never satisfied

[1] An address on 'The Functions of Management' delivered by Sir Charles Renold at a meeting of the London and District Society of Chartered Accountants in London on 17th November, 1948. Published in *The Accountant* (Gee & Co. (Publishers) Ltd.) of 27th November, 1948, page 434.

with the product, upsets production with one modification after another, thus creating havoc with the plans of the drawing office, the works manager and the sales manager, and who, if allowed to go on too long, eventually brings the firm to bankruptcy.

Fifthly, there is the volume-minded manager who concentrates on volume of production, without regard to cost.

Sixthly, there is the price-minded manager who is always convinced that if he can continue to cut his price just below that of his competitors, he will capture the market and sell huge quantities of his product.

Finally, there is the profit-minded manager who represents management in balance. He allots to each of the above points of view the importance due to it in any given circumstances without putting excessive emphasis on one to the exclusion of the others.

It is towards the attainment of this balanced management that the intelligent application of the accountant's techniques of preparing, interpreting and presenting figures can contribute in great measure.

Productivity

The subject of productivity or productive efficiency in industry is at present engaging great attention in this country. Much has been said and written on the subject—some of it wise and some of it not so wise. Having said that, it is perhaps daring to suggest that productivity in industry tends to be regarded from too narrow a point of view.

Why is it that when one speaks of productivity one nearly always discusses the man at the bench, the operator or, it may be, the production engineer? This point is well made in the Report on the Measurement of Productivity—Applications and Limitations,[1] issued jointly by the Institute of Cost and Works Accountants and the Institution of Production Engineers.

An industrial undertaking is a community. In that community there are those responsible for:

Design and product research;
Production;
Selling;
Finance; and
Co-ordination or management.

There cannot be high productivity in any undertaking unless all these functions are being performed efficiently and are in balance in relation to each other. For the reasons already given it is the accountant who,

[1] 'Measurement of Productivity—Applications and Limitations'. Issued by the Joint Committee of the Institute of Cost and Works Accountants and the Institution of Production Engineers and published by Gee & Co. (Publishers) Ltd.

more than anyone else in the organisation, should be in a position to measure the increase or decrease in the effectiveness of the combination and, therefore, in the productivity of the whole organisation.

Information required

The accountant has to supply information to a variety of interests for many different purposes. These are well set out in an article[1] in *The Cost Accountant* of November, 1949, by Mr. F. Leadbetter, F.C.W.A., F.C.I.S.

(a) THE STATE

When considering the kind of accounting information to be supplied to the State one thinks naturally enough of the need of the Inspector of Taxes for information on which he can agree the liability of the concern for income and other taxes—for taxes, like the poor, are always with us and, some may think, are themselves an inexorable feature of the condition of poverty!

The State, however, as well as becoming to an alarming degree a shareholder is in increasing measure becoming also a customer; a customer with, on occasions, dictatorial powers such as the right to investigate the costs of its supplier. Accountants in industry are well aware of these powers and of the need to provide the necessary information for the investigators (themselves often accountants) appointed by the Government department or departments concerned.

Furthermore, nationalisation in Britain has resulted in significant new demands being made by the State upon those responsible for accounting in nationalised industries. The absence of competition makes it more than ever essential to produce effective figures that reveal the extent to which efficiency of operation has been achieved. The issue is complicated by the fact that the public or the nation is at one and the same time a shareholder and a customer and it has been said that 'the nation as a shareholder expects a healthy trading account; as a customer it expects the moon'. It is the job of the accountant to indicate the extent to which one at least of these conflicting objectives has been achieved.

(b) OWNERS

Secondly, there are the owners of the business, or in the case of a company where ownership and management are normally divorced, the shareholders. The day has gone when an attenuated and summarised annual balance sheet, often published some considerable time after the date to which it referred, was deemed sufficient enlightenment for the proprietors.

[1] An article on 'The Function of an Industrial Accounting Department in a Manufacturing Organisation' by Mr. F. Leadbetter, F.C.W.A., F.C.I.S., published in *The Cost Accountant*, of November, 1949.

Accountancy, if it is to fulfil its function, must keep pace with the increasing tempo of industry and its demand for detail. This demand, coupled with the statutory requirements of company law, has led to the provision of more prompt and detailed information for shareholders and owners and to the publication of comparative figures over a period of years giving details of the company's progress, products, factories and future policies.

(c) MANAGEMENT

Management's requirements in the way of information are so extensive and so varied that it is proposed to deal with them in some detail in the section entitled 'Methods and Results'.

(d) EMPLOYEES

For a long time the only information vouchsafed to employees has been that concerning the composition of wages. A more enlightened management outlook has resulted in the provision for employees of information similar to that given to the owners or shareholders. It is open to question whether charts analysing the sales £ do in fact arouse the interest and put over the message they are intended to convey, but they are at least an indication of the willingness of management to give employees a better understanding of their share and participation in the organisation.

Much more information is now given to employees about such things as raw material supplies, orders on hand, future prospects and projects, and while these may be regarded as management rather than accounting matters, the information has, in many cases, to be supplied by the accountant's department.

Advice and information on income-tax (mostly concerning P.A.Y.E. tax), together with details of transactions in all the funds and services created for the benefit of employees, are, of course, almost automatically supplied to employees or their representatives.

It is interesting to note from page 48 of the Management Accountancy Report,[1] published by the team of accountants who recently visited the United States under the auspices of the Anglo-American Council of Productivity, the kind of information which is commonly supplied for the shareholders and employees of firms in that country:

Tonnage or quantity of year's production.
Value of year's sales.
Amount of capital expenditure for year.
Amount charged for depreciation for year.

[1] 'Productivity Report—Management Accounting.' Published by the Anglo-American Council on Productivity, page 48.

Average number of employees for year.
Average hours worked weekly.
Average hourly earnings.
Amount paid in taxation for year.
Net earnings for year.
Percentage earned on total share capital.
Percentage earned on sales.
Amount earned per common stock unit.
Working capital (balance sheet values).
Amount of profits employed in the business.
Reconciliation of opening and closing cash position.

(e) DEBTORS AND CREDITORS

Modern methods of machine accounting automatically ensure the provision at such intervals as are required (usually each calendar month) a copy of the supplier's or the customer's account in the books of the organisation. In the case of the supplier, the information is generally supplied with payment and in the case of the customer it is regarded as a request for payment.

(f) TRADE ASSOCIATIONS

Trade associations are making calls upon accountants in industry (and, of course, upon those in practice also) to provide additional information for members and Government departments for price fixing.

(g) TRADE UNIONS

Trade unions also have realised the necessity for, and advantages of, the services of accountants in promoting the interests of their members and particularly in presenting cases that require figures to substantiate and support them.

(h) INTERNAL AUDITORS

The office of internal auditor normally held, where it exists, by an accountant, is an unusual one since the person holding it, while working within the accountant's department and possibly within other departments, is not generally responsible to the accountant, controller or financial executive (by whatever name this executive is known). He is usually directly responsible to the managing director or to the board and his duties have widened from the function solely of providing an internal check upon records, cash and goods to responsibility for suggesting improvements to the whole office organisation.

Action

Thus far we have considered in some detail the functions and responsibilities of accountants mainly in providing information about past activities and events. Examination of the past, however, is not enough unless it serves also as a means of foreseeing or, it may be, of influencing the future.

Accountancy and figures are not an end in themselves, they are only a means to an end. It is not suggested that the accountant is the one who should take action on his figures (that is the responsibility and prerogative of management), nor is it suggested even that control by accounts is feasible. Accounts and figures are inanimate things and can control nothing. It is the action taken in the light of, and as indicated by, the figures that provides the control.

There are increasing demands, therefore, upon the accountant to provide intelligent forecasts based upon the records of the past. The demand is for facts and reasoned deduction based upon figures, rather than for figures themselves. It is largely upon the extent to which the accountant can fulfil this function that his ultimate usefulness will depend.

It has been said that 'It is often more important to be definite than to be right'; it is obviously better to be both. The most successful businesses are those where decisions are most promptly made and executed. The accountant must have, therefore, a sense of urgency and an outlook similar to that of a commercial manager (in which position, incidentally, it is not unusual to find him). He should persistently seek ways of reducing costs by bringing to the attention of the executives concerned, and by initiating investigation into, facts which indicate that a saving is possible in any of the varying functions and expenses that go to make up cost.

It may be appropriate to conclude this section of the paper by quoting from page 45 of the Management Accounting Report,[1] to which reference has already been made. It says:

'The outstanding feature in American industrial accountancy is the attitude with which the accountant approaches his job. His primary object is to serve management and as a result he has developed an intimate knowledge of the technical and commercial aspects of its problems. He approaches the accounting process with the idea of producing control figures rather than historical records and tries to anticipate the problems that will face management. He is increasingly, therefore, dealing with forecasts and budgets to provide the basis of preventive rather than remedial action.'

STATUS AND POSITION

Whatever may be the functions and responsibilities of the accountant in any organisation it is fair to say that he will not be able to discharge them to the full unless his status and position in the organisation are

---

[1] 'Productivity Report—Management Accounting.' Published by the Anglo-American Council on Productivity, page 45.

such that he holds sufficient authority. He must be recognised as part of higher management, even though as far as management outside his own department is concerned, he holds only an advisory position.

Broadly speaking, the basic facets of management are: design, production, selling and finance. No organisation can prosper unless each one of these functions plays its full part. Good design will fail if production and selling are inefficient while efficiency in production and selling will not compensate for bad design. Nevertheless, even if all these three functions are operating efficiently, it is still necessary to ensure that the product can be made and sold at a price which will recoup the organisation's outlay of revenue and capital and provide it with funds to continue in production. This is the function of finance and the whole position may be summed up in the equation—design plus production plus selling plus finance equals a commercial proposition.

Just as it is necessary for the work of the accountant to be performed within the pattern of a clearly defined organisational structure, so also is it necessary that the accountant in presenting his figures shall follow the plan of the organisation. Mr. E. H. Davison, A.C.A., in a paper[1] published in *The Accountant* of 31st March, 1951, makes this point very clearly when he says:

> 'As control can be exercised only through people the means of indirect control provided by accounting statements are, therefore, the more useful the more closely those statements are identified with the persons responsible for the issuing of orders and the execution thereof and the accounting structure must be wholly conditioned by the structure of the business organisation.'

The primary aim of the accountant in industry is to provide management with facts and figures on which plans and decisions can be made. It is his aim also to see that as far as possible the plan is being adhered to and the decisions correctly interpreted. It is for this reason that the accountant is sometimes known as the controller. He cannot fulfil this purpose adequately unless he is aware of the background against which the decisions are made and the considerations affecting them.

It is accepted by *most* accountants and by *all* managers that the accountant's job is an advisory one but the accountant must nevertheless look at problems in the same way as management. In the Management Accounting Report[2] on page 37 it states that:

---

[1] An article on 'The Accounts Organisation in a Large Industrial Concern' by Mr. E. H. Davison, A.C.A. Published in *The Accountant* (Gee & Co. (Publishers) Ltd.) of 31st March, 1951, page 304.

[2] 'Productivity Report—Management Accounting.' Published by the Anglo-American Council on Productivity, page 37.

'He (the Controller) does not, of course, pretend to be able to solve the problems of production or marketing but he knows their nature and so can discuss in detail with all levels of management the financial implications of the solutions they suggest.'

The accountant is concerned with all the facets of management at all its levels. There is little doubt that in almost any organisation the influence which he holds will depend in no small measure upon his own personality and the extent to which he is able to convince others of his personal ability and integrity. The accountant is often criticised for taking too impersonal and inhuman a view. This objectivity is at once his strength and his weakness; his strength in the ability to arrive at a logical conclusion unhampered by the influence of personalities or personal inclinations; his weakness—sometimes—in his treatment of the human factor and in 'putting over' his findings to others.

This is not always the fault of the accountant; the man who keeps the score is often wrongly held responsible for the score itself. The following quotation from an article[1] by Mr. George Schwartz, first published in the *Sunday Times* and later in *The Accountant* of 3rd December, 1949, illustrates this point admirably:

'The accountant is not a popular figure in life. If economics is the dismal science, accountancy is the dismal practice. A hollow groan goes up when the memorandum for a beautiful scheme is followed by the accountant's observations. Oh for a world in which £ s. d. were really meaningless symbols! Now the accountant does not create accounts; he keeps them. . . . To quarrel with accounting is to quarrel with economic calculation and that is to quarrel with providence itself for not having supplied everything in such abundance that it can be had for the asking. In a world conditioned by scarcity, accounting is the tool of rational choice and action.'

METHODS AND RESULTS

Accountants have spent much time and effort in the reconciliation of cost and financial accounts and figures. This has been a most necessary task. It is disconcerting (to put it in its mildest form) to management to be told during the course of a year that all work is showing a profit and at the end of the year to be faced with financial accounts showing a substantial loss, or vice versa. From the need for reconciliation has grown the realisation that costing and financial statements are, or should be, only different arrangements of the same basic figures and that if these basic figures are properly created in the first place, they should be capable of supplying all the demands made upon them for external or internal uses.

[1] An article entitled 'The Sense of Reckoning' by George Schwartz, originally published in the *Sunday Times* of 13th November, 1949, and reproduced in *The Accountant* of 3rd December, 1949, page 591.

There has been a steady development in this line of thought in British industry, aided, in a large measure, by the use of the techniques of budgetary control and standard costing and by the increasing adoption of perpetual inventories and continuous stocktakings to remove the necessity for an annual stocktaking. The result is that the financial accounts are being prepared more promptly and in more detail and are becoming more useful to management, while management accounts, where they are prepared from properly analysed basic figures, are themselves becoming the source of the financial accounts which, in these circumstances, can be derived almost as a by-product of the periodic or management or cost accounts. We are, therefore, approaching the stage of complete integration of accounting information and the merging of what in this country has been known generally as financial and cost accounting.

Classification of Expense

This integration, however desirable, cannot be successfully achieved unless a sound basis is laid in the design and structure of the code of accounts or expense classification. Fundamentally this classification should be such that the headings required for financial purposes are the natural groupings of the more detailed classification required for cost ascertainment and control. The detailed headings should be such that the cost of departments processes or functions can readily be ascertained and responsibility for them clearly assigned.

The National Association of Cost Accountants in their Research Publication No. 19,[1] entitled 'Assignment of Non-manufacturing Costs for Managerial Decisions', said:

'The accounting plan should start with the determination of responsibilities. The second step would be to set up the necessary functions within each of the major responsibilities. The third step would then be to provide the necessary natural expense accounts to correctly reflect the activities of each function.'

and also that:

'Accountants should devote more attention to cost classification and less attention to cost allocation. . . .'

A specimen illustrating the type of accounts code which might be used for works expense is shown in Appendix I.

Budgetary Control

The term 'costing' takes on a wider significance when it is realised that *control* of cost is at least as important as its *ascertainment*. The

[1] National Association of Cost Accountants' *Bulletin*, May, 1951, Research Series No. 19, 'Assignment of Non-manufacturing Costs for Managerial Decisions', pages 1147 and 1151.

term 'budgetary control' has been applied to this wider application of costing and consists briefly of the preparation of budgets or standards for output and expenditure and the comparison of actual attainment and outlays with these standards.

The variations from the budget or plan and the type of information required to provide the means of control may be illustrated as follows:

Selling (Plan)

(*a*) What products can be sold?

(*b*) To whom can they be sold, e.g. wholesalers or retailers?

(*c*) How many customers are available?

(*d*) What methods can be employed, e.g. agents, distributors, salesmen, advertising?

(*e*) What price can be obtained?

(*f*) How much can be sold at that price?

(*g*) What profit margin is expected from varying prices and sales levels?

Selling (Control)

(*a*) Sales prices obtained compared with budget.

(*b*) Amount of sales compared with budget (analysed in such detail as is required).

(*c*) Cost of selling compared with budget.

(*d*) Comparative costs of different methods of selling.

Production (Plan)

(*a*) What plant capacity is available?

(*b*) What level of output can be attained?

(*c*) What is the expected cost per hour of the plant at normal capacity usage?

(*d*) What is the production layout for each product and what is the production time per unit of output in each department?

(*e*) What therefore is the expected cost in labour and overhead of each product (i.e. the standard cost)?

(*f*) What new plant is available or necessary and what will it cost?

(*g*) What type of power is to be used and what should it cost?

(*h*) What is to be the plant maintenance policy—planned maintenance or *ad hoc*?

Production (Control)

(*a*) Comparison of output and plant usage with budget.

(*b*) Comparison of operating cost per hour (labour machine or process) with budget.

(*c*) Effect on cost and on profit of varying:

Efficiencies;

ALAN S. MacIVER, M.C., B.A.
Secretary of the Congress

Levels of output;

Labour rates;

Over or under expenditure on overheads.

(d) Cost of power and plant maintenance compared with budgets.

Materials (Plan)

(a) What types of materials are to be used—are substitutes available?

(b) What quantity of material is required per unit of production?

Materials (Control)

(a) Material prices compared with budget.

(b) Material usage and yield compared with budget.

Personnel (Plan)

(a) What is the engagement policy and what type of labour is required?

(b) What wages policy is to be adopted, e.g. day work, piece-work, bonus schemes or profit-sharing?

(c) What welfare policy is to be adopted, e.g. canteen, medical and sports facilities?

Personnel (Control)

(a) Labour turnover percentage.

(b) Wages rates earned per hour and percentage bonus earned compared with budget.

(c) Costs of welfare facilities compared with budget.

Finance (Plan)

(a) What credit policy is to be adopted?

(b) What buying policy is to be adopted?

(c) What are the estimated stock and finished goods requirements?

(d) What are the total capital requirements?

Finance (Control)

(a) Credit control.

(b) Stock control.

(c) Cash forecasts or disposal of funds statements.

(d) Comparative balance sheets.

These are some of the types of budgets used for budgetary control purposes and it will be realised that they are illustrative rather than complete and will vary considerably in incidence and emphasis between one industry or firm and another.

K

Standard Costing

It is a short and logical step from budgetary control to standard costing and there is no doubt that the combination of these two techniques and their application have greatly enhanced the service which industrial or management accounting can give to industry.

It is not within the province of this paper either to give a detailed explanation of standard costing methods or to point out all the benefits to be expected from their application. These are well set out in publications by the Institute of Chartered Accountants in England and Wales and the Institute of Cost and Works Accountants.[1]

It should perhaps be emphasised, however, that standard costing basically involves the pre-costing of operations, processes or functions on the assumption that any manufacturing concern is selling the productive *time* of its processes or plant. It follows, therefore, that standard costing does not mean, as is still quite commonly believed, the costing of standard articles. It is costing by function—a much better basis for control than through the ascertainment of the cost of individual products.

This opinion is supported by a further quotation, again from the National Association of Cost Accountants' Research Publication,[2] already referred to, which says, on page 1149:

'When the cost of an individual function is known, management is in a position to study costs of performing the same function in alternative ways and, in some cases, to decide whether or not the function should be performed at all.'

Perhaps the greatest of all benefits to be obtained from the creation and application of budgetary control and standard costing is that they necessitate the closest possible collaboration between management and the accountant in developing a comprehensive and coherent policy, plan or budget that is capable of being expressed in facts and figures.

Marginal Costing

Probably no technique in industrial accounting has provoked more controversy and argument than that known as marginal costing. For those to whom the term is unfamiliar the technique may be described as the segregation of charges or costs into two sections: (*a*) those that are peculiar to any one product or department and which

---

[1] 'An Introduction to Budgetary Control, Standard Costing, Material Control and Production Control', published by the Institute of Cost and Works Accountants, and 'Developments in Cost Accounting'—a report of the Cost Accounting Sub-Committee of the Taxation and Financial Relations Committee of the Institute of Chartered Accountants in England and Wales.

[2] National Association of Cost Accountants' *Bulletin*, May, 1951, Research Series, No. 19, 'Assignment of Non-manufacturing Costs for Managerial Decisions', page 1149.

would cease if the department were closed or the product were not manufactured, and (b) those charges of a general nature which, within wide limits, are not affected by changes in departments or products and which are applied to products for purposes of recovery on a more or less arbitrary basis. This technique is sometimes known also as direct, contributory or comparative costing.

There seems to be no reason why the controversy should be so fierce nor indeed why it should arise at all. Two different techniques are involved. It is an example in support of the theory that different costs are required for different purposes.

It seems that the accountant can never answer such questions as:

What would happen if:
(a) a department were closed?
(b) production were increased?
(c) sales prices were cut by a certain percentage?
(d) certain products were discontinued?
(e) a new product were put into production?

without using the marginal technique, for it is clear that the inclusion in costs of an allocation of general or common expense must obscure the true answer to these questions.

The National Association of Cost Accountants' Research publication,[1] already referred to, says, on page 1163:

> 'Proper application of the contribution margin approach does not constitute disregard of the unallocated expenses, but instead it emphasises the contribution which each segment makes to these expenses.'

Increasing tempo and competition in business life calls for more far-reaching and speedier decisions. Mr. Harry E. Howell,[2] of the National Association of Cost Accountants and formerly controller of U.N.N.R.A. said in a paper on cost accounting, that:

> 'Business decisions usually involve the acceptance or rejection of alternatives. They may involve the taking or rejection of orders; cutting a price on a single order; making a price cut in a competitive market; raising prices; spending additional amounts for promotion and sales to keep the plant running; increasing, curtailing or ceasing production, and many similar choices of vital import to the company. Unless information drawn from cost accounting reports is re-cast and related to many bases not common to cost accounting formulae it will not usually furnish the data needed to make sound decisions. In many cases the routine cost reports give information which is misleading for the purpose of assisting in

---

[1] National Association of Cost Accountants' *Bulletin*, May, 1951, Research Series, No. 19, 'Assignment of Non-manufacturing Costs for Managerial Decisions', page 1163.
[2] Quoted in a paper on 'A Standard Accounting System' by Mr. Ian T. Morrow, C.A., F.C.W.A. Published by the British Institute of Management, page 10.

determining alternate courses of action. Cost reports may show that the sales price of a line or product is below cost, but a conclusion drawn from such figures that a loss equal to the difference would be eliminated by discontinuing the line, would be in error. Included in the cost are elements of fixed and constant costs which would continue whether the product was produced and sold or not, and its elimination might result in adding to the loss because the remaining business would have to absorb the costs which remained.'

The use of the marginal technique is necessary also for the preparation of the break-even chart. The purpose of this chart is to show, with a given volume and mixture of product sales with budgeted contributory margins for each product and in total, the point at which the total margin will be just sufficient to cover the fixed or general overheads of the business. This point can then be compared with the margin obtained from the budget of normal sales and expected contribution, to show the margin of safety of the business. A specimen of a simple break-even chart is given in Appendix II.

In addition, the marginal technique and method of comparison is comparatively simple and thus easily understood by those unacquainted with accounting and costing conventions and methods. It is of particular and increasing importance in view of the tendency in industry for fixed overheads to increase and even a slight reversion or slump might well have much more serious consequences in many firms and industries in this country than is generally realised or anticipated.

On the other hand, opponents of the technique argue rightly that its use in unskilled hands may well lead to price-cutting and disaster. In fixing sales prices it is, of course, essential that the overriding condition of full absorption of overheads should be fulfilled. Commercially it is seldom possible to sell so much at a loss that a profit is eventually made. Subject, however, to this overriding condition, the ratio of the overhead recovery burden as between one product and another may well be as much a commercial function as an accounting one.

Financial Reports

It is not proposed to illustrate in detail the kind of financial or other reports that are produced for management. These will vary to meet the needs of individual concerns but may be said to comprise generally those referring to the assets, fixed and liquid, and the liabilities of the business, with particular reference to the changes that have taken place between the date of the report and the datum or basic period.

Reports for Cost Ascertainment and Cost Control

Again it is proposed to refer only in general terms to the reports required for cost ascertainment and cost control. The minimum requirements which it is suggested these types of report should fulfil are outlined below.

COST ASCERTAINMENT

(a) For any given article or process the material cost must be known.

(b) For any given article the cost shall be available, operation by operation, analysed for each operation into labour and overhead.

(c) The above cost shall be available analysed to that part which is fixed and that part which is variable with output.

(d) There shall be segregated the effect on cost of efficiency of production and of volume of output.

(e) Those products which are profitable and those which are unprofitable and the degree to which they are profitable or unprofitable shall be established.

COST CONTROL

For cost control it seems necessary to produce information:

(a) To measure the level of output as against the predetermined normal and to calculate the effect of variances from it.

(b) To measure the level of performance or efficiency in relation to the target set and to calculate the cost of failing to attain the standard or the gain from exceeding the standard.

(c) To ascertain expenditure and to compare it with flexible budgets.

(d) To control materials and show separately the extent of departures from the standard in regard both to price and usage.

(e) To provide in all the above the means of control at such point of time (which may be anything from hourly to annually) as may be most beneficial over all, taking into account the cost of obtaining the control.

(f) To analyse and present the information (and this is of special importance) by sections of responsibility so that there may be presented to section heads or executives a clear statement of their own departmental results unencumbered by results for which they are not expected to accept responsibility.

In speaking of cost ascertainment it is well to remember that there is no such thing as 'actual cost'; there is only cost under given conditions of output and expenditure. Mr. E. H. Davison, A.C.A., to whose paper[1] in *The Accountant* of 31st March, 1951, reference has already been made, states that 'cost is built up on the basis of a mixture of facts and assumptions' which is indeed a true statement.

The failure by management to appreciate that such arbitrary assump-

[1] An article on 'The Accounts Organisation in a Large Industrial Concern' by Mr. E. H. Davison, A.C.A. Published in *The Accountant* (Gee & Co. (Publishers) Ltd.) of 31st March, 1951, page 307.

tions and allocations have to be made in producing a total cost occasionally leads to misunderstanding. This is well illustrated in the amusing and light-hearted little book entitled *How to Run a Bassoon Factory*,[1] by Mark Spade, which states:

> 'Don't be surprised if your costing department tells you one day that a thing costs £20 and the next day that it costs 4s. 3d. Costing departments always do that and they will certainly be able to produce figures which prove absolutely conclusively that they were right on both occasions.'

Presentation

Throughout this paper it has been emphasised that the ultimate object of all the accountant's work is action—action on the part of those whose job it is to make decisions and carry them out. Information is worth only the benefit obtained from the action taken on it. Confucius is believed to have said: 'Action without thought is dangerous but thought without action is futile.'

If action is required by individuals the reports presented must be prepared in such a way as to excite the interest of, and be understandable by, those who are to use them. For this purpose flexibility is a greater virtue than uniformity.

It is unfortunately true to say that as a rule management does not attribute to figures the importance which is their due. This may well be the fault of the methods of preparation and presentation. It is the author's experience that routine figures that indicate a state of affairs similar to that believed by management to exist usually serve only to increase management's belief in its own omniscience. Only when the figures indicate a state of affairs contrary to that believed to be the case, and after the inevitable criticism has been answered and the figures proved to be correct, will management begin to have confidence in, and take action on, the results shown.

Nevertheless it is the accountant's duty to make his presentations such that the facts are clear, live and understandable. To achieve this, routine reports should be as simple in design and as few in number as possible. Often a verbal report has more effect than a written one and constant personal contact between the accountant and his colleagues in management is much to be desired.

An accounts or cost office is probably more fairly judged by the quality and speed of its special *ad hoc* reports than upon its provision of routine statistics. In preparing special information it is often useful to subdivide the report as follows:

(*a*) Terms of reference.
(*b*) Findings.

[1] *How to Run a Bassoon Factory*, by Mark Spade. Published by Hamish Hamilton.

(c) Recommendations.

(d) Action required by management to implement the recommendations.

Although it is not usually the province of the accountant's department to take action, there should always be a tendency to act more as a 'thermostat' than as a 'thermometer'.

Another useful form of reporting is that used for army operational orders:

Information.
Intention.
Method.
Administration.
Intercommunication.

Often this grouping of a report gives an ideal basis for a comprehensive yet brief statement of the position.

The purpose for which the report is being prepared and the person or persons to whom it is to be presented must always be the principal consideration affecting the design of the statement. Many statistical devices can be used in preparing management reports and some of them are summarised by Mr. Warren G. Bailey in an article[1] in the 1947 Year Book of the National Association of Cost Accountants which lists the following:

(1) Columnar tabulation.
(2) Title headings.
(3) Item descriptions.
(4) Comparisons.
(5) Measurement of increases and decreases.
(6) Special positions.
(7) Special markings.
(8) Ratios.
(9) Averages.
(10) Accumulations.
(11) Sub-totals.
(12) Repetition.
(13) Footnotes.
(14) Summaries.
(15) Graphs and curves.
(16) Special ruling and boxing.

[1] An article on 'Presentation of Accounting Information—within the Management Group' by Mr. Warren G. Bailey. Published in the 1947 Year Book of the National Association of Cost Accountants, page 129.

(17) Heavy and light lines.
(18) Special type.
(19) Special sizes and colours of paper.
(20) Special holders, binders and files.
(21) Special interpretative comments.

Readers will be well aware that there are many other means of presenting information and of emphasising particular points, but the general ideal might be summed up as follows:

Be selective:
> i.e. present to individuals only the information with which they are concerned and concentrate only upon a few (possibly only one) points at one time.

Be simple:
> i.e. exclude matters which although relevant are not the main issues.

Be short:
> i.e. keep the presentation to a minimum if necessary by using appendices for supporting detail.

One of the biggest and commonest bottlenecks in British industry to-day is the executive who has the authority and responsibility for making decisions but who will not exercise his prerogative. If the accountant can help such an executive to make decisions—speedy and correct ones—he will have done great service to industry.

TRAINING

The training of an industrial accountant can, in this country, follow one of two main courses:

First, he may train and qualify as a practising public accountant by becoming a member of certain of the professional bodies who are sponsoring this Congress. In this case his experience, whether serving under articles or not, will be almost entirely confined to professional work.

Secondly, he may enter industry at a fairly early age, either in the factory or in the office and, while obtaining practical experience in costing and related work, study for, and qualify through, the examinations of the Institute of Cost and Works Accountants.

There are advantages and disadvantages inherent in both these courses. The accountant who qualifies in a public accountant's office and who thereafter takes an appointment in industry, has little knowledge of, or experience in, many or even most of the functions which have been referred to earlier in this paper. The tempo and atmosphere of industry are new to him and are different by far from those to which he has been accustomed. As a general rule, therefore, he starts at a disadvantage when he takes up his appointment. Nevertheless, if he is the right man he brings to industry a wide outlook, the high ethical standards to which he has been accustomed in his professional career and an objective and sufficiently flexible mind to enable him, as a rule, to settle down in his new surroundings as an effective member of management.

The accountant who has been trained in industry is familiar with his surroundings and has a detailed knowledge not only of his own subject but also of those related to it and has an industrial background which is of great assistance to him. It may be because of this training that his outlook, though essentially practical, can tend to be more restricted and focused upon detail. The widening of the scope of the Institute of Cost and Works Accountants' examination now in operation should help to correct this tendency, if it exists.

Recently there has been a significant development affecting the training of the accountant in industry. It is the proposed establishment of the fellowship grade of the Institute of Cost and Works Accountants as a qualification in management accountancy. This, as far as it is known, is the first attempt to provide a professional qualification of this kind, although it is noted that following an article[1] by Professor L. A. Schmidt in the *Controller* of January, 1951, there has been comment in the March, 1951, *Journal of Accountancy*.

In announcing the new Fellowship in the October, 1951, issue of *The Cost Accountant*,[2] the Institute states:

'Fellow membership under the scheme will be given to all Associate Members of the Institute and to members of other accounting organisations provided they pass the Institute's Fellowship examination in those subjects not adequately covered by their own examining bodies and comply with the conditions laid down which prescribe a minimum age limit of 26 years, evidence of five years' experience in, and current engagement in, a responsible position in Management Accountancy.'

This step may well be of great importance in developing the technique of management accountancy and in improving the standard and status of accountants in industry.

There are post-graduate courses for public accountants and for those in industry and lately summer schools, held at a university, have come into prominence. In addition, an accountant in industry may, through his firm, attend the Administrative Staff College at Henley and thus

[1] An article on 'Developing To-morrow's Accounting Manpower' by Professor L. A. Schmidt, published in the *Controller* in January, 1951.
[2] *The Cost Accountant*, published by the Institute of Cost and Works Accountants, October, 1951, page 133.

broaden his outlook by mixing with executives performing either similar or different functions in other firms and industries. Such contacts cannot be other than helpful in developing in the accountant the necessary management outlook as opposed to the purely accounting one.

THE PAST AND THE FUTURE

Growth of Accounting

The charge has often been made against accountants in industry and out of it that they tend to live too much in the past; in fact 'that they are marching backwards into the future with their eyes fixed firmly on the past'. The very nature of the accountant's work has tended to expose him to such a charge and it is difficult to see how he could wholly have avoided it. At the risk of adding further evidence let us consider briefly the reasons for, and the nature of, the development of accountancy and the work of accountants in industry.

Financial accountancy has been influenced by a number of factors, chief among which may be reckoned the divorce of ownership from management, the principle of limited liability and the requirements of company and income-tax law.

Cost accounting, on the other hand, has developed as a result of the increasing size of industrial units and through the requirements of management for more detailed and up-to-date information than is provided by the ordinary financial accounts which are available often much later than the period to which they refer. Again, the annual financial statement of profit and loss account, although it displayed a 'true and correct view' of the results, did not always reveal sufficiently clearly the reasons why such results had emerged.

Thus it is perhaps not unfair to say that much of the impetus towards cost or management accounting has come from the pressure by management for figures which were sufficiently revealing, detailed and up-to-date to guide them in the formulation of policy.

Forecasts

To quote again from the Management Accounting Report,[1] in paragraph 6 on page 14, it states:

'American managements are continually looking towards the future. Their policy is to anticipate and influence events by their decisions rather than merely to carry on as before until events force them to make new decisions.'

If accountants are to assist management to this end, they must be interested in the past only as a guide to the future. They must be con-

[1] 'Productivity Report—Management Accounting'. Published by the Anglo-American Council on Productivity, page 14.

cerned with the preparation of forecasts, with budgetary control, with standard costing, with comparative costing and with any form of information which will serve as a guide to policy and action.

It follows that in order to do this intelligently the industrial accountant must be acquainted with the management outlook and must have a working knowledge of technical processes and problems. In this connection it is probably true to say that 'perception' rather than 'precision' should be the watchword. Balance sheet accuracy is not normally essential.

Major Scott, of Tube Investments Ltd., at a British Institute of Management conference,[1] deliberately misquoting Herrick, said:

> 'A slight disorder in industry's dress,
> Kindling in her a liveliness,
> Does more become her than when Art,
> Is too precise in every part.'

The keyword for industry, and for the accountant, is 'liveliness'.

Decentralisation

In this country, as a result of nationalisation and other factors, industry is tending to be concentrated in larger organisations. This concentration brings with it, sooner or later, the problems associated with the need for decentralisation.

Sir Miles Thomas, of British Overseas Airways Corporation, speaking at a British Institute of Management conference, said:[2]

> 'I suppose most businesses start small and centralised. But at a certain stage of their growth there arrives a point at which they must either decentralise effectively or accept a progressive decline in all vital functions. That is the point at which a psychological decision has to be made. It is a crisis at which probably more businesses have come to wreck than any other.'

Decentralisation, if it is to be efficient, must normally work within the framework of a central policy or strategy. The fulfilment of this requirement depends in no small measure upon the accountant or controller who alone can present a comprehensive picture of the extent to which the policy is being adhered to and whether or not it is proving successful.

Integration

It is generally accepted by accountants in industry that integration of accounts is desirable and that it should not be necessary to maintain

---

[1] Comment on a paper entitled 'The Organisational Structure of Large Undertakings—Management Problems' by Sir Charles Renold.

[2] A paper entitled 'Management in Private Enterprise and Nationalised Industry', by Sir Miles Thomas. Published by the British Institute of Management, page 17.

separate sets of accounts for financial and for cost or management accounting. The aim should rather be so to design the basic data that different information for different people for different purposes can be produced from it.

This integration of accounts, coupled with the increasing co-ordination in the training of accountants earlier referred to, gives rise to the thought that in due course the integration of accounts may well bring with it the integration of accountants.

Whatever may be the outcome, it is perhaps not inappropriate to bear in mind the words of the late John Buchan (Lord Tweedsmuir) who said:

'We can repay our debt to the past only by leaving the future in debt to ourselves.'

CONCLUSION

In concluding this paper it is worth repeating that the views expressed in it may well be challenged and opposed. Indeed, to obtain the benefits of discussion it is hoped that they will be.

To this end, the following hypotheses are presented:

(a) That the industrial and public accountant has, in the past, taken too narrow a view of his responsibilities and has failed fully to appreciate and satisfy the needs of management for accounting information.

(b) That the industrial accountant must devote more attention to the interpretation, as distinct from the preparation, of figures.

(c) That the industrial accountant must be more concerned with business forecasts and should have a working knowledge of management and technical problems.

(d) That integration of accounts must lead eventually to the integration of accountants.

The theme of the discussion must be the improvement of the service which the accountant in industry can give to management. It will, however, be appreciated that the paper is written in the light of conditions in this country; of conditions elsewhere the author can claim no knowledge. Perhaps this is a state of ignorance which may be shared by others, and which may be remedied in the course of the discussion.

APPENDIX I

These accounts are for the purpose of analysing and locating works cost. They form part of the nominal ledger.

Where the same account is required in several departments a departmental prefix will be used in conjunction with the account number.

The main headings (e.g. INDIRECT LABOUR AND MATERIALS) form the basis of the financial accounts and comprise the totals of the detailed accounts in the various groups.

In addition to the index given below, there is a list of accounts giving, where necessary, an explanation and the details of the items included or excluded.

No.	Title	No.	Title
400	Works cost control	433	Buildings and fittings
401	Direct labour	434	Roads, grounds, fences and drains
		435	
	INDIRECT LABOUR AND MATERIALS		Depreciation
402	Supervision	436	Plant and machinery
403	Setting	437	Tools, jigs and fixtures
404	Service labour	438	Buildings and fittings
405	Inspection	439	
406	Internal transport		
407	Craning		POWER, LIGHTING AND HEATING
408	Trainees	440	Electricity
409	Overtime premium	441	Coal
410	Night shift premium	442	Coke
411	Lost time	443	Boilers
412	Scrap	444	Gas
413	Rectification	445	Water
414	Consumable stores	446	Fuel oil
		447	Compressed air
	PRODUCTIVE SERVICES	448	
420	Raw material stores	449	
421	Tool stores		
422	Finished parts stores		WORKS EXPENSES
423		450	Rent
424	Sandblasting	451	Rates
425	Welding	452	
426		453	Insurance—General (works)
427	Pattern shop	454	Insurance—national (works)
		455	
	REPAIRS, MAINTENANCE AND DEPRECIATION	456	Holiday pay—works
	R. & M.	457	
430	Plant and machinery	458	Bonus
431	Electrical plant	459	Canteen—works
432	Tools, jigs and fixtures	460	First aid, medical and welfare
		461	

No.	Title	No.	Title
462	Fire brigade	471	Works clerical staff
463		472	Planning
464		473	Progressing
465		474	Time study
466	Travelling expenses—works	475	Shop clerks
467	Carriage inwards	476	Wages office
468	Returnable packages	477	Buying office
469	Sundry works expenses	478	Jig and tool drawing office
		479	Gatemen and watchmen
	WORKS OFFICES	480	Labour office
470	Works management	481	Laboratory

APPENDIX II

BREAK EVEN CHART

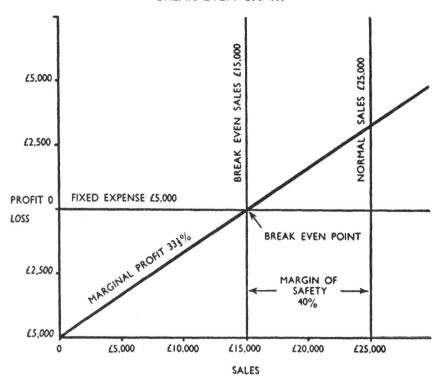

NOTE: The marginal profit is shown as 33⅓ per cent. This percentage may well vary for different products and separate graphs may be drawn for each product or for varying product mixes.

THE ACCOUNTANT IN INDUSTRY

by

CLINTON W. BENNETT, C.P.A.

National Association of Cost Accountants,
United States of America

In attempting to draw a profile of the accountant in industry in the United States it seems desirable to first review briefly the development of industrial accounting and consider the place it occupies to-day in the American industrial enterprise. Against this background the accountant in industry takes on perspective and emerges in more definite form.

HISTORICAL DEVELOPMENT OF INDUSTRIAL ACCOUNTING

Industrial accounting as we know it to-day may be said to have had its start in the United States during the last two decades of the nineteenth century. One who had much to do with this development was the late Frederick W. Taylor, so-called father of scientific management. Dr. Taylor and his associates of that far-away day probably never thought of their pioneering work as industrial accounting, but the big contribution which these men made to the art was the practical idea of setting standards of performance for jobs and of comparing the actual time taken to perform the jobs with these predetermined standards. It is interesting to reflect in these days of highly developed industrial accounting techniques that these pioneers of some seventy-five years ago used all the fundamental principles of the modern standard cost system, with the exception of the continuous control of cost variances through appropriate cost variance accounts.

In the succeeding years and up through the first decade of the twentieth century industrial accounting procedure developed somewhat slowly. Progress seems to have been made more in the area of engineering than accounting. The torch was carried largely by industrialists who experimented with the new methods and found them valuable, and by a small but almost fanatical group of practitioners. The tremendous increase in industrial output brought about by World War I focused attention on the need for industrial accounting methods and procedures. The result was a blending of the work of the scientific management practitioners with that of the accountants. This marriage produced the cost accountant, who operated in an area between and overlapping the work of both the financial accountant and the industrial engineer. The work of the cost accountant usually leaned more heavily on accounting than on engineering techniques and, as a result, the use of job order costs and allocated historical costs came into prominence. However, all during this period a limited but growing number of accountants continued the development of the standard cost or engineering approach to industrial accounting.

During the decade of high business activity in the United States which

281

followed the close of World War I there was a widely expanded acceptance and use of industrial accounting in industry. This coincided with a substantial influx of trained cost accountants into manufacturing positions. Although during this period there was also considerable expansion in the field of management or industrial engineering, which was the successor to the earlier term 'scientific management', the industrial accounting work of that period was largely under the direction of accountants, usually with shop training or experience, rather than engineers. The so-called actual or historical cost concept was widely used and the traditional accountant's love of balancing all cost transactions out to the last penny was indulged in all too often.

The great depression of the early 1930s made it necessary for the business man to re-examine all phases of his organisation to determine whether or not they represented valuable contributions to the business welfare. Those things which could not justify their existence in terms of this test had to be tossed overboard. Industrial accounting naturally had to stand up and be assessed along with all other activities of the business. In many cases the procedures were weighed in the balance and, in the opinion of the executives concerned, found wanting. Not infrequently this elimination or change of methods which was used formerly went too far and, although expenditures were reduced, certain valuable operating information was lost. Out of this crucible, and developed from the white heat of necessity, came a much greater appreciation on the part of the business community of the important contributions which practical industrial accounting can make to the organisation, and a more general understanding of the particular techniques which will best provide management with the tools needed in the day's work. All of this resulted in a greatly expanded use of practical standard cost procedure and a corresponding decline in the use of historical or book-keeping costs. The intense competition of that period had the beneficial result of educating great numbers of executives in the fundamentals of practical industrial accounting, to the great benefit of the business community generally through improved competitive conditions and enlightened operations.

It was well that this broadening of the industrial accounting concept of so many executives took place, otherwise accounting and control problems which were ushered in during World War II and which were phenomenal in scope for most industrial companies might well have been appreciably greater. For nearly ten years prior to the outbreak of World War II, American industry had been operating at low levels of output with price structures geared to these levels. Almost overnight, with the outbreak of the war, came the demand for capacity operations in practically all lines of manufacturing. There was no previous yardstick of measurement which could be used to determine fair prices and probable profits at these new volume levels. In many lines multiple-shift operations were called for where single-shift operations had been the order of the day for many years. Obviously, historical or accounting costs would be of small value to management in its efforts to get fast answers to the pressing problems which were arising on every hand. Hence the experience gained during the lean years in developing practical combined accounting and engineering costs was of utmost value.

MODERN INDUSTRY AND ACCOUNTING

The industrial executive needs two fundamental results from his accounting procedure: (1) a general accounting plan which will record the day-to-day transactions with clarity and in sufficient analysis to make possible the prompt preparation of analytical statements of profit and loss and of condition at the end of each month; and (2) an industrial accounting plan which will show the anticipated cost of all products in the line, the effect of varying volume levels on these costs, and continuously reflect in usable detail any differences which may be found to exist between these anticipated costs and the actual results.

This information is needed particularly by the medium-sized and small American industrial enterprise because, by the very nature of things, the small business has to be more efficient than so-called big business if it is going to compete successfully with giants in its industry.

A few examples will illustrate the practical uses of modern industrial accounting.

An ever-present problem is that of measuring the profitability of the different products which a company makes. Obviously, it is a simple matter to determine the calculated cost of each product and the resulting gain or loss. Therefore why not simply discontinue the unprofitable or marginal products. But unfortunately life is not that simple. Immediately certain questions will arise, such as the effect on the business of the failure to provide a rounded line of products, and the effect on the cost of currently profitable products if they are forced to carry the burden otherwise absorbed by the marginal products. Management is expected to keep the plant busy, which means keeping people employed and earning reasonable profits on the family of products, not necessarily on all specific products. The answer to this question of product-profitability can only be provided by soundly developed accounting and cost information.

When and at what price to sell to a large buyer can pose a serious problem. One of these huge companies may offer the medium-size manufacturer a sufficient volume of business to utilise a sizeable amount of his plant capacity for continuous operation over a long period of time. The buyer will usually want a substantial price concession on the theory that the manufacturer will have practically no selling and little administrative expense. This argument may prove correct provided the manufacturer will discharge people and otherwise reduce selling and administrative expenses commensurate with the desired reduction in price. But unless this is done the regular products will have to bear as additional cost the expenses which will not be recovered in the special price. It is not intended to argue that sales to large buyers of this type are not desirable, but instead to emphasise the fundamental need of adequate industrial accounting and cost information as a means of determining whether or not such business is desirable, as it well may be, and of obviating the possibility of the manufacturer pricing himself out of business.

The industrial executive needs continuous and accurate data in connection with labour costs. Following the great depression of the thirties, labour unions in the United States expanded phenomenally and wages increased substantially. The principle of paying the highest possible wages has been quite generally accepted by American industry for many years. Whether or not any wage can be afforded will depend entirely on whether or not it is earned in terms of production. No wages are too high provided the goods produced can be sold in adequate volume at prices which will return fair profits to the enterprise. Management must have continuous information with respect to the balance that is being achieved between wages and the production received for them.

Not enough attention has been accorded by industrial companies in the United States to the importance of having carefully set up systems of job evaluation to rate the jobs, and merit rating systems to rate the employees who perform the jobs. So-called job evaluation plans are quite generally used, but all too often they fail to do an adequate job. A rather common weakness flows from a confusion of the job as such with the worker who is performing it. An unfortunate result of the industrial system has been the too general failure to recognise the individual as such and to lose him in the mass group of workers simply known as 'labour'. Happily, many industrial companies are recognising this fact and are taking steps to correct it. This can be helped effectively through the proper development and use of merit rating coupled with job evaluation. With this programme in effective operation, the worker, regardless of his job, ceases to be lost in a huge group and becomes recognised as an individual who knows he is under the eyes of management and that good work and loyal service will get commensurate rewards. Probably nothing the accountant can do for his company will be more rewarding than effective work in this important field.

Some Industrial Accounting Techniques

Assistance in obtaining the answers to these and other problems which are continuously arising in industrial enterprises can best be provided by the use of standard costs. But it is not enough simply to have standard costs for all products in the line. The operating conditions which were used as a basis in setting up the standard costs must be definitely known. Fundamentally, the standard costs should reflect the cost of producing a specific product at a given level of output and under an assumed set of circumstances. All of these conditions must be definitely worked out. They represent the time-table of anticipated operations. An essential requirement of the standard cost plan is to provide management with knowledge as to how much can be cut from these standard costs before invading the field of out-of-pocket costs. In other words, in a period of intense competition, what is the point at which the company must stop doing business at a loss in trying to make a profit?

It has been traditional to separate costs into the two divisions of variable costs and fixed costs. To meet the needs of modern business this two-way split is not enough. A three-way cost analysis is essential: (1) out-of-pocket costs; (2) fixed or sunk costs; and (3) semi-fixed costs. Out-of-pocket costs are all those costs which are directly altered by volume—direct material, direct labour and all indirect costs which directly go up or down with the production of goods. The fixed or sunk costs include all expenses and costs which will be present regardless of operating conditions. They include insurance, taxes, depreciation, watchmen's salaries, firemen's salaries, fuel, maintenance and any other kindred costs. Hence, on the one hand will be reflected all costs direct and indirect which vary directly with volume, while on the other will be shown all costs which will be present whether or not the plant is operated. The third element of semi-fixed costs refers to all expenses not allocable to the out-of-pocket or the fixed classifications. These are the salaries and other costs which management believes are essential in order to operate efficiently at the anticipated volume levels, and yet would have to be pruned in case of bad business. It would, for example, be impossible for management to reach a sound conclusion with respect to the advisability of taking special-price business from large buyers as discussed previously without cost knowledge broken down in accordance with this three-way split. This analytical information is also essential if the management is to determine intelligently the profitability of various products in the line.

Management needs monthly profit and loss statements which are co-ordinated with the cost control programme. Cost of sales should be obtained by pricing shipments at standard costs and not as the result of taking inventories. It should be emphasised that this procedure refers to income statements for management purposes and not to those prepared for general financial purposes at the end of the fiscal year or other period. The uses of the two income statements are very different. For financial reporting purposes the income statements should show the results of operating the business. This information is not sufficient for management purposes. Management must know continuously from month to month, not only the results of operations, but, in addition, these results must be known by classes of products costed on the basis of the standard costs which have been based on the management's operating programme. In this way management can determine the operating results that would be provided by the orthodox income statement. But more important, management will also know: (1) how these standards or predetermined costs compare with the sales dollars received for the products; (2) how much this resulting profit on the basis of standard costs will have to be adjusted upward or downward to reflect differences between anticipated and operating results; and (3) reasons for the differences. The reasons for the differences will be obtained from the monthly analysis of cost variances which, under certain operating conditions, may be the most important executive report that management receives.

Many companies operate quite complete and detailed budget systems which start with the sales forecast and follow through the various points of control to the income statement and the balance sheet. Not infrequently these companies continuously co-ordinate operating results with budgeted anticipations to obtain variances in all important phases of operations.

It should be emphasised that these completely budgeted situations are the exception and not the rule. It should, however, also be pointed out that wherever standard costs are used, whether or not they are tied in to the financial books of account, some form of budgeting will be found.

STATUS OF THE ACCOUNTANT IN INDUSTRY

It is obvious from a review of this brief outline that the job of the accountant in industry is an important one and that the person who fills it satisfactorily must have stature. He may, for example, be known in his company as treasurer, controller, chief accountant, auditor, but whatever his title, the chief accountant in industry is a man of importance and if he measures up to his opportunities he is likewise a man of substantial value. As opportunities for the accountant have widened, his responsibilities have naturally kept pace. At times he is in a rather difficult position. He is a member of the management team. In this capacity he is subordinate to the chief executive of the company. Yet he is a professional man, even though all of his time may be devoted to the work of a single employer. Parenthetically, it seems clear that the test of a professional man is the type of work he does and the attitude of mind which he brings to the day's work. The accountant who devotes all of his time to the affairs of a single company may be every bit as much a professional man as his brother who serves a number of companies. So the industrial accountant, although subordinate to the chief executive, is a professional man and as such he has definite responsibilities to third parties who may rely on accounting reports upon which he has placed his approval. The accountant in industry who issues financial statements to be used by third parties, which he knows to be false in any particular or which he should have known to be false had he exercised the care and prudence expected of a trained man, does so at his personal peril, and he could be estopped from pleading in his defence that his superior officer ordered him to take the steps which he took. Hence, more and more, the accountant in industry is in his responsibilities achieving somewhat the same position as the certified public accountant in public practice who must at all times maintain an independent position with respect to all parties. There are some who believe that the chief accountant in industry should report directly to the board of directors and not to the chief executive of the company, since as a professional man he should be independent of the operating management. This idea would obviate the peculiar position of the accountant as referred to above. Theoretically, a good case can be made for the principle of having the chief accountant report directly to the board of directors, but from a practical standpoint the plan is unsound. As a matter of good organisation, the president of the company, or the chief executive, regardless of his title, is engaged by the board of directors and held responsible by the board for his actions and for the results of the company under his direction. It is essential therefore that he have a free hand in all phases of operation, including the hiring and firing of personnel. As a practical matter, therefore, if the chief accountant is part of the management team but, at the same time required to report to the board of directors, he will be placed in an impossible position the first time he takes an important stand with the board in conflict with the ideas of the chief executive. In practice, the only way this procedure would work would be for the board of directors to engage the chief accountant and have him report directly to the board, and in no way be responsible to the chief executive. This would seem to add an unwieldy step to the business organisation and details to the work of the board which ought not to be performed by its members. It seems quite generally accepted practice in the United States for the chief accountant to report directly to the chief executive of the enterprise. If, however, the occasion arises wherein he finds himself faced with instructions from his superior which would require him to do something which he, as a trained professional man, knows he ought not to do, his course of action must be quite clear. He must (1) either convince the superior officer of the necessity for conforming to proper and accepted procedure or (2) resign. Ethically speaking, an accountant cannot compromise on a fundamental issue of this sort and, practically speaking, doing what he knows to be the right thing will prove to be good business. It may keep him out of jail.

Not only is the accountant in industry an important member of the management team but there is an increasing tendency to include him in top management committees and not infrequently on the board of directors. It is also interesting to note the substantial number of chief executives of American industrial companies who started as accountants. With the continuing growth and complexity of American business it would seem reasonable to assume that the accountant in industry will play an increasingly important part in industrial councils and will find ever-widening opportunities for service.

SOME SOCIAL IMPLICATIONS

The accountant in industry is becoming increasingly conscious of the social aspects of his work. With industry operating at high levels of output so essential to mass production enterprises and with competition ever present, the costing concepts of the accountant can have far-reaching effects on the successful operations of his company.

Unsound costing procedure coupled with unsound methods of price determination could well serve to price a company out of a competitive market. Under the most favourable circumstances a delicate balance must necessarily exist between the three fundamental elements of wages, prices and profits. When one of these elements gets out of balance with respect to the others, difficulties develop and as an indication of the magnitude of the troubles which may flow from unbalance in this area it is only necessary to recall the economic history of the not too distant past.

The first and fundamental job of business must be to serve the public interest. There are some who believe that the first job of a business enterprise is to make profits. Obviously, unless adequate profits are earned no business enterprise will long endure. But if the enterprise exists solely to earn profits for the owners, it is most decidedly not carrying its load in the modern social structure. This job of serving the public interest requires that: (1) business constantly strives to get more goods to more people at the lowest possible prices; and (2) to the greatest extent possible provides a job for every person who wants one and at the highest possible wage. All segments of society in the United States are realising more and more that full employment at high wages is essential if the American system of a free economy is to survive in a world that has been drifting toward totalitarianism. Excepting in periods of national emergency there is no place for spread-the-work methods or other imposed limitations on output.

The public attitude towards business is going to depend more and more upon the job that business does in meeting these fundamental, highly important social problems. For the first time in recorded history we are rapidly developing an industrial system that is capable of producing all the things that we need and want, but we have much to learn about how to bring to all the people the high standards of living which this system can make possible. In this tremendous job the accountant in industry has a marvellous opportunity for service and, by the same token, a grave responsibility.

THE ACCOUNTANT IN INDUSTRY

by

A. A. FITZGERALD, B.COM., F.I.C.A., F.C.A.A.

Commonwealth Institute of Accountants, Australia

I. INTRODUCTION

This paper is a brief assessment of the status and responsibilities of the accountant in Australian industry, with some comments on the reasons why management accounting in Australia is not yet fully developed, and on the prospects of progressing towards that ideal.

Australia is a highly industrialised country, and it is steadily becoming even more so. In 1901 manufacturing industry employed 18 per cent. of the total work force: by 1939 it employed 25 per cent., and to-day it employs 28 per cent. This is a higher proportion than in U.S.A. (26 per cent.) or in Canada (24 per cent.), but well below that in the United Kingdom (39 per cent.). Another 37 per cent. of the Australian work force is engaged in building and construction, transport and communication, and commerce and finance. The total work force is 3½ million people.

But Australian industrial units are mostly small-scale. Although there are 37,000 factories, 34,000 of them have 50 or less employees, and only 140 have more than 500. U.S.A. has 3,800 industrial *firms*, the United Kingdom nearly 2,400 *factories*, and Canada 350 *establishments*, with more than 500 employees.

It is, therefore, hardly to be expected that management accounting should be as fully used in Australia as it is in U.S.A., the United Kingdom or Canada. The need for accounting information, and the likelihood that management will be fully aware of that need are naturally greater in countries which have more large-scale industrial units.

Nevertheless, the accounting profession in Australia is well established: modern accounting methods are known and practised and, in recent years, there has been extraordinary improvement in the art of accounting and in the status of the accountant in industry. There has also been a spectacular increase in the number of qualified accountants. Total membership of the five major institutes[1] now exceeds 18,000. Even when allowance is made for the fact that many accountants are members of two or more of the institutes, this is a large number for a country with a population of 8½ million. Since 1919, the number of members of the Federal Institute has grown from 700 to 7,500 and that of the Commonwealth Institute from 1,300 to 6,000.

There is a noticeable tendency for public accountants to transfer to posts in industry. The Institute of Chartered Accountants in Australia was founded

[1] In order of numbers of members, these are: Federal Institute of Accountants, Commonwealth Institute of Accountants, Institute of Chartered Accountants in Australia, Association of Accountants of Australia and Australasian Institute of Cost Accountants.

exclusively for public accountants: members who cease to be engaged in public accounting, either as principals or as employees, are transferred to a 'separate list' of members. In 1939, 18 per cent. of the members were on the separate list: in 1944, the proportion was 22 per cent., and it is now 27 per cent.

The latest report of the Council of the Institute speaks of the tendency for candidates to 'move from the profession to commercial appointments before they have completed their final examination'. This implies that accountants in industry are not in the profession—a view which is unacceptable to the other institutes, each of which has a large number of members who are not in public practice.[1] Eighty-three per cent. of the members of the Commonwealth and Federal institutes, 92 per cent. of the members of the Association of Accountants of Australia and 89 per cent. of the members of the Australasian Institute of Cost Accountants are not in public practice.

The Status of the Accountant in Australian Industry

The belief that the status of the accountant in Australian industry has been raised, and that it is still improving, is shared by several accountants and industrial managers whose opinions have been sought while this paper was being prepared. It is supported also by the conclusions arrived at in recent group discussions within the Australian Institute of Management.

There is, however, some uncertainty as to the scope of accounting responsibility, and as to the precise relationship between the accountant and management.

For example, a research group of the Melbourne Division of the Australian Institute of Management, reporting in 1948, classified accounting as a service department, and budgeting as a staff department. Separation of accounting and budgeting in this way is manifestly based upon a narrow concept of the scope of accounting.

The group thought that 'accounting is a service to line departments which are accountable to the chief executive', but went on to say that 'common delegation of the duty of budgetary control to the accounting department gives that department authority over line departments'.

On the other hand, a discussion group of the Adelaide Division of the same institute in 1950 stated the four major line functions in a typical repetition-engineering plant as Sales, Engineering, Manufacturing and Finance: the responsibilities of the finance department included company finance, secretarial service, cost accounting and control, general accounting, budgeting and internal audit. This concept of the status and scope of accounting was arrived at by the group after discussion extending over several meetings: in the early stages some members of the group contended that there should be only two major line departments—production and sales.

Thus, despite the difference in approach, both groups conceded high status to the accountant, in theory at least. To test the extent to which this theory is

[1] See, for example, N. S. Young: 'The Status of the Accountant in Australia', *Proceedings of the Australian Congress on Accounting* (November, 1949).

applied in practice, some sixty medium- and large-scale Australian industrial companies were asked to supply copies of their management-organisation charts.

About half of the companies intimated that they did not use such charts. Some of these companies, however, commented on the degree of importance which they attached to accounting. Many of the charts supplied by other companies were also accompanied by comments. The comments and the charts showed that, almost invariably, finance and accounting are regarded as a major department, ranking more or less on the same level as Sales, Production and Engineering (methods, research and development), whether it is classified as a line, a staff or a service department.

Typical comments were:

1. *By a public accountant, who is in close touch with many large industrial concerns:*

   'The status of the accountant, particularly in industrial undertakings, is steadily increasing in importance. He is rapidly becoming one of the vital cogs in the wheel of management. His status, function and responsibility would be vastly enhanced if only he were better trained and equipped to assume that superior role. Industry generally wants to make greater use of the accountant: it is up to him to answer that call.'

2. *By a managing director, who holds high office in the Associated Chambers of Manufacturers of Australia:*

   'Each (of the two accounting divisions—general and costing) has number one priority. The cost accounting division takes full responsibility for constant daily check on costs and efficiency: other functional heads look to the cost-accounting department to keep them thoroughly informed on every aspect of the figure work. The Secretary-Treasurer's work is equally important: it includes the preparation of a monthly balance sheet.'

3. *By the managing director of a company incorporated in New South Wales:*

   'As the years go by our accountants will come to enjoy equal status with senior executive engineers and sales executives: the calibre of each accountant must, however, be of such high standard as to justify this recognition.'

4. *By the managing director of a company incorporated in Victoria:*

   'The finance manager, who is in charge of major finance, costing and accounting, is one of the several top-line executives reporting to the managing director or to two assistant managing directors. The work of the internal audit (which in this company is at present a staff function not under the control of the finance manager) is of vast importance, and we are trying to raise its status and to lay it down that it exists not only to check figures and cash beyond the scope of the normal company audit, but to check up on the business methods and practices of the company, its methods of entering into commitments, and so on.'

5. *By a company secretary:*

   'The importance attached by this company to accounting and the value of experience in the accounting department is indicated by the position occupied by the accountant in the organisation chart: it is also indicated by the fact that a number of top-management personnel have been recruited from the accounting department.'

The main features of the twenty-eight charts which were supplied may be summarised thus:

(a) in eighteen instances, the head of the finance and accounting department is directly responsible to the managing director or the general manager;

(b) in thirteen instances, all secretarial and accounting work is combined under the control of one principal officer;

(c) in nine instances, the cost accountant is responsible directly to the managing director or the general manager, in two instances to a finance director, in four instances to an assistant general manager, and in thirteen instances to the head of the finance and accounting department;

(d) in eight instances, financial accounting and management accounting are divided into separate sections at the highest level of the finance and accounting department: in most other instances, this separation takes place at one stage below the highest level; and

(e) internal audit is usually included in the work of the accounting division: in only two instances is it separated from accounting, but in one instance it is divided into two sets of responsibilities, one coming within the scope of accounting (control) and the other within the scope of accounting (records).

The companies selected for this survey may be taken as a fair sample of medium- and large-scale industrial units. Judged by the sample, the characteristic features of the relationship of accounting to boards of directors and to management in Australia are:

(i) usually the company secretary enjoys higher status than the chief accountant: the accountant is often responsible to the secretary and not directly to the managing director or the general manager, and the secretary regularly attends board meetings and often participates, in greater or less degree, in policy discussions, whereas the accountant rarely does so;

(ii) management accounting and financial accounting are usually sharply distinguished from each other; and

(iii) a relatively minor role has so far been assigned to the internal auditor: nevertheless, there is reason to think that his status, and the range of his responsibilities, may rapidly be increased.

Despite the comment by a company secretary which has been quoted above, the accountant in Australian industry normally does not participate to any great extent in policy-making, nor is an accounting training generally accepted as a good preparation for senior managerial posts. There are, of course, many instances of recruits from the accounting department who have become able and successful managers. In such instances, the reason for the accountant's success as manager is probably his strength of personality and his innate managerial ability, rather than his accounting training.

MANAGEMENT ACCOUNTING TECHNIQUE

Methods of management accounting as practised overseas, particularly in U.S.A., are well known to Australian accountants, and they are becoming still better known, even if they are not yet as extensively, or as intensively, used as they might be. A sentence in the report of the Management Accounting Team from the United Kingdom which visited U.S.A. in 1950 could be applied with equal force to Australian conditions:

'The effectiveness of American management and accounting rests not on technical superiority, but on their thorough application of techniques which are as well known in Britain as they are in the United States.'[1]

Standard-cost systems and budgetary control have been taught in the six universities and in the large technical colleges for many years. American and English texts on management accounting are available, in most of the capital cities, in the libraries of the accounting institutes, the Australian Institute of Management and the teaching institutions. There is a small, but steadily expanding, Australian literature of good quality. Active and interested studies are carried on in discussion groups which have been organised by at least three of the institutes. The advantages, and indeed the indispensable need, of cost accounting have been brought well under the notice of manufacturers, through the requirements of price-control authorities, of government procurement departments and, in many instances, of bankers.

Many manufacturers who became accustomed during the war, for the first time, to the use of cost finding as a means of price determination have since learned to use cost analysis for management-control purposes. Wartime conditions provided the opportunity for many Australian accountants to put into practice, and to adapt to Australian conditions, theories which they had studied from overseas text-books.

In 1945, a research group of the Australasian Institute of Cost Accountants made a survey of inventory-accounting practices in Victorian industry. With the assistance of the Victorian Chamber of Manufacturers, the group addressed to a number of members of the chamber a questionnaire covering a variety of aspects of inventory accounting, including the extent to which standard costs were used. Replies received from 248 manufacturing concerns showed that approximately one-third of them operated a standard-cost system.[2] The proportion is probably much higher to-day.

The survey, of course, was confined mainly to the larger firms and did not cover any of the very small units which comprise the great majority of Australian factories. Nevertheless, it showed that, despite the comparative youth of Australian industry, and the fact that for many years most Australian businesses have been operating in a seller's market, in which the pressure of competition has not been strong, one of the most important devices of modern accounting controls is in fairly common use. Budgetary control is even more commonly practised.

The accountant in Australian industry has at least begun to fulfil his

[1] *Management Accounting*, Anglo-American Council on Productivity, page 6.
[2] *Cost Bulletin No.* 2, Australasian Institute of Cost Accountants.

destiny. The use of accounting controls to promote efficiency will doubtless extend rapidly, particularly if pressures on management are intensified within the next year or two, as now seems probable. But there is a long way to go before it can truly be said that management accounting in Australia is fully developed and fully used.

In particular, much remains to be done in providing better education and training for accountants, in designing improved methods and forms of accounting reports to management, in cultivating mutual understanding between accountants and managers, in showing managers how to use accounting reports, and in putting an end to the suspicion with which much of the work of the accountant has hitherto been regarded. In all these directions something has been done, and more is being attempted. But much more is needed.

HINDRANCES AND PROSPECTS

There have been serious hindrances to progress in the use of accounting as an aid to management. In small-scale industrial units, there is usually neither opportunity for full use of accounting services, nor possibility of obtaining such services at a reasonable cost. Moreover, in such units, managers are frequently unaware of the nature, and the range, of the information which accounting can provide, and accountants have done little to enlighten them.

The public-accounting branch of the profession has been preoccupied with difficult problems of general accounting—the form of published financial statements, taxation, auditing, price-control and the like—and has had little time, and apparently less inclination, to interest itself in the development of cost accounting. An especially serious consequence has been that general accounting and cost accounting have come to be looked upon as separate and unrelated, in study as well as in practice. There is an almost complete absence of integration of accounting records and statements, and a deplorable lack of a sense of unity of purpose between public accountants and accountants in industry.

In both branches of the profession, convention has been a strong influence. Australian accountants are naturally conservative: there is a noticeable disinclination to change methods and forms which have been in use for a long time. Some forms of accounting statements, such as the conventional trading 'account', which are ill-adapted to an integrated accounting system, are still in general use. On the other hand, many of the cost-accounting systems which have been installed have been over-elaborate, costly to operate, and productive of little useful information: often, such little information as they have provided has been presented in stereotyped and unimaginative form. In many instances, cost accounting has become a routine process, instead of a flexible and adaptable tool of management.

The professional institutes are uneasy about existing facilities for recruiting, educating and training entrants to the profession. Complaints are frequently heard of the low standard of general education of candidates, of the neglect of candidates to make proper use of the facilities which are available for academic study, and of the lack of adequate means of technical training in modern accounting method.

To outside observers this may seem to be a depressing picture. Possibly, many Australian accountants will think it overdrawn. Fortunately, there are good prospects of improvement in several respects.

In the first place, accounting as a career is becoming more attractive to both teachers and students, so that candidates with good school records are coming forward in increasing numbers. Stimulated by the support of some of the institutes, the universities and technical colleges have raised their standards of teaching and examining, and are planning to raise them still higher.

The Australian Institute of Management, a young and active body with Divisions in several States, is doing valuable work in organising study of the theory and practice of management. The establishment of this institute has provided a means of improving mutual understanding between managers and accountants, through co-operation between it and accountancy institutes.

The accountancy institutes are doing useful work among their members and students through publication of journals and bulletins, sponsoring of text-books, organisation of lectures, conventions and discussion groups, and maintenance of libraries. They could do even better work if their resources—of funds, equipment and leadership—were concentrated.

As this paper is being written (November, 1951) negotiations for amalgamation are proceeding between two of the large institutes. These negotiations seem to have much better chances of success than any of the several abortive attempts which have been made during the past thirty years. It is to be hoped that the amalgamation will have been consummated by the time the paper is presented.

Perhaps the most refractory problem yet to be faced by Australian accountants is how to adapt accounting-control methods to the needs of small-scale industry and how to make those methods available economically to small business units. Probably that difficulty is being experienced everywhere. Australian accountants are anxious to learn all they can of how it is being faced in other countries.

THE ACCOUNTANT IN INDUSTRY

by

H. HJERNØ JEPPESEN
*Foreningen af Statsautoriserede Revisorer,
Denmark*

THE PRINCIPAL DANISH TRADES

Denmark is generally considered to be a typical agricultural country, and it would probably be helpful to quote some figures indicating the comparative size of Danish industries.

In May, 1951, the total number of men in employment in Denmark was 1,898,000. Of these, 438,000 were employed in farming, market-gardening, forestry and fisheries, and 640,000 in handicraft and industry.

The total Danish gross national income in the year 1951 amounted to 24,686 million kr. This figure included: from agriculture, 4,500 million kr.; from industry, handicraft and public works, 7,960 million kr.; from wholesale and retail trade, etc., 4,387 million kr.; from shipping and transport, 2,082 million kr.

From 1st January to 30th November, 1951, the export of industrial articles amounted to 2,018 million kr., while the agricultural export during the same period amounted to 3,000.9 million kr.

A substantial part of the work of Danish 'chartered' accountants is performed for industrial companies but no statistics are available to throw further light on its extent.

THE ACCOUNTANCY PROFESSION AND INDUSTRY

The development of an independent, active accountancy profession in Denmark belongs to this century, and the first 'chartered' accountants received their certificate from the Ministry of Commerce in 1910.

At the beginning of 1952 there were 400 such accountants in Denmark, 90 per cent. of whom were owners or managers of accountancy firms or were employed as assistants in such firms.

In Denmark the basis of the position of accountants in relation to public authorities and to the public is the trade law and a supplementary decree concerning the activities, duties and responsibility of 'chartered' accountants, together with a series of special laws dealing with their employment.

The accountant's certificate is issued by the Ministry of Commerce, upon the applicant's production of evidence that he meets the prescribed requirements, which include an examination by a committee appointed by the Ministry. Before submitting to the exacting test—including a theoretical as well as a practical examination—the vast majority of applicants have acquired the accounting diploma of the Commercial College, which requires a four to five years' study of general theoretical economy as well as a special knowledge of accounting, particularly concerning the problem of internal accounting in industry. According to statistics, the average time of preparation for the examination (i.e. including the accounting diploma) is about ten years and the average age of applicants when passing the final test is about thirty-two years. Before the establishment of their own firms, accountants generally spend some years as senior assistants of an accountancy firm.

The accountancy profession is very much regulated by the Danish law. It lays down specific standards of professional ability and imposes penal regulations as well as regulations concerning the cancellation and suspension of certificates.

The law makes it compulsory that 'chartered' accountants are employed in a number of specified cases, e.g. in the audit of joint-stock companies whose shares are entered at the Stock Exchange, in the audit of banks, savings banks and certain other credit institutions, and in the large unemployment insurance and health insurance societies. They are also employed as a confidence-engendering link between trading companies and shareholders, creditors and the public, to a greater extent than provided for by law. Industry, too, has in a great measure employed such accountants for the modernisation of accounting and calculation, for efficiency improvement in other fields, and also as advisers in numerous cases. As previously mentioned, no less than 10 per cent. of Denmark's 400 'chartered' accountants have deposited their certificates so as to proceed to employment outside the firm of practising accountants, and several of these accountants are in public employment or employed by financial institutions and other non-industrial enterprises. There exists a strong tendency to employ persons who have passed the accountants' examination for filling leading posts within industrial accounting, control and internal audits. Since the difficulties in connection with the establishment of private practices have grown in consequence of the growing number of independent 'chartered' accountants, an increasing number of newly qualified accountants seek employment in industry.

The accountancy profession is, however, represented in industry to a greater extent than the above-mentioned figures would indicate. After a practical training of several years in the profession, and perhaps after passing the theoretical test of the accountants' examination, a considerable number of partially qualified individuals have found employment in industry, preferring to use their practical experience to obtain a safe living at once, rather than facing a period of qualifying service which combines a hard day's work with intensive private study terminating possibly with failure in the final examination.

The accountancy profession possess in the Foreningen af Statsautoriserede Revisorer an organisation which safeguards the professional interests externally and internally, and supervises and contributes to the accomplishment of the general and specific duties of its accountants. The Opinion Committee has given many significant opinions, particularly on subjects concerning industrial accounts, and through its organ *Revision og Regnskabsvæsen* (Auditing and Accounting) the association has in particular been dealing with problems of interest to industrial economy and accounting. The association recently appointed a committee to discuss the terminology of industrial accounting.

The accountants' associations in Denmark, Finland, Norway and Sweden are in close co-operation through 'The Scandinavian Accountants Secretariat' and hold Scandinavian accountants' conferences at regular intervals. The Scandinavian languages are so closely related that conversation and reading require no translation, and experiences and viewpoints concerning industrial accounting and audit affairs, gathered in one country, will immediately become the object of an exchange of opinions with colleagues in the sister nations.

THE ACCOUNTANT'S GENERAL EXTERNAL FUNCTIONS

Regarding his responsibility toward those who read the accounts controlled and endorsed by him (e.g. shareholders, banks, creditors and public authorities), the accountant appointed by the general meeting of an industrial joint-stock company or the accountant appointed by a private manufacturer will be in the same position as in other countries. Only special features of interest to colleagues in some other countries will therefore be mentioned.

The Danish Companies Act dates back to 1930; accountants and people dealing with accounting were not consulted and did not exercise any influence upon its provisions concerning accounting and audit. The provisions did not coincide with progressive viewpoints when the law was enacted, so that the Act must now be considered ineffective and inadequate, particularly in comparison with the German Joint-Stock Companies Act of 1937, the Swedish Act of 1944 and the British Companies Act of 1948. However, certain opinions have been established concerning good accounting and accountantship, which must form the basis of the accountant's decisions.

For example, it is normally considered insufficient to make annual audits only: instead, audits must be carried on in accordance with the prevailing conditions in the course of the year. Special audit records must be kept, to be submitted at the board meetings. The entries made in the course of the year, and when accounts are taken, are often of particular assistance in the board's evaluation of the accounts. These records are not submitted to the general meeting, which only learns the accountant's view on the economy of the company through a brief statement on the accounts.

The management prepares the accounts, which are approved by the board of directors and submitted to the accountant for endorsement. Therefore the latter exercises no influence upon the preparation of the accounts but can, under the provisions of the law, only express his opinion through his endorsement. It sometimes happens that the management does not realise the significance of the publication of facts, and that the accounts do not give the details of the business carried on by an industrial company. The accountant may, however, often enforce a reasonable amplification of the accounts, so that the specific activities of the company are justly reflected in the operations account and balance sheet for the guidance of shareholders as well as

BRIGADIER S. O. JONES, O.B.E., M.C.

Chief Executive Officer of the Congress

employees and workers. As a true and informative summary of the detailed internal accounts, the external accounts ought to give a true statement concerning the operations of the company, as well as indicating its financial status.

If the accountant cannot arrange for an adequate form of statement, and the operations accounts contain only the items of gross proceeds, trade charges, certain depreciations, the net proceeds and their distribution, he will have no proper means of analysing the operational conditions of the company. Since, however, the information that the law requires to be submitted to the interested parties is contained in the above items, he will not have failed in his legal obligation to those who read the accounts by not obtaining the information necessary to enable him to carry out an analysis.

With its constant new installations, maintenance, improvements, depreciations, technical and other experiments, industrial activity offers many taxation problems, especially since taxation legislation does not adopt the principle of caution and conservative tendencies to the same extent as the legislation on joint-stock companies. The accountant's endorsement on the industrial account does not, of course, vouch correctness in respect of taxation, since a statement on that subject will require a closer study of the operational accounts, based on viewpoints other than those relating to joint-stock companies legislation. The skilled industrial accountant may, however, by embarking upon this work and by making a special endorsement or report to that effect, give valuable assistance to his client.

THE ACCOUNTANT'S GENERAL INTERNAL FUNCTIONS

Although considerable reluctance has been demonstrated in respect of expanding external statements of accounts, there has been a great increase in the interest in internal accounts during the last ten to fifteen years. Industrial leaders frequently possess no special training in accounting, but this very fact strongly calls for a clear and unambiguous submission of accounts. Interpretation of the results can best be made by an accountant who not only can familiarise himself with the economy of the industrial company but can also explain it to those whose qualifications or interest lie in other fields. The informative part of the accountant's activities has emerged as a by-product of his dealing with data which must be fully surveyed, if the audit of the accounts is to be successfully undertaken. The accountant therefore makes a thorough study of the technical and administrative organisation of the industrial company; sometimes he must provide a description of the work performed in all divisions for the purpose of preparing the auditing scheme and keeping it constantly up to date. During his audit he takes notes, provides specifications and analyses, and makes comparisons with figures from previous periods, from budgets and possibly also from other companies, e.g. through statistics from trade associations. The independent accountant extracts, during his preparatory work, as well as during the audit itself, a flow of information which it would be natural to utilise for more than the preparation of the figures for a concentrated statement of accounts.

L

Certain fields of the accountant's work are gradually expanded beyond the requirements of his main task, and, through an adequate reporting technique, he makes a productive effort by contributing toward a better utilisation of the accounts as a tool of management.

Many large industrial companies have an internal auditing division. Provided it be sufficiently independent, and its work satisfactory, the external accountant may rely upon it. His work will then consist in determining, in consultation with the executive of the auditing division, the methods and the extent of the work, supervising the proper performance of that work and checking the reports and remarks of the internal audit, including the examination of special conditions. In a large company, the director of accounts and the executive of the internal auditing division will generally prepare many statements and reports, which the external accountant will prepare for smaller companies, but this will rarely mean that there is no need for informative work from the external accountant. Maybe it will make heavier demands on his qualifications, foresight and creative imagination than when he is dealing with smaller businesses; but the possibility will also exist that the external expert can make interpretations and give impulses in fields where the personnel of the industrial company will not be able to utilise facts in the same way.

The accountant takes care that reports on accounting matters are sent regularly to the management, and that the reports can 'stand alone', i.e. be read without prior knowledge, and that they are simple and worded without the use of professional accountancy terminology, which will often not be clear to the board or the technicians, and which is almost always unnecessary. In the preparation of statements, account-like summaries are to be avoided and significance should be attached to clarity. The text should not be worded in telegraphic style but in such a way that oral submission at a meeting is facilitated. It should be the endeavour to standardise the reports so that reference can easily be made from one report to another. Extraordinary factors should be underlined. The reports must be useful; their value is proportional to the amount of work (and expense to the company) which their preparation involves.

In industrial companies, periodical specifications and analyses are sometimes prepared because they once were useful, though they are no longer of any value. The accountant may do good by doing away with or simplifying superfluous forms.

The auditing records prescribed by Danish law are a natural instrument for the submission of information for the management, but should not, as a matter of course, be filled with routine-produced statements. The records must contain such *important* information as the accountant wants definitely to bring to the attention of the board.

Reporting should not only serve the purpose of being some sort of a historical survey. The management is not satisfied to learn that the costs of production amount to this or that, but will ask for the reason; its aim lies all the time in planning developments to the advantage of the company. This should be remembered in wording the report.

SOME OTHER ACTIVITIES

Industries vary so much and the tasks are so different that a few examples may be mentioned of the accountant's activities.

It often happens that the accountant is requested to give his opinion concerning the distribution of costs, or the calculation of cost prices and profit in industrial companies, which perhaps produce different articles in many different divisions. The accounting section, dealing every day with ingeniously invented systems of distribution of costs by means of codes and prescribed formulas concerning the proportion between costs and certain quantities or values, is often inclined to attribute too great a significance to its calculations. The correctness of the results need not necessarily be proportionate to the complexity of the system. The accountant bases his work on the proposition that, in the case of a combined production, no particular method of distribution can claim to be the only correct one. Sometimes he holds quite different views (e.g. concerning depreciation of plant, the use of overhead charges in the calculations, and the significance of external price development to replacements) than those corresponding to the traditions of the company. In Denmark, at any rate, several industrial companies which carefully watch technical development and provide their engineers with the newest results of research, have not let their accounting system benefit by the same watchfulness.

Calculations concerning prices, quantities and costs, particularly in respect of standard rates, the company's 'breakeven point', the problems of utilising capacity, the effect of production for export at other prices than those of the home market, and so on, provide a tremendous field for the accountant's work.

Sometimes the accountant must take a stand on costs and profits from other points of view than those dictated by cost accounting policy. This happens if the Government Price Control Board, with powers conferred by special laws and regulations, establishes ceilings for prices and profits. This applies, for example, to corporations sole or aggregate, whose agreements or practices may greatly influence problems of price, production, turnover, or transportation in the whole country or in particular areas. There may be divergences of opinion between the individual industrial company and the price control authorities concerning the costs which may be included in the calculations of the price of a certain article; since the price control law does not cover export sales, conditions may become very complicated and give rise to several considerations, calculations and interpretations.

The accountant's investigations may include previous financial periods, to ascertain whether price regulations have been violated, or they may serve the purpose of producing material for negotiations concerning the fixation of future prices and profits. Controls may have to be set up to ensure the observance of fixed profits and for this purpose special calculation and accounting systems may be required. It may be one of the accountant's tasks to prepare such systems and to exercise constant supervision.

The accountant's work concerning future financial periods may consist in the preparation of budgets, summaries of financial requirements and other financial plans. Such work requires a very considerable knowledge of all details of the industrial company and will consequently give the best results if the accountant is in close touch with the company. Even if data has to be obtained from several executives, the accountant will be able to give the assistance derived from mastering the technique of analysis and budgeting. The work may also include the fixation of standards to be used in future calculations; here the accountant must often establish close co-operation with the engineers of the company (e.g. concerning time control) in order to find a suitable basis for expressing expectations in figures. The preparation of methods to enable executives to discharge their management responsibilities may lie in the border-land between the respective fields of work of accountants and engineers.

COMPLETE REORGANISATION OF THE ACCOUNTING SYSTEM OF INDUSTRIAL COMPANIES

Improved efficiency in accounting methods may in recent years often have been brought about by the requirements of the price control authorities for more detailed calculations, rather than by the desire of the management itself for better systematisation and control.

The introduction of modern uniform accounting systems has often been appreciated by the staff responsible for the daily routine work of the accounting section, as well as by the management, which benefits by the monthly review of available material. The appreciation has, however, seldom been immediately evident. Often the initial difficulties are considerable, and if the accountant has recommended the transition to a uniform accounting system he will almost always be blamed for these difficulties, even if they may have been caused by an untrained staff. The accountant must never be afraid of suggesting something because reproaches may appear later on—if everybody had acquiesced with the old views and traditions, the industrial era would not have come at all. Human sluggishness must be included in the accountant's consideration concerning the tactics to be followed when—for the benefit of the company—he sponsors a change which may be beset with initial difficulties.

If there exists a uniform accounting system, prepared by the trade organisations for the branch of industry concerned, the accountant will profit by it, but there will generally be so many individual elements that the system can only be used as a basis for further work. In fields where uniformity can be established the standard system should be tried, because useful comparative material between several companies can thus be provided. To companies which are members of cartels or links of concerns, uniformity in the system employed is often so significant that it will be an important task for the accountant to establish uniformity, if this has not already been done.

DEVELOPMENT OF ACCOUNTANT'S WORK IN INDUSTRY

As already mentioned, very few 'chartered' accountants are permanently attached to an individual industrial company and the subject has here been mainly discussed from the point of view of the accountant who runs an independent business and is available for several clients.

However, the growth and concentration of industrial activities, the growing recognition of the significance of the accountant's work, the constant adjustment of the training of accountants to the requirements of industry, theoretical as well as practical, and the increasing number of persons who have received full training, will cause a considerable increase in the number of accountants who fully and wholly enter industry in the future. Among the tasks which will acquire increased significance will be the improvement of administrative efficiency. This field should to a larger extent be the responsibility of accountants, whose education gives them specific qualifications for useful work, frequently in close co-operation with engineers.

Even if a change should take place in the apportionment of tasks between the employees of the industrial companies and the independent accountants, the latter cannot become redundant in the foreseeable future. There will be a special need for an independent evaluation and there will be a need for specialists whose qualifications have been tried in a great number of companies. The accountants have not completed their education by passing examinations which simply inaugurate a new phase; they must, like physicians, lawyers and engineers, keep pace with development in theory and practice, assisted by research in commercial colleges and elsewhere, and supported by their own organisation, for the purpose of offering the best possible service in fields where their life work lies.

THE ACCOUNTANT IN INDUSTRY

by

GEORGE MOLLER, D.JUR., C.A.(CANADA)
Society of Industrial and Cost Accountants of Canada

INTRODUCTION

In presenting a paper on a broad subject, which is also being dealt with in papers prepared by authors in leading positions in accountancy in England, it seems advisable to establish proper demarcation lines within which may be held a subject which invites a review rambling over many adjacent fields.

The justification for this contribution will be sought in its particular emphasis on the description of the historical background, present position and foreseeable future of the accountant in industry in Canada and the neighbouring United States of America, i.e. the North American Continent.

In the 'Accounting Terminology for Canadian Practice' prepared by the Committee on Accounting Terminology of the Dominion Association of Chartered Accountants, issued in 1938, we find 'Accountant' described as 'one skilled in accountancy'. 'Accountancy' is defined as:

'The science (or art, according to individual preference) of recording financial transactions of business or other organisations, preparing from such records statements showing the progress and standing as to worth of the business, analysing such statements and drawing therefrom inferences or conclusions for the information of proprietors and management or others concerned, and determining costs. The term is also used to describe the Accountant's profession.'

We may be permitted to substitute the word 'industry' for the words 'business or other organisations' in this definition and thus derive a description of our subject.

HISTORICAL BACKGROUND

It is self-evident that commerce and finance existed and flourished centuries before industry, based chiefly on machinery, as we understand the term to-day, came into existence and prominence. This applies even to this young continent in its initial colonial farming and fishing era. It may be permissible to state that the use of accountancy for farming and fishing is certainly not older than the imposition of income-tax, which on this continent was a sequence to the First World War. The accountant in commerce and finance and his corollary the public accountant, concerned chiefly with clients engaged in trade, preceded the accountant in industry by generations.

The first organised body of accountants in Canada was the Dominion Association of Chartered Accountants, now known as the Canadian Institute of Chartered Accountants. The leading accountants in industry came, therefore, largely from the ranks of public accountants, whose growing organisations had recognised and taken upon themselves the task of system-

304

atical education for the profession early in this century. There is no doubt that they were largely aided by the experiences of the parent organisations in England.

COST ACCOUNTING

Accountants in industry are largely interested in cost determination. It is therefore only natural that accountants in industry developed cost accounting as their special field. Cost accountants started to organise on this continent about the end of the First World War. The National Association of Cost Accountants in the United States has grown to be one of the most important accounting organisations in the world. Its publications, the N.A.C.A. Bulletin and the annual reproduction of the proceedings of the International Cost Conferences in book form, are one of the important sources of cost information.

At the same time industrial accountants organised themselves in Canada under the name of the Canadian Society of Cost Accountants and Industrial Engineers, which was later changed to the Society of Industrial and Cost Accountants of Canada. Apart from its published literature, the outstanding contribution of this society to the advancement of the accountant in industry has been in the realm of education.

The Canadian Society, in co-operation with leading universities, has organised courses of study and provided for the instruction of students in the field of industrial and cost accounting. Instruction is given through the medium of correspondence courses and evening lecture classes with nineteen universities participating. All instruction is based upon a standard syllabus, and nation-wide uniform examinations are held annually. The Society is, in each province, empowered by government legislation to confer upon its qualifying members the right to use the designation R.I.A. (Registered Industrial and Cost Accountant). To qualify as a registered member, it is necessary to complete the courses of study, pass the prescribed examinations, submit an acceptable cost accounting thesis, and have a minimum of four years' practical experience.

PRESENT ROLE OF ACCOUNTANTS IN INDUSTRY

In defining the role of the accountant in industry we wish to lean on an article by Irving D. Daws, 'Duties and Responsibilities of the Accounting Executive'.[1] According to Mr. Daws, the accounting executive should primarily take *responsibility* proven by his willingness to back his own knowledge and judgment by making decisions and choices on his own initiative instead of referring them to his superiors. His chief qualities should be *accuracy* and *reliability*. On the information produced by the accounting executive the president and board of directors must base their decisions. His knowledge of company conditions must be derived from daily contact with, not only his own department or division, but also with other executives,

[1] N.A.C.A. Bulletin, Vol. XXIX, No. 12, 15th February, 1948.

divisions and departments of his company. For this purpose the accounting executive usually has direct access to all the departments in plant and offices.

The accounting department is a service department and therefore cannot limit its activities to accounting and auditing functions but should at all times *on its own initiative* disseminate information to other departments which should aid these departments in their operations. This will often avoid the setting up of the statistical records and separate recording sections within operating divisions or departments, caused usually by the lack of information coming from the legitimate source, i.e. the accounting department. The accounting executive should be prepared at all times to assume special tasks like examinations and investigations for other departments, thus proving his value as provider of all information which can be derived from records and figures or for which measurements can be set up and explored. The chief executive accountant, who in the United States and increasingly in Canada has the title of comptroller (or controller), should be the ideal co-ordinating link between the heads of the operating and sales and procurement divisions.

A properly organised accounting department should produce statements showing the results attributable to each department for which the department head is responsible. These reports are the basis for comparison between the efforts contributed by the various departments, but also disclose shortcomings often stemming from a lack of co-operation between the various departments. If the chief executive accountant can convince the heads of the departments of the immediate effect their co-operation or lack of co-operation will produce, he has fulfilled one of the main tasks of his position. The accountant in industry has also the permanent task of educating all members of the management team in its largest sense, i.e. from the president down to the last supervisor, foreman and lead-hand in financial matters. Only if he succeeds in convincing every member of the organisation of the necessity of accurate recording, and can persuade them to contribute their share in becoming exponents of accounting in each individual work centre, section and department, can he hope to achieve the ultimate aim of accounting, which is not only reporting of the past, but also ascertaining the present and intelligently forecasting the future.

In an article 'The Accountant's Place in Management', by Ralph C. Mark,[1] the author, who is the director of the cost analysis section of the comptoller's staff of the General Motors Corporation, recalls the time when the accountant was considered as purely a book-keeper and necessary evil whose duty was only to record the financial happenings. According to Mr. Mark, facts still have to be accurately recorded, but the accountant has to be able to analyse those facts to determine their meaning. He must set standards and use them to appraise the present and *forecast the future*. He must be able to simplify his analyses and present them understandably. To quote from Mr. Mark's article, the 'accountant's opportunity is unique in that he is in a position to help to interpret the results of the talent represented in management'. Mr. Mark explores the areas of development and experimental work, both current and long-range, in which the *accountant and engineer are comple-*

[1] October, 1948, issue of *Cost and Management*.

mentary to each other in securing and transmitting information to top management for decision and action. In the field of procurement, the accountant must record the cost of material procured and measure it against the standards included in the price of the product. He should consider whether it would be better to manufacture certain parts than to purchase them at the outset.

In the area of personnel problems, the accountant must furnish management with the effect of increases in employees' earnings and their effect on costs and prices. In an increasing manner or degree retirement and profit-sharing plans become part of the industrial pattern on this continent.[1] It is the accountant's function to explore the possibilities of profit-sharing programmes, and to prepare and support the arguments which prove that an incentive participation in the results of the company's operations will produce increased efficiency and larger net profits after the participation, thereby steadily improving the standard of living through increased production of goods and services. This development is the only real bulwark against the totalitarian assault on a world which wishes to stay free.

In stressing some of the important aspects of the accountant in industrial management, Mr. Mark further states:

> 'Relative comparisons of cost and price trends must be accurately interpreted and furnished to management at a time when something can be done about it, not at a time too late for corrective action. It is particularly important to give top-level management, WITHOUT PROMPTING, data as to how costs and profits will be affected by various factors such as the effect of different volumes of capacity and sales; different methods of manufacturing or marketing; the addition, elimination, or alteration of products; employee analyses as to type of labour performed, labour turnover, labour efficiency; the effect of cutting prices, or raising prices, spending money, not spending money, etc. Finally, the good accountant must have a broad perspective of the business. By developing the management viewpoint he will be better able to recognise and pick out the facts that are especially significant and should be presented to other members of the management.'

For this purpose the executive accountant in industry should have a good knowledge of economics and should be thoroughly schooled in interpreting reports on the economy of the country and the world for their application to the problems of his own enterprise. He should, on the other hand, be also able to produce reports on the function of his own enterprise in such form that statistics of general interest can be derived from these reports and top organisations like the Manufacturers' Association can make country-wide policy decisions based on such reports. There should be a definite 'give' and 'take' in the sphere of reporting in industry.

FROM BOOK-KEEPING TO INTERPRETING AND FORECASTING

The change in the meaning of 'accounting' can easily be seen when one compares a definition of accounting as adapted from Reisch-Kreibigs standard book *Bilanz und Steuer* (Vienna, 1914):

[1] 'The Case for Profit Sharing', Sartell Prentice, Jun., N.A.C.A. Bulletin, January, 1952, Sec. 1.

'Accounting means the total of all records which are intended to prove systematically the status and changes of the fortune of an enterprise as well as its success or failure.'

with the vivid description of accounting given by Professor Carl T. Devine in his text-book, *Cost Accounting and Analysis* (New York, 1950):

'The book-keeping and accounting routine consists of gathering the information from underlying documents, summary sheets, executive estimates, etc.; checking the accuracy of all calculations; sorting the relevant information from these data, recording the information either in intermediate records of original entry or directly to the final summary accounts (ledgers); posting the data to ledger sheets testing the accuracy of the ledgers (and journals); adjusting the books for items which were neglected in detail during the period; preparing fundamental statements and schedules; closing the books; and to some extent interpreting the accounting data. Just where the accounting work in a strict sense begins and where it ends leads to an interesting but fruitless discussion. Some amount of filling in business forms may, if desired, be classified as accounting, and some analytical ability in the interpretation of statements is not too much to expect of the book-keeper.'

It can be easily seen from the comparison of these two definitions that the former entirely historical character of accounting has been improved by adding the *interpreting* phase. This, of course, is by far not enough. The writer thinks that it is fairly accurate to claim that accounting is, in the middle of the century, increasingly looking to the future instead of concerning itself with the past. No one can deny that budgeting and budgetary control have become common tools of executive accountants on this continent. In a recent article by J. W. Gladson, 'The Accountant's Part in Creative Management',[1] the author condenses the questions which the accountant should be able to answer to the manager to the following four:

(1) How have we done up to now?
(2) How are we doing at the present time?
(3) How will we do in the future?
(4) What will be the effect of doing so-and-so?

The third and fourth questions indicate the new trend in accountancy in industry. According to Gladson, the accountant is in a splendid position to make an important contribution to management planning by using the tools he has at his disposition. His presentation may be in the form of detailed budgets of sales costs at different assumed levels of future activity. If the accountant cannot find a basis for a forecast, management has to work out the answer some other way.

The answer to the question, 'What will be the effect of doing so-and-so?' is one of the problems of management and often spells the difference between good and poor management. It is the accountant who will, in most cases, have to answer the question, 'How will this affect us?' The accountant must develop the technique of calculating the isolated effect of major changes in the current business picture in order to be able to show management the current level of estimated profits without waiting for books to be closed. The

[1] N.A.C.A. Bulletin, Vol. XXXIII, No. 1, September, 1951.

same method of specific estimations is used in calculating the effect of proposed changes, new business, plant expansion, etc. When the accountant is constantly called upon to answer the fourth question quoted above, he will be participating in management planning. The following is a quotation from the concluding paragraph of the quoted article:

> 'As a rule, only the very highest levels of management are concerned with all phases of the business. Often only through the controller's or accountant's efforts can all such phases be brought together. The accountant's opportunities in this field are limited only by his imagination, his depth of purpose and his ability to work with other members of management. . . .
> 'By constructive analysis and by co-operation with the segments of the business involved, the accountant or controller can help discover unfavourable spots in the picture and focus constructive suggestion and assistance upon them. . . . The controller or accountant, if he is well qualified, is in one of the most fortunate positions to be able to guide and counsel business management in the major decisions which affect the financial welfare of his company.'

The Anglo-American Council on Productivity report on a tour of the British specialist teams throughout the United States, made the following statement on 'management accounting' as it is practised here in their very interesting report:[1]

> 'Management accountancy is the presentation of accounting information in such a way as to assist management in the creation of policy in the day-to-day operation of an undertaking. The technique of accountancy is of extreme importance as it works in the most nearly universal medium available for the expression of facts, so that facts of great diversity can be presented in the same picture. It is not the presentation of these pictures that is the function of management, but the use of them.'

'Cost consciousness' is described as the outstanding feature of the American industrialist.

Speedy production of figures is a 'must'. This leads to the development of standard costs, predetermined overhead rates, direct costing (often referred to as 'basic costs' accounting),[2] centsless accounting,[3] unit accounting (avoiding all transcribing) and, last but not least, to reporting of exceptional figures only, instead of full statements.

UNIFORMITY IN COST ACCOUNTING

According to the Dean of Accountancy in the United States, Mr. George O. May,[4] accounting is utilitarian and based on conventions (some of which are necessarily of doubtful correspondence with fact) although many accountants are reluctant to admit that accounting is not based on something of a higher order of sanctity than conventions. Accounting procedures have in the main been the result of common agreement between accountants, though they

[1] Anglo-American Council on Productivity, 21, Tothill Street, London, S.W.1.
[2] 'An Appraisal of Direct Costing', by John A. Beckett, N.A.C.A. Bulletin, December, 1951.
[3] 'Penny Elimination in Accounting Records'. A case report by E. C. Jordan, *Cost and Management*, January, 1952.
[4] *Financial Accounting—A Distillation of Experience*, New York, 1943, The McMillan Co.

have to some extent, and particularly in recent years, been influenced by laws or regulations. This is true for financial accounting, but cannot be entirely applied to cost accounting in its predominant role in accounting in industry. It must be admitted that pronouncement on cost accounting terminology and uniform agreements on cost accounting procedures are thoroughly lacking up to this date. Deplorable as this fact may be, it is an invigorating challenge to the accountant in industry and it may be permissible to express the hope that we will see in the foreseeable future statements on cost accounting procedure published by the top organisations in this field similar to the accounting research bulletins issued by the Committee on Accounting Procedure, American Institute of Accountants, or statements on auditing procedure issued by the Committee on Auditing Procedure, American Institute of Accountants, or the accounting or auditing practices statements issued by the Committee on Accounting and Auditing Research of the Dominion Association of Chartered Accountants (now Canadian Institute of Chartered Accountants). Statements of this kind are the sign of reaching maturity in any one profession and it may be admitted without damage to the cost accountant's stature that we are a very young and youthful group which has not yet achieved maturity.

THE FUTURE OF THE ACCOUNTANT IN INDUSTRY

Present trends in both methods and principles of accounting in industry give some indication of what we may expect in the near future.

Mr. Daniel M. Sherhan, Vice-President of the Monsanto Chemical Co., in his address before the 1951 Annual Conference of the Controllers' Institute of America, portrays what seems to be in store for the accountant in industry, if and when the marvellous brain machines now developed chiefly in the United States, but also in Canada, will become available to an enlarged number of concerns at rational costs. Mr. Sherhan states in part:

'Reports which formerly consumed fifty man days in manual preparation are now produced through the use of the so-called ''brain'' or electronic programmed calculator in eight hours. Future electronic equipment may produce them in one hour. The drudgery, the pencil pushing of accounting will be eliminated. Future accountants will devote their time to interpretation of facts and solution of company problems rather than to worrying about records. It is my prediction that through the use of electronic equipment, monthly reports of companies—particularly those of large size—will be available only a day or two after the month's close. It seems possible that by reason of this equipment, controllers will prepare operating reports semi-monthly, or possibly more often rather than only monthly.'

It seems still like reading fiction describing the achievements of future centuries when listening to the remarks made by Mr. Jeming, systems consultant to the Atomic Energy Commission, the Port of New York Authority, Consolidated Edison Co. and other organisations, who stated before the same conference:

'All accounting operations must be planned in advance so they will be parts of an integrated plan—not only on an organisation chart, but also as physical parts of a completely integrated and electrically interconnected accounting system . . . not a conglomeration of individual business machines, but one giant machine which must have built into it the means of doing the whole job. The run-of-the-mill accountant will be displaced by the accountant who will be a planner and an analyst, and who will know how to exploit to the full the operating controls which the electronic accounting system can make possible. The controller will require technical personnel who will know how to maintain the mechanism and to modify the system as the need arises.'

It seems that the controller's department will, in the foreseeable future, become a plant within the plant, operating mostly machines and producing statistical reports and financial statements with the minimum of personal effort in the production, but the maximum of brainwork in their planning and layout. This development will complete the process in which the book-keeping clerk becomes more and more a machine operator in overalls and the accountant becomes a designer and planner and, as such, an active creative member of the management team.

The more conservatively inclined members of our occupation should not become unduly alarmed about these far-reaching prospects in the development of accountancy in industry, because, in spite of the amazing speed with which mechanisation progresses on this continent, it will take not less than one generation to see the process permeating our industrial organisation from the top giant concerns to the small surviving industrial enterprises. Nevertheless, the accountant in industry must be better prepared for this development by educating himself and his successors, recognising the requirements of the present as well as those of the future, which will see him, on this continent, as a full-fledged member of the top-management team.

THE ACCOUNTANT IN INDUSTRY

by

A. PAYRAU

Compagnie Nationale des Experts Comptables,
France

HISTORICAL

Twenty-five Years Ago

Twenty-five years ago, the accountant's function in industry was primarily limited to the historical recording of the financial operations of the business. He was not concerned with costing, which was handled by the factory's technical departments. Most often a self-made man, the accountant was only an accounting practitioner. In the organisation plan, he did not belong to the staff; he had no part in the discussion of the operations, nor in the planning of the general policy of the business.

Of course, there were exceptions to the above description; but, nevertheless, it faithfully pictures the accountant's function in industry in the years 1925 to 1930.

Evolution

Changes in this situation occurred due to various factors.

Among factors related to the accounting profession itself, we can note:

Modern methods of office work and business machines;

Growth of the personality of the accountant: college or university education including a sound law and tax background;

Development and promotion of modern theory and techniques on standard costs, analysis of variances, budget, overhead distribution, etc.; and

Finally, the accountant's own awakening to his responsibilities, especially in the fields of tax, law and finance.

Other factors, although not of an accounting nature, also influenced the accountant's function in industry, among these:

The growth of machinery;

The scientific organisation of production;

The industrial concentration and centralisation;

Economic, social and political evolution of the industrial era;

Evolution in top management's organisation and structure;

Growing complexity of industrial enterprises.

The Necessity of a Doctrine

These various factors, although useful and fruitful, did not bring about the recognition of statutory concepts of the profession and there still has to be worked out a doctrine and philosophy on the accountant's functions in industry and a training programme for those who will fulfil these functions.

312

We will now set forth our views on these three problems of doctrine, methods and training, and consider recent French endeavours in the field of accounting in industry.

ACCOUNTANT'S FUNCTION IN MODERN INDUSTRY

A Twofold Function

The accountant's function is twofold:

First, he records all the company's operations; external transactions as well as all the internal items that can and must be translated into the accounting language, such as, in particular, costs.

Secondly, he interprets, reports and circulates results at all levels of management so that they are put into use.

The Recording Function

For some time, the accountant was expected only to keep records of operations; results were compiled, analysed and issued only at the end of the year as the balance sheet was drawn up.

To-day, it is considered that the recording function is no more than a fraction compared with the administrative charge of the accounting department. This is due to the progress in accounting techniques and methods, in the use of business machines, and to the accountancy profession's own development. Nowadays, this duty is easily dealt with by a properly organised department.

This is not to minimise in any way the importance of the recording function. It is, no doubt, the basis for the accountant's superior functions; but we know that industry has at its disposal plenty of men with the necessary knowledge and experience to take care of the recording, able to surround themselves with the necessary counsellors in the related activities of tax, law, organisation, methods, etc.

But the accountant's function is dual and may be regarded, on the one hand, as 'management of the accounting function', and, on the other hand, as 'accounting for the management function'.

The Management Function

This function combines accounting for management and management by accounting: in other words, it is 'management accounting' or 'controllership'.

From line, the accountant moves up to staff.

From a technical point of view, this function stands midway between the accountant's and the engineer's functions.

It is possible to figure that an engineer could be entrusted with this function; of course he would have to go through the long and difficult road that leads to the mastery of the extensive knowledge indispensable to the public or private accountant.

Methods of compiling cost data are so intimately linked with the methods of using information thus gathered that they cannot be split or dissociated.

Companies where the manufacturing departments, instead of the accounting department, are entrusted with the setting up of operation costs, often suffer disappointing results from errors, lack of co-ordination and lack of self-criticism. The routine work done by the production departments and the statistics they arrive at, duplicate those already worked out by the accounting department for the purpose of setting up the balance sheet.

Although intimately tied to the financial accounting, industrial accounting, which is the science of costs, is a major field in itself. It has its own principles, concepts and techniques, which we will now consider.

Its main purposes are:

> To determine, report and circulate operation costs (the word operation being taken in a general sense of enterprise, plant, department, cost centre, process or detailed production operation);
> To analyse them and to circulate the results of these analyses and researches; and
> To participate in the planning of the company's general policy on the level of general management.

INDUSTRIAL ACCOUNTING METHODS AND TECHNIQUES

The Accountant's Place in the Industrial Enterprise
To fulfil the functions described above, the accountant:

> Must be on the staff level equal in status with the production manager, sales manager, personnel manager, etc.;
> Must be directly responsible to the president, and must be able to make himself heard by the board of directors if and when necessary, and be on a consultative basis, alike with other staff members;
> Must be independent of the production or sales executives;
> Must be considered as a major executive;
> Must be in full charge of the whole of accounting duties, as cost accounting is only one phase of the general accounting.

Ways and Means for the Accountant to Perform his Management Functions
We do not intend to describe here, not even to recall, the various methods of cost computation and recording, but we wish to consider from the special point of view of management some of the adequate techniques to ensure the control of the industrial enterprise.

One can imagine an efficient method from an accounting point of view but worthless from a management point of view. For example, in a factory producing a great variety of products, it is generally much more important to check the efficiency of each cost centre than the cost of each product taken separately.

The activity of the accountant in industry must always be focused on the creation of profits; he must be the most profit-minded man in the whole organisation.

Determination of past and present results is worth while only if it induces management to act and if it projects the future.

The industrial accountant's best means of action are those which prepare for the future.

Amongst the techniques of action of the accountant in industry, we shall give due consideration to standard costs, analysis of variations, reports, budgets, and studies and general researches.

Standard Costs

A standard is altogether a predetermination of costs and, at the same time, the fixation of authorised expenditures within definite limitations, under given conditions.

The standard is in a way a budget—budget of a movement, of an operation, product, a service, etc.

Your plumber works according to standards, without knowing them, when he quotes at £3 a repair job which he figures will cost him £2.

Using a standard is giving up the notion 'How much did this cost?' as a unit of measurement and replacing it by 'How much should it cost?'

The method of standard costing can be adopted practically by all kinds of industries, in all conditions. If difficulties arise, for instance, out of monetary depreciation, these problems are irrelevant of the method itself; they would arise whatever costing method is used.

The foremost advantage of this system is its technique of operational control by what is known as the principle of 'exceptions', applied here through analysis of deviations.

Analysis of Deviations

This technique is designed to figure out disparities between expected results (in terms of predetermined standards) and performance (in terms of actual costs) and to bring the causes of variances to the attention of responsible executives.

Deviations must be analysed in regard to the controlled operation, the component elements of the operation, the causes of variances, and the responsible function.

Deviations are commonly divided into:

Material deviations: prices, quantity (usage);
Labour deviations: rate of wages, efficiency;
Overhead deviations: expenditures, capacity (volume), efficiency.

Each factor of deviation must be isolated and analysed. For example, labour deviation in efficiency may have been caused by time lost due to imperfect materials or lack of materials; or time lost due to machine or tool accidents; or it may have been caused by increased labour due to small series of production or to changes or shifting in methods, etc.

An efficient cost department will endeavour to isolate every possible variance, record it in the books, compare it with an authorised margin and, if proved to be abnormal, it must be brought to the attention of the responsible officer.

For example, in a department with an unfavourable deviation it would be wrong to consider the workshop foreman as responsible if deviations were due to waiting for stock or to imperfect materials (the stock-superintendent or the buyer may be responsible); if they were due to equipment or tool accidents the maintenance superintendent may be responsible, etc.

In short, the analysis of deviations is based upon:

The principle of 'exceptions', i.e. reporting and taking action only when necessary.

Discovery of the causes of variations and the underlying conditions of such causes.

Pointing out responsibilities.

Reports

Preparing and circulating reports is as important as the information they convey.

Their basic qualities rest upon giving as much useful information as possible with the shortest possible delay and with a reasonable maximum of accuracy.

Reports must be 'tailor-made' to meet the needs of the executives to whom they are addressed and should cover only such facts as these persons can account for.

General management must be informed of the achievement of the company's general policy by condensed reports of the type of balance sheet, profit and loss account and supporting schedules.

Reports to executive managers will cover each department's performance in terms of volume, efficiency and contribution to the general profit plan of the business.

Daily reports to foremen will deal in detail with operations of the previous day, especially in terms of labour efficiency.

These reports should be made out:

In terms of money (either exact figures or percentages) for general management, and with charts whenever they make trends and situations clearer;

In terms of money and quantities for executive managers, showing the influence of the performance of their department on the whole organisation; and

In terms of time, volume, weight, etc., for foremen.

The foreman, having no authority on the rate of hourly wages, the amount of social security charges or the price of materials, must be given information in terms of the unit he works with: hours for labour, or weight for materials, etc.

It is important that reports should be prepared in an attractive form, for most of those they are addressed to have no liking for figures. Their form must be clear, as simple as possible, without any useless information. If necessary, they may be completed by spoken comments.

Reports must be impartial. The accountant's function in industry is not to give orders, but information. He shows past and present performance compared with predetermined policies as they were planned and decided upon by the general management.

Budgets

Budgeting and budget control can be described as:

A co-ordinated forecasting of future activities for the purpose of establishing the contemplated final result of all operations, in particular those constituting the profit and loss account.

Systematic comparison at regular intervals (generally monthly) of actual results with expected ones in the various fields of management.

Quick communication of statements at all levels concerned, not only at management's, but at all responsible agents', even on the lowest level of authority.

Budgeting has two main characteristics:

Rational forecasts based not only on past achievements and on plans of management, but also on expected business trends.

Co-ordinated forecasts combining all inter-departmental relations.

The accountant in industry must especially take into account the three following features:

Computation of the break-even point and preparation of profit charts or graphs.

Establishment of flexible budgets which aim to adapt the budget to external circumstances independent of the company's own will (such as wage increases) or internal decisions (such as modification in the sales price policy).

Establishment of variable budgets, automatically adjustable to certain varying factors of cost, such as the volume of sales or of production; the budget must be subdivided in fixed, semi-variable and variable expenditures.

According to certain theories, factors of flexibility and variability should be considered to be identical for they are sometimes quite difficult to discriminate.

The budget must be set up according to the chart of accounts, but this plan must be drawn in view of the desired budget control. The budget is by far the best guide to realise the plans laid for the future by the enterprise; it is not a static, but a dynamic guide.

General and Special Studies

These studies enable the general management to foresee the possible consequences of considered decisions and to size up the effects of a projected policy.

To conduct these studies and researches, the industrial accountant must have a part in management and know the ends aimed at; he must have a general view of the whole enterprise and take an impartial attitude in case of conflicts between the various departments.

It has been said that 'To manage is to foresee', but one could also add that 'To manage is to choose', to select between two or more alternatives. The choice must not be conditioned by decisions based on intuition, personal likes or pride; it must be based on careful studies made in close co-operation with technical departments by the accountant.

For instance, the accountant is logically in the best position to develop all possible information available for solving the following questions:

Should a given product or material be bought outside or produced?

What would be the effects of accepting given orders from customers at a price below production costs or sales costs?

How would it affect production to fulfil orders involving overtime work at higher wage rates?

What would be the consequences of ceasing to manufacture products that show a loss?

What could be the expected effects of plant reorganisation?

These questions and their like are studies of projects.

Other subjects deal with the analysis of actual conditions of operations, such as:

Classifying products according to profitability.

Ratio of non-productive to productive hours, over a long period, in various departments.

Causes and cost of breakdown in machinery and equipment.

These studies based on statistical data deal as much with distribution as with production.

TRAINING OF THE INDUSTRIAL ACCOUNTANT

The Problem

A French statesman is said to have defined culture as 'what is left when everything has been forgotten'. In the same way, we should say that the 'Science of accounting is what is left after everything learned has been forgotten'.

The accounting knowledge for the accountant in industry is the substratum of his 'know' and 'know-how' that enables him to carry out his functions of recorder, of manager of the accounting department.

How should the accountant in industry be trained to fulfil his higher duties of staff member and executive? This is the general problem of education for semi-specialists and semi-'generalists' of the upper brackets.

Education

The industrial accountant needs a strong university education where he must specialise in industrial control and management, either while pursuing his university courses or afterwards..

Besides general education, he must have mastered the science of accounting. He should have specialised by studying as many as possible of the following subjects:

Control practice in industry;
Advanced course of production cost accounting;
Advanced course of distribution cost accounting;
Analysis of economic conditions;
Industrial organisation;
Statistical methods of production and quality control;
Industrial relations;
Principles and problems of management;
Sales organisation and market research;
Plant planning and problems of material handling; etc.

Besides this *ex cathedra* education, future industrial accountants and controllers have to learn how to make sound decisions and bring them into action. It is not sufficient to memorise courses.

The case method is probably the most efficient method of learning how to act, for the student is constantly placed in the situation of a manager whose duty it is, not only to express and judge the facts, but to take decisions relevant to his responsibilities.

Training within Business

The accountant must have a perfect knowledge of the enterprise, know the working of all departments and interaction between the major divisions of the enterprise and know the control points of each of them.

Of all methods of training a man and teaching him to master a problem, the method of job rotation, inter-functional and within the department, is the most simple and efficient.

The accountant's problems are those of management dressed in figures; knowledge of general problems is the basis of his function.

Circumstances and organisation particular to each enterprise will determine the job rotation programme.

Professional Associations

By joining a professional association of industrial accountants, the accountant will be able to compare his own experience with that of his colleagues and their research in common will contribute in selecting techniques that have given the best results in general management of business, in lowering cost, in increasing the workers' standard of living.

Such co-operative activity can be a most efficient factor for development in the science of cost accounting for industrial accountants.

CONCLUSION

This paper does not claim to describe the actual situation of the accountant in industry in France. But our intention has been to examine the main features that would lead the accounting profession to take an increasing part in the top management of business.

How much of this has been done in France?

Under the patronage of administration, especially fiscal, a small group of practitioners has designed a uniform system of accounts, compulsory for some enterprises (nationalised or state-subsidised). This plan is progressively being adopted by other enterprises. This plan stresses the importance of the interrelation of financial accounting with production accounting.

The importance of monetary devaluations has made it necessary, in order to avoid serious disorder in private economy, to revaluate balance sheets. This revaluation of productive assets (buildings, machinery, equipment, tools, etc.) enables the computation of depreciation and their charge to current costs at a more rational value—nearer the replacement value. However, taxation requirements have superseded economic considerations and the aim has been only partially attained.

Incessant monetary devaluations suffered in France in the past fifteen years, exceptional rulings during enemy occupation, and political and fiscal interference in private economy, have discouraged the industry in applying standard costs and budgets. A new trend, based on a national effort to increase productivity, calls attention to the need for sounder scientific methods of management in a more and more complex and competitive world.

Devoted to humanities, France does not easily deviate from purely literary and scientific culture to work out an educational system, both liberal and practical, especially intended to develop leaders in private economy.

As for the accounting profession, public and private accountants, grouped in their professional bodies, can now face the major problems they are entrusted with in the field of management accounting.

The accountant's function in industry provides the most interesting opportunities for development which are likely to contribute to an increased standard of living and national productivity and the preservation of a prosperous and sound private economy.

DISCUSSION

MR. N. R. MODY, B.COM., F.C.A., *Institute of Chartered Accountants of India, the rapporteur, summarised the contents of the papers:*

I consider it an honour to be asked to act as rapporteur on this paper by the Council of the Sixth International Congress on Accounting, the importance of the paper being related not only to the profession but also to industry and trade in general. As you are aware, the original contributions are by Mr. F. R. M. de Paula and Mr. W. S. Risk, and there are five papers on the subject.

Mr. de Paula's paper refers to the development of the profession in the United Kingdom from the last half of the nineteenth century, through the expansion of industry, and of commerce and the conversion of partnerships into companies under the Companies Acts. The objects of the Charter of the Institute of Chartered Accountants in England and Wales focus attention on the work of liquidations and receiverships, and audit work is taken as the last objective. With the growth in the number and size of companies, industry and commerce, however, increasingly relied on accountants for their book-keeping, and it was to the professional accountant that they turned not only to audit their accounts but to prepare them. The increase in the rate of income-tax during the First World War led to further engagement of the services of public accountants. With a low rate of tax the average business man dealt with his own income-tax, as his tax formed a low percentage of his earnings, but the increase in the rate between the wars and the steep rise during and since the Second World War, coupled with the complicated nature of taxing legislation, led him to seek expert advice. Finally, costing, which assumed importance between the wars, and particularly during the last war, led to added responsibilities for the accountant.

From all this developed a further field of activity which has greatly expanded today and is assuming increasing importance, the technique of what is now known as management accounting. The increasing responsibilities shouldered by accountants is leading to more of their number being drawn by industry and commerce to perform functions on a whole-time basis, which were formerly carried out by professional accountants. Thus came into being a demand for specialised accountants to supply the needs of industry and commerce, with an outlook different from that of the accountant in industry of the early days, as well as that of the accountant in practice. Mr. de Paula has given an analogy of a ship's log which, as he puts it, records the happenings of a voyage; from which valuable lessons can be learnt and used by the captain of the ship. But in addition he requires his navigating officer to chart his course ahead and to report whether the ship is on its predetermined course. Similarly, management must know whether the industrial ship is on or off its course, so that prompt remedial action may be taken to prevent her from going on the rocks.

Planning ahead is the essence of management accounting today. Without this, management is not in a position to chart its course of future operations and activities. It is essential, therefore, that information must not only be readily and quickly available but also that it must be unaccompanied by an unnecessary mass of details. How the information reaches management is a matter of organisational set-up, but the ideal to be achieved is centralised control with decentralisation of responsibility along the line. Unless this is achieved, the top command is bound to be clogged with details, and will be prevented from taking action on matters of vital importance.

All the papers are unanimous in this aspect of forward planning by means of standard cost and budgetary control. This involves the laying down of yard sticks under given conditions and the measurement of actual achievement there against. Mr. Payrau has expressed it very simply by stating that using a standard is giving up the question 'How much did it cost?' as a unit of measurement, and replacing it by 'How much should it cost?' The standard must be so fixed that management must be able to prove that the standard can be worked and that it is not based on hypothesis. The setting up of such a system requires the co-operation of all departments—engineering, technical, procurement, sales, etc., and the comptroller comes into the picture to fit in, in a financial form, the details supplied by the various departments. It is he who interprets in one complete picture the information separately supplied to him.

It is agreed generally that in setting up budgetary control and standard cost, the co-operation of every department is essential. Otherwise, the standards set may not have relationship to achievements and the result may be a general distrust of the whole system.

Mr. de Paula's paper outlines in detail the organisational set-up and the part the comptroller plays in it. Briefly, he states—and on this point there is unanimity among the papers—that the finance division must be on equality with the other departments to represent finance at top policy-making level and to give clear expression and advice on financial implications. The finance division would be responsible for finance, costing, accounting, production of periodical reports and annual accounts. Mr. de Paula has given the example of the comptroller of a holding company with ramifications throughout the world. He would be generally responsible for basic principles on which all accounts, cost reports, statistics, etc., should be prepared throughout the whole group, and would lay down the form of presentation of statements for submission to headquarters. The accountant in the divisions and subsidiary companies would report through his chief executive to the comptroller of the holding company. There should be attached to the accounts of each subsidiary a standard questionnaire in a form drawn up by the comptroller, to be completed and certified by the chief accountant of each subsidiary.

The paper submitted by Mr. Risk has concentrated on the functions of the accountant in industry and his utility to the management in general. He has divided the functions of the accountant into two parts—the executive function and the informative function. Under the executive function is

included responsibility for financial and cost accounting, machine accounting, wages control and the operation of agreements arrived at with
labour, such as incentive wages, employee's services in the shape of dis-
bursements for sickness, savings and pension funds and other facilities, and
a knowledge of company law and labour legislation. The informative
function deals mainly with the planning aspect of the accountant's duties
and a comparison of the plan with actuals.

Mr. Risk has drawn attention to the variety of interests for which the
accountant supplies information, and under the main headings may be
mentioned the State, the owners of the business, the management and
the employees. All these relate to the accountant's functions in providing
information on past activities, but, based on the records of the past, forecasts
are required by management for the future.

In order to be able to discharge his duties it is essential for the accountant
to have sufficient authority and for his status to be in line with those of
higher management. Once the forecasts have been made and the standards
laid down and budgeted for, it is the accountant's duty to provide facts and
figures for the management which tell what has happened and whether the
planning has been effective. For the purpose of bringing out variations from
a set standard, the accountant should submit his report in concise form—a
report understood by those sitting round the table who may not be equally
conversant with accounts—and should supplement it where necessary by a
verbal report at the appropriate meeting. An intelligent appreciation of the
variations will enable action to be taken to remedy divergences from the
plan laid down. Mr. Risk has suggested the classification of expenditure so
that the headings required for financial purposes are the natural groupings
of the more detailed classifications required for cost ascertainment and
control. He has illustrated how variations from the budget can be shown
up and the type of information required to provide the means of control,
by setting up 'plan' and 'control' for each department.

The presentation of the report for cost ascertainment and cost control,
with action as its objective, must be such as to convince management. The
figures and the reports must not only be understandable and alive, but they
must also be selective, simple and short.

In commenting on the needs of the industrial executive for a general
accounting plan and an industrial accounting plan, Mr. Clinton Bennett
points out that, for successful competition with the giants in industry,
information is needed as much by the medium and small American enterprises as by the so-called big business. It should be admitted that the size of
a business is relative to each country, and what is medium size for the
United States of America may be a large size business for another country;
but it is interesting to note that, in the relative context of size in the United
States, the medium and small enterprises are interested in the services of the
industrial accountant. The large membership of the National Association of
Cost Accountants is a pointer to the development of industrial accounting and
the use made by industry of the services of such accountants. Mr. Bennett
has rightly pointed out that standard cost reflects the cost of producing

a specific article at a given level of output and under an assumed set of circumstances that are expected to prevail. Variations from these circumstances will obviously upset the forward planning, and it is the task of the industrial accountant to spotlight these variations. Management must have a monthly statement of accounts in order to follow the cost control programme, and for this purpose it is suggested that the cost of sales should not be obtained by the laborious process of taking an inventory of the stock at the end of the month or the given period, but by taking the cost of sales by using standard cost. The obvious purpose of this statement is to compare predetermined costs with actuals. It is generally accepted in the United States that the industrial accountant is considered part of the management team, made responsible directly to the president of the company, who, as the chief executive, is responsible to the board for carrying out the policy laid down by it.

The work of the industrial accountant in Australia, although not as fully developed as in the United Kingdom or on the North American Continent, is assuming importance with the increase in industrialisation. Mr. Fitzgerald states that in Australia industrial units are mostly small-scale, and that is the reason attributed for industrial accounting not being as fully developed as in some other countries. Nevertheless, development appears to be proceeding steadily when one considers that the total membership of the five major institutes in Australia exceeds 18,000 for a country with a population of only $8\frac{1}{2}$ millions. However, it appears that the accountant in industry in Australia has not reached the same status, and although there are instances of accountants having reached managerial status, they are there more by virtue of managerial ability coupled with a knowledge of accounting rather than with accounting ability coupled with managerial qualities.

As stated above, small-scale units predominate, and there is neither the opportunity for the full use of accounting services nor the possibility of obtaining such services at a reasonable cost. A further handicap is that in such units the managers are generally unaware of the uses to which accounting can be put. Finally, Mr. Fitzgerald has suggested that there is lack of unity of purpose between public accountants and accountants in industry, and as a consequence general accounting and cost accounting have come to be looked upon as separate and unrelated in study as well as in practice. Another factor is that convention has played a strong influence in both branches of the profession, and there is a noticeable disinclination on the part of public accountants to change methods and forms which have been in use for a long time. On the other hand, cost accounting systems which have been installed have been over-elaborate, costly to operate, and productive of little information.

In Canada, as Mr. Moller has pointed out, the leading accountants in industry came largely from the ranks of public accountants. The industrial accountants in Canada have organised themselves into a body under the Society of Industrial and Cost Accountants of Canada. The Society in co-operation with the universities has organised courses of practical and theoretical training and instruction based upon a standard syllabus, and uniform nation-wide examinations are held every year. Since accountants in industry are largely interested in cost determination, they have developed cost accounting as their special field. Publications, bulletins, annual reproduction of the proceedings of cost conferences and various literature have contributed to the advancement of the training of the accountant in industry in North America.

Mr. Moller points out that the accounting department is a service department and, therefore, cannot limit its activities merely to auditing functions, but should at all times be prepared to disseminate information on its own initiative to other departments. This will often avoid the setting up of statistical records within the organisation where the information should come from one centralised office, namely, the accounting department. The accountant in industry has also the task of educating all members of the management team in financial matters, and until he succeeds in convincing every member of the organisation of the necessity for accurate recording, then only he can hope to achieve the aim of an accountant, which is not only reporting of the past, but also ascertaining the present and intelligently forecasting the future. The accountant in industry no longer merely records financial happenings as they take place, and although facts must be accurately recorded, he must analyse them to determine the future. He has the tools at his disposal from which he can tell the management not only 'How have we done up to now?' but also 'How will we do in the future?' He must devise means of showing the management the level of estimated profits without waiting for the books to be closed. The top management is where policy is forged and the comptroller is one of the links in this team; it is only by his participation that others can take policy decisions affecting the financial position or, perhaps, the very existence of a company.

Mr. Moller has drawn pointed attention to one aspect that, whereas financial accounting is based on convention, practice and legal aspects affecting each country, such as the Companies Act, 1948, there is a lack of uniformity in the presentation of cost accounting reports. It is hoped that some common approach can be made by statements on cost accounting procedure, similar to the research bulletins of the Committee on Accounting Procedure and the statements of the Committee on Auditing Procedure of the American Institute of Accountants.

Mr. Payrau has stated that the accountant's function is dual—on the one hand, as 'management of the accounting function' and on the other hand, as 'accounting for the management function'. It is only in the last few years that the accountant in industry has come into his own in France, and this is largely due to industrial expansion, complexity of modern industry, and attempted centralisation of authority, coupled with the growth of the personality of the accountant with college or university education including a sound law and tax background.

The position in Denmark appears to be different from that prevailing in other countries from which papers have been submitted. Mr. Jeppesen states that there are only 400 'chartered' accountants in Denmark and 90 per cent. of them are in professional practice or employed as assistants in practising firms. The external accountant is called upon to perform functions not only in connection with the auditing of accounts, but also to report to the board on internal functions. He is responsible for interpretation of results and for bringing out features pertinent from the management point of view, but it would appear that these functions are largely historical in character. Although large industrial companies do employ accountants to guide their financial policies by the preparation of budgets and standard costs, in view of the restricted nature of industrialisation in Denmark this aspect of the work has not developed to as great an extent as in the United Kingdom or the United States of America. There are very few qualified accountants in Denmark permanently attached to one company and, therefore, reliance is placed more on the accountant in practice.

The question of education has been dealt with in some of the papers, and it is admitted that limited facilities exist for practical and theoretical training. Even so, with the growing importance of the industrial accountant, this matter is engaging more and more attention. The Institute of Cost and Works Accountants in England has taken a significant step in the proposed establishment of the fellowship grade for qualification as management accountant. Up to now, the accountant in industry is being drawn largely from one of the professional bodies where he serves articles, and his experience is limited almost entirely to professional work; he may enter industry at a very early age and, simultaneously with practical experience, qualify for the examination of the Institute of Cost and Works Accountants. The accountant who qualifies in a public accountant's office and thereafter takes an appointment in industry has little knowledge of, or experience in, many of the functions which have been referred to in the papers. However, the broad outlook and the high standard of training obtained by him, coupled with practical experience, may lead the right man to be an effective member of the management team. In the field of education, as far as industrial accountants are concerned, it would appear that more facilities exist in the United States and Canada than in other countries. The real problem is not to increase the number of accountants but to secure those of the right type.

Mr. A. A. FITZGERALD (Australia):

I want to refer to a point made in several of the papers, the need for accounting aid to the small business. By way of a footnote, that seems to me to be one of the most valuable services which the accountant can render to society, because for the survival of the system of free enterprise the health and well-being of the small business is essential.

This involves three things. First, it involves the integration of which Mr. Risk has spoken on page 278, an integration not only of so-called financial and so-called cost accounting but an integration of accountants, the development within the profession of a unified outlook towards the purposes, methods and philosophies of accounting.

Secondly, it involves a simplification of cost accounting procedures and a great simplification of cost accounting reports. One of the most helpful signs that progress along those lines is possible is the attention which has been given in the United States of America to direct costing, that is to say, the discovery and analysis of direct costs as distinct from indirect costs.

The third way in which the accountant can and must aid the small business is by shortening the accounting period by making it possible for the small business as well as the large business to get information at intervals of not more than one month instead of waiting until the end of the year to discover what deficiencies have occurred and what damage has been done to the industry by those deficiencies.

If these things are to come about, if the small business is to get the aid, a changed attitude will be necessary on the part of accountants generally. It is for all of us, particularly those like myself, who are in practice primarily as financial accountants, to go back over the history of the development of cost accounting. We shall have a salutary reminder that accountants have at times failed promptly enough to respond to the needs of industry. Mr. Risk has made that point so far as this country is concerned, and it is certainly true in Australia. He says that it is perhaps not unfair to say that much of the impetus towards cost or management accounting has come from the pressure by management for figures which are sufficiently revealing, detailed and up-to-date to guide them in the formulation of policy. I should hope that the profession would take the lead in persuading management to want the information rather than to wait until management has made it clear that the need is urgent.

There are some very trenchant and important observations in the papers on the need for a somewhat different kind of training and education for the accountants of the future. I would particularly direct attention to the comments of Mr. de Paula on page 242.

MR. ERKKI USVA (Finland):

Professor A. ter Vehn, of Sweden, made a lecture trip to Finland after the conclusion of the war, and described the normal accountancy plan of the Swedish Engineering Works Association (Mekanförbundets Normalkonto-plan). This event gave a welcome new impulse to our industrial accounting side by side with its own accounting plans. The Swedish Mekanförbundet's system has been applied primarily in the engineering industry, which has expanded immensely as a result of war reparations.

After the re-establishment of connections with the West, primarily the industrial cost accounting, recently greatly developed in the United States of America, has been paid very considerable attention in spite of the long distances. Thorough studies in this branch have been carried out by Finns in the U.S.A.; this is evidenced by a doctor's dissertation on industrial cost accounting at the Commercial University, Helsinki, made partly as a result of such studies.

A very essential impetus to the development of industrial accounting in Finland was afforded by the new Act on book-keeping passed on 6th July, 1945. It stipulates that anyobdy carrying out industrial activities on a factory scale and any operators of comparable handicraft businesses shall, in addition to double-entry book-keeping, also carry out production cost accounting. This production cost accounting must be comparable to book-keeping and must be amended whenever the values of accounted items or the basis of the accounting undergo a considerable change.

The increase in the number of commercial universities—which now total four, two for Finnish and two for Swedish speaking students—and their expansion have also contributed in promoting and fructifying the development of accountancy in an ever-increasing industry. At the present stage, however, cost accounting is still seeking its definite course, which was somewhat disturbed, for example, by price control stipulations.

Certified auditors, who since 1911 have had their special professional association, have since 1925 been required to possess a basic academic training, in addition to business experience of a certain nature and duration (service in industry, in the first place). The basic requirement is the final examination of the Commercial University ($2\frac{1}{2}$ to 3 years at present), that is, an economist's examination, in addition to which candidates are required to have passed in accountancy with honours, corresponding to the degree of M.Com. or M.Econ., and to have gained a lower mark in commercial law, plus a so-called practical examination in auditing technique, auditing ethics, in the writing of an audit report, and in taxation matters.

Some of the certified auditors are permanently employed in industry as accountants. Some of them teach at commercial schools or hold other public position, undertaking audits in addition to their principal occupation. At present, however, approximately half the certified auditors (totalling approximately 90) work either as independent owners or managers of auditing offices or are employed by such offices carrying out, as their main occupation, audits for industries, commerce, shipping, banking, handicraft, societies, etc. As far as is known, all those having auditing as their main occupation participate in the audits of industrial enterprises also.

The main responsibility of auditors naturally is to inspect the book-keeping and also the administration of firms. The Finnish Joint-Stock Companies Act, for instance, considers inspection of the administration of a company to be of principal importance. Such auditing work has expanded into so-called continuous audit carried out throughout the year, and culminating in the annual audit at the end of the fiscal year. Furthermore, certified auditors assist their clients by discussing with their managements, for example, organisational problems of administration and accounting and development of internal control. It is also customary to take advantage of the auditors' expert knowledge in matters of taxation. By their activities in the various industrial branches auditors acquire abundant experience in industrial problems.

A considerable number of the administrative managers, chief clerks and operation economists, permanently employed in Finnish industry and participating in some way in the lead of accountancy, have a Commercial University degree. They thus possess a fairly thorough knowledge of book-keeping and are familiar with foreign professional literature. Side by side and in consultation with these accountants, the auditors have good prospects of participating in the development of industrial accounting on the correct lines to meet both practical and theoretical requirements.

During the war, in 1943, an Industrial-Economic Association, Teollisuus-Taloudellinen Yhdistys r.y., was established in our country, embodying in its programme co-operation between industrial management engineers and accountants. If this course is also pursued in the other associations, institutes and business firms, the management can be brought close to accounting, and the operation of accounting to management level. In this way we arrive at 'management accounting', responsible for producing quickly-compiled figures, suitably grouped for different purposes, enabling comparison of past achievements with corresponding set targets and the utilisation of data thus collected in projecting future activities. Increased interest in problems of business organisation—both static and dynamic—however, is one of the basic prerequisites for continued revival of industrial accounting.

MR. C. G. BUCK (Great Britain and Ireland):

As the problems confronting the industrial accountant vary, if not fundamentally, at any rate in detail, according to the size and nature of the firm which he represents, it might be helpful to you to know something of the speaker who addresses you. I am from the steel industry and a small to medium-sized firm.

Everything in the sphere of industrial accountancy has since the war been overshadowed by the comparatively recent craze for management accounting. Our economic struggle has thrown the spotlight on the word 'productivity'. We now have the broad picture of the accountant whom we carry in industry as a technical executive whose function it is to provide management with data, statistics, forecasts, etc., for the formulation of policy. It is an attractive picture of the accountant in industry, because he is at once creative. He has now a definite contribution to make, a direct contribution. Management is opposed to the old-fashioned view of an indirect contribution. This will undoubtedly influence the young accountants in entering the sphere of industry. In other words, the 'New Look' in accountancy has arrived, and it has arrived with a fanfare.

My object in addressing the Congress was to strike a note of caution. Where there is light there is shade, and where there is spotlight there is obscurity, and the spotlight has undoubtedly since the war been on the question of management accounting and productivity. There are many other lines with which accountants have to deal, and I think some of them are being subordinated. To give one example, in my home town I know of no fewer than three cases of large-scale fraud perpetrated by very old and trusted employees, and this has been going on for ten years under the noses of the accountants. That is only one example. There are many other fields in which the accountant works and I cannot help feeling that some have perhaps been neglected.

I leave the Congress with this thought. Can it be that we are diverting too much attention to the field of management accounting and productivity research at the expense of the rather dull routine, fundamental but vitally necessary functions which the accountant in industry has also to perform?

MR. A. M. CRAIG (Malta):

Reading through the excellent papers presented to us on the subject, it seems that on the whole the role of the accountant in industry is fairly well established. But it would appear that there still are serious hindrances to the progress in the use of accountancy as an aid to management, especially in small-scale industry. This point was expressed by the Australian contributor to the session, Mr. Fitzgerald. I hope I shall be forgiven if I measure the scope and limitations of industrial accounting in relation to the possibilities of industry as I find it in my country, Malta. Industry in Malta is of the light variety type. There are about 150 factories, but only two employ more than 200 persons, four or five 100 and the rest no more than 30. It may be that there are larger countries whose industries are provided for by the small industrialist such as I know him.

It is for this reason that I feel some concern for the small industrialist and I suggest the establishment of a research committee for the study of the adaptation of some system of standard or management accounting—call it whatever you prefer—to cater for and to be within the means of the small industrialist. He, too, is disinterested in the production of figures showing the position as it was three months or, as is often the case, twelve months ago. Small managers have, up to a point, treated the industrial accountant with a certain amount of reserve. Liaison between the accounting profession and the Institute of Management is most welcome and can do much to foster the spirit of goodwill and is of benefit to the small industrialist.

To deal with some other aspects of the accountant in industry, it seems to me that the fine distinction between cost accountancy and financial accountancy is now a thing of the past. Managers have not the aptitude to digest such fine differentiations. The accountant manager should embrace the whole field of financial forecasting, financial achievement and financial state of affairs at any specified date, either annually or half-yearly or for any other accounting period. In this last connection, he will no doubt bear in mind the complexities of fluctuating price levels, a subject so ably discussed yesterday.

This role is certainly no new adventure. The desire for the departure from the sphere of post-mortems has long been felt. It is now an intensification of activities for the proper diagnosis and the cure of an industrial disease and the preservation of a healthy life leading to industrial longevity. Different schools of thought are prevalent as to who should be the industrial doctor with the best bedside manner, the engineer or the accountant. In my view, we should leave the engineer to devote his time to the solution of engineering problems and the improvement of mechanical aids to industry. By nature he is not inclined to devote much of his time to financial intricacies, albeit that, by and large, he is receptive to good counsel. The accountant who is armed with a fair knowledge of engineering or practical science should be able to provide the right recipe or perform the necessary amputation to prevent the further

H. E. A. ADDY, F.C.A., F.S.A.A.

President of The Institute of Chartered Accountants in Ireland

spread of industrial gangrene or malignant growth provided there is a willingness on the part of the patient.

As to the recruitment and training of such a corps of accountants, perhaps I may be pardoned if I imitate Mr. de Paula who gave us a brief description of the organisation in the smooth running of a man-o'-war by drawing a parallel with the Senior Service in the method of moulding the future naval officer. In that Service the young officer, no matter in which branch he wishes to specialise, receives a full practical training in all branches which contribute to the attainment of such an efficient Service. The training of the future industrial accountant should be as diverse and thorough.

The intention is that a sound all-round knowledge should be imparted to the accountant who intends to specialise in industry in all the complexities of industry in his early training. It would be most beneficial if he were to spend some period in the drawing office and at times accompany sales managers to their various territories. Such training would give him an insight into the complications of production and sales turnover, experience which would be of great help in the intricate task of setting up standards of sales and standard performances. I do not wish to imply that he should be an engineer at the commencement of the week, a chemist during mid-week and an accountant at the end of the week, but it is necessary to provide a background so as to instil not only 'cost-consciousness' but also 'production difficulties-consciousness' as without a combination of these two elements it would not be possible to lay the keystone of the industrial accounting archway, that is, co-operation between manager, technician and the accountant.

MR. J. E. GERMAIN (France):

The accountant has always endeavoured to live up to the problems that were put before him. Industry, developing progressively from craft to the serial manufacturing stage, dragged the accountant along in the wake of its own evolution and shaped him up to a point where he became quite a new specialist, the cost accountant. Thus, it is by the very nature of the problems that were put before him that, on the spot, the industrial accountant was formed.

At the outset of the industrial age the accountant limited his activities to the work he was already performing in trade, namely, continually to deal with the affairs of the company in relation to third parties—customers, suppliers, shareholders and associates. But industrial operations greatly differed from trade operations and the industrial accountant had to face the problem of costing. While in trade the cost price is a concrete entity rather easy to build, in industry it is complicated and is alone insufficient for ascertaining to what extent a company is efficient. It was found that the cost price was an aggregate of various terms not at all independent one of the other. Eventually the industrial accountant had to stop considering his cost prices as such, but he had rather to probe into their actual meaning and then to inform the company executives about the true significance of the operations, so as to pave the way for better company management. It is generally recognised that the part played by the industrial accountant consists in

M

performing the following two duties: developing the cost price and informing and guiding the company executives. So much for the past and the present.

Now we should like to bring into light a slowly developing and novel aspect of the industrial accountant that is, to some extent, a consequence of the nature of the information he can supply. We mean the social part he plays within the company. Various are the provinces in which such social aspect is easily noticed. By analysing and checking production and distribution costs, the industrial accountant is compelled, whichever the cost controls are—simple or budget control—to discuss with the responsible people their outlays and their results, laying his finger on their accurate contribution to the common effort.

Few are the executives or even the people directly responsible who guess how considerable the value of the assets is that they are handling. This is because they do not directly spend the money but merely guide human work, use the material and tools involved and have to work exactly in compliance with the general framework of an organisation whose defective functioning can result in some very substantial labour and material losses. All this, put in terms of cost and commented upon by an aggressive industrial accountant, becomes, for the executives at all levels, a powerful means of professional team-work training. It permits a free correction of errors, often involuntarily committed against this collectivity called 'company'.

An industrial accountant, if active, and if he puts plenty of initiative in his work, becomes, indeed, the corner-stone of company efficiency. On account of his position and his knowledge, will he not become one of the most qualified agents for appreciating by what means can employees become interested in the company's progress? He will have to explain to his colleagues the influence of their performances on the balance sheet and to bring into light for those not initiated some complicated matters as those discussed in the Congress about fluctuating price levels in relation to accounts. In France, similar subjects are already taken up with the 'Comité d'Entreprise', and the discussion shows how difficult the understanding is.

Furthermore, the action of the cost accountant in our country might soon find a positive and ready application as the Government plans to favour, as far as credit and Government contracts are concerned, such undertakings that will work out any kind of incentive plans based on productivity. To achieve this, he will no longer have merely to stick to accurate computations, but he still will have to take stock of psychological considerations which he is most qualified to appreciate if, with the numerous qualities that are required of him, he combines some psychological refinement and a notion of the common good.

MR. A. E. F. GILBERT (Great Britain and Ireland):

It is self-evident on reading through the papers on this subject that all the contributors have presented us with almost a monolith of perfection and I feel sure that there is no aspect of the work of the accountant in industry on which they have failed to comment. The substance of the papers is almost as intractable as a set of multiplication tables and just about as difficult to discuss.

It is therefore with considerable temerity that I am going to enlarge a little on what I consider to be the dominant factor in any organisation of people (and what better example of this is there than the industrial unit?) namely, the human element.

Throughout the seven papers runs this golden thread of the problem of the accountant as he comes in contact with people. He meets, or should meet, face to face in his daily task all types of individuals, shop labourers, foremen, departmental managers, directors, engineers, chemists, salesmen and so on *ad infinitum*, not forgetting those six types of managers so brilliantly personified by Mr. Risk in his description of management in balance. What is his approach to these diverse personalities?

It is my belief that far too many industrial accountants lock themselves up in the seclusion of an ivory·tower, which they are loth to leave except under considerable pressure. I submit that such an attitude cannot fail to have an adverse effect on the fortunes of the companies which are blessed with such monastic specialists. Is it so necessary to remain aloof from the people who are using the figures which, it is presumed, are the product of this ivory tower meditation? True, the management accounting system may be technically perfect to the umpteenth degree; so it should if the accountant concerned devotes practically all his time to this objective, as so many do. How right Mr. de Paula is when he states in his paper, when discussing leadership, 'that the best system in the world, with bad leadership, will probably result in dismal failure'.

Here is a cardinal principle too often ignored by industrial accountants. Let them take their eyes from their text-books, schedules and calculating machines, get on their feet and walk into the factory where they will meet the dominant factor to which I have referred, the people. Then let them talk to these people, get their point of view, reply in plain language, call cotton waste cotton waste and not 'a semi-variable expense'. Let them keep these expressions for the seclusion of their ivory tower. How easy it is to slip into this appalling jargon of ours and do untold harm by using it and leaving in the minds of engineers and the like an irritable frustration. Morale was quite rightly emphasised in one of Mr. de Paula's quotations. Here is but one small example of the influence the accountant can have on this all-important aspect of life in an industrial community.

Again and again we have pleas from management on simplification of control information; of recent years even accountants are saying that this is very important and that we should present information in as simple a way as possible. But how often do we only pay lip service to this vitally important aspect of industrial accountancy? The accountant so often prepares his schedules, column upon column of figures, and then says to himself, 'Ah, I must now simplify this', which he proceeds to do. But—and this is the important point—he simplifies it by his own standards and not those of the people to whom it is being presented. The inevitable frustration then follows.

Surely the answer to this problem can only be found by either finding out what they can understand or teaching them how to understand and interpret the figures presented to them. In practice, a combination of both methods is the ideal, but each of them involves the accountant in talking to the management levels concerned. And how salutary such a discussion usually is. I have never known a case where both parties involved have not ended such a conference very much wiser than when they started. There is no better method of planting the accountant's feet very firmly on the ground. On how many occasions has there been failure to put the thing over correctly? To that extent we are contributing to some of the excess costs of industry.

Let us therefore refuse to accept Mr. George Schwarz's description of accountancy as being the dismal practice. This description can be fallacious if only we accountants inject into it the serum of humanity. This serum could be analysed as follows: tolerance, simplification, plain language and a sense of humour.

I would leave you with Kipling's words, which perhaps are not inapplicable to this aspect of our work:

'If you can talk with crowds and keep your virtue
Or walk with kings nor lose the common touch.'

PROFESSOR H. GREENWOOD (South Africa):

There is not much for me to add to the excellent papers and you have read practically all there is to read about industrial accountants. I shall content myself with stressing a point which does not appear to have been mentioned sufficiently—attitude.

It is not very noticeable, but I have three feet; I have a foot in three different fields. I qualified as an incorporated accountant and I am a public auditor; fifteen years ago I had an interest in management accounting and was a consultant; and in my spare time I am a professor in a university where I have 600 students, 300 of whom will perhaps go into industry as industrial accountants.

As a professor, I dream dreams and see visions of an industrial Utopia and hear soft voices calling for a better land. As a management consultant my only dreams are nightmares and the voices I hear are not soft ones. As an educationist I am a little worried about the tendency to try to turn both types of accountant out of the same mould. I do not think it is possible, and I am in disagreement with some of our speakers about the integration of professional and industrial accountants. I do not think they have very much in common. It is true that they both use figures to express their ideas, but so do women's magazines, with just about as much resemblance to the hard facts of life. They are entirely different in their outlook. The whole attitudes of the professional and industrial accountants are entirely different, and we should not try to bring them together, for by so doing we are only trying to make two birds out of one. Yesterday we heard that the professional accountant resembles the penguin, who walks backwards because it does not want to see where it is going but only where it has come from. That prompts me to define the industrial accountant as an inquisitive bird with a very long neck in the form of a question mark which he sticks out well into the future because he wishes to see round corners before he gets to them. How can you put the two in the same mould?

I have an intimate knowledge of the evolution of a professional accountant into an industrial accountant. The way is hard. Training is very important but experience is far more important. Even if you give a professional accountant all the training and experience in the world, unless he changes his attitude he will still at the end of the time have a professional accountant's outlook and not an industrial accountant's outlook. Therefore, it is essential that we should stress the attitude of mind to the job rather than the technical peculiarities of the difference between the professional accountants and the industrial accountants.

Mr. de Paula asks some questions on page 251 of his paper but does not answer them. When he asks questions which he does not answer, everybody should be wary in trying to provide the answers. He asks, 'Does management accounting represent a new and specialised technique within the field of accounting?' The question is wrongly put. It should begin, 'Does the application of accounting techniques in a wider sphere in the traditional field of accountants. . . .' Mr. de Paula also asks, 'Is it a specialised technique outside the field of general accounting, but embraced within the field of engineering?' It is a specialised technique not required in the normal field of accounting. Therefore, I cannot agree that it must fall within the field of engineering; it keeps its own field entirely and calls upon accounting techniques and engineering facilities for the carrying out of its functions.

MR. A. HARBINSON (Great Britain and Ireland):
There are a few aspects of the subject which appear to me to justify special comment. The first is the attitude of the industrial accountant to costs. It sometimes appears to me that reduction in costs is allowed to become an obsession to the exclusion of other factors in the situation. We must not lose sight of the fact that the objective is a larger net profit and that this can be achieved either by reducing costs or by increasing income. Increased net profit can result from increased turnover even where the cost per unit has increased.

Accountants should give more attention to the effects on income produced by increases in cost before condemning them out of hand. In these matters we must become what Mr. Risk refers to as 'profit minded' rather than 'cost minded'. We can still further enhance the value of this balanced outlook if we apply it to future prospects as well as to present conditions. The management executive is trained to look for new opportunities of developing business. Such opportunities almost invariably call for an initial increase in costs but when the project has got well under way costs can, and frequently do, become lower. The industrial accountant should not lose sight of the fact that by lending his support to such ideas in the early stages, he is playing a much more important part in the success of his business than if he merely contents himself with pointing out the short-term effect on costs, which, if it is accepted as the only criterion, may result in the project never being tried at all.

The second matter upon which I should like to express an opinion is the tendency for accountants in industry to develop into general managers. While in practice many industrial accountants do develop into most successful chief executives, I question whether a person who has the temperament and attributes of a really successful accountant can ever become a wholly successful general manager.

I am in full agreement with the tendency for accountants continuously to widen the sphere of management activities to which they apply their special techniques, but I feel that there are limits beyond which accountants as accountants should not go. The positions of accountant and of general manager call for quite different outlooks and if the industrial accountant endeavours to combine the functions of executive management with those of accountant, then it is my belief that he will fail in one or other, if not in both.

In the final analysis the accountant must essentially remain an adviser and must always allow for the fact that his advice is only one of many different viewpoints that general management must consider. If he goes beyond this, he is endeavouring to take decisions on matters which he has neither the training nor the experience to assess. This applies whether it is a cost accountant reporting to his chief executive or a finance director advising his colleagues on the board.

Finally, I should like to make a plea for the use of a little more psychology in presenting reports to management. Many accountants in industry appear to regard it as their duty constantly to underline the red figures in the reports and to emphasise failures and deficiencies. I suggest that this attitude should be modified according to the overall results reported. When things are going well, then the accountant can be as severe as he likes and the more criticism the better. At such a time the management can take it; but if the general results reported are unfavourable, then the accountant should let the figures speak for themselves and confine his remarks to such favourable items as do appear. Criticism at such a time can become little more than an irritant to all concerned, and emphasising failure can lower management morale just when it should be boosted up. Again, it can very easily destroy that mutual confidence and harmony between the management and accountant which is essential if the accountant is to play his full part in the success of his business.

I do not suggest that we should treat the management executive as a prima donna, but I do suggest that in the training syllabus for industrial accountants we should include a subject entitled 'The Peculiar Psychology of Management Executives' and in this case we might underline the word 'peculiar'.

Mr. A. Holdsworth (Great Britain and Ireland):

I propose to deal with three points, the main theme being that of interdependence and co-operation. My first point is to appeal for awareness of the social good which we, as accountants in industry, can achieve by assisting in and improving the efficiency of management. From increased efficiency should result lower costs and cheaper selling prices, thereby making available to a larger number of our fellow men the material benefits of the products and services that the scientist and the engineer are providing in ever-increasing measurement. Mr. Bennett, in his paper, says, 'The first and fundamental job of business must be to serve the public interest'. The accountant, by serving business, must also serve the public interest.

My second point, following from my first, is to suggest, in support of the remarks made by a French delegate yesterday morning, that there should be some more permanent form of international association of accounting bodies than that afforded by periodic congresses. I see from one of the papers that the Scandinavian countries have some form of liaison. The speaker yesterday mentioned an international council which, with a permanent secretariat, might be charged with the duties of liaison on uniform accounting principles for different industries, liaison on terminology and the dissemination of information and the translation of articles relating to accountancy in different countries.

Mr. Moller in his paper pointed out that agreement on uniform cost accounting principles in Canada is thoroughly lacking up to this date. In spite of several so-called uniform costing systems for different industries in Great Britain the position here is unsatisfactory.

Mr. Risk has stated that 'objective examination and discussion of technique and experience between one form and another and between one country and another can hardly fail to be for the benefit of all concerned'. The question of phraseology and terminology is an important one if we are to fulfil our duty of interpreting facts to management. Mr. Bennett uses the term 'out-of-pocket costs' in an entirely different way from what I have heard it used elsewhere. Mr. Risk has presented the hypothesis that integration of accounting must lead eventually to the integration of accountants. Whatever that may mean, I am sure that Mr. Risk would view his attachment Siamese-twin fashion to a brother accountant with a degree of alarm. Mr. de Paula uses the phrase 'centralised control and decentralised responsibility', a not altogether intelligible phrase since responsibility and control must go hand in hand. It may mean 'centralised policy control and decentralised executive responsibility'.

Not very long ago the Institute of Cost and Works Accountants published a brochure on *Costing Terminology*. Mr. Jeppesen states in his paper that his association recently appointed a committee to discuss the terminology of industrial accounts. It might be possible to use the brochure as a starting point for the discussions of our friends in Denmark and to ventilate our disagreements internationally.

My final point, following my previous point, is the development by internationally agreed uniform costing principles of standards of performance for industries or processes whereby general efficiency can be improved. This further development of control, following Mr. Risk's observation that management is in a position to study performance of the same function or the same function in alternative ways, is a performance control. In the coal-mining industry the output per man-hour is a valid international standard, provided costing principles are uniform in different countries. Other measures for other industries will readily present themselves, and even for processes within industries, which would help in setting standards of achievement—not cost standards but standards of performance—which would tend to raise steadily the productive power of the community.

Mr. JOHN I. MARDER (United States of America):

I read Mr. Risk's paper with great interest, and I appreciate the opportunity of discussing one hypothesis of his, that we have taken too narrow a view of our responsibilities as accountants. It is my belief that in the United States, the only country of which I have any knowledge, accountants are continually branching out and assuming new responsibilities. In public accounting enormous strides have taken place since the first public accounting Act fifty years ago. In costing, only forty years have passed since F. W. Taylor aroused the first interest in the subject, and in private accounting many organisations such as N.A.C.A. and the Institute of Internal Auditors have built up libraries of information on all types of private accounting.

Enlightened top management has taken heed of these developments. Our need, however, is to bring accounting development down to the smaller businesses. There is a reluctance to measure results in small businesses. The little business has to judge a wide variety of trends, ideas and hopes; expediency and opportunism form the basis of many a small business's evolution. We must endeavour to aid management of small businesses by giving direction to its activities rather than allowing the small business man, like Don Quixote, to tilt at windmills.

I feel that internal accountants must to some extent go behind the figures and find out cause and effect. Profit is only a symptom of activity effectiveness and not a cause. Small business managements wait anxiously for their financial statements, because, for the most part, they do not know whether their policies are right or wrong!

Internal accountants must, with the backing of management, be prepared to go beyond financial reporting; they must be prepared to be members of the management team. Accounting is a by-product of management; we were created by management and to some extent we are maintained by management.

Mr. Risk touched upon another subject which is of interest to me. He said that the integration of accounts must lead eventually to the integration of accountants. We need integration of accountants in all countries very much. We are divided as a profession into varied groups, and we must set our house in order if we are to advise others. I believe the Congress represents progress in this regard. If we all work towards uniformity in accounting practices, not by regulation or statute but by objectivity and a factual basis, then our respective countries will benefit.

George Brandes, a famous Danish author, is reported to have said, 'My voice will not be heard in the world—only 3,000,000 people speak Danish'.

We accountants should interchange ideas whatever our language and whatever our country. Sound accounting principles know no international boundaries, and the challenge of philosophies alien to all of us as men of goodwill can be resisted in the business world by honest presentation of facts.

MR. H. NORRIS (Great Britain and Ireland):

I believe in the essential unity of the accounting profession. Unlike Professor Greenwood, I really do believe that accountants in industry and the profession—making an unfortunate distinction—are working together very largely in the same field. The service rendered for the large concern by the internal accountant ought to be rendered for the medium-sized and small business by the outside professional accountant. This is a practice with which I am familiar, and now that I am in industry the fields of my respective employments—professional and industrial—overlap to a very considerable extent. I deal with the accounts of a considerable number of companies and some part of my time bears a close resemblance to the days when I was in the profession.

Saying that is a cover for certain criticisms about the usefulness of the professionally trained man in industry. In industry one is concerned not merely with short period profit and loss accounts. There is a tendency for the professional man on first entering industry to think, 'All I need do is prepare the same kind of figures but more often'. That is far from the case. The more experience I have of industry the less faith I have in periodic reports, which tend to be laid aside as soon as prepared by the people for whom they are intended.

I am a great believer in the special report. It is the accountant's duty to spend more time on special reporting than on periodical reporting. It is very often his duty to file the periodic reports and to make his own special report on the facts which he sees in the figures. It is his duty to analyse the facts in the periodic reports and to add to them such opinion and accounting observations as he thinks will help his management. Mr. Risk emphasised this in calling for a lively approach on the part of the accountant in industry. Liveliness of approach and imagination in the use of figures is exactly what is needed.

It is true, as one speaker said, that accountants in industry do not go out and talk to the people concerned as much as they ought. Managers have many peculiarities, and the same treatment is not common throughout industry. You must study the people with whom you are in contact.

I believe in special reports and I believe that special reports should be built on the principles of good journalism, which consists of some facts with some observations. The principles of good journalism require that the facts should be distinguished from the observations.

An accountant finds that he gets a mixed reception from management. In a large group one can make a comparison because one has to deal with various kinds of managers. One sometimes encounters resistance from people who seem to think we have a restrictive function and view us in the same way as we view the Chancellor of the Exchequer—as a man who says 'No'. The accountant in industry should not be a man who says 'No'; he should be a man who is in right at the beginning when any decision is made and should be consulted for his views.

I have served in the heavy engineering and film industries. They are different industries but they have the same kind of problems. They have the same problem of capacity utilisation whether it is buying expensive machinery or hiring a film star. Engineers are very fond of buying machines and film producers are very fond of hiring film stars. It is for the accountant to advise whether the specialist manager or the film director is doing something to help or whether it is not financially worth while.

MR. L. W. ROBSON (Great Britain and Ireland):

There is general acceptance that there are newer and better management accounting techniques which have been tried and found to be an extremely successful and extraordinarily valuable aid to modern management. As a British accountant, I feel that accountants from overseas would wish me to pay tribute to American accountants for the tremendous amount of development work they have put into the field of creating techniques and methods of budget control and standard costs.

Ten, twenty or thirty per cent. of industrial and professional accountants are not specialists in the application of these techniques. How are we to get this work done? I imagine that despite inflation and high taxation professional accountants are still interested in fees and industrial accountants are still interested in very high salaried posts. The first basic training of an accountant in a professional office is the best start in life. If the accountant then wishes to go into industry he has to specialise in management techniques. I wish we were able to get people to study the technique of financial control as a function in industry. We can never dictate selling prices but the accountant can play his part in management by controlling expense by function.

The United States are on to something in making the accountancy system fit the management pattern. I should like to see highly experienced industrial accounting with a full knowledge of these methods. They are used here in the best firms, as they are in America, but a vast number of firms have to be raised to their level. The professional accountant requires to get some of the vast specialised knowledge of the industrial accountant in order to build up specialist departments, as is being done in the United States and in some practices in this country, in order to bridge the gulf. Cross-fertilisation is needed in order to give us accountancy as a whole. There are two divisions, but they should be integrated.

The papers have established the view that there is a best method of controlling expenditure today. There may be shades of variation but functional control of expenditure by the accountant is the way, having regard to cost and an increase in the cost of living. We all have an important part to play in that in the professional office and in industry.

MR. W. SCOTT (Australia):

Looking recently through a dictionary printed not long before the war one came upon the definition of 'uranium' as 'a hard metal of no particular commercial value'. Is it surprising to find that it is essential for the accountant to re-examine his duties, practices and responsibilities and opportunities in this changing world? It is refreshing to see that the papers give a ready and admirable acceptance of this fact.

I want to comment on three aspects, each of which occurs in virtually all of the papers. I am sure you have been struck by the references to engineering and accounting. Mr. de Paula says that 'the accountant has to approach this whole problem from the point of view of the engineer and thus he finds himself in a new world'. On page 241 Mr. de Paula poses six questions as to the qualifications needed for the introduction of a system of management accounting in view of the fact that the work embraces both engineering and accounting. He follows this up on page 251 with a list of very pertinent questions upon which, being no angel, one is tempted to rush in and express a viewpoint resulting from information gathered from an Australian experiment. Over some two and a half years some very careful observations have been made in an experiment involving accountants, engineers and people with dual qualifications. The accountants are particularly well qualified in all aspects of management accounting and the engineers are highly qualified people, and some of them have a dual degree. A substantial proportion of those involved have had both United Kingdom and/or American experience and Australian experience. A similar experiment has also been carried out in other countries.

As a result of those observations—I am not suggesting that they are any more than just observations at this stage; neither you nor I would be foolish enough to draw any real conclusions from them—one would answer Mr. de Paula's questions along these lines. 'Does management accounting represent a new and specialised technique within the field of accounting?' Yes. 'Is it a specialised technique outside the field of general accounting, but embraced within the field of engineering?' No, subject to qualification below. 'If management accounting is a specialised technique, from what sources should industry draw the necessary specialists for work within industry?' From properly qualified and educated accountants. 'Is there a need for public accountants in general practice, specialised in this new technique to advise industry in the installation of systems of management accounting?' Yes, definitely.

In regard to the related subject of education, the work of the accountants was definitely improved when a number of them were given training in engineering technique or the engineering approach. The work of both the accountants and the engineers was very greatly improved when they were given courses in human and group relations. In the case of the accountants, training in both the engineering approach and the human relations was sufficient to knock down any ivory tower!

I liked the statement that management is the art of raising the standard of living. Surely the accountant has something that he should be doing to help in the raising of the standard of living.

MR. C. OLIVER WELLINGTON (United States of America):

The field of the accountant in industry and the aid that industrial accounting can give to efficient management have been so well covered in the papers that I am merely emphasising a few points.

The question has been raised in several of the papers whether cost accounting should be developed by accountants or by engineers. In my own firm we solved the problem by having on our professional staff both engineers and accountants. We have encouraged them to work together and have urged the engineers to obtain a knowledge of accounting and the accountants to obtain a knowledge of engineering as applied to manufacturing operations.

It seems to me important to stress that cost accounting is accounting and that it should be developed by those with a thorough knowledge of accounting. However, the problems must be approached with the engineering viewpoint, and the accounting must meet the actual shop conditions.

While cost accounting is of value in recording what has happened, its greatest value is for purposes of control, and it must be developed with that idea uppermost. As so well stated in Mr. de Paula's paper: 'The viewpoint of the industrial accountant is from an entirely different angle from that of the accountant in general practice. Whereas the auditor is looking backwards, the industrial accountant is ever looking forward when assisting in the preparation of plans for the future operation of his company and board.'

In the papers there are several references to monthly profit and loss statements. While these are important for financial accounting, they are not sufficient for effective control. A cost system should be so developed as to give daily reports of the more important operations. Otherwise a waste or loss may be going on for over a month without the facts being brought to the attention of the management.

Records and reports are of little value unless they lead to action, and action will be taken by the operating men if they are given the facts. Daily, weekly and monthly reports should go promptly not only to the works manager but also to department heads and foremen. The goal is to make every member of the organisation cost conscious.

Reports should be simple and show variances between the current results and the budgets or standards previously established. A cost accounting plan should be tied-in with the financial accounting so that management can be sure that no items of cost have been omitted. However, practical operating men will not be satisfied with restrictions of financial accounting if such accounting differs greatly from current economic facts. They want costs of materials stated at current prices. They want depreciation of fixed assets stated at fair rates on current values of the assets used in production. They do not want to be charged with depreciation on unused buildings or equipment, but they do want to have included in costs depreciation on assets actually in use, even if such assets have been fully depreciated in the financial accounting.

While there should not be any differences between financial accountants and industrial accountants in their understanding of accounting principles, the industrial accountants must emphasise the uses of accounting reports to management for more effective control of all the operations of the business.

While there has been great progress in the United States, there are still many companies, large as well as small, that are without the benefits of good management control through cost accounting and budgeting, and the accountant in industry can look forward to ever-increasing opportunities and responsibilities.

MR. F. R. M. DE PAULA, *one of the introducers, summed up the discussion:*

We have not had any sharp differences of opinion or a real explosion like we had yesterday morning. Perhaps it is that to many of us this is a comparatively new field and we have not quite made up our minds and got to the stage where we violently disagree with each other. There is general agreement all the way through the papers and the discussion as to our general objectives. We all feel that there is a place for the management accountant in industry and that he is fulfilling a very valuable function. We feel that in this country, and probably in others, this movement will be greatly accelerated by the drive towards increased productivity into which our troubles have drifted us.

Management accounting has evolved over a long period and not solely within the field of accounting. The necessity to understand the engineering side makes the problem a little difficult for the bodies governing the general field of accounting. We must therefore study a wide field. There is undoubtedly need for co-operation between the technical side and the accounting side. The accountant must co-operate and work with a team, and he must know all the facets of the business and how to handle them.

I want to suggest a few thoughts which it might be useful for you to ponder afterwards. The main difficulty at present is to decide exactly who shall do this work. That is why I posed some questions which I did not answer. It is for you in discussions and studies in the future to find out exactly who should do the work and what qualifications he should have. We have the accountant in general practice, the accountant full-time in industry and we have those who specialise in this work and practice. Are they all to do it? If so, each should know what part he is expected to play. If we should try to establish industrial accounting on a professional basis, as I feel we should, I agree that we should begin to have public pronouncements on the principles and procedures and get these spread round the field so that we build up a thoroughly reliable practice which will be successful even in the general field of accountants and auditors.

There is the problem of education. If we feel that this is a new and specialised technique covering a very wide field and having many complications and snags, how should those who take it up be educated and trained? I should be sorry if Professor Greenwood were correct in believing that the practising accountant and the accountant in industry cannot come out of the same mould. Many of us have come out of the same mould and I agree with Mr. Robson that cross-fertilisation is urgently needed. There are clear indications that this is happening. In the English Institute, accountants in industry are not only on the Council but are playing a very important part in the Taxation Research Committee which produces our recommendations on accounting principles, and they have done some very useful work. Mr. Robson is right. Each side should understand the other and they should work as a team. We desire more practical experience of co-operation between the auditor of the company and the accountant in industry.

Then we come to the point of how the education is to be carried out. America is far ahead of us here and most of the rest of us have a lot of leeway to make up. We should do well to study American methods and see what we can introduce into our own countries to make our education and training suitable for producing the men and women who are entering a specialised technique.

The gospel must be spread. We all know first-class systems which have failed because the gospel has not been spread and individuals in management have not understood the system. A system will not succeed unless those in management, from the chief executive to the charge hand, believe in it and use it. I have seen most expensive systems fail because they were not used properly. That is where the human touch comes in. The management accountant should not sit in his office: he should get out and get the confidence of people; he should explain the system and sell it to management.

How can we get techniques of such proved value to industry more widely adopted? The reason why they are not is ignorance. Many in management, even some accountants, regard systems as witchcraft—and the only way to deal with witches is to burn them at the stake! It is ignorance that scares small businesses and makes them say that systems are too expensive and too complicated. Industries large and small must understand that this is a profit earner and not a fixed overhead which will sink them. If it does not save them money and make them money they should not have it.

How can we do this? The Anglo-American Council on Productivity has done remarkably good work with the publication of its report but it is closing down. The only effective way to do it is through accountants. The auditor has the confidence of his clients and, generally speaking, auditors today are more in the confidence of industry than ever they were. That is where Mr. Robson's idea of cross-fertilisation comes in. If auditors have a working knowledge of this field and believe in it and have sufficient knowledge to be able to detect that the root cause of bad spots shown by the figures in the accounts is faulty control and management, they can recommend the calling in of specialists. If we co-operate and survey the field and convince ourselves that it is right, those who have the confidence of individual businesses are the ones to convince the proprietors that they require specialists.

We must spread the gospel so that we are able to produce at the right time the right people with the right education and training.

MR. W. S. RISK, *one of the introducers, also summed up the discussion:*

It is evident that the same problems exist throughout the nations represented here and that there is remarkable unanimity as to the nature of the causes and the steps proposed to solve the problems.

Working in the medium of money, the accountant in industry is the one person able to present an overall picture, whether in the past, present or projected future. He alone is able to express in common terms the wide diversity of facts and assumptions of which industrial accounting is composed.

It is generally accepted that present-day industrial accounting presupposes the use of budgets and standards, and there is agreement on the methods to provide control or the means of control. Control is a function of the individual. It appears to be accepted that the most satisfactory result of the creation of budgets or standards is that such a course necessitates the closest co-operation between the accountant and the technician, and as this enables each to appreciate the problems and the viewpoints of the others it is to their mutual benefit and to the benefit of the industry as a whole.

Much emphasis has been laid on the responsibility of the industrial accountant for forecasts of results, capital and revenue, under known, estimated or hypothetical conditions, a responsibility closely allied to that involved in budgeting and planning. It should be emphasised that such forecasts are the combined results of the estimates of the management and their expression by the accountant. The latter does not pretend to be a crystal-gazer. He is a map reader, normally responsible not for the deviations from plans but for promptly and accurately notifying that such deviations have taken place.

Industrial accounting has a dynamic nature. What is required in a moving picture rather than a still picture is an indication of trend rather than a static viewpoint. It is little wonder that a yearly balance sheet intended to provide a picture at a given moment of time has been found to be not wholly adequate to meet the requirements of management.

As to the status of the industrial accountant, there is a consensus of opinion that adequately to fulfil his functions he must be on a level equal with the heads of the organisations of the other management functions. He will not attain that merely by stating that it is a right or a necessity. That is akin to pulling oneself up by one's bootstraps, a tiring occupation.

Mr. Fitzgerald said that in his country managers are frequently unaware of the range of information that accounting provides and that accountants have done little to enlighten them. It is for the industrial accountant to earn his place in the team by his ability, personal character and integrity, and it is important to bear in mind that the accountant in industry has still a professional standing and should bring to industry, whether trained in it or outside it, high ethical standards of professional conduct and objectivity of mind.

The accountant must not undertake too many tasks. He has to draw the line between being too much of a specialist and spreading his activities over too wide an area. He has to avoid being a specialist who knows more and more about less and less until he knows everything about nothing. He must also not go to the other extreme and begin to know less and less about more and more until he knows nothing about everything.

The human touch has been stressed, and I agree that the accountant must be a psychologist in presenting results. He must give management the facts and show the results of what is believed to be one-sided management.

The aim and object of all accountants in practice and in industry is to give service to industry and management. It is debatable if the present methods are such as to provide the best training for accountants in industry. Mr. de Paula has asked some very pertinent questions and has received some answers. It may well be asked if there is not required more co-ordination and co-operation between the various accounting bodies and between the countries represented here. When speaking of integration it is necessary to stress that what we are looking for is integration of outlook rather than of function. The auditor must always be an independent observer outside industry, but it would be of inestimable value to industry if professional and industrial accountants were pulling together and understood each other's requirements. There are tremendous difficulties in achieving such co-ordination in training and development, and the solution requires statesmanlike minds of breadth and vision.

It is obvious that delegates and members are aware of the facts and their responsibilities. Not long before he died, Field-Marshal Smuts said, 'Civilisation is once more on the move'. It seems that accountancy, too, is on the move. I would remind you that at the service at Westminster Abbey on Monday the Dean of Westminster said, 'What will determine the future is the character of men and women'. The late John Buchan said, 'We can repay our debt to the past only by leaving the future in debt to ourselves'. We are trying as good accountants and as good managers to ensure that in our generation we leave a credit balance in our profit and loss account.

A vote of thanks to the authors of the papers, the rapporteur and those who had taken part in the discussion was accorded with acclamation.

WEDNESDAY, 18th JUNE, 1952

FOURTH SESSION

THE ACCOUNTANT IN PRACTICE AND IN PUBLIC SERVICE

THE ACCOUNTANT IN THE PUBLIC SERVICE

by

A. H. MARSHALL, B.SC., PH.D., F.S.A.A., F.I.M.T.A.

Institute of Municipal Treasurers and Accountants

I. SCOPE AND IMPORTANCE OF PUBLIC AUTHORITIES

For the purpose of this paper an 'accountant in the public service' is regarded as a full-time employee of one of the three main types of public authority found in England. These three kinds of authority are:

(*a*) The central government.

(*b*) The local authorities, which in England are independent administrative units, recruiting their own staff and devising their own financial and accounting procedures (subject to control on some matters from the central government).

(*c*) The public boards or corporations. These are mostly, but not entirely, creations of the present decade, established to operate those vital industries which have been 'nationalised'. The newest of the boards—those responsible for coal mining, transport, gas, electricity and air transport—are large concerns. Answerable to the central government, they are not, however, subject to detailed control by any elected body.

There are a number of smaller boards, e.g. the British Broadcasting Corporation, the Port of London Authority, but they do not present features marked enough to warrant special treatment or mention in this paper.

Most of the boards, large and small, are concerned with trading, and have been treated as such here, though there are some exceptions, e.g. the Hospital Boards and the New Towns Corporations, which rely on direct allocation from the 'votes' of central government departments.

'Mixed' undertakings, i.e. those partly owned by the Government and partly by private individuals or companies, do not figure in English public administration, except to a very small extent. A clear-cut distinction can therefore be drawn between public authorities, which are the subject of this paper, and other kinds of corporate activity.

The first two kinds of public authority—central and local authorities—have greatly extended their activities during the past century, whilst those of the public boards which were established to supply vital services to a highly industrialised community, were of mammoth size at their creation. Together, the three classes account for a considerable proportion of the activities of the community; for example, out of approximately twenty-two million persons employed, about four million, or 18 per cent., are employed by public authorities.

The quality of the accounting work of public authorities is thus of prime importance to the country; and any discussion of the profession of accountancy in England would be incomplete if it did not include a consideration of the role of the accountant in public authorities, and of the organisation of the accountancy and financial work of these bodies. Indeed, the limited competition and the absence of the automatic profits criterion leave the community peculiarly dependent on the refinements of accountancy and costing, because, in so far as tests of efficiency can be applied, they have usually to be based upon advanced accounting and costing technique. Numerical tests of efficiency are in any case difficult to devise and to apply to health, education, amenity and defence services.

II. HISTORICAL

It would be tempting by way of introduction to dwell at length on the historical development of central government accounting. From the foundation of the Exchequer in the very early twelfth century, when the records were dictated by the Treasurer to a scribe who wrote upon specially selected sheepskins, to the burning down of the Houses of Parliament in 1834, because of the overheating of the flue in which the obsolete wooden 'tallies'[1] were being burned, is a long and fascinating story.

Moreover, many historical incidents could be cited which bring into vivid relief the main problems of those who have to handle and account for public money. Thus, for instance, in the reign of Henry VII (1485–1509) an attempt was made to by-pass the normal exchequer procedure for the handling of a considerable part of the king's revenue, only to be followed in Elizabeth's reign (1558–1603) by a reversal to the old practice of more elaborate precaution and division of duties.[2] The two problems of public administration brought out by the incident —the nature of the 'stewardship' or 'accountability' of those who handle public funds, and the determination of the length to which audits, checks, and precautions should be taken—are perennial; and

[1] The tally was a primitive method of giving a receipt widely used in England, from the early twelfth century till 1826. Notches were made in the stick to indicate the amount, and the stick was cut in two, each party to the transaction retaining half. The two could be easily matched up at a future time.
[2] See A. L. Rowse *The Age of Elizabeth*, page 311 ff.

the view which is taken of them very largely determines the pattern of the accountancy of the governmental authorities.

But, in fact, historical discussion, illuminating though it may be from the point of view of principles, has little relevance to the present-day account-keeping of the central government in England which shows hardly any trace of its picturesque medieval ancestry, being a creation of the nineteenth century and the enormous expansion of state activity during the present century. The temptation to pursue the historical aspect must therefore be resisted in so short a paper as the present one.

Similarly with the other class of public authorities which have a long history—the local government authorities—the present-day treasurer or accountant is the direct descendant of the medieval chamberlain, but his duties stem from relatively recent statutes and services. Historical study therefore sheds little light on his position and functions.

Public authorities of the third class—the public boards or corporations—are new, being creations of the last half century.

III. THE NATURE OF ACCOUNTANCY WORK IN PUBLIC AUTHORITIES

Though public authorities, like commercial concerns, must have close regard to their finances, there is an important difference between the ordinary non-trading services of central and local authorities and commercial enterprise. The latter are concerned primarily with the financial result, and with the preservation, and if possible augmentation, of the proprietors' capital. Governmental bodies on the other hand exist to render a service, and they have to be judged by an intangible test—the quality of the service in relation to the amount spent. In those cases where the public authorities run enterprises of a commercial kind, e.g. the Post Office of the central government, the vast trading concerns of the public boards or the trading undertakings of local authorities, the comparison with commercial enterprise is closer. But there are still sharp differences; in particular there are no shareholders, no 'equity' and no competitors, or only limited competitors, e.g. the 'competition' between gas and electricity boards.

The work of the *central* government differs most from that of commerce, because trading undertakings form but a small part of the central government's work, though the number of individual trading concerns is considerable. Examples are: central buying of certain foodstuffs and raw materials, the Forestry Commission, the Mint, the Royal Ordnance Factories, the export guarantee scheme and the Stationery Office.

In the main the central government is concerned with raising money by taxation[1] and disbursing it on objects specifically authorised by Parliament. Government departments therefore think primarily of the 'accountability' aspect of transactions, i.e. all those who handle public funds are thought of primarily as stewards who must 'account' for their dealings with public moneys and properties. Book-keeping is on a cash basis. The departmental appropriation accounts which are presented annually to Parliament show how the actual payments made by a particular department accord with the provision made by Parliament to cover the outlays it has itself authorised through the system of Estimates and Parliamentary grants. For trading departments these cash appropriation accounts are supplemented by trading, manufacturing and profit and loss accounts and balance sheets. The accounts of these activities are published separately from the other Government accounts, and occupy two volumes annually. There are no balance sheets for non-trading services.

The second type of public authority, the local authorities, have set about account-keeping differently; they have modelled their accounts as nearly as possible on those of commercial concerns. Thus they keep accounts on an accruals basis (as opposed to a cash basis), and they keep complete asset accounts and balance sheets—even though the governmental nature of many of their transactions, the intangible nature of some of their assets and the absence of shareholders, limit the significance of the balance sheets.

The third class of public authority, the boards, are usually specifically enjoined in their governing statutes to produce final accounts according to the best commercial practice.[2] Therefore, like the local authorities, they keep complete accounts on commercial principles and, moreover, as their activities are predominantly of a trading nature, their balance sheets are more homogeneous than the consolidated balance sheets of local authorities, which have to reflect both trading and non-trading operations.

The boards expect their accounts, costs and financial statements to do more than emphasise or record the 'stewardship' of those responsible for spending moneys. Or if they think of the accounts as recording 'stewardship' it is from the point of view of accounting for the results of operations, rather than for the spending of sums provided in a budget

[1] The central government and the local authorities together spend almost 40 per cent. of the national income.

[2] Thus for example the Coal Industry Nationalisation Act, 1946, provides: 'the Board shall keep proper accounts and other records in relation thereto and shall prepare in respect of each financial year of the Board a statement of accounts in such form as the Minister may direct, being a form which shall conform with the best commercial standards and which shall distinguish the colliery activities and each of the main ancillary activities of the Board.'

and collected by taxation. The same applies to the trading accounts of local authorities which are kept as near as possible on a commercial basis.

IV. EMPLOYMENT OF QUALIFIED ACCOUNTANTS IN PUBLIC AUTHORITIES

It follows from this brief description of the accounts of English public bodies that a different technique is needed to keep the cash accounts of central government departments than the quasi commercial accounts of local authorities or of the national boards. One would, therefore, expect to find comparatively fewer professionally trained accountants in the central departments than in local authorities or boards, and this proves to be the case.

The central government does not normally experience a need for the accountant with professional background and training, save in a few special instances. Government departments have found it best to recruit suitably qualified staff for their accounting work from the general pool of a selected body of civil servants and to train them for the specialised accountancy of their department. Some of these civil servants become eligible by examination for membership of those accountancy bodies who do not insist upon a period of 'articles' with an accountant in practice, but such action is an act of supererogation on behalf of the official, welcomed, but not required, by the employing department.[1] Even the Exchequer and Audit department (broadly equivalent to an audit department with additional functions) is staffed from civil servants recruited in the ordinary way, though both this department and the branch of the Ministry of Housing and Local Government, which audits the accounts of local authorities, have specialised training schemes and examinations for their staffs.

Professionally trained accountants, recruited to special salary grades, are employed for certain purposes for which their particular knowledge and experience is needed, e.g. for negotiations or contacts with outside accountants where technical matters are involved, for checking

[1] The Society of Incorporated Accountants and Auditors, though it normally requires articles or indentures from intending examinees, allows in lieu (subject to certain conditions) service in some accountancy branches of the public service. An analysis of the society's membership at the end of 1950, kindly supplied by the society, shows the following position:

In practice or with practising accountants	4,832
Central government	318
Local government	668
Nationalised undertakings	328
Industry	1,920
Miscellaneous	711
	8,777

contract prices and charges, for fixing price controls, for Revenue investigations in cases of suspected fraud or evasion of taxation and for preparing the accounts of trading departments. The total number employed is only about 500 and tends to grow less.

These 'professional accountants' as the central government call them, are recruited periodically by open competition from candidates between 25 and 35. The kind of work undertaken by this corps of professional accountants, who stand apart from the administrative officers handling the ordinary departmental financial work, is set out in the form sent to applicants for posts. The following extract from such a notice to candidates illustrates the type of work entrusted to professional accountants in one of the Ministries:

[1]'Ministry of Food:

Maintenance of accounting records for purchases, sales, etc., compilation of final cash account and trading accounts of a commodity or services division; preparation of financial data and returns from detailed accounts, budgetary estimates, payments programmes.

Negotiating claims arising on contracts; correspondence on finance matters generally.

Financial and cost investigations; compilation of statements of profit trends of traders, manufacturers or processors.

Detail audits and their supervision and preparation of reports thereon.

Investigation of books and records of all types of food undertakings in connection with enforcement operations.'

Government service is therefore a potential field of employment for only a few professionally qualified accountants. Some members of the Crick Committee, whose final report on the form of Government accounts was made in 1950, thought that there was scope for a few appointments, at a high level, of professionally qualified accountants with outside experience, to guide government departments in the general organisation of the accountancy work and to make sure that the central government's accounts are of maximum use to the Government and to the economist—an opinion which is now under consideration by the Treasury. If public accountancy is to develop along the lines suggested at the end of this paper, there is much to be said for a corps of central government accountants charged with the task of keeping abreast with developments in accountancy, and continuously reviewing governmental accountancy in the light of current professional practice. In so far as the Treasury must approve the form of the final accounts of the boards, prescribed by the appropriate Minister, a direct interest in up-to-date accounting exists.

The accountants of English local authorities have provided themselves with trained accountancy staffs by establishing a professional

[1] Civil Service Commission, 1951, No. 3436.

association of their own—the Institute of Municipal Treasurers and Accountants (established 1885)—which examines candidates, issues diplomas, organises the profession, provides facilities for research, produces a technical journal and gives the views of the profession on technical matters to the departments of the central government who are concerned with local government. The I.M.T.A. has always required candidates to have a knowledge of commercial practice as well as of local government. This requirement, coupled with the fact that so many local authority accountants have also taken the examinations of the Incorporated Accountants, is largely responsible for the relatively complete final accounts (compared with the central government), and for the importance English local authorities attach to their annual published accounts.

The fully qualified membership of the I.M.T.A. is 2,160, and in addition there are some qualified accountants (usually 'Incorporated') in local government who do not possess the I.M.T.A. certificate.

The I.M.T.A. has welded together municipal accountants into a well organised, closely knit, profession. Students are catered for in a network of students' societies who arrange regular and systematic lectures in all parts of the country, reprint the more important lectures, organise short residential courses, and produce a students' monthly journal. Qualified members are similarly provided for in associates' sections who meet regularly in each area to discuss current professional problems, to carry out small-scale investigations and research work. Finally, chief financial officers in each part of the country meet monthly to discuss their problems.

At its central office the I.M.T.A., like the other accountancy bodies, has organised research work during recent years, in addition to carrying on its traditional functions of conducting the examinations, organising an annual conference and conferring with government departments, associations of local authorities, and kindred societies.

A pleasing feature of the past few years has been the association of other accountancy bodies with the I.M.T.A. in joint research projects. In this way the I.M.T.A. hopes to keep its members in touch with the latest trend of thought in the profession of accountancy generally, and at the same time to place at the disposal of local authorities the benefit of commercial accountancy technique where it is appropriate.

The third type of authority, the boards, are new, and are at present staffed mainly by personnel taken over from the undertakings they superseded. Much of the higher account-keeping is in the hands of qualified accountants. Staff taken from commercial undertakings would usually have a general accountancy qualification—that of chartered, incorporated or certified accountants. Staff taken over from local government authorities (by electricity or gas boards) will have the certificate of the I.M.T.A. The future field of recruitment is not yet determined, but it is unlikely that the boards will be satisfied with less than recognised accountancy diplomas. To meet the case of the Gas, Electricity and Hospital Boards, the I.M.T.A. now includes optional specialised papers for these three services in its examinations.

An indication of the number of qualified accountants employed in the boards may be obtained from the following figures kindly supplied by the officials of the British Electricity Authority which relate to electricity supply:

Chartered Accountants	90
Incorporated Accountants	95
Certified Accountants	120
Members of the Institute of Municipal Treasurers and Accountants (Inc.)	90
Members of the Institute of Cost and Works Accountants	80
	475

The accountants of each kind of board hold regular conferences at which experience can be probed, problems solved, uniformity attained, and inquiries instituted.

The identity of operations in the various regions of the boards, coupled with the statutory requirements have, incidentally, encouraged the boards to produce accounts which are standardised in form and are models of clarity and comprehensiveness, though most of the boards allow to their regions freedom in accountancy methods.

V. The Role of the Accountant in the Public Service

What is the role, be they qualified accountants or not, of those who keep the accounts in the various types of undertaking? To what extent is the keeping of accounts separated from financial administration and financial control? Brief answers to these questions will be given in this section.

In general the departmental accountant in the central government department is also the financial adviser. He is consulted when policy is being formulated, he watches the development of projects from the financial point of view, he should be a party to the drawing up of any contract, agreement or arrangement which may have financial consequences, he represents the department *vis-à-vis* other departments and outside persons on financial matters, and he is the link between the Treasury and the department. (In a few government departments, however, finance is regarded as so closely interwoven with administration that the heads of the divisions are made mainly responsible for finance. In these cases the function of the departmental accountant is restricted.) In the large departments the accountant is an under-secretary, i.e. he comes in the third rank in the hierarchy. He is appointed and removed by the Prime Minister. The departmental accountant, whatever his status in his particular department, has not, however, the supreme departmental responsibility; this resides in the permanent secretary who would resolve differences between the accountant and his colleagues.

The permanent secretary is the accounting *officer*, and in inquiries of the highest importance he appears personally to justify departmental action, e.g. before the Public Accounts Committee of the House of Commons; but usually the accountant acts on his behalf. In cases of differences of opinion with his Minister on a matter of irregularity, the permanent secretary must report to the Treasury—an arrangement which would only be operated in the most exceptional case. (Irregularity would occur where a Minister insists on a payment being made which in the opinion of the accounting officer is not covered by his statutory powers, or is in some other way improper.)

In local government, too, there is complete integration between financial control and accountancy. The chief financial officer, usually called the treasurer, is responsible for advising the committees on the financial aspects of their work as well as for the accounts, just as the accountant in a government department advises the permanent secretary. In addition he acts as cashier, paymaster and internal auditor. He has in law a direct personal responsibility to the ratepayers for the payments he makes, and cannot plead the orders of his council in justification of an illegal payment.

In one respect there is an important difference between local and central government. In the central government the Treasury exercises supreme financial control: the deletion of an item from a department's estimates by the Treasury would be final, except upon an issue large enough to be discussed personally between the Chancellor and the Minister concerned. In local government, all matters of policy are determined by the elected members themselves in committees; the finance department merely draws the attention of the committees of members to the facts, trends and possibilities. Differences of opinion between the chief financial officer and the head of another department are also determined by a committee of the elected members.

The national boards are commercial undertakings of great magnitude, operated over the whole country, and they have all the major difficulties, as well as the opportunities, of large-scale enterprise. One problem is particularly relevant to this paper: it is the point dealt with above in connection with central and local government, i.e. the extent to which accountancy work and financial control is integrated at the top level.

The general practice has been to follow local and central government, and fuse at top level the duties of the chief accountant and the financial adviser. Thus the British Transport Commission have a 'comptroller' and the National Coal Board has a central finance staff organised in three divisions under a director general of finance.

The general conclusion, taking all types of authority together, is that the public authorities normally look to the accountant, whatsoever he may be styled, to produce the accounts, to interpret them and to assume the role of financial adviser. He must therefore be acquainted with money market, the technique of costing, financial and budgetary control, taxation of profits (in the case of local authorities and the boards, who are liable to pay tax on profits in the same way as commercial concerns) and must take an active interest in the affairs of his authority.

The accountant is brought into consultation at an early stage when new projects are proposed, and he is expected to watch the financial aspects of all the activities of the concern, so that the permanent secretary and ultimately the Minister in the case of the central government, the council and its committees in the case of local authorities, the board of management in the case of the boards, have continuous expert financial advice on all aspects of their activities.

Much has been said recently in commercial circles of 'management' accounting. Public authorities in England may fairly claim that they have a well established practice of using their financial data as an integral part of the mechanism of management, though, as the last paragraph of this paper suggests, there are plenty of opportunities for improvement. Budgetary control, which has made such great strides in industry in recent years, is also a device well known to the public services. Indeed, the corner-stone of public finance is the annual budget. None the less the accountants in the public service have much to learn from the more flexible budgetary control of industry, with its continuous adjustment of target figures, and devices to bring home responsibility precisely to an individual instead of rather vaguely to a department.

VI. Comparison of Position of the Accountant in Practice with that of the Accountant in the Public Services

An international audience of accountants will naturally be interested in the relative attractions to the individual of the public service and private practice.

Accountants in practice have more independence. Accountants in the public service are employees, and if they are in a senior position they are subject to the traditional restraints on English public servants, especially abstention from active participation in politics.

Remuneration of the higher posts in the public service might compare unfavourably with the earnings of a principal in a large firm of practising accountants, probably because of the opportunities private practice affords for directorship of companies. On the other hand, as has been explained in Mr. Saunders' paper, salaries paid to subordinates are rather more in the public service.

Pensions are provided in the public service but only to a limited extent in private practice, and hardly at all for principals. The pensions schemes vary in the different forms of public service, but broadly speaking they may be taken as giving in one way or another a pension after forty years' service of roughly two-thirds the salary at retirement. Minimum age of retirement is between 60 and 65 years of age. In the central government the employee does not contribute to his pension; in the local authorities and boards he makes a contribution throughout his career by way of deduction from his salary.

The work in a large professional practice is more varied in so far as it touches many types of business.[1] But on the other hand the accountant in the public service has administrative opportunities (not always confined to finance); he becomes interested in all aspects of his authority's work, and is free from the limitation of the small-scale 'audit' which is the backbone of so much professional practice. Usually his problems of stores control, costing, wages organisation and the like, are of sufficient magnitude and complexity to be interesting in themselves, and sufficiently large to allow him to make use of up-to-date accounting machinery. He also enjoys free exchange of opinion with colleagues in comparable concerns.

Some features apply to private practice only—bankruptcies, liquidations, company accounts, trusteeships, prospectuses (in connection with invitations for new capital). The accountant in private practice may also have opportunities to advise government commissions, to become a company director and to fill honorary public posts. On the other hand, the public services have their own particularly interesting features—problems of raising capital, taxation, rating and the fixing of charges, making of rules (sometimes for country-wide

---

[1] Among the accountants in public authorities, those in local authorities are particularly happy in the variety of their work, for even the smaller local authorities are responsible for so many different kinds of activity—larger trading activities (e.g. local transport and water supply), small-scale trading (e.g. restaurants), education and cultural services, health services, social services, amenity services, protection and regulative services. Many of the larger boards, too, have interesting and important offshoots.

application) and all the opportunities for participating in policy formation and management referred to earlier in this paper.

VII. The Audit of the Accounts of Public Authorities

The financial and accounting organisation of public authorities being usually comprehensive, and controlled by qualified staff, firms of practising accountants are not generally used by the authorities except as auditors. The only continuous point of contact between the professional accountant in practice and the public authorities is therefore in those cases where public accounts are audited by accountants in practice. In the case of the central government even this connection hardly exists, because the auditing is done by the Exchequer and Audit department already referred to, the Government having always regarded it as wrong for there to be any 'external' audit of central government accounts.

The accounts of the central government are therefore audited by the Comptroller and Auditor General, a governmental official who occupies an unusually independent position being removable only on an address from both Houses of Parliament. He operates a continuous audit and is responsible, not only for the accuracy of the accounts, but for calling attention to uneconomical expenditure. His reports are considered by a committee of Parliament called the 'Committee of Public Accounts' to whom the accounting officers of the departments must account. This very important part of the national financial machinery is, however, beyond the scope of this paper.

The accounts of the local authorities are, for historical reasons, partly audited by the District Auditors Branch of the Ministry of Housing and Local Government and partly by practising accountants. An internal audit system is almost universal in all the larger local authorities, the external auditors confining themselves to test checks of routine work and examination of final accounts, matters of principle, and general organisation of the accounts.

The final accounts of the public boards are audited by practising accountants. Sometimes accounts which are kept locally are audited by local accountants, to prevent all the work falling to a few large firms. Nationalised boards are large enough to organise their own *internal* audits, to keep a continuous check on transactions and exercise an oversight over the book-keeping systems in operation. Some functions which were previously done by practising accountants on behalf of clients whose businesses have been absorbed by the boards, have thus been lost to practising accountants. The boards vary considerably in the extent to which they use their outside audit for detailed verification.

VIII. THE EFFECT ON THE ACCOUNTANCY PROFESSION OF THE GROWTH OF THE ACTIVITIES OF PUBLIC BODIES

So far this paper has, inevitably, been mainly factual. By way of postscript I now offer some personal observations on the significance to the profession of accountancy of the growth of the accountancy work of public authorities, and some account of the nature of the challenge which confronts those charged with the duty of looking after the accounts and finances of public authorities. In the concluding section I indicate some of the directions in which the accountancy and financial technique of public authorities is likely to be developed in the next few years.

The transfer to the public authorities of so much of the vital economic activity of the country, coupled with the growth of the work of the central and local government authorities, must, I think, bring about some reorientation in the outlook of the accountancy profession. As has been explained in an earlier paragraph, even the traditional aim of final accounts—to show variations in the proprietors' capital—does not apply to the accounts of public authorities. Nor is private practice now always the goal of those who qualify as accountants; many accountants find their ultimate place in industry (which is the subject of discussion at a separate session of the Conference), or in the service of public authorities.

Accountants in the public service should labour to prevent the disintegration of the profession into a number of specialist interests. To allow the peculiarities of the accounts of public bodies to blind them to the essential unity of all accounting work would be a fatal mistake, for accounts kept by accountants with a detailed knowledge of the affairs of their own concern, but who are out of touch with the profession generally, are likely to be second-rate.

In training staff in specialised branches of accountancy, stress should be laid upon the general principles common to all branches of accountancy, the aim being to give every accountant a generalised skill so that he can readily turn to the keeping of any kind of accounts, commercial or governmental.

For this reason, the profession should not countenance the idea that a diploma which caters principally for the staffs of a particular service, other than the accountancy staff, can confer the right on a successful examinee to hold himself out as an accountant, merely because a subject called 'Accountancy' which tests the candidates wholly or mainly in the accounts or finances of the particular branch of the service, has been added to the syllabus. No solicitor would pretend to be an accountant merely because the Law Society insists that he shall pass in 'Trust Accounts and Book-keeping'.

None the less many specialised techniques, and many important branches of knowledge are called for in the accountancy departments of public authorities, so that in devising training schemes and examination syllabuses for those who are in, or who wish to enter the public services, the specialised needs should be borne in mind, equally with the need for thorough training in general principles.

Those responsible for training and examination might also usefully remember that the considerable proportion of their members who find employment in the public service (and, of course, in industry) need training not only in general accountancy and finance and in the specialised branches of the service, but in administration. Much of the work of the most senior accountants in the public service is administrative, and accountancy is sometimes the gateway to posts which are entirely administrative. Accountancy bodies will doubtless give more attention to large-scale administration and cognate problems in future than in the past. The institution of a diploma in Management Accounting by the Institute of Cost and Works Accountants is recognition of the importance of administration to the industrial accountant. Administration is equally important to the accountant in the public service.

There are also some aspects of training which should be noted by those outside the public service. For instance, there is the possibility that a training in a nationalised industry or in a large local authority may be wider than that in a small practising accountant's office; the accountant trained in some branch of the public service or in private industry is not necessarily more limited in experience than one trained in private practice. To pursue this train of thought would, however, take me beyond the limits of my subject.

Broad initial training is however only the first requirement. To ensure movement of personnel between public authorities and accountants employed in private practice, no large branch of the public service should recruit qualified accountants exclusively from 'within', however thorough its methods of training personnel. It will be for each branch of the public service to determine to what extent, and at what levels, 'outsiders' can be introduced. Whilst it is often easier if outside staff is recruited at relatively low levels, this is not always the case.

Finally, there is the need for continuous exchange of experience by such media as comparative studies in the professional journals and elsewhere of the accounts and finance of public authorities, or by periodical conferences and discussion groups at which representatives of all branches of the public service would meet one another and also representatives of other fields.

These are some of the ways in which I believe the profession of accountancy can be prevented from splintering into specialist branches,

THE RT. HON. LORD LATHAM, F.A.C.C.A.

President of The Association of Certified and Corporate Accountants

and the accountant in the public service can be equipped to meet the challenge of his calling, i.e. the application of the basic principles of finance and accountancy to the transactions of public authorities.

IX. CONCLUSION

Enough has been said in this very short survey to show that accountancy in the public services is a dynamic branch of accountancy. In all three classes of authority there is a realisation of the need for post-entry training schemes, opportunities for research and constant adaptation to the rapidly changing conditions of to-day. Thus, to take two random examples, the central government has recently instituted the inquiry into its accounts which was referred to in paragraph IV, and the Coal Board have engaged a well-known firm of outside accountants to advise them on the possibilities of the introduction of standard costing into the industry.

Of the paramount need to the community for first-class accountancy and financial administration by public authorities, there is no doubt whatsoever. These authorities dispose of a high proportion of the country's wealth; and they control most of the vital services, including transport, coal, electricity and gas.

That there is a fascinating field here for study by accountants is equally undeniable. As public authorities grow in number and importance, a comparative study of the form and contents of their accounts becomes more illuminating and instructive. But most important of all, there are in this field of accountancy and costing, problems of absorbing interest remaining to be solved. Devices to make those accounts of central and local government which relate to non-commercial services indicate whether money is being economically expended; the application of modern costing notions to both trading and non-trading services, methods of breaking down operations into units which allow results to be measured and compared over different periods, and over different regions and areas; methods of analysing results and costs so that responsibility can be attached to individuals; methods of decentralising responsibility so that individuals can really influence the financial results for which they are responsible; methods of compensating for the loose integration of departments, especially in local government —all these and many other problems will keep this interesting branch of accountancy very much alive in the coming years.

N

THE ACCOUNTANT IN PRACTICE

by

G. F. SAUNDERS, F.C.A.
Institute of Chartered Accountants in England and Wales

HISTORY

Introduction

'From writing-master to taxation specialist and financial adviser.' These words might well be used to describe the alpha and omega of the practising accountant over the last two hundred and thirty years. Alas! how many accountants of to-day must wish that the teachings of their earliest counterparts had but found deeper roots.

In recent years, the work of the accountant has expanded considerably. This paper, however, is intended to deal only with the sphere of work of the accountant in practice.

The expression 'in *public* practice' is frequently used to describe the accountant in practice, but as the addition of the adjective 'public' might tend to confuse the subject-matter of this paper with the work of the accountant in public service, I propose to omit any reference to the word 'public' in this connection. Indeed, it is interesting to note that as long ago as 1876 a contributor to *The Accountant*[1] objected to the use of the word 'public' on the grounds that one might almost as justly speak of 'public' bakers or butchers.

The main distinction to be borne in mind is that the accountant in practice is independent, working either on his own account or in partnership with other accountants. He offers his services to the public for reward but is not primarily the servant of any corporation or other body.

There are a number of definitions of a profession, of which Lord Simon's is probably the most complete.[2] He said:

> 'First of all, a profession essentially involves this, that it is based on preliminary study and, it may be, examination on the general principles of the pursuit. In the second place, a profession, I venture to think, essentially involves this, that the profits which may be made from its pursuit do not primarily depend upon the command of great quantities of capital. Thirdly, and most important of all, a profession is a pursuit which is followed not solely as a livelihood, but always subject to overriding duties, prescribed by a code of professional honour involving in an especial

[1] *The Accountant*, 9th September, 1876.
[2] *The Accountant*, 5th May, 1951.

degree the strict observance of confidences, in which the work that we do must be rendered to our clients without stint, in proportion to our clients' need rather than in proportion to the reward which we receive.'

There are many points raised in this definition and I hope to deal with most of them in their appropriate place as this paper progresses.

Ancillary Occupations

The profession of accountancy is, of course, of more recent growth than that of the church, the law and medicine, and in its early stages it was combined with other occupations. At one time accountants appear to have described themselves as 'Writing-masters and practitioners in mathematics' who advertised their willingness 'to rectify accounts or books gone into disorder'.[1]

Their activities in those days would not fulfil the strict definition of a profession referred to above as there was no rule of etiquette against advertising, and their work was essentially of a commercial character. A certain accountant in Liverpool in 1790 had the additional description of 'dealer in tinplates', and for many years the business of stock-broking was carried on by accountants. In Scotland this is still the case with some firms, and in England there remain a few who are entitled to describe themselves as 'chartered accountants and estate agents'.

One of the earliest recorded instances of the appointment of an accountant in the form which is more recognisable to-day, was at the time of the South Sea Bubble, in 1720: Charles Snell was then employed to wind up the affairs of Messrs. Sawbridge & Co., a financial house which was among the many people and firms which became insolvent when the bubble burst.

The rise of the accountancy profession to a standing of its own was not entirely welcomed by the legal profession, a position which is very different to-day, for it was Justice Quain who, in 1875, referring to the Bankruptcy Act, 1869, said: 'The whole affairs in bankruptcy have been handed over to an ignorant set of men called accountants, which was one of the greatest abuses ever introduced into law.'[2]

Although there are records of the exercising of the profession of accountancy in Venice as far back as 1581, it is not until the later years of the eighteenth century that the activities of the profession become noticeable in this country.

Apart from the ancillary occupations to which I have referred, the main work of the practising accountant was in connection with the

[1] *Chapters in History of Book-keeping and Accounting*, by David Murray (Jackson Wylie & Co.).
[2] *A Short History of Accountants and Accounting*, by A. H. Woolf (Gee & Co. (Publishers) Ltd.).

winding up of insolvent estates. This occupation formed an even more important part of an accountant's practice following the Bankruptcy Act, 1869, which provided the foundation for many of the firms practising to-day.

Early form of Articles

Conditions under which the accountant then worked were very different from those of to-day and in most cases, like his brothers in the legal profession, he lived and worked on the same premises.

Twentieth-century articled clerks would find the leisure hours and conditions of their Georgian counterparts very restricted by contrast. This is clearly illustrated by the terms of the articles between one of the founders of my firm, Mr. Harmood Banner, and his son, Mr. Harmood Walcot Banner, dated 6th July, 1830, an extract of which I set out below:

'The said Harmood Walcot Banner of his own free will and consent doth by these Presents, put, place, and bind himself a covenant Servant or Apprentice to the said Harmood Banner from the Day of the Date hereof, during the Term of seven Years thence next ensuing, and fully to be completed and ended. AND the said Harmood Walcot Banner doth covenant, promise, and agree, to and with the said Harmood Banner that he the said Apprentice Harmood Walcot Banner shall and will faithfully serve his said Master his Secrets keep, his lawful Commands gladly obey and do; hurt to his said Master he shall not do, nor suffer to be done by others, when it is in his Power to prevent the same: His Master's Goods he shall not waste or embezzle, the same give or lend without Leave; Day or Night absent himself from his said Master's Service; nor do any other Act, Matter, or Thing whatsoever, to the Prejudice of his said Master but in all things shall demean and behave himself towards his Master as a faithful Apprentice ought to do.'

The obligations were not all one-sided, for:

'the said Harmood Banner doth hereby for himself, his Executors, Administrators, and Assigns, covenant, promise, and agree to teach, inform, and instruct, or cause and procure to be taught, informed, and instructed, the said Apprentice, by the best Ways and Means, he can in the Art, profession or business of an Accountant as now practised by him the said Harmood Banner and also shall and will find and provide the said Harmood Walcot Banner during the said term with Board and Lodging and with necessary and becoming apparel the washing and mending thereof and with physic and surgery in case of sickness.'

The underlying principles of present-day articles are much the same, although they are stated at considerably greater length and no reference is made to the more domestic matters which arose because the clerk lived on the premises of his principal.

Accountancy Bodies in the United Kingdom

The first organised body of accountants to be formed in the United Kingdom was the Society of Accountants in Edinburgh in 1854 and this was followed later by:

The Institute of Accountants and Actuaries in Glasgow. 1855.
The Society of Accountants in Aberdeen. 1867.

These three bodies were amalgamated in 1951 by the absorption of the members of the last two mentioned into the Edinburgh Society under the title of the Institute of Chartered Accountants of Scotland.

The first bodies to be formed in England were:

The Incorporated Society of Liverpool Accountants. 1870.
The Institute of Accountants. 1870.
The Manchester Society of Accountants. 1871.
The Society of Accountants in England. 1872.
The Sheffield Society of Accountants. 1877.

In 1880, the Institute of Chartered Accountants in England and Wales was founded on the petition of the five bodies mentioned above, and whilst the old Institute and the Society were dissolved, the Liverpool, Manchester and Sheffield societies remained in existence and still continue to-day as district societies.

Other bodies of accountants were later formed in the United Kingdom and various amalgamations have subsequently taken place. The present composition of the remaining sponsoring bodies to the Congress is:

The Society of Incorporated Accountants and Auditors. 1885.
The Institute of Chartered Accountants in Ireland. 1888.
The Association of Certified and Corporate Accountants. 1939
(previously The London Association of Accountants 1905
in which was merged:
The Corporation of Accountants. 1891.
The Institute of Certified Public Accountants. 1903).
The Institute of Municipal Treasurers and Accountants. 1901
(following the unincorporated association known as
The Corporate Treasurers and Accountants Institute, founded 1885).
The Institute of Cost and Works Accountants. 1919.

Growth of the Profession

In Fig. 1 is shown a graph setting out the combined growth of all the above bodies.

Although our forbears had the prudence to organise themselves into a learned profession, they could not foresee how far and how wide

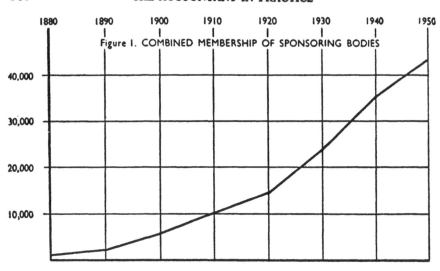

Figure 1. COMBINED MEMBERSHIP OF SPONSORING BODIES

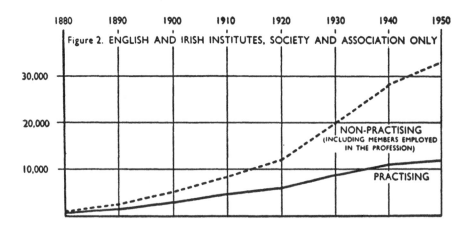

Figure 2. ENGLISH AND IRISH INSTITUTES, SOCIETY AND ASSOCIATION ONLY

NON-PRACTISING
(INCLUDING MEMBERS EMPLOYED IN THE PROFESSION)

PRACTISING

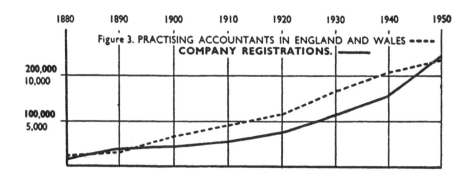

Figure 3. PRACTISING ACCOUNTANTS IN ENGLAND AND WALES ----
COMPANY REGISTRATIONS. ——

their efforts would develop. In June, 1890, a member delivering a lecture was reported in *The Accountant*[1] of that date as having said:

> 'As regards the *distant* future, he would be a bold man who would say that the society of that day would number Accountants among its members. Accountants are the product of present economic conditions the outcome of which cannot be foretold. . . . Without any moral progress we may have economic changes which will render accountants superfluous.'

The economic changes which have come to pass would appear to have had the opposite effects to those expected by the lecturer.

Expansion in Numbers of Non-practising Members

The original Institute of Accountants was composed almost entirely of members in practice, but the position to-day is very different. I set out in Fig. 2 a graph showing the division of the membership between practising and non-practising members from 1880 to 1950. This, however, covers only the membership of the English and Irish Institutes, the Society of Incorporated Accountants and Auditors and the Association of Certified and Corporate Accountants, as full information about Scotland was not available.

Although it will be noticed that the non-practising element has now become the greater proportion of the members of the professional bodies, a substantial proportion of this element is employed in practising accountants' offices.

The graph in Fig. 3 shows the expansion in the practising members of the three English bodies referred to above as compared with the numbers of companies on the English register.

The Institute of Cost and Works Accountants and the Institute of Municipal Treasurers and Accountants are two separate bodies which deal with more specialised sides of the profession.

In my view, it is most important that the practising and non-practising members of the profession should work closely together. Such radical changes have taken place in the work of the accountant in practice over the last fifty years and the expansion of business has so extended the volume of detail encountered in an audit, that their co-operation is essential.

Most of the professional bodies have established research committees on which both elements of the profession are almost evenly represented, and it is surprising what a difference of outlook there is on some of the subjects which are discussed; a feature which is invaluable in thrashing out many of the problems with which the profession is faced, as it helps to prevent the publication of recommendations and memoranda which may be too theoretical.

[1] *The Accountant*, 28th June, 1890.

Milestones in Progress

The activities of the professional accountant have shown a steady expansion over the past seventy years. This expansion is partly due to the increased complexity of modern business, but is very largely caused by the increase in the amount of national legislation which bears upon the daily activities of industry and commerce. Among those which have had an important bearing upon the practising accountant, may be found the following:

(1) The Bankruptcy Act, 1831.
(2) The Relief of Insolvent Debtors Act, 1842.
(3) The Railway Clauses Consolidation Act, 1845.
(4) The Companies Act, 1862.—This was at the time described as 'The accountant's friend'.[1]
(5) The Bankruptcy Act, 1883.—This was the first act in which Official Receivers were established, and the first Principal Official Receiver to be appointed was Mr. R. P. Harding, who was President of the English Institute in the year 1882. On his appointment, Mr. Harding resigned his membership of the Council and retired from the firm of Harding, Whinney & Co., in which he was a partner.
(6) The Bankruptcy Act, 1890.
(7) The Building Societies Act, 1894.
(8) The Companies Act, 1900, which first provided for the compulsory appointment of auditors.
(9) The Companies Act, 1908, which provided for the formation of private limited companies; and finally,
(10) The Companies Act, 1948, which for the first time provided that, with certain exceptions, auditors of limited companies should be members of recognised professional bodies.

It is amusing to record that the first direct recognition of the Institute of Chartered Accountants in England and Wales in a Parliamentary Bill was in the Lunacy Acts Amendment Bill, 1885, under which the accounts of certain institutions registered for the reception of lunatics were required to be audited once a year by a member of that Institute. I cannot trace, however, that this particular clause ever reached the Statute Book.

Taxation is another field which has provided a considerable amount of work for the practising accountant due to the rapidly increasing rate of tax and the complexity of the legislation. In the early days, when income-tax was no more than a few pence or shillings in the £, one finds little record of the subject in contemporary professional journals,

---

[1] *History of Accounting and Accountants*, by Richard Brown. (T. C. & E. C. Jack.)

and it is not referred to in any catechism of the principal occupations of the practising accountant. Indeed, the Finance Act, 1900, contained only one clause dealing with income-tax.

This position has changed over the past forty years. The year 1909 saw the imposition of a super-tax; 1916 the first excess profits duty, and 1939 not only the excess profits tax, but also the increase in the rate of income-tax to 7s. in the £, which subsequently rose to the unprecedented figure of 10s. in the £.

All these increases of taxation have brought with them not only problems connected with the computation of the profits to be assessed, but in addition they have had a serious effect on the moral standards of the commercial community, thereby placing a much heavier responsibility on the accountant, who is usually called upon to compute the profit for assessment.

The progressive expansion of the work of the practising accountant may be traced through the stages which I have set out. From the administration of the Bankruptcy Acts, dealing with the affairs of the private firm, whether from the growing angle of taxation or from an audit standpoint, to the auditing of the accounts of small private companies and the large public corporations which we see to-day.

The tendency in this development has been to remove the intimate atmosphere in which the practising accountant himself previously operated. So much of what is done to-day must be carried out by his managing clerks and their assistants, leaving the accountant to exercise supervision and to deal with points of principle rather than matters of detail.

THE PROFESSION AS IT IS TO-DAY

Nationalised Industries

Whether one accepts the policy of nationalisation or not, it cannot be overlooked that many of the basic industries and utilities of the nation will continue to be operated under public corporations far removed from direct government control.

What part can the practising accountant play in this development? It is ever more vital under such conditions that the results of the public services should be reported on by independent persons who have the knowledge to ensure that a true and fair account of their trading activities is presented to the public—to whom the management is ultimately responsible. Furthermore, it becomes more than ever necessary that the practising accountant should concern himself with matters of principle, leaving the matters of detail to be dealt with by a department of internal audit.

One of the most noticeable features in the development of large-scale enterprise is the shortage of those who are trained to administration on this vast scale. Much of the training which can be acquired in the offices of practising accountants should fit men for this task. With the extension of the public services, it has been the common experience of accountants in practice that many of their best assistants have been drawn away into the public service. I will not, however, develop this theme as it obviously falls more properly within the province of Dr. Marshall who is dealing with this side of the activities of the accountant.

Auditing

The science of auditing has not stood still, but has developed abreast with commercial practice. It is affected partially by legal decisions and partially by changes forced upon the profession by the increasing complexity of modern commerce and by other changes which are necessarily brought about by the adoption of mechanical methods of accounting, which have superseded the older methods.

Of the legal decisions, the most important in this connection is probably the case of the *Royal Mail Steam Packet Co.* (1931) which dealt with the non-disclosure of the utilisation of secret reserves. Up to that time, whilst it had always been regarded as wrong to overstate profits, it was not necessarily considered improper to understate them— indeed, this was regarded as a prudent virtue. It is to-day appreciated that either extreme results in a true and fair view of the profit being distorted, and prevents fulfilment of the requirements of the Companies Act, 1948.

Another important decision was in the American case of *McKesson and Robbins* (1939), which dealt with the verification of the existence of stock-in-trade. Up to now, this aspect of an audit has not been brought into great prominence in this country, but there is a body of thought which feels that sooner or later a great deal more notice must be taken of the duties and obligations of stock verification.

When the audit becomes so extensive that it is impossible for the auditor to carry out his work in the fullest detail, questions of principle take first place, and tests, rather than detailed checking, assume the greater importance. Testing the methods of stocktaking is therefore more likely to become a leading part of the audit programme of the future—even more than it is to-day.

The research committees of the various professional bodies which have been formed over the last ten years have devoted most of their exploration to accounting principles rather than to auditing practice. Those principles which they have laid down have met with a considerable measure of success and have led to an improvement in the all-round standards of accounting.

Auditing is not a matter which can be dealt with in a similar manner: it is essentially a question of experience and judgment and it is not possible to lay down any hard and fast rules for general adoption. It therefore becomes necessary for the accountant to keep his audit programmes under constant review so that, apart from the avoidance of their becoming stilted, he can ensure that his clerks' time is spent on matters which are of value and not wasted on items which are of little consequence. Many points of audit which were essential seventy years ago are unnecessary to-day because of the different methods of book-keeping which have developed since then.

Internal Audit

Not only are the affairs of industry becoming more complicated and involved but, owing to amalgamations, nationalisation and the development of large combines, their activities are more widespread. This all tends to make the work of the auditor more remote from detail than in the past, and a different practice must come to pass if this is to be efficiently carried out in the future. I believe we shall reach the stage when the auditor, as we understand him to-day, will become the auditor of policy and principle. In shaping his certificate he will take into account his views of the functions and the audit programme of the internal auditor, whose duty it will be to ensure the verity of the internal and day-to-day transactions of the business.

With this development, the position of the internal auditor will become more important, and it becomes increasingly essential that he should have a strong professional body behind him and remain actively associated with the practising side of the profession so that he may maintain a position of independence in carrying out his work. The result of such a change would mean that the practising accountant would work with a smaller but more specialised staff who would deal with audits on the basis of principle.

Audit of Management

There have been demands in certain quarters for the accountant to undertake an audit of management. If by this it is intended to mean that he should criticise the activities of the executive this seems to be outside his province. On the other hand, if it is intended to refer to the measurement of efficiency, then it may well be that he can be of service to management by indicating the basis upon which a standard can be set up and comparison made with the similar standards of other units and trades.

I suggest that this line of thought may be developed in the future in conjunction with accountants in industry or in the public service.

Although the accountant in practice cannot be a judge of technical efficiency he can perform a useful function by periodically making an independent report on finance and financial administration. This is particularly appropriate in the case of nationalised industries where the controlling factors of profit and competitive charges are absent. Indeed, it becomes increasingly important, as the work of Parliament to-day is too heavily laden to enable full attention to be given to annual reports of these industries, except to the more outstanding features, and much of the routine detail passes without comment.

Independence

One of the most important characteristics of the accountant in practice should be his position of independence. From this standpoint he is able to present to Government commissions or to the Board of Inland Revenue a dispassionate view of the difficulties facing his clients and of the problems arising out of legislation and its practical application, without these views being tainted in any way—as they frequently are in the case of those who are immediately affected and who naturally look at them from a biased standpoint.

It is also important in his position as auditor. Under the Bill which preceded the Companies Act, 1948, it was proposed to provide complete independence, but this was amended during the passage through Parliament, and in the final Act modifications were made in favour of a partner or an employee of a director being authorised to accept appointment as auditor in certain cases.

In my view, even in the case of a private company, independence is more important than convenience, and it would have been better to have adhered to the original proposals.

This independence is to some degree lost by those who go into industry and public service and it is being lost by other professions, such as the medical profession which, in the United Kingdom, has fallen under the ægis of the National Health Service. Let us hope that this will not be the lot of the accountant, for it is more than ever necessary that a client's interests should be represented by someone who is completely independent and not in any way the servant of the Crown to whose agent the client's profits have to be revealed for purposes of assessment.

In some countries restrictions are placed upon auditors holding shares in their client companies and, although there is no legal restraint in this country, I think that this principle should be regarded as the best practice.

Qualifications of the Practitioner

What are the qualities required by the accountant in practice? Apart from his technical qualifications, undoubtedly the most important is his experience, which should enable him to supervise those who work for him. By his training he is naturally cautious and yet he must be able to take the initiative when required. He should have the ability to concentrate and to sift evidence, to take a realistic view and to inspire confidence. He is more often quiet and of a retiring disposition but, of course, as in all professions, a good personality will be a great asset to him. Above all, he should be patient and understanding and be endowed with tact and determination.

For many years, the principal activity of the practising accountant was the auditing of accounts, but with the growth of modern commerce the proportion of any practice which is devoted to this is very much less. So far as auditing is concerned, this may be of the accounts of companies or public boards when the statutory requirements are defined, or of private firms where the auditor's duties may be restricted by agreement. But, in either case, it is important to realise that the accountant should certify only from his own first-hand evidence and knowledge and not on the basis of information supplied to him by others. It is in the exercise of his judgment in this respect that he either succeeds or fails in his task.

Directors of Companies

It is becoming more and more the practice to appoint accountants to the boards of public and private companies; in many instances they become managing directors or chairmen. In other instances, they are there as part-time directors and bring to the board meetings their knowledge of finance and wide experience of industry or commerce. They are able to regard the proposals which come before the directors from the accounting and financial angle and from the nature of their training they exercise a brake upon any over-optimistic outlook on the part of other members of the board, thus serving as a steadying influence.

Executors and Trustees

The practice of a client appointing his accountant as one of the executors under his will has been found to be particularly convenient. The accountant has probably a greater accumulated knowledge of the deceased's wishes than any one else and, in addition, has the means readily available to administer the trust.

By his personal knowledge of the family of the deceased he can advise and assist them in a less official manner than a trustee corporation.

The trustee departments of the principal banks and insurance companies have entered into this class of work over the last thirty years, but while they offer the advantage of continuity in trusteeship by virtue of their corporate status, the personal approach and intimate knowledge of the deceased's affairs is in most cases more valuable.

This advantage is sometimes more readily appreciated by the beneficiaries under a will than by the testator.

Prospectuses

The certification of profits for prospectus purposes is another important part of an accountant's duties. Until recently, this work was of a very specialised nature, but is now becoming more widespread.

There is no doubt that with the increase in the burden of death duties and taxation, and the resulting necessity for many private family companies to become publicly owned, the outlook for this part of the work of the profession may be regarded as steadily increasing in importance.

Although certain principles are laid down with regard to the preparation of these certificates and the research committees of the professional bodies have issued memoranda dealing with the subject, the ultimate statement rests upon the judgment of the accountant himself. He is frequently called upon to make a number of necessary adjustments so that any changes which may have taken place during the basic period are clearly allowed for, and the profits of the past stated on a similar basis to the recurring profits of the future. The accountant has to remember that in these cases he must deal with the facts as he finds them, avoiding any estimates, especially with regard to future prospects. This is an aspect which frequently appears in a prospectus, but it is a statement which should appear over the signatures of the directors and not form part of the statement of facts which is certified by the accountant.

Taxation

With rates of taxation as high as they are to-day, any new venture which is commenced has to be carefully considered beforehand from the point of view of how taxation will affect the company and its undertaking; in what manner any additional capital that may be required should be raised, and what assessments will arise on the profits which are subsequently made. The accountant, over the past forty years, has acquired great experience and a high reputation for dealing with this part of a company's affairs and for advising the directors on their company's taxation position.

Although this is principally a matter of the application of law, this field has been largely left to the accountant and not so much practised by the legal profession until the stage of appealing to the Courts is reached. Indeed, under Section 137 of the Income Tax Act, 1918, an accountant who is a member of an incorporated body is entitled to be heard on behalf of his client at appeals before the Commissioners, and where the nature of the appeal is a dispute on a question of fact, he is probably the most appropriate person to deal with the matter. On the other hand, where the question of the appeal is based rather more on law and where it appears that the case is likely to go to a higher court before a final decision is obtained, then it is customary for the client to be represented by a solicitor or counsel from the outset so that the case may be handled consistently by the same person throughout the period of the argument.

The settlement of taxation assessments is largely a matter of tripartite agreement between the taxpayer and the Inland Revenue, with the accountant acting as intermediary. He is trusted by his client to make a fair and just settlement and by the Inland Revenue to make a full disclosure of the facts, after which he should and is expected to fight to the best of his ability in his client's interests.

This relationship has been so firmly established and the accountant's reputation for fair dealing so fully accepted by both sides, that taxation liabilities are settled with relatively little recourse to appeal.

When taxation was a few pence or shillings in the £, it was a levy on profits and income for the purpose of running the essential services of a country. But to-day it has become a very different instrument. It is now used for the purpose of transferring wealth from one section of the population to another, with the result that, by the weight of its burden, it controls policy and finance to a degree that cannot be left out of account in considering the management of a business.

The prospect of any change in this respect taking place in the future seems to be unlikely; the profession must therefore accustom itself to this being a permanent feature of its activities and ensure that the best advice that can be given to its clients is available when they require it.

So long as taxation remained at a modest level, it was possible for businesses to continue in the same hands from one generation to another, but now that taxation deprives the shareholder of so large a part of his earnings during his lifetime and prevents him from building up capital invested outside his business to meet death duties, this is not always possible.

Death duties also are at such a high level that the question of the valuation of shares—either for the purpose of assessing the duty, or for the purpose of sale so as to realise the necessary funds to meet the duty—is becoming of increasing importance. The part which accountants, with their experience, can play in this field, will be of great value in the future.

Government Commissions

The contribution which may be made by the accountant as a member of a government commission or trade committee is being increasingly recognised. He brings to this work probably a more practical knowledge than many lawyers who hitherto formed a rather larger part of the personnel of such commissions. The legal mind is, of course, invaluable on many points, but the practical aspect in the production of reports is of vital importance. Such cases as the Monopoly Commission are particularly in point. Government commissions appointed recently to deal in particular with taxation and company law have all had representatives of the accountancy profession on them, who have been able to give a clear indication of the effect of the submissions which were made. Indeed, even apart from the accounting knowledge which the accountant brings to such gatherings, his widespread experience of different businesses also is of considerable value.

With so many trades calling upon their members to provide statistics and returns of their trading for the purpose of agreeing prices with government departments and for other purposes, it is necessary to find some neutral person to whom this confidential information may be entrusted with complete safety. The accountant frequently finds himself faced with such a trust to-day. Many traders who would be unwilling to disclose their affairs are quite prepared to do so when they know the information is to be summarised by a firm of accountants.

Honorary Work

Some of the practising accountant's work is done in an honorary capacity, and there can be few offices where a substantial proportion of time is not occupied in dealing with the affairs of clubs, hospitals, or other charities, although since the National Health Act came into force, the work which the practising accountant was expected to contribute towards the running of voluntary hospitals has ceased and any function which he now performs is in his personal capacity on the management committee rather than work being done by his own staff in office hours. The extent of the voluntary work done by accountants in the past is evidenced by the steep rise which has taken place in the administration costs of hospitals since they were nationalised.

Management Accounting

There are many firms which specialise in advising on management accounting. Not all these firms are accountants in general practice, none the less, the subject is one on which accountants in practice are well able to advise their clients and without difficulty to keep in continuous contact with them, whilst any changes which may have been advocated are being effected. They have the advantage of knowing the personnel with whom they are dealing and they have an extensive knowledge of the past history of their client. At the same time, it is a service which cannot be provided by every small firm as it requires, in the first instance, the whole-time application of members of the account-ant's staff. Not all firms are able to have staff available for this purpose for so long a period.

It behoves the accountant in practice to train himself intensively to become constructive, to make useful contributions towards solving the problems of industry and commerce, and not to be purely critical and negative in his advice.

It will be seen, from what I have said in the foregoing paragraphs, that the accountant performs many services and functions for his clients: he is the architect of a business when it is built, the surgeon or physician during its lifetime in tending its health and diagnosing its difficulties; the policeman protecting the shareholders from those who would misdirect their affairs and ultimately, should the need arise, he fulfils the duties of the undertaker.

The Accountant's Relation to His Profession

Functions of the Professional Body

The functions and activities of his professional body are more important to the accountant in practice than to his colleagues in either industry or the public service, whose techniques and procedures are related to the industries or departments which they serve.

The principal functions of a professional body are:

(*a*) the maintenance of a standard of professional conduct through its disciplinary committee;
(*b*) the admission of members and the maintenance of their standard of qualification through its examination board;
(*c*) to watch over legislation which may affect the professional accountant or his client;
(*d*) to organise facilities for research and post-graduate training; and
(*e*) to advise government commissions and ministers, from an independent standpoint, on proposed legislation, or on the effect of completed Acts.

Etiquette

If the auditor is to carry out his work efficiently, he may find that on occasion he must be prepared to take a strong line and stand out for what he believes to be right. His position is immeasurably stronger if the professional body to which he belongs has a strict code of etiquette. He can then maintain his position in the full knowledge that if his right or judgment is in any way criticised, none of his colleagues would accept any lower standard if threats were made to remove him from his appointment on account of the stand he was taking.

Complaints from time to time will arise on account of audits passing from one accountant to another, but the accountant who is asked to accept nomination should realise that the code of etiquette which is laid down is not only for the protection of the outgoing auditor, but also to prevent the incoming auditor or accountant from being placed in a false position.

This code of etiquette is not always understood and it is sometimes difficult to explain to a prospective client the need for consulting one's professional brethren before undertaking new work.

Special circumstances naturally do exist, but I set out below a pronouncement by the English Institute on this subject, which indicates the code which might be followed by all who are concerned in the prestige of their profession:

'It is the duty of any member of the Institute before accepting nomination for appointment as auditor or professional accountant to a company, partnership or private individual to communicate with the previous auditor or professional accountant.

'The Council indicated in its statement of April, 1937, that such communication should be made with a view to ascertaining the circumstances in which a change of auditor was proposed. Some members appear to have assumed that if the person proposed to be appointed believes himself to be aware of the circumstances in which the change is proposed, then he is relieved from the duty of communicating; the Council therefore wishes to make it clear that the duty to communicate exists in every case. It is essential that the member who is proposed for appointment, whether as auditor or as professional accountant, shall have an opportunity of knowing all the reasons for the change and this requirement can only be fulfilled by direct communication with the holder of the existing appointment.

'Apart from any question of professional courtesy it is important that the legitimate interests of the public and the independence of the existing auditor or professional accountant should be safeguarded and that a communication should take place even though the change is a matter wholly within the discretion of the appointer. The duty to communicate is not confined to cases where the previous appointment was held by a member of the Institute.

'Compliance with the duty to communicate will not necessarily preclude the Disciplinary Committee from considering any complaint which may be made under Clause 21 (3) of the supplemental Royal Charter.

'Where a member is invited to undertake special professional work for a company, partnership or individual, such work being in addition to that already being carried out by the client's auditor or professional accountant and where no question of replacement arises, it is normally desirable, as a matter of professional courtesy, for the member invited to undertake the special work to notify the client's auditor or professional accountant unless the client advances satisfactory reasons for the member not so doing.'

Advertising and Publicity

As accountancy was not recognised as one of the learned professions in its early stages there was no bar to advertising; during the hey-day of the Bankruptcy Act particularly, it was common practice for accountants to tout for work round the various trades and creditors who were involved in the failures. This is now seriously frowned upon and advertising in any shape or form is a discreditable act. A few examples are as follows:

The insertion in heavy type of a firm's name in a directory.

The insertion in the public press (other than the professional press) of notices of changes in partnership or addresses.

The use of an accountant's position as secretary of a trade association for the purpose of securing business.

The addition, in connection with any published article or broadcast, of the member's name with his description as an accountant, or his firm name, after it. Either he writes anonymously as an accountant, or under his own name without any such description. (Exception is, however, made in the case of articles in the professional press.)

Specialisation

Practising as a consultant specialising in a small field of science is developed strongly in many professions, particularly in that of medicine. In the case of the law, the distinction is more clearly maintained between the solicitor in general practice and the barrister. The latter, apart from his general activities in chambers, acts principally in Court and usually specialises in one branch or another, e.g. criminal law, chancery law, and so on.

The accountancy profession, however, has either been slow to develop in this direction or has found other and possibly more satisfactory methods.

Most firms do not specialise in one field or another deliberately, but through accident. In their connections with a particular trade they may become specialists in a certain branch.

Some firms specialise in a particular type of business, for example, underwriting, textiles, engineering, shipping, insurance, etc., or the partners may specialise within their own firm in one plane or another; and do so, shall I say, vertically rather than horizontally, for instance, taxation, insolvency, company work or executorship.

Many of the smaller firms are unable to specialise within the orbit of their own practice, which may be somewhat limited. They may be reluctant to call in those of greater experience from larger firms for fear of losing their client. I am sure that developments along these lines are on the increase, whereby some of the larger firms are consulted by their smaller brethren with the full knowledge that the consultation is only for the purpose of obtaining the specialised advice which is regarded as necessary on a particular point, so that the client may receive the greatest benefit.

A client's requirements from his professional accountant cover such a wide field that it is not unnatural that he prefers to deposit his confidences in one firm, rather than spread them over many firms and individuals. This, again not unnaturally, accounts for the development of amalgamations in the profession, particularly in the larger towns, so that the specialisation may be undertaken under one roof.

Specialisation is the result of particular experience in general practice and not a completely separate field, as in the case of the other two professions which I have mentioned, but that is no reason why changes in this direction should not take place; and it may well be that this is one of the items which will receive special consideration in the future development of the profession.

Research

Research committees which, as I have said, have been set up by most of the professional bodies, have produced great similarity in the problems which have been discussed in different countries, but it must be borne in mind that the purpose of these committees is not to spoon-feed members of the profession, although the results of their deliberations provide a useful backing in arguments with clients. Their primary purpose is to produce the result of the collective thought of members of the profession with the object of improving the standard of accounting, ironing out many of the inequities which arise under the application of legislation, and considering the fresh problems which arise by reason of economic changes.

Although a great deal more is heard of professional pronouncements on such important Acts as the Companies Act, 1948, the Income Tax Act, 1945, and the annual Finance Acts, it must not be thought that this is a new venture. Ever since the establishment of the professional bodies, their views have been expressed from time to time on legislation affecting themselves or their clients. Indeed, at the annual meeting of the English Institute in 1890, the greater part of the business of the meeting was composed of an address by the President to the members on the proposed Companies Bill.

In his early years the accountant should seek a broad experience and refrain from becoming too specialised in his work prior to qualification; the question of post-graduate education or specialisation is an important development which will, in the near future, see many changes.

Chairs of accountancy at the universities are gradually increasing in number, but everyone seeking the opportunity for specialisation in this way will not wish to remain at a university for the rest of his life, but rather to spend a relatively short period after qualification embarking upon research in some particular line of thought, although this might keep him out of touch with current practice whilst he is so doing. The essential need for the practising accountant to be thoroughly conversant with practice and not with theory alone, is one of the primary reasons why practical experience has been so much regarded as an essential in the past and why the opportunities for theoretical study have been more restricted.

If this object is to be achieved, it is important that the accountancy faculties at the universities should be actively supported by accountants who are in practice or in industry, so that the problems do not become too theoretical in their discussion. In this way the research student may devote a considerable number of years to the study of the problems which he has in mind, so long as he does not lose contact with the practical aspect.

To retain continuity, professors or lecturers would have to be whole-time scholars in the university, but through some form of liaison they could maintain close touch with those who are faced with the working problems of the profession.

In accountancy, legislation follows the development of practice rather than that of theory. The best practice is built up by some of the more enlightened practitioners and ultimately followed by legislation bringing the laggards into line. The stage is then set for further advances in practice by those who are thinking ahead, again being followed by legislation, with similar results.

A fair example of this type of progress may be seen in a study of the various Companies Acts from 1908 to 1948. It must be admitted that developments in practice and in legislation are not entirely brought about by improvements in the methods of accountancy, but to some extent by changes in commercial practice, by public opinion, or by financial arrangements which necessarily require a change in the accounting outlook on the problems which they create.

Regulations governing the contents of companies' published accounts are set out in the Eighth Schedule of the Companies Act, 1948.

This form of control is more rigid than it would be if the regulations were governed by the Stock Exchange or a joint committee of the Stock Exchange and the accountancy bodies.

Rigid directions tend to stultify professional progress and I am sure that the science of accounting technique would develop more smoothly if control could be exercised by some less rigid method than detailed legislation.

One of the difficulties of the present time is that the life of the practising accountant has become so hard pressed, and so much of his time is taken up by lesser difficulties, that he is prevented from giving the fullest consideration to some important matters. Although one does not wish to make him the mirror of students of research, none the less, those to whom I have referred in a previous paragraph, who have the opportunity and desire to enter into accounting research, will perform a very useful function in bringing to the notice of the practising accountant some of the developments which, through no fault of his own, he may have overlooked.

Co-ordination

Although the accountancy profession is composed of a number of separate bodies (as set out on page 367), many attempts have been made to co-ordinate the profession by legislation in one form or another. No less than seventeen unsuccessful bills had been presented to Parliament up to 1912 and two further attempts have been made in the last twenty-five years. Most of these bills failed through the difficulty of defining what constitutes an accountant and his activities, and although accountants in Scotland made an early attempt in 1880 to confine the use of the word 'accountant' to members of *their* body, this met with failure, and no other attempt has since been any more successful. In recent years, however, joint action has been taken on many points, in particular through the Accountants' Joint Parliamentary Committee, formed in 1946 and composed of accountants who are members of Parliament or in the House of Lords.

It is recognised that any successful Bill of Registration (or Co-ordination) would bring into the fold many unqualified persons who, at the date of the passing of the bill, were exercising the profession of an accountant. From past experience, this difficulty always appears to be more acute in the present than it does in retrospect, and although it involves an immediate setback in the general standard, it must ultimately achieve its purpose of raising the standard of the whole profession.

Co-operation

Joint action was also taken in dealing with the deferment of accountants for national service during the 1939-45 war and in the formation of the Joint Standing Committee of the Universities and the Accountancy Profession. This committee acts as a liaison body between the universities and the profession in connection with the special courses which are run at certain universities for the purpose of encouraging their graduates to become accountants.

Professional Charges

Unlike solicitors, stockbrokers, and estate agents, who have scale charges which are frequently based upon a percentage of the realisation or turnover involved in the transaction, the accountant's charges are principally based upon the time expended.

As the requirements of clients vary even between those in the same trade, and particularly between the cities and the country districts, it becomes impossible to lay down any particular scale of remuneration for the practising accountant. There are, however, two recognised scales which are used in particular cases:

(a) The Treasury Scale for work done on behalf of government departments.

(b) The Scale for Approved Auditors under the Friendly Societies Acts and the Industrial and Provident Societies Acts.

The revision of these scales from time to time gives an indication of the changes which should be reflected in accountants' charges generally.

Capital Requirements of a Practice

In addition to the knowledge which he has acquired before qualification, the accountant starting practice has other essential needs: the ability to introduce business and monetary capital to cover such items as office furniture, work in progress and debtors. The last two have increased substantially over the last ten years as work has expanded and as costs have increased. The proportion of capital required in commencing his practice may not be large, but will increase as his practice expands. The amount of capital in an established firm compared to its annual fees will vary from practice to practice, but a fair figure is probably from £2,000 to £2,500 for every £5,000 of fees. This excludes goodwill, as the amount which is paid for goodwill does not remain in the practice, but is usually withdrawn by those who are giving up their rights to the profit either in whole or in part. Payments for goodwill are becoming less prevalent, as with the need to attract into the profession those who have ability rather than cash capital, other methods have to be found of paying out goodwill to the retiring partners, an aspect of the problem which calls for more consideration than the payment for goodwill by an incoming partner.

Constitution of a Firm

The size and constituent elements of a partnership will vary from firm to firm. But in considering the number of partners it is important to ensure that they are sufficiently numerous to maintain the personal interest and contact between the accountant and his client. Furthermore, to ensure that a firm maintains its progress from generation to generation, it is necessary to bring in new ideas. It is therefore wiser that future partners, if they be sons of present partners, receive their training in other offices or, at any rate, that some of the future partners are recruited from those who have received a portion of their training elsewhere. Otherwise, a firm which lives on its own ideas and brings in no fresh blood is like a plant which has not been pruned or nourished from time to time.

The development of the size of the firm has been dictated very largely by corresponding developments in commerce. The tendency for amalgamations in commerce, bringing smaller companies under one control, has tended also to produce large firms of accountants who are able not only to provide staff to cope with the greater volume of work, but also to provide a spread of experience and specialisation in the many facets of an accountant's practice. At the same time, whilst this development has been taking place, there has been a tendency to decentralise some of the work which arises, so that medium-sized firms are well able to cope with most types of work. The work of the accountant, like that of his professional brethren, is essentially personal, and in the case of larger firms the advantages to be gained are in consultations between partners, otherwise each partner looks after his own work. At the same time, the client is assured that in the event of the illness or retirement of the partner who has been dealing with his affairs, someone else is available to take over, with full knowledge of his affairs.

The clerks who are employed may be grouped in various ways. They may be allocated to different partners who deal with a particular group of clerks; alternatively, they may be grouped as to a particular type of work which they undertake. In deciding upon a method of grouping, account will be taken of the spread of the work over the year so that each group is continuously employed without too many peak or slack periods in the carrying out of their programme. It is important that too much specialisation or isolation should not occur as the staff of the firm is infinitely more flexible where each group is capable of undertaking any particular type of business and is not restricted to a limited field.

Attraction of Industry and Public Service

It is not the wish of every accountant who qualifies to go into practice; many depart into public service or into industry and commerce, and in the mind of some of them that intention may have been present when they first entered the profession. Many, no doubt, find when they have left the practising side of the profession a certain lack of variety, which they miss. They may find monotonous some of the tasks which they are called upon to fulfil in public service, unless they are fortunate enough to be able to achieve some of the principal posts available to accountants where they are then able to obtain a greater variety of experience.

There are, however, attractions in industry which may withdraw from the practising field many who would have considered themselves as available for practice in previous years. For example, no capital is required in the employ of companies or in the public service. Pensions on generous scales are provided, therefore there is no need to save up for retirement, and in many respects, particularly with the development of the public services, salaries offered to relatively recently qualified accountants are above anything which could be offered by a professional practice, where it must be realised that the rate of remuneration is to some degree regulated by the fees which clients are prepared to pay.

Qualifications of Staff

When considering the staff which he requires, an accountant is faced with the same problem of the attraction of industrial opportunities which I pictured in the previous paragraph with regard to his prospective partners. The qualifications which he requires in his staff, apart from the professional qualifications which they have probably already obtained, are that they should be versatile and, in particular, able to appreciate the points which require especial attention, so that they may pass them on to those who know how to deal with them if they are unable to deal with them themselves. (The knowledge of one's shortcomings is very often as valuable, if not more valuable, than the knowledge of one's own ability.) They will have to be prepared to work irregular hours, as it is a fortunate practice which is able to provide an even load throughout the year without having to work at extreme pressure at certain periods, leaving other relatively infrequent periods when the pressure is much less.

The complexity of modern legislation and modern methods which have affected accountancy generally, have brought about certain changes in the opportunities for clerks in accountants' offices. In the first instance, it is essential that even the junior clerks—and certainly the senior clerks—should have more technical knowledge than was necessary in the past, due to the regulations which have to be complied with and the problems of taxation which affect so much of the commercial community; secondly, the introduction of mechanical methods has eliminated to a large degree many of the routine tasks which, in previous generations, were undertaken by clerks who needed no more than the ability to follow methodically tedious routine without further thought on their part.

Pensions

The attraction of generous pension schemes which industrial appointments hold against those in the profession, is gradually being minimised and m any firms to-day have a pension scheme of one kind or another. In smaller firms, it is probably arranged upon group life assurance principles; in larger firms, where there is a sufficiently broad basis, it may be administered as a privately managed fund. But in all cases, difficulties are presented in that the personnel—particularly the qualified personnel—of an accountant's practice, is of a more fluctuating nature than is similar personnel in industry. In the latter case, they advance from stage to stage until they reach the higher executive positions. In many accountants' offices, however, a large number of those who qualify—indeed, the vast majority—do not remain for the rest of their working life in one office, but either pass on to other accountants' offices, or, more than likely, seek ultimately some occupation in industry or public service; only relatively few remain to attain the position of managing clerk of a practising accountant's office.

Attempts have been made to provide a pension scheme applicable to the profession as a whole, with the advantage that anybody leaving one office and going to another may take all his past benefits with him. This, on the other hand, is not always regarded as an attraction, as it makes the employee more mobile than he otherwise would be and still does not cover the problem of the change-over into industry. An individual scheme providing for the special needs of each firm is probably more satisfactory than a general scheme for the profession.

But none of these methods, however suitable they may be, and however beneficial from the point of view of the employee, are available to the practitioner or principal himself. Unless he is possessed of private means or has heavily insured himself so that on retirement he is able to acquire an annuity from an insurance company, he is obliged to go on working for the rest of his days.

The American Institute of Accountants has, however, adopted a group life assurance plan for principals, but until some benefit can be obtained which costs less than the existing life assurance method, it seems that little relief can be obtained by the practising accountant, and it is hoped that something in this direction will be achieved as a result of the report of the Royal Commission on the Taxation of Profits and Income, which is at the moment considering this point amongst other problems of taxation.

Earlier on, I referred to the fact that many accountants in the early years of the profession combined with their occupation as accountants some other field of work; in many cases they were stockbrokers, but in Scotland they were associated particularly with actuaries and others connected with life assurance, which makes it not surprising that the Edinburgh Institute of Accountants, when it was formed, required not only the payment of an entrance fee, but also an initial contribution of 50 guineas and an annual contribution to their endowment annuity fund. The annual contribution could be augmented voluntarily. The fund to-day is closed, but all those who joined the Edinburgh Institute under those auspices receive at age 65 a capital sum in the vicinity of £500, or an equivalent annuity, the amount being dependent upon age at entry. This, however, is no longer available to new members and other members of the Scottish Institute and I do not know of any other body which has the same privilege.

Retirement

How, then, is the practitioner who has reached the age of retirement to enable himself to make room for those who are coming up after him and at the same time either to take a lesser share in the profits of a practice on account of his doing a smaller portion of work, or to retire completely? I have referred to the fact that it is not possible for him to set aside an adequate pension over the period of his practising life, at any rate by virtue of contributions to any fund other than an insurance policy, and if he is to rely on the payment of a lump sum by any incoming partner when he retires, he may find his choice of that incoming partner very much restricted. Furthermore, when he has received this lump sum, at the present high rates of taxation, the investment of it will provide him with a pension far too meagre to live on and even if this sum is employed in the purchase of an annuity, unless he is of an advanced age, it will not be of sufficient value to cover his needs. The amount which he has been able to save out of taxed income during his professional life has probably been small, and if he has dependants it is more than likely that he will wish to pass something on to them and not to exhaust all his savings in the purchase of an annuity.

It seems, therefore, that from the point of view of both the payer and the payee, the most attractive and most satisfactory method of dealing with this situation is for the retiring partner to receive a pension payable either out of profits or under covenant which is borne by the continuing partners of the business, who are then able to obtain the necessary tax relief on the payments they make and, with his probably lower rate of taxation, the retiring partner is more than likely to find that the sum received in this manner goes further than a payment obtained in any other way. It has the advantage of spreading the burden of taxation more evenly over those who continue the practice and those who retire, and at the same time it avoids the difficulty of any incoming partner having to find a substantial sum for goodwill in addition to the capital he will have to provide to repay the retiring partner.

Conferences

Like most other professions, accountants hold annual or biennial conferences. Such conferences afford a useful opportunity for discussion amongst members of the profession, who are then able to realise and appreciate the fact that their colleagues in other parts of the country are contending with much the same difficulties as those with which they themselves are faced. They are able to discuss in a friendly atmosphere, without fear of criticism, many points which trouble them in their own practices.

Those present on such occasions include many accountants not in practice, although the main participants consist of those who *are* in practice, firstly, because the subjects for discussion are of greater interest to the practising member than his non-practising colleague and, secondly, because the accountant in practice is a freer agent and can make good the time which he has lost by working in the irregular hours which are necessarily associated with practice. He does not have the same difficulty as the member in industry who has other persons to consider and more routine duties to perform. Many accountants, however, do not take advantage of these opportunities for professional and social co-operation and tend to confine their professional activities entirely to their offices. There is no doubt that by so doing they miss a great deal, as these conferences go a long way towards enabling members in the smaller firms and districts to obtain an insight into the wider experience of firms in the larger towns, and also enable those in the towns to appreciate the difficulties of their colleagues in small practices.

Although at the conferences to which I have referred the social atmosphere may be, in many respects, more important than the discussions which take place on the various papers, there are other occasions, such as the summer schools—which are held by most accountancy bodies by courtesy of one or other of the colleges at the universities of Oxford or Cambridge—at which strenuous periods are spent in discussions following papers on technical subjects. The social element on these occasions plays a less important part and the technical discussions are prolonged into the small hours.

This affords an even greater opportunity for the small practitioner and his larger confrère to share their views, exchange their experiences, and discuss in a free atmosphere many of the problems arising out of the development of business and of legislation.

Opportunities of this character are particularly welcome when new legislation is fresh on the Statute Book and when discussion takes place on the various points which will be met in practice.

THE TRAINING OF THE FUTURE PRACTITIONER

Education of Articled Clerks

The extension of the duties of an accountant emphasises the need to give a thorough training to those who will fill the ranks of the future, and so I offer no excuse for referring at this stage to the method of training articled clerks.

The importance of this is clear when it is remembered that—at any rate so far as the Institutes of Chartered Accountants are concerned—the responsibility of training for the whole profession falls upon the members in practice.

In the knowledge that the accountant is going to spend a considerable period over his training before he becomes qualified, there is a tendency to leave school at an earlier age than he otherwise might. This is emphasised under present conditions where the period of compulsory military service has to be added to the period which elapses before qualification is achieved. Nevertheless, the tendency should be decried whenever possible, for, with the wide field which the accountant has to cover in his professional life, it is most important that his vocational training should be based upon a thoroughly sound and broad education beforehand, as this cannot be replaced if its omission is realised at a later date.

Although it is not possible to lay down any hard and fast rules which would be appropriate to all entrants to the profession, in my view, a university education is something which will never be regretted by those who are able to take advantage of it. On the other side, we have the report of the Special Committee on Education for Commerce,[1] which was set up by the Minister of Education under the chairmanship of Sir Alexander Carr-Saunders, which took the view that technical training and practical experience could be sandwiched together and that, to a large degree, entrants to the profession should work in conjunction with those who are training for other callings, many of which are far removed from the profession of the accountant. Whatever method is employed, it is essential that the greatest advantage should be taken of the period of practical experience as, ultimately, the

[1] H.M. Stationery Office, December, 1949.

comparison between one accountant and another goes strongly in favour of that one who has had the greatest amount of practical experience. Examinations may be passed upon book knowledge and cramming, but the inadequacy of this type of learning is frequently discovered when practical application of the knowledge acquired is called for in general practice.

Period of Articles

In so far as the English Institute is concerned, a period of five years' articles is insisted upon, although it is reduced to three years for those who have graduated at a university, and certain concessions were granted to those who had their period of training interrupted by war service. The Incorporated Accountants and the Certified Accountants do not call upon all their entrants to serve a period of articles.

Into the period of articles must be worked not only the practical training in the profession, but also the time which is necessary for study. With the exception of a relatively short period immediately before the examinations, this is usually achieved by evening or week-end study under the postal direction of a tuition college.

Although the practice of articled clerks paying a premium for their training still prevails in many cases, it is rapidly diminishing, with the result that entrance to the profession is no longer restricted to those whose parents can afford to pay a premium and keep their sons for the period of articles during which they will be receiving little, if any, remuneration. On the other hand, in most cases when premiums are received they are repaid in one form or another over the period of the articles. Every opportunity is given to any boy who may have the inclination and ability to become an accountant, whatever his circumstances, the amount of remuneration paid to him being based largely upon the amount of experience which he has obtained.

University Education

For those who are able to receive a university education, it is important that they should get the greatest advantage from the broad, liberal training which a university provides. The course which they take need not be closely related to accountancy or commerce and usually degrees in history, law or economics, as well as the degree of Bachelor of Commerce, provide an adequate basis. It is the training of the mind and brain—the ability to think clearly and to form a sound judgment—which is the ultimate success of a university education and not necessarily the vocational training which a university provides.

A further advantage of a university is the contrast with school life.

At a university facilities are provided to help the undergraduate in his work, but it is *his* decision what work he shall do and, equally importantly, when he shall do it. This encourages initiative and self reliance.

In 1945, three of the accountancy bodies in England and Wales made an arrangement with the provincial universities whereby a special degree course was set up for those who were considering entering the accountancy profession. Under this arrangement they serve a period of articles of five and three-quarter years, of which two and three-quarter years are spent at the university on this particular course, the remaining three years being spent in the accountant's office, partly before going to the university, but mostly, and at least one year, following graduation. One of the attractions of this particular course to those who have been to the university is that they are exempted from the professional intermediate examination. Whether or not this is an advantage is not for me to say, but it does not necessarily mean that this university degree is regarded in all respects as an equivalent standard to the professional intermediate examination, and it is important that any thought of this character should be removed.

From the professional point of view, the advantage is the prospect of attracting into the profession some of the most eligible candidates who have been to the university rather than providing a university training for articled clerks as such. The advantage of exemption from the intermediate examination and three months' shorter articles than is provided by a normal university degree followed by articles is relatively small in the life of a practising accountant, and the benefit of the associations and discussions which arise from a university course is far more important. This advantage is obtained to a greater degree at residential universities such as Oxford and Cambridge, rather than at universities, most of whose students are day scholars.

Practical Training

It is the duty of the principal to train his articled clerk and not to leave that entirely to the professional body, to the state, or to the tuition college. He should see that his pupil gets wide experience (though this may be difficult in some offices) and in particular, he should endeavour to give him experience in such special spheres as executorship, liquidation and bankruptcy. He should receive reports from the senior clerk under whose supervision the articled clerk is placed on his progress, and particularly following the passing of the intermediate examination, he should make endeavours to give particular tasks direct to his articled clerk, which he may bring to his principal personally, so that the latter will have a fair indication of the way in which his pupil is progressing.

Modern methods have eliminated many of the monotonous tasks which it was customary to pass to articled clerks; indeed, there are many of past generations who will remember the long and tedious hours which they spent checking other people's additions. This change, however, is not regarded as purely beneficial, as there can be no overlooking the fact that, tedious though the task may have been, it provided a sound mental discipline which ensured that details were not to be neglected and that thoroughness must be observed in carrying out the work of an audit.

As the greater part of an articled clerk's work in his principal's office is usually auditing, it consists very largely of checking others, and is not work of his own construction. It is therefore important to see that a reasonable balance is observed, because if there is excessive checking of the work of others, the pupil's mind will become passive, and not active as it would be if he were learning to do things for himself, whether it be entering up books, preparing accounts, or handling a particular part of liquidation procedure. During his period of training, too much emphasis should not be placed on the professional aspect and, where possible, every encouragement should be given to the articled clerk to acquire knowledge of the particular work which his clients are carrying out. A tour round the factory is usually welcomed by the client's accountant, as he knows that with this experience the questions which the articled clerk will ask are more likely to be constructive and the answers which he obtains more readily understood.

The practical view cannot be too heavily stressed as it has been the experience of examiners on many subjects that when questions are set which cannot be answered by mere book knowledge, but require the application of knowledge of principle, the answers are in the main disappointing.

Industrial Experience

In 1946, the Institute of Chartered Accountants in England and Wales took power to permit those serving articles to spend a period not exceeding six months in the office of an industrial company, so long as they are under the supervision of a qualified accountant whilst there. This permission has not been sought on many occasions, although the practice is gradually increasing, and there can be no doubt that in many cases it would be an advantage for the pupil to have this experience as it is more than ever likely to provide him with an opportunity of doing something for himself rather than checking the work of others. However it is obtained, it is important that it should not interfere too seriously with a pupil's practical experience in his principal's office, as if there are too many breaks in this, he loses his opportunities.

There has been a clamour from certain quarters that an industrial paper should be included in the professional examination, either as an alternative subject for those who seek their future in industry rather than in practice, or as a compulsory subject as representing one of the most important parts of current practice. Many feel that the training of the embryo accountant up to the stage of his examination should be on broad general principles and not too specialised in one direction or another.

In my view, the field to be covered by the examination syllabus is already so wide that a fresh subject could only be introduced at the expense of some other branch, and the substitution of optional papers would be a mistake. A broad general training, leaving specialisation to be treated as a post-graduate feature, is more important.

This might be incorporated as a means of qualification for Fellowship. Such a suggestion has been made from time to time, but it was only in 1951 that any practical outlet was produced, and this was by the Institute of Cost and Works Accountants, which has now provided that its Fellowship shall go to those accountants who have a qualification the equivalent of its Associateship, and add to it the passing of a special paper in management accounting.[1]

Tuition Colleges

I have referred to the postal tuition which forms the basic examination training of most students. This type of tuition is frequently criticised on the grounds that it takes place in the evening after the student has done his day's work at the office; nevertheless, if the essence of the professional qualification is to be practical training, this must be interfered with as little as possible. It will be appreciated that if an articled clerk attends day classes for tuition and is only spasmodically available at his office, he will not get the opportunity of being given work which requires his attention, not when he is *able* to give it, but when it is *necessary*. This particularly applies to audits. If an articled clerk is frequently away on his studies, he loses a great deal of the value which he can be to his senior or managing clerk, and if that interest is lost, so are the opportunities for practical experience which he seeks to acquire. It is therefore best for the bulk of the examination training to be done by those postal tuition colleges which have been built up over the last forty years with such a wide experience of teaching of this character; and although much criticism may be levelled at this type of tuition, there can be no doubt that the colleges are doing their work exceedingly well, and it would be a great mistake for any change to take place in this method.

[1] *The Accountant*, 29th September, 1951.

o

Students' Societies

A suitable balance in the technical training is provided by the students' societies. Every student in this way has an opportunity of mixing with other students and at the same time finding experienced practitioners who are able to answer many of the problems which he comes across in his courses and which are more readily answered in person.

The lectures which are provided by the students' societies are of two categories. Firstly, those which deal with the examination subjects; these may to some degree overlap the tuition colleges' papers and reading matter, but the subjects are looked at from a more practical standpoint. Secondly, those on general subjects, bearing on different types of trade and current events, all of which help to develop the general knowledge and experience of the student and to prevent him from becoming too theoretical in his outlook.

Another important feature of the work of the students' societies is the debates which are arranged. These opportunities should not be neglected by the articled clerk as they give him the chance of thinking on his feet and expressing himself intelligently, which will stand him in good stead in his later professional life. After all, it is very much easier to have this experience whilst one is training than to try and build up the experience in the hard school of practice, when the cost of making mistakes is much greater. Success in this field enables the student to find many opportunities which would not otherwise be open to him.

A further feature of the activities of the students' societies, which is now being developed, is that of providing residential courses extending over a period of four or five days, a short time before students sit their examinations. These should be timed so as to avoid breaking into the tuition revision courses, but not so far distant as not to give the student the opportunity of tidying up some of the shortcomings which he has experienced during his period of training, and to allow him the opportunity of discussing his difficulties with those of his contemporaries who are similarly placed.

THE ACCOUNTANT'S RELATIONS WITH THE BUSINESS WORLD

Legal Profession

As far back as 1874 attempts were made to provide a distinction between the work which was appropriate to lawyers and that which was appropriate to accountants, but although steps were taken to ascertain how this might be defined, and many other attempts have been made since that date, it has still not been possible to arrive at any decision. None the less, accountants and lawyers in all parts of the world work in close harmony, lawyers endeavouring to avoid incorrect accounting, and accountants to avoid bad legal advice. The accountant should appreciate when to go to a solicitor or to advise his client to do so, and vice versa. This basis probably provides the soundest foundation for co-operation and understanding between the two professions.

Economists

Economists are apt to regard accountants in general, and accountants in practice in particular, as being the repository of much useful information which would help them in their discussions and in the preparation of the statistical statements which they compile. It must be remembered, however, that the accountant in practice holds his knowledge as the secret of his client and if it was felt in any quarter that this information was divulged, in however anonymous a fashion, the relationship of confidence between the accountant and his client would be seriously endangered.

Whilst appreciating the anxiety of the economist to obtain this information for his purpose, we must realise that to some extent he speaks a different language from the accountant—particularly from the accountant in practice. The latter fully appreciates the point of view of the economist, but accountant and economist do not necessarily consider problems in the same light.

Several attempts have been made to bring the two closer together, but the matter ultimately resolves itself into a definition of accounting and economic terms and concepts, and it will be shown how far apart these are when it is mentioned that the report of the Joint Exploratory Committee, which was issued in 1951,[1] was only agreed after deliberations extending over six years. Although this report goes probably a greater way on common ground than might have been expected, it tends to emphasise the difference between the two.

Public View of Accountants

It is sometimes assumed that the principal attribute of an accountant is an extensive knowledge of mathematics and that he spends his life in a world of figures. This is far from the truth; the main article which he has to offer to the public is his certificate—which might be described as his stock-in-trade. This is not sold to the highest bidder, and retains its value only whilst it can be accepted unconditionally and without question. A certificate which cannot be relied upon loses all value immediately.

In the public mind, the accountant is a man of high moral principles, who can be relied upon not only for the accuracy of his work, but also for the soundness of his judgment. To fulfil these high ideals he must be

[1] *Some Accounting Terms and Concepts.* (Cambridge University Press), 1951.

able to go behind the cold statements of fact with which he is presented, and face his problems with a knowledge of the human principles which lie behind them.

Apart from the relations with the Inland Revenue which have been referred to earlier in this paper, the accountant in practice is associated with other government departments. His services are frequently called upon in cases of emergency. One can recollect many instances of accountants being employed during the last war in connection with the food control and other supply departments. They were also employed at the time of the general strike in 1926 in assisting in the organisation of emergency services: again, when the Transport Act of 1947 came on the Statute Book, many accountants were employed and appointed to panels to assist in arriving at the assessment of compensation to be paid to the transport owners in connection with the transfer and nationalisation of their undertakings—and there are many other instances.

These are all occasions on which large numbers of accountants in practice have been employed or their services utilised; but to a lesser degree, selected accountants are called in to arbitrate on questions of assessing compensation. For example, the valuation of the shares of the American associates of Courtaulds Ltd., which were taken over by the Government during the last war, or in settling the distribution of the global sum for division between the owners of the collieries, which were nationalised under the Coal Industry Nationalisation Act, 1946, and there are many other functions of a similar nature where their services are called upon.

In private practice, not only does the accountant perform his functions as auditor and taxation expert, but he becomes the confidential adviser of his client, and is consulted by him on an almost unlimited variety of problems. Indeed, one can recall occasions when spinsters and widows have sought their accountant's advice before embarking or re-embarking on matrimonial seas.

Intelligibility of Accounts

The technique of the presentation of accounts to shareholders has become so involved that few of those who have not been educated in finance have any appreciation of the information they convey. The accountant in practice can perform a useful function in making published accounts more intelligible to the uninitiated.

The presentation of accounts is not a mere exercise in the use of vague accounting terms, resulting in the proof that the account balances and, within certain accepted concepts, reveals the true and fair profit of a given period. They should be set forth in such a manner that even the uninstructed shareholder (and director) can appreciate in a simple way the affairs of his company. If the accountant looks upon his accounts as an architect his building, or an artist his painting, he will attempt to produce them in such a form that they will be clearly understood. This may, of course, be regarded as the field of the accountant in industry, who is primarily responsible for drawing up the accounts of most public companies; but the ultimate arbiter of the accounts is the accountant in practice—the auditor who signs the certificate that they reveal 'a true and fair view', and, in doing so, he should bear in mind those to whom the accounts are issued.

Returning to the analogy of the architect, his drawings take two forms, (a) the ground plan and detailed measurements, and (b) the elevations. His client looks with awe and interest at the first form, but it is the second which reveals the result which he is seeking.

If accountants follow this idea, we shall find that in future the set form of balance sheet and profit and loss account supply the needs of management and the financial expert, whereas the needs of the un-initiated shareholder are met by a supplementary statement setting out the salient features, which are necessary for him to obtain an adequate appreciation of the value of his investment.

Accounting Terminology

The accountancy profession is not adorned by an extensive glossary of technical terms; in fact, accountants have tended rather to employ those already in daily use either in commerce or by the law. In more recent years there has been a tendency in certain quarters to invent a number of phrases and terms, some of which appear to be understood only by their users. Many terms tend to be confused in that as they are dependent upon their context, so does their meaning vary, and although one does not wish the jargon of the profession to become too technical, none the less, it would be an advantage if phrases with well-appreciated meanings, which could be understood by laymen, were used.

Form of Certificates

In most cases, the only communication which the auditor has with his principals—the shareholders who appoint him—is the certificate which he appends to the balance sheet. It is, therefore, important that through this channel his intentions should be abundantly clear. He should not lead anybody to imagine that he has done more than he has done, or that he accepts any greater responsibility than he should.

The length of the certificate required under the Companies Act, 1948, tends to confuse shareholders in that so many positive features are emphasised in a straightforward case that when any negative points are included their presence tends to be overlooked. To assume that accounts are correct unless otherwise stated would no doubt be more satisfactory from the point of view of the shareholder, but this places a heavier burden on the accountant and auditor when he has to raise a specific qualification, which would then stand out in isolation. Nevertheless, the accountant should not shirk the responsibility of doing what he feels to be right, following the dictates of his duty.

Where some of the shorter and non-statutory certificates are given, it must always be appreciated that the accounts so certified may possibly be used for more than one purpose. For example, if accounts are certified for partnership purposes as being in accordance with the books of the firm they may also be used for presentation to the Inland Revenue for agreeing taxation liabilities, or at some future date produced to a prospective purchaser of the business as if they were a completely audited account.

As each of these parties will in their separate ways regard the accountant's certificate as meaning all it conveys to them, it is most important to ensure that nobody is misled; as in the minds of many people the terms 'auditor' and 'accountant' are regarded as synonymous.

Management

What are the relations of the practising accountant with his client or those who manage the affairs of industry? Management as a whole tends to criticise the practising accountant, saying that he is old-fashioned, too conservative and too tied to past ideas. This may be so where the accountant comes in for no more than an audit at the end of the year, or is consulted in some minor field, but it is not the case where the accountant in practice is consulted throughout the year, where he is regarded not merely as the servant of his client, but as one who should advise his client and lead him into proper channels. He should keep his client abreast of developments and bring to his notice all the points which may be necessary in conducting his business, whether it be with a view to forestalling difficulties which might otherwise arise through taxation in years to come on the death of a proprietor, or the penalties which may be incurred through a change in control, either on account of personnel or domicile.

CONCLUSION

I have recorded in some degree the progress and events of the past, the conditions of the present, and the possibilities of the future.

To some of the present generation the past may have no more than an historic interest and their successors may look upon the present in a similar light; but the real value in the consideration of the past is to learn of the progress that has been made and to realise that the accountancy profession, like any other profession, cannot stand still: it must either go forward or slip backwards.

In the certain hope that it is the wish of all those attending this Congress to see the accountant in practice enhance his reputation and service, I pose below a number of questions which might stimulate the Congress to give an indication of the road upon which we might travel in the decades to come:

How will the practising accountant fit into the administration of nationalised industries? Will he find in this a greater or lesser demand for his services? (Pages 371 and 373.)

Is the internal auditor to assume a more directly responsible position? (Page 373.)

Have we been wrong in our method of specialisation; should we have followed the practice of other professions and debarred the specialists from general practice? (Page 381.)

What part should the accountant in practice play in research, or should this become a whole-time occupation? (Page 382.)

How can the opportunity for specialisation and research in accounting technique best be developed? (Page 382.)

Would the progress of accounting technique be more satisfactorily developed under less rigid control than that provided by detailed legislation? (Page 383.)

How can the problems of the continuity of capital and goodwill in the practising firms best be dealt with? (Page 390.)

It is frequently stated that statistics lie; should the accountant accept a greater responsibility for the production or certification of statistical statements, and should this subject take a more prominent place in examination syllabuses? (Page 398.)

Is the stereotyped audit certificate satisfactory? Should this be substituted by a more extensive audit report? (Page 399.)

THE ACCOUNTANT IN PRACTICE AND IN PUBLIC SERVICE

by

T. COLEMAN ANDREWS, C.P.A.
Virginia Society of Public Accountants,
United States of America

It is essential to accurate understanding of public accounting practice in the United States that the source of the practitioner's professional status there be clearly understood.

Contrary to the situation here in the country of our hosts, where an accountant gets his professional recognition from the profession itself, it is traditional in the United States that public practice of accounting is deemed to be an activity affected with the public interest and, therefore, a proper subject of state regulation. Hence, those who engage in public accounting practice get their recognition from one of the forty-eight states, the District of Columbia, or one of the territories or insular possessions. In other words, the public practitioners in my country are 'certified' pursuant to law.

The common title of the public practitioner is 'Certified Public Accountant'. However, in some states there is another class known simply as 'Public Accountants'. In both cases, however, the designation is a legal one.

In general, the designation 'Certified Public Accountant' has been granted only to those who have taken a written test of their knowledge of accounting theory, accounting practice, auditing, and commercial law, although a few states include one or more other subjects.

To explain generally how there came to be two designations, I will illustrate by reviewing the situation in my own State of Virginia, which is fairly typical.

Virginia first adopted legislation regulating public practice of accounting in 1910. This legislation provided that those who satisfied its requirements would be designated 'Certified Public Accountants', but since there were no certified public accountants prior to that time, the initial legislation waived the examination for those who were deemed to be qualified by experience. Hence, the first Virginia C.P.A.s received what we call waiver certificates. These certificates were unqualified and entitled those who held them to full recognition as certified public accountants. The certificates initially issued by most of the states were waiver certificates.

It might be of interest to note in passing that each of the members of Virginia's first Board of Accountancy voluntarily submitted to examination by the other members. Thereafter, only those who took and satisfactorily passed written examinations were to receive the right to call themselves certified public accountants, and the Virginia State Board of Accountancy, which had been created by the Accountancy Act, was charged with giving the annual examinations and otherwise administering the Act. This initial law did not prevent anyone from practising public accounting. It only

402

prohibited anyone from calling himself a certified public accountant if he had not acquired the right to do so as provided by the law.

This procedure prevailed until 1926, when strong protest was made to the General Assembly of the Commonwealth by the uncertified practitioners that their ability to earn a livelihood was seriously impaired by their lack of legislative recognition. The Accountancy Act was then changed to what is commonly called in my country 'two-class legislation'. Under the revised Act those uncertified practitioners who were engaged in practice at the time of the revision were recognised and registered as 'public accountants', but the revised Act closed the door to future registrations and also limited practice thereafter to those holding C.P.A. certificates and those registered as public accountants. Thus the uncertified practitioner became what we call a 'dying class' and the way was cleared for ultimate restriction of practice to those holding C.P.A. certificates. Hence, while Virginia presently has two-class legislation, this legislation will in time become one-class legislation.

At the time of the revision, about sixty practitioners were registered as public accountants. Since then, many of these have passed the examination and become certified, some have died, and others have retired from practice, so that at the present time only a few public accountants are registered and practising. Virginia, therefore, is approaching the time when all of its practitioners will be C.P.A.s.

So much for the difference generally between certified public accountants and public accountants, except to say that some states recognise public accountants as a continuing class.

For several years the examination has been uniform in all but one of the fifty-odd state and other jurisdictions and is taken at the same time in each of these jurisdictions. The one state which holds its own examination has been unable to adopt the uniform examination because of a difficulty presented by this state's accountancy law. It is expected, however, that this difficulty will be overcome shortly and that this state will adopt the uniform examination, so making its use universal.

It should be pointed out, however, that, since public practice of accounting is regulated by state law, each state, the District of Columbia, and each of the territories and insular possessions has its own Board of Accountancy and the decision of each of these boards is final as to whether a candidate who appears before it satisfactorily passes the examination that he or she takes, subject to appeal, in some states, to the courts of those states. The uniform examination is prepared under the direction of the Board of Examiners of the American Institute of Accountants, and is held in each of the fifty-odd jurisdictions in the fall and in some of them also in the spring. In general, each applicant for the C.P.A. certificate files with the Board of Accountancy of the jurisdiction in which he resides, but the laws of some states permit examination and certification of applicants from other states.

History and Growth of the Profession

As is generally known, the origin of public accounting in the United States was British. The investment of British funds in American enterprise was

considerable in the last half of the nineteenth century and the British practitioners followed British capital. This, together with the obviously favourable
outlook for accounting·practice in the States, naturally led to the establishment of offices in the United States by the leading British firms.

However, it was not long before our own people began to develop an
interest in practice and to establish offices, and in 1896 the legislature of the
State of New York enacted the first accountancy law. Schools for the giving
of courses in accounting soon came into being, the teaching of accounting
quickly developed into quite a profession itself, and one by one the state
legislatures enacted accountancy laws. By 1921 such laws had been enacted
by all the states. However, as recently as 1920 there were only 5,000 certified
public accountants in the entire country. But from that point on the number
increased rapidly. By 1940 there were 17,500. By 1948 there were 35,000.
To-day there are close to 42,000.

Organisation of the Profession

The organisation of the profession starts at the state level, each state having
its own state society, institute or association; in recent years many of the
state organisations have also organised local chapters. To illustrate, the
Virginia Society of Public Accountants has chapters at Richmond, the capital
city of the Commonwealth; in the Arlington-Alexandria area, across the
river from the nation's capital; in the Hampton Roads area, embracing
the cities of Norfolk, Portsmouth and Newport News; in the south-
western part of the state, with headquarters at Roanoke; and in the
upper Piedmont section, at Charlottesville, where the State University is
situated.

The membership of the state societies varies from less than a hundred in
the states of relatively small population to several thousand in the states
having large populations. The New York State Society, for instance, has
more than 6,000 members.

Nationally, the organisation of the profession follows to some extent the
pattern of the organisation of the government of the United States, in that
each of the state organisations is autonomous. The American Institute of
Accountants, which is the national organisation, co-operates closely with the
state organisations and maintains continuous liaison with them, but it does
not attempt to control them. In other words, the state organisations as such
are not members of the Institute. Indeed, not all of their members are.
Membership in the American Institute and the state societies is open only to
individuals.

In general, membership in the American Institute of Accountants is open
to all holders of C.P.A. certificates who are in good standing in their respective
states. The Institute is governed by a Council consisting of seventy-two
members chosen from the states generally on the basis of the distribution of
the Institute's membership; nine members at large; the past presidents of
the American Association of Public Accountants (which was the former
name of the American Institute); the past presidents of the American Society
of Certified Public Accountants (which merged with the American Institute

in 1936); and the presidents of the state societies. The Council holds an annual meeting and a spring meeting, the annual meeting at the same time as the annual membership meeting, and the spring meeting usually in late April or early May.

To facilitate the work of the Council, there is an Executive Committee which consists of the officers—President, four Vice-Presidents and Treasurer —and seven members of the Council. The Executive Committee meets as often as the volume or urgency of matters calling for its attention requires. Usually there are five or six meetings a year.

The membership of the American Institute at present is just a little short of 19,000, and because of the Institute's over-all representation of the profession and its consequent ability to finance the greatest possible scope of activities, it has taken the lead in dealing with matters which, for the sake of uniformity, or for other reasons, can be best dealt with at the national level, such as research; formalisation of accounting and auditing procedures; public relations; co-operation with bankers, lawyers and the Securities and Exchange Commission; and the role of the certified public accountant in federal taxation and national defence. That is not to say that important and effective activity is not engaged in with respect to these matters by the state societies. A number of the state societies do, in fact, engage in activities which are closely parallel to those of the American Institute.

Then, as previously indicated, the role of the American Institute in the matter of developing and making available the uniform examinations, and in grading the candidates papers when requested to do so, is of itself a major undertaking. This work is carried on under the direction of a group known as the Board of Examiners and involves the employment of a staff of considerable proportions.

The American Institute also concerns itself extensively with the matter of education for the profession, and in this field not only combines with the teachers of accounting and their respective institutions to improve the choice of academic subject-matter and the organisation of courses, but also seeks to develop positive means of identifying the outstanding characteristics of accountants and discovering those who have these characteristics, and of checking the progress of students and helping them find satisfactory employment upon completion of their studies. The programme of finding positive tests of accounting aptitude, checking the progress of students, and finding employment for graduates has been intensively carried out and has resulted in great benefit to the profession as well as to students.

The American Institute is mindful that, since membership in it is individual, it has a clear obligation to do whatever it can to improve the material status of its individual members. In pursuance of this obligation, the Institute has made available to its members opportunity to participate in a group insurance plan, under which coverage is available up to the amount of $10,000. This opportunity is extended not only to the Institute's members but also to its members' employees, even those who may not be members of the Institute. At the end of 1951 a total of 1,232 firms were participating in this plan with 8,031 persons covered and $41,606,000 of insurance in force.

Other Organisations

In addition to the American Institute of Accountants, there are other organisations which provide focal points of activity for accountants not engaged in public practice, although the membership of each of these organisations includes many public practitioners. Without any implication as to relative rank, these organisations are: American Accounting Association, Controllers' Institute of America, National Association of Cost Accountants.

The American Accounting Association is the national organisation of teachers of accounting.

The Controllers' Institute of America is the national organisation of the controllers and finance officers of the nation's enterprises.

The National Association of Cost Accountants is the national organisation of cost accountants and those who are primarily interested in cost accounting.

Both the Controllers' Institute of America and the National Association of Cost Accountants have great numbers of local chapters which, in each case, are directly affiliated with the national organisation.

At the end of 1951, the approximate memberships of these three organisations were: American Accounting Association, 4,000; Controllers' Institute of America, 3,600; National Association of Cost Accountants, 25,000.

Education for the Profession

In the early days of the profession in my country, the principal source of education for the profession seems to have been the correspondence school; that is, the school which operates from a central location, enrolls students throughout the country, distributes its text material to its students by mail, requires the students to submit written examinations, and grades the papers submitted at the central headquarters. These schools have made a great contribution to the advancement of the profession.

Later the colleges and universities put in courses, often, in the early days, integrating these courses with their schools of economics, though sometimes integrating them with their schools of liberal arts. More recently, there has been a strong trend at the college and university level toward the establishment of schools of business administration and the integration of instruction in accounting with these schools. There already are many such schools.

In recent years, based upon the theory that modern conditions require that an accountant should have something more than a mere vocational education, there has been a strong trend toward the requirement that accounting students precede their specialised study of accounting with some period of basic instruction in the liberal arts, usually for two years. This theory has much to recommend it and it has strong advocates.

If I were to hazard a guess, I would say that this pattern of preparation will in time become the prevailing one. At any rate, from my own observations and experience with staff personnel, and judging from opinions expressed to me by many of my colleagues, I would say that the beginner in the profession who based his study of accounting and related subjects upon a foundation of at least two years of liberal arts education comes to the profession with superior preparation. Such an entrant has the best chance of progressing rapidly and of developing the comprehensive understanding of economic affairs which is rapidly coming to be expected of professional practitioners.

I have no exact data on the subject, but a very large proportion of the colleges and universities of the country now offer varying degrees of instruction appropriate for those who desire to make a career of accounting.

Following World War II, the country embarked upon an extensive programme of education for ex-servicemen, and some idea of the popularity of business administration and accounting can be gained from the fact that I am told that the number of G.I.s who enrolled as business administration and accounting students was greater than the number enrolled for any other course. One would have thought that this would have flooded the accounting profession with a surplus of talent, but it didn't. The G.I. programme has about run out, but in spite of the number of accounting graduates turned out under this programme, and in spite of the fact that the business and accounting schools still are experiencing heavy enrolments, there continues to be a very considerable shortage of personnel trained for the profession. This condition undoubtedly is largely attributable to the high level of economic activity which has resulted from the current defence programme, but the demand for accounting personnel continues to grow, and the time when balance between demand and supply will be reached is not yet in sight.

Factors Contributing to the Growth of Public Accounting Practice

Public practitioners and laymen alike are inclined to ascribe the growth of public accounting practice largely to adoption by my country of income-tax legislation. The first federal tax based upon income was passed in 1909, but we did not get down to income taxation in its present form until 1st March, 1913. It cannot be denied that the adoption of the income-tax and the almost annual extension of the base of this tax created expanding demand for accounting services, and it is a fact, of course, that a good portion of every practitioner's time is devoted to engagements directly or indirectly related to the income-tax. However, I think that the influence of this tax has been greatly overstated.

It is my opinion that fundamentally the profession's almost phenomenal growth has been due to the intensive development of natural resources and the equally intensive extension of industrial activity which has characterised the economy of my country, especially since the turn of the century. It seems to me that this becomes crystal clear when one stops to recall the number of our major industries which have come into being during the last forty years and the proportions of the contribution of these industries to our gross national product.

These industries include such giants as electric power; electrical equipment and appliances; the automobile; truck transportation; radio; industrial chemistry; plastics; rayon; motion pictures; the aeroplane; air transportation; frozen food; television; and synthetic rubber—not to mention the enormous expansion that has taken place in the production of metals, notably steel, copper and aluminium. A good idea of the country's industrial growth can be obtained from the fact that its productive capacity has been far more than doubled since 1939. It was increased about 90 per cent. in the three-year period from 1949 to 1951 alone.

The automobile industry alone directly and indirectly affords employment to 9 million workers, or about one-seventh of the country's entire labour force. The trucking industry, which carries 80 per cent of all the country's inter-state passengers, transports more than 50 per cent. of all workers to their jobs, carries 90 per cent. of all the nation's food to market, and hauls 75 per cent. of all general freight, employs more people than all other forms of transportation combined.

Fundamentally, therefore, while such developments as income taxation, bankruptcy legislation, the control of security exchanges and the issuing of securities, the regulation of public utility rates, and economic controls generally, each has created a large demand for accounting services, the main driving force behind the growth of the accounting profession undoubtedly has been the unparalleled expansion of industry.

Types of Engagements Undertaken by Public Accountants

The backlog of every practitioner's concern is auditing of the books of the country's enterprises and institutions. This is heavily supplemented by tax practice and by engagements involving the installation or revision of accounting systems and procedures. I would say, however, that these other engagements, though many of them are highly important and call for the very highest level of technical judgment and skill, still rank second, even in the aggregate, to auditing.

There has been a recent development, however, that should not be over-looked. The growing complexity of our economic structure, and the burden of complying with an ever-increasing number of government regulations designed to control economic activity, and the exceptional manner in which the public practitioner has met the challenges of practice, naturally have caused clients to look to their certified public accountants for assistance in solving a growing list of problems not originally deemed to be within the scope of the public practitioner's training and experience.

Over the years, business management has found it increasingly difficult to keep costs and expenses down to the point where there would be a reasonable return on investment after the payment of taxes. More and more management has turned to the certified public accountant for help in meeting this problem. As a consequence, many accounting firms have established divisions of their practices to render this kind of service; and be it said to their credit that they have in many situations distinguished themselves highly in this field.

This development is growing and undoubtedly will grow to larger and larger proportions as the years go by, and the certified public accountant will find himself not only an accountant and auditor but also something akin to a business doctor. This is inevitable, because it is a natural evolution. The constantly broadening base of the public practitioner's academic training and experience make it so.

Literature of the Profession

The most widely distributed publication of the profession is the *Journal of Accountancy*, which is published by the American Institute of Accountants. Its present circulation is approximately 67,500. It goes to every member of the American Institute as a part of his membership fee. Thus you will see that there is a circulation of close to 50,000 among others. The other subscribers include, for the most part, business executives, treasurers, controllers and educators.

The American Institute also sponsors from time to time books and other publications on various phases of accounting, one of the most widely circulated of which is the annual publication entitled *Accounting Trends and Techniques*. This is an annual survey by the Institute's Research Department of the published annual reports of corporations. In it are particularly analysed and reported the handling of various elements of corporate financial statements, thus pointing up what is being done in practice about the problems of accounting with which business and the profession, particularly the Institute's Committee on Accounting Procedure and Auditing Procedure, are especially concerned.

Specific technical problems are dealt with from time to time by the Institute's Committee on Accounting Procedure and its Committee on Auditing Procedure. After being thoroughly discussed and reviewed, not only by the respective Institute committees but also by other interested parties and organisations, these problems are reported in the form of Accounting Research Bulletins by the Committee on Accounting Procedure and in the form of Statements on Auditing Procedure by the Committee on Auditing Procedure. Up to this time, forty-one Accounting Research Bulletins and twenty-four Statements of Auditing Procedure have been issued. These statements and bulletins go to all members of the American Institute without charge and are available to other interested persons at nominal prices.

At the moment, the American Institute is engaged in the writing and compiling of what will be called the *Manual of Accounting Practice*. This is perhaps the most ambitious single publication yet undertaken by the Institute and will provide for its members information written by carefully chosen authors concerning every phase of public practice. It undoubtedly will constitute the most valuable of all the many aids to its members that the Institute thus far has developed.

In addition to the publications of the Institute, many of the state societies publish monthly or quarterly reviews of accounting papers and, of course, a great many original papers as well.

Another valuable publication is the *Accounting Review*, which is published monthly by the American Accounting Association. This publication is turned out primarily for the benefit of that Association's members, many of whom are members of the American Institute of Accountants, but, like the *Journal of Accountancy*, it also enjoys substantial circulation among business executives, treasurers, controllers and others.

Further, both the Controllers' Institute of America and the National Association of Cost Accountants put out regular publications dealing primarily with matters of particular interest to their members, many of whom, again, are members of the American Institute of Accountants. Finally, never a month goes by without independently published books on some phase of accounting, auditing, taxes and other subjects of interest to the profession. Altogether, therefore, the literature of the profession in my country is prodigious, to say the least.

Staff Training

There has not been, so far as I know, any nation-wide, or even any state-wide, survey and report on the extent to which staff training is conducted, the kind of training given and the manner in which it is given. However, I have discussed this problem with a great many of my colleagues, and I believe that I can make a fairly accurate statement concerning it.

First, I would say that there is hardly a practitioner in my country who does not recognise the need for staff training, not only as affording the best assurance of establishing and maintaining the highest possible level of competence but also, particularly at this time, as the best possible means of getting beginners up to an adequate level of earnings as rapidly as possible. This is especially important right now, because public practice has been traditionally the training camp from which private industry has drawn much of its accounting personnel. With taxes at their present levels, with the supply of accounting personnel almost acutely short of demand and with salaries subject to strict control, the public accounting profession recently has become the victim of extensive pirating of its personnel by private industry.

Notwithstanding the fact that beginners generally now start in the profession with increasingly better academic training, everyone agrees, including the educators, that there is no substitute for experience. Even the best apprenticeship training during the course of a student's academic work (which is being tried with varying degrees of success, but which is growing) is not now, and is not likely to become, a complete substitute for experience. Consequently, the progressive firm must do everything practicable to hasten acquisition of experience by its junior staff members. Staff training, therefore, is essentially an effort to accelerate the beginner's progress.

Such training varies all the way from relying upon juniors to get the most out of the engagements to which they are assigned, supplemented by study of current papers and articles, to carefully conceived programmes of study and instruction.

For obvious reasons, the extent of in-service training usually is in proportion to the size of the practice enjoyed by the beginner's employer or employers and to his employer's attitude concerning his or their responsibility for the progress of staff members. Some firms, particularly the larger ones, give the instruction themselves. Others arrange to have their staff members attend available extra-curricular classes. Still others, of course, do nothing at all. Some of the larger firms go so far as to put a beginner, regardless of his academic training, through a considerable period of instruction before he is assigned to his first engagement.

There is no question but that staff training is destined, probably very soon, to be extended far beyond its present proportions. In my opinion, this is going to be necessary if the growing firms are to have any hope of keeping the sizes of their staffs equal to the demand for their services. Indeed, I will go even further and venture the opinion that if this is not done, if beginners are not more quickly brought to the point where higher charges can be made for their time and skill, with consequent acceleration of salary increases, the time soon will come, if our economy continues to expand as it has in recent years, when there will not be any but partners left to render the services required by the profession's clients. If this happens, reduction in the size of some firms and increase in the number of so-called small practitioners will be inevitable.

Personally, I should regard this eventuality as being not only unfortunate but also highly undesirable from the standpoints of clients, practitioners and staff members, all three, for the simple reason that the present demand for the services of public accounting firms is so varied that it is next to impossible for an individual practitioner without a fairly numerous staff to render satisfactorily all the different kinds of services now expected of certified public accountants. I do not think it would be good for the profession, for those who require the profession's services, or for staff members for practice to become highly specialised. I believe that if this happens we would find ourselves in the position that the medical profession has reached in my country, where the gradual disappearance of the general practitioner is regarded as a serious problem.

This is not to say that a certain amount of specialisation is not desirable, for such a position could not be justified. However, there is such a thing as over-specialisation, and in my opinion that is more undesirable than no specialisation at all.

Professional Ethics

The recognised authority on ethics in the public accounting profession in the United States is the Executive Director of the American Institute of Accountants, Mr. John L. Carey, who is here at this congress. In 1946, the American Institute published a book on ethics written by Mr. Carey and entitled *Professional Ethics of Public Accounting*. Prior to and since that time, Mr. Carey has spoken extensively on ethics. Mr. Carey believes, as I do, that no profession in our country has a higher code of ethics than the public accounting profession and that the members of no profession are more faithful in their compliance with the rules that they voluntarily have adopted to control their conduct towards the public and themselves.

In a paper read at the Second Inter-American Accounting Conference at Mexico City in November, 1951, Mr. Carey classified and reviewed the rules of ethics that generally prevail in the United States. In this address Mr. Carey divided the rules of ethics into three categories: first, those that are designed to assure and preserve independence and impartiality on the part of the public practitioners; second, those that are designed to safeguard the legitimate interests of clients of the profession; and, third, those that are designed to guide the members of the profession in their relations with each other.

As to the first category, Mr. Carey said:

'. . . the most important rule in a code of ethics for the public accounting profession should be a rule that serves as a guide to right action to the professional accountant in preserving his independence and impartiality and at the same time as a declaration to the public that he will not place himself in positions in which his independence is liable to be impaired.

'Such a rule may be broken down into several parts covering the following points:

(1) The professional accountant acting as an independent auditor accepts the obligation of maintaining independent and impartial judgment in his examination of accounts and in expressing his opinion on financial statements.

(2) He will disclose all material facts which he discovers that have a bearing on the financial position or the results of operations.

(3) He will conduct his examination of accounts in accordance with generally accepted auditing procedures and not express an opinion on financial statements unless he has made an adequate examination.

(4) He will not have any substantial financial interest in the affairs of a company on whose financial statements he is reporting without fully disclosing that interest.

(5) He will not render an opinion on financial statements under circumstances in which the amount of his fee depends on the successful outcome of any venture in which those financial statements may play a part, such as the issuance of securities.

(6) He will not engage in any other occupation simultaneously with the practice of public accounting which might impair his impartiality or objectivity in reporting on financial statements.'

As to the second category, Mr. Carey said:

'. . . the second most important rule of a code of professional ethics for the accounting profession is a rule designed to safeguard the legitimate interests of clients of members of the profession.

'This rule may be broken down into parts to cover the following points:

(1) A practitioner will not violate the confidential relationship between himself and his client.

(2) He will not exploit his professional relationship with the client by accepting commissions, brokerages or other compensation from suppliers whose products or services he may influence the client to purchase.

(3) He will not seek to shield himself behind the corporate form of organization, but will conduct his practice as an individual or member of a partnership.

(4) He will not allow others to practise in his name unless they are in partnership with him or in his employ as an accredited member of the profession and thus subject to his control and supervision. Likewise, he will not sign his name to reports on financial statements which have been prepared by others who are not in his employ or in partnership with him or who, as his representative, are not accredited members of his profession who accept responsibility to him.'

As to the third category, Mr. Carey said:

'. . . the third most important rule in a code of professional ethics for the public accounting profession is a rule to serve as a guide to right action in relations of the practitioner with his colleagues and with his profession as a whole.

'Such a rule might be broken into parts covering the following points:

(1) The professional public accountant will not advertise his professional attainments or services, except as appropriate announcements may be permitted by the rules of his society.

(2) He will not solicit the clients or encroach upon the practice of another professional accountant, although he may properly respond to any request for service and advice which comes without solicitation.

(3) He shall not offer employment to an employee of another public accountant without first informing that accountant, although he may properly employ anyone who of his own initiative applies for such employment.'

Mr. Carey then pointed out that his paper was not intended as an outline of 'a complete code of professional ethics for the accounting profession, but only to suggest the fundamental rules which it is believed should be an essential part of any such code. There are many other aspects of professional accounting practice on which rules or precepts might usefully be written, but the ones mentioned here, in my opinion, are basic and indispensable.'

Finally, Mr. Carey concluded: 'All the points I have mentioned in this paper are now covered, explicitly or implicitly, in the rules of the American Institute as well as some other points which do not seem sufficiently fundamental to warrant consideration at this time', reminding his audience that 'these rules were not all put into effect at one time but have been developed over a long period of time out of the experience of the membership' and suggesting the certainty that 'they will undoubtedly be modified and elaborated further in the future as additional experience may indicate desirable changes'.

Such rules have been adopted by all the state societies, institutes and associations. In some states, the rules of professional ethics have been written into the accountancy laws, either specifically or by reference.

The American Institute enforces its rules continually through its Committee on Professional Ethics, which receives and considers complaints of violations and refers to a trial board those complaints that require disciplinary action. The trial board may admonish, suspend or expel a member who is found guilty after a hearing of the charges made against him. Somewhat the same procedure is followed in one form or another by the state organisations.

Some Current Problems

This paper would not be complete without some reference to at least two problems that currently confront the profession in the United States: first, the question whether it is desirable to define accounting practice; and, second, the question whether those who do not intend to engage in the practice of public accounting should be given C.P.A. certificates.

The first of these questions has been plaguing the profession for years. The second is only beginning to emerge. As to each of them, I desire to make it clear that what I shall say concerning it must be regarded as indicating my own thoughts alone and should not be regarded as indicative of any opinion or conclusion by the American Institute or of any state organisation.

For several years, there has been a growing insistence by certain members of the Bar that certified public accountants, in their practice, particularly in their handling of tax matters, frequently get over into the realm of the lawyer. Some of these gentlemen even go so far as to take the position that certified public accountants are practising law when they do no more than prepare a tax return, and the American Bar Association itself, and some of the state Bar associations, have, through their Committees on Unauthorised Practice of the Law, sought to exclude the certified public accountants from tax practice in one degree or another.

Recently, however, the two professions have agreed upon a tentative statement on this troublesome question through a group consisting of representatives of both professions and known as the National Conference of Lawyers and Certified Public Accountants. A copy of this tentative statement accompanies this paper as Appendix A.

I do not intend to discuss the position taken by the lawyers. I must admit, however, that on occasion, and in varying degrees, members of the accounting profession undoubtedly have gotten over into the lawyers' field. However, I hasten to point out that I have never heard of a single case where the transgression was deliberate and intentional: in every case the accountant has averred (honestly, I believe) that he did not intend to invade the lawyers' province and would be especially careful to avoid repetition of the offence.

The difficulty up to this time has been that the accountants have always been on the receiving end of the complaints, whereas it is perfectly obvious that lawyers frequently invade the province of the certified public accountant. Moreover, lawyers not infrequently (especially where they act as secretary, director or in other close relationships to business enterprises) seek to impose views, not to say orders on occasion, upon the certified public accountant which, if yielded to, would make the certified public accountant guilty of utter and complete violation of his obligation of independence.

It may well be that this problem can be worked out by negotiation, but the lawyers are numerous in our country; it is well known that they are in control of the Congress and practically all state and local legislative bodies. It is entirely possible, therefore, that the lawyers' infringements upon the province of the certified public accountants cannot be solved except by including in the state accountancy laws some definition of what constitutes the practice of accounting, although, recognising that the lawyers are in virtual control of our legislative bodies, this obviously might be a very difficult, if not impossible, undertaking.

However, it is my opinion that if the problem cannot be solved by negotiation, then public interest demands that an effort be made to settle it by legislation. At any rate, I am not willing to concede that the lawyers are Simon Pures and that the accountants alone are sinners, and I think that the accounting profession is too grown-up, and the essentiality of its position in the scheme of things is too well recognised, to warrant its members' allowing it to be picked on, bullied, pushed around and interdicted by another group, no matter how exalted that group may be or in what esteem it may be held by itself and others, including the members of the public accounting profession—and I assure you that we of the public accounting profession yield to no one in our admiration of and respect for our brothers of the Bar individually and as members of a great and most useful profession.

The probable need for defining what constitutes the practice of accounting is not suggested by the encroachment of the lawyers alone, however. We have another group in our country, generally described as public book-keepers, who are not subject to regulation, though there is no good reason why they should be. This group frequently gets over the line into accounting practice, and sometimes with tragic results. For instance, I have seen numerous cases where business people have got into serious financial difficulties, and into such difficulties with the tax authorities as to cause these authorities to assert fraud, because some fellow who fancied himself to be an accountant gave faulty advice as to how books should be kept.

Considering the importance that accounting assumes in a society that is so highly industrialised as that of my country, it seems to me that the giving of advice as to how accounts should be kept is an activity which, like the independence and impartiality of the certified public accountant, acting in the capacity of auditor, is affected with the public interest. I am inclined to believe, therefore, that the time has come for us to insist that the right to give such advice be limited to those who have proven themselves qualified by training and experience to give it.

The question whether C.P.A. certificates should be issued to those who do not intend to follow public accounting as a career is beset with difficulties of equal magnitude, although I do not believe that these difficulties are insurmountable.

The principal difficulty lies in the question what is to be done about those who become certified public accountants and later leave the profession to accept other employment. I would not be so foolish or so unfair as to suggest that in such cases the C.P.A. certificate should be recalled. I do suggest, however, that perhaps the granting of C.P.A. certificates should be conditioned upon demonstration of sincere intention to follow public accounting as a career. It may well be that what I have in mind as a demonstration of this sincerity will not work out in practice, but I believe it will. In any event, I think that the time has come for serious consideration of the problem.

Most of our state laws are founded upon the theory that C.P.A. certificates should not be granted until those who apply for them have acquired some amount of experience, usually from two to three years, on the staff of a C.P.A. or firm of C.P.A.s. But there are many who feel—and this is true of the members of many state legislatures—that anyone who completes a satisfactory course of academic instruction and is of good character should be permitted to take the examination and be given a certificate if he passes. In fact, there are some states that do not impose any experience requirement, and that is exactly what happens in those states.

Based upon my observations and experience over thirty-five years of practice, I think that this is an utterly fallacious view. My own proposition is that anyone of good character who is academically qualified to take the examination should be permitted to do so and that his papers should be graded without regard to whether he has had experience or not. However, I would withhold the issuing of the C.P.A. certificate where the examinee had not had any experience until such time as he gains it, and I would recognise only experience gained under the direction of a C.P.A. or firm of C.P.A.s.

Just how much experience one should have before receiving the certificate need not be discussed at this time. I would say, however, that it ought to be a minimum of three years and perhaps as much as five years, since under such a policy as I have suggested the waiting period ought to be sufficient not only to assure the acquisition of requisite experience, but also sufficient to give reasonable assurance of the applicant's intention to make public accounting his career.

Under the plan that I propose that we should consider, a person who successfully passes the examination and completes the required number of years of experience would be deemed to have demonstrated intention to make public accounting his career and would be given his certificate regardless of whether or not he continues in the accounting profession thereafter.

The C.P.A. certificate was originally conceived as an attestation of fitness to engage in the *public* practice of accounting, and the reasons for this distinction are more compelling to-day than ever. Those accountants who do not choose to go into public practice do not need C.P.A. certificates, and it is a distortion of the purpose of the accounting laws to give them certificates. I know of no surer way to make certain that the designation certified *public* accountant means what it clearly implies than to make the C.P.A. certificate available only to those who demonstrate that they intend to make their careers in public practice.

Conclusion

The outline that was sent to me as a guide for this paper indicated that my subject was to be 'The Accountant in Practice and Public Service'. I have not dealt with the accountant in public service, because that is a separate subject in itself and the problems of governmental accounting are quite different from those encountered by the professional public accountant. True enough, governmental accounting involves the application of special techniques and procedures, but in this respect governmental accounting is no different from many categories of enterprise accounting.

I might say, however, that tremendous advances have been made in governmental accounting in my country during the past twenty-five years, and I think that the professional accountants can claim a great deal of the credit for this, because undeniably it has been the progress of accounting generally that has forced improvement in governmental accounting, and much of this progress has been wrought by professional public accountants who have either temporarily or permanently entered the public service to apply the techniques and procedures that they learned and helped develop in the course of their professional practices.

For instance, our national government has made tremendous improvement in its accounting, especially since World War II, and the leadership in this improvement has been, and is being, furnished without exception by men recruited from the public accounting profession.

APPENDIX A

STATEMENT OF PRINCIPLES RELATING TO PRACTICE
IN THE FIELD OF FEDERAL INCOME TAXATION

PROMULGATED BY THE
NATIONAL CONFERENCE OF LAWYERS AND CERTIFIED PUBLIC ACCOUNTANTS

1. *Collaboration of Lawyers and Certified Public Accountants Desirable.* It is in the best public interest that services and assistance in federal income-tax matters be rendered by lawyers and certified public accountants, who are trained in their fields by education and experience, and for whose admission to professional standing there are requirements as to education, citizenship and high moral character. They are required to pass written examinations and are subject to rules of professional ethics, such as those of the American Bar Association and American Institute of Accountants, which set a high standard of professional practice and conduct, including prohibition of advertising and solicitation. Many problems connected with business require the skills of both lawyers and certified public accountants and there is every reason for a close and friendly co-operation between the two professions. Lawyers should encourage their clients to seek the advice of certified public accountants whenever accounting problems arise and certified public accountants should encourage clients to seek the advice of lawyers whenever legal questions are presented.

2. *Preparation of Federal Income Tax Returns.* It is a proper function of a lawyer or a certified public accountant to prepare Federal income-tax returns.

When a lawyer prepares a return in which questions of accounting arise, he should advise the taxpayer to enlist the assistance of a certified public accountant.

When a certified public accountant prepares a return in which questions of law arise, he should advise the taxpayer to enlist the assistance of a lawyer.

3. *Ascertainment of Probable Tax Effects of Transactions.* In the course of the practice of law and in the course of the practice of accounting, lawyers and certified public accountants are often asked about the probable tax effects of transactions.

The ascertainment of probable tax effects of transactions frequently is within the function of either a certified public accountant or a lawyer. However, in many instances, problems arise which require the attention of a member of one or the other professions, or members of both. When such ascertainment raises uncertainties as to the interpretation of law (both tax law and general law), or uncertainties as to the application of law to the transaction involved, the certified public accountant should advise the taxpayer to enlist the services of a lawyer. When such ascertainment involves difficult questions of classifying and summarising the transaction in a significant manner and in terms of money, or interpreting the financial results thereof, the lawyer should advise the taxpayer to enlist the services of a certified public accountant.

In many cases, therefore, the public will be best served by utilising the joint skills of both professions.

4. *Preparation of Legal and Accounting Documents.* Only a lawyer may prepare legal documents such as agreements, conveyances, trust instruments, wills, or corporate minutes or give advice as to the legal sufficiency or effect thereof, or take the necessary steps to create, amend or dissolve a partnership, corporation, trust, or other legal entity.

Only an accountant may properly advise as to the preparation of financial statements included in reports or submitted with tax returns, or as to accounting methods and procedures.

5. *Prohibited Self-designations.* An accountant should not describe himself as a 'tax consultant' or 'tax expert' or use any similar phrase. Lawyers, simiiarly, are

417

prohibited by the canons of ethics of the American Bar Association and the opinions relating thereto, from advertising a special branch of law practice.

6. *Representation of Taxpayers before Treasury Department.* Under Treasury Department regulations lawyers and certified public accountants are authorised, upon a showing of their professional status, and subject to certain limitations as defined in the Treasury rules, to represent taxpayers in proceedings before that department. If, in the course of such proceedings, questions arise involving the application of legal principles, a lawyer should be retained, and if, in the course of such proceedings accounting questions arise, a certified public accountant should be retained.

7. *Practice before the Tax Court of the United States.* Under the Tax Court rules non-lawyers may be admitted to practice.

However, since upon issuance of a formal notice of deficiency by the Commissioner of Internal Revenue a choice of legal remedies is afforded the taxpayer under existing law (either before the Tax Court of the United States, a United States District Court or the Court of Claims), it is in the best interests of the taxpayer that the advice of a lawyer be sought if further proceedings are contemplated. It is not intended hereby to foreclose the right of non-lawyers to practise before the Tax Court of the United States pursuant to its rules.

Here also, as in proceedings before the Treasury Department, the taxpayer, in many cases, is best served by the combined skills of both lawyers and certified public accountants, and the taxpayers, in such cases, should be advised accordingly.

8. *Claims for Refund.* Claims for refund may be prepared by lawyers or certified public accountants, provided, however, that where a controversial legal issue is involved or where the claim is to be made the basis of litigation, the services of a lawyer should be obtained.

9. *Criminal Tax Investigations.* When a certified public accountant learns that his client is being specially investigated for possible criminal violation of the income-tax law, he should advise his client to seek the advice of a lawyer as to his legal and constitutional rights.

Conclusion. This statement of principles should be regarded as tentative and subject to revision and amplification in the light of future experience. The principal purpose is to indicate the importance of voluntary co-operation between our professions, whose members should use their knowledge and skills to the best advantage of the public. It is recommended that joint committees representing the local societies of both professions be established. Such committees might well take permanent form as local conferences of lawyers and certified public accountants patterned after this conference, or could take the form of special committees to handle a specific situation.

THE ACCOUNTANT IN PRACTICE AND IN PUBLIC SERVICE

by

A. P. C. D'AÇA CASTEL-BRANCO
Sociedade Portuguesa de Contabilidade

THE ACCOUNTANT IN PRACTICE

Modern developments and present-day progress have given to the accountancy profession a very important position both in commerce and in industry, for accounting is an indispensable element in a great business enterprise, which depends on it as surely as the course of a ship relies on the steady touch of the helmsman.

However, it is not always convenient for business firms to maintain specialised personnel on their permanent accounting staffs, because salaries of such specialists have of necessity to be high. Hence the need at times to call upon competent persons who, acting as consultants, are by virtue of the practical and theoretical knowledge acquired through years of experience, able to solve difficulties as they arise.

One problem which can perturb the management of a company, and to a greater degree the members, the great majority of whom are cut off from the day-to-day administration, is that there is available to them only the one opportunity of learning from a condensed annual report the company's current state of affairs, although it is true that Portuguese law puts upon certain companies the duty of publishing half-yearly accounts. Further, it is never possible sufficiently to foresee when the honesty of an individual may cease, so numerous are the influences which may be brought to bear upon him.

But an independent expert, furnished with all the elements indispensable to the fulfilment of his mission, can in the above instances allay possible disquiet and act to the benefit of all members of the concern employing his services. To this end, the expert needs to possess special qualities, the most valuable being absolute integrity, sound knowledge, tact and strength of character.

It is a fact that, usually in the case of a limited liability company (where all the capital is issued in the form of shares) and even sometimes in partnerships (wherein the capital is subscribed by the partners, but where often not all the proprietors take part in the management), the administration is carried on by persons nominated for the purpose, with the acquiescence of the remainder.

There is no doubt that legislators, when they are framing the law, attempt to safeguard the interests of small investors, but this protection is represented in practice by judicial actions, the initiation of which is very expensive. Hence, there come about a hesitancy and a not unnatural anxiety on the part of the average investor due to the lengthy deliberations of the courts and of the consequent embarrassment for business concerns.

But as a result of the verification and auditing work of the accountant, the small investor is not entirely at the mercy of the directors, and so develops a greater feeling of confidence in the security of his capital, invested in a great economic organisation.

It is not possible for the directors themselves to take care of the multiplicity of problems which it is necessary to solve every day. Inevitably they must decentralise and delegate responsibility to subordinates.

In many countries, in an endeavour to counteract the dangers and inconveniences which might result from this delegation of responsibility, business concerns have become accustomed to utilising the services of independent persons who, with special authority to check the books and vouchers of the accounts department, are thereby enabled to formulate and express a detailed and unbiased opinion regarding the activities and the state of affairs of the concern into which they have examined.

Such an expressed opinion brings confidence, on the one hand to investors who take no part in management and, on the other hand, to the management in its subordinates. At the same time, the officials of the enterprise have the satisfaction of knowing that their work is fairly appraised by an independent third party.

We are convinced that, with the utilisation in many countries of these expert services, commerce, banking, finance and industry have become better and more honestly administered. Many states, understanding the benefits which have been brought about, have given to the auditors a well-defined status in law and have even gone so far as to utilise their reports and figures, especially in cases where taxation is based on the true profits of enterprise.

But in order that both states and the general public may confidently rely upon such practitioners, it is necessary that they should possess a certain number of indispensable attributes, in other words, that they merit that confidence. So that, alongside an indisputable competence, there must exist the absolute integrity already referred to, not only in their work itself, but also in all their relations with their clients and their clients' employees and in the reserve to be maintained over the confidential information acquired in the course of their duties, which must at all costs be considered as professional secrets.

We believe that it was in the United Kingdom that professional auditing commenced its evolution and that it owes to the strength of character and foresight of the pioneers that position of trust and confidence which the profession enjoys in every part of the world.

Originally, each auditor would have operated independently, but as clients increased in numbers and problems became more complex, so arose the necessity for several practitioners to pool their resources, thereby giving greater cohesion to the profession and resulting in the bringing together of competent persons assisting each other towards their mutual objectives.

Systems gradually became universal and eventually specialisation came about in different branches of accounting, Accordingly, the auditor, as an expert examiner of accounting records, began to widen his activities, carrying out not only the duties of an efficient auditor as such, but also acting as a financial adviser, an investigator for certain defined purposes, an appraiser of the value of assets and of liabilities, as well as investigating defalcations and frauds, negotiating purchases and sales of entire companies, and reorganising accounting systems. In other words, he became an indispensable unit of a well-organised business community.

We know that in the United Kingdom and in other countries the auditor's report is made available to all of a company's shareholders, and the auditor himself has the right to be present at the annual general meeting; he may be called on to provide explanations required by the members who are present at that meeting. He has profound knowledge of the administration of the business and in the near future, due to developments of commerce, it will be necessary for the accountant to work even more closely with the other specialists who serve the enterprise.

The auditor's attention is mainly concentrated on the most important statements from the accounting point of view: the balance sheet and profit and loss account, as well as the other statements drawn up at regular intervals.

There is no doubt that, in the course of the auditor's rigorous examination of the accounts and records, the whole accounting system of an enterprise is tested, since such an examination requires that the movement throughout the accounting period be audited, from cash entries up to finalised statements. The report on the audit of the accounts—the final guarantee for all interested parties—is the opinion of an expert, given as a result of the direct and profound study which he has had the opportunity to make.

For an audit report to have its full value, long practice is necessary, allied to deep theoretical knowledge. In our opinion a person who completes a technical course cannot undertake efficiently such work without having first perfected his training by some years of practice; further, he must not lack a deep-felt love of the profession. The recent codification of the only professional courses which in Portugal fit students for this work—those of the commercial institutes—determines the necessary qualifications.

It is easily understood that, as in any other calling, a theorist with but little practical experience will not feel himself capable of resolving any serious difficulty which may arise, or any complicated problem put to him by his client. The client will quickly lose his confidence in the specialist who vacillates. Apart from that diplomacy already mentioned, the practising accountant must be able to rely both on confidence being justifiably placed in him by others and on his own confidence in his knowledge, experience and worth. His knowledge he learns at school; experience he learns from his practice; but his full worth is gained gradually during his years of service in the profession.

Returning to other activities, we must mention that the accountant can also become a specialist in initiating book-keeping systems, in negotiating transfers of interests in partnerships, and so on. He can make a valuable contribution to the elucidation of judicial questions, setting out in the Courts, after careful and dispassionate examination the answers to questions which are put before them.

In Portugal, the profession of the accountant has not yet reached the necessary state of development for its value to be fully realised by great financiers or by the general public. However, it cannot be said that the periodical audit of books for informative purposes is entirely unknown to us and many of the more important and progressive firms now recognise its undoubted advantages through its adoption by certain firms, both Portuguese and foreign. A great number of businesses, too, use consultant accountants as periodical or occasional advisers.

The State recognises the usefulness of the verification of the accounts of certain types of company; the National Assembly has already given some attention to this matter and has approved the text of a draft law regarding the audit and control of companies of liability limited by shares. This law envisages the formation of a professional institute to be known as the Council of Auditors of Limited Companies (*Câmera dos Verificadores das Sociedades por Acções*) the members of which are to be qualified persons and for whom Schedule II of the Law establishes the qualifications necessary to permit of a conscientious audit. To this Council the law will allow an autonomy subject only to the limitations of the law itself, so that there is every reason to look forward to dignified and efficient action by the proposed Council.

However, whilst the implementation of this law is still awaited, the examination of the activities of limited liability companies is regulated by the stipulations of the Portuguese Commercial Code of 1888 and amplifying decrees, which require the annual election of a fiscal board from amongst the shareholders. This board, consisting of at least three active members, of whom, however, no academic or professional qualification is demanded, is expected to review periodically the business activity and the accounts of the company and to draw up a report for submission to the annual general meeting of the members, in conjunction with the directors' report.

The Accountancy Rules in the Commercial Code and complementary laws require all commercial bodies to maintain the usual principal accounting records, i.e. ledger, journal, inventory and balance sheet register, minute and other books such as are necessary to show 'plainly, clearly and precisely' the operations they record and the position with regard to the assets and liabilities. All firms and companies must conform to the statutory accounting year, ending on 31st December.

Portuguese accountants, assimilating the results of the development which the science has undergone in other countries, particularly in the United Kingdom, the United States, France and Italy, have succeeded, little by little, in introducing improvements into their accounting procedures, striving always towards perfection.

Portugal was among the first countries in the world to legalise the profession of accountancy, since there is an old enactment, dating from 1594, which determined that all merchants who wished to enjoy the freedoms and privileges due to them as merchants, must first have their names set down and registered in an official 'book'. In 1770, a new law revived and strengthened the previous decree and went further. It prohibited the admission into commercial establishments, whether State- or privately-owned, in the Kingdom or the

Dominions, of persons who, being destined for book-keepers, cashiers, clerks or apprentices, had not frequented a school which was then called the 'Commercial College'.

Modifications of laws through the years have so changed these regulations, that they are now no longer on the Statute Book. In the meantime, Portuguese accountants themselves have not spared their energies to obtain modernisation of the law, and the Sociedade Portuguesa de Contabilidade (Portuguese Accountancy Society), a founder-member of the Union Européenne des Experts Comptables, Economiques et Financiers, and which counts in its membership many of the most important and experienced members of the profession, has contributed by all means in its power towards intensification of interest in the desired codification of accountancy. Our Society has arranged lectures and discussion groups on the advantages to be obtained from the organisation of accountancy on professional lines. In the course of these lectures and discussions, some of the most influential of our members, as well as guest lecturers, professors, industrial accountants, auditors and legal experts, unanimously affirmed the desirability of such an organisation.

THE ACCOUNTANT IN PUBLIC SERVICE

It is obvious that the public service has need of competent accountants, capable of dealing with the multiplicity of problems confronting them; for their solution could favourably or adversely affect the administration of the law.

Nevertheless, it so happens that, by the nature of the service which they are called upon to carry out, they are widely separated from the administration of private business enterprises. An accountant admitted to any particular Ministry occupies a post in a department which confines him strictly to his own sphere, even though he enjoys in that sphere considerable advantages over those who might have higher qualifications. As the law stands at present, the accountant's career is limited to the area of operations of that department, so that his scope is restricted.

In Portugal one General Directorate, subordinated to the Ministry of Finance, directs and carries out the work of public accounts.

The public accounts are based on the State Budget and do not employ the double-entry system, the object being to permit of statistical control of expenses. The accounts are technically straightforward, but must conform to complex legal rules to maintain efficiency with the maximum economy. But whenever any particular government service is operated with a view to profit, or maintained, even partially, out of its own income, then normal double-entry procedure is adopted.

The Directorate-General of Public Accounts superintends the nation's accounting problems through the accounts department of each ministry. (In the Finance Ministry there are three such departments.) But, as has already been stated, each ministry has its own service, either with administrative, administrative and financial, or absolute autonomy not subject to the ministry's accounts department, but conforming to general law and subject to the control of the Accounts Tribunal, which body examines all vouchers for expenditure, as well as the government general accounts.

Further, within the Ministry of Finance there is the Directorate-General of the Public Exchequer, which superintends operations relating to the national and international transfers of moneys, carries through the raising of loans and issuing of Government bonds, and administers the floating debt—internal, external and governmental.

The State verifies the operations of the public accounts, particularly those of the autonomous services, through the Inspectorate-General of Finance, which also periodically examines the various Treasuries of the Public Exchequer.

This same Inspectorate-General examines the activities of private and public companies and firms regarding increases of capital, transfers from reserve funds and transfers of partnership capital. These examinations and inspections extend not only to accounts and associated departments, but also to the analysis of the books of firms connected with the one specifically under review, and have the following main objects:

(a) Appraisal of the results of the period under review, trading and administrative, as well as the treatment of the net profits.

(b) Analysis of the economic position and prospects and financial situation.

(c) Verification of the accuracy of tax returns.

(d) When considering the operating results, separate mention is made of manufacturing and trading expenses, excluding administration expenses, which latter are taken into account in calculating net profits, arrived at after considering expenses of a general nature.

Administrators or directors are in all cases under an obligation to furnish the inspectors with all necessary information.

An important role is played by the Inspectorate-General of Credit and Insurance, responsible for checking banking and insurance businesses. This Inspectorate imposes uniform accounting procedures and scrutinises and checks accounts, which it publishes annually.

The very nature of the public accounting service and its complexity and diversity compel the State to exert considerable care in the recruiting, admission and promotion of personnel. Admission is by public examination, and promotion to higher grades inside the service is based on the results of compulsory examinations. From the foregoing, it will be seen that selection is rigorous and staff must of necessity be worthy and able to fulfil the duties confided to them.

Every individual section of each ministry submits its annual expenditure estimates to the appropriate accounts department by 30th June of the preceding year, and it is the duty of the departments to co-ordinate these estimates and forward the totals to the Directorate-General of Public Accounts by 1st September.

Pending the setting-up of the already approved General Budget Office, it is the Directorate-General of Public Accounts which collates the budget estimates of receipts and expenses of all ministries, and drafts the Budget Law. These documents are submitted to the Ministry of Finance, which presents the proposed Law to the National Assembly by 25th November. The approval of the Budget Law must be voted before 15th December, as this law authorises the Government to collect the taxation and make the expenditure of the following year.

A department may only exceed the budgeted expenditure estimates in the case of absolute necessity and with the higher authority of a governmental decree, and then only on condition there is a compensating reduction elsewhere.

The Government itself has the duty of drawing up each year's accounts for comparison with the original budget estimates.

The organisation of the public accounts service is as efficient as circumstances permit, as is shown by the considerable regularity with which the Government Daily Gazette publishes very detailed extracts of the nation's accounts. The present system provides all parties interested in studying the movement of the national receipts and expenditure with details of the Budget, provisional accounts and finalised public accounts for each year.

The work of the accountant in the public service in Portugal differs considerably from that which he is called upon to carry out in the business world, for the latter requires the more frequent use of special knowledge and experience, to overcome unexpected difficulties. Nevertheless, the accountant in public service does have the opportunity of using his initiative if he is with one or other of the autonomous departments, whilst the Inspectorates-General offer even more of such opportunities.

As we have already seen, accounting criteria are much the same for both officials and professional auditors where the objectives to be attained are identical. But since the main functions of the officials are bound up with the assessment of taxes, their existence does not adversely affect the auditor, whose activities have undoubted economic utility. On the contrary, by intelligent co-operation the official and the professional accountant may contribute to the common advantage of the nation. Even through the activities of the Inspectorates-General there have already come about improvements in accounting technique, both private and public.

Since the Portuguese method of government is that of the Corporate State, there have been set up corporate organisations and organisations of economic co-ordination.

The former are subdivided as to:

Primary organisations: Guilds, labour unions, provincial, countrymen's and fishermen's associations.
Secondary organisations: Unions and federations.

The latter are made up of:

National commissions which co-ordinate and direct certain export goods.
Regulating commissions which similarly treat imported goods.
Institutes which safeguard the origin and quality of export goods.

As a co-ordinator of these various national interests, there is in existence the Corporate Council, whose members are drawn from the various economic and financial activities, and whose task is to report on the laws issued by the Executive and the National Assembly.

Not all the heads of the public departments are accountants, but it is through the persistence and labour of accountants that progress will be made in the direction of ever more clear and accurate accounting, so that it may attain its objective—the accurate portrayal at any given moment of the state of affairs of each and every administrative body.

THE ACCOUNTANT IN PRACTICE IN SOUTH AFRICA

by

PROFESSOR W. J. G. FAIRBAIRN, A.S.A.A., C.A.(S.A.)
Natal Society of Accountants

BRIEF HISTORY OF THE PROFESSION IN SOUTH AFRICA

Accounting as a separate profession first became known in South Africa in the last decade of the nineteenth century. At that time there was no Union of South Africa. Johannesburg was little more than a mining camp. Two of the present provinces—the Cape and Natal—were under British rule. The other two, the Orange Free State and the Transvaal, were Boer Republics.

In 1895 a small body of men in Natal who were interested in accounting mainly as an ancillary to their other vocations, formed an 'Institute of Accountants in Natal'. This was a completely voluntary body; it conducted no examinations and membership appeared to be open to anyone who wished to practise as an accountant, whether in conjunction with some other profession or not. Similar voluntary bodies were formed in the other colonies in the same decade.

The Transvaal was the first colony to give official recognition and status to accountants as a profession. In 1904, when the Transvaal had become a self-governing colony under the British Crown, an Ordinance was passed which provided for the establishment of the Transvaal Society of Accountants and enacted that henceforth no person would be permitted to practise as an accountant and auditor in the Transvaal unless his name was first placed on a register, which was in control of the Society. Natal followed suit in 1908, when the Natal Society of Accountants was established, and the old Institute was incorporated in it. The Cape and Orange Free State continued as voluntary bodies, with the result that Union of the four colonies in 1910 found the profession strictly controlled in only two of the four provinces.

Numerous attempts to bring about unification of the profession in the whole Union followed in the succeeding years. Private Bills were introduced in Parliament on a number of occasions but all failed for some reason or another—mainly because of a lack of unanimity amongst accountants themselves.

The need for uniform standards and examinations in the four provinces became pressing, however, and eventually in 1921, the four provincial Societies set up a General Examining Board, which was henceforth entrusted with the control of all examinations for the profession in the whole of South Africa. The Rhodesia Society of Accountants, which had been incorporated in 1918, subsequently joined the Board. Under the agreement setting up the Board, all four provincial Societies undertook to—and did—so amend their bye-laws that henceforth admission to membership was only by way of service under articles and examination.

P

In the preceding years, however, numbers of accountants with overseas qualifications had come out to South Africa and had commenced practice. Membership of certain overseas bodies automatically entitled such persons to be admitted to the registers in the Transvaal and Natal. Some of these bodies of accountants—notably the Society of Incorporated Accountants and Auditors—had such strong representation in South Africa that they set up branches here. For some years it was possible for an incorporated accountant in practice in South Africa to have a double quota of articled clerks—one set articled through the Incorporated Society and the other through the local Society. That anomalous position was done away with in 1932, when the Incorporated Society agreed that it would no longer conduct examinations for South African candidates, but would accept the examinations of the South African Societies General Examining Board. From that year on, membership of the Incorporated Society for South Africans has only been possible where the candidate has served articles registered with one of the South African societies, simultaneously with articles registered with the Incorporated Society, and has passed a special modified qualifying examination of the Incorporated Society, after passing those set by the General Examining Board.

In 1927 an important milestone for the profession in South Africa was passed. Prior to that year, accountants in the Transvaal and Natal had styled themselves 'Registered Public Accountant'. In 1927 Parliament passed an Act entitled the Chartered Accountants Designation Act. This Act conferred the common designation 'Chartered Accountant (South Africa)' on all members of the four South African societies. The Southern Rhodesia Government followed suit in the following year, providing the designation 'Chartered Accountant (Southern Rhodesia)' for members of the Rhodesia Society.

This was a step in the right direction but the need for complete unified control of the profession in South Africa became more and more evident and pressing. Numerous conferences were held; the Government appointed a Commission in 1934 to investigate and report on the position. That Commission produced a very able and comprehensive report, together with a draft Bill providing for registration of accountants throughout the Union. After further discussions and negotiations the Bill was introduced in Parliament in 1938. The Bill was referred to a Select Committee and actually passed a second reading early in 1940, but was dropped at that stage as the Government had other, much more important matters to deal with, which kept Parliament busy for some years.

In the meantime, over the years, numbers of persons had established themselves in practice as accountants in the Cape and the Free State, without becoming members of the local Societies of Accountants. Particularly in the country towns of those two provinces, numbers of so-called, self-styled 'accountants' had no professional qualifications whatsoever. Several of the younger overseas bodies of accountants admitted such people to membership without examination and thereby acquired some strength. Negotiations towards unification of the profession continually broke down over the claims of members of such bodies to equal status with Chartered Accountants (S.A.).

Eventually, the Government took a hand in the matter and, under pressure from the Treasury, a conference was held in 1947 and was attended by delegates from all organised bodies of professional accountants in the Union. The Chartered Societies were ably represented at this conference and, although some concessions had to be made to those practising accountants who were not entitled to use the designation 'Chartered Accountant (S.A.)', in the main, the Chartered Societies were able to ensure that the high standard that had been attained by them over many years' struggle would be maintained unimpaired. A large measure of agreement was reached at the conference and a draft Bill was prepared. It provided for the establishment of a common register in the Union, to which would be admitted, under certain conditions, members of organised bodies other than the Chartered Societies.

The draft Bill was considered, discussed, amended and re-amended at various conferences in the ensuing two or three years. Eventually it was laid before Parliament in 1951 as an agreed measure and was enacted in that year. It is known as

THE PUBLIC ACCOUNTANTS AND AUDITORS ACT, 1951

Firstly, the Act sets up a body to be known as the Public Accountants and Auditors Board, which is charged with the administration of the Act. The constitution of the Board is such that the four societies, through their nominees, have a bare majority. The remainder of the Board is made up of four Government nominees (to be selected from a panel of high officials such as the Commissioner for Inland Revenue and the Registrar of Companies, etc.), two nominees from the professors or lecturers in accounting at the various universities in the Union, and nominees from the 'other bodies', as the various smaller bodies of accountants operating in the Cape and the Orange Free State, are known.

The Act prohibits any person from practising or holding himself out as an accountant or auditor in the Union unless he is registered as such on the register to be maintained by the Board.

Admission to the register is automatic for Chartered Accountants (S.A.). Members of 'other bodies' will only be placed on the register if they were members of such bodies on 1st January, 1950, and other persons will only be registered if they comply with certain stipulated requirements including five years' practical experience to the satisfaction of the Board.

Once the register has been established, further admissions thereto will only be by way of service under articles and by passing examinations prescribed by the Board. The Act further provides that all articles of clerkship must be approved by and registered with the Board. Very adequate provision is made covering the rights of admission to the register of accountants from overseas who may wish to take up residence in the Union and pursue their profession in this country.

Strong disciplinary powers are vested in the Board, which has power to strike off or suspend any registered accountant who is found guilty of contraventions of the Act or of unprofessional conduct. Furthermore, the Act imposes extensive powers and duties on registered accountants, and does so by way of laying down the circumstances in which an accountant must qualify his report. For example, any statements, balance sheets, reports, etc., must bear a qualified certificate unless, *inter alia*, the audit has been carried out free of any restrictions, proper books and accounts have been kept and so on. Numerous other provisions of the Act will go far to raise the standard of the profession as a whole, to a very high level.

The designation 'Chartered Accountant (S.A.)' has not been taken away from those now or hereafter entitled to it. Those non-Chartered Accountants (S.A.) admitted to the register will only be entitled to the designation 'Registered Accountant and Auditor'.

The establishment of the register has meant the admission to a recognised status of approximately 200 persons, whose qualifications were previously a matter of dubiety. Once this has been done, however, the profession in South Africa will be completely unified and controlled and the only way of entry to it will be by means of articles and examination.

EDUCATION AND TRAINING OF ARTICLED CLERKS

For many years the only means of admission to the Chartered Societies in South Africa has been by way of service under articles and the passing of examinations.

As outlined above, the four provincial Societies set up a General Examining Board in 1922. From that year until 1950, the Board conducted all the prescribed examinations. These examinations consisted of an Intermediate, divided into Sections A and B, and a Final, also divided into Sections A and B. Thus a clerk sat an examination in each of four of the five years of his articles. The examiners and moderators were always practising accountants with many years of experience. The standard of the examinations was always high and compared favourably with those of the leading bodies of accountants overseas. The field of knowledge required of an articled clerk ranged widely. The subjects required in the examinations covered accounting, auditing, cost accounting, taxation, death duties and the law relating to and the handling of deceased and insolvent estates; statutory law relating to companies, taxation, etc., and general commercial law.

The tremendous growth of the profession in South Africa, particularly since the end of the war, led, however, to a number of difficulties in the continued conduct of examinations through a centralised board. The number of candidates increased with every diet. South Africa being a country of long distances between centres, practising accountants found it more and more difficult to devote the necessary time to set examination papers, mark the scripts and finally spend a week or so in conference deliberating on results.

Discussions were accordingly undertaken with various universities in South Africa and the beginning of 1951 saw the introduction of what is known as the Universities Training Scheme. Under that scheme, all articled clerks are now required to sit examinations of one or other of the universities participating in the scheme, in subjects equivalent to all those formerly required by the General Examining Board. Having passed all those subjects, the clerk is still required to write a further examination.

This, known as the Final Qualifying Examination, is still conducted by the General Examining Board. (Incidentally, the latter body has now been re-established as the Examinations Committee of the new Public Accountants and Auditors Board.) The examiners and moderators for this Final Qualifying Examination are still practising accountants and the papers will bring .out the candidate's knowledge of the theory of accounting and his ability to apply it in practice.

All the universities participating in the scheme have Departments of Accounting and Auditing in their Faculties of Commerce, and in nearly all cases the occupants of the Chairs of Accounting are Chartered Accountants (S.A.) who have been and (in some instances) still are in public practice. Although the Universities Training Scheme has only been in operation for just over a year, it is felt that it will bring about a still greater improvement in the standard of training of clerks, in that they will be better grounded than before in the theoretical fundamentals of the various subjects.

CO-OPERATION BETWEEN ACCOUNTANCY BODIES

In 1945, the four South African societies set up what was—and is—known as 'The Joint Council of the Societies of Chartered Accountants in South Africa'. This body was a natural development from the General Examining Board, although it did not displace the latter body, the two working side by side. The functions of the Joint Council are defined as 'to consider and make recommendations to the Council of each Society as to the policy to be adopted by the Societies as a whole, in respect of all matters—which may affect the interests of the Societies as a whole. . . .'

Since its establishment, the Joint Council has undoubtedly done sterling work for the profession. Each of the provincial societies (including the Rhodesian Society) is represented on the Council by two delegates.

All matters affecting the profession on a national basis are first discussed by the Societies, whose delegates carry their views to the Joint Council. The latter thereafter recommends the decided course of action to the individual Societies and in this way unanimity of voice and procedure is obtained.

The Joint Council has taken the lead in a number of matters in which the profession is interested. Memoranda have been presented to and oral evidence given to Government Commissions and Parliamentary Select Committees on such widespread matters as income-tax, company law, the Stock Exchange Control Act and the various laws dealing with insolvent and deceased estates, death duties, etc.

In other directions too, the profession in South Africa has co-operated with other professional bodies. Relations with overseas bodies have always been cordial, particularly with the Society of Incorporated Accountants and

Auditors, which is well represented in South Africa and which for years has had three separate branches operating at Capetown, Johannesburg and Durban.

ETIQUETTE

A high standard of etiquette has existed for years amongst practising accountants in South Africa. While the four societies have power under their bye-laws to deal with cases of breach of etiquette or unprofessional conduct. it is very rarely indeed that they are called upon to exercise their powers. The code in operation is based largely on those of the English societies.

TYPE OF WORK UNDERTAKEN

The use of the titles 'accountant' or 'auditor' having been reserved to members of the Chartered Societies, it follows that the practice of the average accountant in South Africa has been built up largely on accounting and auditing work.

South African company law is based largely on the English law and more or less the same provisions in regard to the appointment of auditors to companies apply in South Africa. While our Companies Act does not specifically state that a qualified accountant must be appointed as auditor, the restrictions on the use of the title, hitherto in the Transvaal and Natal, but now generally throughout the Union under the new Public Accountants and Auditors Act, virtually ensure that only registered accountants can do company audits.

A good deal of the average practice, too, is devoted to accounting for private firms and individuals although there is no legislation governing or requiring such work.

Pure accounting and auditing does not, however, comprise the whole of the average practice in South Africa.

The practitioner must be an expert in taxation matters. Not only is a general income-tax levied by the Union Government but each of the four provinces is permitted to—and does—levy a provincial income-tax. The preparation of returns, checking of assessments and the pursuance of appeals and objections, is all work that is undertaken by practising accountants. There is no restriction by any law on the type or class of person who may do taxation work in South Africa. The Revenue authorities will deal directly with any person authorised to represent a taxpayer, no matter what the profession of the representative. Relations with other professions, particularly the legal fraternity, are very cordial, however, and it has become the recognised custom in taxation problems for the acknowledged expert—the accountant—to be consulted in all phases of the work.

Under the South African Income Tax Act, the first Court of Appeal against assessments is a special court constituted of an advocate of not less than ten years' standing who is President of the Court; an accountant of not less than ten years' standing, and a representative of the commercial community. Different courts are constituted for different areas of the country.

From this it will be seen that even the Legislature recognises the abilities and usefulness of the profession in taxation matters.

The average accountant in practice in South Africa can extend his activities in other directions too. The handling of the estates of deceased persons is one matter where an accountant's expert assistance is much sought after. There is no restriction by law on the type or class of person who may be appointed executor or administrator of a deceased estate. Lawyers, banking institutions and accountants all undertake this type of work. One frequently finds that a testator has appointed, say, a lawyer and an accountant as his executors, realising that each profession has its own special knowledge and experience which can be brought to bear.

The winding-up of companies and of insolvent (bankrupt) estates is another sphere of activities which is confined almost exclusively to accountants in South Africa.

This country is still undergoing an era of industrial development. Many accountants have built up fair practices based largely on cost consultant work. Industrialists and commercial men generally are becoming more and more 'cost-conscious' and it is to the accountant that they turn for help in devising, introducing and maintaining their cost accounting systems. Many practising accountants have established reputations for their abilities as business executives and financial experts. There is hardly a public company or institution of importance in the country that does not have at least one accountant on its board.

Generally speaking, there are many channels through which the practising accountant can exert his influence and extend his practice in South Africa.

PROFESSIONAL CHARGES

There is no fixed tariff for accountants' fees in South Africa. Most practitioners keep accurate records of time spent on normal work and their fees are based accordingly. At one time, two or three of the Chartered Societies suggested a scale of fees which their members should charge. This scale provided for fees for specialised work, for normal work, for qualified seniors and so on. It was not a compulsory tariff, however, and was merely intended as a guide for practitioners.

In regard to estate work, tariffs of remuneration are laid down under the various applicable statutes. These tariffs are all framed to give a fixed percentage on the various classes of asset realised in the estate.

Tendering, in competition with colleagues, for accounting or auditing work is a practice that is not countenanced by the Chartered Societies and, in fact, the invitation of tenders for accounting work is not a practice that is followed at all in South Africa.

FUTURE OF THE PROFESSION IN SOUTH AFRICA

Viewed from all angles the future of accountancy as a profession in South Africa cannot be regarded as anything but excellent.

The profession has now been established on a national basis on very sound foundations. It is recognised by the Government as a profession of importance to the country's economy.

It is accepted, not only in this country but overseas, as a profession of the highest standards, which compare favourably with those in other countries.

There is still scope for tremendous expansion in the profession. Industrialists and commercial men are more and more inclined to use qualified accountants in their businesses as executives and financial experts.

The profession, having achieved a high position in the eyes of the South African world, is determined to keep that position and yet to climb even higher, so that the services which can be offered to the community can be ever widened and extended.

THE ACCOUNTANT IN PRACTICE: A CANADIAN VIEWPOINT

by

C. L. KING, F.C.A.(CANADA)

Canadian Institute of Chartered Accountants

Because of Canada's economic and cultural ties with the United Kingdom on the one hand and its proximity to the United States of America on the other, the accounting profession in Canada, like business practice generally, has been subject to influences from both countries. Many of the founders of the accounting profession in Canada were accountants who had emigrated from the United Kingdom so it was natural that the foundations of the profession were essentially British in nature. As time went on these have been modified to meet Canadian conditions. Mr. Saunders has given a picture of the origin, growth and development of the accounting profession in the United Kingdom, where the profession was born. Much of his paper is applicable to the Canadian scene but there are a few respects in which developments in Canada have taken a different course. In the hope that it may be helpful in understanding the position of the profession in Canada, a few of the points brought out by Mr. Saunders are expanded from a purely local viewpoint.

Under Canada's Act of confederation, the British North America Act of 1867, education was assigned to the Provinces rather than being left with the Federal Parliament. As a result, all professions in Canada have developed first within each of the ten provinces and only as they have matured have they taken steps to create nation-wide organisations. Thus in Canada, a Quebec Institute of Chartered Accountants was formed in 1880, an Ontario Institute in 1883 and a Manitoba Institute in 1886. Other Institutes of Chartered Accountants have since been incorporated, the latest being in Newfoundland upon its entry into the Canadian confederation in 1949. The national organisation of chartered accountants, the Canadian Institute, was incorporated by the Canadian Parliament in 1902.

In addition to the Institutes of Chartered Accountants there are a number of other accounting societies some of whose members are practising public accountants. The Certified Public Accountants Association of Ontario was formed in 1926 and provincial associations have been incorporated recently in Manitoba, New Brunswick and Newfoundland, and in 1951 the Canadian Institute of Certified Public Accountants was formed to co-ordinate the activities of the provincial associations. The General Accountants Association was incorporated in 1913 and until 1949 had members in nearly every province. In the latter year practically all members in Ontario and Manitoba were absorbed by the Ontario Certified Public Accountants Association. The only nation-wide organisation of accountants, other than the chartered accountants, is the Society of Industrial and Cost Accountants which has branches in every province and a national body to co-ordinate the work of the affiliated provincial branches. There are several other organisations of accountants in Canada but their total membership is small. As to chartered accountants, there are slightly over 4,900 in Canada, and of these more than half are in public practice. There are about 800 members in the Certified Public Accountants Associations of whom about 40 per cent. are in public practice. There are about 500 members of the General Accountants Association of whom about 20 per cent. are in public practice and about 2,500 members of the Society of Industrial and Cost Accountants all of whom, with few exceptions, are employed in commerce and industry.

Until recent years there was no legislation in Canada governing the right to practise public accounting, but within the last six years three provinces have passed legislation for this purpose. In Quebec, since 1946, a person can only acquire the right to practise public accounting by qualifying for membership in the Institute of Chartered Accountants of Quebec. To safeguard non-members of the Institute who were in practice at the time the Act was passed, however, those who met prescribed conditions were made members of the Institute and the remainder were granted licences to continue in practice. A member of an accounting organisation in another province is authorised to practise in Quebec only if Quebec accountants have reciprocal rights in the other province. An Ontario Act of 1950 imposed a licensing requirement on the practice of public accountancy. Members of the Institute of Chartered Accountants and of the Certified Public Accountants Association of Ontario are entitled to be licensed upon application and other accountants practising at the date of the legislation were also made eligible for licences without examination. In future, however, persons who are not members of either of the two qualifying bodies must have at least three years' experience in public accounting and pass an examination at least equivalent to the Intermediate examination of either of the two bodies or an examination set by the licensing council. The council has passed regulations authorising non-residents to practise in Ontario without a licence provided the province or state, etc., in which they reside grants the same privilege to Ontario licensees. In Prince Edward Island regulatory legislation similar to the Quebec pattern was enacted in 1949. The legislation in Ontario and Quebec covers approximately two-thirds of the public accountants in Canada.

Technological advances in the world, and the consequences of two world wars and a great economic depression, have enhanced the complexity of the business structure and the need for specialisation in every field. In endeavouring to meet the changing demands of the business community, the accounting profession has developed and expanded at a phenomenal rate in most countries. The change in the concept of service from the seeker-out of fraud and error to the auditor and professional adviser to business is apparent not only in the increased scope of the services rendered but also in the nature of the auditing service itself. The approach to auditing to-day is far more analytical in nature than it was even two decades ago. More emphasis is now placed on the fairness of the overall presentation of financial statements than in mathematical accuracy and it is generally recognised that the auditor's prime responsibility is to render an informed and truly independent opinion.

Apart from public auditing, the profession in Canada has expanded its area of service to include the setting up of accounting systems, financial planning (particularly having regard to taxation), cost accounting, and advice generally in those areas where his knowledge and experience can be of assistance to clients.

It has always been recognised that the members of the profession holding themselves out as public accountants must have the minimum of training necessary to enable them to fulfil the demands placed upon them. To qualify as a chartered accountant in Canada a person must complete a prescribed period of training in the office of a practising chartered accountant and pass the prescribed examinations. For the student without a university degree, but who must have qualified for university entrance, however, the training period is five years. A reduction of one year in the training period is usually given to university graduates holding a B.A. or a B.Sc. degree and of two years to those with a B.Com. degree.

Since educational matters fall under the legislative jurisdiction of the provinces, it is the provincial Institutes of Chartered Accountants which individually determine whether or not a candidate qualifies for admission. Accordingly, for some years each Institute set its own examinations but it was realised that the development of a national profession would be made easier if all members had uniform qualifications. In 1939 arrangements were completed whereby uniform Intermediate and Final examinations would be established by a central authority representing all the provincial Institutes of Chartered Accountants. As an indication of the close integration of the ten provincial Institutes it might be pointed out that members of one Institute can, upon moving to another province, obtain admission to the Institute of that province without examination.

About two-thirds of the chartered accountancy students are required to take correspondence courses of instruction which are supplemented, in some cases, by discussions or lecture periods arranged by the individual institutes. The instruction course has been developed by the Ontario Institute and administered for the Institute by Queen's University. At present this course is used by the Ontario and seven other Institutes. In Manitoba and Quebec students receive instruction at evening classes in the universities. University graduates who have taken courses in accounting, auditing, commercial law and allied subjects are exempted from taking part or all of the courses of instruction depending upon local circumstances.

There is a shortage of student applicants of the proper calibre in Canada to-day. A survey is being undertaken by the Canadian Institute of Chartered Accountants to find the reasons for this shortage and to examine into all aspects of the programme for training chartered accountants. It appears that the length of the training period has deterred many university graduates who might otherwise have considered professional accountancy as a career, and some scheme for the integration of university education and professional training, perhaps along the lines arranged by the Institute of Chartered Accountants in England and Wales, may be the solution.

As mentioned earlier, the Canadian Institute was formed in 1902. While it was originally an organisation separate from the provincial bodies, in 1910 the provincial Institutes and the Canadian body agreed that the latter should act as the co-ordinator of all national, as opposed to provincial, activities. Since that time membership in a provincial Institute automatically carries with it membership in the Canadian Institute. Through it the members publish the monthly magazine, carry out uniform examinations, undertake research, make recommendations on national legislation and provide information and help on inter-related provincial matters.

Steps were taken to set up an accounting research committee in 1939, but the outbreak of war postponed action until 1946, when the chartered accountants established a Committee on Accounting and Auditing Research. The committee does not undertake what might be termed basic research in the fundamentals of accounting or auditing but attempts to deal with topical problems arising out of current practice or with new matters arising because of changing circumstances or law. Of the bulletins issued so far, perhaps the most significant from the Canadian point of view are No. 1, 'A Statement of Standards of Disclosure in Annual Financial Statements of Manufacturing and Mercantile Companies', No. 2, 'A Statement of the Minimum Standards of Professional Practice which should apply in respect of Prospectuses', and No. 6, 'The Auditor's Report'. The titles of Nos. 1 and 2 indicate their content. No. 6 provides that it is the responsibility of the auditor to determine the scope of the audit required to enable him to express an informed opinion, emphasises the importance of independence, and includes a recommended wording for the auditor's report under the Companies Act, 1934 (Canada). While the wording suggested is not entirely what the committee would like to recommend, because of the limitations imposed by the statute, it is believed that a uniform wording will tend to reduce the confusion which results from mere variations in phraseology.

In another effort to reduce the possibility of unnecessary confusion, outside as well as inside the profession, the committee is preparing a revision of the 1936 *Manual of Accounting Terminology for Canadian Practice*. The viewpoint of the profession is also advanced by the committee through meetings with groups such as investment bankers, financial writers, stock exchange officers, and industry. Such meetings also make it possible for these groups to put forward their points of view and lay their problems before the profession. Activities of this sort are also helpful from the standpoint of public relations and more effort is being expended along similar lines.

As in other countries, the profession makes representations on those matters on which it is qualified to speak. For some years the accounting and legal professions in Canada have been making joint recommendations to the Federal Government on the Income Tax Act. This co-operative endeavour has helped the two professions to a closer understanding, and one of its outgrowths has been the creation of the Canadian Tax Foundation. This organisation operates as a clearing house for tax information respecting all countries, and also as a research organisation. While the Foundation receives its main financial support from business organisations, it is controlled by the two professions, one-half of the board of governors being practising lawyers nominated by the Canadian Bar Association, and one-half practising chartered accountants nominated by the Canadian Institute of Chartered Accountants. In its five years of existence the Foundation has done much to promote greater understanding of tax legislation in this country and has created for itself an enviable reputation for independence.

In Canada the future prospects of the profession are encouraging. Business has come to rely more and more on the profession for help in many areas other than pure auditing and accounting. As suggested by Mr. Saunders, the increasing complexities of carrying on business are forcing a trend to greater specialisation. The business man operating on what may be termed a medium or small scale is coming to expect assistance from the profession in an ever-widening area. He relies upon his professional accountant to provide the specialised advice necessary in financial planning, taxation, accounting systems, cost accounting and controls, budgeting, and in the sphere of management generally. In this area the profession, if it fulfils the responsibilities given to it, will assist materially in the preservation of the way of life which has been built upon the concept of the freedom and dignity of the individual. Since the very basis of the professional accountant is his independence, our main objective is to take whatever steps may be necessary to ensure that this independence is always maintained and upheld.

THE ACCOUNTANT IN PRACTICE AND IN PUBLIC SERVICE

by

SVEN-HÅKAN LEFFLER,
Föreningen Auktoriserade Revisorer,
Sweden

Introduction

Auditing has had a long history in Sweden. As far back as the seventeenth century, it was not unusual for a regular audit to be made of the accounts of trading companies and the big manufacturing estates. Sometimes it was prescribed in company by-laws that an annual audit should be made. Legal regulations governing auditing were introduced in the Corporation Act of 1895, which prescribed that every corporation had to have its accounts audited annually by one or more auditors, who were to be appointed at the ordinary meeting of the shareholders. The purpose of this provision was undoubtedly to arrive at an effective system of control of the corporations' accounts, but the trouble with legislative measures is that their effect is not always that intended. Many small and even a number of large companies, even at the end of the nineteenth century, felt no need for the services of an auditor. When, nevertheless, the Act laid down that auditors were to be appointed in all corporations, it became more or less customary to appoint persons without sufficient qualifications for auditing work. Nowadays the circumstances are different. In the present Corporation Act it is laid down that 'an auditor shall have such experience of book-keeping and knowledge of economic conditions as his appointment calls for with regard to the corporation's activities'. There are, of course, no guarantees that this provision will be complied with, and consequently in a number of minor companies the audit arrangements may still be unsatisfactory. (In Sweden the share capital of corporations may be as low as 5,000 kronor.) In the larger corporations, however, as will be shown in detail in the following pages, care is taken to ensure that qualified professional accountants shall take part in the audit.

An important step towards better conditions was taken around the year 1910, when the Stockholm Chamber of Commerce resolved to authorise public accountants. The first authorisations were made in 1912. In succeeding years, chambers of commerce in other parts of the country have also begun to authorise accountants. The total number of authorised public accountants is at present about 250. (The population of Sweden is about seven million.)

A Swedish chamber of commerce is an institution authorised by the Crown. Its object is to look after the interests of economic life; among other things it submits its views on a draft Bill affecting the economic life of the country after it has been returned from standing committee.

Provisions regarding Authorised Public Accountants

In order to become an authorised public accountant a term which, for brevity's sake, will hereinafter be written A.P.A., it is required that the applicant shall have passed his matriculation examination or have received equivalent basic training and that he shall have passed an examination at one of the two universities of commerce in Sweden, obtaining a certificate in those subjects that are of special importance in the work of a public accountant. The course of studies at a university of commerce takes three or four years. As evidence of the fact that the theoretical requirements are of a high order, it may be mentioned that, out of about 600 applicants for admission to the University of Commerce in Stockholm who fulfil the formal requirements for admission, only about 200 can be accepted owing to lack of accommodation. Of these 200, only about 50 students per annum subsequently pass their examination with such a certificate as will enable them to become authorised public accountants. Further, an applicant must have had at least five years' practice as an assistant to an A.P.A. or have had practice comparable thereto. These conditions having been fulfilled, no special examination is required; if the applicant's papers are in order, he receives a certificate as an A.P.A. after having applied therefor to the chamber of commerce in the district in which he is resident. The certificate must be renewed every year. Those who have had no opportunity of studying at a university of commerce may be allowed to take a special public accountants' examination, though applicants very seldom avail themselves of this possibility.

In order that questions regarding the authorisation of public accountants shall be dealt with on uniform lines, they are referred by the various chambers of commerce to a public accountants board common to them all.

The chambers of commerce have issued regulations governing the work of the A.P.A.s. Among other things, it is stipulated that an A.P.A. may not carry on any trading or agency business, nor may he be an active partner in a business firm nor hold any salaried public or private post. The chambers of commerce may make exceptions from this latter rule, but such exceptions are seldom allowed. The chambers of commerce see to it that these requirements are observed. Moreover, they exercise disciplinary authority over the public accountants. They may issue a warning to a public accountant who fails in his duty and, in cases of serious neglect, may cancel the authorisation of the person concerned.

It might be objected, in regard to this system, that the members of the chambers of commerce consist largely of representatives of big business and industrial firms, insurance companies and banks. This implies that supervision over the A.P.A.s is in the hands of some of those very persons whose activities it is the duty of the public accountants to scrutinise. This objection may possibly have some justification in theory; in practice, however, the Swedish system has been found to function well, for the questions of authorisation are handled within the chambers of commerce by persons of sound judgment and with a deep sense of responsibility. The Swedish A.P.A.s have therefore expressed no wish for a change. Besides, their numbers are too small to permit of their dealing with questions of authorisation themselves. The third possibility, that authorisation might be granted by some State-appointed body, is not a question of any urgency, nor has it won any favour.

The chambers of commerce also issue certificates to another category of public accountants, who are called approved accountants. A good knowledge of book-keeping and accountancy problems is required of them (though they are not required to pass an examination at a university of commerce), as well as at least five years' practice of such a nature as enables them to acquire experience in questions regarding auditing and book-keeping. Many of them carry on auditing work in addition to some other employment.

Accountancy Bodies

The A.P.A.s have formed a Society of Authorised Public Accountants. Membership, however, is not obligatory. Out of the approximately 250 A.P.A.s about 180 are members of the society. The society has issued regulations governing the activities of its members—regulations which are somewhat stricter than those of the chambers of commerce. Thus a member of the society may not undertake auditing work in a corporation in which he himself is a shareholder. The board of the society exercises disciplinary authority over the members, who are thus supervised by two bodies, the board of the society and the chamber of commerce concerned. If a member is for any reason excluded from the society, notification thereof must be given to the chamber of commerce which has authorised him.

The approved accountants are members of the Swedish Accountants Association. Other accountants have also joined this association, among them being about ten A.P.A.s. The membership is about 240.

Etiquette

Members of the Society of Authorised Public Accountants are prohibited from advertising except on a very limited scale. There formerly existed other written regulations governing professional etiquette but these are now abolished and have been replaced by a general rule that the members of the society shall observe the professional conduct befitting a good public accountant. How comprehensive such regulations should be is a delicate question. To draw up a code even of such rules of conduct as should be self-evident would hardly serve to enhance the reputation of the public accountants.

Type of Work Undertaken

The work entrusted to the Swedish A.P.A.s is probably of the same nature as in most other countries. Their main task is to perform the annual company audit but they are also employed in carrying out valuations, investigations, organisational commissions, taxation inquiries and assignments as arbitrators. The administration of property, appointments as administrators of estates and as administrators in bankruptcy are of less frequent occurrence. If the appointment of an accountant involves the carrying out of a detailed audit, this is usually done continuously during the year, so as to prevent as far as possible a heavy accumulation of auditing work after the end of the year.

Professional Charges

No regulations or agreements exist as to how the fees of public accountants are to be calculated. It is customary for the time spent on a job to serve as a basis for calculating the fee but the rate of remuneration per day may vary considerably according to the competence of the accountant and the nature of the work.

Types of Auditing Firms

The work of auditing is conducted partly by A.P.A.s working alone, who may have in their employ one or more assistants who are not A.P.A.s, and partly by firms consisting of several A.P.A.s, with their assistants. There are apparently no auditing firms with more than 100 partners and assistants. Each A.P.A. appears to have, on an average, two to three assistants. A number of auditing firms are limited companies. In such cases, it is prescribed that the A.P.A. or A.P.A.s in charge of an audit shall be personally responsible for its performance. Only A.P.A.s may be shareholders or board members in such a company.

Legal Regulations Governing Audits

Legal regulations on auditing are laid down in the Corporation Act, the Insurance Act, the Bank Act and the Registration of Friendly Societies Act. Of these, the provisions of the Corporation Act are the most important. The present Corporation Act took effect in 1948. The principal auditing regulations in that Act are as follows:

For every corporation at least one auditor shall be appointed by a meeting of the shareholders. If the share capital exceeds 500,000 kronor, at least two auditors shall be appointed. If the share capital amounts to not less than 2,000,000 kronor, at least one of the auditors shall be an A.P.A. Even in respect of minor corporations, it is laid down that an A.P.A. or an approved accountant shall be appointed if a request therefor is made by shareholders together holding at least one-tenth of the share capital. It is laid down in the Act that by 'authorised public accountant and approved accountant' is meant a public accountant and an approved accountant authorised by a chamber of commerce.

A.P.A.s are, of course, also appointed as auditors in many companies where such appointments are not necessary by law. An investigation made in 1948 and covering just over 2,000 of the larger corporations showed that 39·7 per cent. of the auditing appointments in these corporations were held by A.P.A.s. It may be mentioned that the corresponding percentage in 1940 was 23·5 per cent. and 7·8 per cent. in 1930.

The Corporation Act contains short regulations laying down what an audit shall cover. Further, it is prescribed in the Corporation Act that the auditors shall issue an audit report, in which they shall give their opinion, *inter alia*, as to:

whether the balance sheet presented by the board should be passed by the meeting of shareholders,

whether the meeting of the shareholders should discharge the members of the board from liability in respect of administration of the corporation during the past financial year, and

whether the meeting of shareholders should pass the board's recommendations for the disposal of the corporation's profits.

Should the auditors be unable to recommend the passing of the balance sheet or the granting of discharge from liability, the reasons therefor must be stated in the audit report.

The provision that the auditors shall in their report express their opinion on discharging the board and the managing director from liability is based on the fact that the work of the auditors includes examining not only the company's accounts with balance sheet and profit and loss account but also the administration of the board and of the managing director. The purpose of this rule is not that the auditors shall scrutinise all the details of the administration. It is the main principles and the important acts of policy to which they should pay attention and which should be examined. For an auditor to be justified in criticising the administration in his audit report and in recommending that discharge from liability should *not* be granted, there must have been gross errors or negligence in the administration of the company.

The Accountant in Public Service

The foregoing observations have dealt exclusively with the accountant in practice. I have not touched upon the second part of my subject, the accountant in public service. As I have already mentioned, the authorised public accountants may not hold any public or private post. Accordingly, in the society to which I belong there are no accountants in public service, and there is no association of accountants in public service. The following brief observations may, however, be made.

The auditing of the ministerial offices is carried out by a special civil service department, Riksräkenskapsverket (the office of the Accountant-General). This audit is of a formal kind. An audit of the State Administration is carried out partly by auditors appointed by the Riksdag (Swedish Parliament) and partly by a civil service department called Statens Sakrevision (State Audit Board). For the purpose of these audits, different sections of the State Administration are selected and examined annually. The main purpose of the audit is to investigate whether the State Administration is organised in a satisfactory manner.

In regard to the towns and municipalities, the major towns frequently have their own auditing departments to perform the audits. A number of towns and municipalities have joined together to form common auditing departments, which have charge of the auditing of their accounts.

Recourse is also had to the A.P.A.s by the public authorities. In several cities the audits are in the hands of A.P.A.s. The City of Stockholm has its own auditing department, which formerly examined the accounts not only of the city itself but also of its public utilities. About a year ago the work of auditing the accounts of these public utilities was transferred to A.P.A.s. There are a large number of State authorities, including fiscal courts and public prosecutors, who employ A.P.A.s for special commissions and investigations. In regard to corporations owned by the State or urban authorities, it is usual to appoint A.P.A.s as auditors, but their auditing duties do not in any way differ from those in respect of corporations owned by private persons.

THE ACCOUNTANT IN PUBLIC SERVICE

by

B. W. RABY, F.A.C.C.A., and A. F. J. SEARS
Federación Nacional de Contadores,
Bolivia

GENERAL

At the present time, Bolivia is a country of limited development, notwithstanding her vast natural resources, which cover products of tropical, semitropical and temperate zones.

Mining is still the basic industry and represents approximately 98 per cent. of her exports. Tin represents the largest part of mineral exports, some 80 per cent. of the total, and is thus the principal factor in the economy of the country, which means that it also has a great influence in Government policy. Other mineral exports are lead, silver, wolfram, bismuth, zinc, copper, etc., though the exploitation of these ores largely depends on favourable world market quotations. Generally speaking, it may be said that the well-being and prosperity of Bolivia is essentially linked to the price of tin.

With an area of some 420,000 square miles, Bolivia is inhabited by 3,500,000 people, the majority of whom live in the Altiplane, or temperate zone, at 12,000 feet above sea level. It is estimated that 55 per cent. of the population are of the indigenous races, 31 per cent. of mixed blood and 14 per cent. of the white races. The broken character of the territory, especially in the mountain regions, together with the vast distances which have to be covered, has given considerable impulse to air travel, thus supplementing the railway services. Both railway and air services are efficiently run.

At one time primary and secondary education were limited to the principal centres, but they have gradually been extended, in accord with the economic possibilities of the country, and rural education is now a reality. Much, however, remains to be done, and this is one of the reasons why the United Nations Organisation considers the country needs technical and cultural assistance.

It may be mentioned here that the government authorities are doing all possible to procure the development of the various activities of the country on a sound technical basis, a desire which has been greatly reinforced by the recent presence of the Keenleyside Mission, named by the United Nations Organisation. To this same end, an important effort was made in 1950 to carry out a really thorough census of Bolivia, to find out the exact composition of the inhabitants, together with a detailed analysis of their activities and mode of life. Complementary to the census of human population was an 'agricultural census', to establish the food resources of the country and the extent to which self-sufficiency existed.

POLITICAL ORGANISATIONS

Bolivia is organised under a central government; it is divided into nine departments, these, in turn, being divided into provinces and cantons.

The President of the Republic and his Ministers of State are the governing body; departmental governments are in charge of prefects; the provinces are ruled by sub-prefects, and the cantons by magistrates. The progress of the cities and towns, as well as the well-being of their inhabitants, is governed by mayors, the heads of the municipal councils.

PUBLIC FINANCES

Until the year 1928, the financial development of Bolivia can hardly be said to have conformed with any standard; isolated legal dispositions were dictated in accordance with the development and increasing needs of the country, both in regard to the securing of income and the procedures of control, accounting, etc. In short, up to that date, no scientific principles were applied, and public finances were in a chaotic state. In view of the resulting financial disorder, the government of President Siles contracted the services of the Kemmerer Mission, a committee of American financial experts. Based on their findings, laws were passed, dealing principally with taxation and the control of public expenditures.

In order better to understand the financial organisation of the country, it is necessary to distinguish between three classes of resources which are related to the different types of governing bodies. These resources, known as national, departmental and municipal, are paid into the respective treasuries and are managed by the national government, the departments and the municipalities respectively, although under the immediate control of the Comptroller-General of the Republic, who is responsible for the perception and management of state funds.

Each one of these three governing bodies has funds allotted to it by means of special laws. Nevertheless, the municipalities may also obtain their own resources through the medium of determined charges for services and patents which are created by municipal ordinances.

TAXES

The taxation system is characterised by its extreme complexity, brought about by the constant necessity of creating new sources of income. This is undoubtedly a serious obstacle to the smooth development of the different activities throughout the country. To give a rough idea of what this means, we give, as an example, the way in which the price of a railway ticket from La Paz to Cochabamba is made up:

(1) Tariff retainable by the railway company.
(2) Percentage for railway servants' pension fund.
(3) Tourist tax.
(4) Local tax for Department of La Paz.

(5) Local tax for Department of Cochabamba.
(6) Road tax.
(7) Tax for La Paz Fourth Centenary Celebrations.
(8) Public health stamp duty.
(9) Stamp duty for La Paz Municipality.

As may be supposed, in this case and in others of a similar nature, private persons or companies (since there would be no other adequate method of collecting these taxes) must carry out the functions of collecting agents. In other cases, such as the liquidation of income taxes, the employers, by law, must act as retaining agents. The taxes collected or retained must be paid in monthly to the respective treasuries, and detailed statements of the collections must be made by the employers or companies concerned.

Unfortunately, this method of tax collection is necessary on account of the peculiar circumstances pertaining in Bolivia; moreover, it has the advantage of considerably diminishing the need of highly trained and competent administrative personnel, apart from producing an appreciable economy in expenses.

Apart from this particular system, used for the collection of certain types of taxes, there are treasuries and other public offices where direct payment of taxes and charges for services are made.

In the case of departmental and municipal resources, payments are generally made direct to the treasuries or collection offices, although some taxes destined for departments and municipalities are collected through the government offices, and in such cases, after the necessary liquidations have been made, transfers are made to the respective authorities.

The creation of taxes in general, in accordance with constitutional precepts, belongs exclusively to Congress, without which authority, theoretically at least, no tax can be legally demanded. Nevertheless, in practice, since the country has been governed at times, for relatively long periods, by 'de facto' governments, there have been cases of taxes being created by government decree (not law) which have been given legal character, although later such taxes have generally been given legal status through the intervention of Congress.

There is no doubt that one of the most serious problems that Bolivia faces is the simplification of tax laws and methods of collection. The elimination of the multiplicity of taxes and the centralisation of collection is certainly advisable, through the adaptation of adequate scientific procedures to the peculiar needs of the country. For, if the factors already mentioned and the different stages of social development in relation to the characteristics of the population are considered, one can say that the direct application of systems which have given good results in more highly developed countries would be impossible.

NATIONAL BOARDS, INDUSTRIES AND CULTURAL INSTITUTES

In addition to the usual government departments and offices, there are several important nationally organised industries and boards. The principal entities are the Fiscal Oil Corporation, the Internal Air Lines, several railways and the Public Works Development Corporation.

Some of these entities are financed entirely by capital supplied by the State, and others by a mixture of private and State capitals.

The agriculture and mining banks, promoted to encourage the activities indicated by their names, are financed entirely by State funds.

The Central Bank, created after the report of the Kemmerer Commission, in 1928, transformed the old National Bank of Bolivia, originally formed with private and State capital, into a State bank. At present, this is the only bank authorised to issue currency.

Although autonomous or semi-autonomous in character, all these organisations are subject to government intervention in varying degrees; however, time does not permit of enlargement on these points.

Mention should be made here of the universities, which are also subject to government control, since their upkeep is financed by special taxes created for the purpose.

BUDGETS—NATIONAL, DEPARTMENTAL AND MUNICIPAL

Preferential attention will be given to the National Budget, in view of its major importance, although we may mention that the economic activities of the departments and municipalities are adjusted to conform with annual budgets, which must fill certain legal requirements, such as their approval by Congress.

The national Budget is prepared and executed in accordance with the provisions of the Budget Law of April 27th, 1928, formed from the counsels and recommendations of the Kemmerer Mission. Amongst the principal provisions affecting the preparation of the national Budget the following may be noted.

The Ministry of Finance has complete control of the financial organisation of the country, and the Finance Minister is directly responsible to the President of the Republic, although Congress has the right to ask for written or verbal information and to question the minister regarding matters under the direction of his department. Thus, the preparation of the Budget is in charge of the Finance Ministry, which has a special dependency for the purpose, known as the Budget Directorate-General.

Income for the period is calculated on the basis of the results of the previous three years. This disposition, applicable to normal times, has suffered modifications in recent years due to periodic monetary devaluations. This difficulty, principally affecting import and export duties, is solved by calculating income at a fixed rate of exchange, afterwards adjusting the figures to the ruling official rate.

The Budget year commences on the 1st of January. There is, however, a supplementary period of three months, from January to 31st March, used for the liquidation of income and expenditure of the previous Budget period, independently of the new Budget year, which must begin on 1st January.

The principal items of income are grouped under the headings of State Property', 'National Services', 'Direct and Indirect Taxes', and

'Miscellaneous Revenue'. The most important of these is the third item, 'Direct and Indirect Taxes', which include export duties on minerals and profits taxes on mining, industrial and commercial enterprises. The other items are of small importance.

The different ministries and government offices make up estimates of their expenditures for the preparation of the Budget, but the Finance Minister has power to reduce these estimates to bring them into line with probable income, and the need of producing a balanced Budget.

The Income Budget for the year 1951 was estimated at Bs.2.214.000.000·00, and expenditure at Bs.3.058.000.000·00, giving an initial deficit of Bs.844.000.000·00. Information from the Finance Ministry indicates that this deficit has been practically eliminated due to a policy of severe economy during the year.

After preparation, the National Budget must be sent to Congress for approval during the first days of August of each year. Once approved, the Budget takes the character of a law of the Republic, but approval is subject to previous study by the Cabinet, which has ample powers to increase or decrease expenditures. If expenses are increased, laws must be passed to provide new sources of revenue to cover the additional expenditure.

As in the case of the majority of Latin-American countries, salaries of public administration personnel constitute the most important item of expense. In the Bolivian Budget about 75 per cent. of expenditure comes under this heading, and only about 25 per cent. is destined for public works, roads, agriculture, school buildings, etc.

During the last ten years there have been no Budget deficits of an extraordinary nature, and any deficitis have been covered by means of loans from the Central Bank. This fact, together with the policy of financing certain public works, national, departmental and municipal, by means of similar loans from the same bank, with Government authorisation, has visibly influenced monetary depreciation.

Apart from the National Budget in the currency of the country, the Finance Ministry prepares a special 'Divisa Budget'. This is a fairly recent practice, designed to ascertain the total foreign currency available to meet the needs of the country.

The major part of foreign currency resources are derived from the U.S. dollar exports of the mining companies, who are obliged to sell to the Central Bank the greater part of their foreign currency income at a rate of exchange fixed by the Government.

Control of Income and Expenditure

As the National Budget covers the receipt of income and provisions for expenses, several government offices have been created to see that the Budget provisions are duly carried out, the following being the most important.

Internal Revenue Offices

These offices, directly under the charge of the Finance Ministry, are to be found in all capitals of departments and some other towns of importance, and receive all taxes except those which, due to their special nature, are paid into other offices. Special auditors or accountants are attached to these offices with the right to inspect the accounts and records of commercial and industrial concerns. Debit notes are drawn in case of delays in payment of taxes, underpayment or fraud. In the case of fraud, fines are generally imposed.

National Custom House

This department and its dependent offices throughout the country, collects duties on imports and exports and certain other taxes. It has the right to impose fines and draw debit notes in cases of fraud, false consular declarations, etc., and, like the Internal Revenue Office, is under the control of the Ministry of Finance.

The National Treasury

This is another dependency of the Ministry of Finance, with offices in the principal cities, which are known as sub-treasuries. The special mission of the Treasury is to centralise all government income in special accounts in the Central Bank and to effect all payments in accordance with the respective Budget items. All government collecting agencies are obliged to deposit receipts in the different special accounts which the Treasury maintains in the Central Bank. Payments in general are made through applications from the various government offices, supported by proper documents. The procedure of payment is subject to a number of controls, some of which are exercised by the office of the Comptroller-General and its dependencies. The National Treasury is responsible for the accounting of the country's income and expenditure.

Comptroller-General of the Republic

The department of the Comptroller-General is directly responsible to the President of the Republic, and the Comptroller-General himself holds the rank of Cabinet Minister.

The organisation includes offices of Departmental Comptrollers in the capitals of the departments and in one or two other important cities. This department, created on the suggestion of the Kemmerer Mission, controls all expenditure and inversions of funds and the correct administration of the National Budget. It also supervises all State properties. To carry out its functions more efficiently the department has inspectors attached to the various government offices and, from time to time, names accountants or inspectors to carry out periodic audits of the accounts of other entities which handle public funds.

In addition to the control of government funds, the department also controls the management of departmental and municipal funds.

Control is exercised in a double sense: *a priori*, which consists of examination and authorisation of payment by a representative or inspector of the department, without which no order can be paid by the Treasury, and *a posteriori*, or later revision and analysis of all documents related not only to payments but also to income. The powers of the Comptroller-General are extremely wide, and he has the right at any time to intervene in anything which comes within the economic interests of the State. In this he is greatly helped by the legal precept that debts and obligations to the State have no time limit.

STATUS AND UTILISATION OF QUALIFIED ACCOUNTANTS IN THE PUBLIC SERVICE OF BOLIVIA

The foregoing observations will have given a rough idea of the present financial organisation of public services in Bolivia, and it is not difficult to see that there is a wide field open to qualified accountants and auditors, not only in government services, but also in semi-government, departmental and municipal offices.

The profession of accountancy in Bolivia is still, however, in a very early and undeveloped stage. There is no true practical training for the profession. Degrees in accountancy, as granted by the universities and associated bodies, are wholly academic and intensely theoretical.

Recognised firms of professional accountants are hardly known.

Two main bodies exist, recognised by law, viz. the Colegio de Economistas and the Federación de Contadores, which, together, form the membership of a national register of authorised accountants, whose privileges and obligation are carefully defined.

Professional qualifications are not widely demanded from accountants in public service, but the bodies named are endeavouring to obtain greater recognition and better standing for their members.

An effort is being made to reorganise the whole of the public service in the direction of the grading of salaries and scientific assessment of staffs, together with a much-needed security of tenure.

Salaries, at present, are not sufficiently attractive for qualified accountants and other professionals, who prefer to enter commerce and industry.

Ways and means of overcoming some of the shortcomings which exist are being constantly sought by the professional accounting bodies, growing in prestige and conscious of their responsibilities, whose aims are wholly in the direction of co-ordinating full compliance with the law and promoting the well-being of their accredited members.

DISCUSSION

PROFESSOR A. M. VAN RIETSCHOTEN, *Nederlands Instituut van Accountants, the rapporteur, summarised the contents of the papers:*

On the above-mentioned subject papers have come in from colleagues in the following countries:

Bolivia	South Africa
Canada	Sweden
Great Britain	United States of America
Portugal	

Only in one of these the accountant in public service has been dealt with in a way that enables me to draw a comparison with the situation elsewhere.

This is the reason why in this summary I can neither aim at a comparison between the parts played in the various countries by the accountant in public service and the development of his professional activities nor at a comparison between the professional development in practice and the one in public service. I shall therefore restrict myself to a few comments inspired by the papers referred to above.

In the English papers the circumstance has struck me that among the accountants in public service functionaries have been included whose role differs from that of the accountant in practice in such a degree as to make it worth drawing attention to. The very name of the professional organisation in which part of these colleagues have united (the Institute of Municipal Treasurers and Accountants) shows that here not exclusively and not primarily does one think of functionaries who are charged with an auditing and advising function to the complete exclusion of any managing function. It seems that with the local authorities in other countries the accountant does not primarily exercise an auditing function either, at least that is what might be gathered from the information obtained from Sweden and Portugal.

In the case of the central government, mention is made of bodies especially charged with an auditing function without managerial activities. But it has not been made clear whether in those bodies the auditing element in the central government has been assembled categorically. The impression has been given that also with the controlling authorities important auditing functions have been put in the hands of functionaries who beside it are charged with managerial functions.

It might be a good thing to investigate in how far this organisation works satisfactorily, all the more so when we consider that mention is made—albeit with regard to local authorities—of the general occurrence of the following combination of functions: financial adviser, cashier, paymaster and internal auditor. According to the papers the characteristic difference between the accountant in practice and the accountant in public service is generally considered to lie in the independence of the former, which naturally cannot exist in the case of the latter. By the side of this I would think that the fact that the accountant in practice is not charged with any form of management in contrast with (generally speaking) the accountant in public service, should be considered of equal importance. It will be interesting to hear what our colleagues who will deal with the accountant in industry will have to say about this matter.

In connection with this it appears to me that the custom developing in England of accountants in practice acting as company directors is open to grave question, especially in so far as it is correct that it is this very director-ship which plays an important part in the income which the accountant in practice is able to earn.

Of special importance is the information from England about the manage-ment form of the nationalised industries, such as of late the coal mines and transport. Is the fact that the final accounts of the boards are audited by practising accountants due to legal regulations? The observation is made that those industries run by the Government present sharp differences with commercial enterprise, in the first place because there are no shareholders. This argument is beyond me. The number of persons concerned in a govern-ment industry is normally much larger than in a private business and I consider their interests to be the same.

Both the accountants in public service and those in practice express in the English papers that it is necessary for the various groups of colleagues to work together and that a disintegration into specialised groups would constitute a danger to the profession. Also in the case of the professional training a stand is made against the introduction of subjects directed towards specialisation.

I do not propose to go into the historical description of the origin, the development of the profession of the accountant in practice and the rules to which it is bound in various countries. Suffice it to say that everywhere there may be perceived a quick and still spreading growth of the need for the services rendered by this profession.

While the various papers agree in emphasising the auditing function I think that by the side of this and second in importance come the services with regard to taxes, which in the last ten years have been increasing enormously. Our American colleague reports on an agreement between certified public accountants and lawyers on a tentative statement as regards the division of work in the field of taxation.

I think a difference in accent may be concluded upon between the English and the American development as regards advice given to enterprises on the subject of effective management. Both reporters draw a comparison with the function of the physician, but whereas the American deals with conviction with the future development in this respect, the Englishman exhorts his colleagues not to be purely critical and negative in their advice.

I will just touch lightly on what our English colleague says about the intelligibility of the financial data, which the accountant is in the habit of judging. In particular I think that in this respect it is important to aim at accounts which can be understood by the uninitiated, because the problems with which business is faced will then be grasped in so much wider circles.

With regard to this, special attention should be paid to the fundamental problem of the assessment of profit which will be discussed in another section of the Congress. Of the financial reports of the last few years it can certainly not be said that they have at all presented to the public in general a picture of the great difficulties which the sharp rise of prices have caused. It is to be feared that the difficulties which will presently proceed from great falls will not be expressed in very helpful terms either.

Meanwhile I also want to draw attention to what has been said by our colleague Mr. Saunders about the wording of the certificate. Does not the fact that Mr. Saunders points out the danger of the positive communication overshadowing the negative qualification point in the direction of a necessary reduction of the positive element in favour of the eventual negative communication which after all determines the certificate? Was not this, by the way, the customary procedure in England before the stipulations in the Companies Act caused the present wording of the certificate?

Characteristic of development is the still growing importance of the professional organisation. It plays the leading part in the training of future colleagues in that it organises the examination, though it is noteworthy that as a rule it takes no part in the training proper. Training has in America, Canada and England always, for a great—and possibly for the greatest—part been postal.

This might be one of the reasons for the development of university training and education which has qualitatively better means at its disposal. The disadvantage of the latter, however, consists of a lesser degree of practical experience in the preparatory stage in the fields of knowledge required for the practising of the profession. The American paper states circumstantially that the qualifications conferred should not exclusively be awarded after the passing of an examination; with this it arrives at wishes which have for the greater part been met by the English institution of a period of articles. Moreover the professional bodies more and more occupy themselves with research into technical problems and they promote the drawing up of reports, the conclusions of which are meant to constitute a guide for the practice of the profession.

At the same time a standard for professional conduct has been set up by the organisations and its observance is supervised by them.

A subject to which in my opinion more attention should be paid by the professional bodies is the threat to the future economical independence of the practising accountant. Is it not striking that problems of a material nature which threaten the future development should arise in a profession whose services are sought after by society in an ever increasing degree?

I have in mind the taxation of those persons who do not enjoy the tax privileges of a labour contract. An important element in this is the impossibility of making material retirement provisions on a level similar to that enjoyed whilst still following the profession.

But even the building up of the capital necessary for the financing of a practice of any size represents a problem under the present circumstances which must be considered of importance for encouraging the young entry.

The increasing number of colleagues not in practice should not be entirely overlooked in this respect either. Our Canadian colleague has in enthusiastic words pointed out the importance of the profession in the part it plays in our way of life built upon the concept of freedom and the dignity of the individual, for which he rightly considers the permanent assurance of independence a *conditio sine qua non*. May his words make us realise that excessive taxation does not only prey upon the material side of our profession but that it is also a direct attack on the independence of our profession and all it stands for.

MR. T. COLEMAN ANDREWS (United States of America):
After having written twenty-nine pages of material on the accountant in practice, I thought I had said all I knew about it! I have one comment to add to my paper; since it was written it has become universal throughout the United States to give the uniform examination prepared by the American Institute of Accountants. That is all I have to add.

MR. A. P. C. D'AÇA CASTEL-BRANCO (Portugal):
May I present my compliments to the Chairman, the Rapporteur and contributors, and all present who, as we all know, are skilled in this science. This is the testimonial from a young man who has benefited much by being here. I take this opportunity to congratulate the sponsors of the Sixth International Congress on Accounting on the success obtained and to express my gratitude for the invitation that was extended to the Portuguese Society which I represent.

In Portugal, we have a special course for accountants and auditors, but, as Professor Van Rietschoten noted, the profession of accountants in practice has not yet reached the desired standard which all conscientious Portuguese accountants seek. Working with enthusiasm we will achieve our end, bearing in mind always the point of necessity for complete independence which is vital for the dignity and integrity of the profession.

At present in Portugal, as I said in my paper, some accountants work for the State as auditors of insurance companies and banks, and in other services of the State. Occasionally they examine the activities of private companies regarding increases of capital, transfers from reserve funds and taxation. Others, such as I, work for British professional firms. As the work of these accountants has proved successful, we hope that this will be the first step towards future development, similar to that which we find in other countries.

The society to which I belong is determined to obtain this standard and every effort is being made in this direction. After such standard has been reached other problems will present themselves, such as the training of young men in the professional life of accounting.

Therefore at this stage I can only bring to the Congress one thing—the *will* and the *hope* of the Portuguese accountants to attain a standard of skill and integrity, comparable to that found today in the leading countries of the world.

MR. B. J. M. BOYS (Great Britain and Ireland):

Mr. Saunders did not make it plain enough that in this country anyone is free to call himself an accountant. Further, though practice in the Companies Registration Office is now stricter, the law would permit persons not knowing a debit from a credit to form themselves into a company holding itself out as an association of qualified accountants and giving its members the right to use certain letters after their names.

Sir Harold Howitt in his Address of Welcome mentioned that persons who are not members of the sponsoring bodies could legally undertake all but very little of an accountant's work, and in most cases they are not governed by any but their own code of conduct. They may seek to obtain clients by touting or advertising or by undertaking work at fees which would be unremunerative to a qualified practitioner. Even the income-tax departments of the banks may be included in that category. I am not suggesting that such persons can ever be more than a minor annoyance to the larger firms of accountants, but to small firms or sole practitioners they can be much more than that.

Mr. Saunders quoted to us Lord Simon's definition of a profession. There is no doubt that the professional man must bring something of altruism into his work but he also depends upon his professional activity for his living. The small practitioner may be faced with competition of a kind which a larger firm will seldom meet and which may be aggravated by financial considerations from which the larger firm will be relatively free.

It might have been gathered from Mr. Saunders' paper that even the smaller firms of accountants had staffs large enough to take advantage of a group pension scheme but there are many qualified practitioners of whom that would not be true and a pension fund for the whole profession is perhaps the only answer.

It may be deduced from the second of the graphs included at page 368 in Mr. Saunders' paper that there are many thousands of members of the sponsoring bodies in practice who employ no qualified assistants. The number of small practitioners is therefore large enough to make them a very important element in the profession in this country. It is upon their integrity and skill that the reputation of the profession depends, as well as on those firms whose names are household words in the business community. The contact of such practitioners with their clients is not only through managers and assistants or by means of their certificate on a set of accounts, but it is active and personal. That personal touch is the one advantage that the small practitioner has over the larger firm.

The small practitioner of whom I am speaking finds that a large part of his work consists of drawing up accounts from 'incomplete records' and thus he is very far removed from the higher planes of accountancy to be met with in the form of published accounts of public companies.

The small practitioner may be a man whose professional training has been received in an office not much larger than his own and whose experience is therefore very limited. To make good that deficiency, the discussion of practical problems in the kind of informal groups which can be organised by the district societies of the professional bodies is of immense value. It is a pity that the busy practitioner does not always appreciate the importance of such meetings to himself and to the profession as a whole.

I agree with Mr. Andrews that the larger part of the practising accountants' time is taken up with accounts and auditing matters. Yet in the vast majority of the small practitioner's cases, it was because the client needed figures for presentation to the Inspector of Taxes that he was prompted, in the first instance, to seek professional help. Afterwards the accountant's knowledge and experience will almost certainly enable him to give advice and help which the client had not at first expected, but the fact will remain that it was taxation which was the original reason for the employment of the accountant. The number of individuals who refer with pleasure to someone they call 'my accountant' increases every year and to the accountant are sent automatically the buff envelopes and their contents which are received from the officers of the Inland Revenue Department. The accountant will not always be able to relieve the client of every anxiety in regard to the contents of the envelopes, but if he can convert a debit into a credit by negotiating a repayment claim, then he becomes a friend indeed.

This country is the home of almost innumerable small enterprises and, but for the small practitioner, the vast majority of such businesses would be deprived of the help of the qualified accountant. For that reason, if for no other, he should receive encouragement and help to improve the service he gives to his clients. The small practitioner would welcome steps which would lead to the closing of the profession, not only for himself but because he knows it to be in the best public interest.

I fear I have been very insular in my remarks, but I have no doubt that the small practitioner and his problems are not peculiar to this country.

MR. D. A. BLOFIELD (Great Britain and Ireland):

We are living in a time of crisis. As Mr. Churchill said last week, our economy stands on a trapdoor and no one can say when it will collapse. Most of us must feel that our thinking and activities are meaningless unless they bear some direct relation to this central fact. There have been many economic crises before but in this one there is a new element—the ideological factor. We are at war—the cold war, which differs only from open war in that the enemy can work openly within our ranks. Industry is at the mercy of difficulties which are not economic and over which it has no control. We should consider what is the accountant's distinctive contribution in this critical time.

The papers written for this session have shown that the accountant in practice has now a large part to play in industry. I have been impressed by the idea put forward by both Mr. Saunders and Mr. Andrews that our role in industry is similar to that of the medical profession in ordinary life. We, like doctors, have to investigate the root cause of industrial disease, to carry out research and to learn how to apply the cure. We need to study the ideological factor if we are to fulfil the demands of this new role.

The latest recommendation on accounting principles issued by my

A. STUART ALLEN, F.S.A.A.

Vice-Chairman of the Council of the Congress

Institute, dealing with fluctuating money values, states that methods to meet the problem so far proposed 'would create issues, social and economic, far beyond the realm of accountancy'. That seems to me to pose a dilemma. How can we deal with problems such as inflation unless we understand the root causes?

General Eisenhower, amongst others, has seen that the cause of the present crisis is moral and spiritual rather than economic. The Dean of Westminster opened our Congress with a challenge which we should consider very seriously. Just think for a moment what would be the effect on my country alone if it were swept by a wave of real honesty, not the sort with which we are all too often called upon to deal, and sometimes to assist—the sort that keeps just within the letter of the law; but the creative, absolute kind which could revitalise our industry. From this platform ten days ago I was privileged to hear many international speakers, including Lord Baden Powell, stressing the need to answer the superficial forces by bringing moral standards into every phase of life, individual, national and international. I heard evidence showing how the application of absolute standards is bringing unity between labour and management in industry.

In one instance, the supervisor of the assembly line of one of our great car manufacturers found the answer to low production and high costs. He applied absolute honesty to his dealings with the men and started by apologising to the chief shop steward for his hatred of him and for his strong-arm methods. This courageous action produced friendship and co-operation between these two men and throughout the department, where before there had been bitterness, and intense antagonism. The result was a large increase in production, increased wages and reduced costs and a considerable speed up in production for export.

In yet another instance, one of the leading American airlines has been seriously damaged by disputes over many years. The superintendent said that two years ago they had 499 grievances. Last year, during which these forces got started, they had only seventeen and this year, so far, only three.

I believe this is the answer to our dilemma. We must study it and apply it immediately, before it is too late. We can cure inflation, reduce and simplify taxation and bring a wholly new spirit into industry. We have the capacity and therefore the responsibility. That is the challenge today—the unique opportunity to fulfil our destiny.

MR. CLIFFORD S. BRISON (United States of America):
Thirty-five years ago there was placed in my hands by a partner in one of the leading firms in London my first permanent file. It was of a brewery located not far from here and it contained a very comprehensive list. I remember it well because about six o'clock, or just before closing time, we used to go down and sample the products.

The file contains fourteen compartments. There are three main classifications, the first being governing or fundamental documents—copy of articles of incorporation and bye-laws of a corporation or of deed of partnership; marked copy of any trust deed *re* funded debt; copies of excerpts of minutes

Q

of continuing and cardinal importance; rescripts or précis of agreements of the first and lasting significance.

The second classification is audit guides. They are: copy of memorandum of client's engagement instructions and representations. This and other components consisting of one or two sheets of paper should be mounted on cardboard so as to withstand continual handling during the course of audit.

Card of accounts and/or copy of client's accounting manual(s). These should be copiously cross-indexed (in green) to corresponding items or persons in components VIII and IX (B).

Seven-year plan of audit. This component might consist of sheets of fourteen-column working paper whereon are listed, in the four left-hand columns, descriptions of the work to be done—these should be double-spaced to allow for emendations (as developed by experience)—and the reasons for changes and dates thereof should be stated in the last three columns headed 'remarks'. This would leave seven columns, headed by the seven years, in which would appear the initials of the assistants and the beginning and ending dates of the work as and when completed by them. A seven-year plan will allow for variations in emphasis from year to year: those items which should be stressed each year being underlined, and those from time to time side scored (and initialed) by the reviewing partner or manager in left-hand ruling of column(s) of the year(s) selected.

Aide-memoire re system of internal check followed by the certificate of the in-charge assistant as to its adequacy and the initials of the reviewing partner or manager.

The first reference to internal check in our language was made somewhere in the fourteenth century by glorious Geoffrey Chaucer writing in London. It is quoted below:

> 'The thridde day this marchant up ariseth,
> And on hise nedes sadly hym avyseth,
> And up into his countour-hous gooth he,
> To rekene with hym self, as wel may be,
> Of thilke yeer, how that it with hym stood,
> And how that he despended hadde his good;
> And if that he encressed were or noon.
> Hise bookes and his bagges many oon
> He leith biforn him on his countyng-bord;
> Ful riche was his tresor and his hord,
> For which ful faste his countour-dore he shette,
> And eek he nolde that no man sholde hym lette
> Of hise accountes, for the meene tyme;
> And thus he sit til it was passed pryme.'

Nearly a quarter century ago, when I designed what was probably the first questionnaire on internal checks to be used extensively in our profession, I was careful to label it an *aide-memoire*, thereby impressing upon its users the fact that it was intended merely as a reminder, and was not in content or emphasis for every type of audit. Mr. Peloubet has made some significant additions to my modest beginning of ninety and nine questions in all.

This component should be cross-indexed to corresponding items or persons in previous components.

Next, charts of (a) Organisation—in the case of a company with subsidiaries; (b) Personnel and duties—these should be cross-indexed with components VI and VIII; (c) Processes—in the case of a manufacturing concern; (d) Statistical comparisons by years. I can recall an instance in which, by comparing some statistics prepared by the sales department with the figures shown in the accounts, a million-dollar error was revealed in the audit of an internationally-known manufacturing concern in New York State.

The above charts would ordinarily be prepared by the client's staff.

Next, copies of (a) tax returns; (b) SEC filings; (c) other returns containing accounting data for government departments.

Next, list of plants, offices, and/or stores, their locations and how to reach them.

The third classification is, Synopses of accounts. First, historical epitome of the accounts. This component might be arranged in the form of a cumulative statement of sources of funds and their disposition from the inception of the concern down to date, arranged in columns which would be sub-totalled by years. Secondly, Master schedules of non-current accounts. This component would be compiled by transferring from the current working papers each year the master (or top) schedule of such as: capital assets, permanent investments, funded debt, reserves, capital, 'excess capital' (capital surplus), and surplus, leaving in the current file the detail of the changes during the year and their verification. Thirdly, Published-accounts file. In the case of a long-established client, this file might well be made ancillary to the main permanent file with only the most recent annual accounts forming the component. Representing, as it does, the *summum bonum* or end result of the accountant's labours, it might well be filed on top of the permanent file with the fundamental documents (as being also least referred to) at the bottom of the file.

MR. E. CALDWELL (Great Britain and Ireland):

I can see little difference between the accountant in practice and the accountant in the public service. The techniques and training, based on similar fundamentals, may be different, but primarily we are concerned with his personality. To be a member of an institute or society pre-supposes that one belongs to a group of persons who believe in tradition, ethical values and cultural development. In the present age of scientific progress, an accountant may become lost in techniques, thereby complicating his position. Soon he must discover, as all creators do, that simplicity is the essence of life. A good accountant is probably fundamentally lazy. In his search he eliminates that which is unnecessary. Unfortunately for the good accountant, in my country the scope of his work is often dictated by Acts of Parliament and other legal requirements. Instead, therefore, of our accountant utilising his leisure in some form of rake's progress, he perforce must spend that leisure in an endeavour to interpret the ever-changing mind of the legislator.

The choice of practice or public service usually depends upon the personal disposition of the individual. Practice offers more personal freedom while public service gives greater recognition and security. All accountants, in practice or public service, must maintain a high sense of ethical values, the more so in a world which now looks upon that which is slick with favour. To a large measure the accountant has assumed in business relationships the position of a priest. In consequence he must of necessity possess judgment, wisdom and understanding. His actions must be guided by the knowledge that trust is the essence of all beliefs in human relationship and without trust the world must perish. If therefore our accountant is the person we look for, he will find in technical and scientific progress a means of expressing himself —but it will be a means and not an end in itself. As an old-fashioned individualist, I believe that my own institution and all the other institutions and societies represented here will increase the respect and freedom which they enjoy if at all times they emphasise personal attributes and cultural development, allowing techniques and the like to make their normal progress.

MR. J. C. CHRÉTIEN (Malta):

I have read the papers with considerable interest, and those of Mr. Saunders and Mr. Andrews are admirable. We in Malta follow the profession in the United Kingdom: all that has been written of the United Kingdom applies to us. I do not agree with the speaker who suggested that there was no difference between the accountant in practice and the accountant in the public service. As in the United Kingdom, in Malta we have government departments with accountants who are general civil servants. They have passed examinations to become civil servants and they study up to the standard of accountancy of the London Chamber of Commerce. They obtain positions as accountants in government departments but all they have to do is to fill in forms. I do not think that is being an accountant.

In our country, the chief accounting officer is the treasurer and he is senior to the auditor. Perhaps that anomaly will be put right later. We have very few accountants in public practice. We follow the profession in the United Kingdom and we have a little bit of everything.

Speakers have said little so far about the continuous or running audit but I have come across it on many occasions. If, after a period of trading, you are presented with a balance sheet, many things have to be checked over the six months and it is difficult to trace certain of the matters—the person concerned may be dead or some of the documents may have been mislaid. I think auditors should do their best to explain to employers that it is better to have a continuous audit, so that better service can be given to our clients. It is better that we should be called in when the disease is at its beginning than that we should be called in to certify death.

MR. J. B. L. CLARK (Great Britain and Ireland):

I propose to discuss the accountant in public service, particularly in the central government. I am one. I was disappointed that there was no reference in the papers to accountants in the public service in the United States. Mr. Coleman Andrews said he would not deal with that aspect of the matter, although he felt that many members of the profession had given part or whole-time service to improving the accounting organisations of his country. I should have liked to hear something of what happened to the Hoover report on the accounting organisation of the United States Government. I understand that at present in the United States the Army, Air Force and, I believe, the Auditor-General have recruited large numbers of professionally trained staffs for work which one would expect to be somewhat similar to that of the practising accountant.

Conditions in this country are rather different. Mr. Marshall makes a distinction between the practice of a local authority and that of the central government, both in methods of accounting and personnel. In this country local authorities maintain their accounts on a basis which produces information very similar to that produced normally by industrial undertakings. They maintain their accounts by means of qualified accounting staffs, at any rate in the supervisory grades. The central government maintains its main accounts on the cash basis—this for historical reasons—and the staff engaged on the work are largely staff trained within the civil service. There are some important exceptions to this.

The central government has a number of functions which to some extent are analogous to those in industrial undertakings—for instance, the Royal Ordnance factories and certain functions of purchasing materials. It is not generally known that the accounts of these undertakings are under the supervision and guidance of professionally qualified accountants.

You will notice I use the word 'qualified' and in this country a distinction is made between the qualified accountant and the professional accountant. This is not merely a question of terminology. It relates to the duties performed. Mr. Marshall refers to some 500 professional accountants and says that tends to grow rather less. These people, spread over various departments, are largely—I almost said 'entirely'—chartered, incorporated or certified accountants—that is, people who received training in professional offices and who are engaged on work very similar to the bulk of that undertaken in most professional offices.

You will gather that the accounting organisation in the central government is distinct from that of the local authorities. One line of thought wishes to form yet another body of accountants to cater for this service. I feel that that would be a mistake. I do not think it would solve any existing problems and is merely likely to create new ones.

MR. H. O. H. COULSON (Great Britain and Ireland):

I want first to thank the authors for having given us such a fine factual survey of the fields covered by our profession. My remarks, like those of the previous speaker, are limited to the public service, although, unlike him, I am not a member of it—but I have so suffered in my time. Mr. Saunders referred in his paper to the independence of the practising accountant. I think he is wrong to limit it to that. Independence is probably one of the virtues of our profession and it is especially desirable in the public service, although it is very difficult to achieve. Quite apart from the question of being rude to one's paymaster, one tends to develop, in a department, a very proper loyalty to the organisation, which may silence the critic who lies under the skin of every accountant. We must ensure that the critic is always kept alive. To some extent we keep him alive but it requires an extraordinary accountant and an extraordinary individual to be independent when it means criticising one's own organisation. It is a very unpopular pastime to follow.

Mr. Marshall referred to the use of accounts as guides to managements. He claimed that local authorities are slow to use this, and I do not know whether the last speaker would agree, but I should say that the central government never do so. The government system of accounting, as was said to the Select Committee on the Estimates some years ago, is not good; the accounts are meticulously audited from a narrow point of view and give as little information as you could possibly imagine. I am speaking after the Committee has sat on the budget and have said in a long report that the present system is a very good one. I feel that the Committee hamstrung itself by interpreting the terms of reference as tying it to present methods. I did not think much of its report.

The growth of State or other monopolies, or near monopolies, tends to remove the comparable criterion of efficiency in those concerns and so far we accountants have not done much to find an alternative. I think we have a duty to find it. So far we have not got much to our credit. It is not an easy subject, and please do not think I am making a plea for more and more statistics. I think, on the whole they are more trouble than they are worth. It lies with the bodies represented here to find the answer. I think the duty lies before us of seeing that independence is fostered in the profession, that we aid management all we can and improve our material relationship in every way possible.

MR. F. C. DE PAULA (Great Britain and Ireland):

It is reasonable to say that we are a young profession, just getting into our stride, and with the growth in size we see a great expansion of the area covered by our work. That expansion is frequently referred to in the papers and Mr. Andrews goes so far as to say that the demand is so varied that it is almost impossible to render satisfactorily all the different services now expected by clients. Mr. King speaks of the increasing complexity of the business structure.

Mr. Marshall says that while they have techniques of their own in the public service, the scope and width of public and local services is now very extensive. Finally, Mr. Saunders refers to training and sounds the ominous warning that the field covered by the examinations for professional societies is itself already so wide that we cannot add any more subjects.

That seems to give a broad picture of a young profession expanding widely and suffering, one might say, from serious indigestion. Mr. Andrews rightly warns of the danger of over-specialisation and says the medical profession are in that danger in America. We must hold together and strengthen the position of the general practitioner in accountancy, just as in medicine.

Perhaps the chief reason for this is set out by Mr. Saunders who says the client likes to deposit his confidence with one firm, but he also says that the small firm are reluctant to call in the services of their larger brother for fear they may lose the job. The first speaker referred to the difficulties of the smaller practitioner and the difficulties he may have in giving satisfactory service to his client. It is clear that as long as every practising accountant tries to get the same work, all are potential rivals, and, not unnaturally, the smaller practitioner does not want to call in his larger brother for fear of falling into the jaws of the tiger. It is pertinent to point to Mr. Saunders' query of whether we should debar specialists from general practice, as in other professions.

I make no statement on that. Let us preserve the essential unity of the profession by universal basic training. We should consider keeping it for all accountants pretty general and reasonably comprehensive, and deal with some of the specialisation on which we are embarking in post-graduate training, and, of course, post practice. By so doing, we could clear the ground lower down and also clarify the atmosphere higher up.

MR. G. B. ESSLEMONT (Great Britain and Ireland):

It has been suggested that one of the essential differences between the accountant in practice and the accountant in the public service is that the first is generally not charged with management. Mr. Marshall refers, on page 362, to the need for training in administration, and that is a point I should like to consider. In the local authority service in which I am engaged the chief financial officer has to be an accountant and in Scotland we have achieved statutory recognition of this. I think England still lags a little behind.

In local authority service, administration has two main branches; you have to deal with the staff and the management of the department but you also have to deal with the problem of putting across to members of the council the general position. This morning someone has spoken of the need to simplify figures. This need for simplification is certainly as necessary in local authority service. The local authority accountant starts with a good foundation on which to build experience of administration but the change from purely accountancy work to administrative work is sometimes rather difficult.

A member of my staff—a first-class accountant, full of initiative—was appointed secretary of an educational body a few years ago. Within a few weeks, he told me he thought he was not earning his pay. Seeing your employer gets value for money is, after all, important. I told him that I sometimes felt exactly the same at the end of a day—there was nothing to show for what I had done; but there were plenty of others who had been able to do good work because of some point that I had dealt with. I am glad to say that this man is now happily settled in his work and that he realises that administration, although there is often not much to show for it, is a valuable part of the work.

May I add a personal note? When you are involved in administrative work you sometimes get out of touch with figures. We therefore feel intense pleasure when some little accountancy problem passes through our hands. I feel sure many of us feel like that in local authority service. We feel that it is some compensation for some of the other things that we have to go through.

MR. BÖRJE FORSSTRÖM (Finland):

The duties of the auditors in Finland are in some respects regulated by the law in such a way that they deviate from the provisions in most other countries and this has influence on the performance of the work and consequently on the building up of the accountant's profession. Therefore, I think it will be of interest for the accountants in other countries to give an outline of the special conditions under which we are working.

The accountant in practice in Finland is an auditor certified by the Central Chamber of Commerce. The auditing of books of companies might be carried out by practically anyone; the company law only states that there must be two auditors. Only when a company's shares are introduced on the Stock Exchange, one of its auditors has to be an auditor certified by the Central Chamber of Commerce, in Finnish, K.H.T.; in Swedish, C.G.R., as we have two official languages.

The auditor in Finland not only examines the books, the balance sheet and the profit and loss statement; he also examines the administration of the company. You will have seen from Mr. Leffler's paper that in this respect conditions are the same in Sweden.

The education of accountants is principally carried out at the universities of economics, of which we have four. After having passed the examination, the graduates go into industry and commerce. To become a certified auditor, a person must prove that he has passed the normal examination in a University of Economics (three years' full day studies), that he has experience in the closing of books, and that he has had good practice in industry and commerce, and also in administration. Thereafter, he has to go through a special examination which is in two parts, one, which is theoretical and similar to a master of economics degree, the other practical—covering auditing, taxation, writing of reports and the ethics of the profession.

The local chambers of commerce also issue certificates to another category of 'approved accountants', who have other employment but who are suitable for carrying out less demanding audits. There are no special examinations required for this category.

The auditors certified by the Central Chamber of Commerce have the right to use assistants. Their number is not regulated but generally one certified accountant has two or three assistants. These assistants have usually passed their examinations at a University of Economics. Only to practise as assistant under a certified auditor is not generally sufficient—therefore applicants to the profession have to go into industry before they qualify as certified auditors. To practise as assistant to a certified auditor is not obligatory, however, and so it is not unusual that persons who have no practice in the field of auditing apply and sit for the examinations required. As auditors in Finland also have to examine the administration of the company, the Central Chamber of Commerce attaches much importance to the applicant's practical experience and his ability to judge administration of companies.

On the other hand, the too slow growth of the profession on account of the relatively high qualifications required and the long distances in a sparsely populated country, which necessarily limits an auditor's clientele, has compelled the Central Chamber of Commerce to give certificates also to persons who intend to carry out auditing work in addition to some other employment. Complete independence on one hand and experience in administration on the other are weighed against one another and the latter is winning, as conditions are now. The K.H.T., or C.G.R., is practising alone, with assistants, in partnerships or in firms registered as limited companies.

The work carried out is in most respects the same as in other countries. The annual company audit which was formerly carried out after the closing of the books, but now more and more being performed as a continuous audit, is the principal task but taxation work and installation and revision of accounting systems are also important tasks.

MR. W. A. HARVEY (Great Britain and Ireland):

My remarks are directed mainly towards the small practising accountant.

In Mr. Saunders' paper appears this excellent counsel: 'It behoves the accountant in practice to train himself intensively to become constructive, to make useful contributions towards solving the problems of industry and commerce, and not to be purely negative and critical in his advice.'

It is under the heading of Management Accounting that these words appear, but it is to a world very far removed from that of budgets and reports to top management that I wish to call the attention of this meeting—to the world of the little man—those electricians, painters, plumbers, etc., whose sole link with the realms of skilled accounting is through the practising accountant—too often, alas, regarded only as a buffer state against the Inland Revenue authorities.

It is truly in the light of experience that I speak of these men, for I spent the years from 1941 to 1947 investigating the costs of ship construction and repair work in a certain corner of these islands and there must be few accountants who have been as fortunate in spending so much time on contracts carried out by very little firms on very little ships. Fine work indeed was done and often at the heavy cost of permanent damage to the health of the proprietors of these businesses, who were here, there and everywhere in all weathers and at all times of the day and night. They knew how long their men should take to do a job and they tolerated no slacking—but how often did they know how much a job had cost? Very rarely, I'm afraid, until their costing records had been overhauled—wages paid and labour charged to jobs pursued their separate paths, materials usage was measured by a look round after the job was finished, while the almost inevitable $33\frac{1}{3}$ per cent.

was calculated on the already inaccurate total of labour and material and added to that total to cover overheads and profit. This was not always done in ignorance, of course, and a long-handled axe was sometimes needed but more than one fine workman has been saved from bankruptcy by a government-sponsored costing system, which he has continued to operate long after compulsion so to do has been removed.

Now the taxation affairs of these men were almost without exception already in the hands of practising accountants and it was to their certified accounts that we turned in order to extract the overhead expenses. It is no exaggeration when I tell you that I have myself seen the owner of such a business take from his safe a sealed envelope containing accounts received six months before, with the remark that he had not yet looked at them. I know there are difficulties and the practising accountant does not willingly overstep his assignment, but it does give a feeling that something really constructive has been accomplished when one of these men has been set on the right road. The type of business I have in mind does not need much; not only an integration, but a coming together, a marriage and a union of the costing and financial records, a strict materials control and the utilisation of the certified accounts to estimate the overheads. As for the recovery of the latter I must not generalise, but where the composition of the working team is constant (and it often is) then there is nothing more suitable than a simple percentage on direct labour with perhaps the odd machine hour rate where necessary.

Our large and medium-sized industrial units have usually their own qualified staff but the little man is wholly dependent on the practising accountant. He plays a vital part indeed in our economy and the more efficiently he plays it the better for us all. And so to those of you who have the opportunity I say, 'Please do your best to help him—he usually deserves it and among the little men today there are at least a few who will be numbered among the big men of tomorrow'.

MR. H. HAYHOW (Great Britain and Ireland):

I want to spend a few minutes on the local authority sector. Reference has already been made to the wide range of functions of the local authority accountant and the many things he has to do. But he has also to be a student of the money market to ensure that the local authority raises capital in the most effective manner and does not rely too much on government sponsored agencies. He does not work through a permanent secretary, chief administrative officer or general manager but is responsible directly to the policy-making body. In England, we have no equivalent of the American city manager or the continental Burgomaster. The finance officer is one of a small group of chief officers who use their specialised knowledge to advise their authorities on many problems that confront them at the present time.

It is essential, therefore, that he should acquire the techniques of management in handling a large department and staff and also some knowledge of administration to enable him to advise the council on policy. The authority, of course, determines policy.

Mr. Marshall referred briefly to the audit of local authority accounts, and here some of us are fortunate in still having practising accountants to audit some part of them. Some part of our accounts is subject to the examination of the district auditor and in some local authorities the whole of the accounts are subject to his examination. He is unique in the public service because he has a power which no other officer in central or local government has—he can disallow and surcharge any sum in the local authorities' accounts which is contrary to the law.

By that, we mean not only that expenditure which is *ultra vires*, without authority and quite illegal, but any legal expenditure which the auditor thinks is too high to warrant its being paid. After an explanation, he can surcharge and disallow it. If he takes such a step, it may be the members of the council who are surcharged, or one of them, or the chief financial officer. Someone must repay that amount. There are means of appealing, of course, but you will see that there is a need for the financial officer to look not only forward and backward, but also over his shoulder so as to ensure that neither the council nor one of its officers take any step which might be outside their power. I wonder what would happen if a commercial auditor had a similar power over companies.

I was interested to read of the practice of the auditor being able to examine the general administration of a company and we have heard that it is also adopted in Finland. Emphasis has been placed on the independence of the practising accountant and Mr. Marshall has suggested that the local authority accountant is not quite so independent. We ought to distinguish between financial independence and independence of mind and courage. Local authorities are subject to income-tax and our computations must be as strict and accurate as any other tax computations. We may be called upon to give evidence at an inquiry or before Parliamentary Committees. We must be as fastidious as any other witness.

I think the municipal accountant in England owes much of his high standing to the existence of the institutes but we like to remember that we are accountants in the broadest sense and, as such, we are happy to take part in this Congress.

MR. T. E. A. KILLIP (Great Britain and Ireland):

I will probably be accused of failure to make any positive contribution to the subject under discussion this afternoon. This failure will possibly be excused, as any contribution I might have made will have been, or will be, covered by the other speakers.

This is the first occasion on which I have been privileged to attend an International Congress. My preconceived ideas were that I would be one of many crusty aged men who would demand reverent attention to more problems than could be solved in the given time. It was, therefore, with surprise and great pleasure that I noticed the large number of younger members present. It gives to the Congress an assurance of continuity. Here we have no problem of 'wasting assets', for wear and tear and obsolescence of the older stock is offset by natural replacement. As these Congresses recur, you younger members will be taking the strain more and more. You will, no doubt, have the temerity, as I now have, of addressing the Congress and making your contribution to international fellowship in matters not only of accountancy, but of human understanding and advancement.

I must claim that these remarks are not entirely removed from the subject of 'The accountant in practice'. As one who has been in that category for nearly forty years, may I claim the privilege on behalf of the older generation to congratulate you on your choice of a career. You will find increasingly as the days go on that you have chosen a career providing wide opportunities in service to your fellow men. It may or may not lead to wealth. But if you use your gifts in the true spirit of service, it will most assuredly lead to happiness.

You will find romance in the profession. That may appear to be an outrageous claim, but I make it most sincerely. Your practice may be mainly concerned with what is known as 'big business', the largest industrial, commercial or financial undertaking. Let your imagination pierce the realm of accounts and statistics to the core of the clients' business, to its place in the social, national and international structure. You will find romance.

But these large undertakings all had a beginning; which leads me to the ordinary practitioner, like myself, whose clients do not come within the category of 'big business'. They are frequently the founders of their business. You will find a thrill in watching their growth. You are witnessing the birth of what may, some day, be a very large concern. You may have the great happiness, springing from service, of helping by your counsel and skill in the romantic achievement of that result.

The future lies hidden. But the older generation has no fears and confidently expects great achievements from the young men and women now qualified and who will later qualify in the profession.

It only remains for age to wish youth a long and happy career in the profession.

PROFESSOR MARY E. MURPHY (United States of America):

In these years of domestic and international crises, the role of the professional accountant is enhanced in importance because of the independent viewpoint he affords business enterprise and the commonweal. Originally concerned with the verification of the accuracy of clients' accounts, the public accountant today has an enlarged perspective. Frequently he is requested, at some time in his career, to serve as a member of a board of directors, or as a controller or cost accountant of a corporation; to install systems of accounts for nationalised industries; to accept appointment to a governmental inquiry committee; to act as witness in cases involving accounting questions; and to supply data for labour negotiations and for regulatory bodies.

These are but a few facets of activity of the modern accountant, and all are compatible with his training and experience. They at least partially explain why the general popularity of private accounting contrasted with public practice has never been stronger than at the present time. Representing a vital aspect of the professional picture, this situation has implications for research and educational programmes of universities and accounting societies, which are called upon to stress accountancy as a tool of management and of the State, equally with the theories, techniques and traditions of auditing. It also impinges on accounting partnerships, which must reconsider staff training, remuneration and pension schemes in the light of private enterprise's serious drain on key personnel.

In the past, attention has been centred upon the refinement of accounting theory to meet ever-enlarging business complexities, with volumes in many languages attesting to the successful efforts of practitioners and scholars to advance professional literature. Insufficient attention, it would seem, has been devoted to the public accountant's contribution to the national and international picture through the integration of audited annual reports with cost analyses, tax returns and government statistics, with the aim of increasing management's, stockholders', labour's and the public's understanding of business enterprise and, in the larger sense, of the nation and the world. The entire field of social accounting, for example, remains virgin territory for investigation, as Mr. F. Sewell Bray has pointed out in several brilliant papers; and the attack on previously undefined areas of theory and practice has been initiated by accountants and economists in Britain, America and other countries, to which Mr. Eric L. Kohler's *Dictionary for Accountants* will provide added impetus.

An International Congress on Accounting offers the matchless opportunity for participants to appraise past accomplishments and to prepare the way for future contributions to the community. In this process, the proper combination of activities commonly associated with an accounting practice and those of a broader, civic nature is revealed as a significant chapter in the evolution of the profession throughout the world. The many responsibilities assumed by the late Lord Plender, who was President of the Fourth International Congress held at London in 1933, are an inspiration to the present generation of accountants who are seeking the path of greater usefulness to the business world and to the State. In the years ahead, this service will be conditioned by the profession's reassessment of its proper place in the national economy, and by its willingness to modify its concentration upon independent auditing to admit an equal emphasis of managerial accounting for private enterprise and of all phases of government service in either a free or a planned society.

MR. V. F. PERRY (Great Britain and Ireland):

I was very interested in the papers, which offer us an insight into the requirements of the various bodies overseas. I noted the suggestion that no one who is academically qualified should be prohibited from taking the professional examination by the organisations concerned, but that a certificate of practice should be withheld until the necessary experience has been obtained. The question of serving articles, as opposed to obtaining experience in industry, seems not irrelevant here. In South Africa the 1951 Act has gone so far as to lay down qualifications for practitioners, which is unusual in the accounting world. Practitioners cannot call themselves such until they meet those requirements and have had that experience.

No specific qualification is laid down in this country, although in the Companies Act of 1948 the requirements for an auditor are laid down; he must be a member of one of four recognised bodies. It is hoped, as the President said, that soon private limited companies will come within the Act. If such experience is accepted in Britain, and in the C.P.A. Association of Ontario, then to promote harmony and co-operation among accountants the position should be made the same. I have just started practising on my own account and it is very hard—perhaps I should not have given my name—but I must say there is a feature of disunity in the profession. It is a question of whether you are a member of one body or of another. Something should be done about that.

We have accountants in banks who carry out tax work, as the Institute has pointed out, and they advertise their accountancy services, while the sole practitioner cannot do so. I do not think that is fair.

Mr. J. E. Germain (France):

I read the contribution of Mr. Miot.

Traditional public accounting is not conceived especially to reflect results in the meaning the word is given in industrial and commercial accounting. Its purpose is to summarise in the administration of finance the amount, by categories, of the receipts and expenditures of a financial year, so as to parallel them with budgets forecasts of the same financial year. That is very far from the company's point of view concerning the results and the profit and loss.

However, public organisations often have some management problems to solve, the economic character of which markedly outweighs the administrative. The management of a patrimony and, to a still greater extent, the capital investment financing problems have led us in France to alter some public accounting rules and adopt some procedures that are currently applied in companies.

The first modification brought to such rules resulted in the adoption of a private property type accounting which, on a permanent basis, shows the position of receivables, property and liabilities of the organisations or departments that show some analogy with industrial and trading concerns.

In the traditional organisation, the patrimonial elements are not altogether neglected but they are accounted for in some documents that do not belong to accounting proper: statements on balance payable, balances receivable, assets, liabilities, inventories. Since there is no link between these various documents, it is difficult to assess the general situation of an organisation or to learn which are its possibilities.

Historically speaking, the first to keep a private property accounting were public concerns having an industrial and commercial character (state-owned Alsatian potash mines, state supervised oil industries, etc.). More recently and in pursuance of some exchange of views that have taken place at the 'Conseil Supérieur de la Comptabilité' between public and private accounting representatives, the particular set-ups that maintain to some extent an administrative character but whose objectives require a more accurate knowledge of their costs and their results (hospices, poor-houses and hospitals, etc.) have been provided with an accounting of such type. Keeping private property accounting requires, first of all, a modification of budget headings, a distinction between ordinary and extraordinary expenses and a discrimination between profits and capital. Most public set-ups maintained, till then, an accounting based on entering merely receipts and expenditures and the results reflected merely the disposable funds position.

Now, the accounts are kept for some public concerns on a charges and proceeds basis and directly reflect in the accounts, without resorting to auxiliary book-keeping, the liabilities and receivable position. This can be done either on a permanent basis when the size of the organisation warrants it or by integrating the balances receivable and payable at the end of the accounting year.

Other noteworthy refinements provide for the introduction of the ideas of provisions, depreciations and reserves, for taking into consideration self-equipment financing which were repeatedly confused with operating. On such various points, the methods adopted are similar to those applied by companies.

In public accountancy, results used to be presented under the form of accounts that give the breakdown by headings for the budget and by accounts for extra-budgetary dealings. It all finally boils down to a remainder that shows the cash balance amount of which the competent controller gives the final appreciation. Nowadays, all the set-ups that keep such new accounting are establishing profit and loss accounts and balance sheets. The competent controller appreciates each balance sheet account.

Among other possibilities, the new accounting should permit of: analysing the appropriation of revenues made available to public organisations; clearly differentiating actual current operating from equipment dealings; facilitating the study of the treasury transactions and, hence, improving financing methods; integrating such accounting within a national economic accounting.

Such a synthesis of public accounting and company accounting methods shows at the same time that a conciliation between the two accountancies is feasible both as to objectives and methods and that French public accounting is flexible enough to permit of necessary adaptations.

MR. L. J. PRATLEY (Great Britain and Ireland):

I want to plead for three points. First, that there should be an international council or committee to advise on and consider research into various accounting problems. Secondly, that there should be a quarterly digest of accounting developments throughout the world and that the bodies represented here should be invited to contribute to it any developments and research which have been made. It should be as concise as possible, and a small pamphlet indicating the more important developments would be a valuable follow-up to the Conference.

The third point is a little more domestic—that the practising accountant should study and be in a position to advise on management accounting. I express my own experience in helping to look after firms in and around London. The practising accountant, the auditor, can give useful advice on such matters if, perhaps, from the more general point of view than the industrial consultant. It is in the smaller type of firm that this sort of advice can be given, without engaging on the more technical aspects.

MR. W. B. McARTHUR (Great Britain and Ireland):

I want to make a plea for the accountant in the public service—central or local government of the nationalised industries. I may be on a sticky wicket, because it is a point of criticism of the political arm in this country. When legislation is being formulated, I plead for greater co-operation with those who have subsequently to operate the legislation. Many accountants must face difficulties in the public service because they have had insufficient time to prepare for the projection of the policy which is being introduced. I know that the Institute and various bodies will have been taken into confidence from time to time by the executive but I feel that sometimes the political point of view, some political argument, increases the tempo of some clauses in Acts which give the Minister the right by regulation to fix a date for the operation of some new scheme. More team work would help accountants to carry out their duties with even more success than has been accomplished in the ever-expanding professional field. Too often they recognise only one colour in the traffic lights—green; and some recognition of amber sometimes might help us considerably.

MR. A. H. MARSHALL, *one of the two introducers, summed up the discussion:*

I was a little disappointed that we did not have more papers dealing with the accountant in the public service in various parts of the world. It may be —I put it no higher—that there is still some co-ordination to be done to bring the accountant in the public service in contact with the accountant in practice more closely.

The rapporteur mentioned the mixture of functions which the financial officer does in England, and although he was polite about it, I feel he thinks it rather odd. We believe in it. It is common throughout the services that the man who keeps the accounts looks after the cash, advises the governing body on policy, too. But the governing body makes the decision. The question was raised of whether we want to give young accountants in the public service some training in administration. The point is this. By the very nature of governmental functions, it is so easy for finance to be forgotten, and it is much more likely to be forgotten if there is a divorce between the accountant and the financial officer. That does not mean that either makes the decision; that is for the policy-making body.

Secondly, it helps the accountant to remember that he is a servant. One effect of running governmental types of organisation is that the profits criterion does not exist, the body suddenly gets into an economical frame of mind, and finance gets too much in the ascendant.

The keystone is that if the accountant is associated with the departmental work all the way through, instead of just keeping the books, he is more likely to identify himself with the administration than if the work were divorced between two people.

The rapporteur also mentioned the audit. The audit of all public authority accounts in England is carried out by independent auditors. It is true that for the central government it is done by a Department of State, but the head of the department occupies a very special status, like that of the judges, so that for all practical purposes what I say is true.

Local authorities and nationalised boards have practising accountants auditing their books, but the central government insists on having its own staff and own separate department. I see from the Swedish contribution that the same thing applies there. One speaker referred to the running audit; that is common in all English services.

I understood one speaker to suggest that he did not think local authority accounts were looked at. Nor do I. I think we have to accept it that accounts will always be for specialists. The high-water mark of published accounts in this country is the efforts of the nationalised boards, and although their accounts are presented in the latest form, I cannot think they make light reading for the public. If you want to bring finances home to the public you must adopt some other way—by summaries and diagrams and so on.

I was pleased to find running through the papers remarks dealing with practice as well as public authority accounts. Everyone realises the need for a broad training in accountancy. If we are not careful we are in danger of splitting our training into a lot of specialised sectors and techniques.

The rapporteur said he did not understand the comment that there were no shareholders in the governmental activities. While in a sense the whole community are shareholders, in the purely technical sense this is the great difference between commercial practice and public authorities. In commerce, there are shareholders with a limited number of direct stakes in the business and control is devised. There is no control in the public service, except the financial officer whispering, or shouting, in the ears of those responsible for policy. When we think of the huge taxation in your countries, you must think accountants have soft voices and are not easily heard.

I was interested to see from *The Accountant* last week that the first Congress concerned itself largely with municipal accounts, and it has been a great privilege for me to present this paper. If I had to summarise the mission of the accountant and financial adviser I would say that we have to try to compensate for the fact that we have no shareholders in the commercial sense and no equity on the balance sheet.

MR. G. F. SAUNDERS, *the other introducer, also summed up the discussion:*

May I first clear up a point in the paper which seems to have caused confusion? On page 395 I refer to the new fellowship of the Institute of Cost and Works Accountants. I seem to have suggested that all that is necessary for that diploma is to obtain a paper in management accounting. That is correct only if the candidate is already in possession of the qualification of the Institute and has taken company law in their examinations. The qualified accountant requires in addition statistics, if not already covered, advanced costing (three papers), management factory and distribution. I should not like it thought that I was making the obtaining of any worth-while qualification appear easy.

The rapporteur, whom I thank for his excellent summary, asked about the desirability of practising accountants holding company directorships. Mr. Marshall has painted in rather alluring colours their importance in the income of the practising accountant. They may not be as important as all that. But the practising accountant can perform a very useful purpose, as I have indicated in my paper, for he brings to the board meeting a completely independent viewpoint. So long as these directorships do not take too much of his time from general practice they are a good thing. It is important that they should be completely divorced from the other sections of the practice.

The rapporteur also raised the point dealing with audit certificates and it occurs to me that there are many shareholders who look at the certificate and by the time they have reached the sixth word, they say, 'I have seen all this before' and go no further. Any qualification is therefore lost. We could consider certifying that accounts comply with the requirements of the Ninth Schedule of the 1948 Act without any further qualification except where it is unusual; then the qualification would stand out, as it is intended to do.

The discussion has had two underlying features—the need for independence and the need for increased efficiency. Both Mr. Boys and Mr. Harvey referred to the smaller firm and I believe that the strength of the chain lies in the weakest link. We know the difficulties of the smaller practitioners, and it is up to the larger practitioners to help them in every way possible. Mr. Boys spoke about co-ordination and although this is not a subject we can discuss here, I would say that when we are considering the competition of unqualified accountants we should consider the efficiency of the service we offer. If our service is efficient and we show our clients what we can do for them, and show that it is really worth while, we need not worry so much about the ultimate reward.

How can we help the small practitioner? Discussion groups have been suggested, and consultation facilities with larger firms when a particular problem arises. The pension issue is under discussion by a committee as a result of conversations held recently.

Mr. Andrews stressed the need for specialisation but not at the expense of the general practitioner. I agree whole-heartedly. It is important that the general practitioner can advise his clients to go to the specialist when the need arises, but his position must be maintained and any specialisation must not be done at his cost.

This morning we discussed the relationship between the practising accountant and the accountant in industry, and there were arguments for integration, on the one hand, and co-operation, on the other hand. I believe that co-operation and cross-fertilisation is the way we should go forward.

But I would also endorse the salutory warning we had from a speaker this morning—that in the search for the future we must not forget the fundamentals of our daily task.

Mr. Killip spoke of the wide variety of the attractions to the profession; we will heed that but we must also be careful that in some cases that wide variety of interests does not unwittingly limit the extent of our allotted span. Let us not be so intoxicated with our enthusiasm for those attractions about which he told us that we bring our own professional life to an untimely end.

When I read the last proof of my paper, I decided that there was one aspect of the life of the practising accountant which I had omitted—his wife and family. That is not a fit subject for discussion now, and I do not say that because our wives are with us, but I feel there must be many here today who are grateful to their wives for the patience with which they endure the all too frequent occasions of grass-widowhood.

A vote of thanks to the authors of the papers, the rapporteur and those who had taken part in the discussion was accorded with acclamation.

FRIDAY, 20th JUNE, 1952

FIFTH SESSION

THE INCIDENCE OF TAXATION

Chairmen

C. H. POLLARD, O.B.E., F.S.A.A., F.I.M.T.A.
President of the Institute of Municipal Treasurers and Accountants
(Morning Session)

S. C. TYRRELL, F.C.W.A.
President of the Institute of Cost and Works Accountants
(Afternoon Session)

Deputy Chairmen

R. D. BROWN, F.P.A.N.Z.
New Zealand Society of Accountants

OLAV C. ILDAL,
Norges Statsautoriserte Revisorers Forening, Norway

Papers
were presented by the following:

R. D. BROWN, F.P.A.N.Z.
New Zealand Society of Accountants

G. B. BURR, F.A.C.C.A.
Association of Certified and Corporate Accountants

THOMAS J. GREEN, C.P.A.
American Institute of Accountants

CONRAD F. HORLEY, F.A.A.(AUST.)
Association of Accountants of Australia

G. P. KAPADIA, B.COM., F.C.A.(INDIA)
Institute of Chartered Accountants of India

THOMAS KJELDSBERG
Norges Statsautoriserte Revisorers Forening, Norway

UNO LÖNNQVIST, M.COM., M.ECON.
K.H.T.-Yhdistys: Föreningen C.G.R., Finland

Rapporteur

PERCIVAL F. BRUNDAGE, C.P.A.
American Institute of Accountants

THE INCIDENCE OF TAXATION IN
THE UNITED KINGDOM

by

G. B. BURR, F.A.C.C.A.
Association of Certified and Corporate Accountants

PART I. THE NATIONAL ASPECT OF TAXATION

'The earliest and most prevalent form of government interference
with the economic life of individuals and business enterprises
is taxation. The right of the chief authority to collect taxes,
and the general policy which determines who is to be taxed,
how much the tax shall be, and for what purposes it shall be
levied have always been controversial issues.'[1]

he weight of taxation and the choice of the shoulders on which the
urden should rest are certainly controversial issues, and the method by

[1] Professor John W. McConnell, of New York University, in *The Basic Teachings of
e Great Economists.*

which national finances are raised varies considerably in different countries. This paper is intended to be mainly factual in its presentation of taxation in the United Kingdom, but with a place for an epilogue in which is discussed the economic well-being of a country in relation to taxation, and in the United Kingdom in particular.

It is hoped to show not only the pattern of various classes of taxation superimposed on the national economy of the United Kingdom, but also to discuss its effects, implications, some anomalies, and possible reforms. By international discussion it may be possible to exert some influence on improving the overall system, often with resulting economic benefit to international trade and good relationships between nations.

THE PURPOSE AND PRINCIPLES OF TAXATION

One of the earliest attempts in the United Kingdom to prescribe principles of taxation in the best interests of the country, and now the classic precedent, is found in Adam Smith's *Wealth of Nations*, published in 1776. Despite the frequency of repetition of these principles, modern taxation practice often deviates so far from these basic requirements that a renewal of their acquaintance may be salutary—even for a Chancellor of the Exchequer. These requirements are:

'(i) The subjects of every state ought to contribute towards the support of the government, as nearly as possible, in proportion to their respective abilities; that is, in proportion to the revenue which they respectively enjoy under the protection of the state.

'(ii) The tax which the individual is bound to pay ought to be certain and not arbitrary. The time of payment, the manner of payment, the quantity to be paid, ought all to be clear and plain to the contributor and to every other person.

'(iii) Every tax ought to be levied at the time, or in the manner in which it is most likely to be convenient for the contributor to pay it.

'(iv) Every tax ought to be so contrived as to take out of the pockets as little as possible, over and above that which it brings into the public treasury of the state.'

Or, in modern form:

(1) Equality of sacrifice.
(2) Certainty.
(3) Convenience in assessment and collection.
(4) Economy of operation.

THE FINANCIAL REQUIREMENTS OF GOVERNMENT

In a profession it is tempting, but futile, to condition one's mind to the burdens of a taxing system and to concentrate unduly upon them, ever pressing for their reduction. This is merely an elaborate and often time-wasting occupation which repeats or reflects the perceptions of the early economists—all taxes are unpleasant.

The first question in considering the taxation burden should be: What is the total of the national fiscal requirements? In this paper we are not concerned with its justification or otherwise, but only with the funds required for the provision of defence, law and order, education, pensions, health services, social services and the other numerous governmental functions, new and old.

Two outstanding factors have increased these functions enormously in the United Kingdom in the last twelve years: the Second World War, and the advent of a Socialist Government in 1945. The yokes of rationing and controls (the latter often amounting to the former by another name) have not been thrown off so quickly or so completely following World War II as they were after the Great War. Rightly or wrongly for the nation's welfare (and this is not the place to discuss either the justification or the errors), the cost of government, controls, nationalisation, departments and redistribution of incomes has grown rapidly. The purposes for which the revenue is raised, and the scope of those services must, therefore, be the background against which the burdens comprising an immense total in the United Kingdom are seen.

Our examination may begin with a glance at the total national requirements, comparing that total with the national income and also the total income of those who, so far as can be ascertained (bearing in mind the impossibility of marking the incomes of those who contribute to such taxes as stamp duty, entertainments tax and estate duty) are most likely to contribute to payment of the national bill.

EXPENDITURE FOR THE GENERAL PUBLIC GOOD: THE BARE ESSENTIALS

Moving from the medieval days, through the times of expensive royal courts to the beginning of the industrial era, one can state the needs giving rise to taxation in brief terms, and perhaps not unreasonably, as primarily covering the following:

(1) Armed forces for the protection of the realm.
(2) Police force and law courts.
(3) Essential public health services according to the medical knowledge of the day.

Many other services, often thought of as Government or quasi-Government undertakings, such as postal services and water supply, are primarily self-supporting, and should make no call on taxation.

'During the nineteenth century taxation was regarded as a necessary evil, not less an evil because it was accepted as necessary. The State was called upon to perform certain functions; in particular it had to provide means of defence, maintain a judiciary, and carry out certain administrative and executive duties arising out of existing laws. It also had to find interest (including sinking fund) upon the national debt. For the rest it was generally held that the State should interfere as little as possible with the lives of the people.

'Taxation was regarded as a real burden, which wise statesmanship would reduce to the minimum consistent with the adequate performance of those duties which were admittedly State duties.'[1]

THE GROWTH OF MODERN REQUIREMENTS

Since the 1939–45 war, we have become accustomed to a national taxation policy embracing at least three main purposes in addition to the elementary ones set out above. These additional purposes are:

(1) To attempt to establish a supply-and-demand equilibrium, by what the early economists would have called the artificial means of taxation; for example, the use of the purchase tax to discourage spending, especially upon certain types of goods.

(2) To play a part in import-export totals, by discouraging imports (customs) and by encouraging exports (relief from purchase tax).

(3) The redistribution of incomes, by taking income from one class of taxpayer and distributing the proceeds in benefits or in cash to other taxpayers.

This last-mentioned process is not a new one or arising out of the war, as will be seen from the following further quotation from a discussion in 1939 on theories of taxation:

'During the present century the attitude of the community towards taxation has been profoundly changed in more than one respect. Several years before the last war (1914–18) it was held that taxation could and should be utilised as an instrument for reducing the inequalities of income.'[1]

(4) The provision of services towards which a contribution is made other than from taxation, and the providing of other services out of a specific tax where the proceeds from the tax exceed the cost of the services for which it is levied. The outstanding example in the United Kingdom is the national health and associated services, whilst the second type is seen in motor vehicle taxation, originally for the purpose of maintaining the roads, but yielding a surplus which is now taken to general revenue account.

DEFINITION OF A TAX

Consideration of the purposes of taxation, and especially the surplus or deficiency on a tax or provision of a particular service, leads one to define one's terms. What is a tax?

Sharply defined though a tax may be in the mind of the average citizen called upon to bear a number of such taxes, it can be clearly

[1] Professor J. H. Jones in *The Accountant* Tax Supplement, 1st July, 1939.

seen from the two examples referred to in No. 4 above—national health service contributions and motor vehicle charges—that the establishment of a true and universally accepted definition is by no means an easy achievement. The correct procedure here, therefore, is to define the word for the special purposes of this paper. Taxes are for this purpose taken to be compulsory payments to the State which are not exactly, or almost exactly, balanced by the value of the services received. This broad definition will be amplified and explained by the actual examination of the large groups or types of taxes.

THE SIZE OF THE BILL AND ITS DETAIL

From the first elementary requirements we move now to present outgoings of a revenue character. These can be extracted from the various parts of the Financial Statement for 1952–53 (the Budget, 1952)—in particular the 'Classified Statement of Estimated Expenditure'—and built up into a summary for our special purpose, as follows:

		Nearest Million £s	
Army	521		
Navy	357		
Air Force	468		
Supply and Defence	116		
	1,462		
Less Sterling Counterpart of Economic Aid	85		
		1,377*	
Civil Defence	111		
Strategic Reserves	61		
		172	
Local Services:			
Education	259		
Housing	61		
Police	35		
Roads	33		
General Grants	64		
Sundry Services	49		
		501	
National Health Service, Pensions and Injuries	445		
Old-age Pensions, National Assistance, Family Allowances and War Pensions	248		
		693	
Tax Collection Costs:			
Inland Revenue	31		
Customs and Excise	11		
		42	
	Carried forward	2,785	

* 1951–52 figure £1,114 million.

Nearest
Million £s
Brought forward 2,785

Various Government Departments and Services:
    Agriculture, Broadcasting, Civil Aviation. Civil
    Defence, Colonial Development, Commonwealth
    and Foreign Services, Employment, Irish Services,
    Prisons, etc., Research, Works, Buildings, Station-
    ery and Information, Miscellaneous   375
Food Subsidies, Rationing, etc.   410
Supply and Trading Services   81
Post Office   14
Permanent Debt Charge   575

£4,240

PART II. SPREADING THE BURDEN: THE GENERAL STRUCTURE

'In regard to the Income Tax, I do not hesitate to associate
myself with the declaration of more than one of my predecessors that an income-tax of a uniform rate of 1s. in the pound
at a time of peace is impossible to justify. It is a burden on
the trade of the country which in the long run affects not only
profits, but wages.'[1]
(Present standard rate of tax, 9s. 6d. in the £, rising to 19s. 6d.
in the £ with sur-tax.)

The main framework of the system of taxation in the United Kingdom
is based upon Adam Smith's first canon of taxation—equality of
sacrifice. This is not surprising in view of the fact that the first income-tax
appeared in 1798—twenty-two years after the publication of Smith's
Wealth of Nations.

EVOLUTION OF THE BRITISH SYSTEM OF INCOME TAXES

It will be shown that the income-tax yield overshadows that of any
other single tax, and short notes on its evolution are of interest.

1798. The first income-tax, introduced by William Pitt in the reign
of George III, based, *inter alia*, upon taxes on horses, carriages and
men servants for the previous year, coupled with window tax and
inhabited house duty, and related to incomes in excess of £60 for the
year.

1799. The first true income-tax on trades, employments, property,
etc. British subjects abroad were chargeable on 'property' in the
United Kingdom. Exemption below £60 per annum. The graduated
rate of tax system on incomes up to £200. The rate of tax was relatively
high—2s. in the £.

1802. A short period of repeal of the income-tax laws.

[1] The Chancellor of the Exchequer, Mr. Herbert Asquith, on the 30th April, 1906.

1803. Deduction of tax at the source of some income, and the now familiar five categories of income, Schedules A, B, C, D and E introduced.

1816–41. After Waterloo, in 1815, the tax was repealed.

1842. The present income-tax system rests upon the Income Tax Act, 1842, which in turn adopted the phraseology of the 1806 Act. Exemption limit £150. Rate of tax, 7d. in the £.

1853. Gladstone carried the Income Tax Act, 1853, imposing the tax for a fixed period of seven years. It was hoped that after this time it could be repealed. The fact that it was not repealed recalls the present-day legal status, under which income-tax ceases automatically if it is not re-enacted.

1874. Before an election, Gladstone promised the repeal of the tax, but he was not re-elected. The new Chancellor of the Exchequer, Sir Stafford Northcote, reduced the rate to 2d. in the £.

1900. The tax had now reached 8d. in the £, but reductions in the rate could be made by 'abatements' on incomes up to £700 per annum.

1907. Differentiation between earned and unearned incomes, based not upon the merits of one or the other, or on class distinction, but on a suggestion by Mr. Asquith, supported by the Dilke Committee, that there should be a differentiation between 'permanent and precarious incomes'—a distinction which it would be difficult to discover in the modern code.

1910. Super-tax, introduced by Mr. Lloyd George, affecting incomes of individuals over £5,000 per annum, but then operating from the £3,000 level at a flat rate of 6d. in the £.

1914. Rising scale rates for super-tax introduced. Rate of income-tax, 1s. 8d. in the £.

1915. Deductions for family responsibilities introduced.

1918. The rising rates of tax in the Great War reached 6s. in the £ for the tax year 1919–20. The Income Tax Act, 1918, consolidated the previous law, back to and including the Income Tax Act, 1842.

1920. In place of a different scale of rates for earned income, a fraction of that income not charged to tax, but with a maximum allowance.

1926. The three years' average basis for profits of trades or businesses abolished (with transitional provisions) in favour of the profits of the year preceding the tax year (ending on 5th April).

1927. Super-tax now known as sur-tax and theoretically an additional income-tax.

1939–45. The rate of tax rose from 5s. 6d. to 10s. in the £ and war-time taxes on trades and businesses introduced: national defence contribution from the rearmament year, 1937, and excess profits tax from 1939, rising from 60 per cent. (12s. in the £) to 100 per cent.

(20s. in the £) from the 1st April, 1940, but allowed as a deduction from income-tax profits.

1946. Excess profits tax ended as from 31st December, 1946.

1952. Income-tax rate 9s. 6d. in the £. Profits tax (the new name for national defence contribution) 17½ per cent. (3s. 6d. in the £) on profits distributed to shareholders, etc., or 2½ per cent. (6d. in the £) on undistributed profits: tax not now allowed as a deduction from profits for income-tax or excess profits levy. Highest sur-tax rate, 10s. in the £, making the individuals' combined income-tax and sur-tax rate in this 'bracket' 19s. 6d. in the £.

THE FULL BURDEN TO-DAY

The full weight of British taxation for the current revenue year 1952–53 and its component parts are best seen and understood by the visual column and section method, shown against a scale in millions of pounds. The corresponding scale (*see facing page*) for the last pre-war year makes an interesting comparison.

DIRECT AND INDIRECT TAXES: THE GROWTH OF THE BURDEN

A tax may be said to be indirect in two senses: (*a*) because it is not ultimately borne by the person on whom it is charged, or (*b*) because it is a tax which can be avoided by not indulging in the activity, purchase or consumption on which it is levied.[1] Often both conditions apply to an indirect tax. The term is perhaps most generally applied to the first category, but in this paper a tax within either description will be regarded as an indirect tax.

A further convenient division into direct and indirect taxes is made for practical purposes by regarding the taxes administered by the Commissioners of Inland Revenue as direct, and those controlled by the Commissioners of Customs and Excise as indirect. This division is often accepted in discussions on taxation.[2]

It will be seen from the foregoing diagram of United Kingdom taxation that just before the war direct and indirect taxes contributed approximately one-half of the total national tax revenue in each case.

'Although total government expenditures have risen steadily during the period 1938–44 ... an increasing proportion of this outlay has been covered by revenue of which direct taxation has contributed a rising share.'[3]

[1] The fact that in some cases, e.g. on tea or sugar, a duty may become part of the cost of an essential commodity in a civilised community does not alter the character of the tax for this purpose.

[2] See, for example, Shirras and Rostas on *The Burden of British Taxation*, 1942.

[3] Mary E. Murphy on England's Experience, in *Curbing Inflation Through Taxation*.

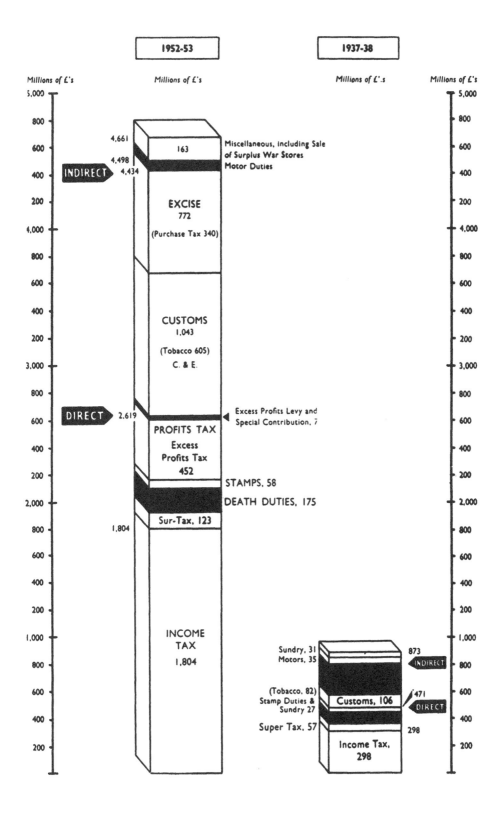

1952-53

1937-38

Millions of £'s

Millions of £'s

Millions of £'s

Millions of £'s

4,661

163   Miscellaneous, Including Sale of Surplus War Stores
Motor Duties

4,498

4,434

INDIRECT

EXCISE
772

(Purchase Tax 340)

CUSTOMS
1,043

(Tobacco 605)

C. & E.

DIRECT   2,619   Excess Profits Levy and
Special Contribution, 7

PROFITS TAX

Excess
Profits Tax
452

STAMPS, 58

DEATH DUTIES, 175

1,804   Sur-Tax, 123

INCOME
TAX
1,804

Sundry, 31
Motors, 35   873   INDIRECT

(Tobacco, 82)
Stamp Duties &
Sundry 27   Customs, 106   471   DIRECT

Super Tax, 57   298

Income Tax,
298

By 1952–53 the proportions had changed to about three-fifths direct and two-fifths indirect, notwithstanding the introduction of purchase tax, yielding no less than £340 million, a figure not far short of half the entire Budget of 1937–38. This tax is chargeable on the wholesale value of a very large number of commodities. An official summary or 'notice' of these goods runs to eighty-four closely printed pages.[1] The rates of tax and the actual yield in the latest report (as distinct from the estimate for 1952–53 dealt with above) are as follows:[2]

	£ million
Goods chargeable at $33\frac{1}{3}$ per cent. ..	217
Goods chargeable at $66\frac{2}{3}$ per cent. ..	41
Goods chargeable at 100 per cent. ..	45
Total, 1950–51	**£303**

We now come to a comparison of total national taxation,[3] as follows:

1937–38 .. £873,000,000
1952–53 .. £4,661,000,000 (including a relatively small amount from the sale of surplus war stores).

The present burden is therefore over *five times* as much as before the war. When offered a cost-of-living index compiled by a government department, showing a percentage increase far below this almost staggering multiplication, one can forgive the citizen for a cynical attitude towards both.

Indirect Taxes

Notwithstanding the huge totals of the income-taxes and other direct taxes, the indirect charges are so large and so far-reaching in their economic effects, as to call for special comment. No attempt can be made at a comprehensive description, but some salient points can be examined.

Amongst the advantages of indirect taxation are:

(1) The tax is not, in general, compulsory: it can be avoided, e.g. the purchase tax or beer duty, by not purchasing the taxed commodity.
(2) It is to a large extent, and at least psychologically, a concealed, or softer, tax than that which requires a cash payment for no direct service in exchange (a direct tax).

[1] Notice No. 78, 'Notice by the Commissioners of Customs and Excise', January, 1952.
[2] Forty-second Report of the Commissioners of Customs and Excise: year ended 31st March, 1951. Command Paper 8449.
[3] The financial statements by the Chancellor of the Exchequer for each of these years.

(3) As will be seen from the table below, large sums are raised by the Chancellor of the Exchequer with comparative ease.

(4) It provides a weapon against inflation, or surplus money.

Its disadvantages include:

(a) Offence against the principle of equality of sacrifice in so far as the burden is often largely borne by persons receiving only relatively small incomes.

(b) Discouragement of enterprise and initiative, the effect of which may remain when economic conditions have changed; e.g. purchase tax, by increasing prices and decreasing demand.

The comparison of total direct taxation with indirect is best shown by the table already given, but the composition of the indirect charges in main groups for 1952–53 is as follows:[1]

		£
Purchase tax	.. .. ..	340,000,000
Tobacco ..	.. .. ..	605,000,000
Spirits, beer and wine	.. ..	399,600,000
General import duties	.. ..	108,900,000
Oil	.. ..	271,000,000
Entertainments tax	.. ..	47,000,000
Other duties	.. .. ..	44,000,000
		£1,815,500,000

NATIONAL INCOME AVAILABLE FOR TAXATION

'We must bear in mind the very great and highly desirable redistribution of wealth that has already taken place over the last few years within our community. To a large extent, this has resulted from the provision of these extended Social Services – services for the less well to do at the cost of the more well to do – thereby making more equal the shares of the national income enjoyed. This has been a purposeful policy, I think most successfully carried through.

'But there is not much further immediate possibility of the redistribution of national income by way of taxation in this country: for the future, we must rely rather upon the creation of more distributable wealth than upon the redistribution of the income that exists. Total taxation, local and national, is now more than 40 per cent. of the national income, and at that level the redistribution of income entailed in the payment for Social Services already falls, to a considerable extent, upon those who are the recipients of these services.'[2]

[1] Financial Statement, 1952–53.
[2] Sir Stafford Cripps, then Chancellor of the Exchequer, in his Budget speech, 6th April, 1949. *Hansard*, col. 2091.

CLOSING SESSION OF THE CONGRESS

The total of the United Kingdom national income, before payment of tax, according to the latest statistics,[1] was nearly £12,000 million (the exact figure was £11,970 million).

To meet the bill for direct national taxation, there are some 20 million citizens with incomes over the exemption limit,[2] of whom over 5 million pay no tax owing to their personal or domestic allowances, thus leaving approximately 15 million persons to share the burden of £4,498 million shown in the Budget for the 1952–53 estimates.

Such a weight of direct taxation yields an *average* for *every one of the 15 million taxpayers*, however small his income, of nearly £300 for the year.

In considering these figures and Sir Stafford Cripps' statement as to 40 per cent. of national income passing away in taxation (including in that case *local* taxation), one must also bear in mind that the contributions range from the first humble 3s. of the person just liable to tax, to 97½ per cent. of the upper slice of the taxpayer whose income exceeds £15,000 for the year.

These condensed figures do, however, convey something of the financial weight being taken by the United Kingdom as a whole.

Two earlier milestones of receipts from direct and indirect taxation (combined) for other financial years make an interesting comparison:

1913–14	..	£175,000,000
1925–26	..	£758,000,000

In all these comparisons, such important factors as the purchasing power of income, the size of the national income, the total population of the country and the number of persons contributing to taxation must be borne in mind. Nevertheless, these total figures, and especially the composition of the taxes in the present national total, shown in the diagram, do tell their own story.

INCIDENCE AND IMPACT

This paper is concerned with the incidence of taxation, i.e. the persons upon whom the charge ultimately rests, and not the person first paying the tax—the point of impact.

The 'rolling' or 'shifting' of taxes between the two stages occurs in many forms, for example:

(1) Most of the customs and excise duties, such as import, beer, wine and spirit duties, purchase tax and entertainments duty.

---

[1] Table 2 of National Income and Expenditure of the United Kingdom, 1946–50. Command Paper 8203, April, 1951.
[2] Table 21 of the Ninety-fourth Report of the Commissioners of Inland Revenue, year ended 31st March, 1951. Command Paper 8436, January, 1952.

R

2) Deduction of income-tax, as in the case of dividends from companies, many types of annual interest, etc., and 'pay-as-you-earn' remuneration, where the employer acts as tax collector.

HIDDEN TAXATION

Very substantial sacrifices are exacted from a modern community in such a form as to be unrecognised as taxes, and even in such circumstances as leave the contributor almost unaware of his burden. For example:

(1) The semi-nationalisation of land, under the Town and Country Planning Act, 1947, which takes away all building or development right from landowners. The compensation is on the indefensible basis of a fixed sum (£300 million), of which a large proportion has already been allocated to priorities, thus reducing the already unknown amount for the individual to something less than it otherwise would have been. Further, although the land was 'frozen' in 1948, except by consent of a government department and the payment of a development charge which is the largest part of the economic value of the land, no payment to the owner is due until five years later, without interest.

(2) The confiscation of other rights under nationalisation or special Acts, such as the National Insurance, for health and other purposes, by which the doctor is not only forbidden to sell his practice (subject to compensation) but even his own house is subject to requisition if desired by a government department.

(3) The patent inequality of two entirely different bases sometimes employed for valuation for the same property, e.g. at a relatively low figure when requisitioned for government purposes, and a full post-war scarcity value in the case of estate duty on the death of the owner.

THE TREATMENT OF CAPITAL IN TAXATION

In the United Kingdom, there are two important taxes upon capital:

1. *Estate Duty.* Payable on the death of individuals unless the net assets left by the deceased do not exceed £2,000. The rate rises from 1 per cent. to the high, if not confiscatory, rate of 80 per cent., payable in cash—hence the sale of large estates and companies, or their break-up, on the death of a wealthy owner. Selected examples of rates are:

Net assets:	Normal	Agricultural
between £2,000 and £3,000	1 per cent.	0·55 per cent.
„ 15,000 and 17,500	10 „	5·50 „
„ 60,000 and 75,000	40 „	22·0 „
„ 200,000 and 300,000	60 „	33·0 „
over £1,000,000	80 „	44·0 „

The Effect of Estate Duty. Although *real* or tangible capital is not destroyed by a tax upon it, there are two outstanding effects of the heavy burden: (*a*) the tendency to break up into smaller units, with consequential effects upon management and organisation; and (*b*) a heavy immediate drain on income, with consequent inflationary pressure.

The yield for 1952–53 is expected to be £175 million.

2. *Stamp Duties* payable on the conveyance of land, investments and other assets, authorised capital of limited companies, etc. The rates of most general application are 2 per cent. of the value of the property passing and ½ per cent. on the authorised capital of companies. The 2 per cent. may in fact be a very large tax on any given property, investment, etc., because it is payable on *every* transfer, no matter how many times this takes place on one asset.

The yield for 1952–53 is expected to be £57½ million.

Losses and Capital Taxation Generally. Notwithstanding the fairly extensive taxation of capital gains in the United States of America, it has, in general, so far been thought in the United Kingdom that the fair and equitable allowance for capital losses, the difficulty of dealing with investment changes, the relatively high cost of collection and low yield of a capital charge, and the existing capital taxation, showed that a general tax on capital would be unfair, unwieldy, unproductive or costly, or all of these things.

Gift Taxes

It will be seen from the above that it is far from true to say that there are no capital taxes in the United Kingdom.

Further, although there is no legislation charging a gift tax, there are similar effects in at least two important aspects:

Estate Duty. This is charged on assets which, though not owned by the deceased at the date of his death, had been made a gift to another person within a period of five years prior to his death.[1]

Income-tax and Sur-tax. Although no longer his income, certain annual payments and many other dispositions of income are nevertheless treated for taxation purposes as income of the donor, for however long a period the gifts may go on, with special provisions for children

[1] Section 38 of the Customs and Inland Revenue Act, 1881, and subsequent legislation.

of the settlor or donor.[1] These statutory provisions apply to attempts to pass on income *as such* to the donee, and not to outright gifts out of taxed income for which no relief is expected: such gifts would normally come from income already taxed, or from capital, and would not be taxed upon the recipient.

The Capital Levy and Capital Gains

Although taxes of this description have been advocated or discussed in the United Kingdom for many years, they have not so far been adopted, except for the effect of the special contribution for the one tax year 1947–48. Some of the reasons for this are given below.

Capital Levy. This may be: (*a*) a straight charge to tax on total capital owned, with an exemption limit; or (*b*) a tax on accretion, rise in value or other fortuitous and unrealised 'profit'.

Capital Gains. By this is generally meant a *realised* 'profit' amounting to the excess of the sale price over the cost of the capital originally.

United Kingdom Treatment. Apart from the special cases of death duties and stamp duties, already referred to, the outstanding principle in the United Kingdom has been *not* to tax capital.

A great deal has been written on these subjects in other countries,[2] and the difficulties of establishing a generally accepted principle of equity are only too obvious from some of these writings.[3]

Some British objections are:

1. If capital gains were charged to taxation, it would be essential to grant some form of relief for capital losses incurred in the same kind of transaction.

2. It might well be found that a tax on this basis would not only cause a great deal of investigation for a very small net yield, but that in the years of depression the tax would yield no revenue at all.

3. The Chancellor of the Exchequer would find it difficult or impossible to budget for income or repayments under this heading.

4. It would lead to claims by the taxpayer to set off these losses against other taxes related to it, such as income-tax, sur-tax and profits tax.

5. It has been admitted by many authorities, including a former Chancellor of the Exchequer, that administrative costs of collection would be high, and the net yield would be comparatively small.

BY WHOM THE TAX IS BORNE

The following summary of the main income taxes payable in the United Kingdom are the latest available 'actual' figures, as distinct

---

[1] See Part XVIII of the Income Tax Act, 1952, as to settlements or gifts generally.

[2] See, for example, *Capital Gains Taxation* (New York) and its substantial list of references.

[3] See the whole of Chapter I of *Capital Gains Taxation*.

from Budget estimates or forecast.[1] They are useful in showing the contribution by different classes of taxpayers.

Tax on Assessments made. Millions of £s

	Income Tax Schedule D (Trade Profits, etc.)	Sur-tax	Profits Tax 1950–51	Excess Profits Tax
Individuals ..	121	121		
Firms	60			
Companies ..	610		258	9
Local Authorities ..	12			
Industrial and Provident Societies ..	10			
	813	121	258	9

It is to be noted that the first column shows tax on trading and business profits only, and not *all* taxes. The whole table represents about three-fifths of the total income-tax yield for the year, the remainder consisting of tax on property (a relatively small fraction of the whole, about one-fifteenth), on government investment income (somewhat less than the property tax yield) and a very substantial amount from employments, appointments, etc.

Thus it will be seen that the brunt of the taxation of profits, and indeed of income of all classes, is borne by companies, for profits tax is now a charge on companies, corporations and societies carrying on a business, and not on individuals.

PART III. THE SCOPE AND OPERATION OF THE TAXES

'INCOME' AND ITS TAX

Notwithstanding the formidable total of Customs and Excise revenue, the income-tax not only overshadows any other single tax for its yield, but its direct and heavy impact is such that it probably stands highest in the mind of the citizen and in its far-reaching economic effects.

What, then, is 'income'? The answer to that question in this paper is not an academic or economic one, but is based on the realities of the taxing system. Its outstanding features as measured for United Kingdom taxation purposes are:

1. It is the sum accruing *before* the tax is paid, i.e. it is *not* the

[1] Ninety-fourth Report of the Commissioners of Inland Revenue, for the year ended 31st March, 1951. Command Paper 8436.

'disposable income' of national income statistics,[1] but is either: (*a*) a fixed amount prescribed by the taxing Acts (as is still to some extent the case for property tax), or (*b*) is 'income' in the accountancy sense, adjusted by specific rules under those Acts.

2. It is *not* necessarily the actual money income either for the tax year or other period.

3. Its measure varies according to the source. Five main categories—so familiar to United Kingdom accountants—determine the basis: i.e. Schedules A, B, C, D and E of the Income Tax Act, 1918, now replaced by the Income Tax Act, 1952, consolidating the 1918 Act and some forty succeeding Acts.

4. It is charged to tax for Government revenue years ending on the 5th April.

THE SCOPE AND MECHANICS OF INCOME-TAX

Property (Schedule A)

By the process of somewhat complex legislation and devious claims for deductions on different bases, land and other real property is assessed on the income of the tax year, but generally differing from the exact cash income. If there is no income (e.g. owner-occupier property and amenity land) a fixed value is assessed, and normally re-assessed every five years, but the war has interrupted the five-year revaluation.

Government (Schedule C) and Other (Schedule D) Investments

Interest and dividends fall into two large groups for income-tax purposes:

1. Tax at the full rate of 9s. 6d. deducted from the income. The 'small' income taxpayer can recover all or some of the tax, according to the size of his income and family or personal allowances for tax.

2. No tax deducted. This is assessed in general, on the same lines as for business profit, but on the amount of the previous *tax* year instead of the accounting year. Personal allowances may be claimed where due.

Profits from Trades, Businesses, Professions and Income from Overseas (Schedule D)

This is the great class of taxpayers which, as will be seen from the table under 'By Whom the Tax is Borne', contributes (including profits tax) over half the total direct taxation of the country.

The basis of assessment is in general the accounting year preceding the tax year (which runs to the 5th April).

[1] National Income and Expenditure of the United Kingdom, 1946–50. Command Paper 8203 (April, 1951).

Companies pay income-tax at the full standard rate (at present 9s. 6d. in the £) on the whole of their profits, whether distributed as dividends or not. On the payment of dividends, the company deducts tax at the full rate, thus acting as collector of taxes on this class of income.

Farmers are now included in the business profits class.

Profits outside the United Kingdom, and profits belonging to persons residing abroad, are dealt with below.

Salaries, Wages, etc. (Schedule E)

Almost all subject to deduction of tax (after calculation of personal allowances due) at the time of payment, under the well-known 'pay-as-you-earn' (P.A.Y.E.) system.

Graduating the Tax

For the tax year 1919-20 a special rate of tax was charged on all the earned income and another rate for unearned income. The rates rose gradually, both for earned and unearned incomes, thus:

Earned Income	*Unearned Income*	*Navy Army and Air Force Pay*
£500 at 2s. 3d.	£500 at 3s. 0d.	
next 1,000 „ 3s. 0d.	next 1,000 „ 3s. 9d.	All at
„ 1,500 „ 3s. 9d.	„ 1,500 „ 4s. 6d.	specially reduced
„ 2,000 „ 4s. 6d.	„ 2,000 „ 5s. 3d.	rates.
„ 2,500 „ 5s. 3d.		

For the tax year 1920-21 and onwards, the system was changed. Personal or 'domestic responsibility' allowances (wife, child, housekeeper, dependent relative, etc.) were allowed as before, but an 'earned' allowance was given first, instead of different rates of tax for different amounts of earned income.

To-day, for the tax year 1952-53, this system can be shown briefly as follows:

Individuals Resident in the United Kingdom

Deduct from the income:

(1) Two-ninths of the income if earned (maximum deduction £450) and a similar fraction, but much more limited, in certain 'small income' cases.

(2) Various personal allowances.

(3) Charge the remainder to tax:
> First £100 at 3s. in the £.
> Next £150 at 5s. 6d. in the £.
> Next £150 at 7s. 6d. in the £.
> All other income at 9s. 6d. in the £.

Individuals not Resident in the United Kingdom

On income from the United Kingdom: All charged at 9s. 6d. in the £, subject to reduction or repayment of tax on allowances to British subjects and certain other categories, in the ratio of United Kingdom to total income.

Companies, Corporations, Societies, etc.

In the case of trades and businesses carried on in the United Kingdom by companies, etc., or where companies are managed ('controlled') here but trading abroad, there is liability to income-tax at the full rate of 9s. 6d. in the £. Both cases are subject to reduction where necessary for double taxation relief (infra).

Complete Exemption

There is no liability to income-tax on individuals resident here if income for the tax year does not exceed the low figure of £135.

'Graduation' Effects

The rise in the tax from 3s. to 5s. 6d., from 5s. 6d. to 7s. 6d., and from 7s. 6d. to 9s. 6d. results in some inequalities and disincentives which will be discussed later, but the recent Budget has provided a much smoother progression of rate than before.

Sur-tax on Individuals

This is in general on the same income as that charged to income-tax, and becomes chargeable when the income for the year exceeds £2,000, starting at 2s. on the first 'slice' of £500 and rising by 6d. or 1s. on increasingly larger slices. The full rates are as follows:

On income of £ £	On the last £	Rates in the £ 1951–52 s. d.
Up to 2,000	—	—
2,001 — 2,500	500	2 0
2,501 — 3,000	500	2 6
3,001 — 4,000	1,000	3 6
4,001 — 5,000	1,000	4 6
5,001 — 6,000	1,000	5 6
6,001 — 8,000	2,000	6 6
8,001 — 10,000	2,000	7 6
10,001 — 12,000	2,000	8 6
12,001 — 15,000	3,000	9 6
15,000 upwards	—	10 0

The maximum rate, on incomes over £15,000 for the year is, on the excess over that figure, 10s. in the £, making, with income-tax at 9s. 6d. in the £, a tax of 19s. 6d. in the £. In other words, TAXATION AT 97½ PER CENT.

In certain companies controlled by five or fewer persons, sur-tax may be charged on the companies' profits or through the companies, whether its profits have been distributed to the members or not.

It is of interest to note that only 783 persons with incomes over the not excessive figure of £20,000 for the year now remain in the whole country, only 147 over £50,000 and 39 with incomes over £100,000.[1]

PROFITS TAX ON COMPANIES, CORPORATIONS, ETC.[2]

This is a tax on profits calculated in a very similar fashion to the method used for income-tax, and is therefore essentially in the nature of an additional income-tax on companies, etc. It was formerly known as National Defence Contribution (1937 to 1946).

The rate of tax is now 17½ per cent. (formerly 50 per cent.) if the profits are distributed to members of the company, and 2½ per cent. on undistributed profits. The tax is not now allowed as a deduction from profits for income-tax or excess profits levy purposes.

There is, however, no liability to profits tax on profits arising outside the United Kingdom, unless made by a corporate body 'ordinarily resident' (i.e. controlled by its directors) in this country.

EXCESS PROFITS LEVY[3]

To assist in the financing of the rearmament programme, an excess profits levy of 30 per cent. is charged on corporate bodies, based on the excess of profits over a 'standard', which is generally the average of the profits of 1947, 1948 and 1949. The tax is not allowed as a deduction in computing income-tax or profits tax.

THE VIEWPOINT OUTSIDE THE UNITED KINGDOM

Trading with Concerns in the United Kingdom

1. There is no liability to income-tax on the mere trading with firms, companies or individuals in the United Kingdom, e.g. purchase here, or sales to concerns in this country; but profits from the establishment of a complete trading concern here, or the receipt of non-trading income arising in the United Kingdom involves liability.

[1] Table 126, for the sur-tax year 1949–50 (tax payable January, 1951), Ninety-fourth Report of the Commissioners of Inland Revenue, year ended 31st March, 1951. Command Paper 8436.
[2] The Finance Act, 1937, as amended by subsequent Acts, notably the Finance Act, 1947.
[3] The Finance Act, 1952.

2. Established agents here, with power to make contracts on behalf of foreign principals, are liable to income-tax.

Double Taxation

Over sixty special arrangements have been made with other countries to give residents in the United Kingdom relief from tax here in respect of tax suffered on income arising in another country. That relief is the amount of the overseas tax or the United Kingdom tax (income-tax plus profits tax), whichever is the smaller.

Certain double taxation relief treaties to which the United Kingdom is a party, provide that residents in the countries concerned who are not resident in this country are exempt from United Kingdom tax on limited classes of income arising in the United Kingdom.

A person not resident in the United Kingdom, whose country of residence has not signed a double taxation relief agreement with the United Kingdom is (with minor exceptions) liable to United Kingdom tax without double taxation relief.

Unilateral Relief

Where there is no double taxation relief, allowance from United Kingdom tax may be made of the full rate of any overseas tax suffered, subject to certain restrictions in specific cases and to a limit of:

1. Commonwealth countries: three-quarters of the United Kingdom income-tax plus profits tax.
2. Other countries: one-half of the United Kingdom income-tax plus profits tax.

Special arrangements are made with the Republic of Ireland for income taxed in that country and in the United Kingdom.

In the least favoured cases, where there is no complete double taxation agreement, tax can be payable at the full overseas rate plus half of the United Kingdom income-tax and profits tax combined— a heavy burden, perhaps consuming almost all the profits.

Nationality

Nationality has no direct effect upon United Kingdom taxation.

Income from Abroad

Income from countries outside the United Kingdom is assessed upon *residents* here, on special bases of assessment and subject to the double taxation and unilateral reliefs already described.

PART IV. THE STRUCTURE UNDER REVIEW: EPILOGUE

'There is widespread agreement among informed opinion that the present burden of taxation is a major factor contributing to this country's economic difficulties. Although individually the various taxes pose separate and different problems, it is widely felt that the root of the problem lies in the sheer weight of current taxation.'[1]

We have seen in Part I, under 'The Purpose and Principles of Taxation', the original, irrefutable and time-honoured basic principles of taxation, and under 'The Growth of Modern Requirements' the new principles so much in evidence to-day. The general wisdom in the choice of the Adam Smith foundations for a tax is not only obvious at a reading, but his principles are perhaps even sounder to-day than they were when written, 176 years ago—a remarkable tribute to Smith's foresight and perspicacity.

It ill behoves us to entertain a slight amusement at the subject of, say, a window tax, if our own taxes are doing as much harm to the national economy and well-being as the window tax did to health and comfort. An examination of the application of the Adam Smith principles to the United Kingdom taxes may be profitable.

Equality of Sacrifice

The zeal of successive Chancellors of the Exchequer in the United Kingdom to build a code of income-tax which will fall upon persons 'in proportion to their respective abilities' had led to a massive structure of a large consolidation Act (1918) plus no less than forty other Acts, nearly all drawn in language and in legislation by reference which is quite incomprehensible to the taxpayer. The Income Tax Act, 1952, consolidating these provisions, has reduced the confusion of so large a number of separate Acts, but has in no way reduced the complications. Some of the many comments on the legal structure of the code are quoted:

'I am told, and rightly told, by the Attorney-General—he understands it as much as anybody—that it is only in this form that legislation can be carried through at all. Then all I have to say is that the price of getting this legislation through is that the people of this country are taxed by laws which they cannot possibly understand, and I must say I think that this is the worst possible example that has ever been put on the Statute Book. ... Therefore, all I say from my point of view is, even the section unamended invokes with Lord Sands my intellectual sympathy with the taxpayer.'[2]

[1] 'The Fiscal Problem in the United Kingdom' in *Tax Bulletin*, January-February, 1952, issued by the Canadian Tax Foundation.
[2] Mr. Justice Rowlatt, in the case of *Lionel Sutcliffe Ltd.* v. *C.I.R.* ([1928] 14 T.C. 171).

'Unhappily the actual language in which many of the statutory provisions are framed is so intricate and obscure as to be frankly unintelligible. Probably no chapter of our legislation has incurred more condemnation from the judiciary for its drafting imperfections.'[1]

On the purpose and equity of a special and extra tax upon a particular class of taxpayers, i.e. the profits tax, charged upon corporate bodies only, it has been said that nobody has ever given a clear and convincing reason for such a tax, from which all other classes of income are exempt.[2]

On the other hand, the advocates of additional corporate or company taxation suggest that it can be more easily borne by corporations than by individuals, and that if it were not charged, the revenue required must inevitably be raised from other taxpayers. The latter is perhaps hardly a justification, but an effect. The former is advocacy of concealed or indirect taxation—an evil which is insidious by its very nature. Moreover, a tax upon a corporation is eventually a tax upon individuals.

'Anything which says to those who organise corporations, "If you should make a profit a large slice of it will be taken in taxes, while if you make a loss that is your hard luck," can have no other consequence than to restrain people from organising and conducting corporate enterprise. This is so simple that I wonder why it is sometimes challenged. Those who do contend that substantial taxation of profits where and when they appear does not diminish the incentives of enterprise must answer this simple question: If taxing profits does not discourage people from initiating or conducting business enterprise, then why not tax them 100 per cent.?'[3]

The reasonable comment here, therefore, is that the approach to equality of sacrifice has been largely successful compared with other countries, but it has been achieved at the cost of extreme complication—not merely as to the form of taxes charged, but as to the rights, reliefs and allowances granted. Such a code, even with the best will on the part of Revenue officials, may be regarded as too high a price to pay for equality of sacrifice.

Certainty

The foregoing criticisms throw up the complexity of the United Kingdom taxing laws, and therefore their offence against this next canon, of certainty of calculation. In considerable numbers of cases of computation of liability to tax, there could hardly be greater uncertainty. The following quotations illustrate that proposition:

[1] The Income Tax Codification Committee Report, 1936. Command Paper 5131, paragraph 20.
[2] Mr. S. P. Chambers, c.i.e., in 'Taxation and the Supply of Capital for Industry', Lloyds Bank *Review*, January, 1949.
[3] W. L. Hearne, Tax Supervisor to the United States Steel Corporation, on 'Does the Present Tax System Discourage Business Enterprise?' in 'How Should Corporations be Taxed?', Tax Institute, New York, 1947.

On Income Tax

'It is a most wholesome rule that in taxing the subject, the Crown must show that clear powers to tax were given by the Legislature. Applied to income-tax, however, this is an ironical proposition. Most of the operative clauses are unintelligible to those who have to pay the taxes and in any case derive such clarity as they possess from the judges who have interpreted them.'[1]

On Profits Tax

'We doubt whether it is realised by those without practical experience how very difficult it is to compute the profits tax payable in any particular case. The difficulty is mainly due to the fact that in effect there are two rates of tax, one on the amount of the adjusted profits distributed by way of dividend, and one on the adjusted profits "ploughed back". (Incidentally the ascertainment of a dividend—"the net relevant distribution"—is often a complicated affair.) The difficulty is accentuated in the case of profits made overseas which are subject to double taxation relief, especially when a deduction is due on account of unrelieved foreign tax. It then becomes necessary to invoke the aid of algebra to solve equations involving several "unknowns". Further complications arise in the case of a group of companies when election has been made to include the profits of subsidiaries in the assessment on the principal company.'[2]

Convenience

Although there is often an exasperating lack of co-operation between the computing and collecting officials in the United Kingdom[3] the vast tax operating machine is an efficient one, involving very little friction with the taxpayer or his agent.

At this point a tribute should be paid to the integrity of Her Majesty's Inspectors of Taxes and their staffs. If at times their approach to a problem seems to be more concerned with technique than with objectivity, their highly specialised training and occupation as agents for the Crown must be borne in mind.

That approach, by the very nature of their occupation, must differ from, say, advising counsel or a judge of the High Court.

Economy

The efficient British system is operated at a very low cost in proportion to the tax collected. For 1952–53 the direct taxes are expected to produce £2,619 million at a cost of only £31 million, or 1·18 per cent. of the amount realised for the Exchequer. The actual ascertained cost for the previous revenue year, 1951–52, was £27 million, being 1·14 per cent of £2,370 million collected.[4]

[1] Lord Sumner, in the case of *National Provident Institution v. Brown* (H.L. [1921] 8 T.C. 57).
[2] The Institute of Taxation in recommendations to the Chancellor of the Exchequer, 1952.
[3] See the representations made to the Committee on Organisation of the Department.
[4] Financial Statement, 1952–53 (Budget, 1952).

Economic Effects of the British System

The modern use of taxation as an economic weapon, mainly for the purposes described in Part I under 'The Growth of Modern Requirements', calls for a most careful review of the whole structure if great harm, often of a long-term character, is not to be done to the economic welfare of the nation.

It is relatively simple to criticise a taxation policy, especially where no immediate reply can be forthcoming, but in suggesting some defects or economic disadvantages of the present British system, some constructive suggestions are made, and the criticisms and questions may well produce better constructive proposals. A sketch of some of the disadvantages of the operation of taxation systems in general, and the British code in particular, may focus attention on possible reforms.

Disadvantages

1. The objections to a system which permits the charging of no less than three taxes (income-tax, profits tax and excess profits levy) and in some cases four (with sur-tax added) on the same income, need no enlargement. Apart from the inconvenience, irritation and heavy burden on the taxpayer, the national man-hours spent upon the computation of the correct liability for these taxes (a concealed but very heavy cost of collection) and the various complications and reactions comprise a monumental waste of economic effort which the country can ill afford at the present time.

2. A high level of taxation, up to $97\frac{1}{2}$ per cent., is the outstanding disincentive to production of our time. The small income man employing two or three assistants in manual work, and perhaps earning profits of some £750 a year, flatly refuses to respond to the call for higher output, whilst the State, in his opinion, relieves him of half of his profits—not an accurate statement, but very nearly true of the higher part of his income. His employees refuse to work overtime after one experience where P.A.Y.E., either correctly, owing to sharply-rising rates of tax, or because of some technical error, took more than half of the hard-earned extra remuneration. The relatively wealthy employer refuses to engage in new enterprises, to launch new inventions or to render some other valuable service to the community, because practically all of the profit will be taken in taxation, with little or no relief if the result should be a loss.

3. High rates of taxation, whether of excess profits levy or sur-tax, result in the well-known attitude of complete disregard of expenses ('the Government is paying') and a consequential nation-wide waste and loss of energy and productive effort.

4. There is no escape from the truism that money cannot be paid in taxes and also be available as capital—the essential equipment of a modern community. The proceeds of taxation are, from a national economic point of view, spent upon revenue outgoings and not capital (productive) undertakings—therefore capital is lost when taxation is levied. The continual demands of the industrialist for more plant, machinery and equipment, and of the farmer for more capital in general, are clear evidence of the shortage of capital largely brought about by the huge slice of national income paid away in taxation, and the inability of industry as a whole to save out of its profits for all its business requirements, including proper reserves.

5. In addition to the loss of monetary capital, high taxation drains away the spirit of enterprise, initiative, the will to create new wealth, and the spirit of adventure.

6. A rate of taxation at 19s. 6d. in the £, however theoretically justifiable in the case of the old rentier or privileged class, is incredibly unwise when applied to men of drive, ability and initiative, who are capable of increasing production, prosperity and employment, and perhaps thereby increasing the microscopic daily British ration of staple, if not essential, food.

7. A tax which leads to such narrow, and sometimes apparently absurd, definitions and distinctions as those employed in purchase tax, with consequent irritation to industry and contempt of the law, is not a well-conceived tax, however large its yield may be. Its huge addition to the cost of commodities without direct knowledge by the final purchaser is also a characteristic of a bad tax.

So much for the disadvantages and economic effects of high taxation. Now to examine queries which may lead to constructive suggestions.

Questions

1. The following table shows the burden of income-tax and sur-tax alone before and after the war on selected earned incomes:

		Tax (nearest £)			
		1937–38		1952–53	
Annual Income		Single	Married 1 child	Single	Married 1 child
£		£	£	£	£
500	..	52	17	63	14
1,000	..	152	117	235	152
5,000	..	1,464	1,429	2,539	2,456
10,000	..	3,897	3,862	6,589	6,506
20,000	..	9,559	9,524	16,114	16,031

Has this impressive scale of taxation, starting with a good artisan's wage, passing to the ordinary small professional man, and including the proprietors of relatively small businesses, come to stay?

2. Is there any good reason, apart from rearmament, why such scales of taxation *should* stay?

3. If the standard rate of income-tax could be reduced between two great wars from 6s. in the £ to 4s. in the £, on a national income so much smaller than it is to-day, is it unreasonable to expect well-managed finances to reduce a standard rate of 9s. 6d. in the £?

4. Is it fully realised by the country as a whole that high taxation means a much lower standard of living than could be attained with lower taxation, and if not, what can be done to bring about a changed and challenging outlook, with eyes upon a fully developed economy rather than the inevitability of the present levels of standards of living, government expenditure, high taxation and limited effort?

5. Should the profit on which tax is charged be the same as for true commercial purposes (e.g. for company law) and should capital replacement values be allowed rather than historical costs? If so, how can the resulting fall in national revenue be made good?

6. If companies or corporations must be taxed at a higher rate than other persons, is there any good reason (even allowing for the difference in rates between distributed and undistributed profits) why the present profits tax should not be replaced by a straight addition to the rate of income-tax in the case of companies—a sur-tax on companies, as in India?

Improvement in the standard of life of the nation and in the operation of the taxes arising out of these questions may possibly come from some or all of the following:

(a) Substantial economies in government expenditure of various kinds—not in odd millions, but in tens or hundreds of millions—not repeating such experiments as the ground-nuts scheme or the South Bank exhibition.

(b) In due time, and as a result of international statesmanship and military efficiency, a reduction in rearmament expenditure.

(c) A gradual extinction of food subsidies by compensating real income benefits through increased production and lower prices.

(d) The possible transference of a state-maintained health service to one more nearly approaching a true and actuarially self-supporting insurance scheme, perhaps of a voluntary nature.

Two things are certain: first, the shape of better living from the suggestions above, or from any other alterations to our fiscal system, must come through our politicians, and ultimately from the will of the nation; and, secondly, we cannot have public expenditure and benefits at the existing rates *and* reduced taxation.

The choice lies before us: there is great space for manœuvre, and the stakes in terms of human happiness on the one hand, or depression and unrest on the other, are high.

THE INCIDENCE OF TAXATION IN THE UNITED STATES

by

THOMAS J. GREEN, C.P.A.
American Institute of Accountants

I. INTRODUCTION AND BACKGROUND

Since the inception of modern government, as we know it to-day, the state has made more and more demands on its citizens for revenue to provide the means for meeting ever-increasing obligations. These obligations have been incurred partly as a result of military necessity, partly because of paternalistic objectives of certain governments, and partly because of increased services, economic and social, expected by the citizenry of the government.

The United States of America has been no exception to these trends. In fact, in military, economic and social spending it has followed a liberal policy heretofore unknown in the world. Accordingly, the United States Treasury has been for some time past a levier and collector of huge amounts of taxes. In addition, through deficit financing and borrowing, it has become a debtor of large proportions.

Where does the burden of these huge, and indeed fantastic, amounts of taxes fall and through what media have they been collected? The answers to these questions are not easy but one simple and paramount fact cannot escape notice. The ultimate incidence of the tax devolves on the individual.

Although superficially it might appear that corporations, perhaps, are bearing the brunt of the total budget or that manufacturers' excise taxes loom relatively large in the total revenues collected, it is a truism that the final tax bill is paid by the individual taxpayer through the passing down to him of the real onus of the tax. This filtering process is not easy to follow through the multiple maze of United States taxes (as will be apparent as this paper develops) but the individual taxpayer is not only the base of the tax triangle but in reality the whole of the triangle.

Perhaps it is all for the best in this state-dominated world that the individual does assume the tax burden. To have the most beneficial effect, however, the citizen must be fully aware of the tax burden he is shouldering. All too frequently, though, the actuality that the real burden is carried by the individual is hidden from him by indirect taxes and so-called 'painless' withholdings. A proper realisation of these facts by more taxpayers might go far to restore to the individual citizen the dignity that is due to him and lead to the assumption of a more active interest in government and its spending with a concomitant improvement in government.

History of Taxation in the United States

The approach to our problem of tax burden in the United States is, perhaps, best understood if a brief sketch of the history of taxation in that country is outlined. Basically, there are two taxing systems in force: (1) the federal or national system, and (2) the state and local systems.

The history of the federal tax system falls into three broad periods: from 1789 to 1861, from 1861 to 1909, and from 1909 to the present time.

From the time the Federal Government was inaugurated in 1789 to the outbreak of the Civil War in 1861, it depended primarily on customs duties for revenue and to a lesser extent on various internal taxes. The first Internal Revenue Act, enacted in 1791, imposed taxes on distilled spirits and carriages, and subsequent early modifications provided taxes on retail dealers in distilled spirits, refined sugar, snuff, property sold at auction, snuff mills, legal instruments, and bonds. In 1798 a direct tax was imposed on real property. By 1802, as the need for additional revenue diminished, internal taxation was abolished. Due to the increased needs of the Federal Government incident to the war of 1812, various internal taxes were reinstated. As the emergency period came to an end, these internal taxes were abolished by 1817, ending internal taxation until the Civil War period.

Thus we see a backing and filling of various internal taxes for a period of about seventy years, the imposition in times of national emergency and the revocation in times of normalcy.

The Civil War caused the introduction of a wider variety of taxes than had ever before been tried in the United States because the secession of the Southern States from the Union placed a greater burden on fewer people (and, of course, the South was faced with a similar problem).

In 1861 a direct tax was levied on real property and apportioned among the States, the first income-tax was enacted, and customs duties were increased. The following year a variety of internal taxes were added, including an inheritance tax, stamp taxes on various documents and products, specific and *ad valorem* taxes on manufactured articles and various products, excises on spirits and liquors, taxes on gross receipts of transportation companies, and various occupational licences and special taxes. Several times prior to 1862 the Bureau of Internal Revenue had been created and dissolved, but in that year was re-established and has since been a permanent branch of the Federal Government within the Treasury department. Starting in 1866, as the need for large revenues lessened, various internal taxes were repealed, and after 1872 internal revenues were derived chiefly from excises on liquor and tobacco and from various stamp taxes. Once again, customs duties bccame the principal source of Federal revenue. In 1894 customs duties were reduced and Congress sought to replace the loss in revenue by enacting an income-tax. This law was held unconstitutional on the ground that it was a direct tax and not apportioned among the various States in conformity with the Constitution, although certain earlier direct taxes not in conformance with the Constitution had been in force but had not been successfully challenged by the taxpayers.

The modern fiscal era for the Federal Government began in 1909 upon the enactment of the excise tax of 1 per cent. on net income of corporations in excess of $5,000. Ratification of the Sixteenth Amendment to the Constitution on 25th February, 1913, gave Congress the power to lay and collect taxes on incomes, from whatever source derived, without apportionment among the several States and without regard to any census or enumeration. In 1913 Congress enacted an income-tax law which imposed a tax on the net income of individuals as well as corporations. An estate tax was enacted in 1916. In 1924 a gift tax was placed on the statute books and remained in force for about one and one-half years, but in 1932 the gift tax became a permanent part of internal revenue taxation. Nowadays the mainstay of our Federal tax system is the income and excess profits taxes supplemented by estate taxes, gift taxes, alcohol taxes, tobacco taxes, manufacturers' excise taxes, retailers' excise taxes, social security taxes and miscellaneous internal revenue taxes. The customs duty, which virtually carried the cost of the Government in the early years, is relatively unimportant today from a revenue standpoint.

State and local taxation is the second of the two taxing systems in force in the United States. During the colonial period of American history land and poll taxes, liquor excises, and customs and tonnage duties were the primary sources of revenue for the States and their subdivisions. Upon the inauguration of the Federal Government in 1789, the several States were forbidden by the Federal Constitution to levy customs and tonnage duties. As the need for additional revenue arose, the land tax was gradually broadened into a general property tax and numerous other levies were introduced. Nowadays the States rely upon the following sources of revenue: corporation and personal income taxes, payroll taxes, general sales taxes, liquor taxes, tobacco taxes, gasolene taxes, motor vehicle licences, inheritance taxes, general and selected property taxes, and various other levies. The various subdivisions of the State, such as cities and towns and counties, rely primarily upon property taxes for revenue supplemented by sales taxes, licence fees, etc., and, in some States, a share of certain state-collected taxes. More detailed discussion of State and local taxes will be found under the heading 'A Study of Present-day Taxation in the United States'.

Enactment, Interpretation and Enforcement of Federal Tax Laws

A bill for raising revenue originates in the House of Representatives. In framing a bill due consideration is given to the recommendations of the Executive Branch of the Government and studies of the Joint Committee on Internal Revenue Taxation. The bill is referred to the Ways and Means Committee and, after extended public and closed hearings, is reported back to the House. A committee report is prepared thereon. The bill is then referred to the Senate Finance Committee and, after extended hearings, is reported back to the Senate with the Finance Committee's revisions. A committee report is also prepared thereon. In the course of the development of a bill, floor amendments may be made in each chamber. The bills are referred to a Conference Committee to iron out differences and a conference committee report is made. After the bill is passed by each chamber it is referred to the President for executive approval or veto. When approved, it becomes law.

A Revenue Act is amendatory of the Internal Revenue Code which embodies the existing law applicable to internal revenue. Prior to 1938, the various Revenue Acts were complete in themselves, each Act superseding in its entirety the prior Act, excepting two Acts which were merely amendatory. Since the enactment of the Internal Revenue Code on 10th February, 1939, which codified the law in force on 2nd January, 1939, each Revenue Act merely amends the Code and is not complete in itself. A number of amendments have been made enacting sections and even whole groups of sections in their entirety, but generally the amendments provide for striking out various provisions and inserting other provisions. As the tax burden reached a much higher level after the year 1939, there has been a marked tendency towards complexity in an attempt to plug loopholes and to adjust and avoid inequities.

The provisions of the Internal Revenue Code are interpreted in various regulations promulgated by the Commissioner of Internal Revenue. Frequently the regulations cover matters too technical and complex to be spelled out in the statute and in those cases the regulations may contain detailed instructions having the effect of administrative extension of the law. Although great weight is given to the administrative interpretation of the law, the regulations are valid only to the extent that they correctly state the legal effect of the statutory provisions. Where a regulation has been long continued without substantial change with respect to an unamended or substantially reenacted statutory provision, it is deemed to have received Congressional approval and may be treated as having the force and effect of law. Where discretionary authority to prescribe regulations is delegated to the Commissioner by statute, for example, with respect to consolidated returns, such regulations have the force and effect of law.

Other interpretations of the law, not having the force and effect of regulations as amended by Treasury Decisions (formal written rulings of the Treasury department), are published bi-weekly in the *Internal Revenue Bulletin* and consolidated semi-annually and printed in cumulative bulletins. These published rulings are designated by a number prefixed by the symbol of the office of the Bureau of Internal Revenue which issues them. Such rulings, which disclose the trend of official opinion, embody the administrative application of the law to specified situations of fact. In many instances opinions of the chief counsel for the Bureau are rendered for internal administrative guidance, and it is not the policy of the Bureau to publish such opinions. Upon request, rulings may also be issued to taxpayers and their representatives upon questions which relate to the character and extent of tax liabilities arising from prospective transactions and, in certain cases, from consummated transactions.

The Bureau of Internal Revenue is charged with the enforcement of the internal revenue laws. A very substantial proportion of all tax controversies are settled at the administrative level, a relatively small percentage being litigated. With respect to tobacco taxes, alcohol taxes, manufacturers' excise taxes, retailers' excise taxes, social security taxes, and miscellaneous internal revenue taxes, the rule of payment first and litigation afterwards prevails. Any additional tax asserted must be paid, and the taxpayer's only remedy is to institute suit in the Court of Claims or a Federal district court for an alleged overpayment. With respect to income and excess profits taxes, estate taxes, and gift taxes, the taxpayer may either voluntarily pay the deficiency in tax asserted and institute suit in a Federal district court or the Court of Claims for the recovery of the alleged overpayment, or contest the deficiency in tax asserted by filing a petition with the Tax Court of the United States for a redetermination of the deficiency. Either party to the tax controversy may thereafter take an appeal to a circuit court of appeals whose decisions are reviewable by the Supreme Court of the United States upon certiorari.

Distinctions between Economic, Accounting,
and Taxable Income and Deductions

Nowadays the Federal Government depends for revenue primarily on taxes measured by income. The average citizen, the economist, the accountant, the tax collector, and the courts have varying concepts of income, and the term defies a common definition that would be acceptable to all groups. The average wage-earner regards as income only take-home pay (i.e. wages less the taxes withheld by the employer). Economists may regard income as the flow of commodities and services accruing to an individual over a period of time and available for disposition after deducting the necessary cost of acquisition, or as the value of a given flow of services excluding appreciation in capital value, or some other concept. Even accountants have their differences of opinion as to concepts of net income in many instances of to-day's complex economy even though in the normal case there would be general agreement. From a federal tax standpoint there are various types and classifications of income which are defined by statute, such as gross income, net income, sur-tax net income, normal tax net income, excess profits net income, adjusted excess profits net income, etc. For example, net income means the gross income computed under Section 22 of the Internal Revenue Code less the deductions allowed by Section 23.

The statute defines gross income as follows:

' "Gross income" includes gains, profits and income derived from salaries, wages or compensation for personal service (including personal service as an officer or employee of a State, or any political subdivision thereof, or any agency or instrumentality of any one or more of the foregoing), of whatever kind and in whatever form paid, or from professions, vocations, trades, businesses, commerce, or sales, or dealings in property, whether real or personal growing out of the ownership or use of or interest in such property; also from interest, rent, dividends, securities, or the transaction of any business carried on for gain or profit, or gains or profits and income derived from any source whatever.'

Since the advent of the income-tax, a marked divergence has developed in the United States as to the concept of income for accounting purposes and for tax purposes. At first, the variations were minor, but as the tax rates rose and the volume of laws and regulations grew, the differences became correspondingly more pronounced. The digression from generally accepted accounting principles has been an ever-widening process.

As specified in the Internal Revenue Code, some of the more important items not includible in gross income for tax purposes are:

(1) Amounts received under a life insurance contract, paid by reason of the death of the insured, whether the proceeds are received in a

single sum or in instalments, are excluded from gross income. Amounts received other than by reason of the death of the insured, e.g. cash surrenders or payments under endowment policies, are not taxable until the total receipts exceed the total premiums or consideration paid.

(2) Annuity payments are included in gross income each year only to the extent of 3 per cent. of the total premiums or consideration paid for the annuity. After the entire cost of the annuity has been recovered free of tax, any further payments are fully taxable.

(3) The value of property received by gift, bequest, devise, or inheritance is excluded from gross income, but the income from such property is fully taxable.

(4) Interest on state and municipal obligations and on certain United States obligations is excludible from gross income.

(5) Amounts received as compensation (*a*) for physical injuries, (*b*) under insurance policies for sickness, or (*c*) under workmen's compensation Acts are excluded from gross income as are also payments received for non-physical personal injuries, such as alienation of affections and injury to personal reputation.

(6) The rental value of a dwelling-house and appurtenances thereof furnished to a minister of the gospel as part of his compensation are exempt.

(7) A corporation may exclude income resulting from the discharge of its own indebtedness if it consents to the regulations prescribed for lowering the basis of the property securing the debt.

(8) Excluded from gross income are recoveries of previously deducted bad debts and taxes to the extent that the original deductions yielded no tax benefits. Recoveries of war losses in general are similarly treated.

(9) Income, other than rent, derived by a lessor of real property upon the termination of a lease, representing the value of such property attributable to buildings erected or other improvements made by the lessee, is excludible from gross income.

(10) Certain exclusions are allowed for pay received by members of the Armed Forces serving in a combat area and for servicemen's benefits, allowances, and allotments.

(11) Payments by the Government to encourage exploration, development, and mining for defence purposes are excludible under certain circumstances.

(12) Under certain conditions, compensation for personal services of a United States citizen resident abroad for an uninterrupted period or a substantially uninterrupted period is exempt.

(13) In addition, the following miscellaneous exclusions are permitted:

(*a*) income of foreign governments received from sources within the United States;

(*b*) income of States derived from public utility or the exercise of any essential governmental functions;

(*c*) certain income received by States from the operation of bridges;

(*d*) amounts received by individual residents of China as dividends from a 'China Trade Act' corporation;

(*e*) receipts (other than interest, dividends and rents) of shipowners' mutual protection and indemnity associations, meeting certain conditions;

(*f*) compensation of employees of a foreign government, of an international organisation, or of the Commonwealth of the Philippines, if certain conditions are met;

(*g*) cost-of-living allowances paid to civilian officers and employees stationed outside the United States;

(*h*) income of bona fide residents of Puerto Rico for the entire taxable year, derived from sources within Puerto Rico, except for services performed as an employee of the United States;

(*i*) income exempt under treaty (the United States now has treaties with the United Kingdom, Canada, Denmark, France, Netherlands, Switzerland and Sweden, and other treaties are awaiting ratification or are under negotiation);

(*j*) income which accrued before 1st March, 1913.

Having had a high-spot look at exclusions from gross income, let us now turn for a moment to the reverse side of the picture to see what, if any, losses or expenses are excluded in arriving at taxable net income. Under American practice, deductions from gross income are a matter of legislative grace.

Accordingly, certain losses and expenses are not deductible in whole or in part in computing taxable net income. Some of the more important items in this category are:

(1) Charitable contributions in excess of the statutory limitations are not deductible. An individual's deduction is ordinarily limited to 15 per cent. of his adjusted gross income, and a corporation's deduction cannot exceed 5 per cent. of its net income before deducting the charitable contributions.

(2) Expenses applicable to exempt income are not deductible.

(3) Net capital losses (capital gains and losses being discussed more fully hereinafter) are not deductible, but may be carried forward to the next five succeeding years and applied against any net capital gains. In the case of individuals, an amount not in excess of $1,000 may be applied to offset ordinary income and the unabsorbed balance carried forward to the next five succeeding years.

(4) Losses on the sale or exchange of securities are not deductible if, within thirty days before or after the date of sale or other disposition, the taxpayer acquired or entered into a contract to acquire substantially identical securities.

(5) Losses sustained on sales or exchanges of property between members of a family and certain other related groups are not deductible. Deductions for unpaid interest and other expenses are disallowed in certain cases involving related groups unless the statutory requirements are satisfied.

(6) Organisation, reorganisation, and similar expenses are not deductible.

No attempt has been made in this discussion to present a comprehensive list of exceptions. The intent has been, rather, to outline a few of the more notable digressions from economic and accounting concepts. However, it may be of interest to note that departure from accepted accounting principles results in the shifting of the year of incidence of income and expense, widening the gap between annual accounting reporting and income-tax reporting. Income received in advance of being earned is taxable in the year of receipt (if no restriction is placed on the use of the money) even though the taxpayer may be on an accrual basis of accounting. Of course, there are a few statutory provisions in the law to afford relief to those whose business is of such a nature that the income received in one taxable year is applicable to a long-term proposition. American taxpayers are cognisant of the fact that most of their difficulties with the tax collector in recent years involve the incidence of expense. The problem of depreciation rates, bad debts, capitalisation of items charged to expense and use of legitimate reserves is nothing more than a question of timing, but the tax collector has found it to be a very fertile field for revision of tax liability.

It must be remembered that our basic tax law was originally enacted to raise only a fraction of the revenue that it is now expected to realise, but as years go on and the cost of maintaining a preparedness economy continue to mount, the taxing authorities, ably assisted by the courts, tend to adopt many a strained construction of the law to obtain the required revenue. A review of recent decisions emanating from our courts is indicative of this trend. Our judicial tribunals of late seem to resolve each case as if similar cases were not previously presented. Precedent and principle are hard to find and may be dangerous to rely on. Our Government requires revenue to support its varied activities and as the costs of these activities rise, so do our taxes. As a corollary, accepted principles of accounting and those of income taxation have had a tendency toward cleavage because the Government has frequently been revenue-minded at the expense, perhaps, of fairness and justice.

II. A STUDY OF PRESENT-DAY TAXATION IN THE UNITED STATES

Having briefly discussed the history and background of United States taxation and the distinctions between economic, accounting and taxable income and deductions, we turn now to a survey of the multiplicity of taxes which are to-day in effect. It would be a gigantic undertaking to list and describe even a small portion of all the taxes to which the United States taxpayer is at present subject and, indeed, it would serve no useful purpose so to do. They may be broken down generally, however, into three categories, as follows:

Local taxes, that is, those imposed by municipalities and counties; State taxes, including those of the District of Columbia; and Federal taxes.

For many decades municipal and county governments were supported almost entirely by local levies on real property and to-day this type of tax is still by far the greatest revenue producer for these political subdivisions. But in recent years a new field of revenue has become more popular as an additional source of local taxes, e.g. the sales and use tax. An impressive number of cities and towns across the nation have enacted this form of tax and, generally speaking, it results in a levy on almost every type of sale at retail. Other types of local taxes include licences, franchises and inspection and other fees.

The rates, bases, exceptions and special provisions with respect to local taxes vary in almost direct relation to the thousands of taxing entities. Few municipalities and counties have identical tax statutes.

It is estimated that these local taxes will produce approximately $9·5 billion of revenue to municipalities and counties for the year 1952.

A discussion of the tax structure of each of the 48 States and the District of Columbia would equally be out of the question here. By way of general summary, however, it may be said that 33 of the States now have personal income taxes; 35 have annual taxes upon the exercise of general business corporation franchises, other than franchise taxes measured by net income; 34 have corporation income taxes, including franchise taxes measured by net income and bank excise taxes measured by income; 26 States levy excise upon the privilege of severing natural resources from the soil; 17 States have chain-store taxes; 16 States have stock transfer or document recording taxes; and 34 States have sales and use taxes. In addition, the following taxes are common to all the States:

(1) Property, or *ad valorem,* taxes.
(2) Organisation fees upon the formation of corporations and fees or taxes in connection with transfer and issuance of corporate securities.
(3) Alcoholic beverage taxes.
(4) Gasolene and motor fuels taxes.
(5) Motor vehicle registration fees.
(6) Cigarette and tobacco taxes (all but four States).
(7) Public utilities taxes (all but four States).
(8) Taxes on gross premiums of insurance companies.
(9) Inheritance, estate or succession taxes.

It is estimated that tax revenues to the 48 States and the District of Columbia will amount to approximately $10·5 billion for the year 1952.

Direct Taxes on Current Earnings—Income and Capital Gains

The most important and burdensome of taxes in the United States are, of course, those levied by the Federal Government. The estimated total for the fiscal year 1952, from all Federal levies, is $63·7 billion.

In order more readily to comprehend the initial incidence of this enormous tax levy, a brief description will be given below of the tax itself and of the manner in which the measure of the tax is determined. This will be limited to the usual and ordinary instances, however, without attempting to present a detailed treatise on all of the exceptions, limitations and unusual features of the Federal tax provisions.

Taxation of Individuals

The income taxes levied directly against individuals account for approximately 41 per cent. of the entire Federal revenue. The measure of the tax is gross taxable income (as to which see discussion under the heading 'Distinction between Economic, Accounting and Taxable Income and Deductions'), less certain deductions specifically authorised by statute.

Ordinary and Necessary Business Expenses

Individuals engaged in a trade or business are entitled to deduct all ordinary and necessary expenses in connection with the operation of such trade or business. These expenses would include reasonable compensation for services rendered to the business by employees, rent, depreciation, bad debts, taxes, net operating losses of the business (which must first be applied against the prior year's income—any not thus used may be carried forward for the next succeeding five years), and other ordinary business expenses.

In addition to these business expenses allowed to individuals, certain other deductions are allowed by statute. There follows a discussion of the more important of such deductions.

Taxes

Taxes imposed by the United States, except Federal income, estate and gift taxes, are deductible. Federal import duties and excise and stamp taxes are not deductible as taxes, but may be deducted as trade or business expenses. Federal import duties and excise and stamp taxes, to the extent that they do not constitute trade or business expenses, may still be deductible as expenses if incurred in connection with the production or collection of income or the management, conservation or maintenance of property held for the production of income.

Taxes imposed by the States or by political subdivisions of the States, except local benefit assessments and estate, inheritance, legacy, succession, and like taxes, are deductible. Unlike Federal income taxes, State income taxes may be deducted.

Taxes on real estate are deductible only by the owner against whom they were assessed. Hence a purchaser of real estate who pays the tax after it has been assessed against the former owner may not deduct the tax but adds it to the cost of the property. If, as is usual, the tax is prorated between vendor and vendee, the vendor gets the entire deduction, but the amount paid by the vendee must be included in the selling price by the vendor for tax purposes.

Interest

Any taxpayer, whether in business or not, may deduct all interest paid or accrued within the taxable year on indebtedness, except (*a*) interest on an indebtedness incurred or continued to purchase a single-premium life insurance or endowment contract, and (*b*) interest allocable to the earning of tax-exempt income.

The indebtedness must be that of the taxpayer, so that interest paid by a corporation on the indebtedness of a stockholder is not deductible by the corporation and interest paid by a husband on a mortgage on property owned by his wife is not deductible by the husband.

Charitable Contributions

Gifts or contributions to certain types of organisations enumerated in the Code (e.g. for religious, charitable, scientific, literary or civic purposes) are deductible to the extent of 15 per cent. of the individual taxpayer's 'adjusted gross income' ('adjusted gross income' being, generally speaking, gross taxable income less certain business expenses and those in connection with real estate rentals).

Casualty Losses

Losses arising from fires, storms, shipwreck, or other casualties, or from theft, though the property lost is not connected with a trade or business, are deductible. The amount of the loss must be reduced by any insurance or other compensation received. The amount of the loss is measured by the difference between the value of the affected property before the casualty and the value immediately afterward, limited to the cost basis thereof.

Medical Expense

Every individual is allowed a deduction for medical expenses including such expenses incurred on behalf of his spouse, and his dependants, in excess of 5 per cent. of the taxpayer's 'adjusted gross income', except that if the taxpayer is over 65 years old, he may deduct the first dollar of medical expenses paid. The deduction is limited to certain amounts, depending upon whether a joint or separate return is filed, with a maximum allowable deduction of $5,000 on a joint return.

Investment and other Sundry Expenses

Payments made by the taxpayer for the production or collection of income, or for the management, conservation, or maintenance of property held for the production of income, are deductible, provided they are ordinary and necessary, having regard to the type of investment and other relevant circumstances. Examples of such expenses are fees of investment counsel, custodian fees, safe deposit box rental, clerical help, etc. Accounting and legal fees in connection with accounting or income-tax matters are also deductible.

Alimony

A husband or wife making alimony or separate maintenance payments under a court decree of divorce or legal separation may, if certain requirements are met, deduct such payments, which must then be reported as income by the spouse receiving them.

In lieu of the foregoing non-business deductions, the individual tax-payer may elect to take a 'standard deduction', by which is meant that if the taxpayer has adjusted gross income of $5,000 or more, he may, without regard to actual deductions, arbitrarily take a deduction of $1,000, or 10 per cent. of his adjusted gross income, whichever amount is the lesser. However, in the case of a married person with adjusted gross income of $5,000 or more who makes a separate return, the 'standard deduction' is limited to $500.

Exemptions

Net income, determined as outlined above, is subject to both normal tax and sur-tax, after deducting the exemptions to which the taxpayer is entitled. The unit of exemption is $600, which sum is multiplied by the number of exemptions claimed.

If a joint return is filed, two exemptions are allowed, regardless of the amount of the spouse's income. If a separate return is filed by a married person, two exemptions are still allowed, provided the spouse has no gross income and is not the dependant of another person. In addition, an exemption is allowed for each dependant with gross income of less than $600, but only if the taxpayer provides at least one-half of the dependant's support. Moreover, an additional special exemption is allowed for taxpayers over 65 years of age, and for taxpayers who are blind. These special exemptions do not apply to dependants.

Tax Rates

United States individual income-tax rates become successively higher in each ascending bracket of taxable net income; for example, the rate is 22·2 per cent. on the first dollar of taxable income, it is 66 per cent. at the $25,000 level, and moves up to 92 per cent. on taxable incomes of $200,000 and over. There is, however, a 'ceiling' upon the tax, expressed as a percentage of net income (after deductions but before exemptions). For taxable years beginning on or after 1st November, 1951, and before 1st January, 1954, the maximum tax liability is 88 per cent. of the entire net income.

The amount of the tax burden on net income (after deductions but before exemptions) in successive brackets, for a married couple with two dependants, filing a joint return, for the calendar years 1950, 1951, and 1952, so that the effect of the amendments made by the Revenue Act of 1951 may be displayed, is shown in the following table:

Net income before exemptions	Amount of Tax		
	1950	1951	1952
$	$	$	$
2,400	—	—	—
3,000	104	122	133
5,000	452	530	577
8,000	1,106	1,174	1,282
10,000	1,417	1,622	1,774
15,000	2,607	2,972	3,236
20,000	4,030	4,552	5,000
25,000	5,672	6,406	7,004
50,000	17,152	19,232	21,088
100,000	47,208	52,640	56,032
500,000	369,645	403,408	411,224
1,000,000	791,430	858,408	871,224

Married individuals may file joint returns and take advantage of the so-called 'income splitting'. A discussion of this provision will be found under the heading 'Unique Features of United States Tax Laws'.

Fiduciaries

The income of a trust or estate is taxable at the same rates as an individual. Its taxable net income is computed in the same manner as an individual except that a further deduction is allowed for amounts distributable to beneficiaries, which are includible in the income of the beneficiaries themselves. The 'standard deduction' is not available to estates or trusts. The exemption is $600 for an estate as for an individual, but it is only $100 for a trust.

Partnerships

A partnership is not a taxable entity. Instead, each partner is taxable as an individual upon his distributive share of the partnership net income. It is required only that the net income of the partnership be determined and reported as a matter of information to the taxing authorities.

For tax purposes, the term 'partnership' includes a syndicate, group, pool, or other joint venture.

Taxation of Corporations

The incidence of income taxes on corporate taxpayers in the United States is demonstrated by the fact that approximately 50 per cent. of all such taxes and 41 per cent. of all Federal tax revenues are now collected from that group. The principles governing the determination of gross income and deductions for corporations are, generally speaking, the same as for individuals. The following differences, however, may be noted. The concept of 'adjusted gross income' and the alimony and medical expense deductions, of course, have no place in corporate taxation, since all the deductions of a business corporation are business deductions. The deduction for charitable contributions is limited to 5 per cent. of net income computed without the contributions deduction as compared with 15 per cent. of 'adjusted gross income' for individuals. Net operating losses (applicable also to individuals with respect to business operating losses) may be used as an offset to income of the previous year and of the succeeding five years.

Corporations are taxed at flat rates rather than progressively as in the case of individuals.

At the present time, corporations are subject not only to income-tax (normal tax and sur-tax) but also to excess profits tax. The latter tax is effective for taxable years ending after 30th June, 1950, and beginning before 1st July, 1953. For calendar-year corporations, this means that, barring further amendments by Congress, the excess profits tax will be imposed for the years 1950 to 1953, inclusive.

The applicable rates, under the Revenue Act of 1951, for calendar-year corporations (there are special provisions for fiscal-year taxpayers, involving, in some instances, an apportionment of the tax at different rates) are as follows:

Normal tax is 30 per cent. for the years 1952 to 1954, inclusive, and 25 per cent. after 1954.

The first $25,000 of sur-tax net income is exempt from sur-tax. On sur-tax net income over $25,000, the tax is at 22 per cent. throughout the years mentioned above. (Sur-tax net income is, in most instances, the same as normal tax net income.) Thus the combined rate is 52 per cent. on taxable income in excess of $25,000.

Excess profits tax is at 30 per cent. of 'adjusted excess profits net income', which is excess profits net income of the taxable year reduced by the excess profits credit.

Excess profits net income is computed from corporate net income by a series of adjustments whose general purpose is to eliminate items of income and deductions which have no proper bearing upon the determination of 'excess' profits, having in mind that the aim of the excess profits tax is to reach profits arising from the accelerated economic activity due to the rearmament programme. Examples of such items are dividends received from other corporations, capital gains and losses, bad debt recoveries, blocked foreign income, etc.

s

The excess profits credit may be determined in one of two ways, whichever results in the lower tax: (a) the income method, and (b) the invested capital method.

(a) The income credit is the sum of (1) 83 per cent. of average earnings of the base period (usually 1946 to 1949, inclusive), (2) 12 per cent. of any increase in capital during the base period, plus or minus; (3) 12 per cent. of the net capital addition or reduction after the base period. In the computation of capital changes, equity capital is taken into account in full, but only 75 per cent. of borrowed capital is included.

(b) The invested capital credit is generally a percentage of invested capital, as determined under the more favourable of two methods, the so-called 'asset' or the 'historical' methods. The 'asset' method of computing invested capital is based simply upon the excess of total assets over total liabilities plus borrowed capital as of the beginning of the taxable year. The 'historical' method takes into account paid-in equity capital and borrowed capital plus accumulated earnings and profits but ignores deficits.

The percentages used to determine the invested capital credit are as follows:

Invested Capital	Credit
Not over $5,000,000	12 per cent.
Over $5,000,000 but not over $10,000,000	$600,000 plus 10 per cent of the excess over $5,000,000.
Over $10,000,000	$1,100,000 plus 8 per cent of the excess over $10,000,000.

The law contains relief provisions granting a constructive base period income, based upon industry rates of return, in the case of: (a) interruption or diminution, in the base period, of normal production, output, or operation because of events unusual and peculiar in the experience of the taxpayer, or depression of the taxpayer's business because of temporary economic circumstances unusual in the case of the taxpayer; (b) substantial change of products or services during the base period; (c) increase in capacity for production or operation during the base period; (d) commencement of business after the beginning of the base period; and (e) membership in a depressed industry sub-group.

In addition to the foregoing relief provisions, favourable alternative methods of computation of the income credit are available to certain eligible corporations which have experienced unusually rapid growth during the base period.

In any event, there is a minimum credit of $25,000 but this amount is applicable only when the credit otherwise computed is less; it is not a specific exemption.

There is a 'ceiling' on the excess profits tax which was provided to prevent the tax from being unduly harsh on corporations with comparatively small excess profits credits; the excess profits tax cannot exceed 18 per cent. of excess profits tax net income. In other words, if the excess profits credit is less than 40 per cent. of excess profits net income, the 'ceiling' is applicable.

Capital Gains Tax

Net capital gains, which will be described under the heading 'Unique Features of United States Tax Laws' later in this paper, are subject to a special tax rate of 26 per cent. if the tax so computed is less than that computed by including the capital gains in other income subject to the normal tax and sur-tax. Such special tax rate applies in most cases for corporations because the normal tax is greater on the first dollar of taxable income—30 per cent. In contrast, in the case of married individuals, filing a joint return, the capital gains rate is beneficial only where net income (including net capital gains to the extent of 50 per cent. thereof) exceeds $28,000, and in the case of single individuals or married individuals filing separate returns, it is beneficial only where such net income exceeds $14,000.

This tax may be optionally computed by all taxpayers realising such gains, whether they be corporations, individuals, estates, trusts or other entities subject to Federal income taxation.

III. Taxes Measured by or with Regard to Prior Earnings or Capital

Taxation of Estates

The Federal estate tax, first imposed by the Revenue Act of 8th September, 1916, is a tax upon the net estate of a decedent. It is in the nature of an excise tax imposed upon the transfer of property from the decedent to others, and is neither a property tax nor an inheritance tax.

The gross estate includes any property or interest therein, except real estate outside the United States, the beneficial ownership in which was in the decedent at the time of his death. This includes all insurance proceeds payable to the estate, and also, where the decedent died after 21st October, 1942, proceeds payable to designated beneficiaries other than the estate, to the extent that such insurance was purchased with premiums paid, directly or indirectly, by the decedent. The gross estate includes also, *inter vivos* transfers made in contemplation of death (and transfers made within three years before death are, in any event, deemed to have been made in contemplation of death and must be proved not to have been so made in order to escape the tax).

The assets in the estate are valued as of the date of death or, at the option of the executor or administrator, as of one year after the date of death.

The taxable net estate is arrived at by deducting from gross estate the following: (*a*) funeral expenses, (*b*) administration expenses, including executors' commissions and attorneys' fees, (*c*) obligations of the decedent, whether or not matured, and interest thereon accrued to date of death, (*d*) unpaid mortgages, (*e*) support of dependants, (*f*) losses from casualty or theft, (*g*) property previously taxed, (*h*) transfers for public, religious, charitable, literary, scientific, and educational purposes, (*i*) the 'marital deduction', and (*j*) the specific exemption.

A so-called 'marital deduction' was introduced by the Revenue Act of 1948 which provides that a proportion of property passing to a surviving spouse is deductible and thus not subject to the tax; such part of this property as remains in the hands of the surviving spouse upon his death is of course then taxable. The deduction is limited to 50 per cent. of the 'adjusted gross estate', which may be broadly described as the gross estate less funeral and administration expenses and claims against the estate.

Determination of the estate tax payable involves two separate computations, both at graduated rates. The first computation is on the basis of rates and the exemptions in effect prior to the enactment of the Revenue Act of 1932, on 7th June, 1932, when rates were quite low comparatively, the sole purpose of such computation being to determine the maximum allowance for State estate, inheritance or succession taxes paid, which may be used as a credit against the Federal estate tax to the extent of 80 per cent. of this tax computation. The second computation (technically called an 'additional tax') is, in effect, the tax actually payable after the State tax credit. As has been previously stated, all States have estate, inheritance or succession taxes. The 'additional' tax rates range from 3 per cent. on the first $5,000 to 77 per cent. on the excess over $10 million.

A specific exemption of $60,000 is allowable to all estates, regardless of size.

The impact of estate taxes will be seen from the following examples of three estates of varying sizes and assumed deductions, after giving effect to the 'marital deduction' to the fullest extent permitted:

Gross estate	$100,000	$1,000,000	$10,000,000
	$	$	$
Specific exemption	60,000	60,000	60,000
Funeral and administration expenses, debts, claims, etc. ..	8,000	65,000	400,000
Charitable bequests ..	1,500	25,000	350,000
Transfers to surviving spouse (marital deduction: 50 per cent. of gross estate, less funeral and administration expenses, etc.)	46,000	467,500	4,800,000
Total deductions and exemption	$115,500	$617,500	$5,610,000
Net taxable estate	None	$382,500	$4,390,000
Total estate tax	None	$99,940	$1,754,900

If the 'marital deduction' were eliminated in the above illustrations, retaining all the other assumptions used in the illustrations, the total tax would be $3,090, $242,040, and $4,519,000 respectively. An accurate comparison, however, between the tax liabilities with and without the 'marital deduction' should take into account the eventual tax upon the wife's estate (barring its dissipation) at her death.

Taxation of Gifts

The gift tax was first enacted in 1924 when heavy estate taxes were in force; it was designed to discourage the transfer of assets in order to escape taxation in the transferor's estate. It remained in effect from 2nd June, 1924, to 1st January, 1926. There was no Federal gift tax from that date to 6th June, 1932.

The rate of gift tax has been geared to the prevalent rate of estate tax at about three-fourths thereof. But since the value of the *inter vivos* gift is removed from the top brackets of the taxable estate and is taxed in the lower gift tax brackets, the gift tax will usually be considerably less than three-fourths of what the estate tax would have been had the gift not been made.

The liability for gift tax is that of the donor, but the donee is required to file an information return and he is liable for the tax should the donor not pay it.

Under the law presently in force, the first $3,000 of gifts (except gifts of future interests) made to any one person during the calendar year is excluded from taxable gifts. This applies regardless of the number of donees. Thus, if a gift of $15,000 were made to one person, $3,000 would be excluded and $12,000 would be a taxable gift. But if the

$15,000 were distributed equally among five donees, there would be no taxable gifts. In addition, there is an overall exemption of $30,000 against taxable gifts which may be taken in one year, or spread over a series of years until it is exhausted.

For the purpose of arriving at taxable gifts, deductions are allowed from gross transfers during the taxable year (which is the calendar year) of gifts to religious, charitable, educational, political, etc., organisations.

Paralleling the 'marital deduction' for estate tax, the gift tax law, by an amendment in 1948, permits the treatment of gifts made by one spouse to anyone other than his spouse, as having been made one-half by each spouse; a similar deduction is allowed for gifts from one spouse to another, except that where the gift is less than $6,000, such deduction is limited to the excess of $3,000 (the donor spouse's annual exclusion).

IV. INDIRECT TAXES

Manufacturers' Excise Taxes

These taxes, which are in effect sales taxes, are levied upon the sale of certain manufactured articles at designated rates, generally a percentage of the selling price. The tax attaches when title passes from the manufacturer to a purchaser, irrespective of the time of manufacture. In the case of credit sales, it is immaterial whether or not the purchase price is actually collected.

The articles taxed and the rates of taxation are shown in the following table:

	Rate
Automobiles:	
Passenger cars (but not house trailers) ..	10 per cent.
Trucks, buses, trailers	8 ,,
Highway tractors	5 ,,
Parts and accessories (except tyres, tubes and	
radios)	8 ,,
Business and store machines (except cash registers)	10 ,,
Cameras and photographic apparatus	20 ,,
Electric, gas and oil appliances	10 ,,
Electric light bulbs and tubes	20 ,,
Firearms, shells and cartridges	11 ,,
Fishing equipment	10 ,,
Gasolene	2c. per gallon
Lubricating oils	6c. ,,
Matches:	
Ordinary	2c. per thousand
Fancy wooden	5½c. ,,
Mechanical pencils, pens and lighters	15 per cent.
Motor cycles	10 ,,
Musical instruments	10 ,,

Rate

Phonographs and records	10 per cent.
Pistols and revolvers	11 „
Radio receiving sets and parts	10 „
Refrigerating equipment (household), including quick-freeze units, air-conditioners, etc. ..	10 „
Sporting goods (except fishing equipment) ..	15 „
Television receiving sets	10 „
Tyres and tubes:	
Tyres	5c. per pound
Inner tubes	9c. „

The questions which arise most frequently in connection with manufacturers' excise tax liability are: (1) whether the person making the sale in question is a manufacturer, as distinguished from a retailer, assembler, or repairer; and (2) determination of the amount of the sales price, where charges for containers or shipping are involved, or where the manufacturer is also a retailer or is affiliated with the retailer.

Statutory exemptions from tax extend to sales to governments, sales for further manufacture, export sales, sales of supplies for vessels and for foreign aircraft.

Retailers' Excise Taxes

Taxes, commonly referred to as 'luxury' taxes, are imposed on the retail sale of cosmetics and toilet preparations, furs, fur coats, and fur articles (exempt if the value of the fur is not more than three times the value of the most valuable component material other than fur), jewellery and similar articles, and luggage.

The rate of tax is 20 per cent. of the price for which the article is sold, except that watches retailing for not more than $65 and alarm clocks retailing for not more than $5 are taxed at 10 per cent.

Exempt sales include sales to states, territories, and political subdivisions thereof, and sales for export or shipment to United States possessions.

Payroll Taxes

Although designated as taxes, the taxes imposed with respect to payrolls under the social security programme are, more properly speaking, in the nature of payments for insurance.

Two kinds of payroll taxes are imposed: unemployment insurance taxes and old-age insurance taxes.

The Federal Unemployment Tax Act levies a payroll tax on all employers of eight or more, except those engaged in certain occupations specifically exempted. The tax base is restricted to the first $3,000 of remuneration paid by an employer to an employee during the calendar year. The rate of tax is 3 per cent. A credit against this tax up to 90 per cent. thereof is allowed for contributions paid under State unemployment insurance laws. Employees are not taxed under this Act. Benefits during unemployment are paid by the individual states and not by the Federal Government.

The Federal Insurance Contributions Act levies three taxes for old-age and survivors' insurance: an employers' payroll tax, an employees' payroll tax, and a self-employment tax.

Every employer who employs one or more employees subject to the Act must pay a tax thereunder. The basis of the tax is remuneration up to $3,600 paid by the employer to each employee during the calendar year. The rates are 1½ per cent. during 1950 to 1953, inclusive; 2 per cent. during 1954 to 1959, inclusive; 2½ per cent. during 1960 to 1964, inclusive; 3 per cent. during 1965 to 1969, inclusive; and 3¼ per cent. thereafter.

The employee's tax is on the same basis and at the same rates as the tax upon employers. It is deducted by the employer from the compensation of his employees and is remitted by the employer along with his own tax.

Beginning with 1951, most self-employed individuals must also pay old-age and survivors' insurance taxes. Liability for these taxes arises if there is self-employment income of at least $400 a year, but it applies only to the first $3,600 of self-employment income or wages, or both. Exemptions are provided for certain self-employed individuals, such as accountants, farmers, doctors, lawyers, etc. The rates of tax are 2¼ per cent. for 1951 to 1953, inclusive; 3 per cent. for 1954 to 1959, inclusive; 3¾ per cent. for 1960 to 1964, inclusive; 4½ per cent. for 1965 to 1969, inclusive; and 4⅞ per cent. after 1969.

Import Duties

Almost every manufactured or semi-manufactured article imported into the United States is subject to an import duty. Most raw materials (in certain instances, limited to a fixed quota) are duty free, including coffee, newsprint and wood pulp, crude rubber, furs, rough diamonds, cocoa and chocolate, raw chemicals and crude drugs, tea, fertiliser materials, and dyeing and tanning materials.

A detailed list of the articles taxed and of the applicable rates is beyond the scope of this paper.

V. MISCELLANEOUS TAXES

Stamp Taxes

A stamp tax is imposed upon the issuance and transfer of corporate stock and bonds, upon conveyances of realty sold, upon foreign insurance policies, upon playing cards, silver bullion, beer, whisky, tobacco and tobacco products.

Admissions and Dues Taxes

A tax is levied on admissions to theatres, athletic contests, swimming pools, dance pavilions, cabarets, roof gardens, etc. The rate at present in force is 20 per cent. A tax at a like rate is also payable upon dues and initiation fees in excess of $10 per annum paid to social, athletic, or sporting clubs or organisations.

Miscellaneous

Taxes at varying rates are also imposed on or with respect to leases of safe deposit boxes, transportation of oil by pipe-line, use of toll telephone, telegraph, radio, and cable facilities, or of leased wire or talking circuit special service, local and other telephone service, transportation of persons or of property, amusement and gaming devices, bowling alleys and billiard and pool tables, machine guns, the processing of certain oils, oleomargarine, sugar, adulterated butter, process or renovated butter, filled cheese, opium, cotton futures, marijuana, and hydraulic mining.

VI. Unique Features of United States Income Tax Laws

There are several provisions in the Federal tax laws which, if not entirely unique, are at least unusual in their application to the determination of the measure of the income-tax (there are also probably many features of state and local tax laws which are distinctive in their application to the taxpayer but it is believed that no purpose would be served by enumerating them; their effect is local in nature). A discussion of some of these Federal tax provisions follows below.

Income Splitting

The significance of the filing of a joint return lies in what is known as the 'income splitting' provisions, introduced by the Revenue Act of 1948. Briefly described, 'income splitting' is accomplished by adding together the gross income and deductions of a husband and wife, deducting their combined personal exemptions and credits for dependants, and dividing such combined net income in half. The tax is computed on this one-half of income and then multiplied by two. Because the tax rate increases as the tax brackets increase, the income-splitting privilege, particularly where one of the spouses has little or no income, produces substantial tax savings. The effect on the tax may be seen in the following example: A husband's net taxable income, after the personal exemptions for himself and his wife, is $15,000; his wife has no income. Without income-splitting, his tax would be $5,286, but because of this provision, his tax is only $4,052, a saving of $1,234.

This privilege is available only when joint returns are filed.

The benefits of income-splitting have been extended to unmarried individuals (other than non-resident aliens) who maintain as a principal place of abode a household in which there resides one or more dependants who, generally speaking, are related by blood, marriage, or adoption and whose gross income is less than $600 per year, provided that the taxpayer furnishes more than one-half of the dependant's support. However, in the case of descendants and step-children the $600 limitation is not applicable. The tax benefits to the 'head of a household' taxpayer are, roughly, one-half of those available to married individuals filing a joint return. For example, if a 'head of a household' has one dependant and has income, after deductions and personal exemption and credit for dependants, of $15,000, his income-tax would be $4,672, as compared with $5,286 which it would be without this special provision, a saving of $614.

Capital Gains and Losses

The special alternative Federal tax on capital gains was previously referred to under the heading 'Direct Taxes on Current Earnings— Income and Capital Gains', above. Assets, the gains from the sale or exchange of which are subject to the capital gains tax, include all property owned by the taxpayer, except for the following:

(a) stock-in-trade or other inventory items;
(b) property held primarily for sale to customers in the ordinary course of trade or business;
(c) property used in trade or business which is subject to allowable depreciation;
(d) discount basis obligations of the United States or a State or political subdivision thereof, payable without interest, if maturing within one year after issuance;
(e) real property used in trade or business; and
(f) copyrights and literary, musical or artistic compositions, etc., by the taxpayer.

Gains or losses from these excepted properties are taxable or allowable, as the case may be, in full, with one further exception to this general rule. With respect to items (c) and (e) above, if they have been held for more than six months, sales or exchanges of these properties which result in net gains are considered as sales of capital assets, and such gains may be treated as capital gains subject to the special alternative tax; so also may gains resulting from compulsory or involuntary conversion (complete or partial destruction, theft or seizure, condemnation, requisition, and the like).

Corporations are required to determine the net result of the sale or exchange of capital assets separately, with respect to (a) assets held for more than six months, and (b) those held for six months or less. If a net gain results from combining these results and such gain is attributable to assets held for more than six months, the alternative tax of 26 per cent. is applicable. If the result is a net loss, no deduction may be taken but the loss may be carried forward for the succeeding five years and applied to any capital gains realised during that period. If a net gain results from both classes of assets, that is, from those held for more than six months and from those held for six months or less, the alternative tax is applicable to the former but not to the latter; this latter gain is taxed at the same rates which are effective for other income.

Individuals determine the net result of the sale or exchange of capital assets in the same manner as do corporations, that is, separately for the two classes of assets. If a net gain results and the assets resulting in such gain had been held for more than six months, he may either include one-half of the gain in ordinary taxable income, or he may compute the separate capital gains alternative tax of 26 per cent. on the whole of the gain. (Obviously, as soon as the graduated rate on total income, including one-half of capital gains, exceeds 52 per cent., it would be advantageous to compute the tax on the entire capital gains at 26 per cent.; the point at which the tax on ordinary income exceeds 52 per cent. is $14,000 in the case of an individual filing a separate return, and $28,000 where a joint return is filed by married individuals.) If the net gain from the sale or exchange of capital assets is attributable to assets held for six months or less, the entire gain is taxed as ordinary income and the special alternative tax is inapplicable. If the gain is 'mixed', that is, partly from assets held for more than six months and partly from assets held six months or less, the gain may be separated, the former being subject to the alternative tax but the latter being fully taxable at the regular rates as ordinary income.

Net capital losses of individuals are also treated differently from those of corporations; an individual may deduct up to $1,000 of such losses (or, if net taxable income is less than $1,000, up to the amount of such net taxable income). Any excess net capital losses not so deducted may be carried forward and similarly deducted, or offset against capital gains, for the succeeding five years.

Depletion of Oil, Gas and Mineral Properties

Income from oil and gas wells and mineral properties may be reduced by taking into account a deduction for depletion of the resources owned. Depletion is allowable in computing the taxable income of all oil and gas wells, mining properties and other natural deposits, and of timber operations.

Generally speaking, the deduction for depletion is determined upon the basis of the ratio of units sold to the estimated total units on the property when it was acquired. For example, assume that at the time an oil property was acquired, at a cost of $1 million, it was estimated, by geophysical and geological surveys, that 10 million barrels of oil were in place. If, in a given taxable year, 2 million barrels of oil were sold from this property, a depletion deduction of $200,000 would be allowable (2,000,000/10,000,000ths of $1 million). The determination of depletion for mining properties, gas wells and similar natural deposits and of timber is similarly made.

While the general rule is as stated above, in order to encourage the development of certain natural resources, a special and often a more advantageous method of determining the deduction for depletion has been provided for in the case of oil and gas wells and practically all types of mining operations. This method consists of computing depletion on the basis of specific percentages of the gross income from the property, limited, in all events, to 50 per cent. of net income from the property before the depletion allowance. These specific percentages (on the major items to which they apply) are as follows:

Oil and gas	27½ per cent.
Sulphur	23 "
Metals, bauxite, phosphate rock, rock asphalt, borax, refractory and fire clay, metallurgical and chemical grade limestone and potash ..	15 "
Coal, asbestos, magnesite, calcium carbonates and magnesium carbonates	10 "
Sand, gravel, slate, stone, brick and tile clay, granite, marble and bromine	5 "

The percentage depletion deduction bears no relation to, nor is it limited by, acquisition cost. For example, assume that an oil-producing company's property cost $1 million and that annual gross income from oil production for ten consecutive years was $1 million (and further assume that other income and deductions resulted in net taxable income of $800,000), the depletion deduction in each of the ten years would be $275,000 (27½ per cent. of $1 million gross income, which is less than 50 per cent. of net income), and the aggregate deductions for this period would total $2,750,000 two and three-quarter times the original cost of the property. However, the cost basis of the property.

in the case of a sale or exchange, would be zero because total depletion deductions had exceeded cost.

The depletion deduction relates only to the natural resources and it is in addition to depreciation on mining machinery and equipment used in production.

Double Taxation of Dividends

The income out of which dividends are paid by a United States corporation is taxed twice because (a) such dividends are not deductible by the payer in determining its taxable income, and (b) they are taxable income to the recipient.

The effect of this double taxation can be seen in the following illustration: Assume a corporation has taxable net income of $1 million and, in order to show the minimum effect of the example, assume that its excess profits credit is sufficiently large to eliminate excess profits taxes. Assume further that it pays its entire income after taxes to individuals whose top tax brackets are 70 per cent. (this rate applies after $38,000 of taxable income). The corporation's tax would be $514,000, leaving $485,500 distributed to the stockholders who would pay $339,850 in tax (70 per cent. assumed). Thus, out of the $1 million of income to the corporation, the individual stockholders had left only $145,650, or slightly over 14½ per cent., after all income taxes, corporation and individual, were paid.

While 85 per cent. of dividends received by one United States corporation from another are not taxable to the recipient corporation (the effective rate thus being only 7·8 per cent., or 15 per cent. of 52 per cent.), such dividends lose their identity as such when paid by the recipient corporation to its individual stockholders and they have left still less after taxes than is shown in the above illustration.

Undistributed Corporate Earnings

In the absence of some penalty device, corporations, particularly family or other closely-held corporations, would naturally refrain from distributing their earnings in order to minimise the graduated tax upon their shareholders and the public revenues would suffer. A provision was enacted, therefore, to make less desirable the unnecessary retention of earnings by corporations. Such provision imposes a penalty sur-tax, in addition to the normal tax and sur-tax, upon corporations annually accumulating earnings in order to avoid the sur-tax upon shareholders. The net income, as determined under this provision and which is not distributed, is subject to a penalty tax at the rate of 27½ per cent. on the first $100,000, and 38½ per cent. on the excess.

The important question in most cases is whether income has been allowed to accumulate beyond the reasonable needs of the business. If genuine business reasons for accumulation of earnings exist, the corporation will ordinarily be immune from the penalty tax. Since the statutory test is one of purpose, the intention of the management is the determining factor and that can be determined only in the light of all the circumstances in the particular case.

Personal Holding Company Sur-tax

As sur-tax rates upon individual incomes increased, taxpayers tried to find ways and means of avoiding the incidence of this tax. One method employed (before the enactment of the personal holding company sur-tax) was to create a corporation and permit the income from investments to accumulate in the corporation and be taxed at what at one time were comparatively low corporate rates. This loophole was closed in the 1930s by the enactment of the personal holding company sur-tax.

This provision provides for a sur-tax (in addition to the regular corporate taxes, excepting excess profits tax) upon the undistributed net income of such corporations at rates of 75 per cent. on the first $2,000 of such income and 85 per cent. on the amount in excess of $2,000. By statutory definition, a corporation becomes subject to this tax if at least 80 per cent., or 70 per cent. depending on certain circumstances, of its gross income is from sources set forth in the law and more than 50 per cent. in total value of its outstanding stock is owned directly or indirectly by not more than five individuals. Personal holding company income consists of income from dividends, interest, certain royalties, gains on securities and commodities transactions, income from estates and trusts, personal service contracts, rents, and mineral, oil or gas royalties under certain circumstances.

The undistributed net income is determined generally after allowing as a deduction from corporate net income, the regular Federal income taxes and dividends paid to stockholders. The effect, therefore, of the operation of this provision of the law is to force a diversion of income out of the corporate shell into the stockholder's personal income-tax return.

By definition, banks, life insurance and surety companies, charitable organisations, and certain finance and lending institutions are deemed not to be personal holding companies.

Because the same results of avoiding the sur-tax could be achieved by taxpayers through creation of a corporation located outside the United States which would not be within its taxing jurisdiction, provisions were enacted concerning the taxation of the income of such corporations. The law provides that if more than 50 per cent. in total value of the stock of a foreign corporation is owned directly or indirectly by not more than five individuals and at least 60 per cent., or 50 per cent. depending on certain circumstances, of the gross income is of a defined class, generally that described in the discussion of 'personal holding companies', then that foreign corporation meets the definition of a 'foreign personal holding company'.

Since the United States has no taxing jurisdiction over foreign corporation, the foreign personal holding company is not taxed. However, it does tax such corporation's stockholders who are residents or citizens of the United States on their aliquot part of the corporate net income whether or not it is distributed. The net income upon which the tax is based is after allowing as a deduction, among other items, Federal income taxes paid to the United States and dividend distributions. In that manner the foreign personal holding company, like the domestic personal holding company, cannot be used as a device to remove an individual's income from the impact of sur-taxes and allow such income to accumulate in a corporate 'pocket-book' subject to relatively lower corporate rates. As corporate rates rise as against personal rates, the expediency of the 'incorporated pocket-book' becomes less evident.

VII. IMPACT OF TAXATION ON THE ECONOMY OF THE UNITED STATES

National Income and the Nation's Tax Bill

The staggering increase in Federal, State and local governmental expenditures, especially Federal, and the concurrent rise in taxation and debt are graphically illustrated in the accompanying tables.

Table I sets forth the relationship between national income and Federal, State and local tax receipts since 1929. Before the outbreak of World War II the annual tax burden was ordinarily less than 20 per cent. of national income and Federal taxation ranged from one-third to one-half of the nation's tax bill. Nowadays the annual tax burden is about 34 per cent. of national income and Federal taxation accounts for approximately 80 per cent. of the nation's tax bill.

Despite the unprecedented increase in the nation's tax bill since 1940, governmental expenditures, primarily Federal, exceeded revenues during the World War II period. It is readily apparent from Table II that during this period of national emergency the Federal debt was increased by more than 200 billion dollars. Since the end of World War II the Federal Government has been reasonably successful in matching its expenditures with tax receipts without resorting to deficit financing on a large scale, but the State and local governments resorted to borrowing to finance capital outlays deferred during the war and the cost of broadened social programmes.

Table III reveals the sources of Federal tax revenues. Until 1913 the Federal Government relied almost exclusively on customs and miscellaneous excises for revenue. Since 1913 the income-tax has been gradually developed as the principal source of revenue. Nowadays, the income-tax provides about 80 per cent. of the Federal tax revenue, of which one-half is borne by individuals and the other one-half by corporations

TABLE I

RELATIONSHIP BETWEEN NATIONAL INCOME AND FEDERAL, STATE AND LOCAL TAX RECEIPTS

CALENDAR YEARS 1929–1952
(in Millions of Dollars)

Year	National Income	Tax Receipts			
		Federal (Note (a))	State and Local (Note (b))	Total	
				Amount	Percent of National Income
	$	$	$	$	%
1929	87,355	3,753	6,552	10,305	11·8
1930	75,003	2,968	6,799	9,767	13·0
1931	58,873	1,980	6,556	8,536	14·5
1932	41,690	1,646	6,352	7,998	19·2
1933	39,584	2,621	5,922	8,543	21·6
1934	48,613	3,493	6,185	9,678	19·9
1935	56,789	3,925	6,659	10,584	18·6
1936	66,941	4,970	7,166	12,136	18·1
1937	73,627	6,986	7,582	14,568	19·8
1938	67,375	6,426	7,765	14,191	21·1
1939	72,532	6,683	7,899	14,582	20·1
1940	81,347	8,623	8,326	16,949	20·8
1941	103,834	15,580	8,782	24,362	23·5
1942	137,119	23,090	8,862	31,952	23·3
1943	169,686	39,399	9,106	48,505	28·6
1944	183,838	41,263	9,331	50,594	27·5
1945	182,691	42,687	9,832	52,519	28·7
1946	180,286	39,374	10,995	50,369	27·9
1947	198,688	43,711	12,678	56,389	28·4
1948	223,469	43,636	14,457	58,093	26·0
1949	216,716	39,285	15,837	55,122	25·4
1950	238,963	50,151	17,643	67,794	28·4
1951 (c)	276,600	72,000	19,000	91,000	32·9
1952 (c)	300,000	82,000	20,000	102,000	34·0

NOTES
(a) Total Federal receipts, less personal non-tax receipts, indirect business non-tax accruals and tax refunds.
(b) Total State and local receipts, less personal non-tax receipts, indirect business non-tax accruals and Federal grants-in-aid already included in Federal receipts.
(c) Estimated.

TABLE II

GOVERNMENTAL REVENUES, EXPENDITURES AND DEBT

FISCAL YEARS 1920, 1930, 1940–52
(in Billions of Dollars)

Year	Revenues			Expenditures			Federal Surplus or (Deficit)	Debt		
	State and Local	Federal	Total	State and Local	Federal	Total		State and Local	Federal	Total
	$	$	$	$	$	$	$	$	$	$
1920	4·201	6·695	10·896	4·824	6·403	11·227	·291	6·900	24·299	31·199
1930	7·916	4·178	12·094	8·223	3·440	11·663	·738	16·900	16·185	33·085
1940	9·063	5·265	14·328	9·252	9·183	18·435	(3·918)	16·660	42·968	59·628
1941	9·425	7·227	16·652	9·138	13·387	22·525	(6·159)	16·665	48·961	65·626
1942	9·758	12·696	22·454	8·850	34·187	43·037	(21·490)	16·138	72·422	88·560
1943	9·810	22·202	32·012	8·379	79·622	88·001	(57·420)	15·144	136·696	151·840
1944	10·089	43·892	53·981	8·151	95·315	103·466	(51·423)	13·931	201·003	214·934
1945	10·337	44·762	55·099	8·686	98·703	107·389	(53·941)	13·144	258·682	271·826
1946	11·429	40·027	51·456	10·012	60·703	70·715	(20·676)	12·451	269·422	281·873
1947	13·179	40·043	53·222	12·999	39·289	52·288	·754	13·281	258·286	271·567
1948	15·289	42·211	57·500	15·923	33·791	49·714	8·419	14·925	252·292	267·217
1949	16·951	38·246	55·197	17·824	40·057	57·881	(1·811)	16·996	252·770	269·766
1950	18·199	37·045	55·244	19·549	40·167	59·716	(3·122)	19·543	257·357	276·900
1951	20·100(a)	48·143	68·243	21·600(a)	44·633	66·233	3·510	21·887(a)	255·222	277·109
1952	21·000(a)	63·600(a)	84·600	22·500(a)	68·400(a)	90·900	(4·800)	23·000(a)	260·000(a)	283·000

NOTE: (a) Estimated.

VIII. Taxation, Philosophies, Goals, and Trends

It has been apparent from even a cursory review of the foregoing statistical tables that taxation, and, concomitantly, government spending, have been on the rise in the United States. This tendency has, of course, been largely stimulated under the compelling pressures of wars and national emergencies. Entirely aside from military spending, however, an important segment of the increase in taxes is attributable to philosophies and doctrines of the national administration which has been in office since 1933. The concept that the Federal Government is the benevolent godfather to its less fortunate citizens, redistributing wealth through the medium of taxation, has been a dominant philosophy in recent American life.

At one time the primary purpose of taxation in the United States was to raise revenue strictly for governmental needs and to some degree regulate imports. Prior to 1913, except in cases of special emergencies such as war, such revenues were raised primarily through liquor and tobacco excises and customs on imports. However, with the expanding need for more revenues, the Federal Government looked to new sources, and in 1913 there was imposed for the first time in peace-time an income-tax. Soon thereafter followed the estate and then the gift tax. As governmental costs increased, the laws were changed to produce more revenues either by increasing the rates or broadening the tax base to include new taxpayers who previously were exempt from taxation. It is safe to say, however, that up to 1933, the role of taxation was to raise revenue. From then on a noticeable change took place in the objectives and philosophies of taxation.

The administration then decided that the taxing medium could be used not only to raise revenues but also to assist in initiating social reforms. The greatest of these was the social security programme. Under the Social Security Acts a tax is levied upon the employers and employees to provide assistance to the unemployed and benefits to the aged and survivors. Unfortunately, the change in objective has not been limited to the effecting of social reforms. Surely there cannot be any objection to the use of the taxing powers of government to maintain a legitimate social assistance programme. Taxation, however, has gone far beyond these objectives. It is now being used to a greater and greater degree as a device for re-distributing the wealth of the citizenry. When the taxing power is thus employed as a leveller, there are sown the seeds of destruction of the private enterprise system.

The impact of this trend in tax philosophy is the gradual elimination of certain segments of our society. Between the high income-tax and the almost confiscatory estate taxes, it is becoming increasingly difficult for an individual to put aside any savings, and savings are the backbone of a capitalistic economy. With the stepped-up income-tax rates in the middle brackets, the middle-class segment of society as America has heretofore known it, is on its way to extinction as the very heart of American economic and social life.

Whether this trend will be halted is difficult to predict. Back in 1819 when the State of Maryland attempted to tax Federal bank notes, the Federal Government brought the case before the Supreme Court of the United States and resisted the State tax on the theory that constitutionally the States had no power to tax Federal agencies. Chief Justice Marshall, in the now famous case of *McCullough v. Maryland*, made the observation that if the State of Maryland were permitted to impose a tax on the agencies of the Federal Government, the other States could do likewise and by concerted action they could tax the Federal Government out of existence since, as he put it, 'the power to tax involves the power to destroy'.

Therefore, while the Federal Government itself has immunity from being taxed out of existence, the American middle-class taxpayers have no such protection from being taxed out of their way of life. The Federal Government has been extending its taxing powers to such an alarming extent that the people are showing signs of restlessness. There is now pending in the legislatures of many States a resolution proposing a constitutional amendment which would limit the amount of taxes the Federal Government may impose.

The movement for a constitutional amendment limiting Federal taxes to 25 per cent. (except in time of war) on individual and corporation incomes, gifts, and estates is being pushed with renewed vigour by its proponents. Although 22 State legislatures (out of a total of 48) adopted the resolution calling for a constitutional convention to propose such an amendment, seven States later rescinded action and in two States the governors vetoed the resolution, so the net score by the end of last year was 13 or 15 States in favour of the amendment, depending upon the effect of the vetoes. On the application of 32 State legislatures, Congress must call a convention for proposing constitutional amendments. Thirty-six States would then have to ratify the amendment for it to become a part of the Constitution. From time to time various prominent individuals advocated the placing of a limit of 50 per cent. on Federal taxes. While this movement is one to be watched with the keenest interest, only time will tell whether it will ever successfully materialise. At this point the outlook for ratification and adoption of the proposed amendment is extremely doubtful.

Undoubtedly, welfare benefits are going to remain a permanent part of the American scene, but as time marches on, the smaller taxpayer is going to assume a larger share of the tax burden than he has heretofore. Even total confiscation of all incomes of $10,000 or over per year would not yield a sum sufficient to produce a ripple in the budget 'pond'. Corporation taxation has reached a level of virtually diminishing returns. This is due to the Congressional fallacy that a corporation, not being a voter, can, with political impunity, be taxed and taxed.

The administration's lip service to a pay-as-you-go policy for the National Government deludes no sound student of finance. At to-day's rate of government spending, it is impossible for the mass of taxpayers to pay annual taxes sufficient to close the gap between revenues and expenses. Deficit financing and long-term borrowing is inevitable. Pay-as-you-go is undoubtedly a sound philosophy in normal times, but in the current emergency period of tremendous spending, it cannot be operable without placing a crushing burden on the taxpayer. The impact of such a load on the taxpayer will be sure to cause political recriminations.

Under the stress of the present emergency it is, of course, futile to speculate too far with respect to future trends in taxation. The cost of defence preparedness must and will be assumed, however complainingly, but it is difficult to envision that the American economy can tolerate any material increase in tax burden over what is currently carrying in the year 1952. Short of an all-out war, top Congressional fiscal policy-makers are disposed to sit tight on present tax rates. On the other hand, it is difficult to detect any possibility of material reductions in the next two years. Come what may, it is essential that non-military expenses be kept to a prudent, business-like minimum so that the lot of the American taxpayer may be made just a little easier.

THE INCIDENCE OF TAXATION

by

R. D. BROWN, F.P.A.N.Z.

New Zealand Society of Accountants

In this brief article, I have confined my comments to some aspects of income taxation as it affects the people of New Zealand. The incidence of other direct taxes (e.g. death duties, etc.) and indirect taxes (e.g. custom duties, sales tax, betting and amusement taxes) cannot be discussed in so limited a paper. I have avoided statistics throughout, and have sought merely to provoke thought and perhaps discussion on a subject that can scarcely be regarded as a cheerful one.

The dictionary meaning of incidence is given as 'the manner of falling'. As applied to taxation I take this to mean 'how taxation falls on those who have to pay it', and that the purpose of this paper is to discuss our present system of taxation, what some of its faults are and what should be done to effect a remedy where experience has shown that defects lie.

That the burden of taxation levied to-day is vastly greater than that of twenty-five years ago is a statement which I know will be accepted without question in all countries. From being a mere annoyance largely disregarded years ago, it has become the greatest single factor in modern business and commercial life; it colours and governs the business man's attitude towards everyday transactions to a degree which calls for serious and thoughtful consideration as to its effect on the national economy and on the national welfare.

Everyone will agree that a high level of taxation was grimly necessary in wartime. Only the politically biased will maintain that taxation in peacetime should be as high. Yet there has been no fall in the demands made on a long-suffering public by the governments of the day since 1945. I think two of the reasons for this are:

(a) The establishment and maintenance of a system of costly and crippling controls; and

(b) The creation of a welfare state—coupled, as it must be, with a falling away in the labour available for production.

Government departments are often referred to as 'the dead hand of bureaucracy'; this is not entirely true—some of our ablest and hardest worked men are bureaucrats—but it is certainly true that the bigger bureaucracy grows, the more deadening its effect, and the more costly. This is not the place for political comment, and it may be that both the controls and the welfare state are good things, but each of them calls for a huge expenditure which has to be paid for and which can only be paid for out of taxation. Ideologies and 'isms' have much to answer for under this heading.

It must be accepted, I think, that taxation will continue (with a little variation now and then, dependent upon the policy of different governments) to be high, and that being so, the question as to the fairness of that taxation—the incidence of it—how and on whom it falls—is of paramount importance.

Public agitation has been strong for a number of years past in my own country (New Zealand) for a review of the whole taxation system, and last year a special Taxation Committee representing all sections of the business and professional community was set up with the following terms of reference:

'To inquire into the present system of land and income taxation in New Zealand in all its aspects, and, having regard to the proposed consolidation of the land and income-tax and social security charge legislation, to report on:

(a) What alterations are considered necessary or desirable.
(b) The relation of taxation to the national economy.
(c) The effect of any proposed alterations on the national economy, the rates of tax and the total yield of land tax, income-tax or social security tax respectively.'

The Committee's report is now available but its recommendations have yet to be dealt with by the Government. The committee has done an excellent job and its findings and recommendations cover a wide field. The following touches on such of the more important recommendations as can be encompassed within the limits imposed on me for this paper.

Land Tax

Whereas in 1892, when first imposed, this tax was a major source of public revenue, and while in its early years it did have as one of its objectives the forcing of large holdings into subdivision, neither of these factors is true to-day. The quantum of tax produced is now comparatively negligible and the large holdings have gone. The Committee rightly condemns land tax as now indefensible in principle and recommends its complete abolition. The incidence here is on a particular class of taxpayer and can no longer be justified on the grounds that he is 'privileged' as the holder of an asset which produces the nation's wealth, or the value of which is created for the owner by the community. The privileges created by present-day controls and licences in many other walks of life have quite eclipsed those of the mere property owner.

Aggregation of Incomes of Husband and Wife

In 1939 the then Government brought in legislation whereby, where the income of each exceeded £200, the incomes were aggregated and taxed as one at higher rates. This was done presumably to deter husbands from transferring income-producing assets to their wives or entering into partnership with them, but was not limited in its application. It embraced all income derived by a wife—including property inherited producing an income, and income earned as a result of her own efforts.

To my mind this is a thoroughly immoral piece of legislation because:
(a) It puts a penalty on matrimony where the wife already has property in her own right or continues to earn an income.

(b) Where the wife's wealth is derived from gifts from her husband, the tax gatherer first collects gift duty from him, then, for the purposes of income-tax, treats the gift as never having been made, and collects again.

It is a precept of good taxation that it should be fair as between members of the community. This tax is grossly unfair—is, in fact, a 'class' tax, and should be abolished.

Farming Income

By far the most important industry in New Zealand is that of farming, on the success of which the whole of the Dominion's prosperity depends. It is natural and proper therefore that the legislature should have particular regard to the many and diverse problems which have faced the industry over the years, not the least of which has been the fairest and most equitable manner in which the man on the land should make his contribution to the public revenue.

Towards the latter end of the nineteenth century, the old property tax was abolished and a system of graduated land tax imposed on land-holders and mortgagees. Income-tax was imposed on all incomes other than those derived from land and mortgages on land. This position held (with certain increases in the graduation in the meantime) until 1915, when the need to finance the war brought income from land and mortgages on land into line with all other taxable income. Land tax was retained, but an allowance of 5 per cent. of the capital value of the land used in the production of the income was made in an endeavour to avoid double taxation. This was only partially successful but the system remained on the statute book until 1923 when the taxing laws were consolidated under the Land and Income Tax Act of that year, when income from land was exempted from tax and only land tax was imposed, with a steep graduation on the larger properties. This exemption did not last long. First, in 1924, 'small grazing runs', i.e. Crown leases whose holders had little land-taxable interest in the land they farmed and consequently paid little if any land tax, were made subject to income-tax, and between 1930 and 1939, first the larger, then progressively the smaller properties were brought in, until finally all those who derived income from any lands became subject to income-tax, and are taxable to this day.

One of the main problems in arriving at the amount of income on which a farmer should be assessed in any year, has always been, and still is, wrapped up in the value to be placed on his livestock at the end of the year. Apart from dealers—who may use current market values—all genuine farmers who breed from their own livestock, are invited to fix a 'standard value' (to approximate the original cost of the flock or herd) and are required to adhere to that value in their income returns from year to year—regardless of market values. Because farmers had first become liable for income-tax in varying years from 1924 to 1939, during which time prices had fluctuated violently, the 'standard' values adopted for balance purposes varied with those fluctuations, e.g. from 10s. to 40s. for sheep and £2 to £10 for cattle. The system works with reasonable fairness, so long as the farmer maintains fairly even stock tallies from balance to balance and does not sell out or die, but in either of these two events, he or his estate is mulcted for income-tax on the difference between his adopted standard value, and the price he gets for the sale of his stock, or the price at which it is valued for probate. With the present-day high prices ruling for livestock (60s. for sheep and £25 for cattle) it will be appreciated that a farmer who adopted, quite naturally, a low standard in the slump of 1930, is faced with a serious problem in taxation should he sell out or die to-day. Recently, some measure of relief has been granted by allowing the book profit arising from these differences in values, to be spread over four years, but in the main, the problem remains. As taxation laws stand to-day, those who die have no option but to leave their beneficiaries loaded with heavy taxation, while elderly farmers who would like to sell out to younger men eager to take up land, refuse to sell while faced with a heavy impost for taxation on what they regard as a 'paper' profit.

Members of the New Zealand Society of Accountants, who are closely associated with farming operations, have long been concerned to find some remedy for this state of affairs. Strong submissions to have the normal winter capacity declared as fixed capital stock (and as such not subject to income-tax) have recently been made to the Special Taxation Committee, which Committee has now recommended the adoption of this principle to the Government. I am hopeful that Parliament will be persuaded to appreciate that livestock, in addition to reproducing itself—thus providing the farmer with an income—is also his fixed capital, and that as such it should be maintained at its full original value from year to year, and that no portion of the proceeds of that capital stock should be subject to taxation on sale or death. Both the United Kingdom and the Canadian Governments have adopted measures calculated to give recognition to the principle that the basic stock is capital, with which principle I am in full accord.

If I have devoted a considerable portion of my limited space to a discussion on farming income, this is because farming is New Zealand's most important industry.

Income-tax and the Shareholder

Certain income in New Zealand (mainly dividends) is referred to, in the hands of the shareholder, as 'non-assessable'—for the reason that it has borne tax at the source before the dividend reaches him. From 1931 to 1941 this non-assessable income was added to the shareholder's other income for the purpose of calculating the tax payable on that other income at a higher rate. There was no particular objection raised to this procedure, but in 1942 the A+B method of assessment was introduced by an amending clause which has become a classic in New Zealand taxation law.

Under this authority tax is first calculated on the total of the 'non-assessable' and the taxable income as if it were all taxable. From this is allowed a deduction of the tax applicable to an income equivalent to the 'non-assessable' income only, this allowance being at lower rates. The effect is, of course, to assess the taxpayer much more heavily than was the case in 1931–1941. Shareholder taxpayers who understood the significance of the

1942 amendment (and those who didn't, but who felt its effect) have long protested their conviction that the effect of the amendment was not clearly understood even in the House by members when it was passed, and they have suffered under the grievance that they have been made the target of a selective and unfair tax. Most impartial people will agree with them and I note with pleasure that the Special Taxation Committee supports this view and recommends the abolition of the A+B system and reversion to the precedure observed from 1931 to 1941. Nothing encourages avoidance or evasion so much as does an unjust tax.

Legal Avoidance

I cannot do better than quote the Taxation Committee on this aspect of taxation:

> 'Legal avoidance takes many forms and is encouraged by high taxation. Tax laws are complex and in some directions inequitable. Human affairs are, of course, most complex, and the law cannot provide for all eventualities. Because of legal distinctions, taxes may fall on one person more heavily than on another with the same amount of income. As the taxing authority insists on payment according to the law, the taxpayer cannot be condemned for following the form of the law to avoid liability for taxation.
>
> 'Tax avoidance does not occur only with larger taxpayers. The spirit of avoidance is evident in those who will not work longer, or try harder, because too much goes in taxes. In a similar spirit, many of those who claim benefits from social security funds make legally permissible adjustments in their affairs to qualify them or to increase their benefits.'

On this last point, as a 60-year-old myself, reasonably healthy and still partially sane, who hopes to remain in active business for another ten years, I say that too many healthy people are being encouraged to retire from active work at 60. The symptoms of laziness and of fatigue are identical and it is easy to mistake the one for the other.

Is High Taxation Anti-inflationary?

The statement has been made from time to time by economists and politicians seeking to justify some increase in taxation, that it serves as a weapon against inflation. This, in my view, is quite fallacious. What happens when taxation is increased? Admittedly, more money is taken from the individual than formerly, leaving him with less spending power. On the other hand, more money comes into Treasury and its spending power is increased. But does a government ever save anything (unless it redeems a debt out of taxation)? It does not; so that the money which the individual might have saved is spent anyway. It has merely found its way back into circulation by a different channel and there will be many who will challenge the claim that a government can spend the individual's money for him to his better advantage than he can himself. Governments generally get less for their money than does the individual; the greater the volume of government spending, the greater the trend towards inflation and higher prices.

The Economic Waste of High Taxation

It is nearly 200 years since Adam Smith laid down certain precepts of good taxation; equity, certainty, convenience and economy. Could Adam, like Rip van Winkle, return to this vale of tears to-day, he would surely be aghast at what he would see. First, he would have to adjust himself to the change from an era of *laissez-faire*, when every man fought the battle of life without aid from or interference by the State, to the present-day era of bureaucracy under which man's money, his movements and his trading, are under some official's control and by licence or permit, and whole nations are strangling themselves with restrictions. Examining the present-day high rate of taxation, and its effect on the nation's economy, I think he would find:

(1) Where a taxpayer company or individual finds that he has reached, or believes he will reach, the top brackets in taxation, that there is a tendency—and this is fairly general—towards recklessness in expenditure of a deductible nature. He feels that if three-fourths of the cost of any expenditure is being paid for by the State, he need not worry overmuch as to the widsom or need for the outlay. He no longer considers whether he could do without for another year or two. The fact that the State will lose and he will save three times as much in taxation as he will lose in net profit is in itself a temptation to spend the money. Any practising accountant handling tax returns for the larger taxpayers will, I am sure, confirm that this is the attitude of a large proportion of his clients in the top brackets and that there is, in the interests of his client, no sound reason why he should endeavour to combat it.

(2) Illegal evasion, as distinct from legal avoidance, has increased to an extent it is impossible to measure. (Nearly £1 million was collected in New Zealand last year as a result of tax inspections.) There can be no doubt that the higher the rate of tax in peacetime, the greater the tendency towards evasion.

(3) But the worst aspect of high taxation is its effect on the business effort of the community. While there are many splendid types who put all they have into personal effort to increase production, there are still more who measure the effort they are prepared to make by the amount of income-tax they have to pay. Incentive and enterprise receive every discouragement under high taxation, and it takes a better than average man to rise above it. This is bad for the economy and recovery of a nation.

Rest in peace, Adam, you're lucky!

THE INCIDENCE OF TAXATION IN AUSTRALIA

by

CONRAD F. HORLEY, F.A.A.(AUST.)
Association of Accountants of Australia

When the invitation to submit a paper on 'The Incidence of Taxation', extended to the Association of Accountants of Australia by the International Congress on Accounting, was passed on to me, I dug back to 1913, before the First World War, to see the exact meaning of 'incidence' in those halcyon days with no thought other than that of being exact, as I was warned that there was a limit of 3,000 words to the paper I was to prepare.

Webster's 1913 edition, which I quote verbatim, gives the following:

INCIDENCE

'(1) An incident or incidental matter (obs. or dialectical).

(2) Act, fact, or manner of falling upon or affecting; also range of occurrence or influence.

"In England and Wales during recent years the incidence of insanity has been as great on women as on men."—*Pop. Science Monthly*.

(3) Physics. The falling of a projectile, ray of light, etc., on a surface—also angle of incidence.

(4) Economics. The falling of a tax upon a person as a burden which he must pay—called specifically the *real* or *final* incidence when he is unable to shift the burden on another.'

My first reaction to this definition was that such is the stamina of the British, that the incidence of insanity, notwithstanding the incidence of taxation, is apparently not greater in 1952 than it was in 1913. I did not expect the definition would allude to the falling of a projectile. I still less expected to find direct reference to taxation in it. However, under 'Definition 4—Economics'—in the days before the economists had put us off the gold standard, and when taxation left us with most of our income intact, 'incidence' was regarded as the falling of a tax upon a person as a burden which he must pay, called specifically the 'real' or 'final' incidence when he is unable to shift the burden on another.

That is as delightfully vague as the economists are to-day, but there is nothing vague in the price we are paying for our planned economy. This shifting of the burden opens up boundless possibilities in the light of to-day's experience. The patriotic efforts of beer drinkers, for example, will contribute this year an estimated £58 million in excise—whereas in the year before the war the figure was £7 million. The annual report of our largest brewery company states that excise now represents about 16s. in the £ of the turnover of draught beer.

In order to tell you in detail about all the taxes that are levied in Australia it would need much more than 3,000 words. There was no Federal income-tax until 1915, and it was introduced as a temporary measure! However, a brief and incomplete summary includes, firstly, the most prolific producer of revenue for needy governments—income-tax, disguised under various names, such, for example, as 'social services contribution'.

In the budget estimates for 1951-52 Federal income-tax on
    individuals is estimated to produce £419,500,000
Company income-tax £135,000,000
and social services contribution £7,500,000

The other large items of revenue are:

Customs £104,000,000
Excise £100,000,000
Sales tax £117,000,000

There are various other taxes which do not amount to much in these days of abounding prosperity. They provide about another £74 million, which is about seven times as much as Federal income-tax in 1938-39, but they are many, varied and ingenious, including the pay-roll tax, land tax, wool deduction tax, estate duty tax, gift duty and entertainments tax. This by no means exhausts the total of imposts by the Australian Federal Government. There are various other forms of taxation by way of licences, etc., which go into the coffers of the Federal Treasury.

Added to these we have the State taxes. In the State of New South Wales, for example, we have motor taxation, various licences and registration fees, various imposts, such as the silicosis levy, which is added compulsorily to the premium paid by all employers on compulsory workers' compensation insurance. There are shire and municipal taxes, licences and imposts. So, from this very brief survey, it will be seen that the 'incidence of taxation' falls heavily on every individual living in or visiting the country.

Examination of the reports of the Commissioner of Taxation, the various year-books, Federal and State, and the Budget estimates lead to the conclusion that recent Budgets invariably underestimate the amounts that taxation will yield, and that collections of taxation are considerably in excess of assessments. The following figures, which are the latest available, will illustrate this point.

Federal income-tax and social services contribution as assessed (figures supplied in the twenty-ninth report of the Taxation Commissioner) amounted to £190,417,020 for the taxation year 1947-48, whilst collections under the same headings totalled £232,900,055. The Federal Budget Estimate of collections of all taxes by the Taxation Department for 1947-48 was £256,150,000, whilst actual collections by the department totalled £301,068,099, or 17½ per cent. above the estimate.

The following table gives the incidence of Federal taxation collections under the various items of revenue for 1947-48 and 1948-49. The taxation year ends 30th June.

Item of Revenue Collected	1947-48		1948-49	
	Amount £	%	Amount £	%
Direct taxes on income ..	232,900,055	77·4	272,346,876	78·6
Sales tax	34,728,579	11·5	39,029,276	11·2
Pay roll tax	16,594,764	5·5	19,802,924	5·7
Land tax	3,640,900	1·2	3,032,316	0·9
Estate duty	4,555,004	1·5	4,740,362	1·4
Gift duty	780,401	0·3	581,463	0·2
Entertainments tax ..	5,198,337	1·6	5,298,677	1·5
Wool contributory charge..	1,423,874	0·5	1,028,882	0·3
Stevedoring industry charge	260,400	0·1	670,219	0·2
Flour tax	985,327	0·4	1,319	
Wool tax	458			
Total Federal Taxation Department	301,068,099	100·0	346,532,314	100·0
Customs and Excise ..	115,605,000	—	126,200,000	—
Other	5,739,901	—	18,080,686	—
Total Federal	£422,413,000	—	£490,813,000	—

The following table gives details of New South Wales State taxation collected during 1947-48:

NEW SOUTH WALES (STATE TAXATION)
COLLECTED DURING 1947-1948

	£	£ s d	Population 3,062,344
Probate	4,610,742		
Stamp duties	2,462,483		
Racing and betting taxes ..	1,066,611		
Liquor licenses	1,073,646		
Other	319,785		
Total Government taxation ..	9,533,267	3 3 4	per head of population
Motor taxes*	3,469,003	1 3 1	,, ,, (397,410 vehicles)
Total N.S.W. State taxation..	13,002,270	4 6 5	per head of population
Local rates including sewerage	11,598,634	3 17 2	,, ,,
Total State and Local N.S.W.	£24,600,904	£8 3 7	

* In 1948 taxes amounting to £414,080 levied on commercial motor vehicles were paid over to the Socialist railway system in New South Wales in an endeavour to discourage road haulage and reduce the annual loss on operating the railways.

The total amount per head of population in Australia collected for the Federal Treasurer in 1948-49 was £62 18s. 8d. and, whilst the Commonwealth Year Book No. 38 tells us that State taxation amounted to £4 13s. 8d. per head, the Official Year Book of New South Wales No. 51 gives the total State and local taxation per head of New South Wales population for 1948 (the latest year available) as £8 3s. 7d., which means that every man, woman and child in that State faced the certainty of having to provide £71 2s. 3d. in taxes, that is, of course, if every one paid the same amount. However, babies in arms obviously were unable to provide their quota, so those who toil must perforce take up the burden.

At 30th June, 1947, the population of New South Wales was 2,984,838, and of these 1,210,000 were employed. Therefore mother and father between them had to do something about the babe in arms and the children at school and the invalids and aged. This meant each person employed had to provide for two and a half others, so that each of the toilers had to face the year 1947-48 with £177 15s. 6d. being taken out of his or her individual earnings, if they all shared the burden equally. However, the burden is shifted again—not this time entirely by the patriotic beer drinkers—but by the civil servants, whose numbers grow apace, and who tell our elected representatives what to do. This is how they faced the problem and shifted the burden so far as income-tax is concerned. The incidence of Federal income-tax in various income groups as assessed for 1947-48 is shown hereunder:

INCOME TAX ASSESSED

FEDERAL INCOME TAX AND SOCIAL SERVICES CONTRIBUTION FOR 1947-48 (INCOME YEAR 1946-47)

Income Group of Taxpayers	No. of Taxpayers	Total Tax £	Average Tax per Taxpayer £ s d
Up to £400 p.a.	1,786,056	38,565,797	21 11 10
£401 to £500 p.a.	302,946	16,036,669	52 18 9
£501 to £1,000 p.a.	261,417	29,232,660	111 16 6
£1,001 to £50,000 p.a.	88,072	53,207,715	604 2 9
£50,001 and over	7	350,615	50,087 17 2
	2,438,498	£137,393,456	£56 6 10

It will be seen that out of a total of 2,438,498 persons and organisations subject to taxation on income, 1,786,056 received a net income of £400 per annum or less in the income year 1946-47 and were assessed to a total of £38,565,797 or an average of £21 11s. 10d. per taxpayer. There were 2,350,419 taxpayers receiving £1,000 or less per year and they paid £83,835,126 in tax, whilst 88,079 received over £1,000 per year and paid £53,558,330 in tax.

On page 555 a comparison is made of the Federal Treasurer's Budget for 1951-52 with the collections of tax during 1948-49, and it is interesting at this stage to give the Federal Treasurer's comparison of United Kingdom taxes on income from personal exertion with Australian taxes. It should be noted that the United Kingdom figures are based on rates declared on income of 1951-52, including national insurance contribution.

Income per annum	Person with no dependants					
	United Kingdom Tax			Australian Tax		
£	£	s	d	£	s	d
100	11	18	0		—	
250	30	8	0	8	1	0
400	63	8	0	24	15	0
500	93	8	0	39	9	0
600	131	8	0	56	16	0
800	207	8	0	99	0	0
1,000	283	8	0	148	10	0
2,000	663	8	0	515	4	0
5,000	2,600	18	0	2,297	4	0

This indicates that the lower-paid groups in United Kingdom are taxed much more severely than they are in Australia.

The following table shows the incidence of income taxation as it falls on classes of taxpayers under four groups. It will be seen that the incidence falls like a very heavy projectile on the non-resident taxpayers.

The income-tax payable by non-resident individuals was 35·6 per cent. of their taxable income, whilst non-resident companies were taxed 31·4 per cent. of taxable income. The non-resident has also to pay taxation in his home country. These conditions discourage the investment of overseas funds in Australian ventures, at a time when Australia is absorbing displaced persons at the rate of approximately 200,000 a year. The City of Newcastle, in New South Wales, had a population approximating 150,000 and an improved capital value rating of £32,325,000 at 31st December, 1946. This suggests new capital requirements of £50 million a year to absorb the migrants.

Our taxation will not permit of overseas capital being used or leave much scope for local investment.

The table covers the same year as the previous table.

Class of Taxpayer	No. of Taxpayers	Taxable Income £	Total Tax £	Percentage Tax to Income
Resident individuals	2,438,498	924,864,273	137,393,456	14·9
Non-resident individuals	2,298	1,813,027	644,756	35·6
Resident companies	16,870	157,582,504	45,815,933	29·7
Non-resident companies	1,212	20,922,257	6,562,875	31·4
	2,458,878	£1,105,182,061	£190,417,020	17·2%

I submit a comparison of the 1948-49 collections of tax with the Federal Treasurer's Budget Estimates for 1951-52:

Item of Revenue					Collections 1948-49	Budget Estimate 1951-52
					£	£
Direct taxes on income	..	..	..		272,346,876	562,000,000
Sales tax	..	..	..	..	39,029,276	117,000,000
Pay roll tax	..	..	..	..	19,802,924	40,000,000
Land tax	..	..	..	..	3,032,316	7,500,000
Estate duty	..	..	..	..	4,740,362	8,500,000
Gift duty	..	..	..	..	581,463	1,300,000
Entertainments tax	..	..	..	..	5,298,677	5,500,000
Wool contributory charge	..	..	..		1,028,882	11,500,000
Stevedoring industry charge		..	..		670,219	—
Flour tax	..	..	..	..	1,319	—
Total Federal Taxation Department				..	346,532,314	753,300,000
Customs and Excise ..		..	..	..	126,200,000	204,000,000
Other ..	..	..	..	..	18,080,686	84,104,000*
					£490,813,000	£1,041,404,000

* Includes railways, post office, broadcasting, etc.

This, no doubt, can be regarded as an 'expanding economy' and we would have differing opinions from our economists as to the correct meaning of 'economy'—it will not be apparent in Government expenditure however.

Extracting the money from the people will no doubt limit individual spending, but excessive Government expenditure will doubtless have an inflationary effect, the net result being merely to deny the individual the right to decide whether he will spend or save his increased earnings and place the privilege of spending them in the hands of the Government.

Incidence of Taxation on Increased Pay.
How Australian workers are worse off with more pay

To make this point clear, it is necessary to outline the basis upon which the Australian Arbitration Court fixes wages and conditions of work. The employer no longer has any individual discretion in fixing rates of pay in respect of workers who come under the jurisdiction of the Arbitration Court. This is practically general, with few exceptions. He may pay more, but he shall not pay less. Therefore, when the weekly rate of pay was increased to £10 per week, it was practically a universal rise—all workers, more or less, rising in like proportion. We also have Prices Ministers in each State and a very wide range of commodities are under price control. Therefore, the increased cost of commodities brought about by wage increases are reflected in increased prices charged to the wage earners for these commodities. The increases are eventually greater than the actual wages cost, because price fixation drives producers out of business, and causes shortages. Also, of course, we have to take more workers out of production to work out prices, exercise controls and police fixed prices.

Now, at £8 per week taxable income under the 1951-52 budget the weekly deduction for taxation is 10s. 6d. per week. That is to say the goods produced

T

are costed on the basis of £8 per week and the worker has to pay these prices, whilst he receives in his pay envelope £7 9s. 6d.

When the wages are raised all round to £10 per week, to meet the increased cost of living, the goods produced and the services, socialist or private enterprise, are costed on a £10 per week basis—must be to retain solvency.

However, the tax deducted from £10 per week is 16s. 6d., so that at the very best and most optimistic reckoning the wage earner is 6s. per week worse off. The higher the award made by the Arbitration Court the worse the net result in the pay envelope. At £12 per week, for example, the weekly tax deduction is £1 3s. 9d.—that is 13s. 3d. per week more than the deduction at £8 per week, and at £12 per week the worker is at least 13s. 3d. per week worse off than at £8 per week, even if we forget the extra cost of the fixers, the controllers and the planners. At £24 per week his tax would be £4 5s. 9d., so that he would then be £3 15s. 3d. per week worse off than he was when his wage was £8 per week. Taxation is not a factor taken into consideration in determining the base rate, and the impact of the substantial increase in taxation flowing from this incidence can be appreciated when it is realised that the base rate has increased from £4 2s. in December, 1939, to £10 7s. per week in 1951, and that over 2,089,000 of the 2,438,498 taxpayers are affected.

And our economists advocate higher taxation as an antidote to inflation.

Double Taxation

Whilst it is not possible to deal exhaustively with the Double Taxation Relief Convention between United Kingdom and Australia, I offer the following observations.

The agreement resulting from the convention dealt with the problem of arranging the taxation systems of both countries so as to avoid double taxation of the same income and to obtain the co-operation of the taxing authorities in both countries in order to prevent tax evasion.

The agreement works satisfactorily so far as certain classes of income, derived from one country by a resident of the other country, are exempt from tax in the former country. These include shipping and air transport profits, certain trading profits not arising through a permanent establishment, patent and copyright royalties, pensions, purchased annuities, and earnings of temporary business visitors.

However, apart from these few classes of taxpayers the provisions are so intricate and highly technical that many taxpayers in Australia who may be entitled to relief from double taxation are not prepared to undertake the preparation of applications under the agreement, unless the amount involved is substantial.

In some cases the agreement appears to create anomalies. For example, persons *who are resident in both countries* are, for double taxation relief, not deemed to be *resident in either country*.

A company which is incorporated in Australia and has the management and control of its business in the United Kingdom is, for tax purposes, resident in Australia and also in the United Kingdom. It is, therefore, neither resident in Australia nor in the United Kingdom in the meaning of Article II (1) (*f*) of the convention.

With taxation at its present almost penal levels, it does not appear that the conventions will go far towards re-establishing international trade and investment.

Although not entirely related to the conventions, the taxation of companies in Australia and the further taxation of the dividends in the hands of share-holders, paid from profits which have been assessed to company taxation, is double taxation, which tends to discourage investment. When, in addition, these dividends are payable to foreign investors and become subject to further tax in the country of the investor's residence, in some cases, there is no residue of income left in the hands of the recipient of the dividends. Whilst such results are possible, an investigating accountant must advise a prospective investor against making such an investment.

From the foregoing brief summary of the incidence of taxation in Australia, it is apparent that it tends to discourage foreign investment, to deter increased production, is inflationary in its effect and provides no incentive to earn more, and, by reducing the value of money, penalises the thrifty.

This observation can no doubt be made of any Dominion or country, and the interest will lie in comparing the incidence of taxation between the respective communities. It is hoped the figures and other material given in this paper will prove to be useful in this regard.

THE INCIDENCE OF TAXATION

by

G. P. KAPADIA, B.COM., F.C.A.(INDIA)
Institute of Chartered Accountants of India

I. THE GENERAL CONCEPT AS TO TAXES AND FINANCIAL REQUIREMENTS OF GOVERNMENTS

The incidence of taxation is a subject which must be considered in relation to the person who actually bears the burden of taxation or, in other words, who pays the tax. Distinctions may have to be made between direct and indirect taxes and the money burden or the real burden. The determining factors may also include the economic condition of the country in respect of which such an examination is made. Before doing so, it is essential to consider the question of the financial requirements of governments. According to the usual concept regarding these requirements, the three main purposes of taxation are:

(a) Expenditure for the common good;
(b) Economic policy;
(c) Services on a basis of contribution equal to, below, or above the cost of those services.

These considerations ignore the fact that in particular types of economy, it is possible that expenditure may not necessarily be incurred for the general public good but nevertheless such expenditure must be taken into consideration in assessing the position in which the country is placed. While the finances of nations in the past could be regulated in a detached manner irrespective of world conditions, the present-day position is that the impact of conditions in other countries is always felt and, out of necessity or otherwise, the tax systems of the different countries are to some extent regulated by world conditions. Normally the financial requirements of government would be determined on the basis of national income and the nature of such income but taking into consideration world conditions, the tax structure need not necessarily be based on the national income concept.

II. TAXES IN ANCIENT TIMES

It was usually felt in ancient times that the controlling authority in any country had to increase or decrease its expenditure in proportion to rises or falls in taxation revenue. In course of time, however, with greater stability obtaining in the governance of countries, the concept that all taxation should be based on the general approval of those governed lost much of its significance and ultimately the raising of public finances became linked with the collective requirements of the people: the financing of governments was for

558

the main purpose of raising taxes for the general public good. It will not be out of place to discuss here the provisions as to the financial requirements of the ruler as found stated in 'Manusmruti', that is, the Code of Manu. We find a mention made about the appointment of tax collectors, who should be clever and should be well versed in the science of augmenting the contributions to the State Exchequer. Such persons were expected to be conversant with conditions of peace and of war. They were also expected to be versed in the languages of the different countries. A distinction was made between the tax collections from the Brahmins and from the Kshatriyas, Vaishyas and Sudras. The king had to protect the country by having armed forces under generals, and there was a provision for the levy of a State charge on commodities for the protection of the individual parts of the State territory. The Brahmins were definitely exempted from any levy of taxation because they were held in the highest respect. The Kshatriyas, as the protectors of the country, had not to bear a high burden of taxation, but the Vaishyas, that is, the trading classes, had to pay taxes which were related to the purchases, sales and expenditure relating to goods, to messing charges and to other expenses including shop and godown rents. These provisions give a clear indication as to income taxation which must have obtained even in those ancient times. Detailed provisions are found as to the method of levy in respect of trading in cattle, trading in gold, trading in food-grains and various other commodities. The basic consideration, however, was that the persons discharging various functions or carrying out various activities should get an adequate compensation for such services and the king had to levy taxes keeping this principle in view. The working classes or the artisans and the manual workers were not exempted, but their contribution to the State taxation was in the shape of compulsory services which they had to give to the State. The king levied taxes on a yearly basis and it was improper to harass the people by heavy taxes. It is clear from the above observations that, even as early as in the times of Manu, there was a clear concept as to public finance and the incidence of taxation. No doubt this concept was not a wide one, as the economy of the Indian sub-continent then was of a totally different character to our present economy and was unaffected by many factors which now concern us. Expenditure by governments was, however, made for the general public good.

III. THE ROLE OF THE STATE AND THE FINANCIAL STRUCTURE

The State in every developed society has to play an important role in economic activity. While the State could not influence the economic life of its citizens in the past, present-day conditions have created such a position that governments in power contribute greatly to the development or curtailment of individual enterprise. Human nature always aims at satisfying its own wants and therefore endeavours to obtain means for the satisfaction of such wants. To extend the analysis made above with regard to conditions obtaining in India, the four main divisions in which society was divided and the castes and the sub-castes which persisted for a number of years give a very vivid example of the contribution of State policy to the creation of a particular economic existence without any planning. Governments normally engaged in the provision of some economic services, directly or by monopolies or other means, create conditions for the performance of such services. They also provide social security for the citizens. It should, however, be mentioned that when comparisons are being made between State enterprises and private enterprises, it is the duty of citizens to see that private business is carried on in the public interest, and to ensure that conditions are created for the proper conduct of private enterprise so that it does not compete with the public interest. With this proviso, the policy of taxation or the raising of finances should not be to strike at the very basic foundation of private enterprise but rather to give momentum to desirable developments.

Questions relating to government services being given in return for contributions equal to, below, or above the cost of those services are difficult to discuss, and State policy cannot be regulated in definite relation to such contributions. In this paper the subject for discussion is rather the actual effect of taxation.

As to the levy of taxes by governments, another important observation which requires to be made is that such taxation cannot be on a uniform basis in different countries: much depends upon the predominant income-producing factors and the sources of income. Thus the economic policy and the taxation structure of a country which is predominantly agricultural would differ from the one which is highly industrialised and further qualifications should be made in respect of partly-agricultural and partly-industrialised countries. Apart from this, the question as to whether a particular country has its own government or is governed by another country is also a very important factor to be considered. To cite the case of India itself, the economic policy and taxation structure during the British regime were modelled with a view to suiting the conditions of the governing country, that is, the United Kingdom, and the attention which the other normal factors deserved did not have full importance.

IV. THE DEFINITION OF A TAX

Tax is a compulsory payment or contribution for the support of the governing authority or for some public purpose. A tax may be raised for defending the State, for regulating or promoting social or other objectives or for the granting of collective amenities. While in ancient times the contribution of the members of society was in the shape of services or contribution of commodities, the concept has so evolved that the members of society now contribute funds for the welfare of society as a whole. A tax may be raised purely for the purposes of revenue or it may be a tax with the twofold object of raising revenue and regulating a particular trade or other activity. Originally the concept of a tax was that it was a voluntary payment and government appealed to the people to make contributions. Thereafter the concept became changed to one of sacrifice, then of an obligation on the part of the taxpayer, and ultimately it evolved into the theory of compulsion.

V. The Structure of the British and American Systems

It is worth noting that the net income-tax which is the mainstay of the British revenue system was first introduced in England in 1798. It became a permanent part of the revenue system in 1842. While in the beginning the tax was proportional and not progressive, the progressive element found place in 1907. Death duties, which were first introduced as stamp duties, were not found productive, and in 1796 they were replaced by the levy of a tax on the transfer of property itself. Owing to strong opposition from landowners this tax was applied only to personal property but finally it was levied on real property in 1853. The form in which this levy is found was given its first shape in 1894.

On an examination of the evolution of public finance in the United States of America, we find that the formative period is linked up with the peopling of the continent, the construction of railroads, the gradual development of industry, the progress of agriculture—its decline and stabilisation. The Federal Constitution which was ratified in 1789 gave the Federal Government ample powers to balance its budget, re-establish its credit and to pay off its war debts including some of the debts which the new Government had assumed. The Federal Government was given the power to levy tariffs and excise, the former being an exclusive right. It may be noted that the American colonies founded their tax institutions upon British experience but some variations had to be made on account of the different conditions obtaining. Public expenditure in the colonial era was modest. There were no social welfare appropriations and public works were unimportant. The direct taxes employed by the colonies were the poll tax, faculty tax, which was the substitute for the property tax and applied to the earning capacity of artisans and of professional people, and the property tax. The general property tax developed in America later on. The inheritance tax was first introduced in the tax system of the State in 1885, but it took its modern and effective form only in the twentieth century. The position is similar with taxes on income. Income-tax was first introduced by the Federal Government during the Civil War but it was discontinued after 1872. The sixteenth amendment to the Federal constitution relating to income taxation was made to clear the difficult position which required the Federal tax to be apportioned amongst the States according to population and the specific amendment provided that the Congress should have the power to tax income from whatever sources derived without apportionment among the several states and without regard to any census or enumeration. It is interesting to note that 'income' was not defined even in this amendment. The power of the Congress to define 'income' subject to the guidance from the Supreme Court remains intact.

It is also significant to note that taxes on income were not altogether foreign to ancient times and such levies can be found in China, Greece, Egypt and India. British income-tax started during the wars with France under the influence of William Pitt. A tax on personal income as indicated by personal expenditures and property was levied in 1798. Income-tax was dispensed with in 1802, reinstituted in 1803, dispensed with for the second time in 1816 and it was ultimately in 1842 that the tax was again restored. As to the United States of America, the Congress enacted an income-tax Act in 1861 but this was drafted very hurriedly and its operation was withheld for the drawing up of a new measure in the next year. Very few deductions were allowed and therefore it was a gross income-tax rather than a net income-tax.

The broad classification of the taxes between (1) income-tax and death duties which are treated as direct taxes, and (2) consumption taxes which are treated as indirect taxes, requires close examination. It is essential that in determining the question whether a particular tax is direct or indirect, the incidence of such taxation should be taken into consideration. A tax on a commodity is presumed to be an indirect tax and may be classified as a consumption tax, but with the complexity of world economy and the post-war effects through which we are passing, it would be difficult to make an assertion one way or the other. With the increasing price of the commodity due to the tax rate paid, it may be that the price increase bears a higher proportion than that reflected by the actual levy of the tax on the commodity and therefore, to that extent, the incidence would be borne to a greater extent by the consumer himself. At the same time the fact that the income gets augmented to the extent of the difference between the tax on the commodity and the price increase being borne by the seller himself, the burden is not necessarily on the consumer. Similarly, for income taxation, with an increase in the rate of tax or the burden of income-tax, there would be a reflection on the commodity prices if the person assessed has a monopoly of the articles, income from which is taxed in his hands. This shifting would, however, be defeated in a controlled economy. One should, therefore, talk in terms of a tax being normally a direct tax or an indirect tax. In this analysis one has to ignore totally the effects of anti-social acts like black-marketing because such factors have altogether a different bearing on the incidence of taxation.

VI. Exemption of Capital

Casual capital gains are excluded in the computation of the income-tax liability in the United Kingdom and only those gains which arise in the regular course of business or a related activity are taken into consideration. In the United States of America, however, capital gains and losses are classed as short-term or long-term. If the disposal of property takes place within six months, the investment is taken as a short-term investment so that the profit or loss on sale or disposal is taken into consideration in determining the income-tax liability and the tax charged is at the usual rates. But in respect of long-term gains, only one-half of the excess is included and the maximum tax rate applicable to this income is 50 per cent. In actual effect the levy is not more than 25 per cent. upon the long-term gains. In India, however, the capital gains levy remained in force for a couple of years, that is, from 1946 to 1948, and the levy was made by subjecting to charge a capital gain if it exceeded Rs.15,000. The charge was not a heavy one and the maximum was only 25 per cent.

In this connection it is desirable to make a distinction between an item of capital gain, an item of income gain, and an item of casual gain. Revenue authorities would aim at treating a gain item as an income gain because that brings the maximum revenue. Failing that, they would try to pin down the gain as a capital gain and the question of a casual gain which is exempted would only arise in cases where the revenue authorities would have no argument. The formula adopted under the United States taxing statutes of differentiating between short-term and long-term investments seems to be equitable for the reason that long-term holdings should not be treated as regular deals or regular activities amounting to business. Usually the argument advanced could be to the effect that the intention at the time of making the investment would be the deciding factor, but the determining factor in actual practice is the date of the disposal, the period of the actual holding and the circumstances under which the disposal took place. Taking these factors into consideration, a proper solution to the matter on an equitable basis would be to make a distinction according to the time factor in respect of the holding.

VII. THE BURDEN OF TAX ON THE NATION AS A WHOLE

The burden on the nation as a whole would be heavy if in relation to the expenditure incurred by the State, the benefits accruing to society were not commensurate with the charge of the tax. Linked with this question is the question of the public borrowings or the public debts. It has been said that the tax structure of a country and its public debt should be so shaped as to leave an equitable burden on the various generations. In other words, it has been argued that one generation should not pay for another. In all such discussion, the complexity of present-day world conditions, and the effects of concentration of material power in the hands of very few nations, are factors which definitely govern the fiscal policies of the various countries, and are ignored. It is not possible for any country to have a detached outlook; there is an automatic shaping of the tax structures of different countries not merely in relation to the particular economy of that country but to the world economy. In fact, the present position is such that the State has to find funds for the carrying out of particular objectives and these objectives are not necessarily related to the services provided for the subjects or to the amenities granted. The collection is not a mere revenue collection but it is a collection based on the economy of the particular country and having regard to world conditions. A country which launches upon industrialisation and a new build-up has problems quite different from those of other countries very much advanced in this respect, and therefore the expenditure on capital outlay bears a higher proportion to the normal services expenditure. With this position obtaining, ambitious schemes for capital layouts cannot come to fruition without a proper borrowing programme. The expansion of the various activities of such countries are therefore regulated by the forces which make such capital available. A well regulated public debt results in an equitable distribution of the burden of taxation. On the other hand, if such a state thought in terms of additional taxes, the burden would fall on the present generation while the benefit would be reaped by coming generations.

So far as the individual taxpayer is concerned, the benefits accruing to him as a result of the tax levy should be commensurate; taxes have an effect on the incentive to work and on private enterprise, which might perhaps not undertake risks to inaugurate large enterprises. In other words, the individual being scared of heavy taxation may not exert himself as he otherwise would. It is therefore necessary that public expenditure should be properly directed so that the burdens of taxation are more than balanced by the advantages accruing from spending. If such a position could be created, the ideal objective of taxation would be achieved, namely, that it would produce a net social benefit on the whole, although it may cause a net social loss to some taxpayers or a particular class or classes of taxpayers.

VIII. The Impact and the Shifting of Income Taxes

A tax on net income is typically not shifted. When one thinks in terms of the shifting of the burden of tax on income, it has to be realised that the tax is payable only if there is a net income and the amount of such tax is in proportion to or gets augmented by the income itself. Moreover, some part of the net income is retained after the payment of taxes. The net amount remaining after the payment of taxes at the different levels of income should be properly regulated according to the cost of living and the normal requirements for expenditure called for in respect of the different ranges. It is doubtful whether as a result of income taxation itself, the taxpayer as a business man would actually sell a smaller quantity in order to obtain a higher price. If such a thing happened, the net income itself would fall; in turn, there would be lower taxes but automatically the net surplus would be lowered. Thus the taxpayer would be left in a worse position by the attempt to shift the incidence of taxation and there could be a shifting, if at all, only in respect of concerns run on a monopolistic basis. The endeavour of every business enterprise is to increase and take to the maximum level the net amount left after the payment of taxes on income, and since marginal revenue and marginal cost cannot change with the application of the net income-tax, the incidence of such tax must fall on the person receiving such income. The higher prices resulting from a rise in demand or a rise in the marginal cost do not necessarily occur as a result of the taxes on income. Taking the other side of the picture, if the tax on income were to be shifted by the increased quantity of sales and the lowering of market price, and in case it is presumed that such factors do obtain before the tax is actually charged, it might be found that these factors did not obtain. All this discussion should lead to one irresistible conclusion, that the taxes on personal income have their incidence upon the person who receives the income and these taxes cannot be shifted.

A distinction may, however, be attempted in the case of the tax on the net income of companies. It may be argued that the tax in this case can be shifted to the shareholders. This is not a correct approach because dividend is a distribution and not the price paid. In other words, the incidence of tax upon a company is, as a matter of fact, an incidence upon the persons who own the company, that is, the shareholders. Because of the payment of the tax by the company, the income is reduced correspondingly and there is so much less to distribute between the owners, that is, the shareholders.

IX. The Evasion of Taxes

Under any economic structure, evasion comes in when the rate of tax passes the limit which can be borne by the taxpayer. In respect of indirect taxes, the burden can be shifted, and therefore the effect is felt when the burden is rather too heavy and the ultimate payer feels that it is beyond his capacity to bear that burden. Even otherwise the evasion element would be there in respect of commodities where the supply is less than the demand. In the case of direct taxes, however, the position is aggravated inasmuch as there is resentment against paying more by way of direct taxation because, after such payment, the residue is very considerably reduced, i.e. in the higher income level, the higher rate of taxation and the higher standard of living reduces the net surplus to a further extent. Naturally, therefore, attempts have been made to conceal income where the rates of income-tax are heavy. Such a concealment may have a twofold disadvantage inasmuch as the State may lose not only on the charge of income-tax, but also on the consumption tax in respect of commodities. As an example, one may cite the case of the sales tax obtaining in India. To evade income-tax, no record would be made of transactions effected and such transactions would take place in cash with the result that sales tax would be lost to government. Again, the problems arising as a result of anti-social acts like black-marketing would also have to be considered and it may be that, with a steep increase in prices and the rates of income-tax, articles in short supply would go into the black market and these would not be dealt with in a proper manner. There is thus a likelihood of a total omission to the extent that there would be no record, and where the article in question is a controlled one, particularly at the production stage, only the controlled price factor would enter into the picture and the balance would go unaccounted for. It is therefore for consideration whether direct taxes which have such an impact on prices and which may encourage evasion, should not be dealt with on a different basis and the taxation policy should not be so revised that the burden of taxation is not extraordinarily heavy. Evasion on a large scale must be dealt with by any governing authority with severe punishment of the tax dodger. Such a process may be adopted either as a deterrent or a corrective. If it is adopted as a corrective the result is the unearthing of huge financial resources which have gone underground. In this connection it will not be out of place to make a reference to the setting up of an Investigation Commission in India whose function it is to make exhaustive inquiries into cases where wholesale evasion of income-tax is suspected. This is not the place to make a critical study of the achievements of the Commission, but the fact remains that huge resources remaining underground have a great bearing on the economic and financial structure of the country. The poser which is raised by post-war conditions and large-scale evasion of income-tax is whether during abnormal times an indiscriminate increase in the rates and levy of taxes on income is justified or not. It may be that an increase which is not so heavy and so extraordinary may not meet with so much resistance and the State would perhaps collect much more with a lesser levy than what it would with a prohibitive one. However, it behoves the citizens of any state to make disclosures if they genuinely believe that the tax structure and economy of the country should be better regulated, and they owe it to themselves to give their own proper contribution as citizens of that state. While it is the obligation of the State to have its economy so regulated as to result in the maximum possible good of the community as a whole, it is equally the obligation of the subjects that they discharge their duties towards the State in a manner which helps the proper regulation of the financial economy and structure of the country. There is a saying in India that in countries where the king is a trader, the people are paupers. To quote a Russian historian, 'the State may swell and the people may shrink'. It is therefore desirable that the State should swell or shrink with the people and that the State so regulates its economy that it does not interfere with private enterprise, does not assume absolute and indiscriminate control thereof and regulates such enterprise only for the common good of society.

X. 'INCOME' AND 'TRADING PROFITS'

No attempt is made in the United States to define income. This definition is left to be determined by the Congress itself under the guidance of the Supreme Court. However, the word 'income' has a definite significance and it has to be distinguished from what is 'capital'. With attempts made to tax capital gains, whether by way of short-term range or long-term range, the word 'income' for the purposes of income-tax loses much of its significance and it has cynically been mentioned that income is something on which income-tax is charged. Leaving aside this interpretation, normally the word 'income' connotes a regular flow or something in the nature of an incoming which is not of an enduring character or something of an exceptional nature or a non-recurring nature. Legislation in various countries and the judicial interpretations make the meaning quite clear and it is more the facts of a particular case which determines the issue whether under the taxing statute a particular item is an item of income or not. The Tucker Committee has simplified the matter to some extent by settling the issue as to what should be included in trading profits and what should not. The findings of this committee should go a long way in clearing up various ambiguities and doubts.

XI. ASSESSMENT OF NON-RESIDENTS—DOUBLE TAXATION RELIEF
AND AVOIDANCE

So far as the assessment of non-residents or their activities are concerned, the United Kingdom legislation makes a clear distinction between trade with the United Kingdom and trade in the United Kingdom. While the latter is definitely brought within the purview of tax, trading with the United Kingdom is left out of consideration. However, the income accruing to a resident or a resident company having its controlling power or brain in the United Kingdom has to suffer taxation on its entire world income. The determining factor is where the real control lies. In India the position is different, and the provisions of Sections 42 and 43 of the Indian Income Tax Act are so wide that transactions which could be rightly termed as trading with India can be included and treated as trading in India. In fact, even principal to principal transactions could be taxed, the only requirement being that there should be a business connection. A very wide interpretation was made in the past but recently executive instructions have been issued whereby, in substance, only trading in India becomes assessable. In India, the question of the residence of an individual and of a company is decided by statutory provisions and is not left to be determined by the background of judicial decisions as in the United Kingdom. A company is non-resident unless the entire control and management of its affairs is in India or more than 50 per cent. of the income arises to the company in India.

The method of the levy of tax on assessees, whether they are individuals or corporations, is on world income basis in most countries and with this position obtaining, the question of double taxation arrangement assumes importance. In fact, the aim now is to have double taxation avoidance arrangements in preference to double taxation relief arrangements, and workable formulas have been agreed to avoid double taxation. With world economy as it obtains to-day, it is necessary that these arrangements should be made. They might be beneficial to very advanced countries having multifarious activities in other countries, but may not be quite suited to countries whose nationals have activities restricted to their own country or whose activities are not spread out so widely.

XII. Economic Considerations

The tax problems of every country are focused on the problem of reducing the restrictive effects of taxation to the minimum, taking into consideration the facilities for raising the necessary revenues. In fact, however, what happens is that in formulating tax policies, the conservation of incentives is overlooked or subordinated to the other objectives which are deemed to be more important. A tax system which creates a position whereby enterprise is impaired and where there is no incentive for the development of new industries, gives results which are both uneconomic and undesirable. Again, there should be an incentive for the existing businesses or enterprises to expand. The higher the rates of tax and the lower the depreciation allowance, the less the amount available for replacement or for expansion. Such a position not only takes away incentive but is a definite deterrent to persons who launch upon new industrial enterprises. Then again there is the question of incentive for the people to invest their savings. Human nature tends towards the retention of a net surplus and it is more beneficial to the economy of any country to direct the surplus savings of the nation to investment in equity capital because it is by such investment that greater expansion can be achieved. This factor also supports the conclusion that taxes on income which are very heavy prevent the investment of surplus moneys. There is also one more consideration and that is the incentive to work. Heavier income-tax takes away the incentive to work and taxpayers would be satisfied to save a little less rather than to put in more strenuous efforts—efforts which would result in only a very small slice of additional income being left with them.

With regard to incentives for new enterprise, a qualification may have to be made in that persons having very large incomes may not be deterred from starting new enterprises, for the simple reason that the new enterprises, if successful, would pay for themselves, whereas if there were a loss, a major portion thereof would be contributed by the State itself. This would apply with greater force to individual enterprises and to some extent to corporate enterprise. For existing businesses it may be that, with heavy tax being imposed, outside capital might be attracted and this may have a major effect on the country's economy. Thus the tax system of any country should be based on considerations which are related to economic incentives and these considerations are very important for the financial structure of such countries. The great majority of the population in most countries falls into the category of investors, and it is of national importance that they should be encouraged to invest their money. The tax structure should therefore take account not only of the risks involved in investment but also the necessity of leaving with the investor an adequate return on his capital.

XIII. The Evolution of the Financial System of India

For a number of years, the Government of India had to rely on income from agriculture. Agriculture being dependent upon rainfall, the incomings were regulated by the monsoon. In 1858 the land revenue was of the order of Rs.15 crores against the total revenue of Rs.30 crores. Income-tax was unknown then and customs yielded a small revenue of Rs.2 crores. Even after the imposition of income-tax the revenue from customs and income-tax was not considerable. In fact, taxes other than those relating to land were considered to be unjustified. This was the position up to 1885. From 1858 to 1919, land revenue, opium and salt taxes and charges showed a decline, while customs and excise increased. The increase after the commencement of the First World War was very noticeable. There was also a change in the economy of the country by reason of industrial expansion. So far as expenditure was concerned, more was spent on security services, and social services came into the picture quite late. This was partly due to the governance of India by a foreign power. Even in earlier times good rulers gave much attention to the social services side and the economy obtaining under the rules of Asoka the Great, Chandragupta of Magadha and Harsha of Kanoj are monumental examples of the rulers spending considerable amounts in the cause of public utility. It is worth noting that defence expenditure which was standing at

Rs.16·7 crores in 1857–58 rose to Rs.54·3 crores in 1930–31. A similar increase was found in the case of expenditure on war, justice and general administration. The increase with regard to education was a very marked one: it was ·2 crores in 1857–58 and it rose to 13·8 crores in 1930–31.

The taxation policy during the period 1877 to 1885 showed marked changes. Famine, war and loss by exchange considerably depleted the finances of the country. It was during this period that customs duties were abolished and free trade having been accomplished in England, it was but natural that India followed suit. The real reason, however, was of a political character inasmuch as cotton textile mills in England wanted this type of preference at the cost of the Indian concerns who were compelled to refrain from the manufacture of finer fabrics. Rapid improvement, however, in the finances of the country was noticed after 1883 but this did not last long. The provincial finances also developed but despite the transfer of certain heads of revenue to the provinces (for example, income from Government estates, stone quarries, excise, stamps, law and justice) the Central Government retained the major share of the increase of revenue. It was found that the revenues transferred to the provincial governments were inadequate and lump-sum contributions had to be made by the Government of India for provincial expenditure. The provinces naturally were indifferent about fostering land revenue and therefore the system of sharing revenues was introduced in 1882–83. A certain portion of the total revenue was allocated to each province. However, posts and telegraphs, mint, and other heads of a central character were kept as 'Imperial' and only those heads which were definitely of a provincial character were marked as provincial.

Being faced with a deficit of Rs.3½ crores in 1894, the Government introduced customs duty again. But even in this imposition of 5 per cent., cotton yarn and cotton fabrics were excluded. Exchange stabilisation came in with the rupee being stabilised at 1s. 4d., and the introduction of the gold exchange standard. A surplus position was then attained and this surplus position remained up to 1901–02. During this period railways showed great development; the total mileage which was 1,587 in 1861 jumped to 25,366 in 1901. Irrigation works were also undertaken, the maximum development being in the Punjab.

The progress of decentralisation of provincial finances continued and by 1905 the provinces had secured substantial powers in finance. But, in spite of increased delegation of financial powers to provincial governments, the control of the Government of India remained intact. There were differences of opinion between the Government of India and the provincial governments but the powers given to the provinces remained of a delegated nature. It is also worth noting that certain provincial governments pointed out to the Decentralisation Commission, which was appointed in England after Lord Curzon had left India, that there was considerable inequality in the distribution of tax burdens between the different provinces.

The next phase of change was between 1905 and 1920. The most interesting feature was found in the position obtaining during the First World War.

The expenditure on defence rose by 300 per cent. As against the figure of £20 million in 1913–14 the figure on this account jumped to £60 million in 1920. No doubt increased prices were in part responsible for the increased expenditure but conditions emanating from the World War were the main cause. With increased expenditure, the prospects for more revenue from indirect taxation were not bright. Imports as well as exports fell and the customs revenue also fell. In 1916 although the general tariff was raised to 7½ per cent., the import duty of 3½ per cent. *ad valorem* on woven goods was not revised. Here again opposition from textile manufacturers in England prevented an increase. This clearly shows that political considerations weighed much in the shaping of the financial policy of this country in those times. The next phase started with the Chelmsford Reforms and the concept of 'responsible government by stages'. With the diarchy in government and the reserved and transferred heads, some divesting of the powers by the ruling nation took place. There was also some relaxation in central control but this was only limited. For the first time in 1922 and as a result of the appointment of the Fiscal Commission, the Government of India became 'free' in that sense of the word from the control of the Secretary of State. However, certain specified heads of expenditure were non-votable by the legislatures and could not be discussed.

Then came the period of depression between 1924–25 and 1935–36. The most critical position arose, however, in 1931, when there was a deficit of Rs.11½ crores. This was the result not only of depression but of political upheaval, which contributed to it to a major extent. There was economic boycott: there were hartals and great political consciousness amongst the people. The year 1935, however, showed considerable improvement and with substantial gold exports, sterling purchases could be made and currency reserves were strengthened. The Government of India Act of 1935 provided for full provincial autonomy but so far most of the expenditure was for external defence and internal security. It was only after provincial autonomy became an accomplished fact that the questions of economic and social services were considered.

The levy of income-tax in 1861 brought in only Rs.2 crores and up to 1915 there was no appreciable change. The figure jumped to Rs.11 crores in 1918 and to Rs.22 crores in 1920–21. There was a gradual decrease subsequently and the collections in 1937 stood at Rs.13 crores. It is interesting to note that agricultural incomes were not exempt from 1860, the year of introduction, to 1873. With the reintroduction of income-tax in 1886, such incomes were exempted and these have continued to be exempt since then.

In the subsequent period defence expenditure showed a further marked increase. From Rs.49·55 crores in 1939–40, this expenditure went up to Rs.360·23 crores in 1945–46. Civil expenditure which stood at Rs. 45·03 crores in 1939–40 rose to Rs.124·34 crores in 1945–46. When this period is considered, it is necessary to discuss taxation during the Second World War. As is usual during such times, the governing authority resorted increasingly to direct taxation. The rates of income-tax and super-tax were increased and excess profits tax was imposed. There was also an imposition of business profits tax and of capital gains tax. The gross tax revenue, which was Rs.80·67 crores in 1939–40 rose to Rs.283·27 crores in 1945–46. It is interesting to note that while taxes on income increased, the revenue from customs declined. From Rs. 45·88 crores in 1939–40, it went down to Rs.26·57 crores in 1943–44 and improved to Rs.39·76 crores in 1944–45. A vital change was brought about with the introduction of the 1947 Budget, which, according to the then Finance Minister of the Interim Government, was prepared with a view to doing away with the glaring contrasts and disparities in the wealth and income of the citizens. Marked increase in the rate of super-tax on higher incomes was provided for and business profits tax was introduced. The result of this extraordinary Budget was fear and frustration and there was considerable lack of confidence, lack of initiative, and lack of enterprise. A change, however, was brought in by subsequent Budgets and various measures of tax relief in the Budgets of 1948–49 and 1949–50 were introduced to generate an atmosphere of confidence and hope, so that private enterprise might not be curbed and the business community could have an interest in the stepping-up of the production of the country. This was the change effected after the partition of the sub-continent.

The present position is quite intriguing. The total revenue, which was Rs.122 crores in 1935–36, has stepped up to Rs.347 crores for 1950–51. Expenditure which stood at Rs.122 crores in 1935–36 has gone up to Rs.337 crores in 1950–51. Customs revenue stands at Rs.106·5 crores, Union excise duties stand at Rs.71·5 crores and taxes on income at Rs.127·4 crores. With regard to expenditure, the amount relating to defence services stands at Rs.168 crores, that for civil administration at Rs.50 crores and the amount in respect of debt services at Rs.36·5 crores. It will thus appear that in comparison to the figures for 1935–36, revenue from customs and excise duties shows an increase of about 300 per cent. while the increase in taxes on income shows an increase of about 700 per cent. These figures should give sufficient indication of the fact that with the expansion of the economy of the country, its political emancipation and rapid industrialisation, direct taxes show a marked increase. The problems facing the country now are of a totally different character. The State has to look to the stabilisation of the financial position and at the same time to provide more and more for social services and to keep pace with industrial expansion. The coming years are bound to show a reorientation of the financial policy so that taxation policy leaves enough scope for private enterprise and at the same time preserves an equilibrium between the various classes of society. The attempt to do away with disparities may result in production being hit and no state can afford to think of a financial policy which hits at the very root of the economic structure of the country. A tax system which 'taxes' the economy of the country and takes away incentive is a method of merely preserving for the time being, the government in power. A balanced system based on the peculiar economy of a country, spreading the burden between direct and indirect taxes, and adding to the momentum of the savings or investment by the subjects in equity capital, would perhaps be an ideal one.

XIV. THE SOVIET ECONOMY

In relation to the different economies of the democracies, it is desirable to discuss the Soviet economy. One important fact to be borne in mind in this connection is that the economy of every country has a definite bearing on its political set-up. In other words, the financial structure of every state is regulated by the nature of its political organisation. The unique feature of the Soviet economic system is that there is State ownership as against private ownership and such ownership is regulated by the dictatorial role of the ruling Communist Party. Not much is known about the internal reactions to the economy in Soviet Russia and it would be guesswork if one attempted to make a comparison and say definitely whether the economy of the democracies of the world is the better one. Because of the peculiar structure of the Soviet economy, and the political set-up, it is but natural that direct taxation in the shape of income-tax has not that regulating effect which it has in equalising the burden between the different classes of society in the democracies of the world and particularly in the United Kingdom and the United States of America. The same observation could be also made about the Commonwealth countries including India. The highest sur-tax in Russia is reported to be only about 13 per cent. as against the very high percentages which leave not more than 13 per cent. in the hands of the taxpayers in other countries. It cannot, however, be denied that the ruling Communist Party in the United States of Soviet Russia have created a unified Socialist State with a definite financial structure. This Socialist State has been in existence for quite a number of years so that even in other parts of the world its influence and impact have been felt, and it may be that in some countries, particularly under Communist influence, it has been copied. The compulsory enlistment of a mass of humanity for a common objective with a set ideal and a dream is more or less enforced by the ruling party in the U.S.S.R. The progress made can be measured by the commodity productions of important items. The output has considerably increased as compared to the figures for the period prior to the First World War. Technical education and training have expanded fully and this progress has been more or less on the same lines as obtained in America during the period of that country's industrial growth. One consideration, however, which should not be lost sight of, is that in the case of democracies where the capitalist system has been in vogue for centuries together, the important factor is the concentration of money power. As against this in Russia, we find the concentration, not of the money power, but of the ruling power itself. Concentration in either case is inevitable and although the Soviet economy may be styled as the one regulated under Communist principles, the capitalist element does exist in a hidden form inasmuch as there is concentration of power as against the concentration of money. There is concentration of power and compulsory regulation of the activities of a mass of humanity; it goes without saying that the different type of political set-up should have a different type of economy and therefore the need for levelling-up of the incomes or the material possessions of the subjects does not arise. The levelling-up is made by the political set-up itself and therefore direct taxation has not that significance in such an economy as it has in the economies of the democracies.

XV. The Ideal of an Independent India and Consideration of the Different Economies of the World

In relation to India, an attempt has been made to level up inequalities. The matter was dealt with by the Planning Commission which was set up in March, 1950, by the Government of India. The terms of reference made clear mention of the fundamental rights as guaranteed by the Constitution of India, which constitution has at the same time

'enunciated certain directive principles of State policy and in particular provided that the State should strive to promote the welfare of the people by securing and protecting as effectively as it may, a social order in which justice, social, economic and political, shall inform all the institutions of the national life and shall direct its policy towards securing among other things that the citizens, men and women equally, have the right to an adequate means of livelihood, that the ownership and control of the material resources of the community are so distributed as best to subserve the common good and that the operation of the economic system does not result in the concentration of wealth and means of production to the common detriment'.

The above enunciation shows a trend towards not only the levelling-up of inequalities in the social and economic structure, but also a definite attempt to regulate the ownership and control of the material resources of the community so that their distribution aims at common good as against individual benefit. It does not necessarily follow that this trend is a trend towards State ownership or State regulation of economy. It is rather a more progressive form of economy for the democracies of the world and it may be taken to be a happy compromise between the existing capitalist structures and the other extreme of the Soviet economy.

While the political set-up or organisation of any state regulates the financial structure or the economy of that country, it is also true that a particular type of economic structure or planning ultimately resolves itself into a different type of political system. While attempts may be made by legislation to change the social or economic structure, the latter may so evolve itself as to actually influence the political system itself. It therefore remains to be seen how far the present political set-up of the important democracies of the world will have an impact on the political set-up of the other countries of the world and their financial economies. It also remains to be seen how far the evolution of different types of economies in the other parts of the world and the Soviet economy itself, which has been described above, will influence ultimately the political set-up of the important countries of the world. While the Soviet economy and its political structure have attracted some attention because of their apparent success in recent times, the democracies of the world and the financial structures and economies flowing therefrom have stood the test of time for centuries together. The enlightened approach made towards the State's obligation for social and economic uplift made in the Constitution of India, leaves a message of hope not only for the democracies of the world, but for all types of political systems and for all types of financial structures.

THE INCIDENCE OF TAXATION IN NORWAY

by

THOMAS KJELDSBERG

Norges Statsautoriserte Revisorers Forening, Norway

I. INTRODUCTION

The constitution of Norway places authority to impose taxes with the Storting (Diet). The only limitation stated is to the effect that taxes may not be imposed for more than one year at a time.

The distinction between direct and indirect taxation follows the usual lines. The more important categories of the latter are purchase tax and taxes on spirits, beer, tobacco and chocolate. Export levies may be classified amongst indirect taxes. They are imposed by the Director of Price Regulations on the authority of a special law. Part of this revenue is used for the general benefit of the trades affected.

Direct taxation comprises two main types, property tax and tax on net capital and income. This summary concerns mainly capital and income taxes, which are payable to the government and to the municipalities.

Property tax is payable to the municipalities as a special tax on real estate. It is assessed on the gross value, disregarding any debts on the property.

In towns, property tax is charged at 0·2 to 0·7 per cent. of the appraised value, surveyed every ten years. In the industries, the value comprises ground, buildings and plant. In rural districts, property tax is based on similar principles.

Property tax is considered an outdated type of taxation and the revenue thereof is of relatively little economic importance. Total assessed revenue in the fiscal year of 1950–51 was 31 million kroner or an average of 10 kroner per head.

II. GENERAL DIRECT TAXATION

Taxes are imposed on net capital and income of persons and corporate bodies, based on the general taxation laws and special regulations by the Storting. The taxation laws—dating from 1911—are practically alike for town and rural municipalities. The main difference lies in special rules for taxation on farming and forestry. Such rules are outside the scope of this summary, which is mainly intended to give a survey of the taxation of commerce and industry run by personal and corporate firms.

1. *Main Principles of the Taxation Law*

Assessment of direct taxation is built on the principle of declaration by the taxpayer, who is responsible for contributing a correct assessment. Persons and firms in the trades must enclose copies of trading and profit and loss accounts as well as balance sheets.

The taxation authorities are not bound, in principle, to follow the taxpayer's valuation of capital. For assessment of trading profit, properly kept accounts should be accepted as to the income and expenses to be taken into consideration.

Taxes are assessed in relation to ability to pay. Taxation of net capital and income, family allowances, taxation of husband's and wife's combined capital and income and the progression in tax rates are examples of the way this is carried out.

The principle of municipal integrity in economic matters is followed in taxation. Within certain limits, the Storting has transferred to the municipal councils authority to impose taxes payable locally. Regulations for distribution of the sources of tax revenue between the municipalities rest on two parallel rules, place of residence and origin of trading results.

Distribution according to place of residence is based on the view that taxation revenues should go to the municipality on which expenses are imposed through the taxpayer and his family. Distribution according to origin of trading results is based on the view that the municipality has a natural right to the revenue from taxation of local business, which enjoys the benefit of municipal installations and other activities. This latter taxation relates to capital in, and income of, real estate and plants and of trading arising therefrom. Other capital and income are taxed by the municipality of residence (for a limited company, by the municipality of its registered office).

Deductions for debts are divided between the municipalities in proportion to the gross capital. Deductions for interest payable is divided in proportion to net income.

There are special rules to safeguard against double *municipal* taxation of the same capital and income. Shareholders in the usual type of Norwegian limited companies do not pay *municipal* taxes on such capital and income, as taxes are imposed directly on the company. Accounts with usual Norwegian banks and interest thereon are not included in the *municipal* assessment, as there is a special tax on such capital and income. This is charged to the account by the bank on 31st December or when an account is closed. The revenue is paid to a central body for distribution amongst the municipalities.

Assessment and computation are carried out through elected municipal bodies. Whilst this system is considered a democratic safeguard, it may, on the other hand, involve a risk of reduced technical efficiency. The above-mentioned consideration of municipal integrity as well as the different scales of family allowances and rates of taxation, are, naturally, obstacles against introduction of taxation of current income ('pay as you earn').

In conjunction with assessment and computation of local taxes, the municipal bodies assess and compute government capital taxes and income taxes. The same declaration is used for both purposes. This work is governed by the general taxation laws unless the Storting decides on exceptions. There are special rules regarding government taxes on limited companies and shareholders therein.

Collection of government and local taxes are effected by two separate organisations.

The taxpayers have two methods of appeal, and the validity of assessments can be dealt with by the courts.

2. *Tax Liability in Norway*

Liability to pay Norwegian taxes is mainly on persons domiciled in Norway, irrespective of citizenship. Minors pay taxes if economically independent.

Persons domiciled abroad pay Norwegian taxes if they own property or carry on business in Norway. In these cases, deduction from gross capital can be claimed only for debts incurred to further the enterprise in Norway, and for a maximum of 50 per cent. of the gross capital. Interest payable is deducted in proportion to the debt. Some fees (for instance of company directors) are taxable in Norway if the recipient is domiciled abroad unless exemption is made through tax conventions with other countries. Persons domiciled abroad pay tax to Norway on dividends received from Norwegian limited companies.

Limited companies pay tax if situated in Norway. Tax on other corporate companies is imposed on the personally responsible partners to the same extent as on persons. Limited companies situated abroad pay tax to the same extent as persons domiciled abroad.

3. *Basis and Extent of Taxation* (net capital and income)

The capital is assessed on the value of taxpayers' fixed and floating property, less debts thereon. Assessment is made as at the end of the calendar year or as at the end of the financial year of the undertaking.

Certain assets are not taxable capital, examples being some conditional rights and the value of dividend and salaries accrued but not yet due for payment. Goodwill in a business is not taxable capital, nor are patent rights, unless acquired by purchase or inheritance. Investments in real estate abroad are not taxable capital in Norway.

The rules for valuation of goods in hand are stated somewhat vaguely, but are generally understood to indicate use of the purchase price as at the end of the financial year. In practice, the rules are not interpreted to the extent of writing up of the value in the case of rising prices. If prices have fallen since the day of purchase, current price is used. In the case of rising prices, actual purchasing price is applied. Generally, the taxation authorities have accepted the taxpayer's valuation, even if the value of goods has been written down. As a rule, 10 per cent. depreciation is sanctioned, even if deduction for non-current goods has been made. The rate of turnover is taken into consideration in the question of depreciation. In the case of commodities expected to be sold in the course of a longer period (or of Norwegian-made goods in competition with goods put on the 'free list'), a reasonable depreciation is allowed. Depreciations should be stated in the declaration.

Gross capital is generally assessed at estimated sales value. Goods in hand are valued exclusive of estimated sales profit.

Taxes imposed, but not yet due for payment, are deductible as debt.

Reserves made for taxes to be imposed on the capital and trading profit of the year under review are not deductible.

Gross Income

Income as defined by the taxation laws is very comprehensive. Apart from interest on capital, pensions, annuities and legacies, etc., it includes all advantages gained through work, capital and property.

There are some limitations in the taxable income. Capital increase through inheritance is not taxed as income, as inheritances are taxed through a special death duty. Profit on sale of shares or bonds is not taxable unless acquired as a natural or necessary part of the enterprise. Profit on realisation of plant or machinery, etc., is exempt from income-tax if used for depreciation on new installations in accordance with certain rules.

Deductions from Income

There are two categories of deductions: (i) expenses to achieve, maintain or safeguard income; and (ii) interest payable and other expenses which are not directly related to a definite source of income. This distinction is of importance in the case of liability to pay taxes in two or more municipalities.

Capital and income taxes are not considered expenses for achieving the income and, thus, are *not* deductible from the income. Property tax is deductible.

Depreciations on plant and machinery, etc., are deductible as from the time the asset is taken into use, based on starting value and with an equal proportion every year. The percentage for depreciation is fixed by taxation authorities according to estimated length of use. Depreciations in excess of 10,000 kroner per annum is, for the time being, deductible only on condition that 10 per cent. of the amount is frozen.

Expenses for upkeep of factories, storage, business and similar buildings are not deductible at more than $1-1\frac{1}{2}$ per cent. annually of the value of the building. This rule was instituted provisionally from the point of view that repairs should be limited on account of the shortage of labour and building material.

It may be mentioned that there is a limited opportunity to make tax-free reserves for renewal of plant and machinery, on condition that the amount is deposited in a frozen bank account.

Assessment of Average Income

In order to reduce fluctuations between profit or loss year by year, assessment of trading income is based on the average of the last three years' result, a loss reducing the average. For personal taxpayers 'average assessment' is applied on trading income only. For limited companies 'average assessment' is applied to all profit and loss except in connection with sales, insurance settlement or renewal of production gear. This regulation is temporarily suspended for business started after 1st January, 1940. There are special rules for municipal assessment of 'average income' in the case of the taxpayer who is taxed in two or more municipalities.

III. Taxation of Limited Companies and Shareholders

In addition to the general government and municipal capital and income-tax, limited companies pay a special 'funds tax' to the government. In principle, this is a tax on the company's profit not paid out as dividend. It is computed on the municipal assessment with the addition of interest on bank accounts and dividend from other limited companies. From the gross amount is deducted dividend paid from the current year's profit and transfer to the company's compulsory reserve fund until this has reached the minimum amount required. In the case of trading loss in the previous one or two years, the loss is deducted from the current year's profit. In the case of dividend being paid from the previous years' undistributed profit, 'funds tax' is refunded accordingly.

This special tax was introduced in 1921, when payment of government capital tax on shares and income-tax on dividends was transferred from the company to the shareholders, as, otherwise, shareholders would not be fully taxed according to their ability to pay taxes.

The 'funds tax' is a logical consequence of taxation on the side of the shareholder. Limited companies do, however, in addition pay capital and income-tax to the government; this is clearly double taxation.

Shareholders domiciled *abroad* pay tax on dividends (at present at the rate of 25 per cent.) unless they are living in a country with which Norway has ratified a tax convention.

IV. Computation of Taxes

The amount of taxes on net taxable capital and income depends on the allowances and tax rates. For local taxation there are nine tables of allowances and for government taxation one table. Allowances increase more than proportionately with the number of dependants. If both husband and wife are earning, allowance for one dependant is deducted from the combined income. Tax-free allowances have been raised in the last ten years, but not in keeping with the rise in cost of living. (*See table on page 584.*) Limited companies and persons domiciled abroad have no tax-free allowances. In the case of persons being taxed by two or more municipalities, the taxpayer can choose where to have the tax-free allowance deducted.

There is a table of tax-free allowance for government taxation, which is applied on incomes up to a certain level. On higher incomes, an amount is deducted from the income-tax—instead of allowances being deducted from the assessed income.

Taxes are computed on both fixed and progressive rates.

(a) Capital Tax

Tax on capital, as well as on income thereon, is charged from the point of view that unearned income can stand higher taxation. Tax is, however, imposed on non-profitable capital as well.

Municipal tax.—Fixed rate, generally 0·4 per cent.

Government tax.—Progressional rates, 0·3 to 0·6 per cent. for persons. A sur-tax equal to four times the computed amount is charged if the taxpayer has taxable capital of minimum kr. 80,000, or a taxable capital of minimum kr. 20,000 besides income taxable to the government.

On taxable capital of kr. 125,000 there is an extra sur-tax. ('Extraordinary capital tax.')

Limited companies pay a fixed rate of 0·2 per cent. capital tax.

(*b*) *Income Tax*

Municipal tax.—On incomes up to kr. 15,000 the rate is fixed (the average percentage in 1949 was 17·35 per cent.). On higher incomes, the assessed taxable amount is increased by 6–30 per cent. before computation according to the rate of tax.

Government tax.—The rates are progressive, varying from 3·9 to 72·8 per cent. for single persons and 3·3 to 67·6 per cent. for taxpayers with four dependants or more. These percentages include a special defence tax, imposed since 1950.

If combined government and local taxes on capital and income on any step of progression exceeds 95 per cent. of taxable income, government income-tax is, on application, reduced or cancelled by the amount which the taxes exceed 95 per cent. This applies to government income-tax alone; the other taxes are not reduced, irrespective of the amount in proportion to taxable income.

Limited companies pay a fixed rate of 30 per cent. income-tax and 10 per cent. 'funds tax'.

(*c*) *Special Taxes*

Old-age pension tax and war pension tax is paid at the rate of 1·3 per cent. of the assessed income for government taxation purposes.

Bank accounts tax is charged at 25 per cent. of interest earned, with a minimum of 0·3 per cent. of the bank balance.

Ship-owning tax is a term for tax on ship-owning and whale-catching companies, payable to the municipalities. These taxes are in several ways different from the taxes usually paid to the municipalities. The government charges a 'tonnage levy' computed on the basis of gross tonnage, irrespective of the ship's earning power. This is in addition to the usual capital and income taxes.

V. THE IMPACT OF NORWEGIAN TAXES

(*a*) As previously mentioned, capital taxes are charged from the point of view that unearned income can bear higher taxation. As they are computed on the basis of the capital and not on the income thereon, the impact of these taxes naturally increases on reduced income. For instance, personal taxpayers pay local and government *capital* tax of kr. 326, 801 and 2,566 respectively on a taxable capital of kr. 50,000 to 100,000 and 200,000 (irrespective of tax on income thereon, though on the assumption that income-tax is paid; see Section IV (*a*)).

Capital taxes in percentage of capital yield are:

Capital yield			Capital in kroner 50,000	100,000	200,000
			Taxes in percentage of yield		
1 per cent	..	..	65·2	80·1	128·3
2 ,,	..	.	32·6	40	64·2
3 ,,	..	..	21·7	26·7	42·8
4 ,,	..	..	16·3	20	32·1

(b) The table in the appendix shows the average *income* taxes for taxpayers in Oslo on income from kr. 5,000 to kr. 200,000, with up to seven dependants. As will be seen, the average income-tax for single persons rises from 17·4 per cent. on an income of kr. 5,000 to 75·6 per cent on an income of kr. 200,000.

(c) An exact comparison of the tax impact between limited companies and persons or personal companies is not possible, because of the special rules in force. On incomes up to kr. 100,000, organisation as a limited company usually results in more tax (company tax and shareholders' tax on dividend). If the income is kr. 200,000 or more, the position is reversed. As will be seen from the table, personal income-tax on kr. 100,000 amounts to 62·8 per cent. when the tax-free allowance is not applicable.

In considering the tax impact in Norway, it must be taken into account that ordinary government and local taxes on capital and income are not considered tax-free expenses, so that tax is paid on the tax amount.

Normal yield on share capital is possible only in the case of irregularly large profits and taxes on company savings amount to more than twice the amount saved. The provisional rules limiting tax-free deductions for *repairs* result in increase of the taxes corresponding to about twice the cost of repairs effected. (See Section II, 3 (c).)

According to statements from the Central Bureau of Statistics, the following direct government and local taxes were paid for the year 1949 (fiscal year 1950–51):

	Million kroner	
Municipal taxes (1·5 million taxpayers)		
Property tax	31·4	
Ordinary tax on capital and income:		
Shipowning companies	36·5	
Other taxpayers	1,030·0	
Local additional taxes	36·8	
Interest tax	21·6	
		1,156·3
Government taxes (about 1·03 million personal taxpayers, 14,800 limited companies and 2,000 other corporate bodies)		
Old-age and war pension tax	97·1	
Ordinary capital and income-tax	780·1	
Extraordinary capital tax	14·3	
Defence tax	23·9	
		915·4
Total		2,071·7

or an average of roughly kroner 670·0 per head.

It may be of interest to give Oslo's share of the total government taxes on capital and income:

Year	Personal Taxpayers	Limited and Corporate Companies	Total
1947	37·0 per cent.	54·13 per cent.	42·79 per cent.
1948	38·61 ,,	50·87 ,,	43·85 ,,
1949	35·48 ,,	49·32 ,,	41·31 ,,

Of Norway's population 13·2 per cent. live in Oslo; 90 per cent. of the taxpayers in Oslo pay government taxes, as against 45 per cent. in the rural districts.

In rural districts, organisation of assessment and computation is not yet sufficiently well built up, which to some extent should explain the above figures. It may also be mentioned that it has been estimated that in 1946 1,000 to 1,500 million kroner were not subject to income-taxes (corresponding to 15–20 per cent. of all taxable income).

In the fiscal year of 1950–51, direct and indirect taxes were:

	Million kroner
Purchase tax .. ..: ..	575·9
Customs duties	178·6
Consumption taxes (spirits, beer, tobacco, chocolate, etc.)	871·3
Death duties	14·6
Other indirect taxes	69·5
Total indirect taxes	1,709·9
Direct taxes (see above)	2,071·7
Total direct and indirect taxes	3,781·6

or approximately kroner 1,220·0 per head.

In calculation of the tax impact, social grants and price subsidies should, naturally, be taken into account.

Whilst complete figures of recent date are not available, the following payments have been estimated:

Old-age pensions about 140 million kroner.

Family grants about 74 million kroner.

Grants to disabled about 9 million kroner.

In the fiscal year of 1950–51, 508·4 million kroner were paid in price subsidies.

If such benefits are deducted from the total of direct and indirect taxes, an average of just below kr. 1,000 per head should be the net result on a population of 3·1 million.

In the current fiscal year, the tax impact will rise considerably. Purchase tax has been raised from 6·25 to 10 per cent. As increases in prices (due in part to higher indirect taxes) have caused increase in wages, direct taxes will, naturally, increase as long as the scales of allowances and rates of progression are maintained.

VI. Closing Remarks

Apart from fiscal purposes, one of the main objects of taxation has been to level personal incomes. There can be no doubt that this has been achieved. As an example, it can be mentioned that in 1948 0·75 per cent. of Oslo's taxpayers paid 23·9 per cent. of the municipal taxes, and 10 per cent. of the taxpayers paid 90 per cent. of the municipal taxes.

In recent years, taxation has also been used as an instrument to relieve purchasing pressure under inflation (for instance, deductions for amounts frozen for subsequent investment, and restrictions on deductions for maintenance of buildings).

Lately, another step has been contemplated, viz. special taxation relief for part of the country. Enterprise in Northern Norway is, for reasons of nature, less developed than in the rest of the country. In connection with a comprehensive plan for development of this area, taxation relief has been proposed to attract capital. The proposal has been met with strong criticism and it has been stated that taxation relief for a part of the country is against the constitution. It is not improbable that the constitutional side of the proposal may be tried by the Supreme Court.

It may be concluded that taxation has reached a level which leaves a reduced incentive for personal savings and which makes it difficult to build up reserves for any future depression or for expansion. By far the majority of the people, however, agree whole-heartedly in facing the economic obligations of the international situation and of post-war reconstruction. There is, as well, general agreement on the assumption that the levelling of spendable income may have contributed towards the steady political development, after four years of occupation and upheaval. On the other hand, opinion is divided on the question of the economic basis for continuation of the present policy and extent of taxation.

APPENDIX

Government and local (Oslo) *income* tax for the year of 1949 (fiscal year of 1950–51) in percentage of personal taxpayer's income (not comprising limited companies):

Assessed Income	Class 1 Single Person	Class 2 One dependant	Class 3 Two dependants	Class 4	Class 5	Class 6	Class 7	Class 8 Seven dependants	Class 0 No pers. allowance
5,000	17·4	14·0	10·0	5·7	–	-	–	–	22·7
8,000	21·1	18·2	14·7	11·7	8·7	5·6	2·4	–	25·1
10,000	24·1	20·2	17·3	14·4	11·3	8·8	6·1	3·2	27·4
12,000	26·7	23·2	19·5	16·5	13·8	11·0	8·7	6·3	29·4
15,000	30·1	26·9	23·3	20·1	17·0	14·3	11·9	9·3	32·3
20,000	35·3	32·3	29·0	26·3	22·7	20·1	17·3	14·3	37·0
30,000	41·9	39·1	36·0	33·8	31·4	29·6	27·7	25·6	43·0
50,000	50·3	47·4	44·4	42·5	40·4	39·3	38·2	36·7	51·0
100,000	62·5	59·1	56·5	55·0	53·5	52·9	52·3	51·6	62·8
200,000	75·6	71·7	70·4	69·6	68·8	68·5	68·2	67·9	75·8

Municipal allowances (Oslo) in 1951 kroner:

1,150	1,950	2,900	4,000	5,250	6,650	8,200	9,900	–

Municipal allowances if there had been full adjustment for rise in cost of living since 1939 level:

1,800	3,230	4,730	6,310	7,950	9,670	11,470	13,340	–

Minimum taxable income government:

2,000	2,100	3,300	4,600	6,000	7,500	9,100	10,800	–

Minimum taxable income, local (Oslo):

1,600	2,400	3,300	4,400	5,700	7,100	8,600	10,300	10

THE INCIDENCE OF TAXATION

by

UNO LÖNNQVIST, M.COM., M.ECON.

K.H.T.-Yhdistys: Föreningen C.G.R.,
Finland

Before the preparation of this paper I was enabled to read the synopsis of the original introducers. I decided that the various kinds of taxes, as well as the development of taxation in Great Britain and in the United States, had been treated by them very exhaustively. To avoid unnecessary repetition I am therefore not going to enumerate various categories of taxes, nor do I think that a detailed statement of the development of taxation in Finland is of great interest to this audience. I wish instead, considering the limited time at my disposal, to bring under discussion aspects of taxation in Finland. As these problems mainly concern the accountant, I hope they may prove to be of some general interest.

The treatment of the subject will be subdivided as follows:

(1) The development of taxation in Finland.
(2) Structure of the Finnish system and peculiar features of Finland's taxation laws.
(3) Some problems for the accountant arising from taxation in Finland:
    (*a*) The influence of inflation upon taxation.
    (*b*) The influence of taxation upon book-keeping.
    (*c*) Observance of taxation and the accountant.
(4) High taxation—cause and effect.

I. THE DEVELOPMENT OF TAXATION IN FINLAND

In Sweden-Finland (as will be known to many in this audience, Finland was united with Sweden until 1809) taxation was originally founded upon free contributions from the citizens but was gradually developed into a permanent duty. In a way it constituted a compensation for the expenditure of the state for national defence and costs of jurisdiction. Taxation was already established in the thirteenth century. The national law code of the 1350s precisely regulated the king's taxation rights. The king was responsible for the entire expenditure of the state and consequently he had at his disposal the income and yearly legal distraints of the state and also additional taxes in specific cases.

Legislation for taxation in Finland, as a separate country, is very young. The 'Diet' of 1863-64 introduced a general revenue duty on a progressive scale. As this duty was not profitable, it was abolished in 1885. By this time taxation on income had been introduced in the cities and 'parishes' and is still in force. During World War I, state taxation on income was temporarily

585

applied in Finland but the first real law on income and property taxation was not passed and applied until 1920. This taxation became a permanent state tax from then onwards. This law was replaced in 1924 by a new law, which remained in force until 1943, when the existing state income and property tax law based upon the place of residence principle was established, i.e. persons residing in this country are liable to full taxation, while those living abroad are bound to pay tax only for income earned in the country and for property situated therein.

II. STRUCTURE OF THE FINNISH SYSTEM AND PECULIAR FEATURES OF FINLAND'S TAX LAWS

As may be seen from the foregoing, there are two permanent income laws in existence in Finland: (*a*) payable to the state and (*b*) payable to the cities and the communes, both laws being based in general upon the extent of the income. Exceptions to this rule include a form of taxation founded on the yield, e.g. taxation of agricultural holdings according to acreage, of foreign insurance companies, etc., according to special rate percentages.

(*a*) State Tax

In Finland, as with other countries, there are both direct and indirect taxes. The relation between these two forms of taxation has varied greatly during the last years, owing to the uncertain economic situation and to the different internal political aims of the various governments. Through the figures in the 1951 Government Statistical Year Book, it is possible to obtain a fairly correct picture of the forms and objects of taxation in Finland. The figures below have been taken from this book.

Total taxes were some 70 per cent. of the state's total income (1949). Of total taxes some 65 per cent. were indirect taxes, and some 35 per cent. were direct taxes.

The purchase tax constituted more than 50 per cent. of indirect taxes. Of direct taxes, the joint-stock companies paid 36 per cent. (1947) (the trade's part of that being 60 per cent. and that of industry 34 per cent.).

As to the relation between the size of the tax and the income, it may be said that some abatements have already been fixed and that for individuals and unlimited companies there is now a progressive scale, which, at the moment of writing, has reached the maximum, i.e. 50 per cent. on an income of 20 million Finnish marks (some £30,000). A proportional scale is applied for the joint-stock companies, the tax amounting to 45 per cent. of the taxable income for 1950.

With regard to *personal income-tax*, the Finnish law, in conformity with modern tax legislation, takes into consideration the ability of the individual. There are three main groups: Group I, single persons; Group II, married persons without children; Group III, married persons who have already educated children or who are educating children.

As to company incomes, the result shown by accounts with consideration taken to cost limitations as prescribed by tax law (e.g. maximum depreciation percentages) is generally regarded as *the taxable income*. The tax scales are drawn up in a way that taxes paid must not be regarded as costs.

In the case of state *property tax*, there is a progressive scale for unlimited companies and private persons and a proportional scale for joint-stock companies and co-operative societies, the percentage of the former being a maximum of 2·5 and that of the latter 0·8 (1951). Theoretically, this tax is intended to be an additional income-tax.

Besides the taxes mentioned above, which are of a permanent character, the following taxes have been imposed during the war and post-war years, viz. *excess profits duty, additional property taxes* and the *property transfer taxes*.

Property Transfer Tax. This tax was used to compensate the one-tenth of the population which lost its property because of the surrender of land to the U.S.S.R. It was applied in and between the years 1939-48 and was charged according to a progressive scale with 5 per cent. in all at the lowest limit and with 35 per cent. in all at the highest: it affected both individuals and companies. Joint-stock companies of a certain minimum size were entitled to surrender their own shares in payment of this tax. To administer the shares a holding company was formed, which issued participating certificates, these being used as part payment to the displaced persons. One-tenth of the shares surrendered were to be re-purchased by the joint-stock companies annually at prices fixed each year by the holding company; these prices were of course also influenced by inflation. The property transfer tax was, in a special degree, peculiar. Not only was ordinary taxable property assessed, but also personal effects such as furniture, clothes, pictures, jewellery, and in fact any marketable possession. The tax was applied only if the property amounted to at least 100,000 marks (about £400) in all. The total yield of the property transfer tax cannot be stated exactly, as the payment occurred during different phases of inflation. It may be mentioned that this tax in the first year, 1941, then at its highest, was three milliard Finnish marks (about £14 million). It provided more than half of all direct taxes and 8 per cent. of the national net income for that year. Full compensation was given to the displaced persons up to a limit of half a million marks (£2,000), and then on a decreasing scale, so that for damage amounting to 32 million marks (£130,000) and upwards the compensation was only 10 per cent.

Double Taxation. In order to avoid double taxation resulting from taxation of the same income both in Finland and in other countries, agreements have been made with Denmark and Sweden. The drafts of similar agreements with England and United States are already prepared.

In Finland income from joint-stock companies is affected by double taxation. The joint-stock companies are, as mentioned above, taxed according to a proportional scale, the rate of which is now fixed annually. The rate for 1950 was 45 per cent. and that for 1951 has not been finally confirmed at the date of writing. This tax must be paid by the joint-stock companies themselves. In addition, the shareholder has to pay tax on dividends paid by the company, this income being treated as other income of individuals and unlimited companies; it is therefore subject to progressive taxation.

U

(b) Municipal and Commune Tax (income-tax only)

Municipal and commune tax, earlier mentioned, is based upon income and is, in the main, calculated in the same way as state income-tax. The rate of this tax varies between 7 and 14 per cent., depending on the financial position of the towns and 'parishes'.

There is a regulation, mainly applied with regard to the municipal and commune tax, that if a company shows no income, or only a small one, tax may be imposed on an estimated income, which is regarded as normal for other companies of the same line and size. This *'size' taxation*, depending as it does on the judgment of the various local taxation authorities, has caused much discussion and trouble. It is one of the most important of the uncertain elements in calculating the tax debts when closing the books of companies in Finland.

The 'size' taxation may in some cases be applied even to state taxation (e.g. foreign subsidiary companies).

P.A.Y.E. Tax. Since the beginning of the year 1944, this tax has been deducted at source, i.e. as to employees the tax is deducted before the payment of wages and salaries, while in other cases taxes are charged in advance and calculated on the basis of the income of two years earlier. At the moment, work on a new tax law is proceeding and it is hoped that it will somewhat mitigate the hardships now arising from double taxation and 'size' taxation.

III. Some Problems for the Accountant Arising from Taxation in Finland

As an introduction to this section I may point out that in the following notes I express my opinions as an independent business accountant.

(a) Influence of Inflation on Taxation

Finland is one of the countries hard hit by the post-war inflation. The general rise in prices can now be said to be fifteenfold compared with 1938. As inflation set in, one of the first taxation measures was to deduct taxes at the source. But apart from that, the taxes increased automatically for all (unlimited companies and individuals) to whom the progressive scale was applied. As nominal income increased at the same speed as inflation, the taxes increased according to this progressive scale; although the purchasing power of the income was unchanged, all prices and costs increased at the same moment as (or before) the income, and compensating allowances in the tax scale were granted only later. Moreover, the indirect taxes increased automatically and proportionally with the prices. As the increased revenue arising from taxation facilitated the financial dispositions of the governments, these factors may have had, together with party politics and other reasons, a negative influence on inflation. On the other hand, the increase of the property tax was undertaken afterwards in relation to inflation. The book-values of the fixed assets were kept unchanged for a long time, and the nominal tax remained for some time unaltered. Gradually the Ministry of

Finance increased the taxation values of the fixed assets according to certain established principles, but not to market value. On current assets, however, firms have been given more freedom. Thus pre-war prices generally were allowed as the basis of valuation of stocks of goods—provided that the same prices were applied consistently every year even if they were, to a considerable degree, lower than the market value. Since the stocks, because of lack of goods, were reduced, and since no amounts set aside for diminution in value of stock were allowed by the taxation authorities, companies were forced, to a considerable extent, to show their concealed reserves as profit. The result was that the economic basis of the companies weakened. In spite of this, I should be inclined to say that if the companies had not earlier been allowed to keep these reserves to fall back upon, many companies would already have gone into liquidation at an early phase of the war. Perhaps, for the sake of clarity, it ought to be said that in Finland it is not permissible to deduct a loss in one year from a profit in another year.

(b) Influence of Taxation on Book-keeping

The opportunities given to the management by a rather free valuation of the current assets for changing the result of the accounts, bring about increased responsibility for the auditor. The higher the taxation, the greater the temptation to the company to show as small a profit as possible. If, in addition, times are uncertain and losses in coming years may be feared, it is fairly obvious that the management will do its utmost to secure the future activity of the firm, even in cases of substantial fall of prices (particularly in relation to the 'size' taxation already mentioned). It may happen that the management will use methods which do not sufficiently comply with the law, good book-keeping principles and fair business ethics (e.g. recording drawings as representing costs; using replacement values instead of cost; invoices at the turn of the year entered in the wrong year, etc.). The higher the taxes, the more closely the accountant has to examine the accounts. On the other hand, he must also ascertain that the company has a solid basis for its continued existence. This he has to do in order to guard the interests of the shareholders.

Before inflation had set in, the book values of the property were used as a basis of the state property taxation. As inflation proceeded, the taxation authorities had to increase the taxation values of fixed assets. But the depreciation on these increased values was not allowed as costs. For that reason, these old fixed asset values were commonly retained in the balance sheets. Later, the fixed asset values were, by some firms, increased in the balance sheets by showing equivalent funds in credit. This was done for special purposes, primarily to increase the share capital by the free issue of shares in order to facilitate higher dividends. The result is, for the present, that balance sheets are published which show:

(a) Fixed assets expressed partly in terms of pre-war value of money and partly that value more or less increased, and finally, various values due to different original values during various periods of inflation.

(b) Current assets expressed in various values depending on the methods of valuation and the time of purchase.

(c) Financial assets expressed in money values in force at the balance sheet date.

As stated above, the taxation authorities in Finland accept depreciation based only on historical value, the result being that depreciation is commonly computed on that value (if the value of the assets have not earlier been increased). To the extent that the firm has had old fixed assets and to the extent that inflation has continued, depreciation has accordingly become too small in relation to the replacement cost. Therefore the profit shown by the books is too high from an economic point of view. Thus the fixed assets and the current assets are treated by the taxation authorities in a different way, and book-keeping has been influenced by that fact. But the various elements work at various strengths in different enterprises.

Both from a general and a book-keeping point of view, it must be regarded as unfortunate that taxation has such a high degree of influence upon balance sheets. The two fundamental requirements of a balance sheet, truth and clearness, are not, in such case secured and the general public's confidence in the balance sheet becomes undermined.

(c) Observance of Taxation and the Accountant

In various respects there are difficulties for the accountant when high taxes are imposed because of the temptation of tax fraud. It may be asked to what extent the accountant is bound to consider matters bearing upon taxation, and to take steps when faults are discovered. A general answer can hardly be given, as action depends on the legislation of the various countries. In my view, the most important factor is the independence of the accountant. He must not be economically dependent upon either the authorities or the enterprise. Thus he can be impartial, and by means of fairness and his professional ability, he gains the confidence of authorities, management, shareholders and the public. In conclusion, I would say that, if an accountant establishes that dispositions have been made which do not correspond to general book-keeping principles and fair business ethics, he ought to point out the possible consequences to the management and, in grave cases, qualify his auditor's report accordingly. In Finland, as in Scandinavian countries, we generally do the auditing during the year as a continuous audit, thus comments can be made as to taxation and corrections can be arranged before the closing of books. So we have little difficulty in this respect. The accountant need not extend his work to comprehend fiscal interests because for almost ten years we have had a special tax-controlling revision department attached to the Ministry of Finance. The tax declarations are, however, examined in a large extent, principally to ascertain that companies have not made mistakes that might result in higher payments than provided for by the taxation laws.

In his routine work, the accountant will find the full confidence of his client very useful. Often he is spared much work, thanks to ready co-operation from the management and officials.

IV. High Taxation—Cause and Effect

It is easy to notice, in Finland as in other countries, that the purpose of taxation has changed considerably since pre-war years. Formerly, it was only to meet the necessary expenses of the state; now the taxes are used for economic and social purposes, the natural result being a substantial increase in taxation. A general democratisation and socialisation can be traced in the charging and use of taxes, which levels the standard of living, controls industry and limits private enterprise. A further result is that capital from private sources cannot be found for new ventures, and thus all commercial and industrial life becomes machinery of the state. Whilst full credit must be given to the improvement in social conditions as compared with the period before the war, there are values at stake which should not be forfeited. The individual loses the greatest incentive to do his best. If the reward is not in proportion to the performance, the individual easily falls into apathy, the result being considerably smaller production, i.e. a lowering of the standard of living. Moreover, the morale of the individual becomes injured; he tends not to feel responsibility for his existence, as the state has taken over the responsibility from him. Instead of working more, he tries to find out means of paying less taxes. The next step—law breaking with all its consequences—is not very far away.

Being an independent accountant serving commercial and industrial life, I can only hope that, in the interests of both individual and state, this period of high taxation will be of a temporary nature. That hope realised, the enormous amount of time now spent on tax calculations, tax control and litigation might be used for more useful purposes.

DISCUSSION

Mr. Percival F. Brundage, c.p.a., *American Institute of Accountants, the rapporteur, summarised the contents of the papers:*

Incidence is defined as the falling of a tax upon a person as a burden which he is unable to shift to another. It was obviously impossible for those who prepared the papers to discuss the ultimate incidence of all of the complex taxes levied in each of the countries they represent. A large part of the total tax burden is levied on corporations in the first instance but must ultimately fall on individuals as Mr. Green points out.

Most of the authors accept the view that redistribution of wealth and income is a conscious purpose of taxation in their respective countries, which means that the heaviest tax burden is borne by the possessors of the larger amounts of income. They point out, however, that the effects of taxation are felt by everyone, even the recipients of special benefits and subsidies.

In studying these interesting papers I was impressed with the similarity of the comments in spite of the many differences in the taxes imposed in the seven countries represented. There seems to be a consensus that in all countries taxes are too numerous, too complex and too burdensome. Excessively high rates are stifling business growth, deadening incentive, discouraging savings and encouraging extravagance in deductible expenditures. Tax evasion is growing. Tax avoidance is universal. The tax aspects of a transaction have become the most important factor in influencing business decisions.

Efforts to increase the material well-being of the lower income groups have resulted in a diversion of effort from production and have impaired the moral standards of the rich and poor alike threatening also their future well-being. This seems to be the prevailing note in the papers we are discussing this morning.

Several of the authors go back to Adam Smith's principles of taxation:

Assessment according to ability to pay.
Certainty of determination.
Convenience of payment.
Economy of operations.

When tested by these rules many of our modern tax systems are found to be wanting.

I was somewhat surprised to find no mention made in any of the papers of Maynard Keynes or of the Neo-Keynsian School which has had so great an influence in the United States during recent years.

In the short time allotted to me to open the discussion I can only comment very briefly on one or two points in each paper.

Mr. G. B. Burr calls to our attention the increase in the Government's needs for funds giving rise to taxation since mediæval times when they were primarily for:

(1) Armed forces for the protection of the realm.

(2) Police force and law courts.

(3) Essential public health services, according to the medical knowledge of the day.

The cost of administration in those days was unimportant and such services as the post and water supply were self-supporting.

In recent years taxation has been employed for the purpose of:

(1) Artificial controls of supply and demand.

(2) Control of imports and encouragement of exports.

(3) Redistribution of incomes.

(4) Levies on special services for the benefit of others.

The present burden of taxation in the United Kingdom is five times that before the war although it was considered high enough at that time. Mr. Burr mentions several kinds of hidden taxation such as semi-nationalisation of land under the Town and Country Planning Act of 1947 which took away all building or development right from landowners for wholly inadequate compensation. He points out that while the British system is administered at a very low cost in proportion to the tax collected, the burdens upon the citizens and businesses is very heavy because of the tremendous amount of time required in computing the correct liability for the various taxes which he says is 'a monumental waste of economic effort which the country can ill afford at the present time'. This I think would be even more true in the United States where the tax departments of large corporations cost hundreds of thousands of dollars a year.

Mr. Burr closes his paper with some very interesting questions which I hope will be covered in our discussion period. Improvement in the standard of life of the nation and in the operation of the taxes, he says, may in the future result from the following:

(a) Substantial economies in government expenditure of various kinds.

(b) Reduction in rearmament expenditure as soon as possible.

(c) A gradual extinction of food subsidies by compensating real income benefits through increased production and lower prices.

(d) The possible transference of a state-maintained health service to one more nearly approaching a true and actuarially self-supporting insurance scheme, perhaps of a voluntary nature.

Both Mr. Horley and Mr. R. D. Brown point out the inflationary effects of high taxation in Australia and New Zealand. This has not been sufficiently stressed in the United States where it is hailed as anti-inflationary. All of the moneys collected by taxation, and more too in several countries, is spent by the governments so there is no lessening of money in circulation, while the tendency of the individual 'towards recklessness in expenditure of a deductible nature' is very noticeable.

Mr. Horley refers to an interesting anomaly in the convention for relief from double taxation between the United Kingdom and Australia. Persons who are resident in both countries are not deemed to be resident in either country. In general, however, considerable progress has been made towards the avoidance of international double taxation through treaties which have been approved since the last International Congress on Accounting.

Mr. R. D. Brown calls attention to the aggregation of incomes of husband and wife where each exceed £200 and taxation as one at higher rates. This is the direct opposite of the income-splitting provision in the United States under which the incomes of husband wife can be added together, divided by two, and the tax computed separately on each half.

Mr. Kapadia gives an interesting illustration of the decreased total yield in India as taxes become excessive. In order to evade the heavy income-tax no record may be made of some of the purchases and sales which are transacted in cash. The result is that in addition to the loss of income-tax—the sales tax also is lost. Cash transactions have unfortunately been utilised for this purpose in other countries as well.

Mr. Kapadia regrets that in formulating tax policies more attention is not paid to preservation of incentives for expansion of industry and the launching of new enterprises.

Mr. Kjeldsberg gives us an interesting account of the authority of municipal councils in Norway to impose taxes payable locally. The principle of municipal integrity in economic matters is followed in income and other taxes. Assessment and computation are carried out through elected municipal bodies. He refers to a recent step contemplated, namely, special tax relief for part of the country, northern Norway, which for reasons of nature is less developed than the rest of the country. A constitutional question has been raised against this special relief. In the United States we seem to have no compunction whatsoever in taxing corporations and citizens of the wealthier states to give relief to the farm areas and inaugurate federal projects like flood control and production of power.

Mr. Lönnqvist brings out the difficulties that the accountant encounters in Finland when high taxes are imposed because of the temptation of fraud. He traces the influence of inflation on taxation, how the tax increases automatically under the progressive scale of rates and accelerates the inflationary spiral. He hopes that the enormous amount of time now spent on tax calculations, tax control and litigation may be used in the future for more useful purposes.

Mr. Green summarises what he aptly calls the 'multiple maze of United States taxes'. With us the Federal tax laws have taken the centre of the scene away from the state and municipal levies both in yield and complexity. Income taxes levied directly against individuals now account for approximately 41 per cent. of the entire Federal revenue. Mr. Green covers certain unique features of United States income-tax laws, the income-splitting for husband and wife to which I have already referred, the complex provisions for taxation of capital gains and losses, the special benefits of percentage depletion for oil, gas and mineral properties, the double taxation of dividends through corporate taxation and individual taxes to the recipient of the dividends, and the complex personal holding company provisions. He refers to the proposed constitutional amendment limiting Federal taxes to 25 per cent., a resolution in favour of which has been passed by a number of state legislatures. He feels that welfare benefits to the unemployed, the handicapped and the aged will undoubtedly continue, but as Sir Stafford Cripps pointed out in the quotation given by Mr. Burr, the yield from taxation of the higher incomes has reached its limit and the burdens are now falling on all of the citizens.

MR. G. P. KAPADIA (India):

In his opening remarks, Mr. Brundage made an observation to the effect that he found uniformity of views in the papers submitted by all the other countries. I wish he had also stated that all governments, whatever their construction, are agreed on one fact, that is, to collect the maximum out of the subjects. Whatever political set-up there may be, direct as well as indirect taxation assumes the high level which we find in various countries. I would particularly invite your attention to the question which I have raised in my paper as to the financial policy and structure of the country having a definite impact on its political set-up. Although the financial structure is shaped by the government in power, as has been pointed out by me in considering the history of the financial evolution of India, the fact does remain that the financial structure and the policy relating to the economic structure of any country would definitely recoil in such a way as to change the political structure absolutely.

I also commented on the Soviet economy, to which no reference is made in any other papers. I did this with a view to comparing the economy of the Soviet with those of the democracies which are so different. In Russia, we find an attempt to collect a mass of humanity for a common objective, and we find a concentration of power itself instead of a concentration of monetary power which is to be found in the democracies. The ideal may be difficult to achieve but it would not be out of place if I referred to the fundamental rights laid down in the constitution of India and to which a reference was made by the Planning Commission in its report. The terms of reference made clear mention of the fundamental rights as guaranteed by the Constitution of India, which Constitution has at the same time:

'Enunciated certain directive principles of State policy and in particular provided that the State should strive to promote the welfare of the people by securing and protecting as effectively as it may, a social order in which justice, social, economic and political, shall inform all the institutions of the national life and shall direct its policy towards securing among other things that the citizens, men and women equally, have the right to an adequate means of livelihood, that the ownership and control of the material resources of the community are so distributed as best to subserve the common good and that the operation of the economic system does not result in the concentration of wealth and means of production to the common detriment.'

In this respect I would add that while Soviet economy and its political structure have attracted some attention because of success in recent times, the democracies of the world and the financial structures and economies flowing therefrom have stood the test of time for centuries. The enlightened approach made towards the State's obligation for social and economic uplift made in the Constitution of India represents a measure of hope.

MR. T. KJELDSBERG (Norway):

It is a general view in Norway that our tax impact is the heaviest in Europe. After reading Mr. Burr's paper I did at first wonder whether this is correct.

How does the tax impact compare in the various countries which co-operate, or compete, with Great Britain? Such a comparison may, perhaps, be of limited value, as several reservations must be made. One should know the size of the national income and how it has been assessed. One should also know the relative internal purchasing value of the currencies and one should take into account the different social and other benefits each country offers in return for the taxes.

The tax impact has risen quite considerably since 1939. The national income in Norway, estimated at 'factor cost' in the years 1939-40 and 1950-51 was about 5,000 and 13,000 million kroner. Total taxes in per cent. of the national income was 19·5 per cent. and 29·2 per cent. respectively. The increase in total taxation revenue amounts to an average of 385 per cent. Figures for the fiscal year ending 30th June, 1952, are, naturally, not yet available. In the national budget, the total tax revenues are assessed at about 4,900 million kroner, or 31·7 per cent. of the estimated national income. This amounts to pretty nearly five times the total taxation revenue in 1939-40. Of the amount of 4,900 million kroner, about 963 million is expected to be paid out in price subsidies.

The greatest increase is to be found in direct government taxes on capital and income. The rate of capital tax has been raised to five times the pre-war level. Regarding income-tax, I may mention that the lowest income on which maximum taxation rate is applicable was 875,000 kroner before the war, as against 275,000 kroner at present. At the same time the taxation rates have risen quite considerably.

In Mr. Burr's paper, there is a table showing the burden of post-war income-tax and sur-tax on selected earned income. Comparison with the table in my paper gives the following result (£1 corresponds to 20 Norwegian kroner):

| | Single persons taxes in per cent. | | Married, one child taxes in per cent. | |
Income	United Kingdom	Norway	United Kingdom	Norway
£500 = 10,000 Kr.	12·6	24·1	2·8	17·3
£1,000 = 20,000 Kr.	23·5	35·3	15·2	29·0
£5,000 = 100,000 Kr.	50·8	62·5	49·1	56·5
£10,000 = 200,000 Kr.	65·9	75·6	65·1	70·4

On all incomes stated, the average percentage of taxation is thus higher in Norway than in Great Britain. For further comparison I may mention that in 1950, the average pay per hour for men working in industry has been calculated at 3s 9d. Taxation of limited companies generally amounts to 73-70 per cent. of the company's surplus (the percentage depending to a certain extent on the relation between capital and income). In order to pay a 5 per cent. dividend, the company must, as a general rule, make a profit of 25 per cent. on the share capital.

When considering the tax impact in Norway, one must take into account all the extra taxes which have been imposed since 1939. During the war, a special tax on increase in incomes was introduced. This was superseded by an increase in the progression of the rates of regular income-tax. Increase in net capital during the war was subject to a special tax as well. A special war damage tax has been applied twice, followed by a special defence tax which has now been incorporated in the regular taxes. These extra taxes have hit owners of capital especially hard, which naturally has not helped to further any interest in saving. As I mentioned in my paper, capital tax is, on principle, a tax on unearned income, but it is imposed on net capital whether or not it yields any income. It comes on top of ordinary income-tax.

Today, direct taxation in Norway also serves a political end in a different way than it did before. Taxation is used as a means to direct activities along the prevailing lines of trade policy laid down. Special taxation rules have been applied to discourage investment. On the other hand, taxation relief has been proposed for Northern Norway to attract capital. Indirect taxation has not been used in the same way. This is due, amongst other reasons, to the fact that indirect taxes are included in the general price index and thus may influence the level of wages.

MR. J. POLY (France):

First of all I must inform the members of the Congress that my remarks on taxation are the summing-up of discussions between Mr. Lauzel, General Secretary of the Conseil Supérieur de la Comptabilité, Mr. Fleury, Director of the Société Fiduciaire de l'Est, and myself.

There are two aspects of taxation which might usefully be emphasised. The first one, which has already been outlined in the papers, is the incidence on economic trend. I shall only give a brief description of what happened in France.

As a result of a constant increase of taxation rates, so much more heavily felt as it has not been related to a corresponding increase of productivity, we can observe, first, a shortening of the tax basis due, on the one hand, to the action of special regulations in favour of such and such categories of taxpayers, and on the other hand to the effect of exceptional regulations bound to the monetary depreciation. Second, the growing complexity of fiscal procedures for the filling of tax returns as well as for their control. Third, the strong incidence on prices.

Some fiscal policy makers felt that an enhancement of taxation could stop the inflation trend by strictly balancing the budget and by reducing the excess in purchasing power. Referring to the classical theory of incidence, they argued that enhancing direct taxes would have but little effect on the price level. In fact, these forecasts have been nullified by experience. Heavy taxation rates have not achieved a sound balance of the budget. They have weighed heavily on prices, contributing to the fear of a rise in prices.

Apart from that, this incidence has been enlarged by the fact that profits tax is not allowed to be deducted from the profits in determining the tax bases. The rise in price has contributed to increasing the burden of the State as the latter was both a customer and an employer; in consequence, there was an increase in the budget deficit.

Taxation has maintained inflation. It is this situation that Mr. Pinay, the French Prime Minister, has decided to fight by the application of a new programme. He gave up all the previous projects of tax increase, practised a fiscal amnesty and used loans more largely, as was easier with the return of confidence.

The second point concerns the influence of taxation on accounting rules. It is a very important matter that gives some trouble, I suppose, to accountants in all countries. A systematic study of the problem in all countries would show some of the ill-effects of fiscal procedures on the evolution of accountancy. Among these effects one might draw attention to the trouble created by intrusion of fiscal rules into accounting and the important waste of time due to new accounts only justified by fiscal considerations.

In France, the Conseil Supérieur de la Comptabilité has settled against the numerous fiscal dispositions disturbing the economical meaning of accounts and hindering the development of uniform systems. It has proposed that, for concerns using the 1947 plan, the profit would be determined according to the rules set up by this plan. The corrections to be made to the figures for fiscal purposes would have to be recorded in a statistical way.

In a letter on 24th May, 1952, relating to the fiscal amnesty mentioned earlier, the Budget Secretary seems to back this thesis. He agreed that the firms which, as a result of amnesty, want to rectify some asset valuations could do so, without recording the rectification in the accounts. In this way, they will have two balance sheets at the same time; the first will be built up from accounts and the second will only have a fiscal character. This solution is not entirely satisfactory. At least, it is less troublesome for the economic value of accountancy than the constant and heterogeneous adjustments inflicted by taxation on book-keeping.

MR. J. F. VAN DER LAAN (Netherlands):

I was disappointed to find that the contributors of the papers at this session have dealt with their subject on such a narrow front. They have all given excellent reports on the *methods* of taxation in various countries, but they have said too little about the *effects* of these methods on the business economy as a whole and the financial position of industrial undertakings in particular. The broad general effects of taxation are surely every bit as important to accountants as the techniques of its calculation, particularly since in most countries nowadays taxation is used by governments as a political instrument to force the economy of the country into a pre-determined direction and to redistribute the national income.

Very few people will deny that every industrial undertaking ought to be able to plough back into the business a substantial proportion of its profits to cover unexpected set-backs, to finance a limited expansion and to replace obsolete plant and equipment, even before it has been fully depreciated. Consequently, when the proportion of profit to be appropriated to tax becomes too large, the financial stability and the productivity of industry must inevitably suffer, whilst, at the same time, management and shareholders alike become more reluctant to assume the risks involved in expanding existing activities and promoting new ones.

This alone is bad enough for the future economic development of a country, but the danger becomes much more serious when the high tax contribution is levied on hypothetical profits and not on real profits. In such circumstances part of the tax has to be paid out of capital, with the result that the capital potential of the undertaking is reduced, even when no, or only small, dividends are paid. Some governments have seen the danger and have allowed companies to calculate taxable profits on the replacement value principle, both in respect of depreciation on fixed assets and stock valuation, but many other governments do not yet accept these sound principles. In these latter countries, industrial progress is bound to suffer and with it the economic position and prosperity of the country concerned. This applies particularly when the government, after reducing industry's capital potential by these means, adds insult to injury by ordering the restriction of capital investment, even for replacement purposes, and emphasises this instruction by making it difficult, if not impossible, for industry to acquire additional finance. The cumulative effect of these measures can have only one result— industrial productivity will lag behind that of other countries, whilst the capital resources of the country are being drained to meet government expenditure of a revenue nature. Under these conditions a country, in the long run, is bound to lose both internal strength and influence in world affairs. Military rearmament by itself cannot correct this development, particularly when it is directed against Communist countries in which capital expenditure for the purpose of increased productivity and expansion of industry is being given high priority, overriding all considerations relating to the immediate standard of living of their peoples.

I believe that it is an important duty of the accounting profession to emphasise persistently and continually the dangers of economically unsound taxation policies, particularly when by way of hidden capital levies, they drain the capital potential of industry. But charity starts at home and for the achievement of results it will be essential for accountants to promote and practise accounting methods which distinguish real profits from artificial profits, and which bring forward the effects of unsound taxation policies. I am convinced that if industry will universally adopt, and the accounting profession encourage and support the application of these sound principles in the presentation of company accounts, public opinion can be influenced to such an extent that no democratic government can, in the long run, resist their adoption in its taxation legislation.

MR. H. A. ADAMS (Great Britain and Ireland):

There are two items of practical interest which deserve our attention today. The first item arises out of Mr. Burr's excellent paper in which he expresses the hope that as a result of international discussion it may be possible to improve the overall system with resulting economic benefit to international trade and good relationships between nations.

In my view, that part of the overall system dealing with visits to other countries is overdue for a comprehensive review. I will quote one case to illustrate my point.

A business man recently visited Pakistan for a period of approximately one month. During this time no emoluments were received by him from Pakistanian sources yet he was obliged—before he could leave the country—to pay Pakistanian income-tax on the whole of his month's salary which was paid to him in London. It is true that the amount involved will be subsequently recovered from the British authorities, but you know, as well as I do, that repayment will not be made without endless correspondence on both sides of the water.

If, as a result of our discussion here today some steps are taken to eliminate the inconvenience, waste of effort and strain of friendly relationships involved in such fantastic legislation, our time will have been well spent, and I am sure that many of you will gladly forego your fees for the morning's work.

My second point comes under the heading of the 'Burden of Taxation', a burden which is far too familiar to us all. I wish to draw your attention to just one section of our national life which is finding this burden too hard to bear; I refer to new companies formed to explore and develop new fields of activity.

In days gone by such companies were not frustrated by high taxation and were able to plough back profits into the business for purposes of expansion. Today, however, we find there is no ploughing back because the tax authorities have done all the 'raking out'. As a result, the world is being starved of certain new ideas and new techniques.

I sincerely hope, and I am sure many of you will share my views, that the organisers of this Congress will continue their good work by making quite sure that our deliberations here today receive the publicity they deserve so that the politicians of all creeds may be sharply reminded of the devastating economic effect of the present high levels of taxation.

MR. J. ANTTONEN (Finland):

Mr. Uno Lönnqvist has given a brief general survey of taxation conditions in Finland. I venture to touch briefly on one special feature in this connection arising from the severity of taxation.

The Finnish taxation law has for a long time contained a stipulation according to which the taxation board of the local government may determine the tax as they deem appropriate if the enterprise has operated at a loss or if its net income is negligible. But the board must pay attention to the nature and size of the enterprise and carefully consider all the aspects of the case as it is expressly stipulated by the law. The stipulation has been interpreted as being exceptional, to be applied in exceptional cases only.

The development has, however, led to the local governments having made this stipulation a rule. In the recent years a similar stipulation has been included also in the state income taxation, but fortunately its application there is much more restricted so far.

If the taxpayer is not satisfied with the taxation, he may appeal. There are three stages in appealing. In the local government stage the composition of the Board of Appeal depends on the relative strengths of the political parties and many appeals are therefore rejected. The decisions of the Supreme Court are, on the contrary, considered as interpretations of the taxation laws.

The idea of the 'size' taxation as such is correct—all those liable to taxation must in any case participate in the common burden by the tax payments—but its application has degenerated almost to an abuse. It can happen that all enterprises are subjected to 'size' taxation, which is very far from the exceptional case.

In these circumstances the business enterprises have begun to work the results of the enterprises entirely with a view to taxation. Attempts have been made to reduce the profits. According to Finnish taxation practice, the stock-taking may be carried out at a reduced value, provided the previous price level is kept approximately from year to year. But some firms have gone much further, thus depreciating the results. Under wartime conditions it happened in many cases that firms disregarded the fact that their expenses increased because their taxes were reduced by these means.

The auditors find themselves in a fairly difficult situation. Finnish professional auditors have adopted the standpoint that they do not wish to be tax inspectors. The state and local governments employ their special inspectors responsible for that.

The new Act in respect of book-keeping in Finland has made the matter much more complicated. The law requires that the auditor should certify below the closing balance sheet that the balance has been made out in accordance with general book-keeping principles and good business usage.

A new taxation Act is being prepared and will be submitted to the Diet probably next autumn. According to that the decisions of the taxation board in the 'size' taxation cases must be made known to the taxpayer prior to the issue of the demand note and he must be allowed to submit his explanations and reply at once regarding this 'size' taxation.

When the law proposal was submitted to the Central Chamber of Commerce for an opinion, the Chamber recommended for adoption that the 'size' taxation should not be resorted to at all so long as the result showed a profit not 20 per cent. below the average yield of the other businesses of the same character. The recommendation is not included in the final bill proposed. With regard to the appeal procedure, the Central Chamber of Commerce made an important announcement. When the taxation amounts are made known, extracts from the divergent resolutions made by the taxation board should be immediately available for appeals. As to the average

incomes, territorial average calculations have recently been started throughout the country at the initiative of the Ministry of Finance.

According to the new law the local and state taxations will be combined
and the taxations be directed into one channel. Also, taxation will be prepared by tax officers. The procedure, we hope, will in the future be more
homogeneous. We auditors hope also that we may rid ourselves of this hot-
house flower of high taxation.

MR. B. M. BERRY (Great Britain and Ireland):

Much was made in the papers concerning the unfairness of high taxation
and various protests were made against the government tendency to expro-
priate earnings because various governments considered that they could
spend money better than we could. I have no doubt that both were justified.
I should have thought that both were fairly obvious, but it may be not
obvious to governments.

However, the thing which strikes me as perhaps being under-emphasised
is the apparent unfairness of incidence between taxpayers—unfairness
which arises in several ways of which I could mention one or two.

One is by varying the rates. Again it is difficult to judge how unfair that
is. Another is by assessing in certain cases profits which in fact are not
profits. The most obvious case of this was the subject of Monday's discussion
and I do not propose to go into that. There are, however, one or two points
which might be made.

There has been a tendency to suggest in some circles that, irrespective of
what goes into accounts, these should be dealt with for tax purposes.
Primarily this is an accounting matter and not a fiscal matter. At the same
time I think that it is dangerous to adopt this habit of having too many
accounts. In one case I came across there were five different tax accounts,
one for internal auditors, one for external auditors and, incidentally, shareholders, the third for the management, the fourth for the fiscal people and
the fifth for the employees. I should hate to think that we really need five
different results to show. After all, profit should be measured sufficiently
accurately to serve all purposes.

The second point I should like to make is in connection with the question
of what I call 'revalorization'. It was said by two or three people on Monday
that to use this meant to tax unfairly the people who were not getting this
kind of relief. It would be true if we were relieved from taxation on what
were in fact profits. To illustrate that, I should be only too happy if the
Inland Revenue said 'We shall take off from your income the cost of replacing
your clothes and the cost of maintaining your house'. If depreciation is to
be allowed at all, it is because it is a business expense and it is necessary to
establish what is a fair figure. This other question is completely extraneous
and to my mind complete nonsense. The people it has been unfair to are the
companies, because they are asked to pay at high rates in a manner which
results in their paying sometimes more money than they in fact have made.

I have two minor points to make. One is that I wish we could avoid calling
income-tax that which is not in fact income-tax. An example of this in Great

Britain is Schedule A which is certainly not a tax on income. It is a property tax. The second point concerns the question of foreign income. I, too, wish that we could convince the authorities that income should not be assessed in both countries.

MR. P. J. DREYER (France):

One of the questions which Mr. Burr asks is, 'Is the scale of taxation to stay?' First of all I should like to try and show you briefly how much we are interested in this question in France. For the year 1952 our budget figures are the following:

Income-taxes, including taxes on wages and on profit for physical persons and companies, approximately 773 million. Death duties, stamps and other duties, 136 million; Customs, 231 million; transactions and purchase taxes, $1\frac{1}{2}$ billion; miscellaneous, including profits in respect of state properties, 294 million. That is a total of $2\frac{3}{4}$ billion. To obtain the full burden of social security we must add another $1\frac{1}{4}$ billion, the total being approximately 4 billion francs.

In order to appreciate the burden of taxation, it is usual to compare the amount of taxation with the national income. The last evaluation of the French national income being 12 thousand billion francs, the burden is about 33 per cent. Incidentally I do not think that the simple formula $\dfrac{\text{Taxation}}{\text{Income}}$ gives a right idea of the burden, and Mr. Laure, the manager of the French Treasury Department, has made an interesting study of this question. He has shown that if productivity falls from 100 to 25 income-tax also falls but from 100 to 5. Therefore, in order to obtain the same tax in a country where productivity is only 25 per cent. of another, taxes must be five times heavier.

To reach the total amount shown above, we have all kinds of taxes and rates, and I think that an example would illustrate the actual incidence in the best manner. Supposing a man managing a commercial or industrial business shows a profit of 100 million francs on a turnover of 1,000 million francs, after having paid 300 million francs in salaries. This business man will pay to the State (in millions of francs)—turnover taxes 173, social security 81, tax on salaries 15, a total of 269. Then income-tax, which is in two parts, the first being a proportional tax which comes to 18, and the second a progressive tax varying from 10 per cent. to 70 per cent. If the man is married without children under the age of 21 years, the figure is 46. Therefore, the State will have received a total amount of 269 plus 64 which is 333 on a profit which should have been 369, before any payment to the State, that is, 90 per cent.

Supposing now that the same business man belongs to a company. The figures are then as follows: turnover, social security, salaries tax (the same), 269. A special profits tax of 34 must be paid in the year when the profit is realised; income-tax, including 18 per cent. proportional tax and progressive tax at rates from 10 per cent. to 70 per cent., has to be paid only when dividends are distributed to shareholders, but the result should be the same as above when the profit is distributed, and when the average rate of progressive tax is 30 per cent., i.e. 18. The total then comes to 333.

Turning to the question posed in Mr. Burr's paper, I am afraid that the answer cannot be given by accountants. If the main purpose of taxation is to cover expenditure for the good of the general public, figures appearing in the reports of colleagues and those given above show that in many countries tax rates have reached such a level that they may be justified only when those countries have to repair war damage, or when they have to protect their freedom. But if it is admitted that the additional purpose of taxation, and particularly the redistribution of income becomes the main purpose of taxation, then I cannot see any good reason why these rates should go down.

MR. A. B. KHAN (Pakistan):

In the first place I should like to reply to an earlier speaker in connection with the point he raised about the tax payable on salaries earned in Pakistan for one month. It is because there is no agreement on double taxation between two countries in certain cases. As the tax is payable on income earned, whether it is payable in the country of origin or in the place where the services are rendered is immaterial. It is on this basis that perhaps the person concerned had to pay tax on salary earned for one month on the basis of total income.

I am very happy to be with you and to say a few words on the incidence of taxation in Pakistan. The pattern of taxation so far has been based on the British model. However, in our recent experiments, after the attainment of independence, we have been trying to develop the method of taxation to suit our people and the needs of our country. The taxation structure in my country is predominately agricultural. We have so far resisted the levy of taxes on agricultural income, except in one state which is moderately industrialised. The following are the main taxes levied in Pakistan: property tax, tax on profits from trade and business, profession, salary, wages and estate duty. Tax on income from industrial undertakings is exempt to a large extent in the form of heavy depreciation. A certain percentage of net income is also exempt for five years based on the amount of invested capital. 'Hidden' taxation such as nationalisation of land which takes away development profits from private owners is still unknown in Pakistan. Double taxation has been completely avoided. However, we have indirect taxation such as amusement tax and sales tax, which is the equivalent of your purchase tax.

The following are the objectives aimed at in our taxation laws: (1) Even distribution of income between the various classes and strata of society. (2) Discouragement of excessive and wasteful spending by thoughtless individuals of the community. (3) Discouragement of luxury imports. (4) Encouragement of national thrift and export. (5) Equality of sacrifices. There is a powerful directive against housing, education, health, social services and in general all the national building projects. Ample provisions have been made for statutory reserves, subsidies, maintenance of administrative and defence services. The birth of my country at a moment when the world is thrown into confusion and chaos has indeed added an extra burden of taxation on our poor economy.

So far as evasion of tax is concerned, I should like to emphasise that the lower the rate of tax the less evasion of it is there; but of course that does not mean no tax, no evasion. In the United Kingdom, as I understand it, the rate goes up to 97½ per cent. after a particular limit. The case is similar in Pakistan. I am sure if the States became a little wiser and reduced the rate of taxation they would realise more tax than they have been collecting. My personal opinion is that in no case should the tax exceed 50 per cent. of the net income. The maximum a man can willingly pay is 50 per cent., but beyond that one grudges, and the principle of evasion occurs. Putting it mathematically, when the limit of taxation reaches 50 per cent. of the net income, in the language of Calculus it works out thus: $DY/DX = 0$ which, in simple language, means the climax is reached and the fall begins. It is at this point where the intention to avoid sets in. Indeed, the very idea of taxation is annoying and I suggest it is high time we substituted a new name for this hated word 'tax'.

MR. A. W. FRYER (Great Britain and Ireland):

Few would deny the evil effects of a high rate of taxation which is clearly a problem of international importance. In his paper Mr. Burr has made an excellent survey of the present system and has also indicated very clearly some of its disadvantages. One point raised by him should, I feel, be emphasised and that is the complete disregard of expenses which occurs when there is a high rate of taxation, as the major portion of this expenditure is, in fact, paid for by the government. The effect of such waste is not easily calculated. There is a direct loss to the nation in the provision of goods and services which, under more normal conditions, would not be required, and an indirect loss in the encouragement of slackness with its consequent detrimental effect on productive effort.

There is apparently no easy solution to the manner in which the rate of taxation may be reduced, and I do not think that we can look simply to an increase in productive capacity to provide any great measure of relief in this direction. The problem of reducing taxation is not made any easier when we remember the opening subject of the Congress—'Fluctuating Price Levels in relation to Accounts'. Many speakers then advocated the calculation of depreciation of fixed assets based upon replacement costs. This view if accepted both for accounting and taxation purposes would involve substantial tax concessions to companies, which would raise the question of the provision of similar reliefs for other classes of taxpayers. Such concessions would not alter the total burden and may adversely affect the incidence on individuals. This point has been brought out by the Institute of Chartered Accountants in England and Wales in its recent recommendation.

It seems to me that for income-tax relief we have to look to a decrease in government expenditure, with which point Mr. Burr has dealt fully. Whilst I should say that there should be rigid economy in all forms of government expenditure, it seems that it would be a retrograde step if a curtailment was made in services such as housing, education and health. The nigger in the woodpile seems to be the expenditure on national defence which is a figure of £1,370 million, or approximately a third of the total national expenditure. It is not within our province as accountants to consider the wisdom or otherwise of the question of national defence, but it comes within the purview of a discussion on the incidence of taxation.

Mr. Burr said that in due time, as a result of international statesmanship, a reduction in rearmament expenditure might take place. I would go further and say that the time is now, that the question of rearmament has been taken too much for granted, and the emphasis should be on peace-making and the progressive reduction of armaments to alleviate many of our difficulties.

MR. J. D. R. JONES (Great Britain and Ireland):

I should like to refer to the part which taxation and its incidence plays in the maintenance of full employment, the avowed objective of most governments today. I do not think that it would be incorrect to suggest that the kind of full employment we have had in Britain from 1945 to date—over-full employment—is synonymous with inflation. That may not be a bad thing in itself. Yet, in order to confine inflation within reasonable bounds, the Government, in addition to imposing a multiplicity of controls, has maintained taxation at a penal level. Such taxation is itself inflationary. In the words of one of the chairmen of our larger companies,'It used to be said that taxes on profits were not inflationary, in that as no tax had to be paid unless a profit were made, the tax did not add to the actual cost of production. When taxes were moderate this was true, but when they are anything like their present level and are accompanied by a general and continued rise in costs they have a definite inflationary effect on prices'.

It has been asserted on innumerable occasions that the way to combat incipient or active inflation, whether it be income or cost inflation, is by greater and more efficient production especially of those goods for which there is a ready overseas market. Ironically enough, the level of taxation imposed on industry, as part of the economic and social policies of the Government, has been such as to leave a wholly inadequate residue to finance the provision of the equipment needed to increase efficiency and productivity. One of the taxes, profits tax, which has been well described as a tax on the tools of industry, discourages the raising of new share capital. Speaking on profits tax, the chairman of another of our large concerns said: 'Profits tax is perhaps the most mischievous tax ever imposed. It is a subtle and cumulative poison in the system of private enterprise, in that it is payable wholly out of profits withheld from distribution and therefore militates against the building-up of a business by the time-honoured process of ploughing-in. It militates also against the raising of capital from outside, because it imposes a fine of 50 per cent. on any dividends paid. It is sapping the strength of British industry and is highly objectionable on that ground alone.' It may be that the new excess profits levy will be less discouraging to the raising of new capital than profits tax by permitting additions to standard profits *pro rata* to new capital raised.

The recently published accounts for 1951 of a well-known industrial company showed a profit allocation of 63 per cent. to taxation, 21 per cent. to dividend, leaving 16 per cent. for reserves. With the advent of the excess profits levy—a thoroughly bad tax no matter how it may be amended by Parliament—that company may find itself paying away as much as 70 per cent. or more of its profit in taxation with a further constriction of the amount it can plough back. That is not an isolated example. I wonder whether there is another country with such an iniquitous three-tier system of taxation of company profits—income-tax, profits tax and excess profits levy—as we have.

Mr. Colin Clark, the distinguished economist, in a letter to *The Economist* in April 1949, expressed the view that taxation at 40 per cent. of the national income could not be maintained for long without intensifying and accelerating inflation. On the other hand, a member of the late government, Mr. Gaitskill, I believe, stated that the proportion of national income absorbed by taxation was not significant. What did matter was how the proceeds of taxation were expended. He did not say anything about wise spending. Which is the right view? If Mr. Colin Clark is correct, is there some ideal ratio between taxation and national income which will enable the economic and social policy of the Government to be fulfilled yet, at the same time, do the least harm to national economy? If the other view is right, its ultimate conclusion, I suggest, is the expropriation of all profits and, after that, what?

MR. D. M. D. McGUANE (Great Britain and Ireland):
While I cannot in the few minutes allotted to me give you a picture of the total incidence of taxation in my country—Ireland—I hope to bring into prominence the uneven incidence of our largest direct tax—income-tax.

Irish income-tax is modelled very closely on the British structure, even though one is primarily an agricultural country and the other an industrial country. The principal taxing statute is still the Income Tax Act of 1918, in itself mainly a reproduction of a body of law enacted more than a century ago and adapted to the economic, social and commercial conditions of that time. Copious amending legislation has been introduced each year but the system has never been overhauled in the light of experience gained or adapted to modern conditions. The same can largely be said of the taxation system in Great Britain but here at least an honest endeavour has been made to preserve a system which will satisfy the requirements of Adam Smith's first principle, even though this has resulted in most complex legislation.

Over the decade ending with the tax year 1949-50, the percentages of income assessable for tax under the several schedules of the Irish Tax Code were as follows: Schedule A (ownership of land) 6 per cent.; Schedule B (occupation of land) 2 per cent.; Schedule C (certain investments) 3 per cent.; Schedule D (profits from trades and professions) 46 per cent.; and Schedule E (salaries and wages) 43 per cent.; total 100 per cent.

An even more illuminating contrast is that shown by comparing the figures of actual income for tax purposes under the above schedules over the period under review. Profits assessable under Schedule D increased from

£24 million in 1939-40 to £48 million in 1949-50; wages and salaries assessable under Schedule E increased from £20·7 million in 1939-40 to £61·1 million in 1949-50, while income derived from the ownership and occupation of land assessed under Schedules A and B increased from £5·5 million in 1939-40 to £6·9 million in 1949-50.

Does this mean that the income of the farming community has remained static while the income of other sections has doubled and trebled? Not at all. It means a far different thing, namely, that the income for purposes of income-tax has remained static. Generally speaking, profits from the occupation and ownership of land are assessed on the statutory valuation of the land. This valuation, which was started in 1852 and completed in 1865, still constitutes, with some exceptions, the statutory measure of the farmers' profits. No allowance is made for the decline in the value of money since 1865.

It is obvious from this necessarily very brief summary that the burden of Irish income-tax is very unevenly shared. A more even incidence of tax on the different sections of the community is necessary to satisfy social justice and to lessen the penalties at present imposed on efficiency and effort. It is easy to devise ways in which this could be done but the responsibility for action rests with the Government.

It seems to me, however, that the accountancy profession has not, in my own country at least—and perhaps in others also—taken a sufficiently positive role in persuading governments that something should be done to redress a position such as I have been describing. The natural tendency for professional bodies is to limit action to providing advice on technical matters and submitting memoranda to committees of inquiry, but something more is called for when the burden of taxation is as heavy as it is at present, and otherwise minor irritants become major anomalies. The various accountancy bodies should not hesitate to issue, preferably on a joint basis, public pronouncements on what they consider to be undesirable in existing or pending tax legislation. In so doing they would be performing a public service and would enhance their own status.

MR. K. T. NEWHOUSE (Great Britain and Ireland):

It is noteworthy that the writers of the papers point out that in their countries the incidence of taxation of profits and of income has reached a level at which the incentive for private enterprise is seriously restricted. This is partly due to a new purpose of taxation. In the past, taxation was exclusively levied to secure revenue for the government. Nowadays in many countries profits and income are also taxed in order to redistribute income. There is a danger that in trying to achieve this objective, taxation is imposed at rates which directly restrict or at least impede economic progress. The high rates of taxation may restrict productivity in many countries so much that a point may soon be reached at which economic decline begins. This problem need not be considered from the point of view of one country alone.

Great developments in the past have been due to international finance. They were made possible by investing capital overseas. The owner of the capital was mostly liable to tax at low rates on his income in his country of residence only. Nowadays, the lender will mostly be confronted with taxation of his income at high rates both in his country of residence and abroad. In other words, the income is taxed in the country where it arises and in the country of residence of the original lender who ultimately has to bear the tax. The lending of funds by the resident of one country, for investment in another country, is in many cases penalised by the imposition of a non-residents tax which may restrict the net return obtainable on overseas investments.

Steps have been taken, in particular since the war, to overcome what is now known as double taxation. Many international conventions have been concluded to relieve the burden of double taxation. The relief obtainable under most of these conventions is unfortunately difficult to assess and rather elusive. The conventions seem to raise many complicated practical problems which concern not only the investor but also his financial adviser and the accountant, and sometimes even the lawyer.

The difficulties which double taxation creates and which are not overcome by the conventions affect a great many taxpayers. It is not only the lonely widow who may not know the effect of double taxation on her personal allowances. Investment companies also have great troubles in ascertaining their true net income.

In drafting the conventions, the rules which Adam Smith formulated have been lost sight of. As is well known, he has stated: 'The tax which the individual is bound to pay ought to be certain, not arbitary. The time of payment, the manner of payment, the quantity to be paid ought to be clear and plain to the contributor and to every other person.' Another of his four requirements is that every tax should be cheap in operation.

There is little in the conventions which makes for economy in administration and for cheapness in computing the relief due. What seems to be required is a more scientific approach to the subject. I submit that the object of the Conventions for the Relief of Double Taxation should be: The avoidance of double taxation so that this does not arise. If tax is not payable twice, the amount of relief need not be computed, claimed and allowed. If this cannot be done then I submit that the provisions for relief should be so clear and simple that relief can be ascertained with certainty as soon as the income arises, so that the lender or the industrialist knows exactly his net income.

Let us hope that when the Seventh Congress meets some conventions will have been redrafted in the spirit of Adam Smith. Simplification should be a small but important step in fostering private overseas enterprise and economic progress. Perhaps this is another subject for consideration by an international committee on accountancy.

MR. C. A. NEWPORT (Great Britain and Ireland):

One or two speakers have suggested that our topic this morning is one which goes back as far as Adam Smith. I wonder whether I might go back a few years earlier to the Greek philosopher Aristotle, who lived about 400 B.C. You will be familiar with the philosophy of Aristotle and you only need reminding that among his various works there is one to the effect that the human mind has a unique capacity in that it is capable, in its higher manifestations, of becoming part of that which it knows. When I consider our papers I feel that there is no danger of the minds of accountants becoming part of the incidence of taxation! We gather from the papers that the incidence of taxation is something the nature of which you can discover if you refer to a dictionary, but apart from that it has no real significance whatever except as part of the general consequences of taxation.

It is rather a pity, I think, that the authors of the papers, particularly those of the United Kingdom, did not, when they wrote their papers, have the benefit of the report of the Government Committee which dealt with taxation on site values, because the report does pay some considerable attention to this question of the incidence of taxation, or the rate of site values which is a comparable subject in many respects. I think that many quite useful suggestions might have been incorporated in the paper if Mr. Burr and his colleagues had had the opportunity of seeing that report before they wrote their papers.

MR. S. P. QUICK (Great Britain and Ireland):

The greatest part of the discussion today is being devoted to the various aspects of direct taxation. Delegates from every country vie with each other in describing in gruesome detail the way in which this monster preys upon its victims; and that emphasis is right, for having spent our student days mastering the intricacies of accountancy, an overlarge proportion of our working life is thereafter spent in trying to reduce the share that this senior partner draws out of each business!

I would, however, invite your attention to the havoc also wrought in the world's economy by the older forms of taxation, namely, excise duties, customs duties and other similar levies. I would class them under the general heading of 'prepayment taxes', taxes paid by businesses sometimes many months before they can be recouped from the individual customer. In times of inflation they increase the inflationary pressure to the detriment of world economy.

In 1952-53, it is estimated that Great Britain will raise approximately £1,200 million from these sources. In the United States of America for 1951 the Federal taxes alone under this head were $7,392 million. In Australia for 1951-52 the yield was estimated at nearly £300,000, well over 25 per cent. of their total budget. These amounts are three or four times the equivalent 1938 figures. It is probable that a similar position exists in nearly every country in the world and year by year our respective governments increase the amounts to be collected in this fashion.

Yet these prepayment taxes are contributing in no small degree to the inflation which besets the world today. Each and every one of us knows of businesses, large and small, which in order to meet the rise in the cost of stocks caused in part by the addition of these taxes, have had to borrow from the banks or other sources in order to maintain their stock position. Consider tobacco in Great Britain. A small shop with a stock costing in 1938 £1,000 finds the same stock today costs nearly £4,000. Your manufacturer finds that £40 million stock has today risen to £130 million. In both these cases the bank is asked to lend money, at least partly secured on the stock value inflated as it is by this rise in tax, that is secured on the very tax for the payment of which it is being borrowed. This is directly inflationary. The individual businesses are thus borrowing capital sums to meet taxes for current government expenditure. Yet in many instances these taxes were imposed to 'mop up expenditure'. These inflationary taxes were imposed in the belief that they were deflationary. What is worse is that they are still being imposed and even increased in the same belief.

You know well I am not quoting isolated cases. The same position is arising in every trade affected by this type of tax. Throughout the whole range of purchase tax we see this damage being done. We are quick enough to tell directors when we think they are not being financially prudent. Are we satisfied that we have given our countries the same unbiased opinion on national financial imprudence with the same weight that we bring to bear on those directors?

To misquote, 'All taxes are bad but some are worse than others'. Whilst we continue to give our major attention to protecting the junior partner, may I suggest that when fighting our other enemy inflation we should examine the inflationary effect of those 'prepayment taxes' when charged to excess and make representations accordingly.

Mr. J. W. ROBERTS (Australia):

A lot has been said concerning the individual aspects of taxation but I feel that one cannot stress over-much the national aspect of taxation. My country is relatively under-developed as compared with other nations in Europe. We have vast areas in the centre of our land which are largely prevented from being developed by the missing links of rail and air communication. Recently it was stated that £19 million was required in order to bridge the gap between the heart and the nearest connecting rail links in Queensland. This money will not come from the funds of corporation and individual taxes. It must come from abroad as well and attention has been called to the fact that in the present state of affairs in Australia, it is not going to be an easy task to convince the industrialists in Britain or America that they should invest very large sums at some not inconsiderable risk with the prospect of having to pay tax on their earnings. How much better it would be, rather than to labour diminishing funds, to say 'We will have a period in which we will make deals with industrialists from abroad who are going to develop certain manufacturing processes and we shall give them the necessary opportunity to develop their industries for the first ten years during which time their tax will be placed in abeyance.

I cannot be specific on so wide a subject but I think that some class of, might I say, 'business seeking' approach is required by the tax collecting authorities. After all, their existence depends more than anything else upon a continuation of the very funds which they tax. Of necessity anything which I say must be general, although as I come from Australia I must relate it to the problem of my own country. Our contribution to defence commitments must be small because our expenditure is very small compared with that of other countries, for instance, the United States. I think that a sane approach based upon the fact that we are still in a stage of development would influence the flow of capital to our country.

MR. R. F. W. SHERATON (Great Britain and Ireland):

I make no pretence to any sort of knowledge of the incidence of taxation in countries other than my own, although I do feel that certain of my observations will apply to conditions prevailing elsewhere. Generally speaking, however, my remarks will be directed towards direct taxation operating in this country at the present time. The question of taxation, as with so many other matters having an important bearing on the life of the community, has been subject from time to time to plausible-sounding catch phrases, which in the minds of many, provide ample justification for the policies which their authors propound in regard to it. For instance,'Payment by virtue of capacity to pay' and 'No taxation without representation' are notable examples which will readily occur to us here today.

There would appear to be little room for doubt that, anyway in this country, the incidence of taxation is governed very largely by political considerations. I venture to suggest that this should not be so. In the interests of the community and of the nation as a whole, taxation should be levied in such a manner as to spread the burden in as just and equitable a fashion as is humanly possible. Today, the doctrine of taxing by virtue of capacity to pay has been carried far beyond the bounds of reason, and we are well aware of the almost insurmountable burdens which certain sections of our people are shouldering. In this regard, many of those whose livelihood is derived from what are paradoxically referred to as 'fixed incomes', i.e. from dividends, pensions and annuities, are bearing, largely as a consequence of abnormal taxation, burdens which, in numerous instances, have become almost intolerable.

It seems now a very long time since the cry first went around that there should be no taxation without representation. At the outset, it was propounded as a precept regarded almost with religious fervour. It is only too clear that the situation today has undergone a considerable change in this respect. Largely as a consequence of the introduction and enormous growth of joint-stock enterprise, we find that taxation is imposed upon many thousands of industrial and commercial undertakings which have no representation—certainly no direct representation—at all. One sees this state of affairs operating not only as regards national taxation, but also by reference to the demands made by local authorities in the form of rates.

I venture to suggest that this is a state of affairs which, in justice, calls for early remedy. It goes, however, further than this, for we have confronting us today a situation wherein there is not only a considerable measure of taxation without representation, but what I submit is even more objectionable—representation without taxation. In other words, we have those directly or indirectly responsible for levying upon others taxation of a character which they themselves bear little or nothing at all. It needs no words of mine to stress the implications of such a condition of affairs.

I should like for a few moments to develop this theme, and in doing so, to submit to you that in many ways the incidence of taxation in this country is not only illogical but it is also extremely unwise and certainly shortsighted.

It has appeared always—anyway to me—a most extraordinary circumstance that industry and commerce, which after all provide us with our means of livelihood, and the results of whose activities enable us to maintain our existing standard of living, always seem to be considered, and treated, by successive governments, as legitimate targets—shall we say 'fair game'— for the imposition of the maximum of taxation. We see large and enterprising businesses, concerns which give employment to many hundreds of thousands of persons, able and willing to enlarge and develop their activities, curbed and frustrated by taxation which is positively penal in its incidence. We saw it in the case of the excess profits tax, and the latest example is at hand in the new excess profits levy. I think it is reasonably clear that those businesses which will suffer most as a consequence of this new impost, are not those without enterprise and initiative, but such as have the spirit and will-power to develop and extend. Here again, apart from being illogical, surely this is altogether unwise? Mr. Burr in his paper very rightly directs attention to the position of the individual. A person with a capacity to exercise his talents and skill, one with the opportunity before him to earn increasing rewards, should not be subjected to excessive taxation by way of imposing upon him such increasing rates of income-tax and sur-tax as ultimately leave him with but sixpence from each pound earned.

I agree unreservedly with Mr. Burr that the incidence of taxation, as it falls today both upon the employer and upon the employee, is doing incalculable harm in restraining productive output. When one remembers that it is of such vital importance to encourage and obtain the greatest possible production, the seriousness of the situation is surely crystal clear.

It was, I believe, Benjamin Franklin, American philosopher and statesman, who ventured the remark that two things in life were certain—death and taxes. That they do not come in that order is to be regretted! Nevertheless, the imposition of taxation does concede to the professional accountant the opportunity for service, and of alleviating to the best of his ability its incidence upon the community generally.

MR. G. H. TAYLOR (Great Britain and Ireland):

I am glad to have this opportunity of voicing my views on this subject as it is to me a matter of great concern. To my mind the incidence of taxation plays too great a part in every-day living. Everything we touch is taxed and it has become a question not so much of what can be collected from the taxpayers as 'what shall be left to them'.

I would like to start with a very debatable point. Should the incidence of taxation be used to control finance and to regulate social conditions? My personal opinion is a very definite no. So used it becomes confiscatory, the benefits accruing cease to have any relation to the contributions made, the total to be raised is greater and avoidance becomes worth while, the taxing statutes become more and more confused as their compilers attempt to leave no loopholes for escape and it ceases to be possible for the general public to understand how they are being taxed. Possibly good for our profession but bad for the taxpayer.

Taxation can be considered as a levy for funds to be spent on objects beyond the scope of individuals, such objects being of two kinds—transient and lasting. A year's transient spending should come from that year's income; lasting spending should be raised by the issue of securities redeemable over a period of years and each year's redemption be provided from that year's income. Capital can be accumulated out of surplus income over a period or it can be borrowed in the first place and repaid out of income thereafter. The primary incidence of tax should therefore be on income, and from the papers on this subject it appears that such a tax comes into being sooner or later in all countries. To tax capital is to my mind essentially bad unless the proceeds are used for a lasting purpose.

Basically we are all individuals possessed of free will and the capability of distinguishing between right and wrong, opinion as to what is right or wrong varying from decade to decade. The expression 'individual' implies a difference from a general pattern and I hold the opinion that no two people will make the same use of any exactly similar opportunity. Thus there can never be equality in a material sense. I believe in spiritual equality, in that we all have the fundamental attributes, the use we make of them being our personal responsibility. There is, however, a growing tendency to deny this right of individuality and attempts are made to impose material equality and the creation of a standard pattern. Along with this has grown a conception of 'The Government' as a distinct entity possessed of personal means in place of the true position of 'The Government' as merely representative of the individual and possessed of no means except what the individual provides through taxation.

If the right of individuality is granted, then it must also be granted that the individual is entitled to reward for his efforts, manual, mental or financial, commensurate to the amount of effort expended and that, further, the individual should be free to do as he pleases with the reward he has obtained. This introduces the question of incentive which must be present except in very rare circumstances. Incentive is basically the need to provide (i) the necessities of life, (ii) improvement in standards of living, (iii) the upbringing of children, (iv) provision for old age, all of which have to be exchanged for effort.

How then does the incidence of taxation link up with individuality and incentive? If the incidence rises steeply the point where the net reward is not commensurate with the effort expended is quickly reached and incentive disappears and with it effort; if the incidence becomes confiscatory and creates dissatisfaction the result is the same.

How should the incidence of taxation be borne? Assuming that it is on income, or recompense for effort expended, then it will be borne by the profits of business and personal incomes, which are actually only part of business profits. These profits have also to provide for the expansion of business and for the repayment of borrowed capital.

I should like to suggest that the incidence of taxation be such as to encourage incentive and to recognise individuality that it should (*a*) fall on personal incomes and business profits only; (*b*) as regards profits left in a business be either nil or at only half the standard rate—this to provide incentive to build up a business; (*c*) as regards personal incomes, be subject to such a scale of allowances for wife and children as would result in the tax cancelled being in close relation to a cost of living per person, slightly above what would be considered reasonable for an average family. Also subject to such a scale that extra earnings did not carry a disproportionate burden. Also subject to relief for savings on the same lines as on profits left in a company, chiefly house purchase and life or endowment insurance. Decrease in savings could be charged at the rate of relief.

I see no justification for a multiplicity of taxes, income-tax, sur-tax, profits tax and the like. There should be one tax and if the incidence of taxation only related to the provision of those services beyond the scope of the individual, e.g. foreign relations, police, army, navy and air force, communications, drainage, water and electricity, these latter being considered not as disconnected immediate requirements but as part of a continuous programme of development, the standard rate should not need to be excessively high.

MR. F. A. COFFEY (Canada):

With regard to the incidence of taxation, it was pointed out that increasing high taxes on business income becomes an indirect tax on consumers. Such tax then becomes inflationary. Mr. Green stated that there was a movement on foot to obtain constitutional amendment in the United States to limit the Federal taxing power to a 50 per cent. rate. Our present Canadian Government has expressed the view that a corporation income-tax of over 50 per cent. is unwise and this year carried out its avowed intention by limiting its income-tax on corporate income to 50 per cent. (tax on the first $10,000 of taxable income is at a 20 per cent. rate). This is coloured a bit by the fact that there has been imposed a separate 2 per cent. tax on income for the old-age pension fund. However, the change is a step in the right direction because the amendment provides as well for a credit of five percentage points with respect to corporations subject to provincial tax on profits. Two of our ten provinces, namely, Quebec and Ontario, levy a 7 per cent. tax on corporation profits. Therefore our tax rate on corporations is 20 per cent. on the first $10,000 and 50 per cent. on the balance plus the additional 2 per cent. pension tax on all taxable income with the extra 2 per cent. for corporations subject to tax in the two provinces mentioned.

Earnings distributed by way of cash dividends are subject to tax in the hands of Canadian shareholders or by withholding tax (5 per cent. or 15 per cent.) with respect to non-residents. A United Kingdom corporate shareholder is not subject to Canadian tax on dividends paid. A Canadian individual receives a credit from tax payable of 10 per cent. of the Canadian dividends included in his taxable income.

Mr. Green also referred to tax on undistributed corporate earnings and we in Canada had in our previous income-tax Act a provision for deeming any undue accumulation of undistributed income as a dividend and subject to tax in the hands of a shareholder, whether or not received. Such a determination by the tax authorities could almost amount to confiscation. Because of this and because of a similar position in which the estate of a large shareholder of a closely-held corporation—not a personal corporation but an active commercial one—would find itself due to the necessity of declaring a dividend in order to pay succession duties, our Government enacted Part 1A.

The Canadian enactment is probably a unique one, providing as it does for the freeing of undistributed income on hand, to the end of the 1949 fiscal year, from any tax in the hands of the shareholders upon payment of a 15 per cent. tax thereon by the corporation and the capitalising of the remaining 85 per cent. As a result of this enactment the Government received almost immediately over $25,000,000 of tax and shareholders received dividends in preference shares which could be immediately redeemed by the corporation. Such stock dividends, I understand, are not taxable in the United Kingdom so this manner of distribution is of particular benefit to a United Kingdom individual shareholder who would in any event be subject to a 15 per cent. withholding tax on a cash dividend which dividend would be subject to tax in the United Kingdom.

There is a continuing feature to this new legislation which in effect allows one-half of post-1949 earnings to be obtained by shareholders at a flat 15 per cent. rate payable by the corporation. The amount to which this provision can be applied is limited to the cash dividends paid from 1949 to the end of the year preceding the year in which election is made to come under the provisions.

It is difficult in a short résumé fully to explain the implications of Part 1A of our Income Tax Act, but such part should be of particular interest to anyone considering investment in an existing or new Canadian company. I might add that the provisions of Part 1A, 'Tax on Undistributed Income' of Section 71A, 'Employees Profit Sharing Plan', of Section 11 (i) (f) and (g), 'Contributions to Pension Plan', the low 20 per cent. rate on the first $10,000 of income (Section 36) and the dividend credit of 10 per cent. (Section 35) combine to enable a small group of persons to obtain the benefits of incorporation with a tax burden not much in excess of what they would pay as a partnership.

Now in respect of multiple taxation, to which Mr. Horley refers, Canada has also taken a forward step to encourage investment in foreign countries. Provision is now made for exempting from Canadian income-tax dividends received by a Canadian corporation from a foreign corporation in which it has at least a 25 per cent. stock interest.

MR. V. SPANG-THOMSEN (Denmark):

Historical facts and details about the taxation of persons in Denmark will hardly be of any particular interest to this international forum. The only thing I should like to say about it is that the amount on which persons in Denmark pay their income-tax is the net income of the year, less taxes and rates paid on income and capital.

The total annual receipts of government and municipalities in Denmark amount to about kr. 4,000 million. About half of this sum is made up of direct taxes and rates, and about 12 per cent. of these are paid by companies. I believe that the taxation of joint-stock companies and holding companies will command a far wider interest internationally. In the following I shall give an account of the taxation of joint-stock companies, particularly holding companies, and in conclusion I shall mention the deliberations that are being made in Denmark on an amendment of the existing rules and regulations regarding the assessment of taxes and rates. In that respect, too, I shall make special reference to the taxation of joint-stock companies and holding companies.

According to the Danish fiscal legislation the following taxes and rates are at present payable by joint-stock companies:

(1) Ordinary income-tax, cf. Act No. 149 of 10th April, 1922, as amended;
(2) Temporary 20 per cent. increase of the tax mentioned under (1), cf. the annual Tax Imposition Acts, the latest being Act No. 109 of 31st March, 1952;
(3) Local rates, cf. Act No. 28 of 18th February, 1937, as amended;
(4) Sur-tax, divided into a 'dividend rate' and a 'remainder rate', cf. the annual Tax Imposition Acts, the latest being Act No. 109 of 31st March, 1952;
(5) Temporary 20 per cent. increase of the tax mentioned under (4), cf. the last mentioned Act, Section 32;
(6) Defence tax which for the current fiscal year amounts to 25 per cent. of the taxes mentioned under (1) and (4), cf. Act No. 111 of 31st March, 1952.

(1) *Ordinary income-tax* is assessed on the net profits earned during each single year, according to an ascending scale, the progressivity being dependent upon the ratio the income bears to the share capital.

When calculating the income, deduction may be made from the net profits of an amount corresponding to the taxes and rates of the categories mentioned under (1), (2) and (3), paid during the financial year just as an allowance of 5 per cent. on the share capital is made. The progressivity is determined *after* the allowance for taxes but *before* the 5 per cent. allowance.

In such cases where part of the income is appropriated with a view to consolidating the enterprise, a reduction of the corresponding taxes is effected upon application being made; such reduction amounts to 25 per cent.

If an amount appropriated for consolidation purposes is later spent in payment of dividend or if, e.g., it is distributed between shareholders upon the winding-up of the company, a penal tax is imposed which is so assessed that half the amount on which the allowance was made in previous years is placed on top of the income for the financial year in which the amount is spent.

(2) *The increase of the tax* mentioned under (1) needs no particular comment.

(3) *Local rates* are levied on a proportional basis, and they nearly always

amount to 5 per cent. of the income. Deduction from the gross income is allowed of taxes and rates as mentioned under (1), (2) and (3), paid during the financial year.

(4) *Sur-tax*. The sur-tax was introduced in 1940. The wording of the Act is rather intricate and has given rise to a very comprehensive set of interpretation rules. I shall not go into details, but here are the main points: the income computed as mentioned under (3) is taxed according to an ascending scale, the progressivity being dependent on the ratio the earnings of the individual years bear to the share capital plus a certain part of the reserves of the company.

'Free reserves', i.e. reserves which may freely be spent in payment of dividends at a later time, including 'balance carried forward to next year', are left out of account when computing such addition. The 'permanent reserves' are also left out of account as far as an amount equal to 50 per cent. of the share capital is concerned. The addition will then amount to half of the remaining permanent reserves as shown by the balance sheet prepared at the beginning of the year.

In order to allow an abatement of one-third of such part of the income as is utilised for consolidation purposes, the computation is made in two stages. First, the 'dividend rate' is computed on such part of the earnings of the year as is not set aside for consolidation purposes (i.e. is not appropriated for the permanent reserve funds). Next a computation is made on the whole income, and from the amounts so found is deducted the 'dividend rate'. The remainder is then reduced by one-third and is termed the 'remainder rate'. Between them the 'dividend rate' and the 'remainder rate' make out the sur-tax.

In such cases where the financial year of the companies does not coincide with the calendar year we sometimes have the awkward state of affairs that the 'dividend rate' and the 'remainder rate' are computed on two different financial years so that the 'dividend rate' deducted upon calculation of the whole income is based on a quite different financial year. No further mention will be made of such absurdities.

(5) The increase of tax mentioned under (4), and

(6) The increase of the taxes mentioned under (1) and (4) require no special comments.

The approximate amount of all the taxes and rates imposed upon joint-stock companies for the current fiscal year will appear from the appendix attached.

Taxation of holding companies

By way of introduction it should be mentioned that—in accordance with a practice that has been retained from previous legislation—a few, rather old companies in Denmark and their subsidiary company, or parent company, as the case may be, are assessed jointly, the concern being regarded as one economic unit. It will hardly be possible to prove that any advantage is derived from this joint assessment and on the whole it must be considered a survival of minor importance.

In addition to the general rules applicable to holding companies referred to later, mention should be made of the provision regarding company earnings through operations abroad. If part of the gross income of a company has been earned through a permanent place of business abroad, the taxes and rates mentioned under (1), (2) and (3), and the 'remainder rate' mentioned under (4), as well as the increases relative thereto, mentioned under (5) and (6), are reduced in proportion to such part of the total gross income as is earned abroad. The provision is of particular importance to insurance companies, but its application is not limited to them.

These general rules concerning abatement in respect of operations abroad will sometimes be made superfluous through provisions contained in the agreements which Denmark has made with foreign countries for the purpose of avoiding double taxation. The inference is drawn from a judgment pronounced by the Supreme Court in 1939 that the provisions of such agreements with foreign countries concerning avoidance of double taxation are always to be applied, but that a company cannot obtain abatement of the tax under both these legal provisions.

The actual legal provisions governing the taxation of holding companies are embodied in the Finance (Taxation) Act, i.e. Act No. 149 of 10th April, 1922, Section 37, subsections (3) and (4), as well as in the other Tax Imposition Acts, the latest of these being Act No. 109 of 31st March, 1952, Section 14, subsection (2).

The provisions apply to all the taxes and rates referred to, with the exception of the rate mentioned under (3), i.e. the proportional 5 per cent. local rate.

The provisions call for a computation, in the first place, of the amount of taxes and rates paid by the subsidiary company on the dividend entering into the profit and loss account of the parent company, and next, of the amount of taxes and rates paid by the parent company on this very same dividend. The parent company will then have its taxes and rates reduced to the extent of the smaller of these two amounts.

Here is an example to illustrate what taxes and rates have been paid on the dividend by the subsidiary company and the parent company, respectively. In the calendar year 1950 the subsidiary company has an income of kr. 50,000, kr. 35,000 of which is paid in dividend to the parent company which is supposed to hold all the shares of the subsidiary company. On the said income the subsidiary company will, for instance, pay taxes and rates in an amount of kr. 16,000 of which $\dfrac{16,000 \times 35}{50} =$ kr. 11,200 falls on the dividend.

In 1951 the parent company has an income in the amount of kr. 160,000, including the sum of kr. 35,000 in question. On its entire income the parent company will pay taxes and rates in an amount of kr. 24,000 of which $\dfrac{24,000 \times 35}{160} =$ kr. 5,250 falls on the dividend of kr. 35,000.

Suppose we consider an out-and-out holding company, i.e. one whose sole business consists in holding and controlling shares of a number of other companies, and whose income is exclusively made up of dividends derived

x

from such subsidiary companies. In that case the parent company would be entitled to abatement on its entire income and as a rule would be exempt from income-tax (still with the exception of the proportional 5 per cent. local rate levied on the income).

It must be admitted that the subsidiary company would have to pay tax on the dividend—such dividend being part of its profit—a year earlier than the parent company. However, in view of the ever-rising taxes during recent years it is probable that the parent company—in the first place—would nevertheless be assessed in rather heavier income taxes and rates on the dividend than those previously paid by the subsidiary companies.

If this is left out of account, and if it is assumed that all the subsidiary companies are running well, are yielding a suitable profit on the capital invested, and are providing for a proper consolidation, then the out-and-out holding company will be quite exempt from paying taxes and rates.

If, according to the scale, all the subsidiary companies are required to pay a larger percentage of their income than does the parent company, the parent company will be exempt from paying taxes and rates, still with the exception of the proportional 5 per cent. local income rate.

A condition for an abatement in respect of holding companies is, in the case of the tax mentioned under (1), and the relative increases, that the parent company, at the time of assessment, holds, and during the whole of the preceding financial year has held, at least 50 per cent. of the shares of the subsidiary company. As to the taxes mentioned under (4), and the relative increases, it will be sufficient for the parent company to have held 25 per cent. of the shares of the subsidiary company at the times mentioned if it is a matter of a holding company proper.

Thus it will be seen that the present taxation system has realised the necessity of preventing the earnings of a concern from being taxed in the hands of both the subsidiary company and the parent company.

In cases where a concern is so organised that the holding company holds shares of the parent company, and the parent company holds the shares of the subsidiary company, the rules referred to above will be applicable both to the assessment of the holding company in respect of dividend from the parent company and to the assessment of the parent company in respect of dividend from the subsidiary company, provided that the provisions as to the percentage of shareholdings have been complied with.

From the point of the subsidiary company the import of these provisions lies in the fact that it is taxed in the usual way and will have to aim at a comparatively constant dividend and an income somewhat larger than the dividend, in order to bring about a sound consolidation. It is of importance that the dividend payable to the parent company can be drawn from the income of the individual year. From the point of view of the parent company or the holding company, the parent company will appear to be practically exempt from paying taxes so long as the profits of the subsidiary company are subject to a higher rate than are the profits of the parent company. The proportional local rate must be regarded as an insignificant supplement to the other taxes, which are far more onerous.

Under the present taxation system the investor should have no great misgivings at subscribing to shares of a holding company since he is assured that the income will be taxed only once (plus a small addition) before the dividend of the holding company falls to him and is taxed as personal income.

However, there is another aspect of the position of the shareholder which merits mention here although it is not particular to holding companies. It is laid down by a certain legal provision (the annual Tax Assessment Acts, the latest of which being Act No. 512 of 21st December, 1951, Section 8) that a shareholder is required to include in his taxable income any yield of shares, the only exception being repayment of the nominal share capital.

A shareholder, therefore, who acquires shares of a holding company at a price of, say, 200, and through a subsequent winding-up of the holding company receives total proceeds corresponding to a price of 195, will have to include in his taxable income an amount corresponding to the 95 points.

The absurdity of this provision has long been recognised, but it has nevertheless been in force these last twelve years. One further provision as to a shareholder's liability to pay taxes should be mentioned here: according to the Danish system of taxation a shareholder resident abroad is not liable to pay taxes in Denmark on dividends paid to him, while shareholders resident in Denmark have to include dividends on shares in their personal taxable income.

I should also like to say that according to the proposals of the committee shareholders, whether residents of Denmark or not, are to pay income-tax on dividends received.

A special suggestion has been made to the effect that holding companies should be exempt from paying the proportional income-tax mentioned under (2), as far as dividends arising from subsidiary companies are concerned.

On the other hand, it has been proposed to levy a dividend tax on dividends going from subsidiary companies to parent companies, and that parent companies are also to pay such a tax on dividends declared. While a number of objections and comments have otherwise been made to the proposals of the Taxation Act Committee, no objections appear to have been raised from any quarters against the double taxation involved. This is presumably due to the fact that holding companies and concerns are not very much in evidence in Denmark. We have no organ to look after the interests of such combinations vis-à-vis the authorities; this has not been of particular importance so far.

If the proposals of the Taxation Act Committee are carried into effect it must be assumed that a holder of shares of a holding company will be left with only a very modest part of the earnings of the subsidiary company. In the first place the subsidiary company will have to pay the proportional tax on the whole of the income (say 40 per cent.) plus an additional tax on the dividend in case it exceeds a certain minimum part of the income (e.g. if it exceeds 20 per cent.). Then the parent company will have to pay dividend tax, since it must be assumed that the dividend cannot be kept within the untaxed part of the income. Finally, the shareholder will have to include in his taxable income the dividend received from the parent company.

How much will be left to the shareholder of the parent company of the earnings of a subsidiary company cannot be estimated so long as the proposals of the Taxation Act Committee do not contain taxing scales. However, as the difference between the net income and the dividend of a holding company will rarely be of any large order, and the progressivity of the dividend tax is dependent on this very factor, the proposals of the Taxation Act Committee must be regarded as a very serious threat against the holding companies and their shareholders.

As I mentioned before, the legal provisions have not yet been amended, and it is to be hoped that the legislators will become aware of the aspect of the matter I have referred to before. No doubt the provision should be incorporated in a new Act on taxation that a parent company is exempt from paying dividend tax on dividends received from a subsidiary company.

Such a provision might be worded almost like the corresponding one in the present Act which provides that the dividend tax of a parent company is reduced by an amount equal to that which has been paid by the subsidiary company on the dividend included in the income of the parent company, provided that the reduction is not to exceed the amount of the tax in which the parent company has been assessed in respect of the same dividend. You will notice that unless such a provision is incorporated the dividends of a subsidiary company will be subject to taxation at three points: first at the subsidiary company, then at the parent company, and finally at the shareholder. As regards concerns which follow the pattern of holding company, parent company, subsidiary company, the dividends will be subject to taxation four times according to the proposals of the Taxation Act Committee. Such a taxation is only likely to put a complete stop to the activities of concerns and will rob shareholders of a holding company of practically all their earnings.

MR. P. LIVINGSTONE ARMSTRONG (Great Britain and Ireland):

In the very admirable papers one aspect is not given consideration: the part accountants can and must play in economic life, in adjusting the incidence of taxation to present-day conditions.

There seem to be two points on this. The first is interpretative—to make clear what the taxation is being used for. This concerns every one of us—whether in our work in public service, in practice, in industry or in commerce, or as private citizens.

Two speakers on Wednesday said they often could not understand public or government accounts. If you, as learned accountants and citizens—I am sure you will not mind if I add, intelligent citizens—cannot understand them, who can? What hope is there for the average taxpayer to do so? It is our duty to insist on having good and clear accounts. If our fellow citizens really understood what our taxation was spent on—and the value received for the expenditure—much might indeed be achieved to reduce it.

The second point is professional unity. Many speakers have referred, wishfully, to the need for government and other public authorities to consult the accountancy bodies before drafting and issuing laws and regulations on accounting matters. This is especially so in taxation and its effect. Some progress has been made in this field, but in my opinion not enough.

Mr. George O. May, in his wise observations on Tuesday, referred to the great increase in the strength of the accounting profession and the need for it to assume greater responsibility. Surely the time has now come for our leaders, together, to press for this right to be consulted and to give advice, on principle and on detail, proved to be so necessary for the cloistered civil servant and overworked politician alike. If necessary, let our leaders say how we can give them the support of this growing strength, so that our professional skill and experience may play a more prominent and effective part in all financial aspects of economic policy.

In conclusion, I would like to tell you a story, a true one. In 1938, government vacillation and delay in placing orders was preventing a large company from starting production on a new line—tooling was expensive and without substantial numbers loss was inevitable. In desperation, after many months, the directors of the company, having confidence in the product, decided to take this risk and production was started, with the hope that government orders would eventually be forthcoming. That production was of the first thousand Hawker Hurricane fighter aircraft. Without that initiative, we might not be gathered here today, in the midst of this great city, for 80 per cent. of the Royal Air Force fighters in the Battle of Britain—on which so much depended—were off that line of Hurricanes.

I do not know the Hawker position today but I very much doubt if equivalent enterprise would now be financially possible in many companies, with taxation draining off liquid resources, especially with profits computed upon historical cost and no adequate alternative field of finance to draw upon.

Although an extreme example, this is in no way an isolated one and is not restricted to Britain. Initiative and enterprise in industry is vital to our life and must be preserved. As skilled and responsible members of this great profession we must not fail in our public duty.

MR. R. STACEY (Great Britain and Ireland):

I should like to comment on one of Mr. Burr's questions on page 506 of his excellent paper. I refer to the question that there should be improvements in the standard of life of the nation by the possible transference of the state-maintained health service to one more nearly approaching a true and actuarially self-supporting scheme perhaps of a voluntary nature. With all possible respect to Mr. Burr, I consider this suggestion—at any rate as applied to England and Wales—both impracticable and unnecessary. Surely, the provision of a comprehensive health service should be the first charge on the revenues of any civilised country, not only from the humanitarian point of view, but from the point of view that people are kept in health so that they can best make their contribution to the welfare of the state.

In England and Wales, the National Health Service is only four years old and it is just beginning to show real benefits. But in any case the structure of the National Health Service in England and Wales is, at the present time, a shared burden between the employees who pay contributions of no small amount, the contributions of the employer and the contribution of the State from taxes. Mr. Burr suggests that the service could be on a voluntary basis but I consider that would be quite unworkable. There are unfortunately many who become ill and who would not become voluntary members of a health scheme; yet they would have to be kept and the cost would fall upon the State.

I submit that the National Health Service is a gilt-edged investment in the nation's health and is money well spent. I would go further and say that the only criticism of it is that we are not spending enough on it. Mr. Burr's summary of the expenditure of the national budget for Great Britain for 1952-53 shows that the National Health Service takes 10 per cent. of the total budget but I would emphasise that the accountants—and particularly those engaged in the health service—can play a very important part in seeing that the money is well spent, particularly in the sphere of budgetary control and comparative hospital costs.

MR. L. KANO (Great Britain and Ireland):

I submit that the incidence of taxation and the rate of taxation are two completely different things. If reform of incidence results, by itself, in a reduction of the revenue, the answer is to increase the rate of tax. It seems to me that if the incidence is made more equitable, it would be easier for governments to raise revenue. Therefore, I regret that professional bodies appear to be content to accept the argument of the Government and to encourage the Government to delay. The professional bodies, instead of recommending what they think should be done immediately, endeavour to accommodate the Government in making revenue suggestions which will not produce the revenue. The incidence of taxation should be amended and made more equitable. Revenue would be maintained much more easily and with less harm to the country and professional bodies should make that clear to the Government.

MR. D. E. COX (Great Britain and Ireland):

I shall attempt to solve the problem of rising prices! This problem has reared its head in relation to taxation, and I shall take the liberty of dealing with it both in relation to taxation and to accounts.

The taxation aspect of the problem will be solved by the Government and not by us, and I feel that it is up to us as accountants to put accounts on to a true basis and let the Government make adjustments afterwards if necessary. The present basis of computing profits is inadequate but new methods which have been discussed have not been found satisfactory. There are many faults and I feel that we must come to the conclusion that no perfectly satisfactory solution will be found. We must do the best we can. It is up to us as accountants to prepare the accounts on a true and fair basis before taxation—and normally profits before taxation are the most important things in accounts.

I suggest that depreciation is the most important factor in oui consideration of inflation. The other principles of inflation are realised by the community but the fact that there is large concealed inflation because of under-depreciation is not sufficiently realised.

I submit that our present accounts are incomplete and unsatisfactory, especially the balance sheet which is the residue of accounts. I suggest that depreciation will consist of two separate items of historical cost and an additional amount of current cost, with separate amounts in the balance sheet for reserves. If you want to know what the current cost of your fixed assets is, you can ring up the supplier and he will give you the necessary information.

With regard to preference shareholders, there are difficulties, but briefly the answer is, I think, to place preference shares which were taken after the adoption of the new principle, under the new considerations and, if necessary, these should be limited or reduced. Preference share dividends issued during the period of inflation should be left to the merits of each case.

Mr. L. Procter (Great Britain and Ireland):
To my mind taxation is necessary for all governments, whether a planned or a free economy. I believe that payment should be welcomed by us all. That is an attribute of good citizenship. But there is such a thing as having the attribute of good government. Expenditure, I believe, should be strictly limited, and the economies practised and moneys raised used for the purpose of improving the morale of a nation.

There is a need for simplification. There should be a balance of receipts and payments and not artificial competition such as we have now. We should also omit stock values from all computations. Lastly, we should ignore the so-called differences between capital and income. I do not appreciate at all why a person who makes £10,000 a year by Stock Exchange transactions should be free from taxation in this country while the humble £10 a week individual should be taxed.

Mr. S. C. Tyrrell, f.c.w.a., *President of The Institute of Cost and Works Accountants, took the chair at 2.15 p.m.*

Mr. P. Busuttil (Malta):
I think that I should be failing in my duty as chairman of the Malta Institute of Accountants if I did not take this opportunity of thanking most heartily the sponsoring bodies of this Congress for the generosity they have shown in extending their invitations to such a small place as my island home, Malta. The opportunity given to me and to others of my colleagues will be of immense benefit to us as I feel sure it will broaden our outlook on the modern world problems facing the accountant.

I regret that in the very limited time at my disposal I am unable to discuss the merits of the papers submitted in connection with the subject before us but I must say that I was particularly impressed with the contents of the papers submitted by Mr. Green, Mr. Brown and Mr. Kapadia. In my opinion, the trend followed by the authors of the papers under discussion is of the same pattern. Each author tried to impress on this Congress the staggering rise in taxation by the government of his country to meet modern requirements.

In the circumstances I think that I am entitled to follow in their strides in order to show that my country, notwithstanding its smallness, did not escape the executioner's axe.

For the year ending March, 1939, taxation in Malta amounted to £767,000. For the year ending March, 1952, it went up to £4,284,000. In spite of this formidable increase and the introduction of income-tax for the first time in the history of Malta, the year 1952 closed with a deficit of £350,000. The incidence and impact of this heavy load is already causing public agitation in the island. The general complaint is that the administration is top heavy and that certain benevolent schemes are beyond the economic structure of the country.

For centuries the economic structure of Malta has been artificial in the sense that it has been based on the invisible export of services which since the political connection with Britain has taken the form of labour on the defence departments of the United Kingdom. The complete absence of rivers, timber, coal, iron and metals of commercial value cannot be changed by human action.

Industrial developments are by no means out of the question, but it does not seem reasonable to expect industrial development of sufficient magnitude to add materially to Malta's national income. The position in a nutshell is as follows. If there is a war on, Malta becomes prosperous. If there is a cold war, the going is fairly good. If it is peace, Malta is heading for a crisis!

From this brief description you can realise how peculiar, precarious and tragic is the fight for survival in Malta. In spite of all this, our administrators have joined the International Congress of their elders in order to distribute the world's wealth more evenly and make people happier.

Although as I have explained there is no power of recoupment in Malta, death duties rise from 1 per cent. to 60 per cent. and income-tax with sur-tax goes up to 10s. in the pound, and then on top of this we have a non-contributory old-age pension scheme in a thickly populated island with a population of 3,200 persons to the square mile. In my opinion, the crushing weight of taxation is the same the world over and unless something is done quickly personal initiative and the will to save will disappear. The results of the attempts made in the United Kingdom since the end of World War II to ease taxation are not very encouraging. The Tucker Committee appointed in June, 1949, took almost two years to recommend adequate initial allowances. As soon as the report was published, the Chancellor of the Exchequer announced that initial allowances belong to the past.

Then a Royal Commission was appointed in December, 1950, to explore almost the same ground as the Tucker Committee with a proviso in the terms of reference to the effect that whatever happens revenue must be maintained. The combination of income-tax and death duties is causing great hardships and tends to impoverish and ultimately diminish the standard of living.

In Malta, death duties account for £150,000 out of a revenue of £6,500,000, which means that the amount collected is out of all proportion to the harm which is done to the financial backbone of the island. In the United Kingdom, I understand it represents about 4 per cent. of the revenue. It should be evident, therefore, to the authorities concerned that if these duties are dropped or reduced considerably, great relief and encouragement can be given to industry at a very small expense. I suggest to the influential personalities of this Congress to work hard on this matter in this direction in order to achieve the same success as the organisation of the Congress.

MR. P. J. TOMBLESON (Great Britain and Ireland):

There is perhaps one aspect of the incidence of taxation on which sufficient emphasis is not being placed at the present time. The currently heavy burden of taxation and its demoralising effect are universally acknowledged. There is also general agreement that inflation has artificially increased taxable profits. It is the projection of this position into a comparison of future taxable capacity with national obligations which merits attention.

One of the preoccupations of the industrial accountant is with the way that fixed charges impinge on varying volumes of revenue. In times of prosperity it is deceptively easy to increase fixed charges but in times of depression their incidence becomes unmanageable. This is how I view the national taxation position.

Since the end of the last war we have experienced a period of unparalleled industrial activity, with profits at a high level accompanied by much overstatement of true earnings due to inflation. In Britain in our post-war optimism we added to our heavy obligations arising from the war the burdens of a welfare state, and now on top we are faced with a heavy rearmament programme. The fixed charges for social services, permanent debt and other essential services run at, say, £2,000 million per annum and the cost of maintaining preparedness for defence once rearmament has been achieved cannot be less than a further £1,000 million a year. Thus our national fixed charges are some £3,000 million a year, or about 65 per cent. of our national taxation revenue. This is not the full story if rating authority taxation is included. On the other hand, 50 per cent. of all our national tax revenue comes from direct taxation on inflated profits and incomes.

It is evident, therefore, that a business recession of any magnitude will mean a substantial deficiency of income-tax, apart from secondary effects on indirect taxation. As a result we may be faced with income-tax at 12s. 6d. or more in the pound, or the alternative of heavy deficit financing, leading to further substantial inflation and still more impossible future burdens. Such a recession may not be far off. In fact, this position can arrive without the occurrence of a recession. It would come about if taxable profits were to be computed on the basis of current replacement costs instead of historical costs. It is possible of course that the damping effects of such calculations on business profits and their distribution might indeed induce a recession.

A situation such as this may more easily be borne by a young and vigorously expanding economy than by a mature and relatively inflexible economy such as exists in this country. Nor is it easy to foresee any solution without a radical change in our present arrangements.

MR. GEORGE L. WEISBARD (United States of America):

The first income-tax law was passed by the Congress of the United States after the adoption of the 16th amendment in 1913. It taxed the income of citizens, residents and domestic corporations regardless of source. On the surface there appeared to be no reason to differentiate the incidence of taxation on the basis of source of income. It was soon realised that the surface equity of taxing income of citizens at the same rate regardless of source was indeed inequitable. Citizens whose income arose from sources outside the United States were subject to double taxation: income was taxed in the country earned and the country of citizenship. Congress moved to alleviate this inequity by providing as a credit against United States income-tax liability the income taxes paid at the source of the income. This was a rough equity from the standpoint of equal contribution to the United States Treasury on account of equal income. While citizens whose income was earned in foreign countries made a total contribution of income-tax equal to that of other citizens, the contribution to the Treasury of the United States was less.

It is thus obvious that other considerations entered into the incidence of taxation on citizens earning income in foreign countries. From economic and foreign policy viewpoints, it was important that American companies in foreign commerce should not be at a competitive disadvantage. Thus to facilitate the sale of American goods in foreign markets and the investment of American capital in foreign countries Congress went even further in its tax concessions to foreign trading corporations.

In 1921, the forerunner to the present Section 251 of the Internal Revenue Code was enacted. Its purpose was to encourage the investment of American capital in American possessions; citizens qualifying under this section are not liable for taxes on income derived from sources, in possessions of the United States.

The China Trade Act, enacted in 1922, exempted income derived from within China to the extent this income is distributed in dividends. Such dividends are excluded from gross income of the stockholder under Section 116 of the Internal Revenue Code, thus an attempt to eliminate the competitive disadvantage of American companies trading in China was made in order to obtain part of that market for American products.

Congress, in 1942, adopted the Western Hemisphere Trade Corporation Act in order to alleviate the tax disadvantage of American companies trading in South America, Mexico and Canada. The specific tax advantage of such corporations is a 27 per cent. credit against normal tax net income before the application of normal and sur-taxes and a complete exemption from excess profits tax. 90 per cent. of the gross income of a corporation must be derived from sources within the designated countries from trading. There is no provision that the trade or business be conducted within the designated countries. Thus there is no attempt to encourage the investment of American capital in the Western Hemisphere country, but merely an attempt to encourage trading.

While the incidence of taxation on traders in certain specified geographical areas is not as great as that of other American citizens, sound competitive and political reasons have dictated the advantage. Any argument as to the inequity of the situation can be answered by the salutary effect such tax concessions have on international trade. Double taxation of profits of international trade could stifle such trade to an even greater extent than high tariffs. New legislation and conventions to alleviate the effects of double taxation should be actively encouraged by all our professional organisations.

MR. P. F. W. SOPER (Great Britain and Ireland):

Mr. Burr in his very valuable paper makes the point that the high taxation in this country means a much lower standard of living than could be obtained with lower taxation and other speakers have supported the contention.

I think, however, that we should examine the reasons which prompted the late Government to introduce this very heavy taxation. They claim—to some extent justifiably—that the greater equality of income towards which redistributive taxation has contributed so much is perhaps the most important of all factors making for full employment. This is a result of the greater purchasing power of the lower paid classes.

But has the high taxation by removing incentive slowed down economic progress? The facts do not appear to support this view. Industrial production in 1950 was about 40 per cent. higher than in 1946 and output per man in industry has risen. I myself have not found that any of my clients are satisfied with their profits and decide that they will slack off because so much of the additional profit goes in taxes. They complain bitterly that they are glad to retain a few hundreds or thousands for themselves and do not work less hard. In fact the effect of high taxes on some people is to cause them to work harder in order to obtain the higher gross income to maintain their standard of living.

Then again the profits tax, particularly that part on retained profits, is said to restrict capital development, but the restriction has been largely physical due to the difficulty of obtaining building licences and the long delivery dates of new machinery. There has been—according to the National Income White Paper—an increase in the value of stocks and work in progress by about £500 millions from 1948-50 as production increased.

While we should all like to see lower taxes and we feel that the present system is unfair on us and on our clients, we must remember that full employment must make for better conditions in industry by reason of the larger market it produces, and it is better to have a small part of a large profit for oneself than all of no profit.

MR. KELVEY (Great Britain and Ireland):

On page 504 of his paper, Mr. Burr refers to the objections to a system which permits the charging of no less than three taxes, and in some cases four. No speaker this morning or this afternoon has referred to a fifth tax, namely, rates. They are, after all, a tax on income and are likely to become even greater in the immediate future.

Another point which struck me was in connection with Mr. Burr's reference to death duties. He mentions the fact that, although real capital is not destroyed, there is a tendency to break up into smaller units with consequential effects upon management and organisation. I think that is a very important point, because you get the effect of the person who is going to inherit an estate investing his money. In the old days he was in a position to provide finance for small businesses and so forth but there does not seem to be anything likely to take its place. The larger financial institutions are more conservative in their outlook, and they are not so anxious to invest their money unless they can see a return. It is quite possible from the economic point of view that the country as a whole is losing quite a considerable amount of potential revenue. I do not think that I could add anything better than to read a quotation from Mr. Burr's paper, namely, 'In addition to the loss of monetary capital, high taxation drains away the spirit of enterprise, initiative, the will to create new wealth, and the spirit of adventure'. That is a thought which we should all consider very carefully.

MR. E. B. WILCOX (United States of America):

Most of you do not know me. Those of you who do, know that I have a habit of being in a losing minority on most subjects and I am about to fulfil that role again today.

There has been talk about taxation being a burden levied by the government on the people. I think that leads us to an erroneous conclusion. Taxation, I think, should be regarded as part of the cost of living of people and if we so regard it, I think we shall abandon the conclusion that there is a percentage limit which the economy can stand.

The point has also been made that taxation is inflationary. I appreciate the point, of course, that it encourages careless spending and the raising of prices but if we assume that a government did spend the money available to it for necessary purposes, taxation which was less than that amount would mean deficit spending, deficit spending means debt increase and increase in debt is more inflationary, I suggest, than any of the other indirect causes of high tax. I think that we should not regard high taxes as one of the causes of inflation.

My next point concerns the question which has been voiced by several people, with respect to goals of equity and simplicity in taxation. I submit that you cannot have both. The more simple you make your tax the more inequitable becomes your incidence, and the more you attempt to make taxes equitable, the more you make them complex. I think that we should be wiser in our approach if the authorities who deal with the problem would address themselves to the more difficult and trying task of seeking an optimum point for excessive complexity and inequity.

With regard to the proposal that the effects of inflation should be adjusted in taxes by adjustment of income determination, I would point out that if any government needs a large sum of money to spend and, for example, increases the lawful charge against taxable income, it must correspondingly increase the tax rate and, overall, we come out where we went in. The objection to that is, of course, that there is clearly an inequity arising from the situation. I submit that the problem of inequities between taxpayers which arises out of this situation is one which should be dealt with by taxation authorities in seeking this optimum point between simplicity and inequity, rather than by attempting to adjust the income determination.

MR. D. A. BLOFIELD (Great Britain and Ireland):

I should like to suggest what may be a new line of approach to this question. I think that we might possibly view high taxation as a valuable indicator—rather like a litmus paper—which shows up dishonesty. I think that we might regard it as such as a quality of our national character under strain.

MR. L. E. GOLDSMITH (Israel):

Israel is a very young country and though taxation of income was first introduced in 1941 (at the time of the Palestine Mandate) it is only since 1948 that the country's budget, including the cost of the War of Independence and the absorption of immigrants, has to be met by the population.

Taxes in Israel, probably similar to all countries, consist of direct and indirect taxes. The portion of the 1952-53 budget which has to be met by income-tax is about 28 per cent. This tax rises under the law at present in force to the high rate of 80 per cent. on incomes over I£2,400 of taxable income and the average contribution per head of the population amounts to a levy of over I£30 per head.

Up to the present the tax law has been largely based on that of the United Kingdom, but experience has shown that that system is not ideal in a country the population of which is as mixed and untrained in tax discipline as that of Israel. Another important factor which has to be considered in the drafting of the tax law is the inflation which has been current in Israel during the past few years and which certainly exceeds that experienced in Great Britain and the United States.

As a result a new Income Tax Bill was proposed to the Knesset late in 1951 and is still under discussion in Committee. Though the system of deductions for dependants, insurance, etc., is proposed to be replaced by a system of tax credits, the incidence of taxation is not basically altered, except for the proposed capital gains tax which is somewhat similar to that tax in the United States. Due to the inflation in Israel one of the objections against that tax raised in Great Britain, i.e. that the fair and equitable allowances for losses might exceed the gains, would not seem to apply in Israel at present.

Inflation has also forced upon the Israeli Government some stop-gap measures which have altered the incidence of taxation a little, e.g. premia on output and the cost-of-living allowance from January, 1952, based on the new index and on the agreement between the employers and employees, are partly exempt from taxation.

Company profits are taxed at the flat rate of 25 per cent., and they are also liable to company profits tax of 25 per cent., after deduction of the small exemption of the first I£250 of profits. The profits of companies are calculated for the purposes of both taxes largely in accordance with principles which are current in the United Kingdom, though wear and tear allowances are based on cost and not the written-down value for tax purposes. There is a provision for double wear and tear allowances for approved investments under the law for the encouragement of capital investments.

The population of Israel is further subjected to a large number of indirect taxes which are levied by the Government on purchases, transfers of property, etc., e.g. luxury tax—a tax on the purchase on a large number of consumer goods—excise duty on tobacco, beer, wines and spirits, stamp duties on receipts, conveyances and other documents.

In addition to the central government taxation there is a levy of tax at the local level. Local authorities collect rates, including special rates for business premises, entertainments tax, etc.

It is obvious from this summary that taxation in Israel has reached a very high level; the saturation point has probably been reached and it is doubtful whether taxes can be raised further without endangering the economy of the country. High taxation reduces the incentive of the worker and increases the temptation of the manufacturer or business man to find legal loopholes to beat the tax collector, apart from draining liquid resources from undertakings which they require for re-equipment. These are problems which face many countries to a larger or smaller extent and one can only express the hope that the law-makers will find a way to levy taxation on 'real' profits only—though we may be a long way off from this Utopia.

MR. NESTOR PAQUET (Belgium):

If the true incidence of taxation could be ascertained, if one could determine to what degree each class of taxation is likely to impose itself upon each class of those who possess the means of work or those who produce, if one could then determine upon whom it is socially and economically the most justifiable to levy public charges, it would be easy to establish the conception of the fairest, the simplest, the most effective, the most convenient and the least costly basis.

But the realisation of this ideal is hazarded by serious impediments, of which the principal are individual liberty and the complexity of the economic factors to which taxation must be adapted.

Individual liberty allows taxpayers the opportunity to escape their liabilities, sometimes by perfectly legitimate means, but more often by making use of the shortcomings of the law, which legislation is unable to curb. Individual liberty also allows the taxpayer, through the perfection and efficiency of these schemes, the classical procedure of hiding every real charge and sacrificing everything with the object of competing against the effective support of public expenditure.

The complexity of modern economy manages to throw back the onus of taxation upon the shoulders of other people. This phenomenon, passing under the name of incidence, has most varied effects.

Generally speaking, one can distinguish between legal and economic incidence.

Legal incidence is only provisional and apparent. The question is resolved by legislation which creates each charge. An example is given whereby the financial contribution due by the proprietor of real estate may be recovered from the occupier, whereas tax on personal estate must be borne by the beneficiary of income.

Economic incidence, of which the effects are most obscure, is definite and real. The legal beneficiary cannot resign himself to support the tax, but strives to transmit the charge to another person. The latter tries to pass on the burden, which is unavoidable, and finally it reaches those people who might have felt themselves protected and whom the law ignores.

Economic incidence does not bow to the direction of the legislator who, instead of being in control of events, is governed by them. It is not due to his wishes that the economic battle ensues; it is owing to a multitude of contradictory and obscure forces and it is impossible to determine in advance with certainty the ultimate bearer of the tax. Values are constantly wavering and unexpected causes sometimes change the incidence in unforeseen ways.

Economists debate the point as to whether repercussion of taxation is subsidiary to the law.

The physiocrats argue that each tax falls back inevitably and necessarily upon the landed proprietor, for land is the only wealth. Some argue that the charge burdens the consumer who cannot pass it on to anyone. Upon whom can a smoker pass on the tax added to the price of tobacco? The answer is definite, for the smoker can refuse the charge by abstaining from smoking. This leads us to the most generally admitted theory which is that incidence obeys the law of supply and demand. Others argue that the question is insoluble. Each tax ends by diffusing itself and reaches those who must support it.

All old taxation is good because the repercussions of it have mellowed it. Each new tax is bad because it must make its own nest and it is said that one never walks better than with old shoes.

Experience allows the formulation of certain rules.

1. Certain taxes escape in large measure from the repercussion of successive legislation.
2. It is the same with light taxation: the taxpayer will not expose himself to the risks and dangers of this repercussion.
3. For other taxes the repercussion is scattered and not responsive.
4. Taxes mature with age. In time they work themselves by settling down and a certain equilibrium is established.

5. The most severe taxes fall upon the weakest link in the chain. The phenomenon of the transfer is a debt between the payer of taxes, the intermediate payers and he who ultimately bears the tax and who is the person who is economically the weakest. It is he who is unable to divest himself of taxable income and who is unable to impose his wishes.

MR. G. B. BURR, *one of the two introducers, summed up the discussion:*

I should like to commence by expressing my appreciation—and, I am sure, your appreciation also—for the work of our rapporteur, Mr. Brundage.

Mr. Green, who is to follow me, has every advantage looked at from the detached point of view, except two. First, I speak before him and therefore leave him the more difficult part, and second, I have an opportunity of referring to him as one of that great concourse of people who are true allies in war and generous friends in peace.

We, as professional accountants, are not concerned only with the reduction of taxation. As I said, all taxes are unpleasant and we hope that the verdict of this Congress will be that suggested by *The Accountant*, namely, 'Characterised by honest thought and unremitting effort'.

I shall divide my summarised comments into four parts: international, technical, inflation and taxation, and industrial and economic effects and repercussions.

At this Congress we have learned—on taxation in particular—a great deal from each other. The striking similarity of national conclusions on rates of taxation and their effects upon the economic well-being of the civilised world is a notable feature in the papers. It runs like a thread not only through the papers themselves but through the discussions. There is that call to return to basic principles—the old ones which we know so well of equality, certainty, convenience and economy and, perhaps most of all, to greater simplicity and less wasting of effort by way of complexity. I am not too sure—and perhaps you are not sure either—that because we have equity we must necessarily have complexity.

On the technical aspect, the papers seem to emphasise that wide disparity between taxation profits and mere profits for commercial purposes. We in this country are working through a Royal Commission towards the closing of that gap. On double taxation agreements, the particular principle of taxation in the country of residence is widely accepted. The point which seems to be brought out in the papers, particularly by Mr. Horley, is as to the restricted class of income entitled to relief. Widening classes and simplifying agreements seem to be the keynote here.

With regard to inflation, we are not economists. We are accountants but economists now play a large part in our work. We have also been told that indirect taxation increases inflation, but the main question seems to be whether purchasing power provided by taxation is still used by the Government instead of by individuals to the best advantage.

Turning to the industrial and economic effects, no one seems to be against the proposition that hidden taxes are a growing evil and that they undermine sound finance and economic health. Mr. Green and I both draw attention to this and Mr. Green also refers to the destruction of private enterprise. Certain speakers have suggested that there should be some kind of overall limit or ceiling to taxation. Mr. Coffey pointed out certain limitations in terms of tax and other speakers have shown examples of a limited ceiling by way of the total percentage of tax raised to the total national income. Mr. Wilcox is against those suggestions.

Realisation by both the main political parties in this country of the great need for some change in taxation policy seems to be shown by many speakers and in connection with that perhaps I should draw attention to these recent remarks. A former minister has said that, if a modern industrial nation does not plough back into industries sufficient increments year by year, that nation is bound to lose the race against other nations. How does that statement compare with another ex-minister who stated that he was doubtful whether the Lancashire problem could be solved without some fundamental changes in the taxation system? Going further back, the late Sir Stafford Cripps stated that there was not much further possibility of the redistribution of national income by way of taxation in this country. For the future, he said, reliance must be placed more upon the creation of more distributable wealth than upon the redistribution of the income which existed. The redistribution of income in payment for social services already falls to a considerable extent upon those who are the recipients of those services. The Inland Revenue report for 1951 shows some 19 million incomes under £1,000 per annum compared with only one million above that figure.

It is impossible for me to sum-up adequately all the interesting points which have been made and I would only conclude by saying that I hope our deliberations will not be lost in the political world nor by the nations as a whole.

MR. THOMAS J. GREEN, *the other introducer, also summed up the discussion:*

Before launching into a summing-up of the incidence of taxation, I want to take this opportunity of expressing my personal appreciation, and that on behalf of the organisation which I represent, for the privilege accorded us, not only of participating so freely in the Congress technical activities, but for the unsurpassable social hospitality of the sponsoring bodies. I should like to note for the record our thanks to the officers and committees of the Congress, particularly the untiring efforts of the President of the Congress. In these days when international unity and co-operation of all the free peoples of the world is more important and more urgent than ever before, it is indeed heartening to observe the manner in which this Congress has tackled its job. May we have many more 'get-togethers' as effective as this one.

I appreciate, moreover, the position of my appearance as the last speaker on the technical programme—a position which I deem to be one of honour. It may be, however, that at the end of a long and exhausting business and social week that you are happy to see me mainly as a representative of the fact that these pleasant but arduous proceedings are coming to a close, and that you can soon get back to the business of earning the wherewithal to pay for your present visit!

I have observed that in the many accounting conferences which I have attended in my time the taxation sessions are held on the last day of the conference. I have frequently inquired why this is so, particularly in the light of being a participant myself in the taxation sessions. The speakers on the earlier programme complete their lectures and are then free to relax and enjoy themselves. The speakers on the tax subject must remain keyed up to the concert pitch ready to deliver their gems of wisdom right up to the conclusion of the proceedings. Perhaps this is as well for the 'tax men' by this means are kept out of mischief!

Some have suggested that the holding of the tax sessions on the last day is a theatrical trick to attract and maintain the interest of all participants. That is very flattering, of course, to my confrères who are tax specialists. I personally feel, however, that while there is some merit in that viewpoint, the real reason that the tax session is held last is to remind us—as was pointed out by a previous speaker—that there are only two certain things in life—death, which comes as the last event in our personal lives, and taxes. In the light of improvements in medicine, taxes are now almost surer than death. Certainly they are more painful, and while death may only occur once, taxes have a habit of increasing repetition!

The papers submitted and the verbal discussions ensuing were of a high order, well thought out, brief, to the point and full of meat. In the language of natural resource prospecting, however, they appeared to me to hit real 'pay-dirt' on two major points. There seemed to be two distinct patterns or keynotes which were obvious throughout all the written matter and the discussions.

One observation is that taxes everywhere are too burdensome and too complex and that, since the ultimate incidence of the tax must fall on the individual taxpayer or citizen, such onerous load can lead to only one result, namely, a certain and depressing lowering of the individual standard of living. Only this morning I read in my newspaper a statement by the chairman of the board of one of your important companies, lamenting the intolerable burden of taxation which his company had to carry in the past fiscal year. As part of his report, the chairman noted that a considerable portion of the profits were realised from stocks of inventories carried at prices far below the cost of replacement of similar goods. He thereby inferentially makes a case for the use of the LIFO method of inventory for tax purposes. The use of LIFO would have materially reduced the burden of the company's tax load. Incidentally, it is my understanding that the authorities have for some time had under consideration the possible adoption of the LIFO method. I am heartily in favour of LIFO as an inventory method in itself and necessarily therefore a more ardent advocate of that method as a proper factor in the determination of net income for tax purposes. To gain the maximum advantage through LIFO, however, care must be exercised in the timing of the adoption of the method since a decline in market prices below the fixed LIFO bases would result in reporting higher earnings than under the conventional method. Realising that disadvantage we have under consideration the use of LIFO under the cost-on-market bases whichever is larger. If the pending Bill covering this method is enacted into law, then a great deal of the possible disadvantage under breaking market conditions would be eliminated. In fact, under such a system a taxpayer could scarcely afford to be on anything other than a LIFO method. I recommend LIFO for your further consideration.

If, then, as generally agreed, the tax burden is so heavy as to be at the point of diminishing returns, what can be done to remedy the situation? The speakers almost unanimously felt that something must be done to alleviate the burden. Just how such reduction might take place was not made too clear or definite.

There must indeed be a general world-wide effort to reduce governmental expenditure. That means not only a reduction in taxes, but the elimination of the tendency toward debt increases, since deficit financing has been a handy tool of spendthrift politicians for a score of years.

If economies are to be made, in what direction may these economies go? It is, of course, easy to indulge in generalities, but when one contemplates the type of world in which we live, we come starkly to the realisation that cuts of too drastic a nature in the military budgets cannot be made without danger to the material security of the countries of the free world. That is not to say, however, that a scientific review cannot be made of the military expenditure field which would result in substantial savings in the United States, for instance, ranging up to estimates from 1 billion to as high as 10 billion out of a total 1953 military budget estimate of 31 billion. Further cuts have been suggested in economic aid to anti-Communist countries ranging from 1 billion to 2½ billion. Little has been suggested as a cut in foreign military assistance expenditure as against the budget. True, every cut is going to do some harm to some recipient, but viewed from the broader aspect there is no time like the present to start making some cuts. In the civilian area subsidies of one kind or another are susceptible to intelligent diminution and wasteful and duplicatory government services of all kinds, civilian and military, must be eliminated.

We, as professional accountants, ought to preach the gospel of governmental reduction to all our friends and neighbours and to our clients and, through them, to our legislators.

A vote of thanks to the authors of the papers, the rapporteur and those who had taken part in the discussion was accorded with acclamation.

OTHER EVENTS OF THE CONGRESS

EXHIBITION OF EARLY BOOKS ON BOOK-KEEPING,
MONDAY, 9TH, TO SATURDAY, 28TH JUNE

INAUGURAL LUNCHEON PARTIES, MONDAY, 16TH JUNE

CONGRESS RECEPTION, MONDAY, 16TH JUNE

LADIES' DRESS SHOWS, TUESDAY, 17TH, AND WEDNESDAY, 18TH JUNE

THEATRE PARTIES, TUESDAY, 17TH, AND WEDNESDAY, 18TH JUNE

BANQUET AT GUILDHALL, WEDNESDAY, 18TH JUNE

VISITS TO PLACES OF INTEREST, THURSDAY, 19TH JUNE

GOLF COMPETITION, THURSDAY, 19TH JUNE

GOVERNMENT RECEPTION, THURSDAY, 19TH JUNE

The Accountant COCKTAIL PARTY, FRIDAY, 20TH JUNE

CONGRESS BALL, FRIDAY, 20TH JUNE

EARLY BOOKS ON BOOK-KEEPING

EXHIBITION AT GUILDHALL

An exhibition of unusual interest was held at Guildhall, London, from 9th June to 28th June, when early books on book-keeping and specimens of that art were among the exhibits shown. This exhibition is believed to have been the first of its kind held in this country.

Among the earliest of the printed books shown was Pacioli's *Summa di Arithmetica . . .*, published in Venice in 1494. Pacioli was the foremost mathematician of his day and the chapter on book-keeping is especially interesting. This was the first work published on the double-entry system and it formed the source-book of the subject for over a century. It was also one of the first to be printed from loose metal type. The copy shown was in so excellent a condition as almost to conceal its antiquity. It was exhibited with a page by page translation which was changed each day.

Other interesting exhibits included sixteenth-century works on book-keeping in English, Dutch, German and Spanish—some of great rarity—from the library of the Institute of Chartered Accountants in England and Wales and items of particular interest from the Society of Incorporated Accountants and Auditors. Christ's Hospital lent the MS Annual Accounts, 1561-1608, partly compiled by James Peele, who was clerk at Christ's Hospital from 1562 until 1585. This item, difficult as it is to read in the contemporary secretary hand, is especially interesting as Peele wrote the first original English work on double-entry book-keeping and is regarded as one of the earliest English accountants. From archives in Guildhall Library came a number of exhibits, among which were an account for cloth supplied by Sir William Turner to Samuel Pepys, the valuation of a Wapping china shop and some early ledgers and accounts.

The exhibition was open to the public and the number of visitors reached the total of 4,217.

INAUGURAL LUNCHEON PARTIES

MONDAY, 16TH JUNE

Prior to the opening of the Congress on the afternoon of Monday, 16th June, the sponsoring bodies extended an invitation to delegates to attend one of several luncheon parties which were organised on their behalf. These luncheons were held mainly at London hotels but two of the sponsoring bodies were able to entertain in their halls. One party was held at the Apothecaries' Hall, by kind permission of the Master and Wardens of the Worshipful Society of Apothecaries of London, and another luncheon was held at the Armourers' Hall, by kind permission of the Master and Wardens of the Armourers and Brasiers' Company.

CONGRESS RECEPTION

MONDAY, 16TH JUNE

Over 1,800 Congress members and their ladies attended the reception in the Royal Festival Hall where they were received by the President of the Congress and Lady Howitt and by the Vice-President and Mrs. Barrowcliff.

Ballroom music was provided throughout the evening by Carroll Gibbons' Band. For the especial benefit of overseas visitors, members of the Royal Scottish Country Dance Society performed an exhibition of Scottish country dancing in evening Highland dress. Their leader, Miss Maclennan, described each colourful dance before it was performed. The pipe music was by Pipe-Major Peter Quinn.

As a contrast there followed a demonstration of square dancing with Mr. David Miller as caller. The guests were then invited to join in and much enjoyment and merriment followed.

A very pleasant evening ended reluctantly at midnight.

LADIES' DRESS SHOWS

TUESDAY, 17TH JUNE, AND WEDNESDAY, 18TH JUNE

With the co-operation of the Apparel and Fashion Industry's Association a dress parade was held in the foyer of the Royal Festival Hall on the afternoon of Tuesday, 17th June, and was attended by more than 300 ladies of delegates, visitors and members.

By arrangement with the Incorporated Society of London Fashion Designers more than 200 ladies were able to attend various dress shows on Wednesday, 18th June, given by member firms of the Society. Among the fashion houses whose collections were on view were the firms of Norman Hartnell, Mattli, Lachasse, Digby Morton, Worth and Victor Stiebel.

THEATRE PARTIES

TUESDAY, 17TH JUNE, AND WEDNESDAY, 18TH JUNE

On both of these evenings delegates, visitors and members, with their ladies, had an opportunity of attending one of a variety of theatre entertainments.

The following productions were available on 17th and 18th June:

Ballet: The Royal Opera House, Covent Garden.
Much Ado About Nothing: Phœnix Theatre.
Seagulls over Sorrento: Apollo Theatre.
Blue for a Boy: Her Majesty's Theatre.

In addition, on 17th June only, seats were available at the Lyric Theatre for a performance of *The Little Hut*.

In all about 1,800 tickets were issued. Every attempt was made to meet the individual preferences of those attending and it was highly gratifying to learn that visitors were so well pleased.

BANQUET AT GUILDHALL
WEDNESDAY, 18TH JUNE

A banquet was held at Guildhall on Wednesday evening by kind permission of the Lord Mayor and the Corporation of London. The principal guests included the Right Honourable the Lord Mayor of London, Sir Leslie Boyce, K.B.E., with the two Sheriffs, Mr. Alderman and Sheriff D. H. Truscott, T.D. and Mr. Alderman and Sheriff C. James Harman; His Grace the Lord Archbishop of Canterbury, the Most Reverend and Right Honourable Geoffrey F. Fisher, P.C., D.D.; the Right Reverend W. White Anderson, M.C., D.D. (Moderator, General Assembly of the Church of Scotland); Mr. G. A. Collins (President, The Law Society); Mr. Arthur Deakin, C.H., C.B.E. (General Secretary, Transport and General Workers' Union); the Right Honourable Lord de L'Isle and Dudley, V.C., A.C.A. (Secretary of State for Air); the Very Reverend Alan C. Don, K.C.V.O., D.D. (Dean of Westminster); Sir Archibald Forbes, C.A. (President, Federation of British Industries); Sir George Hamilton (Presiding Special Commissioner for Income Tax); Sir Patrick Hannon (President, National Union of Manufacturers); Mr. F. Wyndham Hirst, C.B.E. (Public Trustee); Sir Frank Lee, K.C.B., K.C.M.G. (Permanent Secretary, Board of Trade); the Right Honourable Lord Radcliffe, P.C., G.B.E., Q.C. (Chairman, Royal Commission on the Taxation of Profits and Income); Mr. J. Millard Tucker, Q.C. (Chairman, Committee on Taxation Treatment of Provisions for Retirement); and Mr. H. Yates (President, Association of British Chambers of Commerce).

Owing to pressure of Parliamentary duties the following members of Her Majesty's Government were unfortunately prevented from attending: Sir David Maxwell Fyfe, Q.C., M.P. (Secretary of State for the Home Department and Minister for Welsh Affairs); Miss Florence Horsbrugh, C.B.E., M.P. (Minister of Education); Sir Arthur Salter, G.B.E., K.C.B., M.P. (Minister of State for Economic Affairs); and Mr. Peter Thorneycroft, M.P. (President of the Board of Trade).

A full report of the speeches at the banquet is given on page 648 and a list of guests, together with other details, is shown in Appendix C.

VISITS TO PLACES OF INTEREST
THURSDAY, 19TH JUNE

There was no business session of the Congress on Thursday, 19th June. Delegates, visitors and members of the sponsoring bodies and their ladies were given the choice of any one of the following visits, of which brief reports follow:

VISIT TO WINDSOR CASTLE AND HAMPTON COURT PALACE

Nine coaches left Leicester Square at 9.30 a.m. taking a party of almost 300 to Windsor Castle where they arrived soon after 10.45 a.m. As the Court was in residence the State Apartments were not open to view but guides were available to show the party over the Lower Ward and the Cloisters and subsequently the visitors saw something of the magnificence of St. George's Chapel, 'the home of English chivalry'.

After luncheon at the White Hart Hotel and the Castle Hotel in Windsor, the party proceeded to Hampton Court Palace where the visitors were shown over the palace and grounds and those who wished were able to inspect the royal apartments.

Tea was provided at Roehampton Club and the return journey ended at Leicester Square shortly after 6.30 p.m.

TOUR OF LONDON

Promptly at 10 a.m. five coaches set out from Leicester Square, taking about 160 members of the Congress on the first stage of their tour of London —a full tour, which needed careful planning and timing. The first stop was at St. Paul's where could be seen the majesty of Wren's cathedral. After seeing the last few minutes of a morning service, visitors had time to look round the cathedral, though there was not, unfortunately, time to see the Whispering Gallery—there were other places to visit on this all too crowded day.

Next came the Tower of London where the party was able to look over the Tower and view the Crown Jewels.

The journey proceeded over Tower Bridge and past many other places of interest, until arrival for luncheon at the Holborn Restaurant.

The next part of the journey was to Goldsmiths' Hall, where an exhibition of gold plate was being held. It so happened that Her Majesty Queen Mary was due to visit the exhibition later that afternoon and, on the way to the next destination, some visitors saw her car and a few caught a glimpse of Queen Mary herself.

The Houses of Parliament and Westminster Abbey were visited before returning to Leicester Square.

VISIT TO OXFORD UNIVERSITY

The 175 members of the Congress and their ladies who had expressed a wish to visit the colleges at Oxford met at Paddington Station at 9.30 a.m.

In view of the number taking part in this visit it had been decided to divide the party into four groups, with three guides accompanying each group. The visitors arrived at Oxford at 11.20 a.m. and each group was able to visit two colleges before lunch. Mr. H. Garton Ash, a Past President of the Institute of Chartered Accountants in England and Wales, acted as host at a pleasant informal luncheon at the Randolph Hotel. In the afternoon each group was able to visit two more colleges after which the visitors were taken back to Oxford Station in time to catch the 4.30 p.m. train to London.

The following colleges were visited during the day: New College, Merton, Oriel, Trinity, Magdalen and Christ Church. In addition the visitors saw the Old and the New Bodleian Libraries.

Warm thanks were conveyed to Mr. D. Veale, C.B.E., M.C., F.C.A., Registrar of Oxford University, for the excellent arrangements made and for the facilities placed at the disposal of the visitors.

VISIT TO CAMBRIDGE UNIVERSITY

The interesting character of all the visits organised by the Congress Council must have left the guests with a somewhat difficult choice. Those who elected to go to Cambridge had a unique opportunity to see the colleges under most favourable conditions and to have luncheon either in Trinity Hall or in Gonville and Caius College, thanks to facilities kindly afforded by those colleges.

Mr. Bertram Nelson, Vice-President of the Society of Incorporated Accountants and Auditors, was in charge of the party and was assisted by Mr. Douglas Clarke and several stewards, some of whom knew Cambridge well.

One hundred and sixty visitors travelled by train from London (Liverpool Street Station) and on arrival at Cambridge went on a short motor-coach tour, which included The Backs and ended at King's Parade. The first sight of Queens', King's, Clare, Trinity and St. John's from The Backs across the lawns and the river is always a delightful experience.

After some free time the visitors proceeded to Trinity Hall and Caius, where they enjoyed the friendly welcome of traditional college buildings. By kind permission of the Master of Trinity Hall, Professor H. R. Dean, M.D., and the Master of Gonville and Caius College, Sir James Chadwick, PH.D., F.R.S., visitors were able to enjoy the privilege of luncheon in hall. Both colleges extended a most cordial welcome and visitors were given most interesting information about the colleges and their foundations. Time unfortunately did not permit a very lengthy stay.

After Mr. Bertram Nelson and Mr. Douglas Clarke had conveyed the thanks of the Congress for the kindness of the college authorities, the parties were reassembled and conducted to other colleges by members of the Cambridge Guides Association who offered their services for this occasion. For this purpose visitors were divided into a number of groups, all of which saw the glories of King's College Chapel and visited Trinity, St. John's, Christ's, Queens' and Peterhouse. The weather was more than kind throughout the day and contributed much to a programme which for all visitors came to a reluctant end at about 4.30 p.m.

Thanks were extended to the guides and the party was conveyed from King's Parade to the station, arriving at London at 6.45 p.m.

TOUR OF PORT OF LONDON

A popular trip was the cruise down the Thames to London's dockland. Over 150 visitors were aboard two vessels, the S.Y. *St. Katharine*, which was used on a similar trip during the 1933 Congress, and the M.V. *Fordson*. The

St. Katharine, a well-appointed ship, is the inspection vessel of the Board of the Port of London Authority and, together with the *Fordson*, had generously been placed by the Board at the disposal of the Congress.

Embarkation took place at Tower Pier and the two vessels proceeded down the river to Greenwich where the party went ashore to visit the National Maritime Museum. Mr. M. H. Bolton, a member of the Board of the Port of London Authority, travelled with the party to Greenwich. Mr. A. Stuart Allen, Vice-Chairman of the Congress Council, presided at the luncheon, which was held in an open marquee facing Greenwich Park and the Observatory, and among those present were Commander W. E. May, R.N., of the National Maritime Museum and Mr. T. Haworth, F.S.A.A., Chief Accountant of the Port of London Authority. The party then re-embarked and after a tour of the Royal Albert and King George V docks, during which tea was taken on board the two vessels, the party returned about six o'clock. An interesting running commentary was given on both vessels by officials of the Public Relations Department of the Port of London Authority.

GOLF COMPETITION

Golfing enthusiasts spent an enjoyable day at Wentworth by kind permission of the Wentworth Golf Club.

In the Medal Competition, Mr. W. J. H. Rennie, playing from a handicap of eight, returned the net score of 74 to win first prize. Mr. J. L. Somerville was second with a net score of 82. The prize for the last nine holes was won by Mr. J. Chambres with a net score of 28.

Mr. T. J. Green (United States of America) finished first in the Stableford Competition with 35 points. Mr. J. W. Johnstone was runner-up with 34 points. Mr. K. Le M. Carter (Canada) won the prize for the last nine holes with 19 points.

The Scratch prize for the meeting was won by Mr. M. T. W. Easby with a return of 83.

Those successful competitors who were at the Congress Ball on Friday, 20th June, were presented with their prizes by Lady Howitt during an interval.

GOVERNMENT RECEPTION

THURSDAY, 19TH JUNE

A distinguished gathering of delegates and their ladies, together with the President and Vice-President of the Congress, members of the Congress Council and other representatives of the sponsoring bodies, attended the Government Reception at the Tate Gallery. They were received by Brigadier H. R. Mackeson, M.P., Secretary for Overseas Trade.

The choice of the Tate Gallery for this purpose was a particularly happy one and it is difficult to imagine a more perfect setting for such an occasion.

The Congress Council is glad to take this opportunity of recording its indebtedness to Her Majesty's Government for providing such admirable facilities and for sponsoring a memorable function.

THE ACCOUNTANT COCKTAIL PARTY

FRIDAY, 20TH JUNE

All overseas members of the Congress and their ladies, together with officials of the Congress and chairmen of committees, were invited to attend a cocktail party at Grosvenor House given by Mr. Ronald Staples, Editor-in-Chief of *The Accountant*, and Mr. Derek du Pré, the Editor.

The guests were greeted by Sir Harold and Lady Howitt, Mr. and Mrs. C. Percy Barrowcliff and Mr. and Mrs. du Pré. Mr. Ronald Staples was unfortunately not able to be present as he had not fully recovered from a recent accident.

CONGRESS BALL

FRIDAY, 20TH JUNE

The social events of the Congress came to a happy conclusion with a ball at the Savoy Hotel, London, which commenced at 9 p.m. More than 1,700 attended and both the ballroom and the adjoining rooms were fully occupied. A standing buffet was provided throughout and dancing went on until 2 a.m. on Saturday morning. Carroll Gibbons provided the dance music and made a personal appearance at the piano.

The prizes for the Golf Competition held on the previous day were on view throughout and during an interval Lady Howitt kindly presented the prizes to those winners who were able to attend.

BANQUET AT GUILDHALL
Wednesday, 18th June

THE PRESIDENT, SIR HAROLD HOWITT, G.B.E., D.S.O., M.C., F.C.A.,
in the Chair

The loyal toasts and the toast to sovereigns and heads of states represented were duly honoured.

THE CHAIRMAN OF THE COUNCIL (MR. H. GARTON ASH, O.B.E., M.C., F.C.A.), in proposing the toast 'The Right Honourable the Lord Mayor and the Corporation of London', said:

I am privileged to-night, in proposing the toast of the Lord Mayor, Sheriffs and Corporation of the City of London, to speak on behalf of the accountants assembled in London for the Sixth International Congress on Accounting and particularly those gathered together in this historic hall. This toast is indeed a wide one, for the Corporation of London consists of the Lord Mayor, 25 other Aldermen and 206 Commoners, a total of 232 persons. I shall not attempt to deal with them individually!

My Lord Mayor, I need hardly say how very delighted we are that your health has been sufficiently restored to enable you to undertake again some of the very many activities which fall on your shoulders and we take a special delight that you are able to be with us here tonight.

The office of Lord Mayor is of long standing and has been built up by tradition over the centuries. Many here this evening may not know that you, my Lord Mayor, are the six hundred and thirtieth holder of that great office established over seven centuries ago. It is, I think, a mark of the wide outlook of this city that in you we have one who, born in Australia, came to this country some twenty-five years ago and having taken a keen interest in all that pertains to the city's affairs, now presides over our civic parliament. It is, I believe, the first time in history that a son of Australia has been Lord Mayor of London.

The calm confidence and dignity with which you carry out your duties is, I am sure, a great encouragement, not only to the citizens of London, but to that much wider field throughout the world which look to our chief magistrate for example and guidance. Few office holders have to face the exacting procedure by which a Lord Mayor reaches his high office. He must first have been elected an Alderman and then a Sheriff and have been approved by a different body of electors on four distinct occasions. Even then his appointment is subject to the approval of the sovereign. Thus he has been well and truly tried before he is able to take office. No speech submitting this toast could hope to encompass the multitudinous duties and functions with which the Lord Mayor has to deal and we wish him renewed good health to continue in the task.

The next part of my toast concerns the Sheriffs. The office of sheriff is of greater antiquity than any other office in the City. It goes back before the Norman Conquest and is mentioned in Anglo-Saxon laws of the seventh century. It is recorded that the sheriffs of London met William the Conqueror at London Bridge and would not let him enter the City until he had agreed to confirm the rights of the citizens. You will see therefore the power which their ancient office enables them to wield.

Their duties, like those of the Lord Mayor, are exacting. They have the especial privilege of waiting upon the Sovereign on certain occasions and also of presenting petitions to Parliament on behalf of the Corporation.

In Mr. Alderman and Sheriff Denis Truscott and Mr. Alderman and Sheriff James Harman, whom we are indeed glad to have with us tonight, we have two Freemen of the City who are carrying on the high traditions and responsibilities of their office. I should like, if I may, to congratulate Mr. Alderman and Sheriff Harman on his election as Alderman, as recently as 10th June, for the Ward of Candlewick.

I now come to the last part of my toast, the Corporation of the City of London, the full title being 'The Lord Mayor, Aldermen and Commoners of the City of London in Common Hall assembled'. The Aldermen, who are included in this part of my toast, have certain duties both as a separate Court and individually, as well as in the Common Council. An Alderman has the special position that he can on occasions carry out by himself the duties directed to be done by more than one justice. In other words, he can under-take the work of at least two men!

No institution in a free country can for long maintain its existence unless it satisfies the intelligent opinion of the great mass of the people that it exists for the public good. The fact of its continuance shows that this very ancient and long-established Corporation satisfies the country that it does exist for the public good. It can point with a just pride to its liberal and enlightened administration at the present day.

We are most grateful to you, my Lord Mayor, and to the Corporation for the use of Guildhall Library in which historical records on accounting are being exhibited during the Congress. We are also grateful for the privilege of dining together tonight in this historic hall which has been associated over the ages with many great events. Its history shows that it has ever been iden-tified with the maintenance of freedom of thought and action. In the City of London freedom has a special call on our feelings and we use our endeavours and are ever hopeful that true freedom may spread throughout the world.

Over the centuries this City has been a centre of business activity in touch with world-wide conditions. Its community has acquired a unique knowledge and experience of world trade and affairs, and that knowledge and experience is still at the service of all who are able to take advantage of it. Amid the many changes of modern life we are indeed happy to find that the Lord Mayor, Sheriffs and Corporation of London continue to occupy and uphold much the same position that has been occupied for many generations.

I ask you to join me in drinking to the health and continued prosperity of the Lord Mayor, the Sheriffs and the Corporation of the City of London.

THE RIGHT HONOURABLE THE LORD MAYOR, SIR LESLIE BOYCE, K.B.E., in response, said:

On behalf of the Queen's Sheriffs—I say that because they are so often described as the Lord Mayor's Sheriffs, and it is the Queen's Coronation and not mine which takes place next year—on behalf of the Corporation and myself I thank the Chairman of your Council, Mr. Garton Ash, most sincerely for the very interesting, eloquent and generous way in which he has proposed this traditional triple civic toast.

He has told us that I am the six hundred and thirtieth holder of my present office which commenced in the year 1189. Arithmetically that does not add up. The first holder, Henry FitzAilwyn, was Mayor for twenty-five years, and there was Richard Whittington, whom we are all delighted to see at Christmas-time in pantomime and of whom it is said 'Turn again, Whittington, thrice Lord Mayor of London'. He was never Lord Mayor but Mayor of London; and not 'thrice' but four times. It needs this Sixth Congress on Accounting to work out all these complications and to tell me what I am!

Mr. Garton Ash has been good enough to refer to the fact that I am the first Lord Mayor of London to come from the Empire overseas. Canada supplied England with its first Prime Minister from one of the self-governing dominions; Australia supplied London with its first Lord Mayor from a dominion, and I am hoping that perhaps New Zealand will supply what is described in tonight's programme as 'Canterbury, His Grace the Lord Archbishop of'. South Africa might well, seeing the gold reserves she has in Mother Earth, provide a Governor of the Bank of England, and India, Pakistan and Ceylon might also make their contributions in the form of a Lord Chancellor and other equally or nearly equally high officers of State.

Mr. Garton Ash has also referred to the fact that the City enjoys certain special privileges, one of which is to wait upon Sovereigns to ascertain the royal will and pleasure as to the presentation of addresses on behalf of the City, and also to present petitions to Parliament. The last time such an event took place with regard to the presentation of an Address in the reign of His Late Majesty, I happened to be the official spokesman, and the last time a Petition was presented to Parliament I also happened to be the official spokesman and, after sixteen years as a Member of the House of Commons, I made my 'positively last speech' on that occasion. I am glad to say that the present Sheriffs only last month exercised this special privilege to which Mr. Garton Ash referred when they waited upon our present beloved Sovereign to ascertain the royal will and pleasure as to the presentation of an Address which was thereupon presented on behalf of the City.

From the number of times that the health of the Lord Mayor is drunk in the course of a civic year, one might expect that he was going to enjoy perfect health in perpetuity. That, however, has not been my experience. I am particularly grateful to Mr. Garton Ash for the very graceful and charming reference which he made to my recent illness and for his good wishes for my continued recovery. My love of the City and my anxiety to return surpasses that of the young man who wrote to his best girl friend the following letter: 'My dearest Mary, I love you so much that I would climb mountains and fight through storms and snowdrifts to get to you. I would swim through shark infested waters to get to you; I would even face wild animals and cannibals to get to you. Yours lovingly, Jimmy. P.S. If fine I shall come round and see you on Sunday.'

My task this evening is a very simple and a very happy one. It is on behalf of the Corporation of London to extend to your Congress, to every delegate, whether he be present or not, and to the guests a very cordial welcome to this City. Since Queen Elizabeth I opened the Royal Exchange in 1571 this City has been regarded as the commercial centre of the world. What, then, more fitting place could you find for your banquet than in our ancient, historical, battle-scarred and beloved Guildhall?

This great hall is pregnant with historical memory. If our French friends will forgive me, tonight I stand opposite the statue of Wellington, and today is the anniversary of the Battle of Waterloo. I think that Napoleon Bonaparte put up an extremely good fight; but we put up a better one.

Those of us who are engaged in commerce and industry, of which I happen to be one, know only too well that the hardest taskmaster is the profit and loss account. Without integrity, and without the services which your highly skilled and most important profession renders to this City and to the country, we should soon lose our place in the business world. The fact that you come not only from all parts of the Commonwealth and Empire, but also from so many other friendly countries, adds greatly to the pleasure which I have in welcoming you into this City this evening.

There is one thing which I have discovered during my mayoralty. It is said that knowledge comes slowly but wisdom lingers. It is that the only person who likes long speeches is the man who makes them. Therefore, in thanking once again the Chairman of your Council for the very kind manner in which he has proposed this toast, and the exceedingly charming and generous way in which you have received it, I welcome this opportunity to wish you, Mr. Chairman, and all the delegates to your Congress continued success in your deliberations.

THE PRESIDENT:

I have a note in my hands from the President of the Board of Trade, Mr. Thorneycroft, timed as recently as 6.30 p.m. in which he expresses 'my very real regret at being unable to be with you this evening. I have made every effort to leave the House of Commons but I find it is just impossible'. I understand that there is an important division in the House of Commons and, strangely enough, that division takes precedence over this banquet. It has not only robbed us of the pleasure of having Mr. Thorneycroft with us, but also the other Ministers who were to have been here, the Secretary of State for the Home Department and Minister for Welsh Affairs, the Minister of State for Economic Affairs and the Minister of Education. That was a tragedy which was unknown to most of you while you were improving your minds in Festival Hall. Those of us who did know about it have been in somewhat of a flap during the day. At least, we should have been but for a particularly kind gesture which I want to mention.

Y

I rang up Lord Radcliffe at his home last night but I was not able to speak to him. However, I spoke to Lady Radcliffe and on his behalf she said she was quite sure that he would be willing, in an emergency, to switch over from replying to the toast of the guests and instead to propose the toast of the Accountancy Profession. Lord Radcliffe was briefed both ways—without fee in either case—and has held himself free right up to this last moment to speak in either way we wish him to speak. We are deeply grateful to him. The toast of the Accountancy Profession will, therefore, be proposed by Lord Radcliffe.

The Right Honourable Lord Radcliffe, P.C., G.B.E., Q.C., in proposing the toast 'The Accountancy Profession', said:

There is, as you have heard, a slight change in the batting order. I do feel that I owe you an apology for not being the President of the Board of Trade and for not being Mr. Peter Thorneycroft; but it is no good now. I took the false step years ago when I decided to stick to the law and you see there is no moral to this story. There is the President of the Board of Trade being chastised by three line whips of Her Majesty's Government and here I am enjoying your magnificent hospitality in the wonderful setting of Guildhall and the privilege of holding your attention for a brief time this evening.

It has robbed me of one great and to me unusual pleasure. I have had in the course of my life at the Bar many leaders, but I have never been led before by an Archbishop of Canterbury. Until two hours ago I was sitting back as a junior, as I used to sit back in the old days, comfortable in the knowledge that everything properly to be said would be said by one's leader. But for all that, I do in a way welcome the chance as a lawyer to pay a tribute when I propose the health of the Accountancy Profession to those, I think, many accountants whose friendship I have made in the course of my professional experience, and to pay them my tribute for the things which I have learned from them, even with my little knowledge of accountancy. I can see already some faces looking anxious. Have no misgivings. No doubt the people whom I regard as my mentors in accountancy would not recognise the lessons I have learned from them and any opinions I express on that thorny subject will be entirely my own.

I do recognise that the profession of accountancy has much in common today with the profession of the law. We are both, I think, creatures of the modern world. We owe our position to that great rise of commercial and industrial energy which marked the beginning of the modern world as we know it. There were lawyers, of course, before that time and I suspect that there were accountants, but the lawyers who, in those early days, found that their arguments were tending to arrive at a conclusion hostile to that of the governing powers were apt to find themselves in prison, and if you had shown a medieval statesman a consolidated balance sheet and a profit and loss account drawn up in accordance with the requirements of our most recent Companies Act, I think that the accountant would probably have been burnt at the stake for indulging in cabalistic signs or for invoking the improper aids of black magic!

We belong to the modern world as we know it. We belong to a system which is quite recent in the history of the world, of free intercourse, free exchange and free speech. If that system goes down, we go down with it as institutions, and there are few of us in this hall who would wish to survive it. I remember not long ago having to remind your President that when Edmund Burke wanted to signalise the passing of the old order and the coming of the new he said: 'The day of chivalry has gone; that of sophisters, economists and calculators has succeeded, and the glory of Europe is extinguished for ever'. There we are, sophisters, lawyers, calculators, accountants and economists—well economists. You and I this evening can agree that the economists have far outstripped the rest of us. They are indeed the high priests of modern society, talking to each other in a strange cabalistic language which the ordinary man does not understand, making those profound mysteries of modern social life mysteries even more profound in the process. We must leave them to take care of themselves which I have no doubt they are fully capable of doing.

The lawyers and accountants recognise that they have played a part in the last two or three hundred years and that they have a part still to play. We are watch-dogs of society from our respective points of view in a world which has no idea at all where it is going, but which is always anxious to be told where it stands. It is the privilege of the accountancy profession to endeavour, perhaps with somewhat deceptive clarity, to explain to it what that situation is. I think that the world has much to be grateful for to its accountants for what they do. I think that we have come to look to you to do your work as well as it can be done, skilfully, with assiduity and with a fine impartiality; qualities which do not need enlarging upon, which do not need to be referred to too often, but which I think are absorbed by members of the profession half unconsciously because they recognise them as duties. We have come to look to what has become a great profession for the exercise of those qualities. Keep them and exercise them and one stable element in our society is preserved.

I know something about the practice of the law but to me accountants are still somewhat men of mystery. You move, on the whole unostentatiously, about the world upon your important missions; soft black hats upon your heads, destiny in your brief cases, attending to the birth pangs of a new issue or a reconstruction, attending the sad obsequies of liquidation, welcome and respected even when you bring bad news. At least, in the free world about which you move the words 'liquidation', 'reconstruction' and 'reduction of capital' have no sinister political meaning. Liquidation does not mean putting your enemies to death. Reconstruction does not mean a revolution and capital reduction does not mean cutting off the head of your enemy. If a young man who was going to practise law came to me and asked me which he should study, law or accountancy, I should answer unhesitatingly accountancy. After all, he can always pick up the law from the solicitors or from the judges. But a man who can make in court a telling reference to some subject like 'amortisation' is a man marked for success and all the privileges that go with obtaining the higher progressive rates of sur-tax. Many a young man, successful in the law, who has climbed up rung after rung and who has the 19s. 6d. step as his ultimate objective ahead of him, looks back with a sense of pride to some early days when he held the attention of the court, not as in the days of great lawyers of the past with some great piece of oratory or some days spent in analysing the doctrine of conversion—I speak as a lawyer—but to some neat quip about fixed or circulating capital or the proper use of a suspense account.

Well, members of the accountancy profession, I shall quote you one sentence from a very brilliant and interesting paper by Mr. Barrowcliff which I read the other day. 'Events', he said, 'it appears, have caught up with the accountancy profession.' Rather an uncomfortable thought for an after dinner speech.

Here you are, gathered from many corners of the earth, for a brief but determined onslaught upon the great dogmas of your profession. Let me give you an historical reference – the great Council of Trent which met in the sixteenth century to determine what were to be the dogmas of the Roman Catholic religion. A historian states that strong and conflicting opinions were held upon many subjects and that the ten years during which the Council sat were insufficient to resolve those difficulties. Hence there arose the necessity for reticence, equivocation and temporising. They were coping with subjects rather different from that of the principles of accountancy in relation to fluctuating price levels. They were not faced with problems of depreciation allowances or with what you do with reserves. They were faced with other questions such as that of original sin and doctrines of justification. But you have been warned by history. If you do not arrive at the ultimate conclusions for which we are all waiting I, for my part, shall think no worse of you. I shall think of it merely as an illustration of what has been called the 'many-sidedness of truth', and I shall await with some interest to see how many sides truth has. I shall continue to think of you as what I know you to be, a great profession to whom it is an honour to raise one's glass in a toast, and I call upon you to drink in honour of the Accountancy Profession.

THE PRESIDENT, in response, said:

Before I say anything else, may I say what a pleasure it is to see so many ladies of the accountancy profession dining with us here tonight.

I am sure that Mr. Hope and I feel a tremendous pride and responsibility in being called upon to reply to this toast. I am certain that I am speaking for all of you in this hall—qualified accountants from all over the world gathered here in London—when I express to Lord Radcliffe our really deep appreciation for the way in which he took on this toast at short notice, and for the nice things he has said about us. I think that we all feel we should like to be able to produce a speech like that after dinner, only having been briefed at 6.30 the same evening.

Lord Radcliffe, I always feel that it is a little impertinent to ask someone to come to one's dinner and to propose one's health. There is an element of risk about it also. You never know what is going to be said, especially when it is someone like Lord Radcliffe who knows a good deal more about us than he has told us. Many of us present have known Lord Radcliffe for many years at the Bar when he was the person, probably above all others, to whom we turned in times of difficulty. I think that I was the very last person to be cross-examined by him before he went on to the Bench and I remember that case very well. In his address Lord Radcliffe called us 'men of mystery' and then said that he had little knowledge of accountancy. When an eminent Q.C. begins to talk to you that way in the box, that is the time to watch your step. You will find, if you are not careful, that you will be led down the garden of his assumed ignorance and be pulled up with a jolt.

Quite seriously, Lord Radcliffe has been a great friend to the accountancy profession. He is the Chairman of the Royal Commission dealing with a review of all our income-tax problems and in that capacity also has many contacts with our profession. We wish him luck in his very arduous task.

I want to make it clear that I am only responding for the accountancy profession. I am in no sense answering for it. That would be too big a responsibility. I want also to make it clear that in circumstances such as these it is not, I think, for the responder to the toast to eulogise the profession. That has been ably done for us. Lord Radcliffe spoke seriously for a minute or two and I should, therefore, in reply speak seriously for a minute or two.

We do appreciate greatly someone from another great profession coming here and saying such nice things to us as Lord Radcliffe has just said. We do not—and it is not for me at the moment to do so—boost our profession in any way, but I do want to say simply that we are deeply proud of it. We are determined to live up to the high standards which that profession has established. I always wonder at what point it is that a calling in life is entitled to regard itself as being a profession. I always feel that it is not a right that attaches to the members of that calling themselves. It is rather the recognition by the public of that right. I think we can claim, without being boastful, that young as we are, in the present situation of the accountancy profession we are now recognised as a great profession. We are determined to take a careful note of all Lord Radcliffe has said and to live up to the standards which our forbears have established and, if possible, enhance them.

The fundamental truths of accountancy are in a way very simple. They are centred around the vexed and difficult question of trying to make ends meet or knowing if they do not meet. But in these days, with financial problems getting so complicated both nationally and internationally, there is a great risk of those fundamental truths being scrapped, sometimes as a result of wishful thinking. The great problem, as I see it, of the accountancy profession is to keep faithfully to these fundamental truths, to abide by them and yet to retain a receptive mind to be able to march with the times and improve on the standards that we have worked to before. Those are the problems which we are trying to work out at the International Congress in London.

I am very proud to be sitting in this chair supported on either side by the head of the City and the head of the Church. We are indeed being honoured by both Church and State. I suppose that when we think of this Congress week in the years to come, probably two items will stick out forcibly in our minds. Firstly, the service on Monday morning at Westminster Abbey, and in the presence of the Archbishop of Canterbury I should like to thank the Dean of Westminster for the wonderful, delightful and inspiring service and address with which he started our proceedings.

The other memory which I am sure will linger on is that of this banquet in this grand old building. For that we are indebted, as Mr. Garton Ash has said, to the Corporation of London, but it has been made for us by the presence amongst us of London's first citizen. As has been said, this being a gathering of accountants from all over the world, it is very appropriate and fitting that one of the meetings should be in the heart of this great City of London and, in particular, in this Guildhall. Much enterprise, much ability and much pluck have contributed over the ages to make the City of London what it is, and accountancy has played an honoured part in that development. Long may it continue so to do not only in this country but the world over. Long may we as a profession endeavour to hold the balance fairly between man and man and between country and country. As we heard in Westminster Abbey on the first day of the Congress, our business in different parts of the world 'is for the welfare of men in their dealings one with another'. I am sure that it is with ideals no lower than these and with intent to make them good that you expect me to respond on your behalf to this toast to our great profession.

MR. J. WILLIAM HOPE, C.P.A. (United States of America), in response, said:
By virtue of my office as the President of the American Institute of Accountants, the organisation of certified public accountants in the United States with some twenty thousand members, I am honoured and privileged to respond to this toast to the accountancy profession. I am very happy personally that I do not have to make direct response to Lord Radcliffe. I knew that our President would do that adequately as, indeed, he has.

I am fully aware that this gathering in this historic setting is inspiration enough to develop oratory of the highest order and a stately eloquence fitting to the occasion; but it is my purpose, if you will permit me, to speak as I would among friends, for I feel that I am among friends. Like most Americans—indeed, like most visitors to Britain—I cannot feel a stranger to this country. That sense of belonging is due in part, of course, to the gracious welcome extended to us by our hosts. They have been tireless in their efforts to make this meeting one to be enjoyed at the moment and to be treasured as a memory in the days to come. The fact that we have a warm feeling of being among friends is evidence of their triumph.

There is, however, another explanation for our sense of belonging. All of us, and especially those of us who have travelled here from the United States, recognise the great debt which we owe to the accounting profession of Britain. It has taught us much. It has immeasurably enriched our literature; it has enlightened us from the rostrum and in the classroom and, above all, it has sent to our shores men of towering character whose example of integrity has been an inspiration to us. Thus, in visiting this island, we are returning in a way to the half-familiar birthplace of our profession.

Then there is still another reason for our sense of kinship. We are united with you in the common struggle to preserve our threatened liberty. This is a responsibility which rests upon all men who cherish freedom, and the accountant is fully aware of his obligation. Much of the world's turmoil reflects the dissatisfaction of masses of people with their lot. They seek a richer, more satisfying life, and their natural yearning can be a source of strength for democracy if it is properly utilised. It can also have tragic consequences if allowed to become a blind destructive force.

The accountant has a unique opportunity in this situation. He can contribute mightily to the defence of liberty by guiding the economy of his nation with wisdom, guiding it in such a manner as to increase its productivity and thus diminish the discontent which can fatally weaken the free world in this period of dire peril. He must also zealously guard his own professional independence. For it is his status as an independent agent that permits him to provide the information upon which all competing elements in the population can rely. If he should ever compromise his integrity for any personal gain, he will utterly destroy his usefulness. The public's loss of confidence in him will not only mean the end of his profession; it will make it difficult if not impossible to maintain that co-operative spirit between all segments of society which is essential in a democracy.

It is thus the accounting profession looks to us here this evening, and to the toast I respond: 'May we prove to be worthy'. I should like to conclude by recalling the words of another American. Nearly a quarter of a century ago, in this historic hall, Colonel Robert H. Montgomery spoke for the United States delegation at the Fourth International Congress on Accounting. 'We thank you', he said, 'for your cordial greetings and for your boundless hospitality. Our respect and affection for British accountants, which needed no acceleration, nevertheless has been broadened and strengthened.' Those words could be mine tonight. Again, on that other evening back in 1933, Colonel Montgomery concluded 'We hope to come again'. We have done so and now we hope, once more, soon to return for still another visit to you, our friends.

THE VICE-PRESIDENT, MR. C. PERCY BARROWCLIFF, F.S.A.A., in proposing the toast 'The Guests', said:

It is now a very great pleasure for us, the hosts, to raise our glasses in honour of the guests and to assure them that this function would have lost much of its distinction but for their presence. Representing on the one hand almost every important phase of British life, we count ourselves fortunate indeed to have them with us on this unique occasion. They occupy positions of high responsibility in the public life of the country and the wealth of their services showed how well placed that responsibility had been. This country like so many others has been singularly fortunate in the disinterested and public-spirited service rendered to it by its leading men and women.

The printed list attached to the menu is the only practical way of bringing to your notice all our distinguished public men who have placed us so much in their debt. Our friends from overseas must feel, as we do, that it is a gratifying experience to have them with us tonight and the printed list to which I have referred will remain a treasured memento of the gentlemen who have so honoured us by their presence.

We also have a number of distinguished members of the accountancy profession from many parts of the world as our guests and it will be a special pleasure to raise our glasses in cordial greeting and goodwill to them. It is a matter of immense satisfaction to the members of the accountancy profession in Great Britain and Ireland that it has been possible for so many different countries in the world to be represented at this Congress. We are not without hope that our common accountancy problems and our mutual understanding of one another's points of view may make some little contribution to a better understanding and sympathy between the nations of the world.

Peace is in our hearts as it must be in yours. I assure you all from lands near and far that our hearts are warm and our imagination is stirred by your presence here tonight. May you all go away with some understanding of our heartfelt goodwill to you all.

It is my privilege to associate this toast with His Grace the Archbishop of Canterbury. He has surely won the regard and affection of us all by his friendly humanity and spiritual leadership. I would remind His Grace, however, that it was a Frenchman who once said that Englishmen were not spiritually minded and therefore invented the game of cricket to give them some idea of eternity. Was it not also one of His Grace's curates who, the first Sunday after his ordination, when reading the lesson containing the Ten Commandments, concluded in a moment of abstraction—no doubt thinking of recent examinations—with the words: 'And not more than seven of these to be attempted.'

For the benefit of our overseas visitors may I say that His Grace is the ninety-ninth Archbishop of Canterbury—I hope the arithmetic is right— St. Augustine, I understand, being the first in A.D. 593. The title 'Archbishop' was probably introduced into the East in the fourth century, and it was then a distinction implying no superiority of jurisdiction. The first recorded use of the title was when it was given to Alexander as a mark of respect by Athanasius. The present Archbishop I am sure needs no such title as this to mark our deep regard and respect for him.

May I conclude by referring to one of Sir Harold Howitt's articled clerks. A new and pretty comptometer operator had recently joined their staff and one of the other clerks was questioning this articled clerk about this girl. The reply he received was as follows: 'She may not know a debit from a credit, but, oh boy, she certainly adds up!' Our guests certainly add up tonight, and it is our extreme pleasure to welcome you here and we have the greatest possible pleasure in drinking your health.

His Grace the Lord Archbishop of Canterbury, in response, said:

For my own part I am very glad that the batting order has been changed. Had it not been changed I should now have scored a miserable single or two and then had the galling experience of seeing Lord Radcliffe hit the bowling all over the place. As it is, I am last man in and you want to see me out as soon as possible. I shall therefore play my modest innings and go.

May I take this opportunity of saying that the arithmetic was perfectly correct in the case of myself, although not apparently in the case of the Lord Mayor. I am the ninety-ninth Archbishop of Canterbury. I say that with particular emphasis because there are Americans here. When I was in the United States in 1946 I was described as the ninety-seventh, ninety-eighth, ninety-ninth, one hundredth, the hundred and first and the hundred and fifth Archbishop of Canterbury. This so touched me that when I got home I took steps to discover precisely what I was. It is not so easy as you think and an accountant might take a little time to find out. It depends on whether you count one or two Archbishops who were elected but who never took office. One died, for instance, going over the Alps and it is difficult to discover whether he was an Archbishop or not at that time. However, after exhaustive research I made a formal announcement that I was the ninety-ninth. I was sorely tempted—but you cannot juggle with figures—to call myself the hundredth in order to put up a century.

Now I have the privilege of replying for the guests. Though I do not know who they are, I cannot but think that some of them must be surprised to find that an Archbishop of Canterbury should be speaking on their behalf. I reply, of course, as a representative and not as a delegate of the guests, and that is a very important constitutional difference. Our representatives in Parliament are representatives and not delegates. We choose them, thinking that they are the best men, and then we leave them to exercise their own discretion without accounting to us for everything they do. So I shall reply for the guests as a representative allowed to exercise my discretion.

I am sorry to say that this evening as I left the Church Assembly one of my colleagues, having discovered I was coming to this banquet, said, 'What are you doing in company like that?' Personally, I should maintain that there is no company in which it is not fitting for an Archbishop to be present either to encourage or to reprove or both. Anyway, here I am.

I have two reasons for being particularly pleased to be one of your company this evening. The first is this. I was for a considerable period of my life head of a large and important society whose finances were on a considerable scale. I was the headmaster of a school and I had the duty of administering the finances of that body. The governing body was advised by a very excellent and eminent accountant from whom I received the biggest compliment I have ever received. He said to a friend of mine who repeated it to me that if I had entered the accountancy profession I should have gone to the top of the tree. I did have some doubts about his meaning because (as he had discovered) most of my endeavours were to deceive my governing body into thinking they had more money to spend on my projects than they really had and I could not help wondering whether that was why he thought I should get on so well as an accountant.

Let me now make one or two remarks about our hosts whose hospitality we have enjoyed so immensely this evening. First, they are, as we well know and as has been said this evening, an absolutely essential service. It was

Napoleon who said that every army marches on its stomach, but I am bound to say that every modern society rests upon its accountants. Whether we march on them or not I do not know. Second, we regard them as an immensely satisfying service for this reason. There has been a good deal of reference to freedom tonight and the need to preserve that freedom is one of our most urgent and pressing duties; but you must define the conditions of freedom. The accountant gives a demonstration of one condition of true freedom in that he is always the servant of the facts and cannot manipulate the facts to suit his own ends. There are quite a number of people who think that freedom means just that manipulating of facts to suit themselves. You stand as a humble profession—I hope you do—which recognises that it is its duty to be obedient to facts and to exercise an unfailing responsibility to them as servants of truth and not the manipulators of truth.

Third, may I say this. We have been theological this evening. Lord Radcliffe started with the Council of Trent which was followed by references to Alexander and Athanasius. May I say that accountants also demonstrate that there is rooted in men that precise thing to which Lord Radcliffe referred—original sin. If there were not you would not be half as much employed as you are! There is original sin in your clients which you try to restrain and, for all I know, there is some original sin in you. But apart from that, there is the disturbing fact that all experts do tend to wrap up their expert trade, as has been said, to make it a mystery, no longer understood by ordinary people, and that is at once a dangerous situation. It is precisely that which the theologians do. Indeed, by the end of a real theological discourse you have forgotten that religion in essence is a very simple and straightforward practice of a number of duties and obligations. Accountancy, like economics and everything else, has become so intricate that the ordinary person wonders whether it has lost all touch with the simple truths. I am sure that is not the case with you and I am not rebuking you. I am merely saying that which I say of myself and of my own profession constantly, that there is original sin and we have to be careful that it does not affect our own province. The fact is that the only lasting value of things in this world is the relation between persons and how they use things. Things, whether they be figures or anything else, are not ultimates. They are to be made use of by men for their own social purposes. What matters more than the things is how people govern themselves in their personal relations and thus make use of the things which God's Providence has provided. The problem of human relations is the only real problem in this world and in my opinion that problem can never be solved apart from a true solution of the relation between man and God. That leads me to say how much I appreciated the fact that you began your Congress with a service in Westminster Abbey. It is, I believe, a very notable thing that for many years past—going back before the last century—there has been a growing divorce between the secular and the religious. There have been faults on both sides, but increasingly secular thinking has been that men could manage affairs on their own, with man as the sole court of reference, man making his own laws and being his own yardstick. The last few years have, in my mind, borne witness to an increasing drawing together of what has been called the secular and religious, each realising that they cannot get on without the other; that religion is there to help the secular and that the secular is there to conduct its own business with regard to the fundamental truths of religion.

I end by saying that we have at least one phrase in common. Every time I read the Bidding Prayer, I tell the congregation to remember that 'strict and solemn account' that they will have to render before the Judgment Seat of God. You know all about strict and solemn accounts: I remind you of another such account which every man must render to his own conscience and before whatever form of Divine Providence it may be to which he gives his allegiance.

MR. L. VAN ESSEN (Netherlands), in response, said:

I am privileged to have the opportunity to say these few words at the termination of the official toast list.

The organisation of a Congress such as this Sixth International Congress on Accounting is no light task. When we look at the programme—five sessions, thirty-five papers, social events and many others—we are deeply impressed by the enormous amount of work which must have been done to make things run smoothly and make visitors feel completely at home. As far as I can observe, things do run smoothly and visitors do feel completely at home.

Of course there have been various committees and a staff of experienced officers, but there must also be a centre round which all their activities are grouped and that centre is the President, Sir Harold Howitt. We must all be grateful to him that, in addition to all his numerous and important activities, he has been willing to take on his shoulders the burden of the Presidency of the Sixth International Congress.

As we all know, Sir Harold is a Justice of the Peace, a Deputy Lieutenant of the County of London, a member of the Council of the Institute of Chartered Accountants, a member of the tribunal which assesses compensation payable to the owners of coal mines and, last but not least, a partner in the firm of Peat, Marwick, Mitchell & Co. He will know how to spend his time, therefore; yet he has been willing to act as President of this Congress. I know that I am speaking on behalf of all those present and all our colleagues who are not when I wish him health, happiness and prosperity.

MR. MAX ANDRÉ (France), in response, said:

It is with great emotion that I address such a distinguished company in this ancient and beautiful Guildhall, so magnificent in its scars and glory.

First I think that I have a personal account to settle with the Lord Mayor. He mentioned that this day was the anniversary of the Battle of Waterloo, but speaking of anniversaries may I recall that today, the 18th June, is a date which is very dear to French hearts since on that very day in 1940 a very small group of Free French rejoined the British in battle.

Is there much which can be added to that which Mr. van Essen said in such excellent terms about our President, Sir Harold Howitt? I believe that no compliment to him is undeserved. There are many things I like and admire in Great Britain, but I may say that personally I particularly appreciate the way the British delight in understatement. In speaking of Sir Harold it is pleasing to think that one does not run the risk of exaggerating. It is a matter of fact that in all his capacities and in all his activities he has always been at the top. Whether he be carrying out a public duty, or in his profession, or as President of this International Congress on Accounting, he always shows himself to be a true British gentleman—plucky, obstinate and efficient. He even seems to get control over the elements which is just short of miraculous. Therefore, I feel honoured and privileged to associate myself with Mr. van Essen in wishing our President health, happiness and prosperity.

THE PRESIDENT:

This is completely unauthorised. I have only issued one order since I was invited to be President and that was that there should be no toast to the Chairman at tonight's Banquet. I should, however, be less than honest and less than human if I did not confess that I am delighted that the representatives of two friendly countries, the Netherlands and France, should have risen so spontaneously and spoken in such kindly terms. I appreciate it very much indeed and shall not say any more than this, that I feel rather in a false position in accepting the thanks offered in such a kindly way. Thanks are not due to me; they are due to many people to whom I shall have pleasure in referring on Friday. None the less, I am deeply grateful to the representatives of France and the Netherlands for the kind things which they have said.

CLOSING OF THE CONGRESS

FRIDAY, 20TH JUNE, 1952

CLOSING OF THE CONGRESS

THE PRESIDENT:

This has been a great week for the sponsoring bodies and, I hope, a great week for all of you who are visitors. It has also been made a great week for us by the weather.

I see that I am billed for a 'Closing Address' and I did some little time ago endeavour to draft the skeleton of such an address with a view to filling in details in odd moments, but any such moments have been very few. I have noticed during the sessions a certain technique, which I do not think I can emulate. It is a technique in accordance with which you walk up to the microphone with a wad of notes in your hand and, as you approach the microphone, you fold them up and put them in your pocket. That is very good provided you get away with it and I can say that everyone I have seen do it has got away with it. However, I do not think it would apply to me.

I stated in my opening address that it was a pleasure for us to welcome you from all parts of the world. I expressed the hope that you would enjoy yourselves and now I hope that you have. For us it has been a delightful week full of interest and full of the pleasure of meeting old friends and of making new ones.

Our friends from overseas have been over-generous on many occasions, both privately and formally, in expressing thanks to us. I feel as President of this Congress that it should be the other way round and that thanks are due to you, because I have been treated in such a generous manner. The Congress has been made a success chiefly by the cheerfulness and goodwill of all our visitors from the word 'go'.

We all know that, however good organisation may be and however good the scheme may be, it will avail nothing if the human beings concerned do not co-operate. That is the first thing that management knows. I want to say to you straight away that you, as human beings, co-operated right from the first meeting on Monday and have kept it up ever since.

I want to refer on your behalf to a few people whom I know you would wish to thank. May I commence with the Vice-President of the Congress, Mr. Barrowcliff. He has supported me throughout and shared in, and sometimes halved, all the handshaking that I have had to do. Next I want to thank the Presidents of the sponsoring bodies. There are seven of them, again including Mr. Barrowcliff, and I wish to thank them most sincerely for the support which they have given me.

Next I desire to thank on your behalf the Chairmen of the various committees, particularly Mr. Garton Ash, the Chairman of the Congress Council, and Mr. Nelson, Mr. Latham and Mr. House. I know how deeply and keenly over many months those committees have attended to all the problems which have arisen.

I should like, if I may, to say a word in particular about the Ladies'

665

Committee which has provided the human touches which mere men could not have attempted. I have learned more about dress shows in these last few weeks than I ever thought I should learn. However, it is not only dress shows. It is the spirit of goodwill to which they have largely contributed. I have heard my wife on many occasions in the last few weeks say what a joy it has been to her to be allowed to co-operate with such happy, able and cheerful companions as she has had.

Then I want to mention all those volunteers, ladies, members and students, with their little yellow badges, which we know so very well. They have, as liaison officers, contributed to make the Congress a success. They have been the oil which has made the machinery work and without them we should have been sunk. I also desire on your behalf to express our gratitude to the proprietors and editor of *The Accountant*, not only for the support they have given us in our day to day business but for the hospitality which they are extending to us this evening. No effort has been spared by them in their most difficult task so efficiently undertaken.

All those to whom I have referred are, however, very conscious, as indeed we all are, of the fact that the real work of a Congress of this sort falls upon the executive itself, namely, Mr. MacIver and Brigadier Jones.

Mr. MacIver has worked extremely hard during the last few weeks and tonight he will go off for a week's holiday. He confessed to me the other day that at one stage of the proceedings he was tempted to take off his secretary's badge to put off the number of visitors who were following him about. Brigadier Jones took on his job at a time when, unfortunately, we lost by death his predecessor who up to that point was arranging our work. Brigadier Jones took hold of the reins in a masterly fashion and ever since has devoted his time and energy in a way which has won the admiration of us all. At the same time, Miss Hay and all the assistants have put up a remarkable performance. It might interest you to know that a sideline of Miss Hay's is the training of horses. That may account for the very able way in which she has been able to handle us.

We are fortunate to have such a staff. We found that the best thing was to leave the situation entirely to them.

I should like now to take the opportunity—I hope the visitors will not mind—of thanking the sponsoring bodies for the compliment which they paid me in asking me to be President. It is a great honour and I appreciate it very deeply.

Many of your hosts wish they could have entertained you more in their homes, as was done, I believe, at previous Congresses but the spacious days when that was possible (I hope they will come again) are at the moment not with us either here or in other countries; and so I hope you will take the will for the deed.

I am glad to say that at a meeting yesterday, at which all of the accountancy bodies were represented, the general feeling was expressed that a further International Congress should be held on lines generally similar to those of the present Congress, perhaps in about five years time. Generous offers are already forthcoming from potential hosts and the most suitable meeting place will be selected in due course. If the next Congress should be held on the Continent of Europe, the question of language will of course arise as it did at previous Congresses of this series at Amsterdam and at Berlin, and at the Conference at Paris in 1948. I want to make it clear to those who may have had some difficulty this week with our language that practical difficulties, including the question of cost, made it necessary to have one language only. It goes without saying that, when the hosts for the next Congress are selected, any experience which we have gained here will be made readily available to them.

I am not going to attempt to summarise in any way the papers which have been discussed this week. It would be ridiculous for me to try at a meeting of this sort to do such a thing. Indeed, at each meeting the person summing-up has stated that it was almost impossible adequately to summarise all the special points which arose. I am sure that the written record when it is available will be closely studied and all I should like to do at this moment is to thank once again all those who have contributed and, in particular, those who have taken on the difficult role of rapporteur.

As I said at Guildhall on Wednesday, it is not only a privilege but a responsibility to be members of a calling which is now universally regarded as a profession, with all that this implies. It implies integrity, ability, hard work and a very special regard for the interests of one's clients and of the public at large, whether we work in the professional field or in a governmental or commercial career. It requires tact and firmness in dealing with the strains imposed, by inflation or high taxation, on the business ability and even on the commercial morality of normally honest people. It is easy to say these things and they represent qualities required by many people other than ourselves. It is, however, one of the main purposes of professional Congresses to keep such ideals alive and bright. Another and equally important purpose is to foster and to improve international relationship. So I hope and believe that we have succeeded in both objectives.

It was William Shakespeare who said 'Parting is such sweet sorrow', and although with boyhood memories one cannot say that this always applies to 'end of term' proceedings, I hope that it is in some measure true today. It is probably too much to hope that we shall all meet again but I hope that many of us will and that many friendships have been formed which will endure. Subject to the remaining functions this evening, I now declare the proceedings of this International Congress on Accounting terminated.

MR. T. A. HILEY, F.C.A. (Australia):

There is one task which remains before we disperse and it is a task which can only be performed by a visitor who has enjoyed the hospitality of our sponsors. It is on behalf of all the visitors from every country represented here to say to our sponsors how much we have appreciated their boundless hospitality.

London remains a beautiful and glorious city and our hosts during this past week have taken us to their seats of learning, they have shown us the sweet content of a lovely countryside, and for those and countless other material benefits we go away with our hearts filled with gratitude and admiration for the way in which our sponsors have cared for us. But I think that we all go away conscious of something even more. Those material things, magnificent as they are, have been surpassed by something even more rare and even better than those lovely things to which I have referred. I do not think any of us who experienced the feeling which surrounded that opening service in Westminster Abbey will ever forget it. Again, those of us who were privileged to attend Guildhall with its unforgettable atmosphere have experienced something which will live with us as long as life itself.

I say to our hosts that the truest measure of their boundless hospitality has been the way in which they have not only dealt bounteously with us so far as the material things at their command are concerned, but for the way they have unfolded to us those spiritual and emotional vistas which live so long with us.

I think that I speak for the profession throughout the world when I say to our colleagues in Great Britain that they have always commanded our respect and admiration. I say to them now, with the memories of this week living in the minds of each one of us present, that they now command our affection as well. We return shortly to a world of commerce which still wants to know where it is going and in the near future I have no doubt that we shall be busily engaged telling them where they were a few days ago. However, in approaching our task none of us will be able to forget or lightly dismiss from our memories the hospitality which may some day be equalled but never be excelled.

I ask you by acclamation to show to our hosts and sponsors our great satisfaction for the boundless hospitality which they have extended to us during the past week.

MR. G. P. KAPADIA, B.COM., F.C.A. (India):
I should like fully to associate myself with the vote of thanks which has been so ably proposed to our sponsoring bodies and to the President and Vice-President for the hospitality which they have accorded us. The welcome which they have given us has come from their hearts, and it will for ever remain in our memories. We who have come from the East will always retain these memories. We have learned a lot from the Congress and have gathered new experience which will stand us in good stead in the times to come.

S. C. TYRRELL, F.C.W.A.

President of The Institute of Cost and Works Accountants

Photo Turner & Drinkwater, Hull

C. H. POLLARD, O.B.E., F.S.A.A., F.I.M.T.A.

President of The Institute of Municipal Treasurers and Accountants

VISITS TO SCOTLAND AND IRELAND

MONDAY, 23RD, TO WEDNESDAY, 25TH JUNE, 1952

VISIT TO SCOTLAND

One hundred and two delegates and visitors travelled to Scotland at the conclusion of the Congress at the joint invitation of the Institute of Chartered Accountants of Scotland, the Scottish branches of the Society of Incorporated Accountants and Auditors, the Association of Certified and Corporate Accountants, the Institute of Municipal Treasurers and Accountants, and the Edinburgh and District Branch of the Institute of Cost and Works Accountants.

The members of the committee responsible for the arrangements were as follows:

Representing the Institute of Chartered Accountants of Scotland:
Sir David Allan Hay, President,
Mr. John L. Somerville, Vice-President,
Mr. William L. Davidson,
Mr. William Watson.

Representing the Society of Incorporated Accountants and Auditors:
Mr. P. G. S. Ritchie, President of the Scottish Branch.

Representing the Association of Certified and Corporate Accountants:
Mr. William K. Geddes, President of the Edinburgh and East of Scotland Branch.

Representing the Institute of Municipal Treasurers and Accountants:
Mr. Alex. Philip, Secretary of the Scottish Branch.

Representing the Institute of Cost and Works Accountants:
Mr. J. M. Glover, Secretary of the Edinburgh and District Branch.

Sir David Allan Hay acted as convener of the committee and Mr. E. H. V. McDougall, Secretary of the Institute of Chartered Accountants of Scotland, as its secretary.

One of the first decisions taken was that each guest should be able to sleep in the same hotel each night and thus be spared the necessity of moving his baggage. This led to a decision to base the visitors on Edinburgh although it was appreciated that this must reduce the amount of the ground which they could cover during their stay.

Hotel accommodation was reserved only just in time: shortly after the reservations had been made it was announced that Her Majesty the Queen was to pay her first official visit to Edinburgh since her accession during the same week. As there was already another large congress being held in Edinburgh that week hotel accommodation became extremely difficult to secure. For this and other reasons, it was found necessary to put a limitation upon the number of visitors who could take part in the Scottish visit.

Most of the overseas visitors who were to take part travelled North on Sunday, 22nd June. They were met on their arrival at their hotels by Mr. Charles R. Munro, a member of the Council of the Scottish Institute, and Mr. McDougall. It was with some relief that it was ascertained that virtually all of the visitors had arrived: earlier in the day, a message had come from

London which suggested that only about half of the visitors had boarded the train. It was ultimately discovered that they had merely failed to travel in the reserved carriage.

Each visitor received on arrival a letter from Mr. McDougall conveying a welcome from the Scottish host bodies and setting out the revised time-table of the various events. Each visitor was requested to co-operate by being punctual at the various functions as the time-table was somewhat crowded. All the visitors responded magnificently to this appeal and it is impossible to speak too highly of the contribution which they made to the smooth running of the arrangements. As an example, it was announced towards the end of the dinner in Glasgow that the coaches would arrive at 9.15 to carry the party back to Edinburgh. By 9.10 everyone was on the steps of the hotel: at 9.11 the coaches arrived and the whole party was on board within five minutes. The travel agents remarked that they had never experienced such punctuality and said 'We take off our hats to accountants'.

The first event on Monday, 23rd June, was a tour of the City of Edinburgh by motor-coach. The party was shown over the Castle and saw the Royal Mile, the Palace and Abbey of Holyrood House and other features of interest. At the conclusion of this tour the party was received at the George Hotel by Sir David Allan Hay and took luncheon. At the end of the luncheon Sir David addressed a few brief words of welcome to the visitors, and Mr. A. E. Beauvais, President of the Canadian Institute of Chartered Accountants, replied.

Monday afternoon was left free for shopping and further sightseeing or rest, as the visitors preferred. From 8 p.m. to 10 p.m. there was a Civic Reception at City Chambers given by the Corporation of the City of Edinburgh. The Right Honourable James Miller, the Lord Provost, received the guests, who included many representatives of the Scottish host bodies, and made a short speech of welcome to which Mr. Somerville replied. The Castle was floodlit in honour of the occasion.

The following day the visitors assembled at 8.30 a.m. at 27 Queen Street, the headquarters of the Scottish Institute, and boarded motor-coaches for a tour of Loch Lomond, Loch Long and Gareloch. The itinerary included the Forth Bridge and the Field of Bannockburn. Coffee was taken at Stirling, luncheon at Balloch and tea at Helensburgh. Unfortunately the weather was unkind: mist and intermittent rain were encountered all day and many of the features of interest could not be seen. Nevertheless, the visitors retained their good spirits to a remarkable degree. Several times they were heard to say that they had always supposed that Scotland was shrouded in mists and now they were seeing for themselves the truth of what they had been told.

The coaches brought the party to Glasgow in the evening, where there was another reception and a dinner at the St. Enoch Hotel. Sir David Allan Hay was in the chair. There were no formal speeches. After the dinner the party returned to Edinburgh by coach.

The following morning was left free. This gave the visitors the opportunity of joining the crowds gathered to greet Her Majesty when she drove along Princes Street on her arrival in the City. At 1.30 p.m. the party assembled at 27 Queen Street and drove by motor-coach to Dryburgh, where the Abbey was visited and tea was taken, and to Melrose. There was nearly a crisis at this point, as the party did not return to Edinburgh until almost 6.30 p.m. and they were due, after having changed, at 7 for 7.30 p.m. at the North British Hotel for the formal dinner which was to conclude the Scottish visit. The crisis did not, however, occur as the visitors rose to the occasion and most of them had been received by Sir David and Lady Allan Hay before 7.15 p.m. and dinner was in fact served almost exactly on time. After the dinner Mr. I. W. Macdonald, from Glasgow, proposed the health of 'The City and Royal Borough of Edinburgh' and Bailie F. H. N. Walker (who represented the Lord Provost, who was in attendance on Her Majesty) replied. Sir David Allan Hay, who was in the chair, proposed the health of 'The Guests' and there were replies from Mr. Edward B. Wilcox, a Past President of the American Institute of Accountants, and Mr. Gösta Björfors, President of the Svenska Revisorsamfundet, and in addition an extemporary reply by one of the Danish representatives. Mr. C. F. Horley, President of the Association of Accountants of Australia, then proposed the health of 'The Chairman' and the chairman replied.

The evening concluded with a group of songs by Mr. John Tainsh, tenor, accompanied by Mr. McGrogan at the piano, and an enjoyable evening was brought to an end when Mr. Tainsh led the gathering in singing 'Auld Lang Syne' and 'God Save the Queen'.

The following is a list of those from overseas who took part in the visit to Scotland:

Mr. and Mrs. N. O. Barkland
Mr. and Mrs. A. Emile Beauvais
Mr. and Mrs. Arthur B. Beynon
Mr. and Mrs. Gösta Björfors
Mr. and Mrs. I. Boesberg
Mr. and Mrs. R. D. Brown
Mr. and Mrs. A. Busch-Sørensen
Mr. and Mrs. Paul Busuttil
Mr. Ö. Cassel
Mr. and Mrs. S. A. Christensen
Mr. and Mrs. Veli Colérus
Mr. and Mrs. Arthur M. Craig
and Miss Craig
Mr. Dilip Kumar Datta
Mr. and Mrs. Niels Hansen
Mr. and Mrs. M. Hermann
Mr. Alfred R. Herning
Mr. and Mrs. Anson Herrick
Mr. Ernst Hinst and Miss Hinst
Mr. and Mrs. Magnus Holm
Mr. and Mrs. Conrad F. Horley

Professor and Mrs. George R. Husband
Mr. and Mrs. C. J. Idman
Mr. Willi Ihne
Mr. and Mrs. Tore Isakson
Mr. Vilh Jensen
Mr. K. Katagiri
Mr. C. L. King
Mr. and Mrs. Franz Kinnebrock
Mr. and Mrs. Thomas Kjeldsberg
Mr. and Mrs. C. N. Langkilde Larsen
Mr. and Mrs. Kaj Larsen
Mr. and Mrs. Sigurd Löfgren
Mr. and Mrs. J. Loos
Mr. and Mrs. John I. Marder
Mr. and Mrs. J. M. Mehra
Mr. Shigeru Morita
Mr. L. Müller
Miss E. Neumann
Mr. and Mrs. Christian Nielsen

Mr. Maruo Okamoto
Mr. Harry L. Pearce
Mr. and Mrs. V. N. Raiji
Mr. and Mrs. Reidar Rösjö
Mr. and Mrs. Oscar
      Schmidt-Pizarro
Mr. and Mrs. Hans-Th. Schubert
Mr. and Mrs. H. Schultheis
Mr. and Mrs. Walter Scott
Mr. and Mrs. A. F. J. Sears
Mr. A. Serpollet and
      Miss Serpollet

Mr. A. Solz
Mr. and Mrs. J. Angus Steven
Mr. and Mrs. A. A. Surber
Mr. John Tengström
Mr. O. Thies
Mr. and Mrs. Olav V. Thiesen
Mr. and Mrs. Erkki Usva
Mr. H-K. von Weitershausen
Mr. and Mrs. Edward B. Wilcox
Professor B. J. S. Wimble

VISIT TO IRELAND

A party of thirty-five persons from overseas accepted the joint invitation of the Institute of Chartered Accountants in Ireland, the Society of Incorporated Accountants and Auditors in Ireland, the Irish Branch of the Association of Certified and Corporate Accountants and the Dublin and District Branch of the Institute of Cost and Works Accountants, and visited Dublin after the Congress from the 23rd to 25th June.

The arrangements were undertaken by a committee consisting of the following:

Representing the Institute of Chartered Accountants in Ireland:

Mr. P. Butler, Vice-President,
Mr. E. P. O'Carroll,
Mr. W. E. Crawford, Secretary,
Mr. H. E. Green, Assistant to the Secretary.

Representing the Society of Incorporated Accountants and Auditors in Ireland:

Mr. M. Bell, Past President,
Mr. W. L. White, Past President,
Mr. J. Love, Honorary Secretary.

Representing the Association of Certified and Corporate Accountants (Irish Branch):

Mr. M. F. MacCormac, Past President,
Mr. Matt J. Kenny, Honorary Secretary,
Mr. R. Christopher, Honorary Treasurer.

Representing the Institute of Cost and Works Accountants (Dublin and District Branch):

Mr. J. C. Tonge, President,
Mr. E. Mullen, Past President,
Mr. T. F. V. Jackson, Honorary Secretary.

The Right Honourable Alderman Senator Andrew S. Clarkin, P.C., Lord Mayor of Dublin, welcomed the visitors on their arrival on Monday, 23rd June, at a reception in the Mansion House and, with the Lady Mayoress, attended the luncheon which followed in the Shelbourne Hotel, at which Mr. Mervyn Bell, Past President of the Society of Incorporated Accountants and Auditors in Ireland, presided. After luncheon the visitors made a tour of the city by motor-coach in the course of which they saw the famous Book of Kells in the library of Trinity College, spent a short time in the Botanic Gardens and also visited Phœnix Park. In the evening the party attended the Gaiety Theatre and enjoyed the first night of the Dublin Musical Society's presentation of *The Desert Song*.

On Tuesday, 24th June, the visitors left Dublin at 10.15 a.m. by motor-coach for a full-day tour through County Wicklow, by Dun Laoghaire and Killiney to Glendalough where luncheon was taken at the Royal Hotel. The Vale of Avoca and Bray were visited on the return journey and a halt was made at Greystones for afternoon tea on the lawn of the Grand Hotel. Proceeding via Ballybrack, Dun Laoghaire was reached at 7.30 p.m., where dinner in the Royal Marine Hotel—presided over by Mr. J. C. Tonge, President of the Dublin and District Branch of the Institute of Cost and Works Accountants—completed the day's programme. At the dinner Mr. Carl E. Dietze, a delegate from the United States of America, who had to leave Dublin the following day, took the opportunity of saying how pleased he was to be able to visit Ireland and thanked the host bodies for the welcome and hospitality he and the other visitors had received.

Following a free morning on Wednesday, 25th June, the visitors were entertained to luncheon in the Shelbourne Hotel—Mr. M. F. MacCormac, immediate Past President of the Irish Branch of the Association of Certified and Corporate Accountants, presiding—before proceeding on a motor-coach tour of the Boyne Valley. At the luncheon a visitor from New Zealand, Mr. B. H. Wood, who with his wife was flying back to London that evening, thanked the sponsoring bodies for all they had done to make their visit so enjoyable and interesting.

Mr. P. Butler, Vice-President of the Institute of Chartered Accountants in Ireland, presided at the farewell reception and dinner in the Shelbourne Hotel at which the guest artists, Miss Angela O'Connor and Mr. Robert McCullagh, vocalists, with Mr. J. R. Cowle, pianist, provided an excellent musical programme, visitors and hosts alike joining in the choruses. A feature of the evening was the unexpected and talented contributions by two members of the host bodies—Mr. Mervyn Bell and Mr. T. F. V. Jackson. Mr. Bell's duets with Mr. Robert McCullagh 'Watchman, What of the Night?' and 'The Merriest Fellows are We' (from *The Gondoliers*) were much appreciated; the visitors from Germany were particularly pleased and impressed by his rendering of Bach's 'Bist du Bei Mir'. Mr. Jackson played his own accompaniment to some German folk songs and had no difficulty in persuading the delegates and visitors from Germany to join in the choruses. Miss O'Connor then paid a graceful compliment to the French visitors by singing a Parisian song which was acknowledged by Messrs. Henri Kontzler and Louis Réchard of France.

On behalf of their respective bodies the following representatives of each country expressed in the most sincere and graceful terms their thanks for and appreciation of the generous entertainment provided by the sponsoring bodies and spoke of the very pleasant and unforgettable memories they would always have of their visit to Ireland:

Mr. Otto Bredt (Germany)
Mr. A. A. Fitzgerald (Australia)
Mr. Henri Kontzler (France)
Mr. C. W. Mavor (Canada)

Mr. E. Moberg (Finland)
Mr. Kurt Schmidt (Austria)
Mr. J. Thorbjörnsen (Norway)

Mrs. Mavor, speaking on behalf of the ladies, mentioned particularly how much they had appreciated and been touched by the thoughtfulness of the organisers in providing the beautiful flowers which had welcomed them on arrival at their hotels and the chocolates presented to them at the theatre.

It was nearly midnight when the proceedings terminated and visitors and hosts had taken their reluctant and regretful farewells, with many expressions of hope that opportunities would occur in the future for continuation, or renewal, of the friendships which had been formed.

The following is a list of those from overseas who took part in the visit to Ireland:

Mr. and Mrs. R. Bechinie	Mr. and Mrs. C. W. Mavor
Mr. and Mrs. Otto Bredt	Mr. and Mrs. Albert Meier
Mr. and Mrs. Ingolf Bryn	Mr. and Mrs. A Melchner
Mr and Mrs. Wilhelm Dieterich	Mr. and Mrs. F. Merkle
Mr. Carl E. Dietze	Mr. and Mrs. W. Minz
Mr. and Mrs. W. Elmendorff	Mr. and Mrs. E. Moberg
Mr. and Mrs. A. A. Fitzgerald	Mr. Louis Réchard
Mr. and Mrs. F. E. Gercke	Mr. Kurt Schmidt
Mr. Karl Hax	Mr. and Mrs. J. Thorbjörnsen
Mr. Henri Kontzler	Mr. and Mrs. B. H. Wood

The following members of the host bodies with their ladies took part in the entertainment of the guests:

The Institute of Chartered Accountants in Ireland

Mr. Patrick Butler, Vice-President, and Mrs. Butler	Mr. and Mrs. H. H. Forsyth
	Mr. and Mrs. C. F. Smith
Mr. and Mrs. E. T. McCarron	Mr. H. W. Robinson
Mr. and Mrs. G. Francis Klingner	Mr. L. Chance
Mr. and Mrs. D. McC. Watson	Mr. W. E. Crawford, Secretary

The Society of Incorporated Accountants and Auditors in Ireland

Mr. Mervyn Bell, Past President, and Mrs. Bell	Mr. R. A. Kidney
	Mr. and Mrs. R. S. Baskin
Mr. A. H. Walkey, Past President	Mr. and Mrs. C. J. Dalton
Mr. and Mrs. R. L. Reid	Mr. A. P. Carey
Mr. and Mrs. W. A. Kenny	Mr. and Mrs. S. A. Matthews
Mr. R. J. Kidney	Mr. C. D. Shannon

The Association of Certified and Corporate Accountants (Irish Branch)

Mr. M. J. McNally, President, and Mrs. McNally	Mr. P. Callan
	Mr. W. Pearson
Mr. M. F. MacCormac, Past President, and Mrs. MacCormac	Mr. Matt J. Kenny, Honorary Secretary
Mr. and Mrs. J. Bannon	

The Institute of Cost and Works Accountants (Dublin and District Branch)

Mr. J. C. Tonge, President, and Mrs. Tonge

Mr. E. Mullen, Past President, and Mrs. Mullen

Mr. and Mrs. T. J. Murphy

Mr. and Mrs. T. A. Egan

Mr. and Mrs. P. E. W. Burgess

Mr. T. F. V. Jackson, Honorary Secretary

APPENDICES

A. LIST OF OVERSEAS DELEGATES AND VISITORS BY COUNTRIES.

B. ALPHABETICAL LIST OF MEMBERS OF THE SPONSORS OF THE CONGRESS

C. BANQUET AT GUILDHALL: MENU, TOAST LIST AND LIST OF GUESTS.

APPENDIX A

LIST OF OVERSEAS DELEGATES AND VISITORS BY COUNTRIES

ARGENTINA
Delegate *Organisation*
VIACAVA, A. M.   Federación de Colegios de Doctores en Ciencias
                             Económicas y Contadores Públicos Nacionales

Visitor
BECKETT, A. H.

AUSTRALIA
Delegates
FITZGERALD, A. A.   Commonwealth Institute of Accountants
HARDIE, J. M.   Institute of Chartered Accountants in Australia
HILEY, T. A.   Institute of Chartered Accountants in Australia
HORLEY, C. F.   Association of Accountants of Australia
PROSSER, C. H.   Commonwealth Institute of Accountants
SAVAGE, E. W.   Institute of Chartered Accountants in Australia
SCOTT, W.   Commonwealth Institute of Accountants
STEELE, R. M.   Institute of Chartered Accountants in Australia
SUMMERSON, E. D.   Institute of Chartered Accountants in Australia
YOUNG, S. G.   Commonwealth Institute of Accountants

Visitors
AIRD, W.   Australasian Institute of Cost Accountants
ATCHESON, Myrtle M. N.   Australasian Institute of Cost Accountants
CRUST, R. H.   Institute of Chartered Accountants in Australia
GAZE, A. E.   Commonwealth Institute of Accountants
GREEN, G. A.   Commonwealth Institute of Accountants
HEWITT, C. L. S.   Commonwealth Institute of Accountants
KELLIE, F. H.   Institute of Chartered Accountants in Australia
LORMER, G.   Commonwealth Institute of Accountants
MATHEWS, R. L.   Commonwealth Institute of Accountants
ROBERTS, J. W.   Institute of Chartered Accountants in Australia
SHIRLEY, P. H.   Institute of Chartered Accountants in Australia
SMITH, M. C.   Institute of Chartered Accountants in Australia
WHITE, T. H.   Institute of Chartered Accountants in Australia
WILSON, E. L.   Institute of Chartered Accountants in Australia

AUSTRIA
Delegates
BECHINIE, R.   Kammer der Wirtschaftstreuhänder
SCHICK, H.   Kammer der Wirtschaftstreuhänder
SCHMIDT, K.   Kammer der Wirtschaftstreuhänder

681

AUSTRIA (—*continued*)

Visitors	*Organisation*
HALPERN, R.	Kammer der Wirtschaftstreuhänder
HOLLER, F. R.	Kammer der Wirtschaftstreuhänder
RAZELSDORFER, H.	Kammer der Wirtschaftstreuhänder
REICHART, Maria	Kammer der Wirtschaftstreuhänder

BELGIUM

Delegates

PAQUET, N.	Société Royale Chambre Belge des Comptables à Bruxelles
VANHOUTEGHEM, A.	Institut Belge des Reviseurs de Banques
VAN IPER, R. J.	Collège National des Experts Comptables de Belgique

Visitor

NEUMAN, H. O.	Commission Bancaire

BOLIVIA

Delegates

RABY, B. W.	Federación Nacional de Contadores
SEARS, A. F. J.	Federación Nacional de Contadores

BRAZIL

Delegates

CAMPOS, E. S.	Federação dos Contabilistas do Estado de São Paulo
D'AURIA, F.	Federação dos Contabilistas do Estado de São Paulo
DE LA MANO, J.	Federação dos Contabilistas do Estado de São Paulo

BURMA

Delegates

MACQUEEN, A. T.	Burma Accountancy Board
MAUNG, Maung	Burma Society of Accountants
SHEIN, Wunna Kyaw Htin	Burma Society of Accountants

CANADA

Delegates

BEAUVAIS, A. E.	Canadian Institute of Chartered Accountants
BURKE, T. V.	Institute of Chartered Accountants of Quebec
CARTER, K. Le M.	Canadian Institute of Chartered Accountants
COFFEY, F. A.	Institute of Chartered Accountants of Quebec
CRAIG, I.	Institute of Chartered Accountants of Quebec
CURRIE, G. S.	Institute of Chartered Accountants of Quebec
DALGLISH, K. W.	Canadian Institute of Chartered Accountants
FARISH, D. H. M.	Institute of Chartered Accountants of Quebec
FIELD, R. C.	Canadian Institute of Chartered Accountants
GROVER, F. J.	Institute of Chartered Accountants of British Columbia
HUTCHISON, T. A. M.	Institute of Chartered Accountants of Alberta
KING, C. L.	Canadian Institute of Chartered Accountants

CANADA (—Delegates—*continued*)   *Organisation*
LEVER, H. A.   Institute of Chartered Accountants of Ontario
McDONALD, W. L. L.   Canadian Institute of Chartered Accountants
MAPP, K. A.   Institute of Chartered Accountants of Ontario
MAVOR, C. W.   Institute of Chartered Accountants of British Columbia
RATHJEN, T. H.   Institute of Chartered Accountants of Manitoba
RISING, P.   Institute of Chartered Accountants of British Columbia
SHULMAN, J. J.   Institute of Chartered Accountants of Ontario
SNYDER, K.   Institute of Chartered Accountants of Ontario
WILSON, J. R. M.   Canadian Institute of Chartered Accountants

Visitor
TURNER, J.   Institute of Chartered Accountants of Ontario

COLOMBIA
Delegate
IRELAND, N. M.   Instituto Nacional de Contadores Públicos

DENMARK
Delegates
BUSCH-SØRENSEN, A.   Foreningen af Statsautoriserede Revisorer
HÆRNING, M.   Foreningen af Statsautoriserede Revisorer
JEPPESEN, H. Hjernø   Foreningen af Statsautoriserede Revisorer
NIELSEN, A.   Foreningen af Statsautoriserede Revisorer
VELLING, A. C.   Foreningen af Statsautoriserede Revisorer

Visitors
ALLUM, E.   Foreningen af Statsautoriserede Revisorer
BOESBERG, I.   Foreningen af Statsautoriserede Revisorer
CHRISTENSEN, S. A.   Foreningen af Statsautoriserede Revisorer
GLYTTING, M.   Foreningen af Statsautoriserede Revisorer
HANSEN, N.   Foreningen af Statsautoriserede Revisorer
HOUD, O.   Foreningen af Statsautoriserede Revisorer
JENSEN, V.   Foreningen af Statsautoriserede Revisorer
JESPERSEN, J.   Foreningen af Statsautoriserede Revisorer
KLEVEL, J. V.   Foreningen af Statsautoriserede Revisorer
LANGKILDE LARSEN, C. N.   Foreningen af Statsautoriserede Revisorer
LANGKILDE LARSEN, K.   Foreningen af Statsautoriserede Revisorer
LARSEN, K.   Foreningen af Statsautoriserede Revisorer
MARHOLT, J. O.   Foreningen af Statsautoriserede Revisorer
NIELSEN, C.   Foreningen af Statsautoriserede Revisorer
NIELSEN, C. M.   Foreningen af Statsautoriserede Revisorer
NIELSEN, E.   Foreningen af Statsautoriserede Revisorer
NIELSEN, K.   Foreningen af Statsautoriserede Revisorer
NISTED, V. O.   Foreningen af Statsautoriserede Revisorer
OLSEN, C. O.   Foreningen af Statsautoriserede Revisorer
SPANG-THOMSEN, V.   Foreningen af Statsautoriserede Revisorer
THIESEN, O. V.   Foreningen af Statsautoriserede Revisorer
WILLADS-HANSEN, E.   Foreningen af Statsautoriserede Revisorer

EAST AFRICA
Delegates   *Organisation*
LAWRIE, A. A.   Association of Accountants in East Africa
REED, G. C.   Association of Accountants in East Africa

FINLAND
Delegates
ANTTONEN, J.   K.H.T.-Yhdistys: Föreningen C.G.R.
FORSSTRÖM, B.   K.H.T.-Yhdistys: Föreningen C.G.R.
GRANDELL, A.   K.H.T.-Yhdistys: Föreningen C.G.R.
IDMAN, C. J.   K.H.T.-Yhdistys: Föreningen C.G.R.
LÖNNQVIST, U.   K.H.T.-Yhdistys: Föreningen C.G.R.
USVA, E.   K.H.T.-Yhdistys: Föreningen C.G.R.

Visitors
COLÉRUS, V.   K.H.T.-Yhdistys: Föreningen C.G.R.
KETTUNEN, M.   K.H.T.-Yhdistys: Föreningen C.G.R.
KIVISTÖ, E.   K.H.T.-Yhdistys: Föreningen C.G.R.
MOBERG, E.   K.H.T.-Yhdistys: Föreningen C.G.R.
STEINER, L.   K.H.T.-Yhdistys: Föreningen C.G.R.
TENGSTRÖM, J.   K.H.T.-Yhdistys: Föreningen C.G.R.
TIKKANEN, T.   K.H.T.-Yhdistys: Föreningen C.G.R.

FRANCE
Delegates
ALEXANDRE, J.   Ordre National des Experts Comptables et des
                                  Comptables Agréés
ANDRÉ; M.   Fédération des Associations de Commissaires de
                                  Sociétés Inscrits par les Cours d'Appel
BENVENISTE, R.   Union Professionelle des Sociétés Fiduciaires
                                  d'Expertise Comptable
BERGEON, P.   Compagnie Nationale des Experts Comptables
BOULY, F. L.   Compagnie des Chefs de Comptabilité
BOUTIN, F. J.   Société de Comptabilité de France
CIBERT, A.   Conseil Supérieur de la Comptabilité
CLOSON, F. L.   Conseil Supérieur de la Comptabilité
DEFOSSE, A.   Chambre Nationale des Experts-Comptables
                                  Diplômés par l'Etat
DREYER, P. J.   Chambre Nationale des Experts-Comptables
                                  Diplômés par l'Etat
DUCHESNE, L. R.   Société de Comptabilité de France
GOLDSCHILD, A.   Ordre National des Experts Comptables et des
                                  Comptables Agréés
HÉNAULT, A. G.   Chambre Nationale des Experts-Comptables
                                  Diplômés par l'Etat
LAUZEL, P.   Conseil Supérieur de la Comptabilité
LE BRIS, M.   Chambre Nationale des Experts-Comptables
                                  Diplômés par l'Etat
MARTIN, H.   Ordre National des Experts Comptables et des
                                  Comptables Agréés
MÉRIGOUX, A.   Compagnie des Experts-Comptables près la Cour
                                  d'Appel de Paris

FRANCE (—Delegates—*continued*)   *Organisation*

PAYRAU, A.   Compagnie Nationale des Experts Comptables
POLY, J.   Conseil Supérieur de la Comptabilité
RÉCHARD, L.   Société de Comptabilité de France
REYDEL, A.   Chambre Nationale des Experts-Comptables
                      Diplômés par l'Etat
RICHARD, F. M.   Compagnie Nationale des Experts Comptables
SERRES, E.   Compagnie Nationale des Experts Comptables
VEYRENC, A.   Compagnie Nationale des Experts Comptables

Visitors
CARDON, L. C.   Fédération des Associations de Commissaires de
                      Sociétés Inscrits par les Cours d'Appel
DANET, R.   Ordre National des Experts Comptables et des
                      Comptables Agréés
FLEURY, J.   Conseil Supérieur de la Comptabilité
GERMAIN, J. E.   Conseil Supérieur de la Comptabilité
GRIVEL, A.   Ordre National des Experts Comptables et des
                      Comptables Agréés
HERMANN, M.   Ordre National des Experts Comptables et des
                      Comptables Agréés
HERNING, A. R.   Fédération des Associations de Commissaires de
                      Sociétés Inscrits par les Cours d'Appel
KONTZLER, H.   Ordre National des Experts Comptables et des
                      Comptables Agréés
LABOURIER, R.   Comité National de la Productivité
MARIE, C.   Chambre Nationale des Experts-Comptables
                      Diplômés par l'Etat
MAUGRAS, P.   Ordre National des Experts Comptables et des
                      Comptables Agréés
MAZARS, R.   Ordre National des Experts Comptables et des
                      Comptables Agréés
MIOT, P.   Conseil Supérieur de la Comptabilité
NOCLAIN, M.   Compagnie Nationale des Experts Comptables
PAUL, B.   Ordre National des Experts Comptables et des
                      Comptables Agréés
ROUILLON, R.   Ordre National des Experts Comptables et des
                      Comptables Agréés
SERPOLLET, A.   Ordre National des Experts Comptables et des
                      Comptables Agréés

GERMANY
Delegates
BEHRENS, K. C.   Bundesverband der Vereidigten Buchprüfer
BREDT, O.   Institut der Wirtschaftsprüfer
DIETERICH, W.   Institut der Wirtschaftsprüfer
ELMENDORFF, W.   Institut der Wirtschaftsprüfer
HAX, K.   Institut der Wirtschaftsprüfer
HEIZMANN, H. F.   Bundesverband der Vereidigten Buchprüfer
KNORR, E.   Institut der Wirtschaftsprüfer
MEIER, A.   Institut der Wirtschaftsprüfer
MEIER, W.   Bundesverband der Vereidigten Buchprüfer

APPENDIX A

GERMANY (—Delegates—*continued*)   *Organisation*

MELCHNER, A.	Institut der Wirtschaftsprüfer
MERKLE, F.	Institut der Wirtschaftsprüfer
WINKER, P.	Bundesverband der Vereidigten Buchprüfer
ZIEGLER, F.	Bundesverband der Vereidigten Buchprüfer

Visitors

ADLER, H.	Institut der Wirtschaftsprüfer
BARTH, K.	Institut der Wirtschaftsprüfer
DOBLER, E.	Institut der Wirtschaftsprüfer
DREISS, W.	Institut der Wirtschaftsprüfer
GERCKE, F. E.	Institut der Wirtschaftsprüfer
GRIESEL, P.	Bundesverband der Vereidigten Buchprüfer
HELLER, E.	Institut der Wirtschaftsprüfer
HERZFELD, K. S.	Institut der Wirtschaftsprüfer
HILLMEISTER, L.	Institut der Wirtschaftsprüfer
HINST, E.	Institut der Wirtschaftsprüfer
HOFFSCHMIDT, R.	Institut der Wirtschaftsprüfer
HUPPERTZ, H.	Institut der Wirtschaftsprüfer
IHNE, W.	Institut der Wirtschaftsprüfer
JÜNGER, H.	Institut der Wirtschaftsprüfer
KALENDER, H.	Institut der Wirtschaftsprüfer
KENNTEMICH, R.	Institut der Wirtschaftsprüfer
KINNEBROCK, F.	Institut der Wirtschaftsprüfer
KRAUS, W.	Institut der Wirtschaftsprüfer
LAU, W.	Institut der Wirtschaftsprüfer
LOOS, J. P.	Bundesverband der Vereidigten Buchprüfer
LOOS, Marianne	Bundesverband der Vereidigten Buchprüfer
MAERTEN, H.	Institut der Wirtschaftsprüfer
MINZ, W.	Institut der Wirtschaftsprüfer
MÜLLER, H.	Institut der Wirtschaftsprüfer
MÜLLER, L.	Institut der Wirtschaftsprüfer
MÜLLER VON BLUMENCRON, K.	Institut der Wirtschaftsprüfer
RAPPMANN, B.	Institut der Wirtschaftsprüfer
RÄTSCH, H.	Institut der Wirtschaftsprüfer
REMIEN, P.	Institut der Wirtschaftsprüfer
REUSCHEL, H.	Institut der Wirtschaftsprüfer
RIEMER, W.	Institut der Wirtschaftsprüfer
ROBENS, H.	Institut der Wirtschaftsprüfer
ROSSBERG, C.	Institut der Wirtschaftsprüfer
ROSSBERG, Susanne	Institut der Wirtschaftsprüfer
RÖVER, Maria	Institut der Wirtschaftsprüfer
SCHIFFMANN, C. W.	Institut der Wirtschaftsprüfer
SCHUBERT, H. Th.	Institut der Wirtschaftsprüfer
SCHULTHEIS, H.	Institut der Wirtschaftsprüfer
SCHÜRER, K. K.	Institut der Wirtschaftsprüfer
SOLZ, A.	Institut der Wirtschaftsprüfer
STRACK, W.	Institut der Wirtschaftsprüfer
STÜTZ, G.	Institut der Wirtschaftsprüfer
THIES, O.	Institut der Wirtschaftsprüfer
TROMMSDORFF, E.	Institut der Wirtschaftsprüfer
VON DER TANN, K.	Institut der Wirtschaftsprüfer

GERMANY (—Visitors—*continued*) | *Organisation*

VON WEITERSHAUSEN, H-K.	Institut der Wirtschaftsprüfer
VOORS, W.	Institut der Wirtschaftsprüfer
WELLAND, K.	Institut der Wirtschaftsprüfer
WÖHL, K.	Institut der Wirtschaftsprüfer

INDIA
Delegates

AIYAR, S. V.	Institute of Chartered Accountants of India
FRANCIS, J.	Institute of Cost and Works Accountants (India)
GHOSE, S.	Institute of Chartered Accountants of India
KAPADIA, G. P.	Institute of Chartered Accountants of India
MODY, N. R.	Institute of Chartered Accountants of India
OJHA, S. K.	Institute of Cost and Works Accountants (India)
SAHGAL, A. L.	Institute of Chartered Accountants of India

Visitors

BATHGATE, G. M.	Institute of Chartered Accountants of India
BYRAMJI, S. T.	Institute of Chartered Accountants of India
DANDEKER, S. B.	Institute of Chartered Accountants of India
DATTA, D. K.	Institute of Chartered Accountants of India
KHANNA, K. C.	Institute of Chartered Accountants of India
LAKHIA, C. R.	Institute of Chartered Accountants of India
MARFATIA, N. M.	Institute of Chartered Accountants of India
MEHRA, J. M.	Institute of Chartered Accountants of India
MENZIES, Sir Robert	Institute of Chartered Accountants of India
RAIJI, V. N.	Institute of Chartered Accountants of India
RANE, D. R.	Institute of Chartered Accountants of India
SHAH, N. J.	Institute of Chartered Accountants of India

ISRAEL
Delegate

BAWLY, L.	Association of Public Accountants and Auditors in Israel

ITALY
Delegates

ANTOLINI, F.	Consiglio Nazionale dei Commercialisti
BISHOP, P. W.	Mutual Security Agency
CARTER, P. S.	Mutual Security Agency
DE DOMINICIS, E.	Istituto di Ricerche Economico-Aziendali: Università degli Studi di Torino
D'ERCOLE, E.	Istituto di Ricerche Economico-Aziendali: Università degli Studi di Torino
GIANNINI, A.	Istituto di Ricerche Economico-Aziendali: Università degli Studi di Torino
LA FORGIA, M.	Istituto di Ricerche Economico-Aziendali: Università degli Studi di Torino
ONIDA, P.	Istituto di Ricerche Economico-Aziendali: Università degli Studi di Torino

z

JAPAN
Delegates   *Organisation*
HAYASHI, R.   Nippon Keirishi Kai
KATAGIRI, K.   Nippon Keirishi Kai
MORITA, S.   Nippon Keirishi Kai
MURASE, G.   Nihon Konin Kaikeishi Kyokai
OHYAMA, Y.   Shadan Hojin Nihon Keirishi Kyokai
OKAMOTO, M.   Nihon Konin Kaikeishi Kyokai
SHIMOJI, G.   Nihon Konin Kaikeishi Kyokai
TATSUMI, S.   Nihon Konin Kaikeishi Kyokai

Visitor
YAMASHITA, K.   Nippon Keirishi Kai

MALTA
Delegates
BUSUTTIL, P.   Malta Institute of Accountants
CHRÉTIEN, J. C.   Malta Institute of Accountants
CRAIG, A. M.   Malta Institute of Accountants

MEXICO
Delegate
CASAS-ALATRISTE, R.   Instituto de Contadores Públicos Titulados de
                                  México

NETHERLANDS
Delegates
DE BRUYNE, A. L.   Nederlands Instituut van Accountants
DEMENINT, A. L.   Vereniging van Academisch Gevormde Account-
                                  ants
GOUDEKET, A.   Nederlands Instituut van Accountants
KASTEIN, A. Th. E.   Nederlands Instituut van Accountants
KRAAYENHOF, J.   Nederlands Instituut van Accountants
LIMPERG, Th.   Nederlands Instituut van Accountants
LINDNER, J. A. M. F.   Vereniging van Academisch Gevormde Account-
                                  ants
VAN ESSEN, L.   Nederlands Instituut van Accountants
VAN RIETSCHOTEN, A. M.   Nederlands Instituut van Accountants

Visitors
BOLHUIS, P.   Nederlands Instituut van Accountants
BRACKEL, G. J. L.   Vereniging van Academisch Gevormde Account-
                                  ants
BRANDS, J.   Vereniging van Academisch Gevormde Account-
                                  ants
BREEK, P. C.   Nederlands Instituut van Accountants
DE JONG, A. A.   Vereniging van Academisch Gevormde Account-
                                  ants
DE JONG, A. C. J.   Nederlands Instituut van Accountants
DE JONG, J.   Nederlands Instituut van Accountants
DE JONG, K. J.   Nederlands Instituut van Accountants

NETHERLANDS (—Visitors—*continued*)   *Organisation*

DE LEEUW, H. D.	Nederlands Instituut van Accountants
DE TOMBE, W. J.	Nederlands Instituut van Accountants
DE VRIES, H.	Nederlands Instituut van Accountants
DE ZWAAN, D.	Nederlands Instituut van Accountants
DIEKEMA, T.	Nederlands Instituut van Accountants
ENGELGEER, A. G. C.	Nederlands Instituut van Accountants
FOPPE, H. H. M.	Nederlands Instituut van Accountants
FRESE, G. W.	Nederlands Instituut van Accountants
GERBERS, P. W. Th.	Nederlands Instituut van Accountants
KEUZENKAMP, J.	Nederlands Instituut van Accountants
KONING, J. A.	Vereniging van Academisch Gevormde Accountants
KOPPENBERG, W. C.	Nederlands Instituut van Accountants
LOOS, J.	Nederlands Instituut van Accountants
LYRE, J. H.	Nederlands Instituut van Accountants
MEIJER, C. J.	Nederlands Instituut van Accountants
PIMENTEL, M.	Nederlands Instituut van Accountants
RANKEMA, G.	Nederlands Instituut van Accountants
REDER, H. R.	Nederlands Instituut van Accountants
REINOUD, H.	Nederlands Instituut van Accountants
RINSMA, F.	Nederlands Instituut van Accountants
STEK, H. C.	Vereniging van Academisch Gevormde Accountants
STOUTHANDEL, A.	Nederlands Instituut van Accountants
STRAATEMEIER, A.	Nederlands Instituut van Accountants
SURBER, A. A.	Vereniging van Academisch Gevormde Accountants
SWART, H. R.	Nederlands Instituut van Accountants
TIMME, D.	Nederlands Instituut van Accountants
TIMMER, G.	Nederlands Instituut van Accountants
TREFFERS, H. C.	Nederlands Instituut van Accountants
VAN BORK, W. H.	Nederlands Instituut van Accountants
VAN DEN BOSCH, H. L.	Nederlands Instituut van Accountants
VAN DE REE, J.	Nederlands Instituut van Accountants
VAN DER LAAN, J. F.	Nederlands Instituut van Accountants
VAN DER VEEN, G.	Nederlands Instituut van Accountants
VAN DER VELDEN, J.	Vereniging van Academisch Gevormde Accountants
VAN DER WERF, S. J. G.	Nederlands Instituut van Accountants
VAN DER ZANT, H. J.	Nederlands Instituut van Accountants
VAN DOORNE, F. F.	Nederlands Instituut van Accountants
VAN DUIN, W. J.	Nederlands Instituut van Accountants
VAN EIJDEN, J. W.	Nederlands Instituut van Accountants
WAANDERS, W.	Nederlands Instituut van Accountants
WIERSUM, K. A.	Nederlands Instituut van Accountants

NEW ZEALAND
Delegates

BELLRINGER, N. B.	Incorporated Institute of Accountants of New Zealand
BROWN, R. D.	New Zealand Society of Accountants

NEW ZEALAND (—Delegates—*continued*)   *Organisation*

FORSYTHE, J. G.	Incorporated Institute of Accountants of New Zealand
HOGG, J.	Incorporated Institute of Accountants of New Zealand
LEESE, G. L.	New Zealand Institute of Cost Accountants

Visitors

AVERILL, J. C.	New Zealand Society of Accountants
BATTISTON, J. A.	New Zealand Society of Accountants
BECKINGSALE, A. B.	New Zealand Society of Accountants
BENNETT, E. D.	New Zealand Society of Accountants
DALZIEL, R. T.	New Zealand Society of Accountants
DAVIS, D. D.	New Zealand Society of Accountants
EDGAR, G. C.	New Zealand Society of Accountants
GENTLES, J. L.	New Zealand Society of Accountants
HAY, H. G.	New Zealand Society of Accountants
ILOTT, J. V.	New Zealand Society of Accountants
JOHNSTON, T. R.	New Zealand Society of Accountants
MATTHEWS, G. J.	New Zealand Society of Accountants
ROSSER, D. C.	New Zealand Society of Accountants
SINCLAIR, B. S.	New Zealand Society of Accountants
SPOONER, Joan C.	New Zealand Society of Accountants
STARKE, L. J. R.	New Zealand Society of Accountants
TAILBY, W.	New Zealand Society of Accountants
WICKHAM, J. H. D.	New Zealand Society of Accountants
WILLIAMS, P. G. E.	New Zealand Society of Accountants
WOOD, B. H.	New Zealand Society of Accountants
WOOLCOTT, Mrs. E. E.	New Zealand Society of Accountants

NORWAY
Delegates

AMUNDSEN, I. W.	Norges Statsautoriserte Revisorers Forening
BIRKELAND, A.	Revisorforeningen i Oslo
GLOMSTEIN, A.	Norges Statsautoriserte Revisorers Forening
ILDAL, O. C.	Norges Statsautoriserte Revisorers Forening
KJELDSBERG, T.	Norges Statsautoriserte Revisorers Forening
THORBJÖRNSEN, J.	Norges Statsautoriserte Revisorers Forening

Visitors

BAKKE, K.	Norges Statsautoriserte Revisorers Forening
BERGE, E.	Norges Statsautoriserte Revisorers Forening
BRYN, I.	Norges Statsautoriserte Revisorers Forening
CARLSON, E.	Norges Statsautoriserte Revisorers Forening
CORNELIUSSEN, O.	Norges Statsautoriserte Revisorers Forening
ENG, A.	Norges Statsautoriserte Revisorers Forening
FAUSKE, G.	Norges Statsautoriserte Revisorers Forening
GRAN, T.	Norges Statsautoriserte Revisorers Forening
HARR, J. C. C.	Norges Statsautoriserte Revisorers Forening
HOLM, M.	Norges Statsautoriserte Revisorers Forening
JENSSEN, A.	Norges Statsautoriserte Revisorers Forening
KLYVE, C.	Norges Statsautoriserte Revisorers Forening

NORWAY (—Visitors—*continued*)	*Organisation*
KVALSTAD, A.	Norges Statsautoriserte Revisorers Forening
LÖKEN, R.	Norges Statsautoriserte Revisorers Forening
RIEKER, L.	Norges Statsautoriserte Revisorers Forening
ROSENLIND, F. E.	Norges Statsautoriserte Revisorers Forening
RÖSJÖ, R.	Norges Statsautoriserte Revisorers Forening
RUDBERG, F.	Norges Statsautoriserte Revisorers Forening
SKREEN, O.	Norges Statsautoriserte Revisorers Forening
SUNDBYE, E.	Norges Statsautoriserte Revisorers Forening
TISTHAL, B. Th.	Norges Statsautoriserte Revisorers Forening
VON KROGH, G. F.	Norges Statsautoriserte Revisorers Forening
WULFF-PEDERSEN, E.	Norges Statsautoriserte Revisorers Forening

PAKISTAN
Delegates
BRAY, J. P.	Pakistan Council of Accountancy
CHAUDHURY, M. H.	Pakistan Council of Accountancy
KHAN, A. B.	Pakistan Council of Accountancy

PERU
Delegates
BEZER, G. R.	Colegio de Contadores Públicos del Perú
CALLIRGOS, B.	Instituto de Contadores del Perú
SCHMIDT-PIZARRO, O.	Colegio de Contadores Públicos del Perú
SMITH, F. E.	Instituto de Contadores del Perú ·

PHILIPPINES
Delegates
DE LA ROSA, R. L.	Philippine Institute of Accountants
PICKUP, M. H.	Philippine Institute of Accountants
VILLA, O. J.	Philippine Institute of Accountants

PORTUGAL
Delegate
CASTEL-BRANCO, A. P. C. D'A.	Sociedade Portuguesa de Contabilidade

RHODESIA
Delegates
MUSTO, C. R.	Rhodesia Society of Accountants
UNDERWOOD, A.	Rhodesia Society of Accountants

SOUTH AFRICA
Delegates
EDMUND, M.	Transvaal Society of Accountants
GREENWOOD, H.	Cape Society of Accountants and Auditors
GRIEVESON, R. E.	Transvaal Society of Accountants
LEWIS, P. R. B.	Transvaal Society of Accountants
PORTER, C. B. I.	Natal Society of Accountants
WALKER, R. S.	Institute of Municipal Treasurers and Accountants, South Africa
WIMBLE, B. J. S.	Transvaal Society of Accountants

SOUTH AFRICA (—*continued*)

Visitors	*Organisation*
Britz, G.	Transvaal Society of Accountants
Horvitch, J. U.	Transvaal Society of Accountants
Levien, J. H.	Cape Society of Accountants and Auditors
Morris, A. I.	Cape Society of Accountants and Auditors
Vieler, D. E. G.	Transvaal Society of Accountants

SWEDEN

Delegates

Ahrén, C. E.	Föreningen Auktoriserade Revisorer
Barkland, N. O.	Svenska Revisorsamfundet
Björfors, G.	Svenska Revisorsamfundet
Cassel, Ö.	Föreningen Auktoriserade Revisorer
Karlgren, N.	Föreningen Auktoriserade Revisorer
Montelius, H.	Svenska Revisorsamfundet
Orreby, E. V.	Föreningen Auktoriserade Revisorer
Rybeck, E.	Föreningen Auktoriserade Revisorer
Samuelsson, S.	Föreningen Auktoriserade Revisorer

Visitors

Andersson, C. S.	Föreningen Auktoriserade Revisorer
Gentele, H. L.	Föreningen Auktoriserade Revisorer
Isakson, T.	Föreningen Auktoriserade Revisorer
Kannesten, R.	Föreningen Auktoriserade Revisorer
Kollén, I.	Föreningen Auktoriserade Revisorer
Löfgren, S.	Föreningen Auktoriserade Revisorer
Magnusson, R.	Föreningen Auktoriserade Revisorer
Norgren, L. E.	Föreningen Auktoriserade Revisorer

SWITZERLAND

Delegates

Engel, P.	Schweizerische Kammer für Revisionswesen; Verband Schweizerischer Bücherexperten
Fahrni-Lenz, Ad. R.	Schweizerische Kammer für Revisionswesen; Verband Schweizerischer Bücherexperten
Giroud, E.	Schweizerische Kammer für Revisionswesen; Verband Schweizerischer Bücherexperten

Visitor

Zweifel, J. J.	Schweizerische Kammer fur Revisionswesen; Verband Schweizerischer Bücherexperten

UNITED STATES OF AMERICA

Delegates

Adam, P. J.	Missouri Society of Certified Public Accountants
Andrews, T. C.	Virginia Society of Public Accountants
Arthur, J. F. S.	Texas Society of Certified Public Accountants
Bailey, G. D.	Michigan Association of Certified Public Accountants
Barton, M.	Society of Louisiana Certified Public Accountants
Beynon, A. B.	Texas Society of Certified Public Accountants

UNITED STATES OF AMERICA (—Delegates—*continued*)

Organisation

BLOODSWORTH, A. J.	Michigan Association of Certified Public Accountants
BOYNTON, W.	Massachusetts Society of Certified Public Accountants
BREIMO, M.	Arkansas Society of Certified Public Accountants
BROAD, S. J.	American Institute of Accountants
BRUMIT, J. L.	National Association of Cost Accountants
BRUNDAGE, P. F.	American Institute of Accountants
CAFFYN, H. R.	American Institute of Accountants
CAREY, J. L.	Rhode Island Society of Certified Public Accountants
CLARKE, E. A.	Ohio Society of Certified Public Accountants
COLLINGE, F. V.	Wisconsin Society of Certified Public Accountants
CONICK, M. C.	Pennsylvania Institute of Certified Public Accountants
DICKERSON, T. M.	National Association of Cost Accountants
DIETZE, C. E.	Wisconsin Society of Certified Public Accountants
DOHR, J. L.	American Accounting Association
ESKEW, S. W.	Kentucky Society of Certified Public Accountants
FEDDE, A. S.	New York State Society of Certified Public Accountants
FOYE, A. B.	New Jersey Society of Certified Public Accountants
GREEN, T. J.	American Institute of Accountants
GREGORY, R. H.	National Association of Cost Accountants
HARROW, B.	New York State Society of Certified Public Accountants
HERRICK, A.	California Society of Certified Public Accountants
HILL, G. M.	Texas Society of Certified Public Accountants
HIMMELBLAU, D.	Illinois Society of Certified Public Accountants
HOLLINGS, W. J.	California Society of Certified Public Accountants
HOPE, J. W.	Connecticut Society of Certified Public Accountants
HUSBAND, G. R.	American Accounting Association
INGLIS, J. B.	American Institute of Accountants
JONES, J. W.	Maryland Association of Certified Public Accountants
KOHLER, E. L.	American Accounting Association
LINDSAY, A. J.	Colorado Society of Certified Public Accountants
MARDER, J. I.	National Association of Cost Accountants
MARVIN, J. A.	New York State Society of Certified Public Accountants
MATHER, C. R.	New Jersey Society of Certified Public Accountants
MAY, G. O.	American Institute of Accountants
MILLER, E. O.	Pennsylvania Institute of Certified Public Accountants
MOONAN, W. J. P.	Ohio Society of Certified Public Accountants
NEILL, J. W. F.	New York State Society of Certified Public Accountants
O'HARA, J. B.	Pennsylvania Institute of Certified Public Accountants
PARKER, H. W.	Institute of Internal Auditors

UNITED STATES OF AMERICA (—Delegates—*continued*)

Organisation

PEARCE, H. L.	California Society of Certified Public Accountants
PENNEY, L. H.	California Society of Certified Public Accountants
POWELL, W.	New York State Society of Certified Public Accountants
PRYOR, O. K.	California Society of Certified Public Accountants
ROBINSON, J. R.	Institute of Internal Auditors
ROSSDUTCHER, C.	Kansas Society of Certified Public Accountants
SATCHELL, G. E. H.	Oregon Society of Certified Public Accountants
SCHAFFER, W. L.	Pennsylvania Institute of Certified Public Accountants
SCOTT, DR	American Accounting Association
SCOVILL, H. T.	American Accounting Association
SHAPIRO, S. G.	Maine Society of Public Accountants
STEWART, A.	American Institute of Accountants
STEWART, J. H.	Massachusetts Society of Certified Public Accountants
TALBOT, C.	Oklahoma Society of Certified Public Accountants
WAGNER, G.	Georgia Society of Certified Public Accountants
WALMSLEY, E. C.	Institute of Internal Auditors
WEISBARD, G. L.	Illinois Society of Certified Public Accountants
WEISS, L. C.	Ohio Society of Certified Public Accountants
WELLINGTON, C. O.	Massachusetts Society of Certified Public Accountants
WILCOX, E. B.	Illinois Society of Certified Public Accountants
YAVERBAUM, I.	Pennsylvania Institute of Certified Public Accountants

Visitors

BIEGLER, J. C.	American Institute of Accountants
BRISON, C. S.	American Institute of Accountants
CAINE, N. R.	American Institute of Accountants
FORBES, H. W.	American Institute of Accountants
HANNER, P. V. A.	American Accounting Association
MURPHY, Mary E.	American Institute of Accountants
MURPHY, R. J.	American Accounting Association
SIMPSON, H. B.	New York State Society of Certified Public Accountants
STEVEN, J. A.	American Institute of Accountants

URUGUAY
Delegate

STARICCO, A. J.	Colegio de Doctores en Ciencias Económicas y Contadores del Uruguay

VENEZUELA
Delegate

LANG, E. H.	Colegio Nacional de Técnicos en Contabilidad

APPENDIX B

ALPHABETICAL LIST OF MEMBERS
OF THE SPONSORS OF THE CONGRESS

Sponsoring body or bodies of members are denoted in the column headed 'Organisation(s)' as follows:

The Institute of Chartered Accountants of Scotland	1
The Institute of Chartered Accountants in England and Wales	2
The Society of Incorporated Accountants and Auditors ..	3
The Institute of Chartered Accountants in Ireland	4
The Association of Certified and Corporate Accountants ..	5
The Institute of Municipal Treasurers and Accountants ..	6
The Institute of Cost and Works Accountants	7

Name	Organisation(s)	Name	Organisation(s)
AARONS, N.	5	ATKINSON, W. O.	6
ADAMS, H. A.	2	AUSTRIN, E. C.	6
ADAMS, W. G.	3	AYLETT, S. I.	2
ADDINGTON, P. B.	2		
ADDY, H. E. A.	3/4	BACON, A. F.	2
AITCHISON, J. F.	2	BACON, J.	4
AITKEN, W. E.	2/3	BAILEY, J.	2/4
ALBAN, Sir Frederick J.	3/6	BAILEY, W.	3/6
ALEXANDER, R. S.	3	BAIRD, J.	3
ALLEN, A. S.	3	BAKER, D. W.	3
ALLEN, C. A.	2	BALDRY, E.	3
ALLEN, J. A.	3	BALLANTINE, J.	2
ALLISON, T. B.	1	BALLARD, D. G. W.	2
ALLSOP, E. T.	5	BALMFORD, A. M.	2
ALLSOP, F. J.	2	BARBER, C. A.	2
ANDERSON, B. H.	1	BARKER, G. L.	5
ANDERSON, E. A.	3	BARLOW, E.	7
ANDERSON, W. H.	4	BARR, W. A.	1
ANGUS, H. M.	1	BARRELL, F. J.	1
ANTHONY, J. K.	3/7	BARRETT, Madge	5
APPLEYARD, G. R.	2	BARRINGER, P. A. O.	5
ARCHER, L. C.	3/6	BARROWCLIFF, C. P.	3
ARIS, D. H.	3	BARROWS, W. L.	2
ARMITT, A.	3/6	BARSHAM, A. J.	2
ARMSTRONG, P. L.	2	BARTHOLOMEW, E.	2
ARNOLD, F. V.	3	BARTON, Sir Harold M.	2
ARNOLD, H.	2	BATEMAN, R. D. R.	2
ASH, H. G.	2	BEAVER, D. W.	2
ASTBURY, H. A.	2	BECK, M. R.	7
ASTBURY, R. M.	5	BEDFORD, R.	2
ASTON, C. W.	2	BEDWORTH, T. E.	2
ATKINSON, C. R.	2/3	BEEVOR, E. A.	2

Name	Organisation(s)	Name	Organisation(s)
BELL, E. S.	2	BREWSTER, S. P.	3
BELL, H. F.	3	BRIGHAM, M. G.	2
BELL, N.	1	BRITTAIN, J. S.	2/3
BENGTSSON, M.	1	BROCK, G.	4
BENSON, H. A.	2	BROOKS, W. J.	5/6
BENTLEY, A. W.	2	BROOME, E. P.	2
BERGER, S. J. D.	7	BROWN, D. L.	3
BERLAK, H. L.	3	BROWN, H.	3/6
BERLANNY, S. S.	1	BROWN, O. M.	2
BERMAN, M.	3	BROWNE, B.	3
BERRINGER, F. W.	3	BROWNE, H. L. K.	2
BERRY, B. M.	2	BROWNE, L. W.	5
BEST, C. V.	3	BRYDEN, J. A.	2/3
BEST, Minnie M.	3	BUCK, C. G.	2
BEVAN, W. H.	2	BUDD, W. M.	3
BIDWELL, M. J.	1	BUNDY, A.	5
BIGGS, L.	2/3	BURKE-SCOTT, J. P.	2
BINDER, Sir B. H.	2	BURLEIGH, J. C.	1
BIRD, H G.	5	BURNET, R. A.	1
BIRLEȝ, O.	5	BURR, G. B.	5
BISSET, Helen F.	5	BURTON, J. V.	3
BLACKIE, L.	2	BURTON, R. N.	2
BLACKMAN, R. E.	3	BURTON, Vera M.	2
BLAGG, Barbara H.	3	BUSCH, C. T.	2
BLAKEY, J.	2	BUTLER, P.	4
BLOFIELD, D. A.	2	BUTTERFIELD, A.	2
BLUMER, J. C.	2	BUTTERICK, S.	5/7
BLUNDELL, Kathleen	5	BUXTON, H.	7
BODY, J. F.	2		
BOLTON, H. J.	5	CAIRD, D. E.	2
BOND, T. J.	2	CALDWELL, E.	2
BONNER, F. E.	3/6	CALDWELL, W. B.	2
BOOTH, W. R.	2/3	CALDWELL, W. G.	3
BORSAY, J.	7	CALLABY, F. A.	5/7
BOSTOCK, C. I.	2	CAMPBELL, W. G.	2
BOSTOCK, E.	2	CANN, G. H.	2
BOURNE-PATERSON, R. A.	2	CAPPS, R. A.	5
BOWDEN, J. B.	2	CARLESS, S. J.	3
BOWIE, I. M.	1	CARNELLEY, W. E.	2
BOWMAN, J.	2	CARPENTER, P. F.	2
BOYCE, C. W.	2	CARRINGTON, W. S.	2
BOYD, A. S.	4	CARROLL, E. J.	2
BOYD, F. E.	4	CARTER, R. G.	2
BOYD, H. C.	4	CARTNER, J.	2
BOYLES, E. E.	2	CATCHPOLE, A. M.	3
BOYS, B. J. M.	2	CATTO, J. I.	2
BRACE, J. W.	1	CHAMBERS, R. P.	2
BRAIN, M. B.	2	CHAN, K. C.	5
BRAITHWAITE, S. E.	7	CHANNON, E. H.	2
BRAY, F. S.	2/3	CHAPMAN, A. N.	2
BRAZIER, L. H.	3	CHAPMAN, K. P.	2

Name	Organisation(s)	Name	Organisation(s)
CHAPMAN, W. B.	2	DALTON, E.	5
CHARLES, F. W.	2	D'ALTON, E. D.	2/3
CHARTREY, W. L. D.	5	DANIEL, B. H. J.	2
CHEYNEY, L. F.	3/6	DANNREUTHER, I. A.	1
CHITTS, M. H. G.	5	DA SILVA, L. M. G.	3
CHRISTMAS, F. H. C.	2	DAVEY, B. E.	2
CHUBB, S. J.	3	DAVID, L. C.	2
CHURCH, A. G.	2	DAVIDSON, C. R. M.	5
CITRON, A.	2	DAVIDSON, L. L.	3
CLARIDGE, J. L.	1	DAVIES, H. V.	7
CLARK, J. B. L.	2	DAVISON, E. H.	2
CLARKE, D. A.	2	DAWSON, A. E.	4
CLAY, H. J.	5	DAWSON, A. M.	6
CLAYTON, J.	2	DAWSON, G. W.	5
CLEMENCE, I. W.	2	DEEKER, H. A.	2
CLEMENCE, L. A.	2	DENSEM, W. G.	2
CLEMENTS, J. W.	2	DE PAULA, F. C.	2/7
CLEMINSON, L. P.	2	DE PAULA, F. R. M.	2
CLIFTON, S. C.	3	DEWAR, G. D. H.	1
COCK, H.	2	DICK, J. C.	1
COCKE, J. W. G.	2	DICK, J. K.	2
CODLING, J.	2	DICKER, A. S. H.	2
COHEN, H.	3	DICKINSON, A. C.	2
COLE, M. C.	2	DILLON, G. D. F.	2
COLES, W. A.	2	DOBSON, R. W.	1/7
COLLIER, D. H.	2	DONALD, W.	1
COLLINGS, Christine M.	2	DONALD, W. C.	1/7
COMBRIDGE, D. L.	2	DOODSON, N.	3/6
COOPER, V. R. V.	2	DOWDY, E. W.	2
CORBETT, J. T.	2	DRAGE, S. M.	2
CORBISHLEY, P.	3	DRAKE, F. G. F.	2
CORMACK, W. M.	1	DRESSER, T. W.	3
CORNWELL, S. W.	2	DRUMMOND, J. M.	3/6
COTTIER, D. J.	7	DUBUIS, H. F.	2
COULSON, H. O. H.	2	DUDMAN, G.	3
COWAN, J.	7	DUNCAN, G.	1
COWIE, C. R.	1	DUNCAN, S. M.	2
COX, C.	7	DUNKERLEY, R.	7
COX, D. E.	2	DUNLOP, R. L.	2
CRAFTER, W. J.	3	DUNN, N.	2
CRAIG, I. A. F.	3	DUNN, P. H.	3
CRAIG, J. S.	1	DYBALL, L. B.	2
CRAWFORD, R. N.	4	DYER, S.	2/5
CROOK, S. K.	3/6		
CROWHURST, K. B. S.	2	EASBY, M. T. W.	2
CROWTHER, J. V. F.	2	EDEN, H. A.	7
CUCKOW, P. E.	3.	EDGCUMBE, S.	2
CULLING, C. R.	2	EDIS, D. C.	7
CULLIS, A. E.	2	EDWARDS, W. F.	3
CULSHAW, L. J.	2	EDWARDSON, F. C. H.	2
CURTIS, S. R.	2	ELCOMBE, L. R.	2

Name	Organisation(s)	Name	Organisation(s)
ELGAR, S. N.	2	FYNN, B. M. L.	2
ELLICE, C.	2		
ELLIOTT, E. C.	3	GAIRDNER, C. D.	1
ELLIOTT, N. C.	2	GALPIN, G. F.	3
ELLIOTT, S. J.	3	GAMMELL, J. G. S.	1
ELMAN, C.	2	GANTEAUME, L. E.	5
ELVEN, W. W.	3/6	GARDNER, F. J. B.	2
EMMERSON, B. F.	2	GARETY, H.	1
EMMERSON, R. F.	3	GARNER-STEVENS, A.	5
ENGLISH, F. W.	2	GARRAWAY, C. S.	3
EREAUT, P. A.	6	GARRETT, A. A.	3
ESSLEMONT, G. B.	1/6	GARRETT, E. F.	2
EVAN-JONES, C. A.	3	GATENBY, L. W.	2
EVANS, W. B.	3	GEE, L. G.	3
EVERETT, N. A.	2	GIBB, W. K.	1
EWEN, P.	2	GIBBS, L. P.	2/3
		GIBSON, C. H.	5
FABES, S. A.	2	GILBERT, A. E. F.	7
FALKNER, A. C.	2	GILBERT, H. R.	2
FARRELL, R. W.	5	GILES, C. G.	2
FEA, W. W.	2	GILL, H. C.	2
FELL, J.	1	GILL, W. T.	1
FELTHAM, C. B. J.	5	GINNINGS, D. J.	2/3
FENDICK, D. R.	2/3	GIRDWOOD, J. G.	1
FERGUSON, T. L.	1	GLENCROSS, J. C.	2
FIELDER, L. B.	1	GLENDINNING, R.	1/7
FIELDHOUSE, A.	5	GODFREY, J.	2
FISH, F. J.	2	GOLD, R.	2
FLEMING, A. R. C.	2	GOLDSON, P. S.	5
FLETCHER, C. E.	2	GOODMAN, A.	2
FLINT, D.	1	GOODWIN, C. R. P.	2
FLYNN, F. G. A.	2	GORDON, J. A.	2
FOLEY, K.	3	GOULT, G. G. G.	2
FORD, J.	2	GRAHAM, J.	4
FORD, R. H.	2	GRANGER, E. T.	2
FORREST, T. W.	5	GRANGER, P. F.	2
FORRESTER, R.	5	GRANT, M. L.	2
FORSTER, K.	2	GRANVILLE, J. W.	3
FOST, H. T.	2/7	GRAVES, B. W.	2
FOSTER, D. U.	2/7	GRAY, L. G.	5
FOWLER, F. D.	3	GRAY, W. M.	5
FOXON, C. M.	3	GREENE, A. C.	2
FRANKLAND, L.	2/7	GREENHALGH, R.	2
FRATER, W. A.	1	GREENHILL, E.	5
FREEDMAN, H.	5	GREENSHIELDS, R. G.	1
FREEMAN, G. R.	2	GREENWOOD, H.	3
FREEMAN, S.	2	GRIFFITH, T. H.	3
FRYER, A. W.	3	GRIFFITHS, J. A.	3
FURLER, J. S.	3	GRIMSHAW, L. E.	3
FURNESS, H. J.	7	GRIMSHAW, W. G. P.	2
FURNIVAL-JONES, O.	2	GUILFORD, P. A.	5

Name	Organisation(s)	Name	Organisation(s)
HAINES, V. C.	2	HOLLAND, A. H. D.	2
HALL, C. E.	2	HOLLWEY, J. D.	4
HALL, G. E.	3	HOLMAN, W.	3
HAMLYN, Dora N.	2	HOLT, E.	5
HAMMOND, R. W.	2	HOLT, W. B. P.	2
HANDEL, F.	3	HOOPER, J. E.	2
HARBINSON, A.	3	HORN, D.	2
HARDAKER, W. C.	5	HORTON, H. E.	7
HARDING, K. W.	7	HOSKIN, P. W.	2
HARDING, T. G.	2	HOUGH, J. W.	3/6
HARPER, A. N.	4	HOUGHTON, G. S.	5
HARPER, G. S. C.	2	HOUSE, D. V.	2
HARPER, J. P.	1/7	HOW, T. H.	2
HARRALD, W. G.	3/6	HOWARD, H. C.	2
HARRIS, E.	2	HOWELL, G. R.	7
HARRIS, J.	6	HOWELL, N.	7
HARRIS, J. E.	5	HOWITT, A. W.	2
HARRIS, L. G.	3	HOWITT, Sir Harold G.	2
HARRIS, P.	2	HOWSON, A. G.	5
HARRISON, E. T.	2	HUGHES, B. L.	2
HARRISON, H.	3/6	HUGHES, R. E.	6
HARRISON, H. W.	3	HULTON, W. S.	1/7
HART, J. B.	1	HUMPHRIES, A. P.	2
HART, N. B.	2/3	HUNTER, F. T.	2/7
HARTLEY, E.	2	HUNTER, G. N.	2
HARVEY, L.	5/7	HUNTER, V. W. S.	2
HARVEY, M. G. J.	2	HUSSEY, A. V.	3
HARVEY, W. A.	1/7	HUSSEY, F. V.	2
HASLAM, E. M.	2	HUTTON, C. I. R.	1
HAWORTH, T.	3	HYMAN, L. D.	2
HAY, Sir David Allan	1		
HAYES, L. J.	3/7	IDLE, A. E.	2
HAYHOW, H.	3/6	INGLE, W. G.	7
HEALD, A. J.	2/5	IRONS, P. D.	2/7
HEALD, R.	2		
HELLYAR, C. D.	2	JACKMAN, D. A.	2
HENDERSON, R. C. R.	2	JACKSON, C. D.	2
HERD, J. J. S.	1	JACKSON, J. A.	2/3
HEYNES, G. A. A.	1	JACKSON, W.	5
HICKS, I.	2	JACKSON, W. J.	3/6
HIGHAM, F.	5	JACQUES, D. E.	5
HIGHAM, R.	7	JAMES, P. G.	3
HILL, E. G.	3	JAMES, W. C. W.	5
HILL, J. R.	3/6	JARVIS, C. V.	5
HILL, N. K.	1	JARY, H. J. A.	5
HILLYER, S. G.	2	JEANS, H. T. W.	2
HININGS, P. H.	2	JENNISON, L.	2
HIRSHFIELD, D. B.	2	JEWELL, A. J.	5
HITCHINS, E. F.	7	JEWERS, D. F.	2
HODGSON, H.	2/7	JOHNSON, B. M.	7
HOLDSWORTH, A.	5/7	JOHNSON, H. O.	3

Name	Organisation(s)	Name	Organisation(s)
JOHNSON, I.	3	LATHAM, The Lord.	5
JOHNSTON, L. R.	1	LATIMER, R. L.	2
JOHNSTONE, J. W.	1	LAURENCE, J. K.	1
JONES, A. A.	4	LAWRENCE, C. N.	7
JONES, E. B.	3/6	LAWSON, W. H.	2
JONES, G. C.	3/6	LAYTON, H. L.	2/3/5
JONES, H. L.	7	LEA, C. B.	2
JONES, J. D. R.	3	LEACH, R. G.	2
JONES, Marjorie S.	2	LEDSAM, F. C. A.	2
JONES, S. C.	5	LEDSAM, H. J. R.	2
JUDD, H. G.	1	LEITCH, J. R.	1
JUDGE, W.	3	LE MAISTRE, J. V.	2
		LEPPARD, A. H.	2
KAHN, D. H. E.	2/3	LERSE, A.	2
KANO, L.	5	LESTER, H. J.	3
KEABLE, Phyllis G.	2	LEWIN, O. M.	2
KEEBLE, R. M. L.	5	LEWIS, W. S.	2
KEELING, H.	6	LINDEMANN, K.	7
KEEN, N. H.	2	LISTER, C.	3/6
KEENS, Sir Thomas	3	LISTER, T.	1
KENNEDY, J. A.	1	LIVOCK, Dora M.	2
KENNEDY, R. D.	1	LOCKE, P. E. F.	5
KENNETT, L.	5	LODGE, W. F.	3/6
KENNY, M. J.	5	LOKER, H.	3
KERMODE, E. R.	6	LOLLAR, E. J.	2
KETCHLEE, B. J.	2/3	LORD, F. A.	2
KETTLE, Sir Russell	2	LORIMER, T. D.	4
KEYS, F.	3	LORYMAN, L. W.	5
KILLIP, T. E. A.	5	LOVE, J.	3
KILPATRICK, J.	1	LOVEDAY, C. H. S.	2
KING, A. L.	5	LOVICK, J.	3
KING, F. W. E.	3	LOWE, G. R.	2
KING, H. R.	5	LUMB, S. W.	5
KING-FARLOW, A. R.	2/3	LUSCOMBE, C. N.	2
KIRK, D. H.	3		
KIRK, H. V.	3	MCALLISTER, C. H.	2
KIRK, R.	7	MCARTHUR, W. B.	3
KITCHEN, J.	2	MCAULEY, C.	2/3
KNIGHT, A. T.	2	MACBEATH, A.	1/7
KNIGHT, J. S.	7	MCCRUDDEN, M. J.	4
KOCH, F. E.	5/7	MCDANELL, F. A. M.	2
		MACDONALD, D. R. F.	2
LAIDLAW, Jean	2	MCDONALD, H.	2
LAMBARD, E. G.	2/3	MACDONALD, I. W.	1
LAMBERT, A. J.	2	MACDOUGALL, D. C.	1
LANCASTER, M. W. H.	2	MCDOUGALL, E. H. V.	1
LANE, F. C. T.	2	MCGRATH, J. C.	3
LANGE, Stella G.	3	MACGREGOR, D.	1
LANSLEY, A. W.	6	MCGUANE, D. M. D.	4
LATHAM, J. A.	2	MCHAFFIE, A. N. E.	1
LATHAM, J. C.	3/5	MACINTOSH, A. M.	1

Name	Organisation(s)	Name	Organisation(s)
MacIver, A. S.	2	Miller, Dorothy H.	2
Mackay, A. G. A..	1	Milne, J. W.	1
McKell, J.	1	Milroy, H. D.	2
Mackenzie, A.	1	Mistry, D. M.	3
Mackenzie, J. B.	1/7	Mitchell, A. G.	1
Mackenzie, J. R.	3	Mitra, S. K.	3
Mackenzie, J. S.	2	Moll, V. R. .	6
Mackenzie, T.	1	Mont, C.	2
Mackie, W. E.	1	More, R. H.	5
McPhail, R. T. M.	1	Morgan, S. S.	3
Maddison, A. S.	2	Morgan-Jones, G. P.	2
Magrath, H. W.	2	Morgan-Jones, P.	2
Makin, S.	2	Morris, E. J.	3
Maltby, E. E. P.	2	Morris, G. A. J.	2/3
Mann, J. H..	2	Morris, J.	2
Manners, J. L.	2	Morrish, G. E.	2
Manning, B.	2	Morrow, I. T.	1/7
Margetts, J. W.	2	Morton, S. S.	2
Marsh, A. R.	5	Mott, G. C..	5
Marshall, A. H.	3/6	Mottram, J.	2
Marshall, F. D.	1	Muirie, J. R.	1
Marshall, T.	3	Murison, A. B. L.	2
Martin, A. J.	5	Murray, A. G.	1
Martin, E. H. R.	3	Murrells, F. S. B.	3
Martin, P. J.	5	Murtagh, Marion	5
Maskell, J. R.	3		
Mason, D. H.	3	Nairn, H. W.	1
Matheson, N. S.	1	Napier, I. C.	1
Mathias, N. J.	2	Neale, Amy J.	5
Matson, J.	2	Nelson, B.	3
Matthews, R. P.	2	Neville, A. J.	2
Maurice, C. J.	2	Newby, J. G.	2
Maurice, G. M.	2	Newhouse, K. T.	2
Mayer, H. C.	5	Newman, J.	2
Maynard, B. A.	2	Newman, T. O. W.	5
Maynard, G. T.	5/7	Newport, C. A.	5
Maynard, H.	2	Newth, J. S.	2
Maze, A.	4	Newton, C. N.	2
Mead, C. H.	2	Nicholas, P. N.	2
Mearns, S. H.	1	Nicholson, C. H.	4
Mee, J. W.	3	Nicholson, E. R.	2
Meikle, A.	1	Nicholson, J. A.	2
Meredith, E. R.	2	Nicholson, R. G.	1
Merriman, C. O. H.	2	Nicholson, T. H.	3
Metcalf, G. M.	2	Nickson, F. I.	2
Meyer, G. F.	3	Nicol, J. A.	2
Meynell, A. C. S.	5	Niven, T. G.	1
Middleton, A. E..	3	Norman, H. W.	2
Milburn, W. J.	2	Norman, J. R.	5
Millar, T. F.	1	Norman, L. H.	2
Miller, A. A.	2	Norris, H.	2

Name	Organisation(s)	Name	Organisation(s)
NORRIS, V. L.	2	PERFECT, J.	2
NORTCLIFFE, A.	3/6	PERKINS, E. L. B.	3
NUNN, G. W.	5	PERRY, V. F.	2
		PHILIP, J. D. M.	3
O'CALLAGHAN, G. J.	3	PHILLIPS, J. S.	2
OFFORD, E. J.	5	PHILP, R.	2
OLDAK, P. V. A.	2	PICKARD, T. W.	2/3
OLIVANT, H. F.	2	PICKETT, F. G.	2
OLIVIER, W. H.	2	PITT, M. L.	2
OLSEN, F. M. L.	2	PLATT, A. J.	2
OPPENHEIMER, W.	2	PLEWS, P. H.	2/3
ORANGE, H. D.	3	POLLARD, C. H.	3/6
OSBORN, F.	7	POMEROY, S. J.	2
OSBORN, H. E.	1	POWELL, C. H. W.	2
OSBOURN, F. C.	5	POWELL, T. R.	5
OSMOND, E. E.	3	POYNTER, K. R.	2
OSMOND, L. J.	2	POYNTON, T. L.	6
OUTHWAITE, J. V.	5	PRATLEY, L. J.	2
OWEN, E. C. W.	2	PRATT, D. W.	4
		PRIMOST, S.	3
PARKER, A. R.	2	PRINCE, E. S.	2
PARKER, W. E.	2	PRIOR, F. A.	3
PARRY, F. L.	2	PROCTER, L.	5
PARTINGTON, J.	5	PROCTOR, C. ST. C.	3
PATERSON, I. C.	2	PROCTOR, F. B.	2
PATON, R. L.	2	PURTILL, P. J.	3/4
PATTERSON, J. T.	2/3	PYKETT, G. F.	2
PAUL, A. J.	3		
PEAKE, E. L.	2	QUICK, S. P.	2
PEARCE, B. H.	5	QUINNEN, J. N.	2/7
PEARCE, C. T. W.	2		
PEARCE, J. C.	3	RABAGLIATI, D. N.	1
PEARCY, B. E.	2	RABEY, R. R.	1
PEARS, S. J.	2	RAINBOW, J. W.	2
PEARSON, A. G.	2	RAVENHILL, A. P.	2
PEARSON, A. M.	2	RAYNER, A.	2
PEARSON, G. E.	2	READ, J. E.	2
PEARSON, R. H.	2	REDDISH, K. W.	5
PEAT, C. U.	2	REEKIE, J. D.	2
PEAT, H.	2	REES, P. M.	2
PEAT, Sir Harry	2	REID, E. B.	1
PEAT, J. R.	2	REID, R. A.	1
PEAT, R. M.	2	RHODES, C. N.	1
PECK, G. E.	7	RICHARDS, D. G.	2
PECKHAM, E. T.	2/3	RICHARDS, G. E.	2
PEGLER, R. G.	2	RICHARDS, J. C.	2
PEIRSON, E. T.	2	RICHARDSON, E. C.	1
PEIRSON, K. S.	2	RICHARDSON, J. N.	3
PENTELOW, J. O.	7	RICHMAN, S.	5
PENWILL, S. W.	2	RICKARD, R. Y.	3
PERCIVAL-SMITH, J. B.	7	RIDDLE, A. B.	2

Name	Organisation(s)	Name	Organisation(s)
RIDGWAY, Phyllis E. M. .	3	SHERATON, R. F. W.	2
RISK, J. M. S.	1/7	SHORT, H. C.	5
RISK, W. S. .	1/7	SILLEM, S. G.	2
RITCHIE, T. N.	1	SIMPSON, J. L.	2
ROBATHAN, P. E.	1/3	SIMPSON, R. .	3
ROBERTON, W. E. .	1	SIMPSON, R. M.	3
ROBERTS, G. G.	2	SINNOTT, E. .	3/6
ROBERTS, P. V.	2	SKINNER, P. W.	3
ROBERTS, R.	7	SKLAR, V. .	2
ROBERTS, R. W.	3	SLADE, C. O. G.	5/7
ROBERTSON, D. W.	2	SLATER, G. P.	7
ROBINS, W. T.	3	SLATER, J. McI.	1
ROBINSON, H. W. .	4	SMALLEY, P. C. A. .	2
ROBINSON, J. R.	7	SMEETON, A. G.	2
ROBSON, L. W.	2/7	SMITH, A. C.	1
ROBSON, P. L.	1	SMITH, Sir Alan Rae	2
ROBSON, T. B.	2	SMITH, A. MacC. .	1
ROGERS, J. F. S.	2	SMITH, F. O. M.	2
ROLT, G. E. .	2	SMITH, H. E. .	2
ROMER-LEE, C.	2	SMITH, H. G.	3
ROOKE, C. W.	2	SMITH, J. M. A.	2
ROSS, D. .	1	SMITH, L. W.	3
ROTHSCHILD, H. J. J.	5	SMITH, N. A.	2
ROUNTREE, A. F. .	2	SMITH, N. P. .	5
ROWE, D. N.	4	SMITH, P. E. .	2
ROWETT, G. C.	2	SMITH, R.	2
RUDERMAN, W.	5	SMITH, S. B. .	2
RUSSELL, G. .	5/7	SMITH, V. A. .	2
RUTTER, C. J.	7	SNELGROVE, W.	3
		SNELL, H. A.	2
SADD, M. J. G.	2	SOLOMONS, D.	2
SANDERS, H. J.	2	SOMERVILLE, Helen M.	1
SARSON, A. W.	2	SOMERVILLE, J. L. .	1
SAUNDERS, F. W. H.	7	SOMERVILLE, J. M. .	5
SAUNDERS, G. F. .	2	SOPER, P. F. W.	3
SAVAGE, R. A. W.	7	SPALDING, W. L. .	1/7
SAWBRIDGE, C. J. B.	2	SPARSHATT, A. E. .	5
SAYERS, E. C.	2	SPENCE, J. D.	1
SCOTT, A. G. W.	2	SPENCER, E. .	5
SCOTT, Beatrice L. .	2	SPENCER, M. C.	2
SCOUGAL, J. .	3/6	SPENCER, W. R.	3
SCRUBY, J. T. W.	1	SPICER, R. E.	5
SEWARD, H. W. S. .	2/3	SPOFFORTH, S. A. .	2/3
SEWELL, B. E.	2	SPOORS, J. E.	3
SHAH, J. S. .	3	SPROULL, R.	1/7
SHARP, L. G.	3	STACEY, R.	5/6
SHAW, J. P. .	5	STAGG, E. H.	5
SHEARER, J. F.	2	STANBURY, C. G.	2
SHEASBY, H. B.	2/3	STATHAM, R. W.	5
SHEPHERD, E. T.	2	STEELE, D. .	2
SHEPHERD, G. D. .	2	STEPHANY, G. M. .	2

Name	Organisation(s)	Name	Organisation(s)
STEPHENSON, J.	3	TULLY, W. S. C.	2
STEPTO, W. E.	5	TURNBULL, R.	2
STEVENS, G. P.	2	TURNER, D. G. A.	3
STEVENS, H. L.	2	TURNER, E. G.	2
STEVENSON, H.	4	TURNER, J. L.	2
STOBY, W. S.	7	TURNER, O. L.	2
STOCKLAND, J. M.	2	TYRRELL, S. C.	7
STOUGHTON-HARRIS, G.	2		
STRACHAN, H. F.	2	UNDERWOOD, L. W.	2
STRAKER, N.	2		
STRAUB, F. L.	2	VINCENT, T. H.	3/6
STREDWICK, C.	5		
STRONG, W. B.	1	WAINWRIGHT, J.	5
STUART, N. K.	2	WALKER, A. D.	2
STUBBINGS, R. J. W.	2	WALKER, H.	3
SUDLOW, E. W.	7	WALKER, J.	1/4
SUMMERSCALE, N. T.	2	WALKER, J. A.	1
SUMNER, R. F.	2	WALKER, T. D.	2
SUTTON, R. A.	3	WALKER, W.	5
SWABY, R. A.	5	WALKER-ARNOTT, C. D.	2
SYLVESTER, Sir Edgar	2	WALLER, J.	3
		WALLER, R. L.	2
TANFIELD, D. E. T.	2	WALLIS, Joan M.	2
TANGYE, Gladys L.	3	WALLIS, S. I.	3
TAPLEY, W. D. T.	2	WALMSLEY, J. A.	2
TATE, L. F.	3	WALTON, R.	3
TAYLOR, C. J.	7	WALTON, T.	2
TAYLOR, E. D.	2	WARBURG, G. A. S.	2
TAYLOR, G. H.	2	WARD, A. H.	5
TAYLOR, L. R.	2	WARD, D. A. J.	2
TAYLOR, R. R.	7	WARD, J. R.	2
TAYLOR, W. F.	1	WARLOW, R. E.	2
TEALE, H.	2	WARNER, L. E.	5
TEMS, J. S.	2	WARREN, A. F.	3
THOMAS, R. C. L.	3	WATERHOUSE, Sir Nicholas E.	2
THOMPSON, F.	2	WATLER, E. J.	7
THOMPSON, G. McC.	4	WATSON, A. J.	1
THOMSON, H. C.	1	WATSON, H. J.	2
THOMSON, R. J.	1	WATTS, Ethel	2
THOMSON, W. E. S.	5	WATTS, H. S.	3/6
TILLEY, R. G.	2	WAYNE, F. T.	2
TODD, G. A.	1	WEATHERLEY, L. H.	2
TOMBLESON, P. J.	2	WEBB, J. R. L.	5
TOOTHILL, P.	3	WEBBER, D. G.	3/6
TOUCHE, G. L. C.	2	WEEKS, F. J.	2
TRIPP, D. A.	2	WEIR, C. J.	1
TROY, J. G.	4	WELLS, H. F.	7
TRUE, C. H.	5	WEST, A. L. A.	6
TUCKER, A. S.	5	WHATMORE, W. R. T.	2
TUCKER, F.	3	WHINNEY, D. H.	2
TUDBALL, V. A.	2	WHINNEY, E. F. G.	2

APPENDIX C

BANQUET AT GUILDHALL

MENU

Wines	Clear Turtle
SHERRY Domecq La Ina	★
★	*Salmon Bellevue* *Sauce Mayonnaise*
PUNCH Madeira	
★	★
RHINE WINE Liebfraumilch (Hanns Christoff Wein) 1949	*Duckling Bordelaise* *New Potatoes* *Garden Peas*
★	★
CHAMPAGNE Bollinger 1943	*Strawberry Melba* *Petits Fours*
★	
PORT Warre's 1937	★
★	*Dessert*
BRANDY Bisquit Dubouche 1904	★
★	*Coffee*
LIQUEURS	

THE ROYAL ARTILLERY ORCHESTRA
By kind permission of
The Officers, Royal Artillery

Conducted by
Mr. K. ELLOWAY, A.R.C.M., p.s.m.
707

APPENDIX C

TOAST LIST

THE QUEEN

Proposed by THE PRESIDENT
(Sir Harold Gibson Howitt, G.B.E., D.S.O., M.C., F.C.A.)

QUEEN ELIZABETH THE QUEEN MOTHER, QUEEN MARY, THE DUKE OF EDINBURGH AND OTHER MEMBERS OF THE ROYAL FAMILY

Proposed by THE PRESIDENT

SOVEREIGNS AND HEADS OF STATES REPRESENTED

Proposed by THE PRESIDENT

THE RIGHT HONOURABLE THE LORD MAYOR AND THE CORPORATION OF LONDON

Proposed by THE CHAIRMAN OF THE COUNCIL
(Mr. H. Garton Ash, O.B.E., M.C., F.C.A.)

Responded to by THE RIGHT HONOURABLE THE LORD MAYOR
(Sir Leslie Boyce, K.B.E.)

THE ACCOUNTANCY PROFESSION

Proposed by THE RIGHT HONOURABLE THE LORD RADCLIFFE, P.C., G.B.E., Q.C.

Responded to by THE PRESIDENT
and MR. J. WILLIAM HOPE, C.P.A.

THE GUESTS

Proposed by THE VICE-PRESIDENT
(Mr. C. Percy Barrowcliff, F.S.A.A.)

Responded to by HIS GRACE THE LORD ARCHBISHOP OF CANTERBURY
(The Most Reverend and Right Honourable Geoffrey F. Fisher, P.C., D.D.)

LIST OF GUESTS

A

Aarons, N., A.A.C.C.A.

Adam, P. J., C.P.A. (*U.S.A.*)

Adams, H. A., A.C.A.

Adams, W. G., F.S.A.A.

Addington, P. B., F.C.A.

Addy, H. E. A., F.C.A., F.S.A.A. (*President, The Institute of Chartered Accountants in Ireland*)

Ahrén, C. E. (*Sweden*)

Aiyar, S. V., F.C.A. (*India*)

Alban, Sir Frederick J., C.B.E., F.S.A.A., F.I.M.T.A. (*Member, Congress Council*)

Alexander, J. R. W., F.C.I.S. (*President, The Chartered Institute of Secretaries*)

Alexander, R. S., F.S.A.A.

Alexandre, J. (*France*)

Allen, A. S., F.S.A.A. (*Vice-Chairman, Congress Council*)

Allen, J. A., F.S.A.A.

Amundsen, I. W. (*Norway*)

Anderson, E. A., F.S.A.A.

Anderson, The Right Reverend W. White, M.C., D.D. (*Moderator, General Assembly of the Church of Scotland*)

André, M. (*France*)

Andrews, T. C., C.P.A. (*U.S.A.*)

Angus, H. M., C.A.

Antolini, F. (*Italy*)

Anttonen, J. (*Finland*)

Archer, L. C., F.S.A.A., F.I.M.T.A.

Arnold, F. V., F.S.A.A.

Arthur, J. F. S., C.A., C.P.A. (*U.S.A.*)

Ash, H. G., O.B.E., M.C., F.C.A. (*Chairman, Congress Council*)

Atkinson, W. O., M.B.E., F.I.M.T.A.

Austrin, E. C., F.I.M.T.A.

Aylett, S. I., A.C.A.

B

Bailey, G. D., C.P.A. (*U.S.A.*)

Bailey, J., F.C.A. (*Member, Congress Council*)

Bailey, W., F.S.A.A., F.I.M.T.A.

Baird, J., F.S.A.A.

Baldry, E., F.S.A.A.

Bankes, R. W., C.B.E.

Barker, G. L., F.A.C.C.A.

Barkland, N. O. (*Sweden*)

Barlow, E., A.C.W.A.

Barrowcliff, C. P., F.S.A.A. (*Vice-President of the Congress; President, The Society of Incorporated Accountants and Auditors*)

Barrows, W. L., F.C.A.

Bartholomew, E., A.C.A.

Barton, Sir Harold M., F.C.A.

Barton, M., C.P.A. (*U.S.A.*)

Bawly, L., F.A.C.C.A. (*Israel*)

Beauvais, A. E., C.A. (*Canada*)

Bechinie, R. (*Austria*)

Beer, H., C.B. (*Under-Secretary, Insurance and Companies Department, Board of Trade*)

Behrens, K. C. (*Germany*)

Bell, E. S., A.C.A.

Bell, H. F., F.S.A.A.

Bell, N., C.A.

Bellringer, N. B., F.P.A.N.Z. (*New Zealand*)

Bengtsson, M., C.A.

Benson, H. A., C.B.E., F.C.A.

Benveniste, R. (*France*)

Bergeon, P. (*France*)

Berger, S. J. D., M.C. (*Member, Congress Council*)

Berlanny, S. S., C.A.

Berman, M., A.S.A.A.

Best, C. V., F.S.A.A.

Best, Minnie M., A.S.A.A.

Beynon, A. B., C.P.A. (*U.S.A.*)

Bezer, G. R., F.C.A. (*Peru*)

Binder, Sir B. H., F.C.A.

Bird, H. G., F.A.C.C.A.

Birkeland, A. (*Norway*)

Bishop, P. W., F.C.A. (*Italy*)

Bisset, Helen F., A.A.C.C.A.

Björfors, G. (*Sweden*)

Blackman, R. E., A.S.A.A.

Blagg, Barbara H., A.S.A.A.

Blakey, J., F.C.A.

Blofield, D. A., F.C.A.

Bloodsworth, A. J., C.P.A. (*U.S.A.*)

Blundell, Kathleen, A.A.C.C.A.

Borsay, J., F.C.W.A.

Bostock, E., F.C.A.

Boston, W. T. (*The Sword-Bearer*)

Bouly, F. L. (*France*)

Boutin, F. J. (*France*)
Bowman, J., F.C.A.
Boyce, C. W., C.B.E., F.C.A. (*Member, Congress Council*)
Boyd, A. S., F.C.A.
Boynton, W., C.P.A. (*U.S.A.*)
Bray, F. S., F.C.A., F.S.A.A.
Bray, J. P., R.D., A.C.A. (*Pakistan*)
Bredt, O. (*Germany*)
Breimo, M., C.P.A. (*U.S.A.*)
Brewster, S. P., A.S.A.A.
Brittain, J. S., F.C.A., F.S.A.A.
Broad, S. J., C.P.A. (*U.S.A.*)
Broome, E. P., F.C.A.
Brown, H., O.B.E., F.S.A.A., F.I.M.T.A.
Brown, R. D., F.P.A.N.Z. (*New Zealand*)
Browne, L. W., A.A.C.C.A.
Brumit, J. L. (*U.S.A.*)
Brundage, P. F., C.P.A. (*U.S.A.*)
Burke, T. V., C.A. (*Canada*)
Burleigh, J. C., C.A. (*Joint Honorary Auditor of the Congress*)
Busch-Sørensen, A. (*Denmark*)
Busuttil, P. (*Malta*)
Butler, P., F.C.A.
Butterfield, A., A.C.A.

C

Caffyn, H. R., F.C.A., C.P.A. (*U.S.A.*)
Callirgos, B. (*Peru*)
Campbell, W. G., F.C.A.
Campos, E. S. (*Brazil*)
Canterbury, The Lord Archbishop of
Capps, R. A., A.A.C.C/A
Carey, J. L. (*U.S.A.*)
Carpenter, P. F., F.C.A.
Carrington, W. S., F.C.A.
Carter, K. Le M., C.A. (*Canada*)
Carter, P. S. (*Italy*)
Casas-Alatriste, R. (*Mexico*)
Cassel, Ö. (*Sweden*)
Castel-branco, A. P. C. d'A. (*Portugal*)
Catchpole, A. M., A.S.A.A.
Chan, K. C., F.A.C.C.A.
Chapman, K. P., D.S.C., A.C.A.
Charles, F. W., C.B.E., F.C.A.
Chaudhury, M. H. (*Pakistan*)
Cheyney, L. F., F.S.A.A., F.I.M.T.A.
Christmas, F. H. C., F.C.A.
Chubb, S. J., F.S.A.A.
Cibert, A. (*France*)
Clarke, D. A., F.C.A.

Clarke, E. A., C.P.A. (*U.S.A.*)
Clayton, J., A.C.A.
Clemence, L. A., F.C.A.
Clifton, S. C., A.S.A.A.
Closon, F. L. (*France*)
Coffey, F. A., C.A. (*Canada*)
Collinge, F. V., C.P.A. (*U.S.A.*)
Collings, Christine M., F.C.A.
Collins, G. A. (*President, The Law Society*)
Conick, M. C., C.P.A. (*U.S.A.*)
Cooper, V. R. V., F.C.A.
Crafter, W. J., F.S.A.A.
Craig, A. M. (*Malta*)
Craig, I., C.A. (*Canada*)
Craig, I. A. F., O.B.E.
Craig, J. S., C.A.
Culling, C. R., A.C.A.
Currie, G. S., C.M.G., D.S.O., M.C., C.A. (*Canada*)

D

Dalglish, K. W., C.A. (*Canada*)
d'Auria, F. (*Brazil*)
David, L. C., F.C.A.
Davidson, L. L., F.S.A.A.
Dawson, A. E., F.C.A.
Deakin, A., C.H., C.B.E. (*General Secretary, Transport and General Workers' Union*)
de Bruyne, A. L. (*Netherlands*)
de Dominicis, E. (*Italy*)
Deeker, H. A., F.C.A.
Defosse, A. (*France*)
de la Mano, J. (*Brazil*)
de la Rosa, R. L. (*Philippines*)
de L'Isle and Dudley, The Lord, V.C., A.C.A. (*Secretary of State for Air*)
Demenint, A. L. (*Netherlands*)
Densem, W. G., F.C.A.
de Paula, F. C., T.D., A.C.A., A.C.W.A.
de Paula, F. R. M., C.B.E., F.C.A.
d'Ercole, E. (*Italy*)
Dewar, G. D. H., C.A.
Dickerson, T. M. (*U.S.A.*)
Dieterich, W. (*Germany*)
Dietze, C. E., C.P.A. (*U.S.A.*)
Dillon, G. D. F., F.C.A.
Dobson, R. W., C.A., F.C.W.A.
Dohr, J. L., C.P.A. (*U.S.A.*)
Don, The Very Reverend A. C., K.C.V.O., D.D. (*Dean of Westminster*)

Donald, W. C., C.A., F.C.W.A.
Dreyer, P. J. (*France*)
Duchesne, L. R. (*France*)
Dudman, G., A.S.A.A.
Duncan, S. M., F.C.A.
Dunkerley, R., F.C.W.A.
Dunn, N., F.C.A.
Dunn, P. H., A.S.A.A.
du Pré, D. (*Editor, 'The Accountant'*)

E

Edis, D. C., A.C.W.A.
Edmund, M., C.A. (*South Africa*)
Elcombe, L. R., F.C.A.
Elliott, E. C., F.S.A.A.
Elliott, N. C., A.C.A.
Elmendorff, W. (*Germany*)
Emmerson, R. F., F.S.A.A.
Engel, P. (*Switzerland*)
Eskew, S. W., C.P.A. (*U.S.A.*)
Esslemont, G. B., C.A., F.I.M.T.A.
Evan-Jones, C. A., M.B.E.

F

Fahrni-Lenz, Ad. R. (*Switzerland*)
Falkner, A. C., A.C.A.
Farish, D. H. M., C.A. (*Canada*)
Fedde, A. S., C.P.A. (*U.S.A.*)
Fell, J., C.A.
Ferguson, T. L., O.B.E., C.A.
Field, R. C., C.A. (*Canada*)
Fieldhouse, A., F.A.C.C.A.
Fitzgerald, A. A., F.I.C.A., F.C.A.A. (*Australia*)
Fletcher, C. E., F.C.A.
Flint, D., T.D., C.A.
Forbes, Sir Archibald, C.A. (*President, The Federation of British Industries*)
Forrester, R., A.A.C.C.A.
Forsström, B. (*Finland*)
Forsythe, J. G. (*New Zealand*)
Foster, D. U., A.C.A., F.C.W.A.
Foxon, C. M., F.S.A.A.
Foye, A. B., C.P.A. (*U.S.A.*)
Francis, J., A.C.A., A.I.C.W.A. (*India*)
Frankland, L., A.C.A., F.C.W.A.
Freeman, G. R., F.C.A.

G

Gammell, J. G. S., M.B.E., C.A.
Garraway, C. S., F.S.A.A.
Garrett, A. A., M.B.E.

Gedge, M. L., Q.C.
Ghose, S. S., F.C.A. (*India*)
Giannini, A. (*Italy*)
Gibb, W. K., C.A.
Gilbert, A. E. F., A.C.W.A.
Gill, H. C., M.C., F.C.A.
Gill, W. T., C.A.
Giroud, E. (*Switzerland*)
Glendinning, R., C.A., F.C.W.A.
Glomstein, A. (*Norway*)
Godfrey, J., F.C.A.
Goldschild, A. (*France*)
Goldson, P. S., F.A.C.C.A.
Goodwin, C. R. P., F.C.A.
Goudeket, A. (*Netherlands*)
Goult, G. G. G., F.C.A.
Grandell, A. (*Finland*)
Graves, B. W., F.C.A.
Gray, W. M., F.A.C.C.A.
Green, T. J., C.P.A. (*U.S.A.*)
Greenhill, E., F.A.C.C.A.
Greenshields, R. G., C.A.
Greenwood, H., F.S.A.A., C.A. (*South Africa*)
Gregory, R. H., C.P.A. (*U.S.A.*)
Grieveson, R. E., M.B.E., F.S.A.A., C.A. (*South Africa*)
Griffiths, J. A., A.S.A.A.
Grover, F. J., C.A. (*Canada*)
Guilford, P. A., A.A.C.C.A.

H

Hærning, M. (*Denmark*)
Hamilton, Sir George (*Presiding Special Commissioner for Income Tax*)
Hannon, Sir Patrick (*President, The National Union of Manufacturers*)
Harbinson, A., A.S.A.A.
Harman, Alderman and Sheriff C. J.
Harris, J. E., A.A.C.C.A.
Harris, L. G., F.S.A.A.
Harrow, B., C.P.A. (*U.S.A.*)
Hart, J. B., C.A.
Harvey, L., F.A.C.C.A., A.C.W.A.
Hax, K. (*Germany*)
Hay, Sir David Allan, K.B.E., C.A. (*President, The Institute of Chartered Accountants of Scotland*)
Hayashi, R. (*Japan*)
Hayes, L. J., A.S.A.A., F.C.W.A.
Hayhow, H., M.B.E., F.S.A.A., F.I.M.T.A.
Heald, A. J., F.C.A., F.A.C.C.A.

Heizmann, H. F. (*Germany*)
Hénault, A. G. (*France*)
Herd, J. J. S., C.A.
Herrick, A., C.P.A. (*U.S.A.*)
Heynes, G. A. A., C.A.
Higham, F., A.A.C.C.A.
Hiley, T. A., F.C.A. (*Australia*)
Hill, G. M., C.P.A. (*U.S.A.*)
Hill, J. R., O.B.E., F.S.A.A., F.I.M.T.A.
Himmelblau, D., C.P.A. (*U.S.A.*)
Hirst, F. Wyndham, C.B.E. (*Public Trustee*)
Hodgson, H., A.C.A., F.C.W.A.
Hogg, J., O.B.E., F.R.A.N.Z. (*New Zealand*)
Holdsworth, A., A.A.C.C.A., F.C.W.A.
Hollings, W. J., C.P.A. (*U.S.A.*)
Hollwey, J. D., A.C.A.
Holt, E., F.A.C.C.A.
Hope, J. W., C.P.A. (*U.S.A.*)
Horn, D., A.C.A.
Hough, J. W., F.S.A.A., F.I.M.T.A.
Howard, H. C., F.C.A.
Howell, G. R., A.C.W.A.
Howitt, A. W., A.C.A.
Howitt, Sir Harold G., G.B.E., D.S.O., M.C., F.C.A. (*President of the Congress*)
Howson, A. G., A.A.C.C.A.
Humphries, A. P., A.C.A.
Hunter, F. T., A.C.A., A.C.W.A.
Husband, G. R. (*U.S.A.*)
Hutchison, T. A. M., C.A. (*Canada*)
Hutton, C. I. R., C.A.

I

Idman, C. J. (*Finland*)
Ildal, O. C. (*Norway*)
Inglis, J. B., C.P.A. (*U.S.A.*)
Ireland, N. M., C.A. (*Colombia*)

J

Jackson, J. A., F.C.A., F.S.A.A.
Jackson, W., F.A.C.C.A.
James, P. G., F.S.A.A.
Jarvis, C. V., F.A.C.C.A.
Jeppesen, H. Hjernø (*Denmark*)
Jewell, A. J., F.A.C.C.A.
Jewers, D. F., A.C.A.
Jones, J. D. R., F.S.A.A.
Jones, J. W., C.P.A. (*U.S.A.*)
Jones, S. C., F.A.C.C.A.

Jones, S. O., O.B.E., M.C. (*Chief Executive Officer of the Congress*)
Judd, H. G., C.B.E., C.A. (*Joint Honorary Auditor of the Congress*)
Judge, W., A.S.A.A.

K

Kano, L., F.A.C.C.A:
Kapadia, G. P., F.C.A. (*India*)
Karlgren, N. (*Sweden*)
Kastein, A. Th. E. (*Netherlands*)
Katagiri, K. (*Japan*)
Keeble, R. M. L., F.A.C.C.A.
Keens, Sir Thomas, D.L., F.S.A.A.
Kennett, L., F.A.C.C.A.
Kenny, M. J., F.A.C.C.A.
Kermode, E. R., A.I.M.T.A.
Kettle, Sir Russell, F.C.A.
Khan, A. B. (*Pakistan*)
Killip, T. E. A., F.A.C.C.A. (*Member, Congress Council*)
King, C. L., C.A. (*Canada*)
King, F. W. E., F.S.A.A.
King-Farlow, A. R., F.C.A., F.S.A.A.
Kjeldsberg, T. (*Norway*)
Knorr, E. (*Germany*)
Kohler, E. L., C.P.A. (*U.S.A.*)
Kraayenhof, J. (*Netherlands*)

L

La Forgia, M. (*Italy*)
Lang, E. H., A.C.A. (*Venezuela*)
Lange, Stella G., F.S.A.A.
Latham, J. C., D.L., F.S.A.A., F.A.C.C.A. (*Member, Congress Council*)
Latham, The Lord, F.A.C.C.A. (*President, The Association of Certified and Corporate Accountants*)
Laurence, J. K., C.A.
Lauzel, P. (*France*)
Lawrie, A. A., A.S.A.A. (*East Africa*)
Lea, C. B., F.C.A.
Le Bris, M. (*France*)
Lee, Sir Frank, K.C.B., K.C.M.G. (*Permanent Secretary, Board of Trade*)
Leese, G. L., A.R.A.N.Z. (*New Zealand*)
Lester, H. J., F.S.A.A.
Lever, H. A., C.A. (*Canada*)
Lewis, P. R. B., C.A. (*South Africa*)
Limperg, Th. (*Netherlands*)
Lindner, J. A. M. F. (*Netherlands*)
Lindsay, A. J., C.P.A. (*U.S.A.*)

Link, C. E. (*Past Chairman, City Lands Committee*)
Lister, T., C.A.
Livock, Dora M., A.C.A.
London, The Lord Mayor of
Lönnqvist, U. (*Finland*)
Loryman, L. W., F.A.C.C.A.
Love, J., F.S.A.A.
Loveday, C. H. S., A.C.A.

M

McAllister, C. H., A.C.A.
MacBeath, A., C.A., A.C.W.A.
McDanell, F. A. M., F.C.A.
McDonald, H., F.C.A.
Macdonald, I. W., C.A.
McDonald, W. L. L., C.A. (*Canada*)
McDougall, E. H. V.
MacGregor, D., C.A.
McHaffie, A. N. E., C.A.
Machin, G., D.F.C.
MacIver, A. S., M.C. (*Secretary of the Congress*)
Mackay, A. G. A., C.A.
McKell, J., C.A.
Mackenzie, J. R., A.S.A.A.
Macqueen, A. T., C.A. (*Burma*)
Magrath, H. W., C.B.E., M.C., A.C.A.
Mann, J. H., M.B.E., F.C.A.
Mapp, K. A., C.A. (*Canada*)
Marder, J. I., C.P.A. (*U.S.A.*)
Marker, E. H., C.B.
Marshall, A. H., F.S.A.A., F.I.M.T.A.
Martin, E. H. R., F.S.A.A.
Martin, H. (*France*)
Marvin, J. A., C.P.A. (*U.S.A.*)
Mather, C. R., C.P.A. (*U.S.A.*)
Matheson, N. S., C.A.
Maung, Maung (*Burma*)
Mavor, C. W., C.A. (*Canada*)
May, G. O., F.C.A., C.P.A. (*U.S.A.*)
Mayer, H. C., A.A.C.C.A.
Mearns, S. H., C.A.
Mee, J. W., F.S.A.A.
Meier, A. (*Germany*)
Meier, W. (*Germany*)
Melchner, A. (*Germany*)
Menzler, F. A. A., C.B.E. (*Past President, The Institute of Actuaries*)
Mérigoux, A. (*France*)
Merkle, F. (*Germany*)
Meyer, G. F., M.C., A.S.A.A.

Meynell, A. C. S., F.A.C.C.A.
Middleton, A. E., F.S.A.A.
Milburn, W. J., F.C.A.
Miller, Dorothy H., F.C.A.
Miller, E. O., C.P.A. (*U.S.A.*)
Mitra, S. K., A.S.A.A.
Mody, N. R., F.C.A. (*India*)
Montelius, H. (*Sweden*)
Moonan, W. J. P., C.P.A. (*U.S.A.*)
Morgan-Jones, P., F.C.A.
Morita, S. (*Japan*)
Morrish, G. E., A.C.A.
Morrow, I. T., C.A., F.C.W.A.
Muirie, J. R., C.A.
Murase, G. (*Japan*)
Murtagh, Marion, A.A.C.C.A.
Musto, C. R., F.C.A., C.A. (*Rhodesia*)

N

Neill, J. W. F., C.A., C.P.A. (*U.S.A.*)
Nelson, B., F.S.A.A. (*Member, Congress Council*)
Nicholson, C. H., A.C.A.
Nicholson, T. H., C.B.E., F.S.A.A.
Nielsen, A. (*Denmark*)
Norman, J. R., F.A.C.C.A.
Norman, L. H., F.C.A.
Norris, H., A.C.A.
Nunn, G. W., A.A.C.C.A.

O

O'Callaghan, G. J., F.S.A.A.
O'Hara, J. B., C.P.A. (*U.S.A.*)
Ohyama, Y. (*Japan*)
Ojha, S. K. (*India*)
Okamoto, M. (*Japan*)
Olivant, H. F., A.C.A.
Olsen, F. M. L., A.C.A.
Onida, P. (*Italy*)
Orange, H. D., A.S.A.A.
Orreby, E. V. (*Sweden*)
Osbourn, F. C., M.B.E.

P

Paquet, N. (*Belgium*)
Parker, H. W., A.C.A. (*U.S.A.*)
Parker, W. E., C.B.E., F.C.A.
Partington, J., F.A.C.C.A.
Paterson, I. C., A.C.A.
Payrau, A. (*France*)
Pearce, H. L., C.P.A. (*U.S.A.*)
Pears, S. J., F.C.A.

Peck, G. E., F.C.W.A.
Penney, L. H., C.P.A. (*U.S.A.*)
Perfect, J., F.C.A.
Phillips, J. S., F.C.A.
Pickup, M. H., A.C.A. (*Philippines*)
Pollard, C. H., O.B.E., F.S.A.A., F.I.M.T.A. (*President, The Institute of Municipal Treasurers and Accountants*)
Poly, J. (*France*)
Pomeroy, S. J., A.C.A.
Porter, C. B. I., C.A. (*South Africa*)
Powell, W., C.P.A. (*U.S.A.*)
Pratt, D. W., A.C.A.
Primost, S., F.S.A.A.
Prosser, C. H., F.I.C.A. (*Australia*)
Pryor, O. K., C.P.A. (*U.S.A.*)
Purtill, P. J., F.C.A., F.S.A.A.
Pykett, G. F., M.C., F.C.A.

R

Rabagliati, D. N., C.A.
Raby, B. W., F.A.C.C.A. (*Bolivia*)
Radcliffe, The Lord, P.C., G.B.E., Q.C. (*Chairman, Royal Commission on the Taxation of Profits and Income*)
Ralph, H. R., O.B.E., F.S.A.A., F.I.M.T.A.
Rathjen, T. H., C.A. (*Canada*)
Rayner, A., A.C.A.
Réchard, L. (*France*)
Reed, G. C., M.B.E., A.C.A. (*East Africa*)
Reydel, A. (*France*)
Richard, F. M. (*France*)
Richardson, E. C., C.A.
Richman, S., F.A.C.C.A.
Ridgway, Phyllis E. M., F.S.A.A.
Rising, P., C.A. (*Canada*)
Risk, W. S., C.A., F.C.W.A.
Roberts, P. V., A.C.A.
Robertson, D. W., F.C.A.
Robinson, J. R., A.C.A. (*U.S.A.*)
Robinson, J. R., A.C.W.A.
Robson, L. W., F.C.A., F.C.W.A.
Robson, T. B., M.B.E., F.C.A. (*President, The Institute of Chartered Accountants in England and Wales*)
Ross, D., C.A.
Rossdutcher, C., C.P.A. (*U.S.A.*)
Rothschild, H. J. J., A.A.C.C.A.
Rowe, D. N., A.C.A.
Russell, G., F.A.C.C.A., F.C.W.A.
Rybeck, E. (*Sweden*)

S

Sahgal, A. L. (*India*)
Samuelsson, S. (*Sweden*)
Satchell, G. E. H., C.P.A. (*U.S.A.*)
Saunders, F. W. H., F.C.W.A.
Saunders, G. F., F.C.A.
Savage, E. W., F.C.A. (*Australia*)
Savage, R. A. W., A.C.W.A.
Schaffer, W. L., C.P.A. (*U.S.A.*)
Schick, H. (*Austria*)
Schmidt, K. (*Austria*)
Schmidt-Pizarro, O. (*Peru*)
Scott, A. G. W., A.C.A.
Scott, DR (*U.S.A.*)
Scott, W., F.I.C.A. (*Australia*)
Scougal, J., F.S.A.A., F.I.M.T.A.
Scovill, H. T., C.P.A. (*U.S.A.*)
Sears, A. F. J. (*Bolivia*)
Serres, E. (*France*)
Shapiro, S. G., C.P.A. (*U.S.A.*)
Shein, Wunna Kyaw Htin (*Burma*)
Shepherd, E. T., F.C.A.
Shepherd, G. D., M.B.E., F.C.A. (*Member, Congress Council*)
Shimoji, G. (*Japan*)
Short, H. C., F.A.C.C.A.
Shulman, J. J., C.A. (*Canada*)
Sillem, S. G., A.C.A.
Simpson, R., A.S.A.A.
Simpson, R. M., F.S.A.A.
Sinnott, E., F.S.A.A., F.I.M.T.A.
Skinner, P. W., F.S.A.A.
Slade, C. O. G., F.A.C.C.A., F.C.W.A.
Smith, Sir Alan Rae, K.B.E., F.C.A.
Smith, F. E. (*Peru*)
Smith, F. O. M., F.C.A.
Smith, N. P., A.A.C.C.A.
Smith, S. B., F.C.A.
Smith, V. A., A.C.A.
Snell, H. A., F.C.A.
Somerville, J. L., F.R.S.E., C.A. (*Member, Congress Council*)
Somerville, J. M., A.A.C.C.A.
Spalding, W. L., C.A., F.C.W.A.
Sparshatt, A. E., F.A.C.C.A.
Spencer, E., F.A.C.C.A.
Spicer, R. E., F.A.C.C.A.
Spoors, J. E., F.S.A.A.
Sproull, R., C.A., F.C.W.A.
Stacey, R., A.A.C.C.A., A.I.M.T.A.
Staricco, A. J. (*Uruguay*)
Steele, D., F.C.A.

Steele, R. M., F.C.A. (*Australia*)
Stephany, G. M., A.C.A.
Stepto, W. E., F.A.C.C.A.
Stevens, H. L., A.C.A.
Stevenson, H., F.C.A.
Stewart, A., C.A., C.P.A. (*U.S.A.*)
Stewart, J. H., C.P.A. (*U.S.A.*)
Strong, W. B., C.A.
Sudlow, E. W., F.C.W.A.
Summerson, E. D., F.C.A. (*Australia*)
Swaby, R. A., A.A.C.C.A.

T

Talbot, C., C.P.A. (*U.S.A.*)
Tapley, W. D. T., A.C.A.
Tatsumi, S. (*Japan*)
Taylor, R. R., A.C.W.A.
Thomas, R. C. L., M.C., T.D., F.S.A.A.
Thompson, F., F.C.A.
Thomson, W. E. S., F.A.C.C.A.
Thorbjörnsen, J. (*Norway*)
Touche, G. L. C., F.C.A.
Troy, J. G., F.C.A.
Truscott, Alderman and Sheriff D. H., T.D.
Tucker, J. Millard, Q.C. (*Chairman, Committee on Taxation Treatment of Provisions for Retirement*)
Turnbull, R., A.C.A.
Turner, J. L., A.C.A.
Tyrrell, S. C., F.C.W.A. (*President, The Institute of Cost and Works Accountants*)

U

Underwood, A., F.C.A., C.A. (*Rhodesia*)
Usva, E. (*Finland*)

V

van Essen, L. (*Netherlands*)
Vanhouteghem, A. (*Belgium*)
van Iper, R. J. (*Belgium*)
van Rietschoten, A. M. (*Netherlands*)
Velling, A. C. (*Denmark*)
Veyrenc, A. (*France*)
Viacava, A. M. (*Argentina*)
Villa, O. J. (*Philippines*)

W

Wagner, G., C.P.A. (*U.S.A.*)
Walker, A. D., F.C.A.
Walker, J., C.A., F.C.A.
Walker, R. S., A.S.A.A., C.A. (*South Africa*)

Walker, W., F.A.C.C.A.
Waller, R. L., A.C.A.
Wallis, Joan M., A.C.A.
Walton, R., A.S.A.A.
Walton, T., F.C.A.
Ward, A. H., A.A.C.C.A.
Warlow, R. E., T.D., F.C.A.
Waterhouse, Sir Nicholas E., K.B.E., F.C.A. (*Member, Congress Council*)
Watson, A. J., C.A.
Watson, H. J., A.C.A.
Webb, J. R. L., A.A.C.C.A.
Weir, C. J., C.A.
Weisbard, G. L., C.P.A. (*U.S.A.*)
Weiss, L. C., C.P.A. (*U.S.A.*)
Wellington, C. O., C.P.A. (*U.S.A.*)
Wells, H. F., F.C.W.A.
West, A. L. A., F.I.M.T.A.
Whinney, E. F. G., F.C.A.
Whitehead, W. A., F.A.C.C.A.
Whittle, J., A.C.A., F.I.M.T.A. (*Member, Congress Council*)
Whyte, A., A.C.A.
Wilcox, E. B., C.P.A. (*U.S.A.*)
Wilkinson, F. M., A.C.A.
Williamson, J. B. P., F.C.A.
Wilmot, H., C.B.E., F.C.W.A.
Wilson, F., O.B.E., F.A.C.C.A. (*Member, Congress Council*)
Wilson, I. S., C.A.
Wilson, J. R. M., C.A. (*Canada*)
Wimble, B. J. S., F.S.A.A., C.A. (*South Africa*)
Winder, H. J., A.C.W.A.
Wingrove, E. C., F.A.C.C.A.
Winker, P. (*Germany*)
Witty, F. R., F.S.A.A.
Witty, R. A., F.S.A.A.
Wood, J., C.A.
Workman, E. W., F.A.C.C.A., F.C.W.A.
Wright, E. K., F.C.A.
Wright, W. B., F.I.M.T.A.

Y

Yarwood, F., F.C.A., F.C.W.A.
Yates, H. (*President, The Association of British Chambers of Commerce*)
Yaverbaum, I., C.P.A. (*U.S.A.*)
Young, S. G., F.I.C.A. (*Australia*)

Z

Ziegler, F. (*Germany*)

APPENDIX C

The Accountant
Congress Official Reporter
The Exchange Telegraph Company
The Financial Times

The Manchester Guardian
The Press Association
The Times

INDEX